A SHORT HISTORY OF
WESTERN CIVILIZATION
To 1776

A SHORT HISTORY OF
WESTERN

John B. Harrison
Richard E. Sullivan
MICHIGAN STATE UNIVERSITY

CIVILIZATION

FIFTH EDITION

VOLUME ONE: To 1776

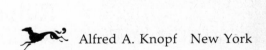 Alfred A. Knopf   New York

FIFTH EDITION

987654321

First Edition published 1960
Second Edition published 1966
Third Edition published 1971
Fourth Edition published 1975

Library of Congress Cataloging in Publication Data

Harrison, John Baugham.
  A short history of Western civilization.

  Includes bibliographies and index.
  1. Civilization, Occidental—History. I. Sullivan,
Richard Eugene, 1921–   joint author. II. Title.
[CB245.H32 1979b]   909'.09'821   79-21373
ISBN 0-394-32438-2 (v. 1)
ISBN 0-394-32439-0 (v. 2)

Manufactured in the United States of America

Design: James M. Wall
Cover Design: Gene Krackehl
Photo Research: Roberta Guerette
Cover Photo Credit: Monet, *Rouen Cathedral in Full Sunlight.* 1894. Courtesy, Louvre, Paris.
Photo: Editorial Photocolor Archives, Inc.

CREDITS FOR PART OPENING PHOTOS

PART I Ralph Mandol/DPI   PART II Elizabeth H. Burpee/DPI   PART III Anderson/
Giraudon   PART IV The British Museum   PART V Epreuve D'Archives/Rapho/Photo
Researchers   PART VI The British Museum   PART VII The Granger Collection
PART VIII   Alinari/EPA   The maps were executed by Jean Paul Tremblay, Francis & Shaw,
Inc., Dyno Lowenstein, and Vantage Art, Inc.

to Mary and Vivian

BIBLIOGRAPHICAL NOTE

In compiling the bibliographies the authors have made no attempt to supply an exhaustive list of the latest titles. Books have been selected chiefly for their readability. Brief descriptions have been supplied for each title to guide the reader. Note that many older classic works, although cited here with the original publishing data, have been reprinted in recent years. A special effort was made to utilize to the fullest the numerous inexpensive books now available. All books published in paperback or inexpensive hardback editions have been designated by an asterisk (*). The series in which each volume has been published (Meridian, Penguin, and so on) has also been noted.

PREFACE

Twenty years have passed since the first edition of this book was written. Much has changed during these years; but, as is increasingly clear, much more has remained the same. The aspiration of many dedicated teachers to encourage their students to expand their capacity to cope with the present and the future by learning about how their world came to be what it is has not changed. Nor have American citizens changed much; many continue to appreciate how an engagement with the past can illuminate the troublesome present, as they have demonstrated by their response to any search for their roots or to the glories of an ancient Egyptian pharaoh's tomb or to a genuine threat to the American Constitution from an imperial president. Even students have changed very little; many entering college freshmen still hate history on principle but nearly always become fascinated with the past once they engage in a serious study of its complex relevance to their present.

The authors still hold to the basic conviction that first inspired our effort two decades ago: that a carefully crafted textbook structured with the needs of both teacher and students in mind is the most indispensable aid to anyone who would teach or learn about the past. We have again concentrated on the features that we have always thought are essential to an effective survey of the history of Western civilization in its world setting: accuracy, clarity, brevity, and specificity. In preparing this new edition we have given close attention to factual details in order to ensure accuracy. Knowing full well that the story of Western civilization is immensely complex, we have tried to be clear and direct in our writing and in organizing our material in a way that will help students comprehend the interrelationships that give the evolving Western experience continuity and cohesion. We have continued our struggle to keep our account brief enough so it offers our primary audience — our student readers — a realistic opportunity to absorb an overview of the essentials of the history of Western civilization. Finally, we have continued to tell our story in terms of specific details about the past, believing that generalizing and philosophizing about the past mislead students unless they possess a body of factual knowledge. We hope our emphasis on specific data will continue to be helpful to teachers by ensuring that their students have sufficient familiarity with the record of past events to prepare them for what the teacher can best give them: an interpretation that gives meaning to the facts.

Despite the fundamental similarity of this edition to earlier editions, we have made some significant changes. Realizing that so much has happened in the last two decades that must be treated as a part of the entire Western tradition, yet reluctant to make our book longer, we have reorganized the material formerly covered in the first four chapters into three new chapters and have expanded the last chapter of earlier editions into two new chapters covering in greater detail the world scene since World War II. We have tried to give more attention to other civilizations, especially in terms of their increasingly important interactions with the Western world. In many places throughout this edition we have tried to reflect the most recent historical scholarship by altering our approach to issues and our choice of material for inclusion. Most of the maps and illustrations have been redone or replaced. We have included new interpretative essays featuring points upon which historians disagree, hoping thereby to encourage our readers to develop a healthy skepticism toward accepted generalizations about the past and to learn to ask questions about the meaning of historical investigation. The suggested reading lists have been revised and updated; special attention has been given to works available in paperback editions. We have given particular attention to sharpening the broad perspectives offered in the introductory and retrospective essays at the beginning and the end of each of the twelve parts of the book.

While making these changes, we have held firmly to the one feature that we have been told distinguishes this book: a structure that takes into account the practical realities of the academic calendar. In most universities and colleges there are ninety class meetings during the year in a Western civilization or humanities course, the typical class meeting three times a week. We believe that the most effective way to teach the typical course is to ask students to prepare for two weekly classes by mastering manageable reading assignments. For this reason we have maintained in this new edition an organization that tells our story in sixty chapters. Believing that brevity is a virtue in a textbook, we have limited these chapters to ten or twelve pages. Our organization, requiring students to master textbook material to prepare for two classes a week, provides the instructor with some flexibility to use the third meeting to conduct discussion sessions focusing on issues raised by the textbook, to encourage additional readings drawn from our suggested reading lists, to utilize audio-visual presentations, and to organize activities that will develop student skills in oral and written expression. We hope that the completely revised instructor's manual and student workbook will serve to guide students and teachers alike in the best possible use of the flexibility designed into this book.

For all that can be said about what is the same and what is different in this fifth edition, we must still say one more thing: our debt to others is even greater than before. Our obligation to a legion of historians whose industry and wisdom have helped us understand the past is immense. We are especially in the debt of a select group of our fellow teachers who, after using our book in their classes, have been willing to share with us their invaluable insights into how to improve our book. We have called on our colleagues from many departments at Michigan State University to help us clarify our thinking; they have never failed us. We are especially in the debt of our co-workers in the Department of History and the Department of Humanities for their assistance. Finally, we thank our students and other students who have written to us from many parts of the country for their incisive comments on our effort; they have taught us a great deal about how to do better what we have tried to do — to make the past speak meaningfully to the present.

J.B.H.
R.E.S.

East Lansing, Michigan
AUGUST 1979

CONTENTS

VI   The Late Middle Ages 1300-1500

VII   The Beginning of Modern Times   Fifteenth and Sixteenth Centuries

VIII   The Age of Royal Absolutism   Seventeenth and Eighteenth Centuries

Where Historians Disagree

Maps

A SHORT HISTORY OF
WESTERN CIVILIZATION

I

The Ancient Near East
4000-300 B.C.

This book will seek to explain the evolution of Western civilization by describing the numerous ingredients that combined over a long period of time into its basic features. While the emergence of civilized life on this planet occurred over immense ages, the crucial "roots" from which Western civilization developed began to grow about 6,000 years ago in a particular area of the world known as the Near East.

This first section of the book will concentrate on developments occurring there over a long era stretching from about 4000 B.C. to 300 B.C. After a few introductory remarks concerning the long era of human history that preceded the emergence of civilization in the Near East, we shall focus on the amazing activity that occurred in two river valley systems in the Near East: the Tigris-Euphrates in Mesopotamia and the Nile in Egypt. For it was in the challenging environment of these river valleys that human communities developed the first complex patterns of institutions, techniques, and ideas that can be called "civilizations." What was achieved in this setting established the foundations upon which Western civilization was to grow. Beyond characterizing the main features of the early civilizations of Mesopotamia and Egypt, we must consider the beginnings of a process as important to the history of the Western world as was the original creation of civilized life—namely, the beginning of the expansion of the river valley civilizations into a large area of northeast Africa and southwest Asia. Not only did this process permit new peoples to raise the level of their existence, but it also created a cultural setting in which they made their own unique contributions to the broadening stream of civilization. Until at least 500 B.C. the peoples of the Near East were on the forefront of the civilized world. This creative population fashioned a priceless heritage that was later exploited by other peoples participating in the shaping of Western civilization.

TIME CHART OF WESTERN CIVILIZATION

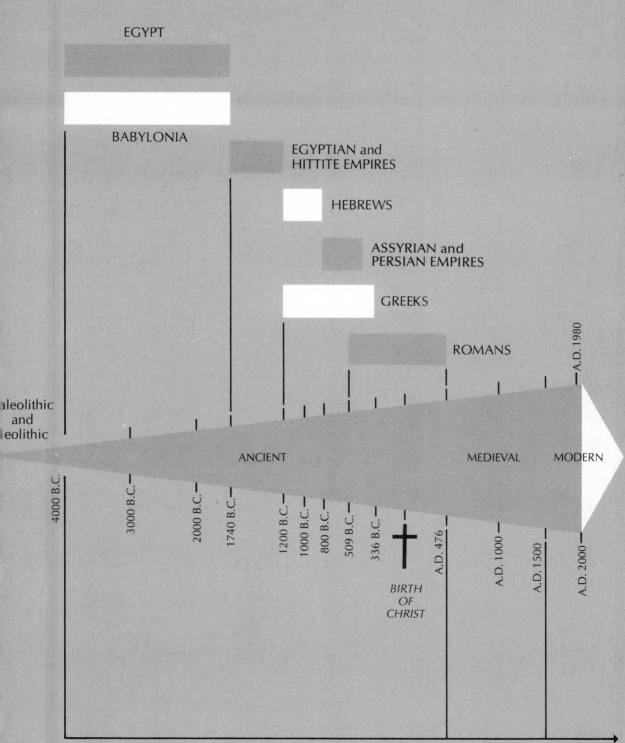

EGYPT

BABYLONIA

EGYPTIAN and
HITTITE EMPIRES

HEBREWS

ASSYRIAN and
PERSIAN EMPIRES

GREEKS

ROMANS

Paleolithic
and
Neolithic

ANCIENT   MEDIEVAL   MODERN

4000 B.C.

3000 B.C.

2000 B.C.

1740 B.C.

1200 B.C.

1000 B.C.

800 B.C.

509 B.C.

336 B.C.

BIRTH
OF
CHRIST

A.D. 476

A.D. 1000

A.D. 1500

A.D. 1980

A.D. 2000

It is now generally agreed that a great leap forward in human history occurred shortly after 4000 B.C., allowing people occupying the Tigris-Euphrates Valley in Mesopotamia and the Nile Valley in Egypt to make a spectacular advance from primitive agricultural life to complex urban civilization. The causes of this transition are still an issue of considerable debate among historians, anthropologists, and archeologists. Some stress the natural evolution of complex city life out of simple village culture. Others speak of technological advance, particularly the use of metal, as decisive. Still others argue that an environmental change gripping the entire Near East generated a spurt of creative activity that resulted in radical changes in life style. And not a few authorities stress the instrusion of new peoples into the area as the vital stimulant. There is evidence to support all these views. Whatever the explanation, major changes occurred in the river valleys that pushed the level of human existence far beyond anything witnessed on earth before.

1. THE BACKGROUND

The preparation for the appearance of higher civilization in the Near Eastern river valleys extended over an immense period. The story of prehistoric man is badly known and much debated. In very simple terms, it was an immensely long history involving two interconnected

THE RIVER VALLEY CIVILIZATIONS: MESOPOTAMIA AND EGYPT, 4000–1750 B.C.

themes: the biological development of the human species and the evolution of cultural patterns that allowed humans to improve their survival powers in the face of the forces of nature.

The physical origin and development of the human species must be deduced from a meager collection of skeletal remains found quite by accident at various places on earth. Some of these remains suggest the existence of man-like creatures well over 2 million years ago. It was not, however, until about 40,000 years ago that the human species assumed its present physical form. Whatever had happened during the long ages before *homo sapiens* (= wise man) finally appeared on the scene, he was endowed with a combination of physical traits that gave him an advantage over other creatures with which he shared the earth. Especially important were an upright posture, stereoscopic vision, a voice mechanism capable of producing a wide variety of sounds, a large and complex brain, a unique hand structure, and a digestive system capable of utilizing almost any kind of food.

The evolution of the human species was accompanied by developing patterns of culture shaped by humans themselves. Across most of prehistory, the culture of primitive peoples was much alike everywhere on earth. This culture has been given a common name, *paleolithic* (Old Stone), derived from the fact that most tools were fashioned from stone. Paleolithic peoples lived in small groups as hunters and food gatherers. They were perpetual wanderers, their lives controlled by the movements of animals on which they depended. They sheltered themselves in caves, in holes covered with skins, or in fragile tents and covered themselves with clothing made from skins. At best, their existence must have been precarious, and improvement in the human condition was slow and faltering. Perhaps the major accomplishment of paleolithic peoples was the development of an increasingly complex set of stone, wooden, and horn tools which enhanced their capabilities as hunters and food gatherers. They learned how to put fire to their service and perhaps developed ways of organizing group activities more effectively. Scanty pieces of evidence suggest the beginnings of religious life centered on a belief in the existence in all things of spirits susceptible to human control, on the regenerative powers of nature, and perhaps on life after death. The amazing cave paintings found at Altamira in Spain and Lascaux in France, as well as crudely shaped human figures, decorated hunting weapons, and jewelry scattered wherever paleolithic groups lived, suggest an urge to express ideas and feelings about the world and to soften the rigors of life by adding elements of created beauty.

Not until about 10,000 years ago did hunting life begin to disappear in a few parts of the world; elsewhere it persisted much longer, with feeble survivals even today in Alaska, the Pacific islands, and Australia. The revolutionary change which began to end paleolithic culture was the invention of agriculture, involving the domestication of plants and animals. This change ushered in the *neolithic* (New Stone) age. The best evidence suggests that agricultural society first developed about 8000 B.C. in the foothills of the mountain ranges ringing the Tigris-Euphrates Valley on the west, north, and east. This area was especially favored at this time by climatic changes occurring as a consequence of the retreat of the ice caps at the end of the last ice age. This change gave much of Europe and parts of Asia heavy forests and produced the deserts of North Africa and Western Asia. These areas, formerly strongholds of hunting societies, grew inhospitable to those pursuits. In the zone between, the changing situation brought regular rainfall and a mild climate, both conducive to grass and cereal grain growing. Here hunting communities learned — probably after considerable trial and error — to plant wheat and barley seeds and to tame wild sheep, goats, pigs, and cattle as means of feeding themselves. During the next few thousand years, agriculture appeared over most of the earth, sometimes borrowed from the original inventors and other times "invented" anew by groups faced with difficulties in sustaining a food-gathering economy.

The development of agriculture revolutionized primitive man's way of life. He settled permanently in villages and produced new tools and techniques, such as houses, hoes, sickles, pottery, and weaving. Accumulations of wealth became possible to hedge against the terrors of nature. Larger social groupings and specialization of labor became possible. More complex systems of village governance, based on tribal groupings each directed by a village chief and a council of family elders, developed to organize communal efforts to meet problems of defense, justice, and worship. Neolithic men also had to expand their minds to cope with their new condition. Their religion, which increasingly centered on the worship of the forces of nature believed to control fertility, challenged them with ideas more complex than those associated with the animal spirits so central to the lives of

earlier hunters. The response was to place more trust in religious experts — priests — and to dedicate more energy and wealth to the worship of the spirits that nourished crops and protected villages.

Neolithic society marked a great advance in the level of human life, but it had serious limitations. Men had to find ways to go beyond it in order to create higher civilizations. Such a leap forward occurred in the river valleys of the Near East about 4000 B.C. — and somewhat later in comparable settings in China and India. Before we turn our attention to the development of higher civilizations in the Near East, it might be well to recognize the debt owed to those hunters and simple farmers of old. Because of them, it was already decided that civilized life would be supported by an agricultural economy. They had realized that man was a social being and had developed institutions attaching the individual to other men. They had perfected crude but effective tools which gave them considerable control over nature. Through their religious beliefs and practices, they had begun a search for understanding and control of the mysteries that surround life. Their achievements served as the basis upon which higher civilization was built; without them, further human advance would have been impossible.

2. THE RIVER VALLEY ENVIRONMENT

The great transformation that occurred in the Near East — which began about 4000 B.C. to create urban civilizations — resulted primarily from a new relationship between simple farmers and their environment. These farmers learned how to organize their efforts so that they could construct irrigation systems which allowed them to utilize the waters of the Tigris-Euphrates and the Nile to support a more intensive agricultural system than was possible in neolithic times.

The Tigris-Euphrates and Nile rivers have many features in common. Both systems originate in areas that provide a fairly regular supply of water and then course through territory that is lacking in natural rainfall. The Tigris and Euphrates have their sources in the Armenian highlands, whence they flow southward in roughly parallel courses to the Persian Gulf. After traversing a semiarid plateau in their upper reaches, the rivers enter a flat alluvial plain about 300 miles north of their mouths. This relatively small area, called Mesopotamia (a word of Greek origin meaning "the land between the rivers"), is immensely fertile as a result of the silt regularly supplied by the flood waters caused by the thaw of snow in the Caucasus Mountains. The Nile arises in the mountains of equatorial Africa, whence it traces a narrow, cliff-lined trough seldom more than 10 miles wide through bleak desert almost devoid of rainfall. As it nears the Mediterranean, the Nile fans out into a series of channels to form the Delta, a triangle of rich land about 120 miles on each side. The Nile floods with even more predictable regularity than the Tigris-Euphrates rivers to create what the Egyptians called the "black land" of the narrow valley and the Delta, which they contrasted with the dreaded "red land" of the desert.

The gifts these river valley systems had to offer were not easily possessed, which explains why early farmers so long avoided them. The annual floods were capricious, especially in the Tigris-Euphrates Valley; too much water could destroy crops and settlements at a stroke, while too little left the crops victims of the burning sun. The fertile soil, capable of producing yields of grain far in excess of dry-land farming, was useless in the near-desert climate of the valleys without a dependable water supply. To assure such a supply demanded a tremendous output of human labor and large-scale planning invested in cutting canals, building dikes and reservoirs, and regulating the flow of water to the fields at the proper time during the growing season. In brief, the successful exploitation of the agricultural potential of the river valleys required a level of planning, organization, and technology much more complex than was needed to sustain life in the neolithic villages dotting the Near East. A response to that challenge produced the first higher civilizations.

While the basic physical characteristics of the Tigris-Euphrates and Nile valleys were essentially alike and required similar efforts to assure their control, there were differences that gave the patterns of life which developed in each unique features. The flood season in the Tigris-Euphrates Valley was less regular and predictable than the Nile floods, and the maintenance of an irrigation system in the broader plain area of Mesopotamia was more difficult than in Egypt. As a consequence, an everlasting threat of flood, drought, and famine hung over the inhabitants of Mesopotamia, creating an attitude of uncertainty and fatalism that is reflected in literature and art. The more predictable and easily manageable Nile inspired confidence and optimism among the Egyptians, who had good reason to sing: "Hail to Thee, O Nile, that gushest forth from the earth and comest to nourish Egypt!"

No less important was the role of geography in dictating the relationship between the inhabitants of the two river valley systems and the world beyond. No natural barriers protected Mesopotamia. As a consequence, those who first mastered the Tigris-Euphrates Valley were constantly attacked by tough herdsmen who lived in the Zagros Mountains to the east, by formidable nomads of the Arabian Desert to the west, and by hardy farmers from the plateau land along the upper reaches of the rivers to the north. The constant assaults of these peoples had a significant effect on Mesopotamian society, but they also made possible the spread of Mesopotamian influence outward into these more primitive areas. By contrast, the Nile Valley was shielded from invaders by forbidding natural barriers. The deserts flanking it, the rapids (cataracts) that block river traffic about 700 miles south of its mouth, and the Mediterranean combined to isolate the valley. The only readily accessible entry into Egypt was a narrow, easily defensible passage connecting the Delta to the Sinai Peninsula and Asia. This isolation gave Egypt security but limited opportunities for contacting and influencing outsiders.

3. MESOPOTAMIA: POLITICAL, ECONOMIC, AND SOCIAL LIFE

The development of higher civilization in Mesopotamia began about 4000 B.C. when a new people, called the Sumerians, settled in the southern

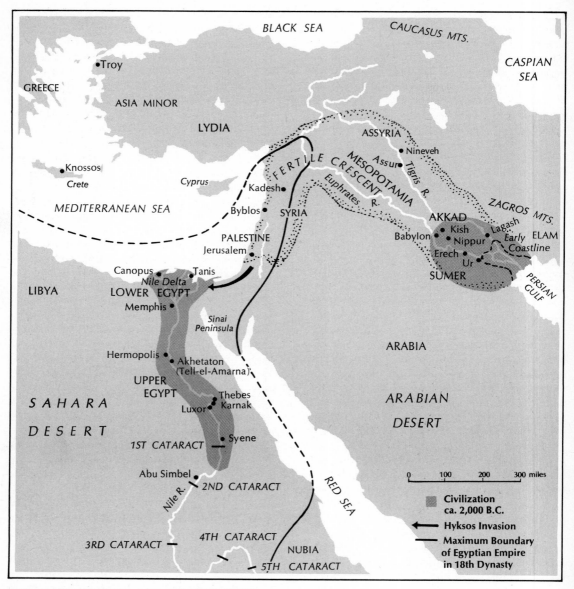

BLACK SEA

CAUCASUS MTS.

CASPIAN SEA

GREECE

•Troy

ASIA MINOR

LYDIA

ASSYRIA

•Nineveh

MESOPOTAMIA

Assur•

Tigris R.

ZAGROS MTS.

•Knossos

Crete

Cyprus

FERTILE CRESCENT

Euphrates R.

AKKAD

•Kish   •Lagash

Babylon• •Nippur   Early ELAM

Coastline

MEDITERRANEAN SEA

Kadesh•

Byblos•

SYRIA

•Erech

•Ur

PALESTINE

SUMER

PERSIAN GULF

Jerusalem•

Canopus•   •Tanis

LIBYA

Nile Delta

LOWER EGYPT

Memphis•

Sinai Peninsula

ARABIA

Hermopolis• •Akhetaton
(Tell-el-Amarna)

UPPER EGYPT

ARABIAN DESERT

S A H A R A

D E S E R T

•Thebes
Luxor• Karnak

•Syene

1ST CATARACT —

Abu Simbel•

Nile R.

2ND CATARACT

RED SEA

3RD CATARACT —

4TH CATARACT

NUBIA

5TH CATARACT

0   100   200   300 miles

Civilization
ca. 2,000 B.C.

Hyksos Invasion

Maximum Boundary
of Egyptian Empire
in 18th Dynasty

EARLY MESOPOTAMIA AND ANCIENT EGYPT

part of the Tigris-Euphrates Valley, named Sumer after the newcomers. The Sumerians began almost immediately to create an agricultural system based on irrigation. Their efforts were successful, resulting in a growing population, a need for more farm land, and pressure to

extend the irrigation system. The challenge was met by the organization of relatively large and complex city-state communities in which the authority to plan and manage an extensive, irrigation-based agricultural system was concentrated in the hands of a small circle of rulers. By 3000

B.C., many rich and populous city-states had been built on the swampy, flood-threatened land of Sumer; among the most prominent were Ur, Lagash, Erech, and Umma. During this same period, another group of people, speaking a Semitic language, began migrating from the Arabian Desert into the area called Akkad, located between the rivers north of Sumer. Imitating their more advanced Sumerian neighbors, the Semites too developed thriving city-states.

The governance of these city-states was grounded in religious belief. The Sumerians believed that each city-state was created by a god who had rolled back the primeval flood, made the earth appear, and fashioned the city and its inhabitants out of the mud. The city therefore belonged to the god, and its citizens were his slaves. At an early date, the responsibility for making the decisions by which the will of the divine owner of the city would be carried out was concentrated in the hands of a single leader. This agent of the patron god, called *ensi* or *lugal*, centered his activities in a palace-temple complex located in the heart of the city-state. From there flowed orders coordinating the numerous communal activities required to till the lands of the patron god. Back to the palace-temple came a huge income gathered from the lands reserved for the support of the god, his house (the temple), and his agents (the priest-king and his aides). Around the palace-temple complex and supported by income from the city-state's agricultural establishment developed specialists whose skills were needed to conduct the numerous rituals honoring the god and to plan and oversee the city-state's economy. Here, too, were cultivated the arts, architecture, writing, learning, and trade—all serving to glorify the patron god and his city and to lift the level of life far above that prevailing in neolithic villages. In the early history of the Mesopotamian city-states, the temple and its priestly community dominated city life. Gradually, the priest-king began to divorce his activities from the temple to assume a more secular status. The king did not surrender his role as agent of the patron god. But he exercised his power more independently by creating a circle of nonpriestly agents to assist him and by drawing many functions away from

the temple to his palace. In this transformation lies the roots of a type of government, sometimes called *Oriental despotism*, destined to play a major role not only in the history of the Near East but also in other parts of the world long after the Mesopotamian city-states of Sumer and Akkad had vanished.

The changing character of early Mesopotamian city-state government was probably related to new political problems emerging after about 3000 B.C. By then, the city-states were solidly established, but they were plagued by lack of stability resulting from the attacks of outsiders attracted by the riches of the valley communities and from violent intercity rivalry for land and power. The solution was eventually found in the formation of *empires* built by conquest and ruled by powerful kings who developed new techniques for keeping peace and order. In the course of this search, Oriental despotism, grounded in early Mesopotamian political experience, took mature form.

The first attempts at shaping a new political order were made by Sumerian cities. At various times between 3000 and 2400 B.C., strong kings from Ur, Erech, Lagash, and Umma used military force to establish mastery over other cities, but these "empires" were short-lived. Ultimately, the Semites proved more talented in uniting Mesopotamia. The first great Semitic empire builder was Sargon I, ruler of the city of Akkad. About 2400 B.C. he led his Semitic warriors in campaigns that not only subdued the more advanced city-states of Sumer but also extended Akkadian rule into the Zagros Mountains to the east and as far west as the Mediterranean Sea. Sargon's empire was sustained by his descendants until about 2200 B.C., but then it collapsed, chiefly as a result of internal resistance from the proud Sumerian city-states that cherished their ancient local independence.

By 2000 B.C., a new people began to rise to prominence; they were the Amorites, recently settled in Mesopotamia from the Arabian Desert. Their day of greatness came with Hammurabi, ruler of the city-state of Babylon. His reign (about 1792 to 1750 B.C.) was distinguished first of all by his military exploits. He repeated the conquests of Sargon I, creating a large empire

Hammurabi's code. The relief, which shows
Hammurabi receiving his code of laws from a god,
is carved at the top of a cylinder carrying the laws in
cuneiform symbols. *Photo: Giraudon*

based in Mesopotamia but stretching in a great
arc from there to the Mediterranean. Babylon
became a great city, the seat of a government
that maintained peace over a broad territory and
spread the fruits of Sumerian civilization to
many different peoples. For all its brilliance, the
Amorite Empire was relatively short-lived.
Shortly after 1700 B.C., outside attackers, such as
the Hittites and Kassites, began to batter its
frontiers (see chapter 2). Eventually, the Kassites conquered Mesopotamia. Never again did
the people of "the land between the rivers"
create a strong political power, although they
and their rich land would serve as a base for
large empires built by future conquerors.

The empire builders who dominated Mesopotamian history between 2400 and 1700 B.C. instituted several new ideas and practices in government that proved to be among the greatest of all

Mesopotamian contributions to civilization. The
challenge facing these rulers was to use political
power to create common bonds among peoples
who were otherwise divided. Hammurabi's career exemplifies some of the means used to meet
this problem.

One of Hammurabi's achievements was the
exaltation of the figure of the ruler, the "king of
kings," as he called himself. The king was the
sole agent of the gods in determining the destiny
of the community over which he ruled; in his
own right he was judge, lawgiver, military
leader, and spokesman to the gods. The vast
display of the riches of his court at Babylon and
the splendor with which he presented himself to
his subjects made him the symbolic center toward which his subjects from "the Four Quarters
of the World" looked for their well-being. The
priestly caste that had once held a monopoly on
power in the early Sumerian city-states was now
little more than an adjunct to the majestic king.

But Hammurabi's power was more than appearance. His authority was based on a well-
organized army ready to curb threats to peace in
his empire. He established a centralized bureaucracy in Babylon with specialized departments of finance, public works, justice, and
defense. He subdivided his empire into local
units and sent out royal servants to collect taxes,
raise troops, and administer justice. He sought
to create a common religion in his empire, based
on the worship of Marduk, once the patron god
of the city of Babylon but now presented as chief
of all gods by virtue of having conquered them
in a series of heavenly wars which gave him the
right to rule their lands on earth.

Perhaps Hammurabi's most significant measure was the issuance of his famous code of law,
which he claimed was handed down to him from
the gods. Hammurabi's code was a synthesis of
earlier Mesopotamian legal codes. It was obviously intended to provide his subjects with
common rules for property, wages, marriage and
family affairs, crime, commerce, and inheri-
tances. Here was a practical way of unifying his
subjects and maintaining a civilized order. A
modern reader is taken aback by the brutal
punishments prescribed for lawbreakers: death
to a builder whose construction falls and kills its

owner; loss of a hand for a surgeon whose patient dies; loss of an eye for anyone who puts out another's eye. But the code is better characterized by its common-sense, humane approach to basic human problems: protection for women, children, and slaves; fairness in commercial exchange; protection of the property of soldiers on duty; standard procedures for adjudicating disputes; debt relief for the victims of flood and drought. On the whole, the code probably represented an enlightened concept of justice that drew people to accept the rule of a king who claimed he issued the code "to destroy the wicked and the evil, so that the strong may not oppress the weak."

Undergirding these political developments, yet dependent on them, was a remarkably unchanging economic system. The material base of Mesopotamian society was provided by a carefully organized agricultural system that allowed the irrigation of the rich lands between the rivers in a way that returned bountiful harvests of cereal grains and food for animals. Aside from the irrigation system — a technological miracle in itself — agricultural techniques made some advance, especially as a result of the invention of the wheel and the use of copper and bronze to replace the basic agricultural tools previously made of stone. Agriculture was an enterprise that still depended chiefly on human labor, although oxen and asses were harnessed to assist in the most arduous farming operations — ploughing and hauling. The prime agricultural unit was the large farm tilled by gangs of laborers, some semifree peasants and others slaves, working under the careful supervision of a landlord or his agents. This labor force also spent much time repairing dikes and canals, cleaning away the troublesome swamp growth that came with the floods, and dredging out the silt that threatened the irrigation system. Although there were some small independent farmers who farmed their own lands, land ownership was confined to a small segment of the population. In early Mesopotamian history, the temple priests nearly monopolized land ownership. Although the myth persisted that all land belonged to the patron god, by Hammurabi's time, a nonpriestly aristocracy — chiefly soldiers and royal officials —

had gained possession of much of the land, usually by grant from the king.

The basic agricultural economy of Mesopotamia was greatly enriched by a flourishing trade and industry. A major incentive to trade in Mesopotamia was a lack of crucial raw materials, especially metal and stone. But need itself did not produce trade or manufacturing. These were consequences of the ability of priests and kings to extract surplus wealth from agriculture that could be used to support traders who sought out materials from far-off places and to employ artisans sufficiently skilled to turn these materials into fine clothing, pottery, jewelry, metal tools and weapons, and monumental buildings. Almost from the beginning, traders and artisans played a prominent role in the economy of Mesopotamian cities. Their efforts greatly enriched the cities for which they labored. And they demonstrated an amazing ability to perfect the techniques conducive to their pursuits. By Hammurabi's time, traders had evolved significant aids to commerce, including complicated contracts, standard weights and measures, credit buying, lending for interest, deeds, and promissory notes. And artisans were no less inventive in developing their skills to convert raw materials into products that made easier the control of nature and more comfortable the basic conditions of life.

It hardly need be said at this point that the organization of irrigation-based agriculture and of urban life was accompanied by the emergence of a dominant aristocracy of priests, landowners, and royal servants. This class benefited most from Mesopotamia's material wealth and created a glittering life for itself. At the same time, the aristocracy performed an absolutely crucial function by directing the efforts of a large lower class in the cooperation needed to control the rivers, to plant and harvest the crops, and to develop all the specialized skills required to sustain city life. Nor were these aristocratic masters totally forgetful of other classes. Hammurabi's code embodied the principle that nobles should be punished more severely for certain crimes than other members of society. It was also careful to state the rights and duties of slaves, peasants, merchants, and artisans. Mesopotamian society indeed favored its aristocracy, but it was understood that each social class had a role in society that must be respected and protected.

4. MESOPOTAMIA: CULTURAL LIFE

The advances in government, economy, and social organization described above were accompanied by equally impressive developments in cultural life — in religion, literature, the arts, and sciences.

Central to Mesopotamian culture was a set of religious beliefs and practices that influenced every facet of life and thought. It was a religious system that is not easy for modern people to understand, chiefly because its origins lay in a remote, inaccessible past and because it was never given precise definition by its practitioners. But its main features are fairly clear.

Mesopotamian religion was *polytheistic*, that is, based on the worship of many gods. Perhaps the most basic belief shared by all Mesopotamians was that every occurrence in the universe was caused by spirits living in all things. Especially awesome were the spirits that controlled the forces of nature. These deities provided the major focus of religious life: Anu, the sky god; Enlil, the god of air; Enki (called Ea by Semitic-speaking peoples), god of the earth and waters; Nanna (Sin in Semitic), the moon god; and Utu (Shamash in Semitic), the sun god. One of these powerful gods was usually accepted as the founder and present owner of a city-state. Another deity almost universally worshiped was the goddess of fertility, whose munificent power renewed all nature each spring. This great mother, called Inanna by the Sumerians and Ishtar by the Semites, had a special appeal to the ordinary people who lived close to the soil. Sharing the universe with these great gods and goddesses were legions of lesser spirits, each of whom controlled some aspect of the multitude of activities that surrounded human existence and could bring blessings or misfortunes to men and women in all stations of life.

During the long period of Mesopotamian history under review, considerable intellectual effort was spent attempting to clarify the nature and powers of these deities and to spell out their relationships to one another and to the human community. The fruit of this effort was a rich and intriguing body of mythology. That body of "knowledge" about the gods ascribed to them a style of life very similar to that of men. The mythologists also struggled to spell out the hierarchy that prevailed in divine society, a task made difficult not only by such fundamental questions as which force of nature took precedence over others but also by the fact that earthly affairs seemed to spell the rise and fall of some deities. Particularly troublesome was the fate of a god whose earthly city-state was conquered by another city-state, a not infrequent event in Mesopotamia. Usually this resulted in a myth about a heavenly war between the gods, with one conquering the other and reducing him to a subordinate rank. The victorious god was usually accepted by the people of the conquered city-state as their chief deity. The most splendid warrior god was Marduk, originally god of Babylon, who won wars in heaven comparable to those of King Hammurabi on earth and who, as a result, became universally recognized as master of the universe, just as Hammurabi was recognized as king of kings on earth. Mesopotamian mythology also tried to explain how there came to be order in the world. The result was a series of elaborate creation stories describing how a powerful god, such as Marduk, subdued the primeval chaos, fashioned the families of gods, created and positioned the heavens, the stars, the land, and the seas, and filled the universe with living things. Change also intrigued the mythologists. A favorite way to explain change was in terms of floods sent by angry gods. Especially appealing was the rich mythology that had developed by Hammurabi's time explaining how the goddess Ishtar and her lover, Tammuz, managed to assure the renewal of life each spring. As a body, this primitive "theology" is an impressive attempt to answer some basic questions that face man. It became a rich storehouse from which later peoples drew their religious ideas.

Man's place in the god-filled universe was not easy. He was viewed as a slave of the gods, bound to carry out their will and open to their angry, vengeful tempers. Man bore a terrible burden in trying to keep these unpredictable masters happy. Their care and feeding was crucial in winning their favor. To this end, magnificent temples were built and supplied with lavish furnishings and endless offerings of food and drink. Troops of priests and priestesses were supported by society to attend the deities. Great public festivals were regularly organized to please the gods, while people offered prayers and gifts at countless shrines in homes, fields, and streets to win the favor of the hordes of spirits that controlled life. No project, great or small, was undertaken without an effort first to ask the favor of the gods and then to thank them for its success. Always anxious to find out what the gods might be planning, men and women developed a whole battery of predictive techniques involving dream interpretation, reading the stars, and interpreting animal entrails. Those skilled in predicting the future, especially astrologers, were powerful figures in society.

In a real sense, then, life at all levels in Mesopotamia was lived as a ritual aimed at pleasing the gods. What the Mesopotamians expected in return was the material gifts the gods had to give — the safety and prosperity of the city-state, the family, and the individual. From what surviving records tell, it appears that most men and women were never sure that their powerful gods would smile on them. A tone of pessimism and fatalism permeated their view of life. This may in part have been due to a lack of any moral dimension in Mesopotamian religion. The Mesopotamians had no god who placed ethical demands on his believers; as a consequence, moral issues played little part in religion. Neither did concerns about immortality. Mesopotamians believed that the dead passed on to a "land of no return" somewhere underground "where dust is their feed, clay their sustenance; where they see no light and dwell in darkness." Without a chance to please the gods through good behavior that would result in rewards after death, perhaps there was reason for pessimism about the ultimate value of life.

A major product of the effort to know and please the gods was an impressive literature, art, and science that marked a considerable advance over peoples living in the area before the advent of Mesopotamian life. By and large, the Sumerians were prime creators in cultural life. The Semitic peoples, who played a decisive role in political history, were usually cultural imitators. In the course of time, the two peoples merged culturally, so that a common pattern of culture rooted in ancient Sumer embraced all of Mesopotamia.

One of the greatest Sumerian achievements was the development of a writing system during the fourth millennium B.C. The original form of Sumerian writing employed actual pictures of what was being communicated (pictographs), but gradually a system of symbols representing sounds was developed. These symbols were pressed into soft clay with a wedge-shaped stylus and then the tablets were baked; thus the writing is called *cuneiform* (from a Latin word meaning "wedge"). By the time of Sargon I, the Sumerian written language began to be replaced by a Semitic languaged called Akkadian, but learned men continued to study Sumerian texts much as modern men learn ancient Greek, Latin, and Hebrew, so that a considerable body of Sumerian literature survived to inspire writing in Akkadian.

While a large part of Mesopotamian writing was devoted to record keeping, talented men learned to use it for more creative purposes. The most impressive literary productions were magnificent religious epics, of which the *Creation Epic* and the *Epic of Gilgamesh* are the best examples. The *Creation Epic* describes how Marduk won supremacy over the spirit world and created earth and man. The *Epic of Gilgamesh* recounts the fruitless struggle of a legendary hero, Gilgamesh, ruler of Erech, to find immortality, a venture that leads him through numerous encounters with angry gods and the forces they create to destroy him. The Mesopotamians also wrote hymns, chronicles of the deeds of great rulers, and letters. The literary forms, themes, and styles developed by the Mesopotamians not only enriched their own culture but also helped to shape the literature of later peoples, as is so clearly evident in the Mesopotamian influences reflected in Hebrew scripture, written a thousand or more years after the Mesopotamian works from which it borrowed.

From the beginning of their civilization, the Mesopotamians were skilled and creative artists. Their major architectural works were the temple complexes that were built in every city to honor its patron god. The crowning feature of the temple complex was the temple tower, called a *ziggurat*, designed as a series of terraces one on top of another, each successive layer smaller than the one below. A sanctuary remote from the world was placed atop the final terrace. Around the *ziggurat* there usually developed an elaborate complex of lesser shrines, offices, dwellings, storehouses, and workshops, all comprising a sacred precinct where the gods could be served. Hardly less elaborate or impressive were the palaces where the kings and their courts lived. The palace at Mari, an important city in the Amorite Empire, covered 6 acres and contained more than 250 rooms. A lack of stone in the Tigris-Euphrates Valley resulted in the use of clay bricks as the chief building material. Architects knew how to use the column, the dome, the arch, and the vault, but given the limitations in building materials at their disposal, they did not apply these techniques very extensively.

The Mesopotamians were skilled sculptors, although this art, too, was restricted by the shortage of good stone. Most three-dimensional statues are portrayals of gods and kings. Sculptors took some pains to give a distinctive character to the faces of their subjects but concerned themselves little with a realistic rendering of the bodies. Their work, strongly influenced by ideal geometrical forms — cylinders and cones — is solid, stiff, motionless. More realistic and animated scenes were created by sculptors working in low relief. These *steles*, usually depicting historic events or divine exploits, accentuated action. The most exquisite carving was done by seal makers, who wrought miniaturized scenes on stones that could be used to press an identifying mark into clay. The same fine skill is also illustrated in the jewelry, metal work, and decorated pottery produced in abundance by numerous artisans working in temples, palaces, and individual workshops. Much of the excellence of this work resulted from the specialization permitted by a highly organized, carefully directed society.

Chiefly as a result of their efforts to cope with the gods and with the rivers, the Mesopotamians produced a body of knowledge that can be called science. They devised a system of time reckoning based on a seven-day week, on months tied to the moon's cycles, and on a year derived from the sun's movements. They developed a standard of weights and measures almost universally used by Hammurabi's time. Their numbering system combined a decimal system and units of sixty. They were able to add, subtract, multiply, and divide and to perform simple geometric functions, such as finding the area of a plane surface or the volume of a cylinder. A body of medical knowledge, mixing practical observations and religious lore, was developed. The Mesopotamians compiled a considerable store of geographical knowledge, based chiefly on their travels as conquerors and traders. Inspired by an urge to foretell the future, the Mesopotamians gathered accurate information about the movements of the stars, thus laying the basis for astronomy. While the Mesopotamians were seldom concerned with knowledge about the natural world for its own sake, the information they compiled about nature in the course of meeting practical problems and in dealing with gods was passed on to later peoples, particularly the Greeks, to provide a base for theoretical science.

Taken together, the cultural achievements of the Mesopotamians suggest a few general characteristics of the outlook that predominated in this ancient society. Certainly religion was the integrating force in intellectual life. It supplied the basic assumptions that governed all thought and expression and provided the great overarching truths about existence that gave meaning to every intellectual activity. Because the prime aim of religion was to sustain earthly life in the face of powerful, capricious divine forces, Mesopotamian thinkers and artists were basically practical men. They focused their talents on keeping the gods happy and protecting the status quo. There was little room for free expression, experimentation, individual fancy, and speculation. The creative person was conservative, given to saying and doing over and over what had already been proved effective. There is a notable absence of evolution in artistic styles and themes across the 2,000 years we have reviewed. Mesopotamians were also basically pessimistic, seldom hopeful that the burdens imposed on the slaves of the gods would lighten in an unstable and uncertain cosmic system. Finally, they were anxious, their minds alert for signs that man's efforts were attuned to the forces that governed existence. Perhaps this anxiety supplied the adaptability that made Mesopotamian civilization durable.

5. EGYPT: POLITICAL, ECONOMIC, AND SOCIAL LIFE

Not long after higher civilization took shape in Mesopotamia, a similar leap forward occurred in Egypt. While there is some evidence that Mesopotamian influences played a role in forming Egyptian civilization, the basic developments in the Nile Valley were indigenous and assumed their own unique form.

Probably as early as 5000 B.C., neolithic agricultural settlements were established on the fringes of the Nile Valley, perhaps by peoples migrating from the deserts developing to the west and east. During the next thousand years, these original settlers found the courage and the skills to master the rich valley land by developing an irrigation system that controlled the floods and supplied water for the bounteous crops that could grow in the fertile soil. By 4000 B.C., village settlements had spread throughout the Nile Valley. For reasons that are not clear, these villages did not unite into city-states, as was the case in Mesopotamia. However, with the passage of time, small kingdoms did emerge, perhaps as a consequence of the efforts of aggressive leaders in certain villages who forced their authority on weaker neighboring villages. As larger units were formed, it probably became obvious that cooperation on a larger scale brought greater benefits to everyone.

The era of the formation of small kingdoms, called the Predynastic Age, ended suddenly about 3100 B.C., when all Egypt was united under a single ruler, called the *pharaoh*. Egyptian tradition ascribed this feat to Menes, who founded the first dynasty of pharaohs and

opened an era called the Old Kingdom. Certainly the process of unification had begun before Menes' time, for he already ruled a larger kingdom in Upper (southern) Egypt before he subdued Lower (northern) Egypt. Still, Menes preceded Sargon I by nearly seven centuries, and when Hammurabi built his Amorite Empire, Egypt had enjoyed about thirteen centuries of unity.

During the Old Kingdom (3100–2200 B.C.), Egypt was ruled by six dynasties of pharaohs. The rulers of the first two dynasties were concerned chiefly with coercing or persuading Lower Egypt to accept unification and with developing a royal administration capable of effective governance of the entire valley. Success in this venture set the stage for the glorious third and fourth dynasties, the golden age of the Old Kingdom. From their capital in Memphis, these pharaohs asserted a beneficial authority that brought peace and order to the entire valley and extended Egyptian influences into the Sinai peninsula, Syria, and Nubia. The splendid pyramids built at Gizeh by the powerful pharaohs of the Fourth Dynasty, Menkure, Kephren, and Khufu (Cheops), reflect the immense wealth of a society unified in exploiting the Nile and the great power of the rulers who controlled that unified effort.

The key to that success was the political system that had taken shape by the time of the Third Dynasty. Its central feature was the absolute power of the pharaoh. Indeed, he was a special kind of ruler, a god sired by the sun god Ra and destined to eternal life along with the other gods. The pharaoh owned Egypt and her people. Every person was his servant, subject to his unchallengeable law. Despite their lofty status, most of the pharaohs of the first four dynasties were active statesmen, well trained for their role and constantly occupied in overseeing the irrigation system, giving justice, directing building programs, and sponsoring trade. Their power was supported by a highly developed administrative system centered in the royal palace at Memphis. There the pharaoh gathered a trusted circle of officials to whom he assigned important responsibilities. Among the high officials prominent in the records of the Old Kingdom was a chief minister, a treasurer, a chief of irrigation, recordkeepers, and high priests, each assisted by numerous state servants of lesser rank. Egypt was divided into forty-two administrative units, called *nomes*, each controlled by royal officials held closely accountable in Memphis. Every nome was divided into villages, where the mass of the people lived and where royal officials appeared regularly to enforce the pharaoh's commands and to collect taxes.

During the Fifth and Sixth Dynasties, this splendid system faltered. Royal officials, provincial governors, and priests began to usurp the pharaoh's authority and to exercise power for their own benefit. The causes of this decline are not clear. There is no evidence of any sudden catastrophe. Perhaps the pharaohs grew lax in tending to affairs and granted too much power to their officials. Perhaps the administrative machine had become too large and complex for one man to control. There is some evidence that the pharaohs impoverished themselves by overgenerous grants of land and power to their officials, especially the priests. And the rulers may have discredited themselves by imposing too heavy a burden on their subjects for such costly, nonproductive projects as the great pyramids. In any case, by the end of the Sixth Dynasty, Egypt entered a period of anarchy called the First Intermediate Period (2200–2050 B.C.). The pharaohs of this era (seventh through tenth dynasties) were shadowy, ineffectual figures. Political power rested in the hands of innumerable local rulers whose pursuit of their own interests brought internal wars, lawlessness, injustice, and economic depression.

About 2050 B.C., the princes of Thebes, previously an insignificant city far to the south in the valley, undertook the task of reunification, perhaps in the name of the god Amon, heretofore only a minor deity. After a fierce struggle, these princes (designated as the Eleventh Dynasty) established what is known as the Middle Kingdom (2050–1750 B.C.). It reached its peak during the Twelfth Dynasty. Some of these rulers, especially Amenemhet I and Senusret III, remind one of the great pharaohs of the Fourth Dynasty. They restored many of the political institutions characteristic of the Old Kingdom —

the divine power of the pharaoh, the centralized bureaucracy, the provincial administration — and labored to revive the economy, reclaim land from the desert, and maintain order. Once again, Egypt's influence was felt in Syria, the Sinai region, and Nubia.

However, the divine character of the pharaoh was no longer so predominant. One authority has suggested that the pharaohs of the Middle Kingdom might better be called "good shepherds" than gods. The word *ma'at* (justice) provides a key to the spirit animating their government. They were especially concerned with providing *ma'at* for the lower classes, defining their place in society, ensuring their rights and welfare, and protecting them from greedy and oppressive officials. It appears that the grim experience of the First Intermediate Period had heightened the moral sensitivity of the Egyptians and generated a sense of individual rights. The strongest pharaohs of the Twelfth Dynasty did modify the government to some extent by decreasing the power of the old nobility and giving greater authority to a class of professional civil servants, called *scribes*, to carry out the multitude of functions associated with directing a centralized state.

After nearly 300 years of orderly government and prosperity, the Middle Kingdom also began to decline. Its end was hastened by the emergence of a threat for which the Egyptians were not prepared. About 1750 B.C. a barbarian horde called the Hyksos swept out of Asia and seized control of the Nile Valley. Lawlessness and violence replaced orderly government. This interlude is usually called the Second Intermediate Period (1750–1580 B.C.). Eventually Egypt recovered from this catastrophe, but that story is a new chapter in the history of the Near East and must be reserved for later.

Like Mesopotamian civilization, the brilliant achievements of the Old and Middle Kingdoms rested on a carefully controlled agricultural system that took full advantage of the rich soil and the bountiful waters of the Nile. The backbone of this economy was the peasant population, living in small villages in mud huts and devoting their lives to an endless round of labor required to keep the irrigation system working and to plant and harvest the crops of wheat, barley, flax, vegetables, and fruit. To this was added the incessant demands for extra labor on the immense building programs of the pharaohs, the priests, the royal officials, and the landowners. The peasants' labors were rigorously controlled in the service of the pharaoh, and they enjoyed material rewards barely sufficient for survival.

Although Egyptian civilization rested chiefly on agriculture, a considerable number of artisans and merchants also added to the wealth. They produced primarily luxury goods, working directly for the pharaoh, the rich nobles of his court, or the powerful provincial nobility. Every great household and temple had its own shops where artisans made a variety of items and from which merchants went forth to exchange goods and procure raw materials. In some cases, such as stone quarrying, copper mining, and brick making, production was organized on a large scale. The social status of the craftsman and merchant was usually much like that of the peasant. They were bound to an overlord, granted little freedom of action, and rewarded for their efforts with little more than subsistence.

Like Mesopotamia, Egypt was dominated by a relatively small aristocracy. At its summit stood the pharaoh and his family, enjoying command over all elements of society and control over the total wealth of the state. The rest of the aristocracy consisted of those to whom the pharaoh chose to give high status and reward with wealth. The priestly class enjoyed an especially high rank, but hardly more than great royal officials and local landowners who played a prime role in organizing the labor of the peasants, artisans, and traders. This aristocracy enjoyed the full range of the gifts that the Nile had to offer. Yet without their talents for organizing the efforts of millions of people, no one would have been able to tame the river. Aristocratic leadership and dominance of society was to remain a keynote of civilized life long after Egypt and Mesopotamia had declined.

6. EGYPT: CULTURAL LIFE

Success in unifying Egypt's population and conquering the Nile was accompanied by a brilliant and sustained flowering of intellectual and artistic life. To this day, the early Egyptians' cultural achievement impresses the world as one of the great accomplishments of man.

Egyptian culture was rooted in powerful religious forces that inspired and shaped every aspect of thought and expression. Writing in the fifth century B.C., the Greek historian Herodotus concluded that the Egyptians were the most religious of all peoples. From at least some perspectives, the modern student is forced to agree. Certainly few peoples had to contend with more gods; their numbers reached into the thousands. This vast array of spirits was conceived in a confusing variety of forms—as animals, humans, birds, plants, inanimate forms, abstractions, and mixtures of any two or three of these forms. These gods lived everywhere and roamed freely through the heavens and across the world; they were likely to be present wherever and whenever humans were at work or play. While their powers to control human affairs were great, the Egyptians never developed a very clear definition of the nature or the powers of these gods. Perhaps their willingness to tolerate this confusion stemmed from the fact that the Egyptians conceived their gods as basically benevolent and kindly disposed toward humans. In contrast to the Mesopotamians, they did not live in constant fear of the gods; rather, they shared the world comfortably and confidently with them.

However, over the centuries, certain gods did achieve universal prominence in Egypt and were conceived as having unusual power. The efforts to explain the role of these deities resulted in a rich body of mythology. During the Predynastic and Old Kingdom periods, there was a tendency to exalt the gods of the victors in earthly wars. For instance, when Menes unified all Egypt, the falcon god Horus, formerly the god of Upper Egypt, became the chief public deity of the entire kingdom. Even as late as the Middle Kingdom, the relatively unknown god of Thebes, Amon, was elevated to a major role following the successes of the princes of Thebes in reuniting Egypt. By the end of the Old Kingdom, the sun-god, Ra, demanded reverence from all as the supreme power in the heavens. The effort to understand how things came to be resulted in special prominence for some gods; such was the case of Ptah, brought into prominence by the priests of Memphis as the prime creator of the universe. Especially significant was the emergence of Osiris, who was believed to possess the power to grant a happy life after death. But even as gods like Ra and Osiris came to be accepted by all Egyptians, never were the innumerable local gods eliminated from the scene as important forces in human affairs.

Another indication of the validity of Herodotus' statement, noted above, was the effort devoted by the Egyptians to please these gods and win their favors. An elaborate set of ritual practices was established early in Egyptian history and changed little over the centuries. To the pharaoh belonged the prime responsibility for bringing the favor of his fellow gods upon his land and people; no small part of the activities of a typical pharaoh was devoted to religious worship. He was aided by a numerous and powerful priesthood. Their efforts centered on the many temples that dotted the land; in each of these temples an elaborate round of rituals took place designed to please the gods with food, gifts, song, prayer, and dance. Acts of worship and sacrifice also took place at tiny chapels and in homes. A rich array of magical practices evolved to attract the attention of the good gods and to drive away evil spirits. The surviving records suggest that the Egyptians were convinced that their constant concern with the gods was worthwhile. The abundant harvests, peace, and security proved to most of them that the gods were happy with their earthly subjects.

Besides earthly benefits, the gods held another precious gift for deserving Egyptians — a happy life after death. Concern with immortality was a unique aspect of Egyptian religion and was the source of some of its most dynamic features. From early times, Egyptians believed that every man had a *ka*, a double for his body that lived on after death in some kind of close association with the divine spirits. The *ka* had to have all it needed to keep it happy after death. In early Egyptian history, that end was met in a rather crude and materialistic fashion. The body was preserved by mummification so that the spirit could return to it. A tomb that would last forever was built to shelter the spirit. Elaborate arrangements were made to ensure that the spirit would have food, drink, luxuries, companions — everything it had enjoyed in life — to make immortal life tolerable. Perhaps only the pharaoh could afford proper provisions; but at least he was willing to help some others live eternally so that they could continue to be his companions and servants. He therefore built tombs for his wives, his children, his officials, and his friends close to his own great tomb. By the end of the Old Kingdom, many nobles were constructing their own tombs. The fate of the common man in this early period is not clear, but one must presume that some kind of afterlife was his lot too, even if he could not make the proper preparations.

Gradually, the expectation of gaining immortality was democratized and universalized until the gates of heaven were open to all Egyptians. The critical moment in this radical transformation came in the troubled First Intermediate Period and was probably part of the moral outrage generated against the materialism and greed of the Old Kingdom's ruling class. The new concept of immortality found its focus in the worship of Osiris, which by the period of the Middle Kingdom had advanced to a central place in religious life and was embodied in a touching myth. Osiris, a good god associated with life forces and the Nile, was murdered by his wicked brother, Seth, who dismembered his body and scattered the parts over the face of the earth. Osiris' wife, Isis, patiently gathered them up, and when her task was finished, Osiris returned to life. Thereafter, he had the power to raise everyone from death to life. When any Egyptian died, he appeared before Osiris and a panel of judges in the other world. Osiris placed the dead man's heart on one pan of a balance and a feather on the other. If the heart was weighted with evil, the dead man was not fit for eternal happiness and was tossed to a ferocious beast. If it was buoyant with goodness, he was allowed to live forever in a heavenly place very much like the earthly Nile Valley.

The radically new element in this concept of immortal life is the idea of the moral worth attached to each man. Osiris was concerned with

This Egyptian funerary papyrus from the tomb of a princess shows some of the steps in the transition to afterlife. In the center, the gods weigh her heart in a balance against the figure of the Goddess of Truth. Ca. 1000 B.C. *Photo: The Metropolitan Museum of Art*

goodness in evaluating a man's eligibility for eternal life, not with his wealth and social position. In articulating a moral basis for human life, the Egyptians were far in advance of other ancient peoples. This is not to imply that all of Egyptian life was transformed by this birth of conscience and moral sense. Egyptians continued to provide for the material welfare of the dead, although from the Middle Kingdom onward the emphasis was less on the grandeur of the tomb and more on its decoration—a record in pictures and writing to convince Osiris that the occupant had indeed lived a "good" life; and in time, men came to busy themselves devising clever formulas to conceal their moral faults. Still, Osiris worship heightened moral awareness in a way that was unknown in Mesopotamia, and it provided a meaningful place in the cosmic order for all men.

The constant effort to understand, please, and thank the gods inspired an impressive literary and artistic activity, remarkable not only for its high level of technique but also for its unity and coherence. Egyptian literature in the proper sense was preceded by the development of a system of writing, called *hieroglyphic*, which made its appearance about 3200 B.C. Like cuneiform writing, it began as pictographs. Gradually symbols representing sounds were perfected, and these were combined to form words. The first use of writing was probably in recordkeeping and letter writing in connection with the pharaoh's court, but it was not long before more artistic uses were found for writing skills. Much of the creative writing was devoted to religious themes. The pyramids were repositories of some of this literature. On their walls are carved hymns, prayers, magical incantations, moral exhortations, and bits of mythology, all intended to influence the gods in some way. Some of this writing reflects deep feelings and sophisticated ideas. Also written on these walls were accounts of the splendid deeds of the pharaohs who built them—clearly an early form of history which contains material not only illustrating religious thought but also describing Egyptian society. Aside from these pyramid texts there survive writings of other kinds, set down either on stone or papyrus (a writing material made from the pulp of the papyrus plant pressed into flat sheets). The Egyptians apparently liked collections of maxims and wise sayings, often presented in the form of instructions given by a father to his son or a teacher to his pupil. Lyric

clearly. In all its forms, Egyptian art mirrors what may be the keystone of Egyptian civilization: the ability to work for long ages with set forms and subjects without loss of freshness and vitality. These artists created for eternity in full confidence that the existing order was the right order. Their work mirrors a stable, unemotional, proud people, impressed by what they had achieved and eager to maintain it.

Architecture was the queen of all the arts in Egypt, most of the other forms serving to adorn it. Architects worked in many materials, including mud, reeds, brick, and wood, but the most monumental work was in stone. The first flowering of stonework occurred in the early years of the Old Kingdom and was devoted chiefly to tomb building, which reached its apogee in the construction of the pyramids. The pyramid of Khufu (about 2600 B.C.) stands as one of the great construction feats of all time. It measured 755 feet on each side at the base, falling short of a geometrically perfect square by about 8 inches of difference between the north and south sides and by less than ½ inch of difference between the east and west sides. The pyramid was 480 feet high and contained over 2 million blocks of stone averaging 2½ tons each but weighing as much as 30 tons. The outside of the structure was covered with polished stone. Most of the stone was precut, probably with copper saws and wedges, in quarries many miles away and floated down the Nile to the pyramid site, a procedure that entailed tremendous planning. The huge blocks were probably elevated into position up dirt ramps built alongside the pyramid. The labor was performed by hand with almost no mechanical aid. The passages and rooms that honeycomb the interior were skillfully vaulted. Pyramid building continued for many centuries, but later architects never equaled those of the Old Kingdom. Shifting con-

poems were written, and laments expressing disgust with the world circulated in difficult times. Perhaps most appealing today are the marvelous tales of fancy and romance recounting the adventures of travelers, shipwrecked sailors, and soldiers. On the whole, Egyptian literature is gay and confident in mood. It is more varied and versatile than Mesopotamian literature but less profound; the Mesopotamians never developed lyric poetry, romances, and tales of fancy, but the Egyptians produced nothing comparable to the *Epic of Gilgamesh.*

It is through the visual arts that the character and quality of the Egyptian genius shows most cepts of immortality militated against such massive, complex undertakings as the pyramids at Gizeh.

Although the surviving evidence is not so impressive as the pyramids, it seems quite certain that architects had arrived at the basic forms for temples and palaces by the end of the Old Kingdom; by the Middle Kingdom they were building impressive structures. The basic temple style was the hypostyle hall, consisting of a roof on columns. Typically a high-ceilinged central hall was flanked by side halls, each covered with a roof on columns shorter than the central hall's. The builders achieved splendid artistic effects by modeling their columns after plants — the palm tree, the lotus plant, the papyrus plant, the reed. Within the temple, numerous chambers were grouped to serve as the sanctuary, which was the living place of the god. Before the temple was an open court surrounded by a columned portico and entered by a massive gateway. In the center of the court often stood an obelisk in honor of the sun god. The palaces of the pharaohs were undoubtedly as splendid as the temples and probably utilized the same basic architectural forms.

Egypt's sculptors matched her architects in skill. At a very early date sculptural styles became fixed, and they changed little over most of her history. Sculpture was the handmaiden of religion. The chief subjects of three-dimensional works were the gods, the pharaohs, their families, and their companions, the statues being intended for tombs and temples. Human forms were usually massive, stiff, unemotional portrayals following fixed proportions, but the face was another matter. Here the sculptor tried to show feeling and purpose: the power of a god, the majesty of a pharaoh, the devotion of a royal servant. He was concerned not with realistic portrayal of a particular individual but with a semblance of the perfection that the individual embodied. Thus the face of a typical statue gazes straight out at the viewer as an embodiment of an ideal. Although the sculptor worked within highly conventionalized canons, each face is different — a reflection of the dynamic quality of the Egyptian achievement in art.

Egyptian sculptors were also skilled at relief work. Inside the tombs and on the pillars and walls of temples, endless series of scenes tell us more about daily life in Egypt than does all Egyptian writing. Again, the sculptor seldom tried to be realistic. He let the space he had determine the size and shape of his figures, and he often used conventional designs to represent objects. The human shapes are distorted, the feet and faces usually being shown in profile while the main trunk of the body faces the viewer. Many of the reliefs were painted to heighten the effect. Painting, most of which survives in tombs, bears a striking similarity to relief work in terms of subject matter and form. The artist sketched an outline of the scene to be pictured, often in red, and then filled it in with strong colors of one tone.

The Egyptians made advances in technology and practical science that rivaled the work of the Mesopotamians. They recorded a great deal of information about the movement of the stars, from which they developed an accurate time reckoning system based on the annual appearance of the star Sirius and a calendar of twelve thirty-day months plus five days added at the end of each year. They developed a system of numbers that permitted them to perform basic arithmetic functions and to calculate areas and volumes. Egyptian scientists accumulated considerable information about the properties of metals and about plant and animal life. In medicine they developed surgical techniques and learned to use a wide range of drugs. Their understanding of anatomy was extensive, undoubtedly a result of observations made in the process of mummifying the dead. Egyptian medicine was far in advance of that of other Near Eastern people. However, like the Mesopotamians, the Egyptians had little interest in pursuing knowledge about nature for its own sake. Once they had found a practical solution for a problem of engineering, metallurgy, or medicine, they sought no further. Religion provided them with the basic answers about the fundamental secrets of nature.

By about 1750 B.C. a new day was dawning in the Near East, in large part because of the amazing achievements that had occurred in the unique environment of the Tigris-Euphrates and

Nile valleys during the preceding two millennia. As we have seen, the peoples who mastered those valleys invented higher civilization. By 1750 B.C., the wonders they had wrought began to influence a wider world, and so our focus must shift beyond the river valleys. But the shifting scene must not hide the fundamental heritage prepared by the Mesopotamians and the Egyptians during the centuries stretching from 4000 B.C. to 1750 B.C.

Suggested Reading

Overview

Will Durant, *Our Oriental Heritage* (*The Story of Civilization*, Vol. I, 1935).

*Sabatino Moscati, *The Face of the Ancient Orient* (Anchor).

Jacquetta Hawkes, *The First Great Civilizations* (1973).

*James Mellaart, *The Earliest Civilizations of the Near East* (McGraw).

*Chester G. Starr, *Early Man: Prehistory and the Civilizations of the Ancient Near East* (Oxford).

*W. W. Hallo and W. K. Simpson, *The Ancient Near East: A History* (Harcourt Brace Jovanovich). This and the preceding five titles will provide a broad survey of the material covered in this chapter in varying degrees of detail.

*C. W. Ceram, *Gods, Graves, and Scholars: The Story of Archaeology* (2nd ed., Bantam). A splendid introduction to a science that has contributed greatly to our understanding of ancient Near Eastern history.

*Ignace J. Gelb, *A Study of Writing* (rev. ed., Phoenix). An invaluable guide to a subject critical to man's ability to develop higher civilizations.

Paleolithic and Neolithic Cultures

*Robert J. Braidwood, *Prehistoric Man* (8th ed., Scott Foresman).

Richard E. Leakey and Roger Lewis, *Origins* (1977). These two books will provide good introductions to the diverse and always changing interpretations of human prehistory.

*Wayne M. Bledsoe, ed., *The Advent of Civilization* (Heath). An excellent collection of essays by leading authorities on the problem of transition to higher civilization.

Mesopotamia and Egypt: Political History

*H. W. F. Saggs, *The Greatness That Was Babylon: A Sketch of Ancient Civilization of the Tigris-Euphrates Valley* (Mentor). The best general survey of Mesopotamian civilization, providing a good summary of political history and topical discussions of social, economic, and cultural developments.

*Alan H. Gardiner, *Egypt of the Pharaohs* (Galaxy). A well-organized survey of Egyptian political history.

*H. Frankfort, *Kingship and the Gods: A Study of Ancient Near Eastern Religion as the Integration of Society and Nature* (Phoenix). A brilliant study of the nature of Mesopotamian political institutions and the forces that shaped them.

*John A. Wilson, *The Culture of Ancient Egypt* (Phoenix). A perceptive analysis of the interaction between political and religious life in ancient Egypt.

Mesopotamia and Egypt: Economic and Social Life

*Georges Contenau, *Everyday Life in Babylon and Assyria* (Norton).

*Adolph Erman, *Life in Ancient Egypt*, trans. H. M. Tirard (Dover). These three works provide a wealth of detail about how people of all classes lived in ancient Mesopotamia and Egypt.

Mesopotamia and Egypt: Religion and Culture

*Henri Frankfort et al., *Before Philosophy: The Intellectual Adventure of Ancient Man* (Penguin). A series of essays summarizing the basic outlook on life which dominated thought in Mesopotamia and Egypt.

*Thorkild Jacobsen, *The Treasures of Darkness: A History of Mesopotamian Religion* (Yale).

*Henri Frankfort, *Ancient Egyptian Religion: An Interpretation* (Harper Torchbook).

Jaroslav Cérny, *Ancient Egyptian Religion* (1952). This and the preceding two titles will provide a thorough introduction to all aspects of religious ideas and practices in the river valley civilizations.

---

*Works available in paperback or inexpensive hardback editions are marked with an asterisk.

Anton Moortgat, *The Art of Ancient Mesopotamia* (1969).

K. Lange and M. Hirmer, *Egypt: Architecture, Sculpture, Painting in Three Thousand Years* (4th ed., 1968). The preceding two titles provide splendid introductions to all phases of Mesopotamian and Egyptian art; both are well illustrated.

*I. E. S. Edwards, *The Pyramids of Egypt* (2nd ed., Penguin). A fascinating description of these marvelous structures, characterized by its clarity and grasp of technical details.

*Otto Neugebauer, *The Exact Sciences in Antiquity* (2nd ed., Dover).

Henry Hodges, *Technology in the Ancient World* (1970). This and the preceding volume provide full details on the Mesopotamian and Egyptian accomplishment in science and technology.

Sources

The Epic of Gilgamesh: Prose Version, trans. Nancy Sandars (Penguin).

James B. Pritchard, ed., *Ancient Near Eastern Texts Relating to the Old Testament* (1955). A splendid collection of literature representing the accomplishments of the Mesopotamians as well as other peoples of the ancient Near East.

*Miriam Lichtheim, *Ancient Egyptian Literature: A Book of Readings*, Vol. I: *The Old and Middle Kingdoms* (California).

Joseph Kaster, *Wings of the Falcon: Life and Thought in Ancient Egypt* (1968). These two works offer a rich sampling of Egyptian literature which will illuminate some of the ideas and values that animated Egyptian society.

2

THE DIFFUSION OF NEAR EASTERN CIVILIZATION, 1750–800 B.C.

By the beginning of the second millennium B.C., the institutions, techniques, and ideas that had been formed in the river valleys during the preceding two thousand years had already begun to spread outward. For about the next thousand years, the process of cultural diffusion quickened and became the central theme in Near Eastern history. As a result, the zone of higher civilization was considerably expanded, and new peoples came to share both the fruits and the burdens of civilization with the Mesopotamians and the Egyptians.

1. INVASIONS AND DIFFUSION

Cultural diffusion in this era was a complex process. Traders, travelers, soldiers, and diplomats were prime carriers of ideas and techniques. Imitation of the superior ways of the river valley civilizations by peoples long settled on their fringes was common. Especially important as a catalytic force was the impact of invaders intruding into the civilized zone to upset the existing order and create new states eager to match the glories of Mesopotamia and Egypt. The invaders washed over the Near East in two great waves, the first about 1800 B.C. and the second about 1200 B.C. Each resulted in a major political realignment.

Two groups of people spearheaded the invasions. One was the Semitic-speaking inhabitants of the Arabian Desert, with whom we are already familiar as intruders into Mesopotamia prior to 2000 B.C. After 1800 B.C. these vigorous, seminomadic desert dwellers continued to pour out of the desert to play a major role in the history of northern Mesopotamia, Syria, Palestine, and Egypt. The other people were the Indo-Europeans, who were newcomers in the Near East. Although some have argued that these newcomers (sometimes designated as Aryans) represented a physical type contrasting sharply with the more ancient inhabitants of the Near East, the only sure significance of the term "Indo-European" is linguistic. The newcomers brought with them a new language from which later evolved Sanskrit, Persian, Greek, Latin, and most modern European languages. The Indo-Europeans moved into the Near East from the Eurasian steppes north of the great mountain chain that stretches across Europe and Asia to divide each into two parts. By 2000 B.C. they had developed a settled agricultural life in their homeland, but their general cultural level was far below that of most Near Eastern peoples. In only one sense did they have the upper hand: a superior military system, based on horse-drawn chariots and a skilled warrior class, which ultimately permitted them to establish political dominance over extensive areas of the Near East.

Beginning about 2000 B.C., the Indo-Europeans began to move southward from their ancient homeland on an immense front. Their impact was felt in Central Europe, Italy, Greece and the Aegean Islands, Iran, and India. Their first settlements in the Near East were concentrated in a belt stretching from the upper Tigris-Euphrates valleys westward into Asia Minor, where the newcomers established a series of small principalities led by petty warlords. Gradually, these principalities coalesced and expanded by conquering native populations to create large kingdoms modeled on the river valley monarchies, especially the Amorite Empire of Hammurabi. One group, the Kassites, first established in the mountainous area east of the Tigris, crushed the Amorite Empire in about 1600 B.C. and established a domination over Mesopotamia that lasted four centuries. In the upper Tigris-Euphrates area the Mitanni built a strong kingdom. The Hittites occupied eastern Asia Minor and began to thrust to the east and the south. Amidst this shifting scene there was a considerable movement of Semites, particularly into Syria and Palestine, where the invaders established several flourishing city-states. In that area also emerged the Hyksos, perhaps a mixture of Semites and Indo-Europeans, whose attacks on Egypt ended the Middle Kingdom.

The era following these disturbances (about 1600–1200 B.C.) witnessed the establishment of stability in the Near East, with these new kingdoms playing a major role. In the process, the new masters absorbed major elements from the techniques, cultures, and religions of the old civilizations. As a result, not only was higher civilization extended over a much larger area but also some of the new peoples were able to rival the old as major forces in the civilized world. The main foci of this new order were the Kassite kingdom, the Hittite kingdom, Egypt, and the island of Crete. Of the Kassites, little need be said; their role in Mesopotamia was both uneventful and undistinguished, although a high level of civilization continued there as a source of imitation for many other peoples. More needs to be said about the other three centers.

2. THE EGYPTIAN AND HITTITE EMPIRES, 1600–1200 B.C.

Egypt was thrust into a new role as a result of her reaction to the Hyksos invasion. The Hyksos' presence lasted about two centuries (ca. 1750–1580 B.C., a period called the Second Intermediate Period). Although Hyksos kings claimed the powers of the pharaohs (they are counted as the Fourteenth, Fifteenth, and Sixteenth Dynasties), they never in fact ruled more than the Delta region. Most of Upper Egypt escaped their control, although considerable chaos existed there as a result of the collapse of effective central government. The chief result of Hyksos rule was a revulsion against foreigners in Egypt, which eventually generated a revolt led by the princes of Thebes, who established the Seventeenth Dynasty. Revolt turned quickly to a war of liberation and then a crusade to smash the hated "shepherd kings," as the Egyptians contemptuously called the Hyksos rulers, on their home base in Palestine. Ahmose I (ca. 1580–1546 B.C.), founder of the Eighteenth Dynasty, crowned this resurgence with a crushing defeat of the Hyksos in Palestine. His reign opened a third period of glory in Egypt's history — the Egyptian Empire or New Kingdom (1550–1280 B.C.).

During the first century of the Eighteenth Dynasty, a succession of able pharaohs devoted their energies to restoring internal order, "cleansing" the land of the taint of foreign domination and reestablishing the ancient system, and they succeeded remarkably well. The administrative machine, agricultural regime, tax system, foreign trade connections, religious order, and artistic and intellectual life all revived in patterns closely parallel to those of the Old and Middle Kingdoms. Especially notable was the religious fervor of the age, which manifested itself in the worship of the sun god, Amon-Ra, whose priests became ever more powerful.

Amid the restoration, there was a new factor at work, challenging the Egyptians' long-standing sense of superiority: a haunting fear of new invasions. The first pharaohs of the Eighteenth Dynasty responded to this sense of insecurity by conducting raids to the south and into Syria-Palestine. These raids not only restored confidence but also demonstrated that the exploitation of foreigners could be profitable. Fear, pride, greed, and internal strength slowly combined to breed imperialism.

Thutmose III (1484–1447 B.C.) launched the

policy of conquest and occupation of foreign lands. He led a series of brilliantly executed campaigns into Syria-Palestine, Nubia, and Libya that crushed all resistance to Egyptian domination. The Egyptians had learned the use of the horse and chariot from the Hyksos, so that their armies proved more than equal to the foreign forces they met. Thutmose's diplomats made Egypt's might felt beyond the area of actual conquest, forcing powers such as the Hittites, Mitanni, Kassites, and Assyrians to seek to remain on friendly terms with her. He marshaled Egypt's internal resources, both material and human, to support the enlarged army, and he established an administration to ensure Egyptian domination over conquered lands. For a century Thutmose's successors pursued his policy and kept Egypt the dominant power in the Near East.

Successful imperialism brought Egypt a new period of magnificence. Her government reached peak efficiency in exercising absolute control over the population. Agriculture and trade, coupled with heavy tribute extracted from foreign subjects, produced unprecedented prosperity. Artistic and intellectual life blossomed again, inspired by pride in Egypt's power and supported by her great wealth. The greatest landmarks of Egyptian artistic vigor were magnificent temples built at Luxor and Karnak in honor of Amon-Ra, the chief god at this time. Like the pyramids built a thousand years earlier, these giant pillared structures, brilliantly decorated with carvings and paint, illustrate the Egyptian genius for building. However, artists looked back to earlier times for models, thereby maintaining the static quality in Egyptian art.

Nevertheless, the cultural activity of the New Kingdom kept alive and vital an ancient and rich cultural tradition. And the influences of that culture were felt in a positive way throughout the eastern Mediterranean world. In Nubia huge temples were built in the Egyptian architectural style in honor of Egyptian gods; on their walls were written prayers and hymns in the Egyptian language. In Syria and Palestine artisans began to imitate Egyptian styles and techniques in the manufacturing of pottery, metalwork, and jewelry. The petty princes of this area, many of whom were educated at the Egyptian court, aped

the royal style of the pharaohs, as is evident in the considerable body of diplomatic correspondence that has survived from the period (the Amarna letters, discovered in 1887 in the ruins of that city). Egyptian manufactured products were exported in quantity to Mesopotamia, the Hittite kingdom, and Crete. Here was cultural diffusion at work.

Despite the successes of the New Kingdom, imperialism had its price. One burden arose from controlling conquered peoples and protecting the imperial frontiers from outsiders. Egypt sought to govern her conquered subjects by a policy which permitted native rulers to continue in power under the terms of treaties which called for pledges of loyalty, regular tribute, and hostages to be held in Egypt as security for peace. She tried to hold these intricate alliances together by establishing garrisons abroad, organizing periodic displays of military might, and sending diplomats abroad to monitor the semi-independent princes. The system demanded constant vigilance, for each subject prince was a potential rebel. Particularly dangerous was the encouragement given to these princes by foreign powers who feared Egypt's might. For the Egyptians learned that expansionism did not assure safety from foreigners; indeed, it increased their hostility and invited their attacks. Holding her empire thus imposed on her the burden of foreign wars against formidable enemies.

A second problem emerged internally. The demands of war caused an increasing regimentation of the lower classes by the pharaoh's government. The concerns of empire distracted the pharaohs from careful attention to the welfare of their subjects. Their officials grew increasingly heartless and grasping. Especially rich and powerful were the priests of Amon-Ra, who amassed immense wealth and even challenged the authority of the pharaoh for the right to approach the gods. New ideas and styles of life, often brought in by foreigners, raised questions about the validity of ancient ways. Excessive wealth vulgarized life and eroded long-established social values. Tensions and doubts mounted in a society long accustomed to stability and respect for time-honored traditions.

These problems plunged the New Kingdom

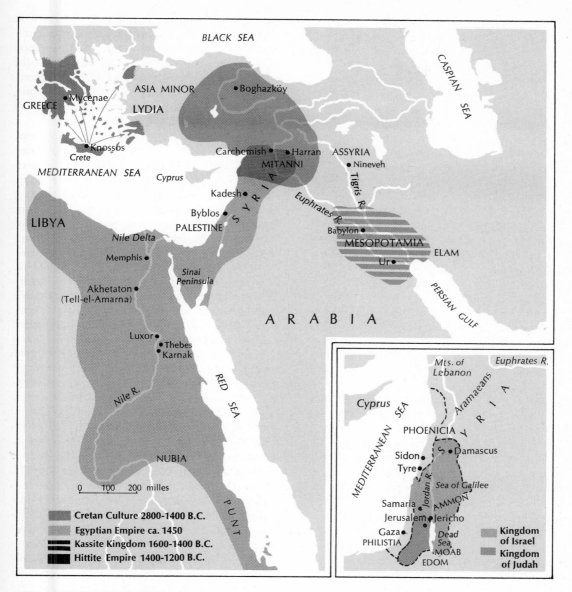

THE ANCIENT NEAR EAST, CA. 1450 B.C.

into a crisis about 1400 B.C. Egypt's foreign subjects, especially in Palestine and Syria, became more difficult to control. In that area, already restive subject princes were encouraged to revolt by a formidable external foe, the Hittites. Of all the "new" peoples who emerged from the Indo-

European invasions, the Hittites enjoyed the most success. Their history began in eastern Asia Minor about 1800 B.C., when invading Indo-European warlords imposed their rule on the natives of the area and formed a series of small Hittite kingdoms. By about 1600 B.C., sev-

Akhenaton with his wife, Nefertiti, and one of their daughters are shown making an offering to Aton, represented by the sun disc pouring its rays on the worshipers. The artistic style is much more natural-istic and free than the traditional Egyptian style. *Photo: The Metropolitan Museum of Art*

eral of these were united into a consolidated kingdom with its capital at Hattusas (modern Boghazköy in Turkey). The unified kingdom developed an advanced culture, brought to light by modern excavations of Boghazköy and by the decipherment of Hittite writing. Hittite political institutions, religion, literature, and art were strongly influenced by Mesopotamian models; the Hittite kingdom was a cultural outpost of an older civilization and a prime example of cultural diffusion. But the Hittites did add native elements to what they borrowed.

Once the Hittites had established a firm base in Asia Minor, they were able to expand their influences to the south and the east. They drew the Mittani into their sphere of influence and attacked the northern fringes of the Egyptian Empire in Syria. By 1400 B.C., they were actively engaged in encouraging and supporting rebellion among Egypt's numerous subject states throughout Syria and Palestine. Their presence threatened disaster for the Egyptian Empire.

At the critical moment of test, Egypt was torn by an internal crisis, brought on by the accession in about 1375 B.C. of the Pharaoh Amenhotep IV, an intriguing individual who sought to solve the internal tensions mounting in Egyptian society by instituting a new religion based on the worship of the sun god Aton. By Amenhotep's order, Aton was decreed the sole god of Egypt, master of the universe, the cause of all things, and the only deity to be worshiped. To dramatize his break with the old order, Amenhotep IV changed his name to Akhenaton (= It pleases Aton) and abandoned the old capital at Thebes for a new one called Akhetaton (modern Tell el Amarna). The worship of the old gods was forbidden, their temples destroyed, and their priests demoted. New rituals and a new art, fresh and naturalistic, were developed to honor and portray Aton. Akhenaton, his beautiful Queen Nefertiti, and his five daughters were deeply involved in the new cult and became symbols of a renunciation of imperialism, ostentatious wealth, bureaucracy, and staid modes of thought and expression.

A storm of protest, led by the priests of Amon-Ra, broke over Egypt and for a decade consumed the energy of all society. This reaction doomed the reform. Even before Akhenaton's death (about 1365 B.C.), his foes had forced him to abandon his reforms. His successor, Tutankhamon, sealed the reaction by a vigorous restoration of the old order in religion, art, and

Akhenaton the Enigma

Every student of history must learn to recognize generalizations about the past and to view them with a healthy skepticism. One such generalization appears in the section of this text on Akhenaton, where it is argued that he was an innovator seeking to move a tradition-bound, proud, self-centered society wallowing in wealth and power into a new world, larger and more complex than the accustomed one. But was this enigmatic figure a leader of this order? A quick glance at the surviving portraits of him may even raise some doubts: His long-faced, pot-bellied, thick-legged figure does not bespeak vigorous, forward-looking leadership. Indeed, not all who have studied his career accept him as he is presented in this book.

Akhenaton's contemporaries were extremely harsh on him. To most of them, he was a heretic who denied the ancient gods in his pursuit of a false deity. His defection bred internal strife and external disaster, as one would expect. The other gods, especially the almighty Amon-Ra whose worship had become dominant in Egypt in the two centuries prior to Akhenaton's reign, would surely display their anger. Even before the end of his reign, Akhenaton's mother, Tiy, took the lead in halting his religious reforms and restoring the old order. The pharaoh spent his last years in isolation at his holy city of Akhetaton, while a co-ruler was installed at Thebes to represent the real authority in Egypt. After his death the very name of the "criminal Akhenaton" was dropped from the list of pharaohs, and all traces of his religious ideas were erased from the books and chiseled from the stones (with the exception of some tombs at Akhetaton). Not until these tombs were unearthed in the nineteenth century was the existence of Amenhotep IV, renamed Akhenaton, even known to historians.

The initial reaction to the discovery of Akhenaton's existence and his religious ideas was to exalt his role in history. The American Egyptologist James Henry Breasted gave wide popularity to this view. He saw the pharaoh as a sensitive, intelligent man of great individual talent with a new religious vision for which he became a prophet. Steeped in the trends of religious development working in imperial Egypt and offended by the pedestrian, routine religious concepts and practices represented by the traditional priesthood, his seminal thought drew him to monotheism. The unlimited power that was his as pharaoh prompted him to impose this exalted religion on his subjects. The formulation of the new faith was his personal achievement, a witness to his intelligence and depth of feeling. Here then was the first monotheist. Breasted's Akhenaton soon promoted others to see the first monotheist as the teacher of Moses, whose career in Egypt came about a century after his reign. In *Moses and Monotheism,* Sigmund Freud argued that Akhenaton was really the progenitor of Hebrew monotheism.

Not all scholars are persuaded that the evidence points where Breasted and Freud thought. Some have found evidence that Akhenaton was an irresponsible, bigoted religious zealot who insisted on imposing his religious "fads" on a populace that had no desire for innovation and when this did not work withdrew to his own little paradise where he could work his will on his docile retainers, leaving the empire to drift toward ruin. Others see him as demented; perhaps he was a victim of disease, since recent studies of his mummified body suggest he suffered a pituitary disorder that led to physical and mental deterioration. The most careful studies of Akhenaton's religious ideas strongly suggest that he was not a monotheist, but rather the propounder of a faith that proclaimed a new god for the pharaoh to worship while insisting that everyone else worship the pharaoh. This may have been a political ploy: the restoration of the pharaoh's absolute power, the focusing of attention on royal splendor as a key to control over the empire, the curbing of the power of the rich priests. These basically conservative goals would make the pharaoh not even a heretic, much less a religious revolutionary.

Like all significant men in history, Akhenaton will undoubtedly continue to provoke differing viewpoints. Each one must draw his own conclusions on the basis of all information he can gather about one of the first "individuals" to emerge in human history.

politics. Although the forces at work in this strange interlude are by no means clear, the violence of the reaction against Akhenaton suggests that he had posed a fundamental question to Egyptian society: Was it ready to move forward with the times or remain backward looking? Akhenaton tried to direct his people toward the worship of one almighty god who demanded moral goodness in place of continued obeisance to a welter of gods who asked material offerings. He was trying to reduce the power of a rapacious priesthood and to divert intellectual and artistic talents into fresh channels leading beyond a sterile worship of the past. In short, he sought in a new religion a means of arousing Egyptians to take the lead in exploiting the more cosmopolitan currents that were running strong in the Near East in this era of the mixing and mingling of cultures.

However noble were the motives that inspired Akhenaton, the disturbances caused by his reforms were fatal to the Egyptian Empire. Neglect of military affairs during the internal crisis encouraged widespread revolt in Syria and Palestine. Unfortunately for Egypt, Hittite power was at its peak at this critical moment. Under their able king Suppilulimas (1375–1355 B.C.), the Hittites openly attacked and promoted rebellion everywhere in Egypt's holdings. The early rulers of the Nineteenth Dynasty, especially Seti and Rameses II, acted with some success to redress the balance in Syria and Palestine, but at a heavy price. Incessant warfare sapped the strength of both powers. Although they agreed on a peace settlement in about 1270 B.C. that assigned each a sphere of influence in the embattled area, both empires were approaching the end of their greatness.

Decisive in the final destiny of these empires was a new wave of Indo-European invaders, especially formidable because they possessed iron weapons, who spilled over Asia Minor, the Aegean Sea area, and the waterways of the eastern Mediterranean. Their assaults were abetted by new movements of Semitic nomads from the Arabian Desert. The Hittite Empire was completely destroyed about 1200 B.C. by Indo-Europeans and Semites. Egypt's fate was not quite so drastic. However, attacks from Nubians

Libyans, and the "People of the Sea," seafaring marauders probably from Asia Minor, forced her back into her old boundaries and from time to time put foreigners on her throne. These blows greatly weakened Egypt internally and limited her capacity to influence the course of Near Eastern history.

3. THE MINOAN WORLD

The diffusion of the higher civilizations originally based in the river valleys was felt as far away as the island of Crete, which witnessed a remarkable surge of creative activity during the period 2000–1400 B.C. as a result of its contacts with the centers of civilization to the east. While the Cretans owed a great deal to their borrowings from the Near East, their pattern of civilization assumed many unique features. In part this was a consequence of the contrasting physical environment. Crete was endowed with fairly reliable but limited agricultural resources. But its inhabitants had the seas. Not only did they provide the island with security from more powerful neighbors, but they also gave access to a wider world from which the Cretans could buy and borrow products and ideas to enrich their lives. The people of Crete advanced to a high level of civilization as a consequence of their ability to turn the seas to their advantage at a moment in history when the processes of diffusion were particularly powerful. Their achievement was of special importance in history because their civilization provided a link between the ancient Near East and the world to the west—especially Greece—where new peoples would eventually add fresh elements to civilized life.

The foundations upon which the development of higher civilization in Crete was based lie in the late fourth millennium B.C., when a flourishing neolithic farming culture developed over a wide area embracing Crete, Greece, the Aegean islands, and Asia Minor. This pattern of life apparently reached Crete about 3000 B.C., probably imported by invaders from Asia Minor; it dominated life on the island for the next thousand years. Life centered in agricultural villages. There was change, however, generated in part by the creative talents of the Cretans themselves and in part by newcomers who continued to migrate to Crete from the north. Technical skills advanced steadily, especially with the introduction of bronze. Larger social groupings evolved, permitting more effective farming and a high level of specialized craftsmanship in pottery and metal working. Most important of all, the Cretans learned to sail the seas. As a consequence, they came in contact with Egypt and Asia. These contacts resulted in an influx of techniques and ideas which permitted the Cretans to outstrip the peoples with whom they had shared a relatively simple neolithic culture.

The emergence of Crete as a leading center of advanced civilization came about 2000 B.C. That civilization has been named Minoan by modern historians, after a legendary Cretan king whom the Greeks called Minos. The new age was heralded by the appearance on Crete of several full-fledged city-states, especially Knossos, Phaistos, and Mallia. These city-states were centered on magnificent palaces, whose ruins have been excavated only within this century and from which we derive most of our knowledge of Minoan civilization. Not only do these palaces bespeak great wealth and technical ability, but they also give evidence of consolidation of society under the direction of kings who had perfected techniques for administering larger areas and numbers of people. The city-states coexisted apparently without any serious conflicts; and their energies were devoted largely to overseas trading — in Egypt, Syria, Asia Minor, the Aegean islands, the Greek mainland, and even the western Mediterranean — and to the manufacturing pursuits that supplied this trade. The Minoan thrust into the Greek peninsula was particularly strong and marked a significant period in Greek history to which we will return in a later chapter.

With time, Knossos seems to have outstripped the other cities of Crete and established dominance over them peacefully. Knossos reached the peak of her power between 1600 and 1400 B.C., when she dominated Crete and held sway over a wide circle of the eastern Mediterranean. Then suddenly about 1400 B.C. the city was badly damaged, as were other important Minoan cities, and Minoan culture began to decline. Some evidence suggests a disastrous earthquake as the cause of the destruction, but there are also signs of an invasion of Crete by a Greek people called the Mycenaeans, who had been powerfully influenced by the Minoans.

The nature of Minoan civilization must be derived chiefly from archeological remains. Not long after 2000 B.C., the Minoans did develop their own unique system of writing which modern scholars call Linear A; this writing has not yet been deciphered. Linear A was replaced in about 1450 B.C. by another system, called Linear B; its recent decipherment has proved that it is an early form of the Greek language, perhaps brought to Crete by invaders from mainland Greece. The documents written in Linear B, chiefly business records, provide only limited information about Minoan civilization.

From the evidence we have, we know that a well-developed system of monarchy had developed based upon orderly recordkeeping and bureaucratic administration. Royal power appears to have depended on religious sanction and on the wealth the kings derived from overseas trade, rather than on military strength. A powerful nobility grouped itself around the kings and helped uphold royal authority. A productive agriculture sustained society, but trade and industry contributed considerable wealth. Innumerable artisans plied their talents in the workshops of the palaces and the cities. Especially skilled were the potters and the metalworkers. Merchants carried these goods abroad in fleets owned by the kings and brought back a variety of raw materials and manufactured goods. Little is known about the condition of the lower classes, but the nobility enjoyed a luxurious life in fine city houses. The Minoans worshiped a variety of gods representing the forces of nature, chiefly the goddess of fertility, whose life-giving powers were evoked by prayer, ceremony, and sacrifice. Religion played an important but not dominant part in Minoan civilization. No great temples were built, nor was a numerous priesthood maintained; worship was carried out on hillsides and in groves with considerable popular participation. There was a belief in an afterlife and some attention was given to the care of the dead, but never on the scale that occurred in Egypt.

The genius of the Minoans was in the arts, which also convey best the character of their civilization. Their considerable architectural skills were lavished on palaces and private dwellings rather than temples and tombs. The immense palace at Knossos was a marvel of technical ability and mixed architectural forms. Palaces and houses were decorated with paintings and carvings that emphasized nature and humanity. Often the artist sought to capture the action of living things in his work, so that Minoan art is mobile, free of stylization, intense, energy-filled. Minoan decorated pottery reflects a fine sense of form, great ingenuity in decoration, and love of color. In its general character, Minoan art reflects a civilization that was gay, worldly, lacking in fear, eager for change, pleasure loving, and amazingly free. Its spirit contrasts sharply with that underlying Mesopotamian and Egyptian civilization, although the Minoans borrowed considerably from both. It points not east but west toward a world yet to come — to Greece and Europe.

4. THE ERA OF SMALL NATIONS, 1200–800 B.C.: PHOENICIANS AND ARAMEANS

The collapse of the Hittite and Egyptian empires around 1200 B.C., coupled with the decline of Minoan power, left the Near East without a dominant power center for about four centuries. Several small groups seized the opportunity to establish their independence. The changed political order emerging between 1200 and 800 B.C. did not, however, constitute a break in the broad pattern of historical development. The diffusion of culture remained the basic characteristic of the era. As the small nations struggled to establish and maintain themselves, they borrowed from Mesopotamian and Egyptian cultures. Their efforts resulted in the continued spread over the Near East of ideas and institutions that had originated in the great river valleys.

Two small nations stand out especially as borrowers and disseminators of the older civilizational patterns — the Phoenicians and the Arameans. Both were Semitic in origin, the products of the numerous migrations from the Arabian Desert that had been in progress for many centuries before 1200 B.C. These migrants were repeatedly conquered and strongly influenced by Mesopotamians, Egyptians, and Hittites. Consequently, by 1200 B.C. they were already highly civilized peoples, and when Egyptian and Hittite power collapsed, they were able to establish political independence. The Phoenicians, located in the narrow band of territory lying between the Mediterranean Sea and the mountains of Lebanon, developed a number of independent city-states, chief of which were Byblos, Tyre, and Sidon. The Arameans were located east of the Lebanon Mountains between the northern fringes of the Arabian Desert and the Euphrates River. There they organized a number of small kingdoms, centering on Damascus, Kadesh, and Palmyra. For about four centuries, these city-states and principalities were among the chief states in the Near East. Their independence was finally crushed by the Assyrians in the eighth century B.C.

The Phoenicians and the Arameans derived most of their wealth from trading ventures. The Phoenicians took to the seas and established a virtual monopoly on trade in the Mediterranean. Their merchants carried manufactured goods from the whole Near East to the backward peoples of Greece, Italy, North Africa, Spain, and southern France, and brought the raw materials of these areas back. From these merchants many barbarian peoples got their first taste of higher civilization. The Phoenicians, not content to trade, also established colonies abroad, notably the North African city of Carthage, which became one of the leading centers of civilization in the western Mediterranean after 800 B.C. The Arameans were land traders; they exploited the trade routes that linked Egypt, Mesopotamia, Asia Minor, and points beyond. Both Phoenicians and Arameans reaped a rich reward from their trading ventures which was, in part, devoted to patronizing the arts and learning. Neither people was particularly creative, but the Phoenicians did perfect an alphabet that later served as a model for the written languages of the Mediterranean world.

5. THE ERA OF SMALL NATIONS, 1200–800 B.C.: THE HEBREWS

The most significant of the small nations for the history of Western civilization was that of the Hebrews. To do them justice in a brief account is virtually impossible, for few people have evoked greater interest or more intensive study. We are aided in telling their story by a magnificent literary record they created: their Bible (called the Old Testament in the Christian world). Composed over a long period of time out of a mixture of historical traditions, legal enactments, moral exhortations, and speculation, this book raises innumerable problems for the historian. But it does provide an historical record far superior to that produced by any other ancient Near Eastern people. The main outlines of the story it tells have been corroborated by other literary documents and by archeology, and it can be read as a serious introduction to Hebrew history.

The Hebrews originated as Semitic nomads who migrated from the Arabian Desert to Mesopotamia, perhaps as part of the Amorite movement. About 1800 B.C., roughly in the time of Hammurabi, some of these migrants, led by the patriarch Abraham, left Mesopotamia in search of a new homeland in the Syria-Palestine area. Some traditions buried in the Bible suggest that at even this early date, the wanderers had already borrowed significant religious and legal ideas from the Mesopotamians; for example, the flood story in the Bible closely parallels Mesopotamian accounts of great floods, and some aspects of Hebrew law are akin to Hammurabi's Code.

In Palestine the newcomers encountered the well-established and highly civilized Canaanites, themselves Semitic speakers, whose culture showed heavy Egyptian and Mesopotamian influences. While some Hebrews quickly adopted Canaanite civilization, others, forced to settle in semiarid parts of Palestine, retained their ancient desert way of life. Grouped into small tribes under patriarchal leaders such as Isaac and Jacob and often seminomadic, they sustained a fierce sense of independence and an egalitarian social order.

Some Hebrews made their way into Egypt to escape famines in Palestine, perhaps as part of the Hyksos invasions or as Egyptian prisoners. There they were assigned lands in the Delta region (the Biblical land of Goshen), and some, like Joseph, even enjoyed great favor in the pharaoh's court. Eventually, however, life in Egypt became intolerable, probably because the Hebrews became victims of the increasing oppression of the late Eighteenth and Nineteenth Dynasties. This set the stage for a major turning point in Hebrew history—the Exodus from Egypt, which occurred shortly before 1200 B.C.

The familiar story of the Exodus and of Moses' effective leadership of those Hebrews who fled Egypt does not need detailing here. During forty trying years spent wandering about the Sinai peninsula, Moses' followers underwent a religious experience that laid the basis for a Hebrew nation. The origins and development of Hebrew religious concepts up to the Exodus are extremely obscure and open to debate. The Bible probably distorts this development by projecting backward into this early period ideas that developed much later. It cannot be said for sure that the Hebrew tribes had a common religion during the age of the patriarchs; but at least some gave particular allegiance to Yahweh. Yahweh was a powerful and somewhat terrible nature god, capable of caring for the material needs of followers who courted his favor with sacrificial offerings and prayers. The tribes that worshiped him did admit that other gods existed. Therefore, prior to 1200 B.C. some Hebrews appear to have developed *monolatry*, that is, belief in one god for a given community while recognizing other gods proper to other groups. A true *monotheism*, that is, a religious system based on the belief that only one god exists in the universe, had to await further developments in Hebrew history. But even monolatry set the Hebrews apart, for no other Near Eastern people —with the possible exception of the ill-fated circle around Akhenaton—had as yet propounded such a belief.

During their stay in the desert, however, the followers of Moses pledged themselves to the worship of Yahweh and accepted certain ideas about that god and their relationship to him. Prompted by the inspired leadership of Moses, the Hebrews of the Exodus entered into a covenant, or contract, with Yahweh: They pledged themselves to worship only him, and in return, he promised that he would care for them under any circumstances, just as he had done during the escape from Egypt. The Hebrews also accepted from Yahweh a set of laws, enshrined in the Bible as the Ten Commandments, that were to govern the way each follower conducted himself toward Yahweh and toward his fellowmen. By the acceptance of these ideas, Moses' "mixed multitude" became a "nation," the Israelites, bound together by the exclusive worship of one god. The gradual refinement of these concepts and their adjustment to new historical situations led ultimately to the great contribution of the Hebrews to the history of the world—Judaism.

The first task to which the newly formed Hebrew nation turned was to renew the search for the Promised Land. Armed with the Ark of the Covenant, a wooden chest containing Yahweh's commands, this impoverished band turned again toward Palestine, where considerable confusion reigned in the wake of the collapse of the Egyptian and Hittite empires. Shortly after 1200 B.C., they crossed the Jordan to capture the Canaanite city of Jericho. For the next hundred and fifty years, the Hebrews devoted their energies to establishing their dominion over Palestine. Usually they were successful, although their own disunity made the task difficult. Only in periods of great crisis were they able to overcome tribal jealousies for a united effort. As their control over Palestine widened, the Hebrews enjoyed increasing prosperity. The primitive culture of desert dwellers was greatly modified by the higher culture of settled farmers, which the Hebrews borrowed from the conquered Canaanites.

The worship of Yahweh gained new adherents during the period of conquest, probably because Yahweh seemed to be fulfilling his promise to watch over the interests of those who worshiped him. The Hebrew system of law, still closely allied to the worship of Yahweh, continued to expand and to serve as a common bond among many Hebrew tribes. Another common tie developing in this era was a shared set of religious practices directed by an emerging priesthood and centering around the Ark of the Covenant, which appears to have been located at the town of Shiloh. However, Yahweh worship was still not accepted by all the Hebrews. During the period of conquest, there was a series of leaders who tried to rally backsliding Hebrews to return to the worship of Yahweh. These leaders, called "judges" in the Bible and represented by figures like Gideon, Samson, and Samuel, sought to convince the Hebrews that their many military setbacks were punishment for their failure to serve Yahweh and for their tendency to fall under the spell of the Canaanite gods, the Baals.

Although they succeeded in overpowering the Canaanites, the Hebrews eventually met a foe they could not handle so easily. Shortly after 1100 B.C., they began to clash with the Philistines, a part of the already mentioned "People of the Sea," who had settled along the Mediterranean shore of southern Palestine after having been rebuffed in an attempt to seize Egypt. By 1050 B.C., most of the Hebrews had been conquered by the Philistines. This disaster eventually proved a blessing for the Hebrews because it forced them into a political union. As a step toward ending Philistine overlordship, several Hebrew tribes agreed to accept a single king. The person they selected for that honor was Saul.

The reigns of Saul and his successors, David and Solomon (about 1020 to 930 B.C.), mark the high point of Hebrew political history. These kings smashed Philistine power and subdued many other enemies around Syria-Palestine, making the Hebrew nation the leading power in that area. A centralized government developed at Jerusalem, and diplomatic relations were established with most other nations of the Near East. Hebrew traders brought prosperity to the new kingdom. The royal court at Jerusalem patronized the arts and letters. There was occasional dissidence, often in protest against the personal conduct of the kings. Saul's jealousy of the youthful David, David's passion for other men's wives, and Solomon's heavy expenditures outraged the feelings of some Hebrews. For a time, however, the kings were able to curb the dissatisfied elements and to maintain a unified kingdom enjoying power and prestige.

The reigns of Saul, David, and Solomon repre-

sented a significant chapter in the history of
Judaism. These kings were all active champions
of Yahweh, claiming they had been anointed to
lead the Hebrews to the victory promised in the
Covenant. Nearly all Hebrews now accepted
Yahweh worship. David moved the Ark of the
Covenant to Jerusalem after he captured that city
and made it the seat of his power. Solomon
completed the process of making it the religious
center of the nation by building a splendid
temple. The ritual practices devoted to Yahweh
took on elaborate form under the guidance of an
expanded priesthood richly supported by the
kings. A body of religious writings, much of it
later to be incorporated in the final form of the
Bible, was set down at this time. Yahweh worship was becoming a full-fledged religious system.

Even while Solomon reigned in all his glory,
however, deep-seated economic, political, and
religious dissension threatened the Hebrew nation. Many Hebrews, remembering their tribal
freedom, hated the autocratic methods used by
the kings to hold the kingdom together. The old
social equality characteristic of tribal life began
to be undermined as the Hebrews became more
civilized, and a definite aristocracy emerged and
sought to subdue the masses. This social and
economic inequality was anathema to many Hebrews. As for their religion, many Hebrews
resented the non-Hebraic ideas and practices
that had slipped into the rituals at the great
temple in Jerusalem. Furthermore, they deplored
Solomon's tolerance of the religions of his many
non-Jewish wives, for such forbearance of the
alien appeared to compromise Yahweh worship.
Immediately after Solomon's death, this discontent ended the short-lived unity of the nation.
The northern part of the kingdom refused to
recognize his son as king and formed a new
kingdom called Israel, with its center at Samaria.
The southern Hebrews formed a kingdom called
Judah, under kings descended from David.

Israel and Judah proceeded steadily toward
destruction, both victims of internal disturbances and misrule that sapped their will to
resist foreign attack. In 722 B.C. Israel was destroyed by the Assyrians. Her people were carried off to captivity, to become known hence-

forth as the Ten Lost Tribes. Judah survived
until 586 B.C., when the Chaldeans captured
Jerusalem and took large numbers of Jews to
Babylon as captives. Thus ended the political independence of the ancient Israelites. The Persians did liberate some of the Babylonian captives in 538 B.C., allowing them to return to
Jerusalem and to reestablish the Jewish religious
community, but this meant only that Hebrew
priests were given permission to exercise limited authority over religious life in Palestine,
always under the supervision of Persian political
authorities.

As Hebrew political glory faded in the centuries after 900 B.C., Hebrew religious life took
on new depth. During the period of the divided
kingdoms and foreign conquests, religion became the sole force that sustained a sense of na-
tionhood and uniqueness among the harassed
Hebrews. The priests fashioned a sober, austere
cult that cut away much of the magic and superstition surrounding other Near Eastern religions. Much more significant was the fresh
reformulation of the basic concepts of Hebrew
religion by a series of powerful religious leaders
known as the *prophets*. Several of these rank
among the world's greatest spiritual spokesmen:
Elijah (ninth century), Amos and Isaiah (eighth
century), Jeremiah (seventh–sixth centuries),
Ezekiel and the anonymous second Isaiah (sixth
century), and Haggai (late sixth century). As a
group, they represent a unique type of religious
leader in the ancient Near East. They spoke forth
as individuals, often of humble origins, who
raised their voices out of personal conviction
and spiritual insight. They all proclaimed a common message that the Hebrews were abandon-
ing their covenant with Yahweh and would be
punished for their sins. Their prophecies were
based on concepts firmly rooted in Hebrew tradition, but they spoke with such passion and
such depth of spiritual understanding that collectively they formulated in nearly final form a
set of religious ideas that became the essence of
Judaism. Their reformulation of Judaism, put
into writing in the prophetic books of the Bible,
established a base for much of the religious development of the future.

First of all, the prophets proclaimed a true

monotheism. They made Yahweh the only god and denied that any other gods existed. Second, they proclaimed a whole new concept of Yahweh. He was a god outside nature, not existing in any natural object; he was a god of justice, acting according to a definite law instead of his own fancy; he was omnipotent, controlling the whole universe and causing everything in the past, present, and future to happen; he was a god with a plan for the world; his will would be worked out in the history of the world. He was a god of righteousness, pleased by those who did good, vengeful toward those who did evil. This was truly the most exalted concept of deity yet expressed in the Near East.

Third, the prophets defined a new basis for human conduct. Just as Yahweh treated men with righteousness and justice, so also must each individual treat his fellowmen according to these same principles. God had handed down to men a code of law (called the Torah) that must serve as the basis for earthly society. Transgression of the law would bring down his punishment on the offender. Decent treatment of other men became a major obligation of each Hebrew. The religion of the prophets thus emphasized ethical concepts far above ritual practices.

Finally, the prophets proclaimed that the Hebrews were the people chosen to carry out Yahweh's will on earth. No matter what disasters might befall them at a given moment, they would ultimately emerge victorious over the other peoples of the earth, and through them the one god would eventually be worshiped by all. Yahweh would aid in this venture, since it was his plan for the world, and eventually he would send a Messiah to lead the Hebrews to victory. While awaiting that final victory, the Hebrews must retain their ties with one another. If they could not all live in an independent kingdom, they could rely on their common religious beliefs as a binding tie. The Hebrew "nation" would live on as a religious community, awaiting its victory over the non-Hebrews.

By the fourth century B.C., when the ancient Near East was conquered by Alexander the Great and its civilization submitted to heavy Greek influences, the Hebrews had made no progress toward winning the world to worship of their god. Near Eastern peoples were too accustomed to a multitude of nature gods, their elaborate mythology, and splendid rituals for winning divine favor to listen to Hebrew concepts of a single almighty god living outside nature and expecting men to live by a law requiring high moral standards. But although few men then paid attention to these ideas, they had tremendous impact on later civilizations, serving as the base upon which Christianity and Islam would be built. Despite modest success in the total setting of ancient Near Eastern history, the Hebrews had written one of the great chapters in man's spiritual and moral history.

Suggested Reading

Indo-European and Semitic Invaders

V. Gordon Childe, *The Aryans: A Study of Indo-European Origins* (1926). An objective treatment of a much discussed subject.

*Sabatino Moscati, *Ancient Semitic Civilizations* (Capricorn). An excellent survey providing a balanced discussion of the role of Semitic peoples in establishing Near Eastern civilization.

The Egyptian Empire

*George Steindorff and Karl E. Seele, *When Egypt Ruled the East* (2nd ed., Phoenix). This detailed history of the period of the New Kingdom will add to the material provided by the general histories of ancient Egypt cited in Chapter 1.

Minoan Civilization

Sinclair Hood, *The Minoans: The Story of Bronze Age Crete* (1971). A brief, readable treatment solidly based on archeological evidence.

M. P. Nilsson, *Minoan-Mycenaean Religion and Its Survival in Greek Religion* (2nd ed., 1950). A clear description of the main features of Minoan religion.

Hittites, Phoenicians, and Arameans

*O. R. Guerney, *The Hittites* (2nd ed., Penguin). The best general survey of Hittite history and culture.

*C. W. Ceram, *The Secret of the Hittites: The Discovery of the Ancient Empire* (Schocken). Provides a well-balanced picture of the nature of Hittite civilization and tells a fascinating story of how it was found by archeologists.

Sabatino Moscati, *The World of the Phoenicians*, trans. Alistair Hamilton (1968). The best survey of the history of this fascinating people.

A. T. Olmstead, *History of Palestine and Syria to the Macedonian Conquest* (1939). Although somewhat out of date, this work will be helpful in describing the role of the Arameans.

Hebrews

*Stanley Cook, *Introduction to the Bible* (Penguin). This excellent study is useful in interpreting the Old Testament as a historical source.

*Harry Orlinsky, *Ancient Israel* (2nd ed., Cornell). A concise but well-done survey of the early history of the Hebrews.

*William F. Albright, *The Biblical Period from Abraham to Ezra* (Harper Torchbook). A provocative treatment by a famous archeologist that does an excellent job of reconciling archeology and the Old Testament version of Hebrew history.

Salo Wittmayer Baron, *A Social and Religious History of the Jews* (2nd ed. rev., 12 vols., 1952–67), Vol. I: *Ancient Times: To the Beginning of the Christian Era*. A masterful longer history of the ancient Hebrews.

*Roland de Vaux, *Ancient Israel: Its Life and Institutions* (2 vols., McGraw-Hill). Rich in details about Hebrew society in Old Testament times.

Th. C. Vriezen, *The Religion of Ancient Israel* (1967).

Helmer Ringgren, *Israelite Religion*, trans. D. E. Green (1966). This and the preceding title are excellent in tracing the development of ancient Judaism and highlighting its unique features.

3

THE GREAT EMPIRES:
ASSYRIA AND PERSIA, 800-300 B.C.

During the ninth century B.C., the rising might of Assyria heralded a new era in Near Eastern history. The ground had been prepared in the previous millennium for a cosmopolitan civilization and a universal political order. The diffusion of the river valley cultures had provided large numbers of men with common techniques and ideas. The formation of new political entities, even though many of them were small, had established local stability and order and had created political building blocks out of which great empires could be shaped. Expanding trade had knit distant communities together with common economic interests. These developments invited attempts at political consolidation, and adventuresome men were at hand to respond to the opportunity.

1. THE ASSYRIAN EMPIRE

The Assyrians were a people of Semitic origin who migrated out of the Arabian Desert as early as 3000 B.C. and settled on either side of the upper Tigris Valley. They eventually spread out toward the Zagros Mountains and into the plateau highlands between the Tigris and Euphrates rivers. For centuries after 3000 B.C., the main lines of their history are extremely vague. Perhaps the chief development during this period was the powerful influence exercised by Mesopotamian civilization over the Assyrians. In fact, so intimate were the cultural ties

that many historians treat the two areas as having one history. At times, such as under Sargon I and Hammurabi, the Assyrians were politically incorporated into empires based in the lower Tigris-Euphrates Valley. However, Assyria never lost her identity completely, and when the Amorite Empire declined after 1750 B.C., Assyria continued as an independent nation.

The era from 1750 to 1000 B.C. was the testing period for Assyria. In an age of general confusion, she was subjected to great pressure from beyond her borders, her location making her a constant target for the invading Kassites, Hittites, and Mitanni, all of whom assaulted Assyria at one time or another, as did new hordes of Semites from the Arabian Desert. The hardy farmers of Assyria met this challenge by subordinating all other interests to a defense of their homeland, and they developed one of the best military forces in the Near East, especially after they adopted the new iron weapons introduced in the late second millennium. The incessant struggle for survival produced a prime motive for later expansion: fear for the safety of the ancestral homeland which encouraged preventive wars against potential enemies.

In the ninth century B.C., a series of capable leaders emerged who harnessed the warlike sentiments of the tough Assyrian farmer-soldiers to launch a wide-sweeping series of raids on surrounding nations. The Hebrews, the Phoenicians, the Arameans, the Mesopotamians, the

This carving from an Assyrian royal palace represents Jehu, King of Israel, bowing before his Assyrian conqueror, King Shalmaneser III. It conveys the awe which the Assyrian rulers struck in the victims of their conquest. *Photo: The Granger Collection*

mountaineers to the north and east of Assyria, and the nomads of the northern part of the Arabian Desert all felt the lash of Assyrian might. No one was capable of standing up against the Assyrian armies, siege engines, and strong cavalry units. They increased the effectiveness of their military machine by pursuing a deliberate policy of terrorism. The annals recording their exploits are filled with some of the most incredible examples of brutality and inhumanity ever perpetrated by man in his long career of mistreating his fellowmen. Victorious Assyrian kings proclaimed their feats as a matter of course in terms such as these: flaying conquered chiefs to death, covering the walls of conquered cities with the skins of the captured populace, impaling victims on sharp poles, cutting off the ears, noses, fingers, and legs of prisoners, spanning a river with corpses so as to make a bridge, turning cities into pastures. So awesome did the Assyrian reputation become that many peoples refused to resist, preferring to "embrace the feet" of the conquerors.

These ninth-century forays were primarily tribute-collecting raids, not empire-building expeditions. They demonstrated a second powerful motive generating Assyrian expansion: the desire for a larger sweep of territory from which to exact tribute as a way of enriching life in a hard, poor land. The Assyrians were still predators, little concerned with the fate of their victims as long as they turned over their wealth. There thus began a vast flow of wealth from all over the Near East to the modest kingdom astride the Tigris, and the fortunate recipients began to adopt a grandiose style of life. Perhaps the Assyrians would have remained mere predators if the methods employed by their ninth-century rulers had been permanently successful. This was not the case. Rebellion and refusal to pay tribute occurred as soon as the Assyrian armies departed from any pillaged territory, requiring repeated expeditions that strained the never abundant Assyrian manpower resources. The system seems to have set off internal struggles for the division of the booty and bred resentment against the ruler for his distribution of the wealth produced by the new national industry. This internal disarray was so serious that during the early eighth century the raiding nearly stopped.

Shortly after 750 B.C., a ruler who was the real founder of the Assyrian Empire appeared. He was Tiglath-Pileser III (745–727 B.C.), and his policy was twofold: Internally, he imposed a new order by strengthening the hand of the king against the great nobles who had been troublesome earlier. Externally, he initiated a policy of establishing permanent, organized, systematic control over conquered subjects. A succession of able kings continued his policy from 722 to 631 B.C.: Sargon II, Sennacherib, Esarhaddon, and Ashurbanipal III. These five rulers, several of whose arrogant visages still stare out from the remarkable stone reliefs wrought by Assyrian artists and all of whom left boastful accounts of their exploits, built the first genuinely ecumenical empire in the Near East.

Tiglath-Pileser III and Sargon II shaped the heartland of the empire. They led the Assyrian armies on a series of expeditions that destroyed the chief political powers from southern Mesopotamia around the great sweep of the Tigris-Euphrates Valley into Syria and Palestine. Only the tiny kingdom of Judah escaped, but at a terrible price in tribute. Assyrian governors were sent to rule the conquered lands and ensure the delivery of tribute. The central administration in Assyria was enlarged to supervise the conduct of imperial affairs, and effective means of communication were devised to keep the royal court informed of affairs in the empire. The army stood ready to crush all signs of resistance, continuing its brutal habits.

Once this base of power was established in the Fertile Crescent, Sennacherib, Esarhaddon, and Ashurbanipal devoted their energies to dealing with outsiders who insisted on interfering with Assyrian rule. Egypt was attacked and forced to accept overlordship. The last remnants of local independence in southern Mesopotamia were crushed. Assyrian influences were extended into Asia Minor. Semibarbaric peoples in northern Arabia, the Zagros Mountains, and the highlands to the north of Assyria were beaten into submission. By 650 B.C. the whole civilized Near East accepted for the first time a single master, the great king of Assyria, "ruler of the four rims of the world."

The Assyrian state, however, was not so strong as its size indicated. The terrorism had aroused an irreconcilable hatred among subject peoples, nowhere better reflected than in the writings of the later Hebrew prophets. Constant warfare depleted Assyria's manpower and eventually forced her armies to rely on levies from conquered subjects, who made much less efficient soldiers. Some of the later Assyrian rulers were more inclined to enjoy the fruits of victory than to exercise the active leadership needed to hold their empire together. Worst of all, Assyria encountered the plague of all empire builders— enemies beyond the frontier, aroused by the threat of absorption. Assyria's enemies included the Medes, living east of the Zagros Mountains; Semitic tribes pushing into the lower Tigris-Euphrates Valley; and barbarians pouring into territory north of her.

The Assyrians began to suffer setbacks during the time of Ashurbanipal; they mounted in fury after his death in 631 B.C. The Egyptians successfully revolted and caused discontent among the Assyrian subjects in Syria and Palestine. A Semitic group, the Chaldeans, raised the standard of revolt in southern Mesopotamia. Assyria committed most of her strength to checking this particular liberation movement, weakening herself beyond repair. Then the Medes, who had learned a great deal by imitating Assyrian military techniques, struck out of the east. In 612 B.C. they and the Chaldeans destroyed the Assyrian capital at Nineveh. Assyria's power vanished immediately, leaving her empire at the mercy of her many foes.

No one in the Near East lamented her passing. The Hebrew prophet Nahum spoke for all the world: "All who hear the news of you clap their hands at your downfall." However, Assyria's bad reputation should not conceal her contributions to history. She broke new ground in trying to create a single state out of many different peoples. Her attempt to erect a centralized monarchy was to be imitated by others. She wiped out many artificial political boundaries that kept small groups at sword's point. She at least briefly imposed a beneficial peace on the Near East, protecting it for nearly three centuries against barbarians who might have destroyed its civilization had they succeeded in seizing control.

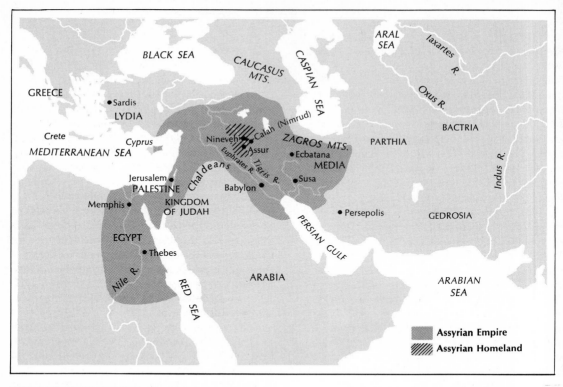

THE ASSYRIAN EMPIRE, CA. 662 B.C.

Economically, the Assyrian regime had significant results. The Assyrians themselves added very little to Near Eastern economy, but they encouraged trade and assisted it by breaking down barriers against the movement of goods. People like the Arameans, the Phoenicians, and the city dwellers of lower Mesopotamia seized this opportunity: Through their efforts goods flowed freely across the Near East, and technical skills associated with production spread widely among peoples still technologically backward.

In cultural activities, the Assyrians also made a notable contribution. Their efforts were not creative, but their imitations resulted in the continuation of cultural activity. This can be seen best in architecture and sculpture. Assyrian kings were avid builders, constructing the great cities of Nineveh, Calah (modern Nimrud), and Ashur as monuments of their power and glory. In these cities earlier Mesopotamian architectural styles were followed closely and thus kept alive. Temples and palaces were decorated with massive sculptured pieces and with excellent stone reliefs. The vigorous application of traditions from the past gave the Near East a new period of artistic glory. In literature, the Assyrians devoted a great deal of effort to collecting and copying older works in Sumerian and Akkadian. One of Assyria's kings, Ashurbanipal, built a huge library at Nineveh as a repository for thousands of copies of cuneiform tablets. Aside from administrative and economic records, most of the writing in Assyrian was merely a re-rendering of earlier literary works, especially the religious epics and creation stories so dear to the Sumerians. The Assyrians did show some originality in compiling accounts of their innumerable military campaigns, thereby making a contribution to the art of historical writing.

Assyrian religion was likewise strongly colored by borrowings from earlier Mesopotamia. The great state god of Assyria, Assur, was very similar to the Amorite Marduk. Assyrian rituals, prayers, and priesthoods are almost indistinguishable from those of the earlier Mesopotamians. Despite the derived character of their religion, there is considerable evidence that the Assyrians were deeply religious. Perhaps even their imperialism was motivated by a genuine desire to assert Assur's dominion over other gods. In all these ways the Assyrians kept alive some of the most precious cultural traditions in the Near East, and their conquests helped to spread those traditions throughout a vast region.

2. SUCCESSORS OF ASSYRIA, 612–550 B.C.

Assyria's sudden collapse opened a brief but spirited era of competition for the spoils of her empire, a struggle that ended when another empire builder, Persia, crushed the other contenders for power.

Egypt was one nation that seemed destined to benefit by the fall of Assyria. Foreign rule had again had the effect of uniting her under a single pharaoh, Psammetichus (also known as Psamtik; 663–609 B.C.), who founded the Twenty-sixth Dynasty. Egypt again briefly enjoyed internal order, prosperity, and international prestige, but she was incapable of meeting the needs of the new era. Her pharaohs had to rely on foreign mercenaries (chiefly Greeks) to man the armies. These troops, thoroughly hated by the antiforeign Egyptians, caused internal trouble. Egyptian artists and writers failed to produce anything new that would establish the Egyptian reputation abroad. The priests were even more reactionary, using religion as a means of resisting necessary changes. Old age had gripped Egypt, making her unable to check Persia. She fell to Persian armies with almost no struggle in 525 B.C.

In Asia Minor, the small kingdom of Lydia, which first emerged after the fall of the Hittites, was the chief beneficiary of Assyria's fall, and she quickly established control over nearly all of Asia Minor. Her rapid rise was especially significant in Greek history, since Lydia lay as a link between the Near East and Greece. During the reign of Croesus (560–546 B.C.), this greatest Lydian king ruled many Greeks living in Asia Minor. However, Lydian power was shaky, succumbing in 546 B.C. to one blow by Persia.

Still another contender for the Assyrian power was Media. The Medes had long been restless dependents of Assyria, and they furnished most of the armed might to destroy her. Once she was defeated, the Medes seized control of a large part of the northern empire and built up a vast state in the Iranian plateau. However, the state was poorly organized. One of the Median vassal princes, Cyrus of Persia, succeeded in deposing the Median king and laying successful claim to old Median territory.

The most spectacular of all Assyria's successors was the empire of the Chaldeans, a Semitic people who had entered lower Mesopotamia while it was under Assyria's rule. On her decline, the Chaldean princes seized some of the most valuable parts of the conquered territory. Under the one great Chaldean ruler, Nebuchadnezzar II (605–562 B.C.), all of Syria-Palestine was joined with the Tigris-Euphrates Valley in a single empire. Among the victims of his conquests was the kingdom of Judah. Jerusalem was destroyed in 586 B.C., and many of its citizens were carried off to Babylon as captives.

Nebuchadnezzar not only prided himself on being a conqueror, but also a champion of culture. In fact, the Chaldean interlude in Mesopotamian history was marked by a cultural renaissance strongly oriented toward the ancient past. The jewel of this revival was Nebuchadnezzar's rebuilding of Babylon as his capital. Its massive walls, its beautiful temples and palaces, its fabulous hanging gardens, and its impressive sculpture and painting made it one of the most splendid of ancient cities. Even the redoubtable Hebrew prophet Jeremiah, amid his lamentations over the calamities that had befallen his people at the hands of Nebuchadnezzar, had to admit that "Babylon was a golden cup in the hands of Yahweh" (Jer. 51:7). A religious revival in this period brought all the ancient Mesopotamian gods, above all Marduk, again to the center of the stage.

Nonetheless, Nebuchadnezzar's empire was not strong. It was guilty of worshiping the past, and its military resources were limited. Nebuchadnezzar's heirs were weak and little interested in political problems, and when the Persians captured Babylon in 539 B.C., the Chaldean state collapsed immediately.

3. THE PERSIAN EMPIRE, 500–328 B.C.

The final victory in the competition to succeed Assyria fell to a people who hardly seemed in the running—the Persians. They were of Indo-European origin, their ancestors having migrated to the Near East about 2000 B.C. from north of the Black Sea. The original Persians settled in the barren plateau of Iran, becoming simple farmers and herders. For many centuries they maintained their own political independence. During these long years, civilizing influences penetrated Persian society, especially from Assyria, so that the Persians began to be drawn into the orbit of the cosmopolitan civilization emerging in the Near East. However, they did retain significant aspects of their old Indo-European pattern of life, especially in religion and language. In the seventh century they were forced to accept the overlordship of the Medes, who were closely akin to them in language and culture. But in 550 the Persian king, Cyrus, overthrew the Median ruler and began to call himself "king of the Medes and the Persians." This event launched the Persians on their spectacular career as masters of the Near East.

Cyrus' accession to power resulted immediately in a rapid extension of Persia's boundaries. Cyrus and his successors Cambyses and Darius (collectively 550–486 B.C.) destroyed all other powers in the Near East. Cyrus was the most successful conqueror, taking first Lydia, the key to control of all Asia Minor, and then the Chaldean Empire, which made him master of the Tigris-Euphrates Valley and of Syria and Palestine. During his last years he subdued various nations in eastern Iran, pushing Persian power to the borders of India. Cambyses conquered Egypt. Darius extended Persian power into Europe by conquering a territory west of the Black Sea. However, this expansion was checked by the Greeks in 490 B.C. in a war we shall describe later. When Darius died in 486 B.C., the Persian Empire stretched from the Aegean and Mediterranean seas to India and from the mountains bounding the Near East on the north to far south in the Nile Valley. It was one of the largest empires ever created.

The first rulers were intelligent statesmen as well as conquerors and laid the basis for sound government of their huge holdings. Cyrus established a good reputation for Persian rule by practicing a policy of tolerance toward defeated people. He avoided slaughtering captured kings, preferring to proclaim himself the legitimate successor of the conquered local dynasty. Especially meaningful was the respect he showed for the religious systems of his conquered subjects, making their gods his own and contributing to their worship with his resources. He earned himself a hero's role by allowing the Hebrew exiles to return to Jerusalem to rebuild the temple of Yahweh. These actions convinced most peoples in the Near East that the Persians did not intend to continue the terrorism and brutality of the Assyrians.

Darius was the most constructive of the Achaemenid dynasty, as this line of rulers was called. Borrowing and adapting old ideas and practices in government, he laid the basis for one of the great political systems of all history. He established himself as absolute ruler, claiming full authority to make laws, to judge, and to command the services of his subjects. At his court in the capital cities of Ecbatana, Susa, and Persepolis, he created a magnificent court etiquette intended to impress upon everyone that he was, as he proclaimed himself, "The Great King." He surrounded his position with powerful religious sanctions, claiming that he was the divinely selected representative of the great Persian god, Ahura-Mazda. Darius gathered around him numerous officials and servants, assigning to each a specific task. These servants, usually of Median or Persian origin, became a kind of aristocracy fanatically devoted to maintaining Persian power.

Darius' greatest political innovation lay in the techniques he devised for ruling widely scattered possessions inhabited by many different peoples. He divided his empire into twenty large districts, called satrapies. Over each he appointed a governor, usually a Persian and often a member of the royal family, who was given power sufficient to make him a king in his own right. These satraps were removable at the will of the great king and were held strictly accountable for the administration of their districts. An excellent road system was developed binding

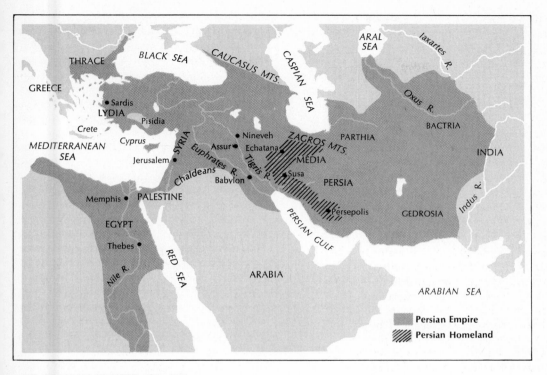

THE PERSIAN EMPIRE, CA. 500 B.C.

the satrapies to the capital, and a constant stream of correspondence flowed to and from the royal court. Periodically, Darius sent out inspectors to investigate the administration and report back. Spies in his pay swarmed through the empire to keep him informed. Contingents of the royal army under trusted commanders were garrisoned in strategic spots. Careful tax records were kept at the capital as a means of accounting for each governor's administration. By these methods Darius managed to create twenty semi-independent governments and still keep an eye on each in a fashion that coordinated policy over the whole empire.

In the final analysis, the armed forces were the key to Darius' power. The Persian army was built around a corps of professional soldiers recruited from the Persians and the Medes and was rounded out with contingents supplied by the conquered peoples in vast numbers that made the Persian armies awe inspiring. The Persians also commanded excellent naval forces,

composed largely of hired Phoenician, Egyptian, and Greek ships and crews. In view of this military might, very few peoples were willing to challenge the Persian king.

Darius' imperial system endured about 150 years. The history of Persia after his death contains few events worthy of our attention. There were wars with outsiders that the Persians seldom won; on the other hand, they did not lose much territory. Rebellions occurred within the empire, only to be smashed eventually by the superior power of the king. Perhaps the most significant aspect of this period was the slow erosion of royal power. The Persian royal family declined in vigor and political intelligence, and the court became corrupt, torn by intrigue among the friends and officials of the king. Several later Persian rulers spent more time trying to survive the plots of their many wives and children and ambitious servants than administering their empire. The satraps could not resist the temptation to try to overthrow the king. Often they raised a rebellion by putting themselves forward as champions of subject peoples or by promising great rewards to anyone who would follow them against the king. The only protection against these rebellions was rigid control over the satraps, which the Persian kings were unable to maintain. With the passage of time the Persian army also declined in strength. By the middle of the fourth century B.C., all that was needed to destroy Persian power was a strong attack from the outside. It was soon forthcoming, led by a Macedonian king, Alexander the Great, who was driven in part by an urge to destroy the Persian menace that had haunted the Greeks since the reign of Darius the Great. Alexander was able to take possession of the whole Persian Empire before his untimely death in 323 B.C.

The Persians, emerging suddenly to master the Near East and confronted constantly with the problem of holding their empire together, devoted most of their talents to administrative and military affairs. As a consequence, their contributions to cultural development in the Near East were not spectacular. In general, they played a role similar to that of the Assyrians, borrowing from the cultural treasure that already existed. They utilized already developed written languages, especially Aramean, for administrative purposes. Their kings were lavish in their patronage of the arts, the results showing chiefly in the royal palaces built at Susa, Persepolis, and Ecbatana. They continued the Assyrian practice of commissioning artists to render in stone pictorial records of their military exploits. The Persians welcomed in their cities men who were schooled in the literary and scientific traditions of the past and thereby helped to keep alive ancient traditions. Their tolerant attitude toward the many different cultural elements in their empire is of inestimable importance in the history of Western civilization, because it was from the Persians that the Greeks derived and transmitted westward a knowledge of many ancient Near Eastern ideas and institutions.

The Persians did make one outstanding contribution to Near Eastern history. They created a new religion, Zoroastrianism, and aided in the spread of some of its ideas. Its beginnings seem certainly to have rested on beliefs held by the Persians before they became the rulers of the Near East. Early Persian religion centered around the worship of several gods who represented forces of nature, including especially a god of the sky and a god of fire. Along with the chief gods, the ancient Persians believed in innumerable lesser spirits who were capable of doing both good and evil. A complicated ritual, including sacrifices, magic, and prayer, had developed as a means of winning the favor of the gods and the spirits. A group of priests called the Magi played a prominent role in the early religious life of the Persians.

Out of this setting came one of history's great religious reformers, Zoroaster (Zarathustra in the Persian language), a worthy member of that potent breed of men who by the vigor and freshness of their insights into man's spiritual nature have left an indelible imprint on other men's minds. Legend has clouded Zoroaster's career, but it seems likely that he lived in the seventh or sixth century B.C., prior to the emergence of the Persians as masters of the Near East. According to tradition, he spent the early part of his life in contemplation in the desert, finally receiving a revelation of the true way from Ahura, the god of the sky. Fortified by his vision, Zoroaster returned to the world as a preacher urging all to become converts to his beliefs. At first he enjoyed little success and even suffered persecution, but eventually he began to win adherents, and his religion was implanted in Persian society just prior to the emergence of Persia as a world power.

Zoroaster's exact teachings have become as blurred by the passing centuries as are the details of his life. The essence of his religion is contained in a sacred book called the Avesta, compiled over many centuries and consisting largely of interpretations and refinements of his original doctrines. It seems certain that Zoroaster cast his new message in terms of a protest against existing Persian religious beliefs. His central tenet, repudiating the old polytheistic system and the superstitions surrounding it, was monotheism. In this conviction, Zoroaster resembles some of the Hebrew prophets, whose concepts of the divine nature were taking final shape at about the same time. The only god was characterized as the all-powerful, all-pervading lord of creation, Ahura-Mazda (Lord of Wisdom). This good and benevolent spirit presides over human destiny, emanating and personifying such qualities as justice, pure thought, integrity, devotion, good intentions, and immortality. But the good Ahura-Mazda is opposed by the diabolical Ahriman, who struggles to blot out justice, light, wisdom, and good. The warfare between good and evil, going on since the beginning of the world, constitutes the essence of existence. Eventually, in a final day of judgment, Ahura-Mazda will prevail, but in the meantime, the conflict will continue, extending into every soul and demanding that it choose whether to join the good or the evil. On the final day of reckoning, those who have chosen good will be rewarded with perfection and eternal happiness, while those who have elected the way of Ahriman will be damned to eternal misery. This concept of dualism provided fertile ground for discussion in Zoroastrianism and produced a rich vein of spiritual speculation in later centuries.

By postulating the goodness of Ahura-Mazda and the evil of Ahriman as fundamental to the cosmos, Zoroaster made man's basic obligation clear. Only good conduct could win favor in the eyes of Ahura-Mazda. The worship of the old gods, magic, sacrifices, and priestly intervention were irrelevant and constituted surrender to evil because they diverted attention from doing good. Zoroaster spelled out a vigorous moral code for his followers, derived in its particulars from the qualities of goodness surrounding Ahura-Mazda and including a clear concept of sin. Certainly none of the religions in the world that the Persians were soon to rule, except Judaism, gave such emphasis to ethical issues— and not even Judaism placed the burden so squarely on each individual. Zoroaster did not associate goodness and righteousness with a particular chosen people; his message was aimed at all mankind.

Although the record is again vague, it appears that Zoroaster's religion took hold among the Persians and the Medes after the prophet's death and that it became in some fashion the official religion of the rulers of the Achaemenid dynasty at least from the time of Darius the Great on-

ward. But the Avesta shows that the Zoroastrianism of the Persian Empire was not the religion proclaimed by Zoroaster. Ritual practices aimed at pleasing Ahura-Mazda and warding off Ahriman's evil influences grew increasingly prominent. Polytheism crept back into religious life. Ahriman was elevated to the status of a god, standing equal to Ahura-Mazda in the cosmic order. Many of the old gods reappeared and hosts of angels and devils joined the eternal war between good and evil. The whole concept of the struggle between good and evil tended to associate good with purely spiritual things and evil with material things. This version of dualism had the effect of belittling the practice of virtue in everyday life and of exalting flight from the world to a secluded life. These new currents dulled the sharp edge of monotheism and ethical purity and drew Zoroastrianism back toward the patterns of ancient Near Eastern religions.

The conquest of the Persian Empire by Alexander the Great represented a setback for Zoroastrianism. Although the Achaemenid dynasty had never supported it fanatically, still Zoroastrianism was the official religion and it suffered from that association when the dynasty collapsed. The general policy of tolerance in the empire had meant that other faiths had maintained their hold, and thus Zoroastrianism did not have a very large base. Despite this defeat— and others in the future—Zoroastrianism survives today; its modern adherents, called Parsees, are located chiefly in Iran and India. During the twenty-five centuries of its existence it has not only satisfied its adherents but has powerfully affected other religions, including Judaism, Christianity, and Islam.

The ignominious end of the Persian Empire must not detract from an appreciation of its importance. The enlightened and tolerant rule of the Achaemenids built a universal empire in the ancient Near East, one that brought all kinds of people at many levels of civilization into a viable community. The benevolent, cosmopolitan Persian spirit permitted local elements to persist while providing instruments through which all could mix and fertilize each other. The resulting amalgam was a fitting climax to a long chapter in history.

Suggested Reading

Assyrians

*Georges Roux, *Ancient Iraq* (Penguin). Provides a clear chronological survey of Assyrian history, treating it as an extension of earlier Mesopotamian civilization.

*A. Leo Oppenheimer, *Ancient Mesopotamia: Portrait of a Dead Civilization* (Phoenix). Covers much of the same ground as the previous work with a stronger emphasis on cultural history.

André Parrot, *Arts of Assyria* (1961). An excellent guide to the Assyrian accomplishment in all of the arts.

Persians

*A. T. Olmstead, *History of the Persian Empire* (Phoenix). A detailed survey that presents a rich picture of the Persian accomplishment.

*R. N. Frye, *Heritage of Persia* (Mentor). A recent study emphasizing the intellectual developments in ancient Persia.

R. C. Zaehner, *Dawn and Twilight of Zoroastrianism* (1961).

*R. C. Zaehner, *The Teachings of the Magi* (Galaxy). These two works present a full description of the nature of Zoroastrianism and of its historical evolution.

R. Ghirshman, *The Arts of Ancient Iran* (1964). An excellent guide with splendid illustrations.

Retrospect

When in 330 B.C. Alexander the Great stood in triumph over the body of Darius III, a great chapter in the history of the world had ended. The Persians ruled a world that was old and tired, while their youthful conquerer was a fitting symbol of a new world, a world filled with vitality, emerging on the western periphery of the Near East. Before shifting our focus to that new setting, at least an epitaph on the civilizations of the ancient Near East is in order.

For the purposes of this epitaph, let us view the Persians as the last scions of a great family whose origins are rooted in simple neolithic villages and whose members include all the peoples whose history has been reviewed in the preceding pages. The first thing that strikes one is that this family had in the course of five or six millennia put together a great and varied patrimony for the future. The family fortunes had grown especially rich after about 4000 B.C., when men had learned to exploit the river valleys and had adjusted their whole life style to that environment. Their treasure included impressive techniques for controlling larger groups of people: absolute monarchy, complex tax systems, effective military establishments, organized bureaucracies, recordkeeping systems, legal codes—all representing great advances in government. These same peoples had devised effective systems for wresting sustenance from nature: organized agriculture, skilled technology, trade, transportation. They had developed complex social systems by which large numbers of individuals could relate to other individuals in an orderly and productive fashion. They had learned to enrich their lives through a magnificent art. They had devised writing systems and put into a permanent record descriptions of their daily activities, their thoughts, and their knowledge about themselves, animals, plants, the stars, and all other matter of things. It is indeed an insensitive man who can view this patrimony in all its shapes and forms without being convinced that the peoples of the ancient Near East were amazing creators, a testimony to the ability of the human species to turn the world to its own support and pleasure. Out of this ancient world had come achievements in government, economics, social organization, art, literature, and science from which all men of future ages could draw. And men of succeeding ages did draw on this treasury and thus did not have to do over again what men in the Near East did so well the first time. In one sense, world history is a story of the diffusion of ancient Near Eastern achievements across much of the face of the earth.

But the Near Eastern patrimony was more than a jumble of things to be borrowed from piecemeal and looked back upon in wonder. The peoples of that area had interrelated the elements of their lives in a pattern that gave meaning to their actions. In a higher sense, the most impressive part of the Near Eastern patrimony was its intellectual component. Men in the ancient Near East had learned how to reflect on the human endeavor and the setting in which it took place. Their reflections resulted in an understanding of the human condition and a sense of its destiny. In the ancient Near East the integrative, unifying, sense-giving aspect of civilized life was supplied by religion. Religion penetrated every facet of life, providing reasons that things happened and justifications for all that was done. All the Near Eastern religions (except Judaism and Zoroastrianism) posited a universe totally occupied and completely directed by powerful cosmic spirits to whose demands men had to adjust in every facet of their existence. Men—even the most powerful—were slaves in this cosmic system, bound forever to repeat in their government, labor, prayer, sacrifice, art, writing, and thinking those kinds of actions and thoughts demanded to sustain harmony in the cosmos. If they acted the part of good slaves, then life went on; the proof that obedience to the established order paid off was the wealth and splendor achieved by the Mesopotamians, the Egyptians, the Persians, and all the rest. The confidence and sense of sureness this approach to existence generated was the vital spark pushing the people of the ancient Near East on to their accomplishments.

Viewed from such a perspective, the achievements of that world were magnificent. Why then did the society grow old and lifeless? Men have for centuries wrestled with the causes of the decline and fall of civilizations. Most great theories on the theme have been discarded soon after their initial expression in favor of newer theories. Here we cannot expect to do more than point to certain limitations on the pattern of civilized life that developed in the ancient Near East by way of suggesting some factors in its decline. The environment imposed a set of limitations, for aside from the river valleys the Near East had limited potential in terms of material resources. Technology imposed another limitation. We must not let the spectacular advances of the last century or two blur a basic fact: Technological advance through most of history has been slow and painful, hindering man's ability to expand his control over nature. The ancient Near East suffered too from the overpowering influence of the river valley peoples. What succeeded so remarkably in early Mesopotamia and early Egypt became the model of civilized life for every people in the Near East. Although they benefited from imitation, those living beyond the valley floodplains became prisoners of modes of life that were creative only in a small geographical setting. This problem became especially serious when the direction of Near Eastern civilization passed from the people of the valleys to the people from the outside—the Hittites, the small Semitic kingdoms, the Assyrians, the Persians. Slavish imitation of the river valley pattern of civilization brought people to a certain point—and then stopped them from further advance. Still another limitation on the ancient Near Eastern world was its waste of human resources. It was a world directed by small elites who achieved wonders but who ultimately failed to call forth fresh creative talent. The social structure was too inflexible, too closed, to permit genius to break through from unexpected sources.

However, the greatest constriction on ancient Near Eastern civilization and the ultimate cause of its stagnation lay in the minds of men. The world view encased in the great religious systems made it extremely difficult for men to use to full capacity their greatest asset: the power to reason. Instead of freeing them to reflect on the nature and potential of themselves and the things around them, the ancient Near Eastern world view required that men pour their intellectual energies into acts of conformity with the directive forces of the cosmos. Because rationality was smothered, men failed to discover themselves. They were reaching in this direction, as the Hebrew prophets and Zoroaster testify, but they never broke through the formidable barriers imposed by the assumptions upon which their civilization was based. Only someone outside their world still had the freedom to discover what man really was. When that discovery was made, the Near Eastern peoples had to surrender the leadership of civilization to others.

Here then is the epitaph of the ancient Near East: It was a world that knew men not well enough.

II

Greco-Roman Civilization

200 B.C.-A.D. 200

While the civilizations of the Near East were reaching maturity under the political sway of the Assyrians and the Persians, a new civilization was appearing in the lands around the Aegean Sea. It began to emerge about 1200 B.C. and reached its most creative phase in the fifth century B.C., when the city-states of Greece produced literary, artistic, philosophical, and scientific works that departed radically from those of the Near East. The great intellectual and artistic outburst of fifth-century Greece was nourished in a political and social order that was likewise revolutionary.

From its Aegean center the new civilization exerted a powerful influence over other peoples. The Greeks themselves propagated their style of life through trading and colonizing ventures that ringed the Mediterranean with their city-states. More significant was the role played by non-Greeks as missionaries of Greek civilization. In the latter part of the fourth century, the Macedonians under the meteoric Alexander the Great joined with the Greeks to burst out of the Aegean basin and overrun the old centers of civilization in the Near East. All across this vast area Greek ideas and institutions made a profound impression, and in the territory bordering on the eastern rim of the Mediterranean, the Greek way of life became supreme. In the third century B.C. the Romans, just emerging as a world power, became enamored of Hellenic civilization and turned their energies to absorbing and spreading it. The Romans eventually conquered Greece and the Near East but were themselves mastered by the ideas and culture of their victims. The empire that they forged became the setting for a further extension of the Greek pattern of life so that much of Western Europe and North Africa fell under Greek influence. Roman political genius combined with Hellenic cultural patterns to forge a vast community of men living around the

Mediterranean and a civilization that ranks as a great achievement in human history.

In tracing the complex evolution of Greco-Roman civilization through fourteen or fifteen centuries, one should try to identify in an orderly way the main stages of development and the actors responsible for each new stage. One should comprehend the essential ingredients of Greco-Roman civilization, many of which became a permanent part of the total human accomplishment. But perhaps most important, one should grasp the extent to which the Greco-Roman world discovered and unleashed a new range of human talents and turned them to creative ends. To many historians, the key to this chapter of human history was the discovery and development of the idea expressed by the Athenian dramatist Sophocles in his *Antigone:* "Many are the wonders of the world, and none so wonderful as Man."

Greco-Roman civilization was born in a group of small, independent communities around the Aegean Sea. No one can understand that civilization until he grasps the unique nature of these communities, which spurred their inhabitants to creative activities radically different from any that had preceded them. However, no Greek city-state sprang full-grown from a void; each was a product of long experimentation and sometimes painful growth. This chapter will trace that evolution and seek to reveal the nature of these communities by showing how they came into being. After a look at the general pattern of development, a closer study will take Athens and Sparta as examples of city-state society.

Greco-Roman civilization had its origins in the setting provided by the Aegean Sea—the lands to its west, north, and east and the innumerable islands on its surface. The sea and the land merge intimately, so that no inhabitant is far from the sea, and none using the sea is far from land. The whole area is blessed with beneficent climate, marked by mild winters and long, dry summers, which permits men to sail the Aegean in relative safety and to live on the land without expending great amounts of energy to clothe and house themselves. But its resources are not overabundant. The topography, especially of Greece proper, is dominated by mountains, valleys, bays, and peninsulas that cut the land into many small pockets of tillable soil and create barriers

4

THE ORIGINS AND DEVELOPMENT
OF THE GREEK CITY-STATE POLITY

against political unification. The limited amount of tillable soil was poor in quality, subject to erosion, and ill-suited to cereal production. As the Greek historian Herodotus said, "Greece has always poverty as her companion."

This restrictive environment might have doomed its inhabitants to a modest historical role had there not been an avenue of escape: the sea. The Aegean provides excellent harbors, and it is tideless, is relatively calm, and has good sailing winds. It thus became a roadway especially to the east and the north. This was an important factor because it drew the Greeks toward the higher civilizations of the Near East.

1. THE MYCENAEAN AGE, 2000–1200 B.C.: GREEK ORIGINS

The emergence of a unique Greek civilization occurred over a long period and under circumstances not yet fully understood. There is evidence of paleolithic culture in the Aegean world, but perhaps the first important step toward civilization was made when neolithic culture was introduced in the area late in the fourth millennium B.C. During the ensuing centuries, agricultural villages developed everywhere in the Aegean area and typical neolithic institutions emerged to create a basis for future growth. About 2000 B.C. this primitive order was profoundly affected by the intrusion of Indo-Europeans into the area; these newcomers were

a part of a larger movement that disturbed much of the Near East and produced such peoples as the Hittites and the Kassites. In the Aegean world, the invaders imposed their political system and their language on the native population. However, they borrowed from these natives the basic features of agricultural life. For the next four or five centuries, Aegean history centered on the activities of a large number of small principalities dominated by aggressive warlords and their retainers.

Although we cannot reconstruct the course of events during these centuries in detail, it is clear that significant developments occurred. By about 1500 B.C., the kings of some of these small principalities in southern and central Greece were able to build huge fortress-palaces. The most impressive was located at Mycenae, which has given its name to this phase of early Greek history. These impressive structures indicate not only a notable advance in the material level of life but also a concentration of power in the hands of the rulers who built them. The key to their success appears to have been what they learned from their growing contacts as pirates and traders with the more advanced societies of the Near East and Crete. Especially from Crete, where Minoan civilization was reaching its apogee, came a great influx of technical skills, art forms, religious ideas, and political techniques. The rulers of Mycenae and other important centers established well-organized bureaucracies capable of imposing strong control over the populations living in the areas surrounding their fortress cities. A written language, which modern scholars call Linear B, was perfected chiefly to record the kings' dealings with their subjects. The decipherment of the language in 1953 furnished proof that the Mycenaean world spoke Greek and that its people must be given a place in Greek history.

Mycenaean culture reached its peak about 1300 B.C. As it matured, it appeared to move toward assimilation with the larger pattern of civilization developing all across the Near East; the process of cultural diffusion so actively at work seemed destined to link the Aegean world to the Near East. However, that process was cut short about 1200 B.C. by the collapse of Mycenaean culture. The causes are not entirely clear. Perhaps the collapse of Minoan civilization after about 1400 B.C. cut off a vital source of inspiration. The vast movements of peoples that disrupted the Hittite and Egyptian empires about 1200 B.C. very likely cut the trade routes essential to the material well-being of the Mycenaean kingdoms. This, in turn, caused the Mycenaean kings to react to their shrinking world by turning on closer neighbors and on each other in destructive ways. It was in these difficult times, for instance, that warriors from several mainland cities under the leadership of King Agammenon of Mycenae attacked and destroyed Troy. These troubles were compounded by a new wave of Indo-European invaders, called the Dorians, moving into the Aegean area from the north during the eleventh century B.C. These barbarians destroyed many of the great fortress cities that were already badly weakened by changing conditions in the Aegean world. With the fall of the Mycenaean world ended the first chapter of Greek history. Its memory lived on in myth and legend, but its passing required the rebuilding of society in the Aegean area on a new basis.

2. THE DARK AGES, 1200–800 B.C.: THE FOUNDATIONS OF GREEK SOCIETY

From one perspective, the decline of Mycenaean society and the Dorian invasions were

catastrophic. The Mycenaean establishment— the bureaucratic kingdoms, the palaces, trading connections with the outside world, technical skills, art, writing—were swept away. The Aegean world entered a dark age that lasted nearly four centuries and was marked chiefly by poverty and disorder. However, this era had another side: It witnessed the establishment of a new Greek culture. Although that new culture borrowed elements from the wreckage of the Mycenaean world, it was basically different in form and spirit from its predecessor and would serve as the basis for future Greek greatness. Our information about the dark age depends largely on archeological remains and is both spotty and confusing. However, at the very end of the period two literary masterpieces, the *Iliad* and the *Odyssey* of Homer, were set down. Combined with the archeological evidence, these poems provide us with sufficient information to permit us to understand the basic features of the new culture.

The dark age witnessed a considerable movement of peoples in the Greek world. Not only did the invading Dorians spread over a large part of the Greek mainland, but also considerable numbers of already established Greeks migrated to the Aegean islands and the coast of Asia Minor. This movement created the geographical base of future Greek development and set the stage for future interaction between the Greeks and the peoples to the east. A common language (with several dialects) spread over the area. A new writing system, based on the adaptation of the Phoenician alphabet to accommodate the Greek spoken language, was perfected to a level that made possible the magnificent Homeric epics. A common pattern of religion, clearly delineated in the *Iliad* and the *Odyssey*, was shared by most Greeks. This emerging society was based on a simple agricultural system, but by the end of the dark age the Greeks had adopted iron-age technology, developed remarkable skills in pottery making, and began to engage in extensive trading activities, especially in the eastern Mediterranean area. The basic political unit was the small kingdom ruled by a chieftain who led his people in war, judged their disputes, and represented them before the gods.

In marked contrast to the Mycenaean age, the power of these kings was limited by a powerful nobility whose authority was based on patriarchal family ties and personal followings and on extensive landholdings. In each kingdom, the nobles met regularly as a council to advise the king on matters of common interest. Peasants and artisans possessed honorable status by virtue of their membership in a clan, and even participated to a degree in political life through an assembly where they could shout their approval or disapproval of the decisions of the king and the council of elders.

By 800 B.C. kinship and personal ties still provided the chief cohesive force in this simple society, but already people were being drawn into another entity that transcended the clan. The communal bonds found their focus in the physical center of each kingdom, all of which were so small that every citizen had access to that center. There the king's residence was a fortress where all could gather in times of danger. There temples were built in honor of the gods shared by the members of the kingdom. The same center served as a meeting place for the clan leaders when they gathered from their rural estates to advise the king. A market developed around the fortress. Little by little this "city," called the *polis* by the Greeks, became the center of communal life. Those who became increasingly identified with the *polis* became its "citizens"; *citizenship* constituted the total set of conditions that gave a man membership in a *polis*. Participation in military, religious, political, and economic activities at a single center slowly ingrained in men's minds a sense of belonging to a larger group than their kin group. This combination of physical and psychological involvement in the city-state provided the dynamic element in the Greek world.

Perhaps the Dark Age produced another development as unique and important as these institutional patterns, a development that ultimately allowed the citizens of the *polis* to do something creative for it. On the basis of Homer's epics and the artistry of the pottery fashioned during the later stages of the age, one might venture that the Greeks had assumed a new mental posture. In simplest terms, these sources portray a view of the world that placed a high value on human capability and that took joy in human activity. Moreover, each work shows a sense of harmony, proportion, balance, and order, the product of one of man's special powers, his reason. Dare we suggest that, amid the darkness at the beginnings of Greek history, humanism and rationalism were somehow born, opening wide vistas to men increasingly inclined to serve the *polis?*

3. THE ARCHAIC AGE, 800–500 B.C.: GROWTH AND DEVELOPMENT

By 800 B.C. the foundation was laid for a new civilization; in the succeeding three centuries, the edifice was largely completed. These were centuries of rapid change which produced more complex institutions and ideas. The cultural, intellectual, and religious aspects of growth will be treated later. Here the focus will be on the evolution of the *polis*, which provided the basic stimulus for most other changes.

A fundamental change affecting all but a few Greek city-states occurred during the eighth century, with the replacement of kingship by a system of government where the decisive authority rested in a council of wealthy, high-born nobles and the execution of council decisions was entrusted to elected officials from the same noble class. Aristocratic domination of most *poleis* persisted at least into the sixth century B.C. Although they were often greedy and jealous of their power, the aristocrats promoted a variety of activities that expanded the influence of the *polis* over which they ruled on the lives of all people associated with it. They formulated in their own ranks an ethos that emphasized civic concepts and responsibilities, and lent their wealth and talents to the propagation of these ideas in art, literature, and education, so that other elements in society caught a sense of the larger community. Most important of all, these aristocratic masters of most city-states were ultimately willing to take political action to resolve basic problems affecting the entire population.

One change of great significance in broadening the base of participation in civil life occurred in the military organization of most city-states.

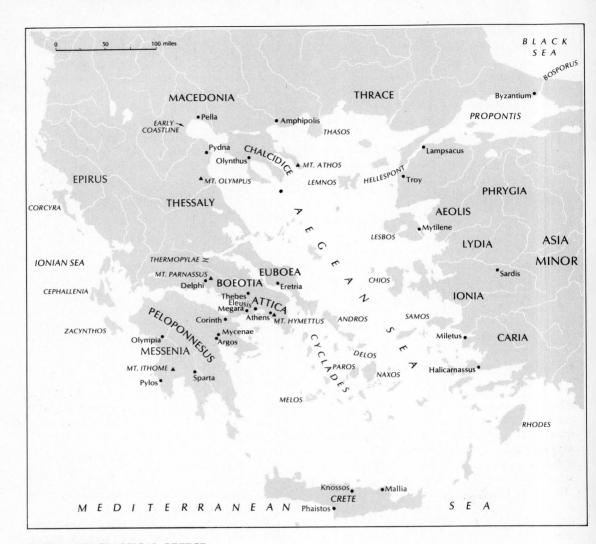

EARLY AND CLASSICAL GREECE

Chariot warfare, which gave rich aristocrats able to afford horses and expensive equipment a virtual monopoly on military might, was replaced by a military organization based on the *phalanx*, a massed formation of heavily armored infantrymen, called *hoplites*. This change not only brought larger numbers of citizens into the service of the *polis* but also placed a premium on disciplined, purposeful action of men of modest means, on whose shoulders rested the safety of the city-state.

Even more significant in increasing the role of the *polis* were the actions taken by aristocrats to cope with a major economic crisis that began to grip the Greek world early in the Archaic Age. As reflected so clearly in the lamentations of the eighth-century poet Hesiod, most Greek city-states began to feel the pinch of poverty. The causes were deep-seated and many: the basic poverty of the Aegean soil, increasing population, aristocratic exploitation, and a growing urge for economic gain, driving men to compete

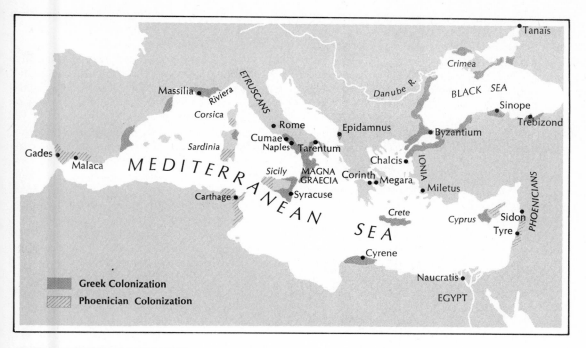

GREEK COLONIES ABOUT 500 B.C.

for limited resources. Especially threatened were the modest citizen-farmers, who were being forced into dependency or slavery; their repression threatened to destroy the bonds that linked these common people to the *polis* and thus to weaken its fundamental character.

The economic crisis was in part resolved by overseas settlement. Bold leaders, often of aristocratic origin, and impoverished followers took to the seas in search of new land that would assure their livelihood. Often these ventures were civic undertakings, sponsored and organized by the aristocratic rulers of the mother city. Especially heavily colonized were southern Italy and Sicily; this area was so completely Hellenized that it was long called Magna Graecia (Greater Greece). Numerous Greek settlements were also established on the northern shores of the Aegean and around the Black Sea. Important Greek settlements were even planted in southern France, Spain, and the area of North Africa that is today Libya (called Cyrenaica then). This amazing burst of activity greatly expanded what the

Greeks called Hellas—the area dominated by Greek peoples and their culture. The new communities founded by the emigrants from the Aegean area were not colonies in our sense. Rather, they were independent *poleis* with their own governments, citizens, laws, and civic pride. Their foundation marked a massive extension of the sway of the *polis*.

More significant in reducing the economic pressures was a great expansion of trade and industry. The colonizing undertakings played a part in this by opening opportunities for trade between overseas Greek cities and the homeland. From this kind of trading activity it was but a short step to involvement in the larger trading world already mapped out in the Near East, especially by the Phoenicians. The Greeks proved energetic and enterprising, and by 500 B.C. they had become the leading traders in the Mediterranean world. Trade nourished manufacturing, particularly of excellent pottery. Even the old agricultural system was altered by expanding trade opportunities. Enterprising farmers abandoned the raising of grain in favor of raising grapes, olives, and livestock, all of which found profitable markets overseas and in the Greek cities. Thus for merchants, artisans, and commercial farmers alike, the center of economic life shifted to the marketplace in the city, creating new ties between citizen and *polis*.

The social structure changed under the impact of economic change. Some aristocrats became involved in trade and industry, either as entrepreneurs or as supporters of growth through political action. This development weakened their solidarity as a class and bred disagreement among them. Men from the lower ranks of society succeeded in amassing wealth through trade and industry and became rivals of the landowning aristocracy for power and prestige. Small farmers, unable to engage in capitalistic farming and unwilling to become dependents of great landowners, moved to the cities. This change dissolved ancient family ties, weakened the control of the clan leaders over the populace, and thrust upon public authorities the burden of controlling socially displaced groups.

By the seventh century B.C., these basic changes produced in most city-states tensions and disorders that threatened their very existence. Aristocratic governments reacted by deliberate political actions that had the overall effect of expanding and strengthening the ties binding the total populace to the *polis*. Each city-state ended up with its own unique institutions, but a broad pattern was discernible throughout the Aegean area and even in the city-states established by migrations.

In general, aristocratic regimes tried to relieve mounting tensions by "reforms" that did not require surrender of their monopoly on political power. They enacted codes of law that defined rights and responsibilities and limited the arbitrary administration of justice. They encouraged overseas settlement and the expansion of trade. They granted relief to debtors and protection to small landowners. The aristocrats were undoubtedly motivated in part by self-interest, but another force also shaped their conduct: patriotism, born of a realization that steps must be taken to retain the allegiance and services of valuable artisans, soldiers, sailors, shopkeepers,

and farmers who, each in his own way, made a contribution to the welfare of the *polis*.

As important as they were in strengthening the *polis*, aristocratic "reforms" were not usually sufficient to maintain stability. The growing attachment of men of all levels to the city generated demands for greater political participation that the aristocrats were unwilling to grant. Usually, force was required to unseat the nobles. The revolt against them was spearheaded in many city-states by individual leaders called *tyrants* by the Greeks. Tyrants were often men of noble origin and great wealth, acquired in many cases by trading ventures, who were zealous for personal power and pursued policies that would ensure they held it. Once established in control of a *polis*, the typical tyrant struck at the wealthy nobles who were the greatest threat to his power. Nobles were taxed severely, sometimes deprived of their lands, and often driven into exile; most important of all, they were deprived of control of political life. Tyrants usually sought to please the poorer elements in society by creating economic opportunities for them, spending huge sums on beautifying the cities, and increasing trade and industry. Although their political methods were brutal and oppressive, they did increase the economic stake of the common citizen in the *polis*.

The period of tyranny was brief in most cities, chiefly because tyrants had seized power illegally and were incapable of carrying out the changes in political institutions that would prolong and legitimize their rule. The aristocrats who had been their chief victims took the lead in unseating them but were seldom able to restore their old monopoly. In progressive city-states the end of tyranny was accompanied by radical changes in the political system that allowed the total citizen body to take control of civic affairs and to decide for themselves what was in their best interest. With all citizens entitled to participate in government, the last knot binding them to the *polis* was tied.

The perfection of a democratic polity provided the setting for the Golden Age of the Greeks — that glorious era centering in the fifth century B.C. that witnessed the flowering of literature, art, philosophy, and science. Beyond doubt the full participation of citizens in political life provided a major stimulant to the burst of artistic and intellectual energy that made the fifth century a golden age; indeed, the democratic *polis* was one of the prime features of the Golden Age.

4. ATHENS

The history of Athens provides a case study illustrating the process by which a collection of people grew into a democratic *polis*. Athens was a center of modest importance in Mycenaean times, and the region called Attica, of which it was the center, was populated by a Greek-speaking population. Attica seems to have escaped the worst effects associated with the collapse of Mycenaean culture and the Dorian invasions. However, during the Dark Age the level of life in Attica reverted to a primitive state, centering on a number of small, independent agricultural villages led by clan leaders. With the passage of time and under circumstances that remain a mystery, these villages coalesced into a single unit centering on Athens to constitute an embryo *polis* embracing about 1,000 square miles — the largest city-state in ancient Greece except for Sparta. The emerging *polis* was ruled by a hereditary king assisted by a council of clan heads called the *Areopagus*. A popular assembly, called the *ecclesia*, also existed but its role was limited. For political and military purposes, the clans were grouped into four tribes, each of which was divided into three brotherhoods (*phratries*, whence is derived our word "fraternity"). Citizenship was established by admission to a brotherhood, which, in turn, was based on identification through blood ties with a clan.

About 750 B.C. monarchy was abolished, and an elected official, called an *archon*, took over the functions of the king. Within a short time, the chief archon came to share his power with lesser elected officials, the chief of which was the *polemarch*, chosen to lead the army. These officials were elected annually by the *ecclesia*, but only wealthy men of noble birth were eligible. The directive power in the *polis* rested in the Areopagus, composed of ex-archons who passed from service as elective officials to life membership in the Areopagus. The wide range of powers entrusted to this aristocratic group, including supervision of the archons, formulation of proposals submitted to the *ecclesia*, direction of foreign affairs, and final jurisdiction in all cases appealed in the courts, was sufficient to assure its complete control of political life in Athens.

This aristocratic political system, formed in the eighth century B.C., persisted with only minor changes for two centuries. However, across these centuries there were mounting internal tensions. In large part, strife arose from economic problems resulting from the exploitation and enslavement of small farmers by a greedy aristocracy. Unlike many other city-states, Athens did not engage in overseas settlement to relieve her economic problems. However, there was a steady growth of trade and industry that caused shifts in the distribution of wealth and the development of new social groups which did not fit easily into the ancient clan structure, rooted in landowning, and which found little support for their interests from the ruling aristocrats. Within the governing aristocratic circle there developed factions whose rivalries sharpened the tensions. By about 630 B.C. the situation had become so serious that a would-be tyrant nearly seized power.

Ultimately, the ruling aristocracy responded to these pressures by introducing changes in the political system. In 621 B.C. a reformer named Draco was able to codify the law in a way which curtailed the power of aristocratic judges to use the courts as a tool of oppression. Shortly after, there appeared a more significant reformer named Solon. Elected archon in 594 B.C., Solon was given extensive power to restore order. Although an aristocrat by birth, Solon was a man of broad vision, deep intellectual interests, and strong patriotism, all reflected in surviving fragments of his poetry. His reforms seem to have emerged from a conviction that Athens was endangered by aristocratic oppression of the poor and by the lack of opportunity for many citizens to improve their economic lot.

In his effort to aid the poor and the oppressed, Solon struck down the ancient debt laws that permitted landlords to extract exorbitant returns from small farmers who fell into debt and even to enslave them. Many who had fallen into bondage were freed, and some who had fled Athens because of debt were repatriated. Steps were taken to encourage new forms of agriculture, especially the production of olive oil, a product which could be sold abroad. Solon was especially concerned with promoting trade and industry as a means of enriching Athens and offering new opportunities to the poor. To this end, he introduced a new coinage system and recruited skilled artisans from abroad.

To check aristocratic abuses of power, Solon made changes in the structure of government. As a means of offsetting the power exercised by aristocratic families through their domination of the brotherhoods, he reorganized the entire citizen body into four classes, each defined in terms of income derived from land. This classification system opened the way for a wider and more regular involvement of all citizens in political life. Only those from the first two classes—the wealthy—could hold the chief elective offices from which they passed to life membership in the Areopagus. The two lower income groupings were given a place in the *ecclesia,* which began to take on greater importance in Athenian governance. To assist the *ecclesia* Solon instituted a new body, called the *Council of Four Hundred,* made up of one hundred citizens selected from each of the four tribes. This body's main functions were to prepare matters for the *ecclesia*'s deliberations and to provide recommendations on what actions that body should take. While the Areopagus, controlled by the rich, still had the final authority in most matters, the new Council of Four Hundred could play an important role in shaping decisions. Solon also took a major step in curbing abuses in the administration of justice by making the *Heliaea* instead of the Areopagus the final court of appeal. The *Heliaea,* theoretically composed of all citizens sitting in the *ecclesia* but constituted in practice as a large panel of that body selected by lot, now had the power to correct inequities perpetrated in the tribal and brotherhood courts which were totally dominated by powerful family heads. All of these changes in the political system still left the governance of the *polis* in the hands of the aristocrats, but together they gave the citizenry as a

whole the means to prevent abuses of power that worked against their interests.

Although Solon's reforms provided means of checking abuses and helped to strengthen the economy of Athens, they did not bring stability. Strong factionalism, with noble families in the forefront, marked political life during the first half of the sixth century B.C. These struggles opened the way for tyranny.

Athens' first tyrant was a nobleman, Pisistratus, who finally established control in 546 B.C. after two earlier abortive attempts. He held power until his death in 527, and his sons continued the regime until 510. Pisistratus came to power by force, using foreign mercenaries paid out of his own wealth and the contributions of foreigners hostile toward Athens. He and his sons made no changes in the constitutional structure of Athens, but they did direct the overall policy of the government toward safeguarding the interests of the poor. They promoted a foreign policy that greatly expanded Athenian commercial and industrial interests to the advantage of the merchants and artisans. They patronized public works and the arts with vigor, thereby providing jobs for many and making Athens prominent as a cultural center.

Tyranny was overthrown in Athens chiefly through the efforts of the aristocrats whose power had been curbed for thirty-five years; their cause was abetted by help from Sparta. But they had no chance to restore their old monopoly. Another reformer, Cleisthenes (archon in 508 B.C.), took the initiative in establishing a democratic regime in which power rested with the total citizen body. He carried out this important reform by abolishing the political functions of the twelve brotherhoods and the four tribes they constituted, although leaving them their ancient religious and social functions. To replace the old clan-dominated system, he divided the whole city-state into territorial units called *demes.* All freemen living in a *deme* were registered as citizens, family connections making no difference. The *demes* were combined into ten new tribes. In forming the tribes, Cleisthenes made a special effort to conciliate clashing economic and social interests. Over the years Attica had developed three distinct geographical regions in which special interests prevailed — the hill country, where poor farmers lived; the plain, where the land was most fertile and the great noble families were based; and the coast, where the artisans and merchants of the city proper predominated. Each tribe was composed of *demes* drawn from each of these districts; as a result, each of the basic units of political life contained a cross section of the population. Each *deme* and tribe was a political unit in its own right with officials, courts, taxes, and military forces allowing a wide range of opportunity for direct political participation by local citizens.

Cleisthenes then rearranged the main organs of government to fit the new tribal organization. The Council of Four Hundred was replaced by a Council of Five Hundred, fifty citizens of each tribe selected by lot for annual terms. No one could serve on this council more than twice in a lifetime. This body, however, did not have the final authority, which rested with the *ecclesia* made up of all male citizens over eighteen years of age voting by tribe. It met at least once a month and decided upon matters prepared for its deliberation by the Council of Five Hundred. Thus the citizen body, consisting of perhaps 30,000 or 40,000 males, had the final power in the state. The citizens were further involved in governing the city through the Heliaea, which remained as Solon had constituted it. Finally, Cleisthenes ensured popular control over the *polis* by introducing the practice of *ostracism*, through which a majority of citizens in the *ecclesia* could vote an individual dangerous to the state and exile him for ten years. Cleisthenes did not disturb the Areopagus, although it now lacked the authority to guide crucial decisions, and the elected archons remained the executive officers of the city-state. They were elected by the *ecclesia* and were still usually from aristocratic backgrounds, but now they had to win the support of the total body of citizens. Cleisthenes thus provided political equality for the citizens and devised a way whereby a majority of them could decide all matters. This was democracy.

Cleisthenes' system of government was not much changed in later years. It did require some time for the citizenry to become accustomed to the full exercise of its power. Not until the time of Pericles, the chief political figure in Athens from 461 to 429 B.C., did Athenian democracy reach its full bloom. Pericles was not primarily a lawmaker, although he did enact measures stripping the Areopagus of its last remnants of power. More important, he introduced payment for service in the Council of Five Hundred, the Heliaea, and the elective magistracies. This enabled the poor to engage in political life without sacrificing their livelihood. Pericles' real importance lay in the encouragement he gave to citizens to participate in political life. Although aristocratic by birth and the companion of the leading intellectuals and artists of his day, he felt no fear in entrusting the political destiny of Athens to the common citizens. His own exemplary conduct as a leader convinced nearly all citizens that public life was a dignified, responsible, and rewarding activity.

In discussing the nature of fifth-century Athenian democracy, we must make one important reservation. Participation in political life was confined to citizens, a severely limited group in Periclean Athens. Only those whose ancestors had been citizens could qualify for that precious right. Large numbers of foreigners (called *metics*) and slaves did not and thus took no part in political life. Since metics and slaves outnumbered citizens, a minority of the population actually governed the city.

5. SPARTA

Many Greek city-states followed a pattern of development similar to that of Athens, ending with a system that encouraged participation in civic affairs by all citizens. But not all, as Spartan history illustrates.

The city-state of Sparta emerged as a result of the coalition of several small agricultural villages founded by the Dorians when they invaded southern Peloponnesus about 1100 B.C. As the city-state developed during the early part of the Archaic Age, its institutions differed little from those of other city-states. Ruled by its kings and a powerful landed aristocracy, Sparta played a considerable role in the mainstream of Greek life down to the seventh century. There was one difference, however. When the Spartans began to feel

Sparta's policy led to consequences which caused a complete reorganization of the city-state. The Messenians rose in revolt in about 640 B.C. After a desperate struggle lasting twenty years, the revolt was suppressed. In its wake, Spartan society was radically restructured to assure military strength sufficient to retain control over the city's subjects. The reform was attributed to a great lawgiver, Lycurgus, a legendary figure given credit for changes carried out by several leaders over several decades in the late seventh and early sixth centuries B.C. The most fundamental feature of the new order was the division of the population into three classes, each with responsibilities rigidly defined in terms of serving the city-state. First were the *Spartans,* comprising a relatively small portion of the total population and all considered as social equals. The members of this class—the real citizens—dedicated their lives to soldiering; no other occupation was permitted to them except preparedness to subject the rest of the population. Next were the *perioeci,* a class charged with whatever trading and manufacturing were necessary to sustain the state. Finally, there were the *helots,* state slaves who served as laborers on the land or as personal servants. Membership in each class was hereditary, and there was little movement from one class to another.

The so-called Lycurgan reforms prescribed a regimen to be followed by each Spartan to prepare him for his life's service as a soldier. At birth each child of a Spartan citizen was inspected by state officials for physical fitness. If the child was defective, the state ordered death by exposure. If allowed to live, the child lived with his mother until the age of seven. Then the males were sent to barracks, where severe military training, stressing physical fitness, discipline, simplicity of life, obedience, and patriotism, was given them until the age of twenty. Females were likewise rigorously trained to become the mothers and wives of future soldiers.

At twenty, the Spartan male became a regular soldier, deriving his income from a piece of land that the state assigned to him along with enough helots to farm it. He could marry after he was twenty, although he was not permitted to live with his wife until he was thirty, when he was

This bronze statue of a Spartan warrior, about 6 inches high, dates from the late sixth century B.C.
Photo: Courtesy Wadsworth Atheneum, Hartford

the economic stresses that gripped most of the Aegean world in the Archaic Age, their solution was to conquer their neighbors and force them to labor for Sparta's benefit. Especially crucial was the conquest of Messenia, lying to the west of Sparta, a step which made Sparta the largest of all city-states in terms of territory.

also allowed to take part in political life. At sixty he could retire from military service.

The helots and perioeci escaped this regime, but they too were carefully disciplined. Every year the state formally declared war on the helots so that any troublemaker could be killed on the spot. The perioeci had greater freedom, even being allowed to govern themselves in some cases, but they were excluded from decisions affecting the policy of Sparta and therefore never had a chance to command a leading position in Spartan society.

This rigid social order was held in place by a governmental system derived in large part from earlier political institutions. The government was formally headed by two kings, but the real power of these co-kings was slight. Actual power rested in the *gerousia,* a council of elders made up of the two kings and twenty-eight men over sixty years old elected to serve for life. This body formulated all legislation, judged the most important cases, and acted as an advisory body to the administration of the state. Its decisions had to be presented to an assembly made up of all male Spartans over thirty. Theoretically the assembly had the power to repudiate any policy, but one can well imagine that this assembly of citizen soldiers, peopled by men taught from childhood to obey orders and to let their superiors do the thinking, was seldom able to render an independent decision. The execution of laws was entrusted to a board of five *ephors,* elected annually by the assembly, which conducted foreign affairs, supervised military training, policed the helots, and handled all matters of military preparation. Throughout most of Spartan history the ephors exercised virtually dictatorial powers, especially if, as was usually the case, they agreed with the thirty-member *gerousia.* Sparta was thus ruled by an oligarchy of military commanders.

Once the new system was completed, it proved effective. Sparta enjoyed an internal stability that was envied by many other Greeks. While the system was not conducive to intellectual and artistic pursuits, it did provide Sparta with the most powerful military force in Greece. By 500 B.C. she had forced most of the city-states in the Peloponnesus to join the Peloponnesian League. The member cities were allowed independence but were forced to follow Spartan leadership in foreign affairs. Her armies and her allies prepared Sparta to play a major role in Greek history after 500 B.C.

6. THE CHARACTER OF THE POLIS

The two or three hundred other city-states that had been shaped by the fifth century each considered its institutions as excellent and as typically "Greek" as those of Athens and Sparta. In fact, there was infinite variety in the structure of the Greek *poleis;* the Greeks spent much intellectual energy — and sometimes blood — debating the merits of various political systems. But more significant in the grand historical picture are the features common to all *poleis.*

The city-states were all small, intimate organisms, embracing a territory seldom as large as an American county and a populace often less than that of a modern university. In each *polis* life focused on a spot — a town — familiar to all, where were concentrated political, religious, economic, and cultural activities bearing directly on all. Each made citizenship a distinctive and precious condition of life that involved direct and active participation in civic affairs. What the Greek historian Thucydides credited Pericles with saying of Athens can serve as a fundamental characterization of all *poleis:* "We alone regard a man who takes no interest in public affairs, not as harmless, but as a useless character." Whatever its constitutional form might be, the *polis* drew the individual out of himself, his clan, his calling, his class to make him a participant in a community enterprise. It made him, as Aristotle put it, a political animal. Active involvement nourished a psychological state in the political animal, breeding patriotism — fierce pride in and love for his *polis.* Every *polis* was then a pressure chamber compelling men to discover and exercise their talents in the interests of something larger, more enduring, and more splendid than themselves. As such, the *polis* nourished an intensity of life seldom witnessed in history and brought forth achievements which sometimes seem almost superhuman.

Suggested Reading

General Surveys of Greek History
*Antony Andrewes, *The Greeks* (Norton).
M. I. Finley, *The Ancient Greeks: An Introduction to their Life and Thought* (1963).
*H. D. F. Kitto, *The Greeks* (Pelican). Any of these three books will provide a stimulating short introduction to the history of the Greeks.
N. G. L. Hammond, *A History of Greece to 322 B.C.* (1959). An excellent longer account, treating all aspects of Greek development.

The Mycenaean, Dark, and Archaic Ages
C. G. Starr, *The Origins of Greek Civilization* (1961).
R. J. Hopper, *The Early Greeks* (1976). Two excellent surveys of early Greek history, based on the most recent research.
J. T. Hooker, *Mycenaean Greece* (1976).
*John Chadwick, *The Mycenaean World* (Cambridge).
*Emily Vermeule, *Greece in the Bronze Age* (Phoenix). Three excellent studies on a phase of early Greek history that has undergone significant reinterpretation in recent years.
*M. I. Finley, *Early Greece: The Bronze and Archaic Ages* (Norton).
T. D. Seymour, *Life in the Homeric Age* (1963). This and the preceding title are excellent on the history of the Archaic Age.

The Polis and Its Evolution
*Alfred E. Zimmern, *The Greek Commonwealth: Politics and Economics in Fifth-Century Athens* (Galaxy). A classic treatment of the fundamental nature of the city-state.
*Kathleen Freeman, *Greek City-States* (Norton). A more recent work than Zimmern's, especially good for the information it provides on city-states other than Athens and Sparta.
*W. G. Forrest, *The Emergence of Greek Democracy, 800–400 B.C.* (McGraw-Hill).
C. Hignett, *History of the Athenian Constitution to the End of the Fifth Century, B.C.* (1952). Two excellent studies of the evolution of the Athenian political system.

A. H. M. Jones, *Athenian Democracy* (1957). Especially useful for understanding the operation of the Athenian system of government.
*W. G. Forrest, *History of Sparta, 950–192 B.C.* (Norton). A good study of Spartan development.
*A. Andrewes, *Greek Tyrants* (Harper Torchbook). Provides a clear picture of the role of tyrants in Greek history.

Economic and Social History
*Chester G. Starr, *The Economic and Social Growth of Early Greece, 800–500 B.C.* (Oxford).
Hendrik Bolkestein, *Economic Life in Greece's Golden Age* (rev. ed., 1958). These two works present a full picture of material factors shaping Greek society.
Robert Flacelière, *Daily Life in Greece at the Time of Pericles,* trans. Peter Green (1965). A good portrayal of how the Greeks lived.
*John Boardman, *The Greeks Overseas* (Penguin). A full account of an important aspect of Greek development.

Sources
*Homer, *Iliad* and *Odyssey* (many editions; an excellent one is the translation by E. V. Rieu, Penguin). Essential for understanding the origins of a unique Greek society.
Hesiod, *Works and Days,* trans. H. G. Evelyn-White, Loeb Classical Library. A picture by a contemporary of the economic and social stresses of eighth-century Greece.
*Aristotle, *On the Constitution of Athens,* trans. K. von Fritz and E. Kapp (Hafner).
Xenophon, "Constitution of the Lacedaemonians," in *Scripta Minora,* trans. E. E. Merchant (1925). This and the preceding work provide descriptions by two Greeks of the constitutions of Athens and Sparta.
*Plutarch, *Lives* (many editions). Presents short biographies of Lycurgus, Solon, Themistocles, and Pericles that offer insight into the careers of key political figures associated with the evolution of Greek city-states.

5

WAR, POLITICS, AND THE FAILURE OF THE GREEK CITY-STATE POLITY

In its full bloom in the fifth century B.C., the *polis* was a marvelous institution for spurring its citizens to expend their talents for the internal well-being of each city-state. Much of the history of the Golden Age, as the fifth century B.C. is often called, centered on the continued development of the city-state system. But increasingly, another issue became critical: the problem of the relationships among the numerous, small, fiercely patriotic communities, each struggling to strengthen and to enrich itself in a world of limited resources. At the beginning of the century, a threat from outside the Greek world demonstrated the value of cooperation, but that spirit could not in the long run be sustained. Progressively the city-states surrendered to their parochialism and became engaged in a succession of intercity struggles that destroyed not only their material prosperity but also their internal energies. These struggles greatly weakened the ability of the Greek city-states to assert their leadership over the civilization of the Mediterranean world.

1. THE PERSIAN WARS, 490–479 B.C.

Prior to 500 B.C. the Greeks were often engaged in war with each other, but these wars were generally on a limited scale. The Greeks poured their energies into shaping the political and social institutions of their city-states, building settlements overseas, strengthening their economic position, and creating impressive cultural monuments. In fact, certain trends suggested that the city-states were becoming more interdependent. A major pan-Hellenic force was religion, which gave the Greeks a common set of gods and promoted such pan-Hellenic festivities as the Olympic Games, created to honor these deities with splendid ceremonies and athletic competition. Most Greeks shared a common language, which became the vehicle for a literary tradition shared by all the city-states. Increasing commerce led to increasing economic interdependence. Some progress had even been made toward political unions, such as the already noted Peloponnesian League.

The practical need for strong pan-Hellenism was dramatically posed at the beginning of the fifth century by the threat posed by the Persian Empire. For nearly two centuries prior to 500, the Greeks had been increasing their commercial and cultural contacts with the Near East and had benefited greatly from this highly civilized world. Some of the Greek cities on the Ionian coast of Asia Minor had even been incorporated into the Lydian Empire while it was the dominant force in Asia Minor. But the sudden emergence of Persia after 550 B.C. created entirely new relationships between the Greek world and the Near East. Persian expansion engulfed the Lydians and brought the Greeks of

Asia Minor under Persian rule. That rule was not unduly harsh, especially under Darius I, but it seemed burdensome to the Greek city-states, long accustomed to independence or the easy overlordship of Lydia. The city-states in Europe sympathized with their captive fellow Greeks and viewed the Persians as a threat to the independence of all Greek cities. They became particularly alarmed when Darius invaded Europe in 512 and established his rule in an area lying north of the Aegean called Thrace.

Hostility between Greeks and Persians grew rapidly after 499, when the Greek cities in Asia Minor revolted against the Persians. The rebels called on the European Greeks for aid and received it from Athens and Eretria. Darius crushed the rebellion, however, and determined to punish those who came from Greece to make trouble in his empire. He was encouraged to believe that this might be an easy task by political factions—usually antidemocratic—in many city-states who saw the Persians as potential allies in their struggle for power and by the neutrality proclaimed by several key city-states. He did not realize, however, that there were equally potent forces emerging in the same cities who saw in the Persians a threat to the new Greek way of life just coming into bloom.

In 490 B.C. Darius sent a fleet bearing a moderate-sized army across the Aegean, ostensibly to punish Athens and Eretria but perhaps to begin the conquest of the Greeks. After destroying Eretria, the Persian army landed in eastern Attica near Marathon, probably expecting that pro-Persian elements in Athens would launch an internal revolt to open the way to the city. But the Athenians, although outnumbered, decided on an attack. Under the brilliant leadership of Miltiades, they mauled the Persian army at Marathon and forced it back to its ships. The Persians then sailed around to Athens, but by the time they arrived Miltiades had marched his army from Marathon and was ready to defend the city. Since Spartan help was already arriving, the Persians sailed back to their bases in Asia Minor while the Greeks rejoiced over their triumph.

The Persians, not yet ready to accept defeat, were prevented from a new attack for ten years, chiefly because of internal disturbances accompanying the accession of Xerxes in 486 B.C. as successor to Darius. The Greek city-states, meanwhile, made better preparations than they had before Marathon. Athens was especially fortunate with the emergence of Themistocles as its leader. A staunch supporter of democracy, he stabilized the internal order of the city and persuaded its citizens to make a major increase in the size of the Athenian navy. Sparta took the leadership in 481 B.C. in forming a league of thirty-one city-states that agreed to pool their armies and navies into a joint force commanded by Spartan leaders. Despite this show of unity, many cities, especially in northern Greece, remained neutral or allied with Persia.

Early in 480 B.C. Xerxes was ready to attack. This time he chose to trust the Persian cause to a huge land army that could be supplied by the Persian navy. He moved this force into Europe across the Hellespont and marched it slowly around the northern Aegean coast and then southward toward the centers of Greek strength. The Greek League decided to make its stand at Thermopylae, where a narrow pass would allow the smaller Greek army to check the massive Persian forces and where the narrow sea lanes between the mainland and the island of Euboea could be advantageously blocked by the Greek fleet. It seemed that the plan might succeed. The Greek fleet fought the Persians, weakened by severe losses suffered in storms, to a standstill, and the Greek army threw back attack after attack in the pass. But a local traitor showed the Persians a trail around the pass. When the Greek commander, King Leonidas of Sparta, discovered what had happened, he sent the bulk of the Greek army south while he and three hundred Spartans fought to the death to delay the Persians. Once past Thermopylae, the Persians flooded into central Greece. Athens was captured and burned, atlhough her citizens fled to safety.

At this point, Themistocles exercised a deciding influence. There was strong pressure in the council of the Greek League to withdraw the armies to the Peloponnesus and the fleet to the Gulf of Corinth. Seeing clearly that the issue would be decided by sea power. Themistocles

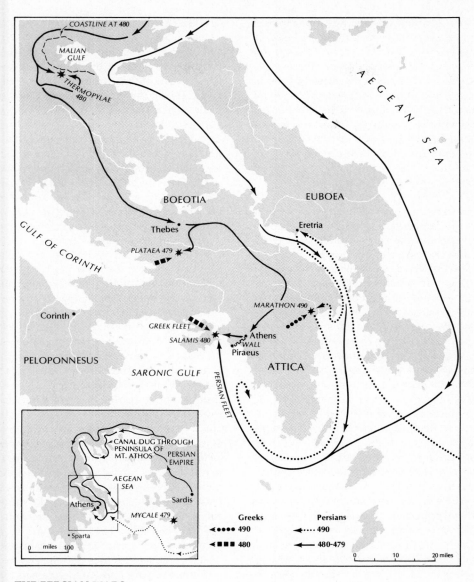

COASTLINE AT 480

MALIAN GULF

THERMOPYLAE 480

AEGEAN SEA

BOEOTIA

EUBOEA

Thebes

Eretria

PLATAEA 479

GULF OF CORINTH

MARATHON 490

Corinth

GREEK FLEET

SALAMIS 480

Athens
WALL
Piraeus

PELOPONNESUS

SARONIC GULF

ATTICA

PERSIAN FLEET

CANAL DUG THROUGH
PENINSULA OF
MT. ATHOS

PERSIAN
EMPIRE

AEGEAN
SEA

Athens

Sardis

MYCALE 479

Sparta

0   miles   100

Greeks	Persians
◄●●●● 490	◄·····490
◄■■■ 480	◄——— 480-479

0   10   20 miles

THE PERSIAN WARS

combined persuasion and threats of Athenian withdrawal to convince the league to face the Persians in the waters off Attica. In late September 480 B.C., he maneuvered the Persians into an engagement in the narrow strait between Attica and the island of Salamis. Caught where they could not use their full strength effectively, the Persians suffered a shattering defeat. Since the winter season was close at hand, Xerxes ordered his fleet back to Asia Minor and the withdrawal of his armies to northern Greece, for they could not survive without sea support.

Xerxes undertook a new campaign in the spring of 479. This time a sizable Greek army moved out to meet the Persians and defeated them at Plataea. In the meantime the Greeks sailed boldly across the Aegean and destroyed what was left of the Persian fleet at Mycale. This was a signal for the Greek cities in Asia Minor to revolt once again. Xerxes could do nothing but recall his armies from Europe; the Greek fleet could now cut the path of escape in the straits. The jubilant Greeks had demonstrated their vitality against even so great a foe as Persia.

2. CONFEDERACY OF DELOS

The Greek victories in 480–479 had been magnificent, but the Persians were still a threat. This realization kept alive the spirit of unity among the Greeks, although leadership passed into new hands. The Spartans, who had directed the league in the critical days of 480 and 479, grew increasingly unwilling to commit their limited strength to projects remote from the Peloponnesus. Athens took the lead in summoning a meeting of Greek cities on the island of Delos in 478. It was quickly agreed to form the Confederacy of Delos to continue the war against Persia. Policy decisions were to be made by representatives of all the cities meeting annually in an assembly, with Athens executing the decisions. The members pledged to contribute ships and money according to their abilities. And the cherished independence of each *polis* was protected; no city-state was required to surrender its sovereignty.

The confederacy immediately swung into action. An Athenian, Cimon, was placed in command of its forces and enjoyed immediate success against the Persians. Within about ten years, all the Greek city-states in Asia Minor had been freed from Persian rule, while the Aegean and the straits area were cleared of Persian naval power. Athens was obviously the most powerful city in the league, but she conducted herself with marked restraint in her relations with her fellow city-states. Cimon's policy was conciliatory even toward nonmembers such as Sparta. Seldom before or after did the Greek world present a more unified front than during the first years following the victory over the Persians.

3. THE ATHENIAN EMPIRE

This happy condition did not last long—and Athens was responsible for altering the situation. As the danger from Persia receded, some members of the confederacy desired to withdraw. Athens was unwilling to allow this to happen. Her leaders and many of her citizens saw that Athenian sea power, developed to check the Persians, could be turned to commercial advantage. Athens slowly began to convert the league into an empire under her control. She refused to allow members to withdraw, used territories won by league forces to establish her own colonies, and forced cities not in the league to join.

Athenian imperialism reached its full tide with the emergence of Pericles as the leader of the city in 461 B.C. He came to power in the wake of the downfall of Cimon, who had tried to restrain Athenian imperialism to a degree. We have already noted the role Pericles played in strengthening democracy in Athens. With overwhelming popular support, he launched a two-pronged drive to spread Athenian influence. In Greece he used every method available to force more cities into the confederacy under Athenian control. He supported revolts against nondemocratic governments, tried to entice the members of the Peloponnesian League to abandon Sparta, and used Athenian sea power to bottle up such trading powers as Corinth. Meanwhile, he renewed the assault on Persia, carrying the struggle into the eastern Mediterranean. In both offensives, he enjoyed some success. But about 450 B.C. it became obvious that Athens was overextending her power, and in spite of popular opposition, Pericles arranged peace treaties with both Persia and Sparta. In a treaty of 449 B.C. Persia and Athens agreed to respect each other's spheres of influence; and in the Thirty Years' Truce of 445 B.C., Sparta promised to refrain from interfering in the affairs of the Confederacy of Delos while Athens agreed to halt her aggressive policy among free Greek cities and especially those in the Peloponnesian League.

These treaties left Athens with a considerable empire, consisting of about three hundred city-states in the Confederacy of Delos. She continued to collect tribute annually, although the Persian danger had vanished. The money was now used in Athens for whatever the Athenians chose. Athens forced many of the league members to institute democratic governments in the hope that such governments would be more manageable. She forced subject cities to use her money and her weights and measures. By any standard of judgment, she treated these formerly independent cities as her subjects. And she did this for her own profit.

The profit was indeed great and very beneficial to Athens. At the height of the Periclean Age, she had grown to a population of perhaps 400,000, about 160,000 of these citizens and the rest alien artisans (metics) and slaves. The tribute money and the wealth from commerce made her richer than all others. A considerable part went to the citizenry as payment for the service in the many political agencies of the Periclean system of democracy. And it was liberally used to beautify the city and support the writers and artists who made Athens the "school of Hellas." The master hand of Pericles guided this great polis with sureness, purpose, and total trust in the citizens, and to his guidance they responded with good judgment and restraint. But fifth-century Athens would not have been the jewel of Hellas had it not been for the price she exacted from her "allies."

The subject city-states, of course, shared the fruits of increased commerce and the security that came from the imposed peace. Still, their hatred for Athens grew steadily. Its source was political. Athens had usurped their one valuable privilege, political independence. She had become an oppressor, endangering liberty everywhere. Even some of the Athenians felt moral aversion at destroying the liberty of any polis and raised their voices in protest. But the mass of the people, aware that the economic welfare of Athens was related to imperial power, overrode these voices.

Athens made no attempt to compensate her subjects for limitations on their freedom. They were not permitted to become citizens of Athens, and they were allowed no representation in the Athenian government. Gradually, anti-Athenian feeling spread throughout the Greek world. These city-states now began to look toward Sparta as a champion of freedom. This was a rather strange development, considering Sparta's own record of domination over the cities of Peloponnesus. The anti-Athenian sentiment heralded a serious war in which Greek assaulted Greek, unmindful of the many things the city-states had in common.

4. THE PELOPONNESIAN WAR, 431–404 B.C.

The uneasy peace in the Greek world was finally shattered in 431 B.C. by the outbreak of the Peloponnesian War. Its immediate cause was the success of a few cities, especially Corinth, in convincing Sparta that Athens was violating the Thirty Years' Truce, thereby threatening the independence of all Greek cities. Athens was not unwilling to join the issue, probably feeling that a showdown was inevitable. She had a large fleet and huge financial resources to pit against the superior land forces of Sparta and her allies. Pericles was confident that the Spartans were incapable of a campaign that would strike at the real sources of Athenian power—her maritime empire.

The first ten years of the war were indecisive. Athens refused to commit herself to a land war with Sparta; Pericles persuaded the populace to withdraw within the city's impregnable walls and let the Athenian fleet hold together the empire which the Spartans were ill-equipped to attack. This disciplined strategy proved too much for the Athenians, especially after a plague decimated the cooped-up population in 429 B.C., claiming Pericles among its victims. The restless populace demanded bolder military action; a new leader, Cleon, answered by leading Athenian armies outside Attica. The Spartans produced a leader named Brasidas, who persuaded them to use their military forces to encourage revolt among the subject cities of the Athenian empire rather than waste energy attacking the walls of Athens itself. However, before the new struggle reached a decisive point, Cleon and

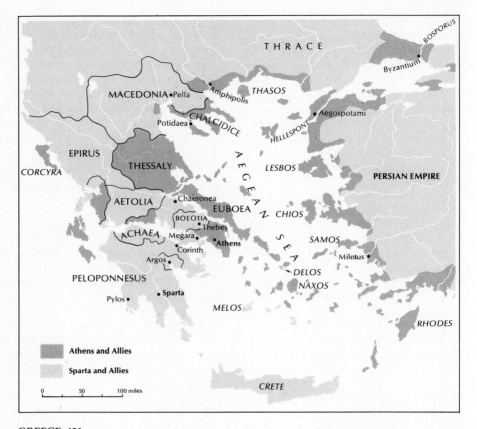

GREECE 431 B.C.

Brasidas were both killed in 422. This gave powerful peace elements in both cities a chance to end the war. In 421 B.C. they agreed to a Fifty-Year Truce, which returned their relations to what they had been before the war.

The truce lasted only until 415. Again, Athens was responsible for ending it. Led by the brilliant and popular but overly ambitious Alcibiades, she launched an ill-conceived expedition against the great Greek city of Syracuse in Sicily, where the Athenians suffered a disastrous defeat after a two-year campaign. Worse, her attack on Syracuse provoked Sparta and her allies to renew the war against an Athens seriously weakened by the Sicilian venture.

After 413 the fortunes of Athens declined steadily. The main theater of war shifted to the Aegean Sea, where the Spartans, brilliantly led by Lysander, proceeded to destroy Athenian sea power while encouraging the cities of the Confederacy of Delos to revolt. At the same time, Sparta allied herself with the Persian king, who supplied money and ships in return for Spartan permission to reestablish Persian control over the Greek cities in Asia Minor. Athens occasionally won an isolated victory, but the net of Spartan-Persian power continued to close around her. Finally in 404 B.C. she surrendered. The victors forced her to tear down her walls, to destroy all but twelve of her ships, and to submit to a government of oligarchs who were guarded by a Spartan army stationed in the city. Although these Thirty Tyrants, as the Athenians called them, were ousted in 403 and democratic government was restored. Athens never recovered her former power.

5. THE DECLINE OF THE CITY-STATES, 404–336 B.C.

The defeat of Athens in no way solved the problem of intercity rivalry. The Peloponnesian War, which left a legacy of deep hatred, had caused other problems as well. Trade had been badly disturbed, and numerous areas of Greece had been laid waste. In many cities the declining economy bred serious class struggles. Often the lower classes were prevented from stating their case because democracy had suffered a heavy blow with the defeat of its champion, Athens. Many Greeks, especially intellectual leaders, grew pessimistic and sought escape from their civic responsibilities in individual pursuits.

The majority of Greeks failed to realize what was happening. They persisted in engaging one another in fruitless struggles that merely compounded the problems. Sparta, now the greatest power in Greece, behaved even more dishonorably than had Athens. She pursued a reactionary policy of imposing oligarchic government on any city-state she could bully into submission. When the Greek world protested her narrow and often brutal policy, she turned to Persia for help, which only increased Greek hatred of Spartans.

The resentment against Sparta led to a new series of wars. Thebes now became the champion of city-state independence. Under her one great statesman, Epaminondas, Thebes smashed the declining power of Sparta in a single battle in 371 B.C. She established a new league under her control, but was never able to extend it to all Greece. She too succumbed to the lure of Persian money in the attempt to ensure her own supremacy, but even Persian assistance was insufficient. A new coalition of cities, led once again by Athens, inflicted a fatal defeat on Thebes in 362 B.C.

The incessant warfare went on, but none of the city-states was able to establish the predominant position that might have meant peace. Instead, struggles prompted by the smallest issues continued to waste human and material resources and put the citizens of all the city-states under constant strain. Civic life was being sapped. The engulfing weakness and discouragement were especially dangerous at this moment. For on the northern fringe of the Greek world a powerful giant, the semibarbarous Macedonian kingdom, was casting greedy eyes on the seething turmoil to the south; and in the west Carthage and Rome were stirring.

Some Greeks became aware of the dangers of intercity warfare and raised eloquent appeals for some kind of union that would stop it and protect Greece from foreigners. Some of them, like the Athenian orator and statesman Demosthenes, argued that Athens should take the lead in forming a confederation, but his appeal was not effective in view of Athens' past conduct. Others urged that the Macedonian king serve as the head of a Greek league, but this idea was widely looked upon as treason. In general, political pan-Hellenism was a lost cause. The Greek city-states were too accustomed to total independence to surrender their sovereignty to a super-organization. Such great philosophers as Plato and Aristotle, who lived during the fourth century, vigorously maintained that only the traditional small city-state was fit for the Greeks. With this attitude, the Greeks did nothing to put a stop to their quarrels.

6. MACEDONIAN CONQUEST OF GREECE

The Greek city-states, unable to check their feuding, grew increasingly ripe for conquest. The conqueror rather unexpectedly turned out to be Macedon. The Macedonians had not had a particularly brilliant history before the fourth century. The land was poor and inhabited by an unruly, semibarbarous people who long resisted efforts to organize them. However, the situation changed rapidly under the leadership of Philip II, king from 359 to 336 B.C. This masterful ruler showed considerable skill in welding his wild subjects into a disciplined and loyal army and in reorganizing his kingdom internally to support that army. From this increasingly strong power base Philip turned his attention to the Greek world, to which he was drawn by ambition and a deep admiration for all things Greek.

The expansion of Macedonian influence into Greece involved a complex play of political forces. Many Greek city-states engaged in war with each other sought Philip's support to give them an advantage over their Greek enemies. He was not above intriguing to incite wars in Greece so that his services would be called upon. Wherever he became involved, Philip ended with the upper hand. Gradually the confusion in the Greek world began to clear as the Greeks realized the strength of Macedon and as Philip's growing mastery made itself felt. Athens emerged as the champion against Macedon and tried desperately to rally the rest of the Greeks to that cause, but the struggle was one-sided from the beginning. Demosthenes, whose eloquent pleas to the Athenian population to wake up to the threat from the north can still be read in his *Philippics,* did succeed on occasion in persuading the Athenians to send aid to Greek cities besieged by Philip, but usually too late and always too little. Demosthenes' efforts to form a Greek union fared little better. Slowly Philip advanced, finally forcing the Athenian alliance to commit itself to battle at Chaeronea in 338 B.C. In a single engagement the last strength of the Greeks was destroyed by Philip's well-trained army. Greece lay at his feet to be dealt with as he chose.

Philip II treated his victims with extreme mildness. He did, however, end the old order in Greece. One of his first moves was to call a meeting of all Greek city-states in 338 B.C. and form them into a Hellenic league, formally called the League of Corinth. Members of this league were theoretically entitled to complete independence, but in fact crucial restrictions were placed upon that freedom. No city was allowed to change its existing form of government, and without freedom to change its government a city-state certainly was no longer the city-state of old. The league held regular meetings at which each city had representatives to debate and decide league policy. Finally, a common army and navy were created, with each state contributing according to its ability. Although Macedon was not a member, Philip required that the league sign a treaty of alliance with her, thereby giving the Macedonian king an important voice in its decisions.

Philip dictated the first undertaking of the League of Corinth: a war on the Persian Empire,

a goal most Greeks could approve. But he did not live to lead the union of Greeks and Macedonians in an Asian campaign. One of his own nobles assassinated him in 336 B.C., perhaps at the behest of his wife, who did not fully approve of Philip's lack of respect for the institution of marriage.

Philip II was certainly one of the most far-seeing statesmen of the fourth century. He was aware of the folly of the rivalry that had kept the Greek cities in a state of warfare for nearly a century. To end this, he used the superior strength of Macedon to force them into a union sufficiently strong to check the strife, and he sought to divert the martial characteristics of the Greeks into a war against Persia. These policies mark a turning point in Greek history. Philip II has seldom been given full credit, for his son, Alexander, put into practice the policies Philip had conceived.

7. THE SIGNIFICANCE OF THE CITY-STATE

The fateful course toward self-destruction followed by the Greek city-states during the fifth and fourth centuries B.C. is hardly inspiring. It may seem that the history of this period involves a contradiction. Much has been made of the unique vitality and strength of the *polis* — but in view of its precipitous decline, could it have been so great an institution? There can be no doubt that the city-state generated self-destructive warfare. It obviously limited the political capabilities of the Greeks to regulate relations among independent, proud, self-contained political units. But we should recall that man has always had grave difficulty restraining himself from warfare and from the destruction of his best handiwork. The generalization that inter-city warfare was the nemesis of the Greek *polis* may be too obvious and too easy.

The study of Greek history in this period leads one to suspect that the fatal flaw in the *polis* lay in the superhuman demands it made upon the frail creature that man is. It demanded of its citizens a willingness to recognize the problems of others, to judge these problems rationally, and to sacrifice self-interest in the name of a higher good. Perhaps for brief periods men are capable of such conduct, but in the long run they cannot sustain it. Individuals and classes could not sustain the rational, detached posture—what the Greeks themselves defined as the aristocratic view—demanded to keep the *polis* alive. They descended in human fashion to self-seeking and self-interest and to irrational warfare. It was a failure of men, not institutions, that doomed the *polis*. The city-state suffered from what was perhaps the nemesis of the whole of Greek civilization—too high an estimate of the capabilities of men.

Whatever its flaws, the Greek city-state was amazing, at least for a brief period. For the first time in history, large numbers of people were virtually compelled to rise above themselves to search out and put to work whatever talents they might have. The age-old system of masses of men bent before the will of a few masters was challenged and found wanting. The typical Greek *polis* demonstrated that even the most ordinary man could do remarkable things if he had the freedom.

This scene from an Attic pottery cup (ca. 480 B.C.) shows an Athenian woman helping her husband put on his arms—perhaps to fight the Persians at Marathon. The painted vase was one of the finest of Greek art forms, employed by skilled artists to represent a wide variety of scenes ranging from mythological themes to portrayals of everyday life. *Photo: The Granger Collection*

Suggested Reading

Fifth- and Fourth-Century Greece

M. L. W. Laistner, *A History of the Greek World from 479 to 323 B.C.* (3rd ed., 1957).

N. G. L. Hammond, *The Classical Age of Greece* (1975). This and the preceding title are excellent detailed accounts of the political history of the era.

*A. R. Burn, *Persia and the Greeks* (Minerva). An interesting study of the Persian Wars.

*A. R. Burn, *Pericles and Athens* (Collier). Will help to evaluate the policy of Athens in the heyday of its empire.

Russell Meiggs, *The Athenian Empire* (1972). A full description of the subject.

Sources

*Herodotus, *The Persian Wars,* trans. Aubrey de Selincourt (Penguin). A stirring account of the encounter between Greeks and Persians; one of the great classics of historical writing.

*Thucydides, *The Peloponnesian War,* trans. Rex Warner (Penguin). Another classic describing the bitter struggle between Athens and Sparta.

*Plutarch, *Lives* (many editions). The short biographies of Themistocles, Aristides, Cimon, Pericles, Alcibiades, Lysander, and Demosthenes will add color to the history of this era.

6

GREEK CULTURE

Our examination of the Greek *polis* as a political, social, and economic institution revealed it as an instrument capable of evoking from its citizen members intense activity, activity generally creative and beneficial but sometimes destructive. We must now approach the *polis* from another, more difficult perspective. It provided the setting for one of the most creative cultural outbursts in all history. Living within its confines and interacting with others according to its rules, men were stimulated to modes of thought and expression that still seem amazing for their variety, their quality, and their durability. We must try in this chapter to grasp a sense of the "miracle" of Greek thought and expression as revealed in literature, art, philosophy, and science. It was in this realm that the *polis* produced something shared by all Greeks, something "Hellenic," as they would have said, to balance the divisiveness bred in political life.

1. AN OVERVIEW

The roots of Greek culture lie far back in the history of the Aegean world, the seeds having been planted by neolithic men, early Indo-European invaders, Minoan influences, and Mycenaean achievements. During the long Dark Age, that inheritance was shaped within the isolated Aegean world to produce a uniquely Hellenic culture. The first fruits of this new culture emerged in the eighth century in highly original

pottery decoration and in the Homeric epics. From the eighth through the sixth centuries B.C., the Archaic Age, the new culture developed rapidly, its unique characteristics being nourished by the changes in society which marked the development of the *polis* and by increasing contacts with the outside world resulting from overseas settlement and expanding commerce. New poetic forms, large-scale architecture, and three-dimensional sculpture evolved. By the end of the period, the first signs of rational philosophical inquiry and mature prose literature had appeared.

During a relatively short period in the fifth century B.C. extending from the beginning of the Persian Wars through the Peloponnesian War, Greek culture reached its Golden Age, with Athens as the chief center. The esthetics and ideas shaped in the Archaic Age were honed to perfection by a remarkable group of artists and thinkers who reflected a strong civic and religious sense but who were powerfully animated by a rational impulse and an increasing concern with the individual. This was the age of tragic and comic drama, the poetry of Pindar, the history of Herodotus, the architectural and sculptural masterpieces of the Acropolis in Athens, the science of Hippocrates, and the philosophical inquiry of a succession of brilliant thinkers. However, by the end of the fifth century, signs of transformation and decline had appeared. The Sophists and their relativistic concepts, Socrates and his questioning, the dramatist Euripides and his critical attitudes, the historian Thucydides and his disillusionment set the tone of this age. By the fourth century B.C., classical Greek culture had clearly passed its peak. The literature and art produced between the end of the Peloponnesian War and the triumph of Philip of Macedon were undistinguished. Only in philosophy, dominated by Plato and Aristotle, was there still vitality. The ground was being prepared for a new phase of culture, which is called Hellenistic, one derived from the Hellenic experience but more cosmopolitan, individualistic, and personal.

2. GREEK RELIGION

A description of the cultural achievements of the Greeks must begin with their religion, for their lives were permeated with religious forces and their main cultural achievements were rooted in religious beliefs. The origins of Greek religion are buried in the earliest stages of Greek history. By the time the first clear statements on religious life were made—in the writings of Homer and Hesiod at the end of the Dark Age—an elaborate mythology and a complex set of rituals already existed. These myths and rituals represented an amalgam of concepts and practices drawn from neolithic, Indo-European, Minoan, Mycenaean, and Near Eastern sources. However, these diverse borrowings had been combined into a religious system that was uniquely Greek.

The Greeks, first of all, were polytheistic. Most of their many deities were conceived as having human forms and as conducting themselves much as earthly humans, except that the gods were immortal and infinitely more powerful than human beings. Among the vast array of gods were certain remote and abstracted forces—such as fate, death, justice, and procreation (Eros = love)—which provided the basic and unchangeable order governing the universe. More conspicuous and appealing was the tumultuous family of major deities living on Mount Olympus under the authority of Zeus, whose position resembled that of an earthly father of a noble household. From an early date, artists created visual portrayals of this pantheon in stone and paint, and writers told of their activities—their feats, their intrigues, their love lives, their incessant intrusions into the lives of men and women, their special likes and dislikes. Thus they came to be known and honored by all Greeks, and their worship provided a powerful common element in the Greek world. To many of these Olympian gods were ascribed special roles: Zeus was the father of the Olympian family, the controller of the forces of nature, and the ruler of other gods and humans; Hera, his wife, was the protector of marriage and the family; Athena was the goddess of wisdom; Apollo was the bringer of light and the patron of the arts and of prophecy; Ares was the god of war; Poseidon was the god of the seas; Aphrodite was the goddess of beauty and love; Hermes was the protector of merchants and thieves; and so forth. Several deities had among their duties the protection of particular city-states, so that the worship of the Olympian pantheon provided the basis for civic religion. However, the Olympian gods and goddesses were not the only divine forces in the Greek religious system. Myriad lesser spirits—nymphs, satyrs, muses, demons, spirits of departed heroes and ancestors—populated the world and meddled constantly in human affairs.

Although there came to be some doubters, most Greeks believed that the gods controlled all human affairs and therefore that individuals, families, and city-states had to attune their activities to divine will. Their attitudes about what to expect from the gods were mixed. There were fear-inspiring aspects to Greek religion. Underlying all Greek thought was a strong sense that a certain iron-clad order controlled by divine forces governed the universe and imposed conditions which none could escape; this view imposed a certain fatalism on Greek thought. Most Greeks viewed the Olympian deities as capricious, unpredictable, and amoral with respect to human beings, as exemplified by Zeus' insatiable lust for earthly maidens; such gods and goddesses could cause all kinds of troubles in life. There was a terrible concern among Greeks that their actions might make them victims of some kind of taint, some awful pollution that would alienate the gods and plague offenders and their offspring for generations. Yet, on the whole, the Greeks viewed their deities as basically benevolent, approachable, concerned with human well-being—in short, good. The gods and goddesses were too full of life, too "human" to inflict a burden of terror and helplessness on human beings. If men and women took care to learn the ways of the gods, bent to their will, and refrained from a prideful usurpation of their powers, they could expect divine support in filling life with what was good and perhaps even in gaining an honorable place in the company of the gods after death.

The Greeks devoted considerable energy and talent to pleasing their gods. Prayers, sacrifices, and gifts were offered according to carefully defined rituals in shrines maintained in each home and by each clan. More impressive were the splendid civic cults, for which great temples were built and maintained at considerable expense to the city-states. Large numbers of people from all walks of life participated in these civic religious activities, as is so dramatically illustrated in the sculptured frieze decorating the Parthenon in Athens portraying the annual procession of citizens in honor of Athena. On occasion, the entire Greek world joined in honoring the Olympian pantheon; the Olympic Games, held every four years from 776 B.C. on, represented a pan-Hellenic celebration honoring Zeus. Almost every kind of human activity was acceptable as a way of praising the gods—athletic contests, poetry reading, song, dance, dramatic presentations, gift offering. As a consequence, religious ceremonies were also cultural and social events. There were no elaborate priesthoods in Greece; fathers conducted rituals in households and clan centers, and elected officials served as priests for civic ceremonies. The Greeks spent considerable energy seeking advanced information about divine intentions: They interpreted dreams, studied the stars, and read the entrails of animals in search of clues. But most of all, they relied on *oracles*, who were especially gifted people through whom the gods spoke. The most famous oracle was at Delphi, where innumerable Greeks went to implore Apollo to send them messages through special priestesses, who would tell them

how to solve problems ranging from personal matters to great political issues. While the priestesses at Delphi often spoke in perplexing ways, they gave many Greeks assurance that things would work out favorably.

From a rather early date, there developed in Greece another stream of religious belief and worship to complement that centering on the Olympian deities and the civic rituals. This movement tended to respond to personal and emotional needs not fulfilled by the group-oriented civic religion strongly colored by aristocratic values. It produced what are called *mystery* religions, rooted in the ancient worship of the regenerative forces in nature and influenced by an influx of ideas and practices from the Near East. The mystery cults centered on a belief in a god or goddess who died and then arose to become a savior for individual believers properly initiated into the cult. Often such religions emphasized the power of the resurrected deity to give a happy afterlife. The youthful wine-god Dionysus was the center of such a religion throughout much of Greece. His worship, based on a belief that he had been torn to pieces by evil gods and then reborn, involved his devotees in a highly emotional initiation ceremony and in ecstatic rites accompanied by wild dancing, drinking, and the eating of raw flesh. Another mystery cult, with its center at Eleusis near Athens, developed around the worship of the fertility goddess Demeter and her daughter Persephone, raised from the dead by her mother's efforts. Over time, the mystery cults grew more subdued, as is illustrated by a poorly understood movement called Orphism, which modified Dionysus worship by emphasizing the need for an austere life and a high level of ethical conduct as a way of pleasing Dionysus and winning an escape from the material world into a happy hereafter.

Greek religion was a powerful force shaping politics, war, and daily life in every city-state. However, in the context of this chapter, it had another dimension: Religion provided the framework and the stimulus for intellectual and artistic growth. It encouraged men and women to try to understand, explain, and please the gods through literature, art, and philosophy, each of which served as a form of religious expression. To create in a cultural sense was to serve a special group of goddesses, the Muses, in a way that would bring rewards to the artists and the communities to which they belonged. Consequently, religion provided the prime inspiration for art and thought, and supplied both with a basic store of themes out of which was shaped a variety of masterpieces that still awe and intrigue thoughtful people.

3. LITERATURE

Greek literature is a magnificent artistic creation emerging from a substratum of religious themes. Most of it demands a familiarity with Greek mythology, for literary artists played upon this material to give it new vitality and meaning in terms of the human situation.

Greek literature was born in glory with the two epic poems of Homer, the *Iliad* and the *Odyssey*, probably set down in the eighth century B.C. Behind them lay a long tradition of oral poetry sung by professional bards in aristocratic courts to tell the deeds of heroic figures who lived in Mycenaean times. Homer, who according to tradition lived in Ionia, drew these oral threads together into unified compositions characterized by great artistry and dramatic force. His language is masterful and his verse form reveals a mature esthetic sense. The *Iliad* recounts the feats of a circle of heroes during a brief period in the war which the Mycenaean Greeks waged against Troy to avenge the theft of a Greek woman, Helen, by Paris, the prince of Troy. Its central figure is Achilles, whose inflated pride and misdirected anger threaten to destroy the Greeks before he is brought to his senses and takes his place as a great warrior able to turn the tide of battle. The *Odyssey* is an adventure story celebrating the clever talents of one of the heroes at Troy—Odysseus, who needs ten years to overcome a variety of obstacles preventing his return from Troy to his homeland and his patient, long-suffering wife, Penelope. Not a little of the appeal of these epics lies in their gripping plots; but they have other dimensions. They create a heroic picture of men endowed with courage,

nobility, and a deep love for life; in portraying men in such heroic proportions, Homer wrestles with the thought-provoking problem of the relationship of these demigods to the real gods. His epics enshrined a view of gods and men that provided Greeks of all ages with an ideal of heroic greatness.

The epic style of Homer was imitated long after his death, but for all its richness, this one literary form could not contain the Greek literary genius. In about 700 B.C., the poet Hesiod wrote his *Works and Days*, a bitter reflection on the poverty of small landowners and the injustice of the rich and powerful. It is filled with a search for some deeper understanding of divine justice as an antidote to human misery. Hesiod's work pointed the way to an outburst of lyric poetry in which several poets developed new verse forms to express their personal reactions to man, nature, political developments, the gods, love, and a wide variety of other subjects. Among the best were Archilochus of Paros, Alcaeus of Mytilene, and above all the poetess Sappho of Lesbos. Aside from the new literary forms they developed, including the elegy and the choral ode, these lyricists made literature a vehicle for the forceful expression of deep thought and a personal reaction to life. The nobility and force of Greek lyric poetry were perhaps best exemplified by Pindar of Thebes (ca. 518–441 B.C.), most of whose works took the form of choral songs to honor victorious athletes at great religious festivals. His poems set forth the classic view of aristocratic (in the Greek sense of "the best") man in terms seldom equaled in poetry. He convinces one of what many Greeks believed —that great poetry can inspire ordinary men to rise above their own limits to the greatness of the athletes who struggled for personal and civic glory and for the honor of the gods.

The burgeoning poetic talent reflected in epic and lyric poetry reached full fruition in the fifth century with the development of tragic drama, perhaps the greatest literary achievement of the Greeks. The drama was written and produced for large audiences and paid for by the state from public funds. In this respect, it is a product of the democracy of the fifth century. Its profundity and artistry suggest an articulate, sensitive, thoughtful populace that speaks well for the power of democracy.

Tragedy originated in religious ceremony and never lost touch with its seedbed. It began in the dramatic choruses and hymns developed to honor the god Dionysus. By the sixth century B.C., the dramatic element in these rituals had grown increasingly important, providing opportunities for poets to portray the deeds of the gods and heroes enshrined in Greek mythology and to comment on the meaning of these deeds through choral interludes interspersed with the dramatic action.

This developing dramatic art suddenly burst forth in full maturity during the fifth century in the work of three of the world's greatest masters. The first was Aeschylus (525–456 B.C.), a writer of deep religious convictions and strong aristocratic sentiments. He wrote about ninety plays, only seven of which survive. His tragedies spell out with great power the consequences that follow human transgressions of the dictates of the divine powers. His most impressive surviving work is a cycle of three plays called the *Oresteia,* which traces the tragic fate of the family of Agamemnon resulting from its crime of spilling the blood of its own kinsmen. Aeschylus had a genius for making his suffering characters noble and admirable, capable of bearing their burden of punishment with dignity and even with understanding.

Sophocles (495–406 B.C.) was less conservative. During his long life, centered chiefly in the period of Athens' greatest power, he produced a large number of plays, all but seven now lost. His dramas remained closely bound to the traditional themes provided by myth and religion, but his interest is more human, more intent on searching out the psychological effects of suffering on men who ran afoul of the gods. He portrayed suffering as an experience that uplifted and purified man. Many would argue that Sophocles' *King Oedipus* is the greatest tragedy ever written. Essentially it is a drama that reveals the measure of man by showing his response when he is trapped by fate into committing an act for which the gods must destroy him. Much more than Aeschylus, Sophocles celebrates the greatness of man.

Euripides (480–406 B.C.) was a dramatist profoundly touched by the growing disillusionment, skepticism, and pessimism of the later fifth century — the generation of the Peloponnesian War. He utilized tragedy as a vehicle for posing profound questions, arousing the suspicion that human powers are limited. His plays, especially *Medea,* represent a search for some understanding of the full nature of man, especially his dark and frightening emotional qualities. Again and again he casts doubt on conventional moral values and accepted religious beliefs. But from this incessant probing emerges a picture of man that is fuller and subtler — if not nobler — than the portraits by Aeschylus and Sophocles.

While the tragic drama was developing, the Greeks also perfected comic drama to a highly effective level. Comedy, like tragedy, began as a part of public religious ceremonies, especially the worship of Dionysus. Its origins were rooted in ribald songs evoked by the joy and good humor that apparently surrounded religious feasts. By the fifth century, comedy became independent of religious ceremony and was performed as a distinct art that educated audiences about current affairs by making them laugh. The greatest user of this form was Aristophanes (ca. 445–385 B.C.), a conservative Athenian who despised nearly all the developments of his society. His comedies held up for scorn politicians, artists, democratic institutions, and Athenian social mores. Typical is his play *Lysistrata,* based on the efforts of Athenian women to deny their husbands any pleasures with them until the men gave up warfare.

Prose literature in Greece was long overshadowed by the immense influence of poetry. Its first use came in the sixth century in the works of early philosophical and scientific writers, and it was thus closely associated with emerging rationalism in Greek life. The best Greek prose in the fifth century was historical literature, a form particularly well suited for serious reflection on the human condition. Two outstanding men, Herodotus and Thucydides, not only produced great literature, but also introduced scientific history to the world.

Herodotus (ca. 484–425 B.C.) wrote a history of

the war between the Greeks and Persians. To make his account as accurate as possible, he traveled extensively and searched through written records for evidence concerning the causes and the events of the wars. Herodotus usually tried to sift his material to arrive at the truth; however, he was too good a storyteller to leave out colorful material whether true or not. His finished work was therefore spiced with hundreds of anecdotes and stories, many quite fantastic, intended to illustrate the qualities of the two peoples involved in the war.

Thucydides' masterpiece was a *History of the Peloponnesian War*. With great industry and complete objectivity, he searched out the details of the military campaigns and the political maneuvers associated with the war in which he was personally involved and which he was convinced was the greatest in Greek history. He tried to let the events illustrate the folly, the nobility, the chicanery, and the bravery of which men under stress are capable. His presentation leads one to the inevitable conclusion that the Athenians lost because of their own mistakes, their pride, their bad judgment; humans emerge as responsible for their own destinies. By successfully illustrating what war in any age can do to men and to political institutions, Thucydides did what every modern historian yearns to do: to make the truth about the past enrich our understanding of men in the present.

4. ART

"Painting is silent poetry; poetry is painting that speaks." Greek art drew its basic themes from the same sources as literature — religion and mythology. Artists labored toward the same ends — to discover man and place him meaningfully in the larger cosmos. Artists found their audiences where writers did; and they poured into their work the same talents. Certainly nature provided them with some of the finest materials in the world, especially marble, and with dramatic sites upon which to place their buildings, such as the Athenian Acropolis, but it was their genius that produced the magnificent works that reveal the Greek spirit.

The art of the Golden Age was the product of a long evolution. During the Mycenaean era, a flourishing art, strongly influenced by Minoan models, had developed on mainland Greece. With the onset of the Dark Age, Mycenaean art styles and technical skills were largely lost, although remnants survived to provide a starting point for a uniquely Greek art. The first signs of this new art appeared near the end of the Dark Age: finely executed pottery decorated first with geometric patterns and, by the eighth century B.C., with human forms. These works established the basic themes for painters and set conventions for representing humans and animals in action. During the Archaic period, architects developed a basic style for temples and other public buildings: a rectangular form with surrounding columns and low-pitched roofs; toward the end of the period, most of these structures were being built of stone. At the same time, sculptors were perfecting a unique style of portraying the nude male and the draped female figure. Architects, sculptors, and painters received increasing support from the city-states, whose leaders and citizens were deeply interested in beautifying the cities and in elaborating civic religious ceremonies.

By the beginning of the fifth century, the long apprenticeship was over, and Athens had become the focal point for artistic excellence. Her monuments offer the best examples of Greek art. Unquestionably, the city's crowning glory was the Acropolis, a hill upon which were built three major temples, the Parthenon, the Erectheum, and the temple to Victorious Athena. A splendid gate and stairway, called the Propylaea, gave access to the Acropolis.

The Parthenon, portions of which still stand, was the noblest of the temples. Built in honor of Athena, this structure is of moderate size, measuring 228 by 101 feet. The inner chamber is surrounded by simple, unadorned columns (called Doric columns), seventeen on each side and eight on each end, which support the roof. A series of dignified statues and stone reliefs added a harmonious decorative touch. Many devices were employed by the architects to achieve harmony, balance, and unity. The columns all lean inward slightly and are thickened in the middle to offset the optical illusion that

Hermes with the infant Dionysus. Most likely the work of the famed sculptor Praxiteles, this statue is an excellent example of Greek artistic canons; the gods are taken as subject matter and portrayed in an idealized human form that emphasizes physical perfection rather than spiritual qualities. *Photo: Hirmer Verlag*

same features. The only basic departure is the slightly more slender and ornate columns (in the Ionic style), which add a grace lacking in the rather severe Parthenon. Similar temples were built in other cities, although none quite equals the Acropolis group for total effect. The many public buildings constructed in the *poleis* incorporated the principles employed in temple construction, adding to the beauty of the cities.

Greek sculpture was primarily dedicated to the adornment of temples. The most representative sculptors are Phidias (ca. 500–432 B.C.), Polyclitus (ca. 452–412 B.C.), and Praxiteles (ca. 400–320 B.C.). Phidias designed the sculpture adorning the Parthenon and executed some of the individual pieces. His statues in the round have been lost; all the surviving Parthenon sculpture is relief work, and it is difficult to tell whether any particular piece is the work of Phidias or of someone working under his direction. Polyclitus devoted his talents chiefly to shaping bronze statues of young men. Praxiteles created splendid versions of the gods in human form. The work of all these sculptors concentrated on the idealized human body; their figures are dignified, quiet, and beautifully proportioned. When looking at any of the statues of Greek sculptors, the viewer feels that he finally sees man as he should be, although he is aware that he has never seen such perfect men.

Little has survived of Greek painting, except for pottery decoration, which had perhaps passed its peak by the fifth century. However, it remained a significant art during the Golden Age. There is evidence from literary sources that artists rendered large-scale paintings to decorate temples and public buildings. For example, the painter Polygnotus decorated a colonnade in the Athenian *agora*, which was the section of the city where major political meetings and market activities took place, with scenes from the Trojan Wars. We may suspect that Greek painting reflected the same idealizing traits seen in sculpture and drew heavily on mythology for its themes.

5. PHILOSOPHY

The Greeks leaped furthest beyond the achievements of earlier cultures in the realm of philo-

makes a straight column viewed from below seem to tip outward. The middle of every long horizontal line is slightly higher than the ends to avoid the impression of sagging.

The other Acropolis temples and the Propylaea, all built after the Parthenon, incorporate the sophical and scientific speculation. They left a heritage that has shaped thinking in the West up to the present. Until the sixth century B.C., most Greeks were content to accept the explanations of mythology for the nature of the universe and man's place in it; Homer and Hesiod provided the basic ingredients of their world view. Then during that century, just when the *polis* was reaching maturity, thinkers began to move beyond these limits, initiating one of the great intellectual revolutions in the history of the world. Fundamentally, the new modes of thought were by-products of a growing faith in man's capabilities and of the freedom nourished in the atmosphere of the *polis*. So bold and so cogent was this activity of the mind that the fifth and fourth centuries B.C. are still regarded as the most productive in the entire history of philosophy.

The prime concern of speculative thinkers during the sixth and fifth centuries centered around the explanation of the fundamental force lying behind and giving unity to the universe. Rejecting traditional religious explanations, a series of philosophers tried to give rational answers. One school of thinkers developed a materialistic approach and concluded that such obvious elements as fire, water, and air were the basic substances out of which all other things came. This materialistic tradition continued to be refined until in the early fourth century Democritus expounded an atomic theory, according to which the universe is composed of tiny atoms floating at random in space. By mere chance these atoms compose themselves into beings and objects and by the same chance decompose into floating particles again. Another school of philosophers rejected materialism and sought the key to the universe in some nonmaterial force. Perhaps the source of this approach was the sixth-century thinker Pythagoras, whose career combined deep scientific interest with a strong religious bent. He argued that the key to the universe lay in a numerical relationship among its many parts. Equally influential in shaping this school was Heraclitus (flourished ca. 500 B.C.), who insisted that change was the essence of the physical, material world and therefore that no physical explanation of the universe could have meaning. This whole school of thinkers ultimately concluded that a nonma-

terial, changeless being, endowed with perfect intelligence, supplied the creative force of order in the universe.

About the middle of the fifth century philosophical inquiry shifted from speculation about the fundamental nature of the universe to an examination of man's nature and his place in that universe. The Sophists, although they were primarily teachers whose interest in philosophy was a by-product of their ideas on education, led the way into this fresh realm of thought. Protagoras (485–410 B.C.), a famous teacher in Periclean Athens, was chiefly responsible for articulating their precepts. He rejected speculative philosophy on the grounds that the many contradictory schemes put forth by the speculative thinkers proved objective truth to be nonexistent. Man was the measure of all things. Human reason, he said, should be dedicated to a search for the kind of knowledge that would be useful to man in his quest for a comfortable, safe, happy life. He therefore spent his time instructing Athenians in those things that would fit them for citizenship in a democratic society — public speaking, politics, grammar, and the art of being respectable. Greece soon swarmed with his disciples. They delivered withering attacks on all things that were accepted as the truth, preaching that truth was relative and encouraging their audiences to live by any rules of conduct that proved beneficial and workable. The Sophists as a group were condemned, with partial justice, as skeptics, troublemakers, and destroyers of morality. But they made the Greeks more aware of human problems than had earlier thinkers, and they prepared the way for the greatest Greek philosophers, Socrates, Plato, and Aristotle.

Probably no one was better known in Athens just before 400 B.C. than a homely, dumpy little stonecutter named Socrates (ca. 469–399 B.C.). Socrates left no writings. He set forth his ideas orally; the Athenian *agora* provided him an ideal setting. Here he locked horns intellectually with anyone interested. But Socrates was more than a street-corner debater. His pupils, especially Plato, recorded enough of his ideas to permit us to grasp the basic thrust of his thought. He believed that objective truth did exist and that man was prevented from discovering it by his own ignorance, which Socrates made it his business to enlighten. The Socratic method consisted of asking questions until the error of those who claimed to know something was exposed and then leading the mind through further questioning to the truth by way of precise definition and exact logic.

Socrates attracted an eager following of youths, including the scions of several of Athens' noblest families—and he earned the anger of many of the elders of his society. His annoying questions finally got him into trouble with the state. In 399 B.C., amid the bitterness surrounding Athens' defeat in the Peloponnesian War, he was accused of corrupting youth and sentenced to die. Although given a chance to escape, he chose to abide by the state's decision of death by drinking hemlock, still convinced that the highest virtue consisted of pursuing knowledge, no matter what the consequences.

Plato (427–347 B.C.) carried on the work of Socrates, his master. He was an Athenian whose career spanned an era filled with defeats for Athens and constant civil strife, all of which discouraged him. Most of his life was spent as a teacher in a school called the Academy, which he founded. His voluminous works, elegantly written in dialogue form, offer a complete although sometimes confusing record of his thought. Plato was a philosophical idealist; his work brings to a conclusion that nonmaterialistic philosophical movement that had begun with Pythagoras. He argued that the fundamental realities in the universe are *ideas*, or abstract forms, the chief of which is the good. The so-called realities that man perceives with his senses are but imperfect reflections of the perfect universal forms. The justice practiced in Athens was only a shadowy reflection of perfect transcendental justice; a man is but a pale image of higher reality, humanity. The intellect, by reflecting on the imperfect earthly embodiments of ideas, opened the path to contemplation and comprehension of the ultimate, unchanging realities of the universe.

Much of Plato's writing centers on a search for perfect understanding of universal ideas and an effort to make that wisdom and insight applicable to the problems of human existence. His best-known dialogue, *The Republic*, illustrates his idealism, his method, and his earnest concern for the human condition. This work is devoted to governance. Plato assumes that the purpose of the state is to achieve justice, the ideal state being an earthly embodiment of the perfect idea of justice. He concludes that justice consists in each man's doing that for which he is best fitted. The ideal state is one in which every man holds that station and does that job for which he is qualified. Such a state, Plato argues, must be ruled by a philosopher-king who will be wise enough to know and recognize the talents of his subjects and put these talents to work. A completely socialistic economy controlled by the wise king must be instituted so that each will be rewarded according to his merits and so that competition and greed can be eliminated from society. In short, the perfect society is a dictatorial state. In his other dialogues Plato conducts a comparable search for an understanding of the nature of love, friendship, courage, the soul—in fact, virtually the whole range of those elements that constitute the ultimate reality, perfect good.

Aristotle (384–322 B.C.) was Plato's most brilliant and productive pupil. As a youth, he came to Athens from northern Greece to study at the Academy. After Plato's death, he spent some time as tutor to young Alexander the Great. He then returned to Athens and founded his own school, the Lyceum. His followers were called the Peripatetics because Aristotle often walked about while lecturing.

During his career, Aristotle produced a massive body of philosophical work ranging across the whole spectrum of human knowledge. Perhaps typical of teachers in all ages, he had a passion for systematizing and organizing knowledge, so that his works constitute a kind of encyclopedia of the total learning of the ancient world. Imbedded in his massive scholarship, however, is a basic philosophical position. Aristotle was certainly influenced by Platonic idealism, but his approach is basically different. In his seminal *Metaphysics*, he argues that reality consists of a combination of matter and form (or idea). The form makes the object what it is but has no reality except when it exists in matter.

The Irrational in Greek Culture

Every historian who tries to reconstruct the grand sweep of history in an account of reasonably modest proportions quickly becomes aware of a disturbing consequence of his effort. He finds himself distorting the past by concentrating on what is dominant in any era at the expense of many facets of a society that in his judgment are less momentous.

Our treatment of Greek culture provides an example of the distortion of selection: We have repeatedly and emphatically stressed that the central and crucial mode of Greek thought and expression was rationalism. Ours is, of course, no new insight. Across long ages, Near Eastern potentates, Roman aristocrats, medieval churchmen, Renaissance artists, early modern scientists, American revolutionaries, and modern intellectuals have all paid obeisance to the Greek confidence that man is preeminently a thinking creature capable of utilizing his rational faculties to make the world into what he "thinks" it should be.

But was what later admirers and interpreters—all in one way or another historians—focused on the whole story? Did all Greeks perceive all things from a rational perspective? Was even the most sophisticated and intellectually enlightened Greek convinced that man was primarily a rational being? Is it possible that the legions of students of the Greek "mind" have been blinded to significant dimensions of the Greek cultural experience as a consequence of their eagerness to make the Greeks models of that desirable human trait, reasonableness?

Investigations of Greek culture have been broadened and deepened over the past century by valuable insights and techniques supplied by social scientists. Especially illuminating has been the work of anthropologists investigating religious life among existing primitive societies and of psychologists seeking to comprehend the nonrational aspects of human behavior. The whole thrust of this approach to the nature of Greek culture has been to cast doubt on the conventional generalization that rationalism is the key to that culture.

One of the most perceptive and learned of contemporary classical scholars, E. R. Dodds of Oxford, has brilliantly posed the issue of the irrationality of Greek civilization and has suggested a viable response in his book *The Greeks and the Irrational* (1951). Dodds begins by asserting a fundamental postulate established by modern anthropologists and psychologists: In the intellectual behavior of all people in all ages there is a powerful element of the primitive mentality, a mentality that often manifests itself in religion. He argues that, in the main, interpreters of the Greek experience have failed (or refused?) to take this fact into account. Quite rightly he asks: "Why should we attribute to the ancient Greeks an immunity from 'primitive' modes of thought which we do not find in any society open to our direct observation?" He thinks the attribution is erroneous, and sets out to demonstrate that the Greeks were not "quite so blind to the importance of nonrational factors in man's experience and behavior as is commonly assumed."

Dodds succeeds in demonstrating persuasively that Greek literary and philosophical spokesmen were always aware of irrational factors governing human conduct and that they expressed their awareness in religious terms. For example, he finds in the Homeric epics, usually interpreted as reflecting no deep religious concepts, significant evidence that Homer saw irrational conduct among his heroes as a case of "psychic intervention" by an outside divine agency. He discerns the sense of despair and insecurity in the Archaic Age as stemming from a conviction that the divine forces were hostile toward man. This religious strain bred a sense of guilt, often associated with the idea of pollution. He examines Greek concepts of madness, positing that to many it represented a state of blessedness because it indicated the infusion of the divine into man. Dodds finds evidence to suggest that the "enlightened" views of the great cultural heroes of the fifth century B.C. were looked upon with suspicion by many intellectuals, who felt that the rationalist concepts being promulgated did not encompass man's whole existence, and by the great mass of the Greeks, who reacted violently by persecuting the intellectuals. Extending his view beyond the Golden Age through Plato to the Hellenistic era, Dodds concludes that the irrational grew increasingly important in accounting for man's actions.

Dodds' powerful synthesis forces us to realize that only a few Greek thinkers affirmed that man was a rational creature, and in the long run their belief was buried under a belief in man as irrational. When one adds to this the obvious fact that the great mass of Greeks always accepted a religious interpretation of man, believing his existence dependent on divine forces, the generalization about rationalism as a key to Greek culture becomes exceedingly suspect.

Thus it turns out that the historian who stresses rationalism as a major feature of Greek culture is overlooking a dimension that had immense importance to the Greeks. This sounds dishonest. Yet in fitting the Greeks into the grand sweep of history, their rationalism is of greater significance than their irrationalism. Their consciousness of man's rational powers marked a fresh insight into human nature, while their awareness of the irrational aspects of human behavior simply provided the common bond with most other societies in history that have tried to cope with the monumental problems of living.

Every object has some purpose in a larger universal order, and its perfection consists in serving that purpose. Behind the wilderness of individual objects lies an ultimate "cause," a higher force that animates everything. The philosopher's path is from the study of nature toward the formulation of concepts about the entire universe.

In most of his works, many of which deal with scientific subjects, Aristotle pursued the course laid down in the *Metaphysics*. His *Politics* supplies an illustration of his method. On the basis of a study of the history and organization of more than 150 Greek city-states, he concluded that the state is a natural grouping of men for the purpose of promoting virtue. Man is a political animal and cannot fulfill his true nature unless he is a member of a state. In his *Ethics*, Aristotle asked how man should conduct his individual life and argued that happiness is the proper goal of every human action. Man is happy and therefore good if he controls his passions by use of his reason and if he seeks a mean between extremes. Although Aristotle's principal method is inductive and although he was the most influential exponent of that method among the Greeks, he is also the founder of formal logic, a deductive discipline. The last great thinker of Greece, Aristotle was the most comprehensive.

6. SCIENCE

Aristotle's scientific works were the culmination of a sustained and highly significant interest in science reaching back at least two centuries before him. Because the Greeks made no clear distinction between science and philosophy, it is difficult to treat science as a thing apart. Nearly all thinkers derived their conclusions from observations of nature, but they also borrowed extensively from ancient Mesopotamia and Egypt.

Hippocrates (460–377 B.C.), a leading physician to whom is attributed the famous oath defining the responsibilities of a physician which we still know today, typifies Greek interest in observation. He insisted that nothing could be known about sickness except through observation of sick people and through a search for the natural causes of illness. He repudiated

the traditional belief that sickness was due to evil spirits and taught that it was a result of natural causes. Hippocrates had numerous followers who took the same approach and accumulated an extensive body of knowledge about the human body and its workings.

The collective efforts of Greek astronomers, physicists, geographers, botanists, and zoologists allow us to credit the Greeks with the invention of the scientific method, which relies on observation as the source of knowledge about nature. But of course they lacked precision instruments; and they often made glaring errors in interpreting their discoveries. Moreover, few were interested in using their knowledge for practical purposes. Scientific knowledge was employed chiefly by philosophers who sought to illustrate the operation of the universe by observing how it worked.

7. THE GREEK MIND

Any review of the brilliant work of the Greeks in literature, art, philosophy, and science raises one final question: Did all the leaders of Greek cultural life, whatever their specific interests, share any common ideas that characterize the Greek approach to life? The following basic concepts are offered in answer.

Greek thought was intensely *humanistic*; it placed man on a pedestal for admiration and idealization. Most Greeks believed that the world had been created for man's happiness. They therefore were certain that man was *in harmony with nature* and had no need to struggle against it, try to escape it, or shrink from it in fear. The Greeks were *rationalistic*; they placed a powerful trust in man's ability to understand nature's mysteries through his own intelligence and to act on the basis of his sound judgment to solve any problems that might beset him. The Greeks insisted upon *restraint* and *balance*; nothing was worse than excess in any shape or form. Their *spirit of inquiry* constantly pushed them into new fields in every aspect of life and added an element of *boldness* to their endeavors. Most Greek intellectual leaders were *politically oriented*, ready to offer their talents to the community instead of pursuing individual and introspective ends. Finally, the Greek mind sought *order* and *symmetry* in all things.

No one would insist that the ideals expressed by a few intellectual and artistic giants were attained by all Greeks. Probably most Greeks, engaged in the routine of daily life, seldom paused to think about what their civilization really meant to them, just as most modern men seldom dwell on this question. But even so, at least Greek ideals were presented to them in poetry, drama, history, sculpture, architecture, and philosophy. Thus values ingrained in the great artistic and philosophical works of Greece became a model of civilized life for numerous peoples who rose to prominence in the Mediterranean area after the Greeks had lost their position of political predominance.

Suggested Reading

General Cultural Histories
*Edith Hamilton, *The Greek Way* (Norton).
*C. M. Bowra, *The Greek Experience* (Mentor). This and the preceding title represent two splendid introductions to the general features of Greek culture and its underlying spirit.
François Chamoux, *The Civilization of Greece*, trans. W. S. Maguinness (1965). A general survey that is enriched by splendid illustrations.

Religion
*Robert Graves, *The Greek Myths*. 2 vols. (Penguin). The best starting place in understanding Greek religion is to discover what the Greeks believed about their gods as these beliefs were set forth in mythology; this work provides a full treatment.
M. Hadas and M. Smith, *Heroes and Gods* (1965).
*W. K. C. Guthrie, *Greeks and Their Gods* (Beacon). Either this or the preceding title will provide a description of the content of Greek religious belief and the nature of religious practice.
A. J. Festugière, *Personal Religion Among the Greeks* (1960). Touches on aspects of Greek belief that are sometimes overlooked.

Literature
*M. Hadas, *A History of Greek Literature* (Columbia).
*Albin Lesky, *A History of Greek Literature* (Apollo). Two clearly presented surveys, especially useful in assessing the contributions of individual authors.
*C. M. Bowra, *Ancient Greek Literature* (Galaxy). Another survey that provides more interpretation than the preceding titles.

Art
*J. Boardman, *Greek Art* (Praeger). An outstanding general description.
*J. Barron, *Greek Sculpture* (Dutton).
*A. W. Lawrence, *Greek Architecture* (Penguin).
*P. Devambez, *Greek Painting* (Compass). This and the two preceding titles will provide excellent introductions to specialized aspects of Greek art; all are well illustrated.
John Travlos, *Pictorial Dictionary of Ancient Athens* (1971). A masterful guide to the art of Athens, highlighted by impressive illustrations.

Philosophy and Science
*Rex Warner, *Greek Philosophers* (Mentor).
*W. K. C. Guthrie, *Greek Philosophers: From Thales to Aristotle* (Harper Torchbook).
*F. Copleston, *History of Philosophy*, Vol. 1: *Greece and Rome* (Image). Any of these three works will provide a clear account of the development of Greek philosophy and an assessment of its accomplishments.
*Marshall Claggett, *Greek Science in Antiquity* (Collier). An up-to-date summary of Greek scientific accomplishments.

Sources
*W. H. Auden, ed., *The Portable Greek Reader* (Penguin).
*Michael Grant, ed., *Greek Literature: An Anthology* (Penguin). The most fruitful way to get at the spirit of Greek culture is to read Greek literature. These two anthologies will provide a rich sampling. From this sampling, many may wish to read individual

authors in their entirety; especially suggested are Homer, Herodotus, and Thucydides, whose works were cited in earlier chapters.

*L. R. Lind, ed., *Ten Greek Plays in Contemporary Translations* (Riverside Editions). Contains representative works of Aeschylus, Sophocles, Euripides, and Aristophanes.

*Scott Buchanan, ed., *The Portable Plato* (Penguin). Provides a good selection illustrative of Plato's philosophical position and method; especially worth studying are his dialogues *Protagoras, Phaedo, Symposium,* and *The Republic.*

Richard McKeon, ed., *The Basic Works of Aristotle* (1941). Offers *Politics, Nicomachean Ethics, Metaphysics,* and *Poetics* as representative of Aristotle's philosophical works.

7

GREEK IMPERIALISM: THE HELLENISTIC WORLD, 336-31 B.C.

To many Greeks, the coming of the barbarian Macedonians spelled doom. But, as is so often the case when men judge their own age, they were wrong. The Macedonian conquest set the stage for a new chapter in Greece's history. The Greeks were about to discover what one of their own philosophers, Democritus, had argued: that the native land of great souls is the whole earth. Under Macedonian leadership, they exploded out of their Aegean-centered world to establish their mastery over a wide circle in Asia and Africa. Their genius and their traditions began to mix with Near Eastern civilizations to produce a new culture that historians have called "Hellenistic."

1. ALEXANDER THE GREAT

The military and political genius of Alexander the Great was chiefly responsible for launching the Greeks on this new phase of their history. Endowed with numerous powers—intelligence, ambition, industry, imagination, physical attractiveness, boldness, an iron will—Alexander has never ceased to fascinate students of history. Although Macedonian by birth, he was a Greek in spirit. His education under Aristotle had instilled in him a fanatical admiration of Greek civilization.

Alexander was twenty when his father was murdered in 336 B.C. Philip had charted the immediate future for his son. Besides being king of

Macedon, Alexander was master of the Greek city-states by virtue of his control of the League of Corinth. Philip had prepared for a war against Greece's ancient foe, Persia, perhaps hoping to win the approval of all Greeks by rallying them in a crusade. It was this war that absorbed Alexander's interests.

In 334 B.C. he led his Macedonian-Greek army into Asia Minor in order to attack Persia. Although Persia possessed a huge empire, a rich treasury, and a large army and navy, Alexander was victorious from the beginning. Mindful of the role naval power had played in the long struggle between Greeks and Persians, his first campaigns were aimed at depriving the Persians of control of the coastal cities of Asia Minor and Phoenicia, whence came the chief source of Persian naval power. Shortly after entering Asia Minor, Alexander overpowered a major Persian force at a battle on the Granicus River; this victory assured control of the Greek cities along the east coast of the Aegean Sea. From there he moved into Syria, and in 333 B.C. won a brilliant victory at Issus against a much larger Persian force. This victory opened the way for his conquest of Syria, Palestine, and Egypt. Then he marched on the center of Persian power in Mesopotamia and in the spring of 331 B.C. destroyed the last major military strength of the Persians at the battle of Arbela. Following this victory, he occupied the major centers of Persian political power, including the capital city of Persepolis, and hunted down the fugitive King Darius III, who was finally murdered in 330 B.C. by his own officials as Alexander closed in on him.

The conquest of the Persian Empire did not satisfy Alexander's ambition. During the next five years he drove on eastward. Battling vast distances, native resistance, and defection among his own troops, he relentlessly destroyed pockets of resistance led by Persian satraps in the regions of Parthia and Bactria. Then he pushed across the Hindu Kush Mountains into the rich land drained by the Indus River, a venture that brought the Greeks into direct contact with Indian civilization. All this territory he claimed as his, and sought to assure his control by founding cities as centers of Greek power. Beyond the Indus Valley his troops refused to go. Alexander therefore turned back westward through southern Persia and into Mesopotamia, where he fell ill and died in June 323 at the age of thirty-three. Tradition has it that he was planning new conquests, including Arabia, Carthage, and Central Asia.

A career so short and so completely occupied with military campaigns left Alexander little time to face the problems of ruling his vast conquests. Probably he had no definite plans when he launched his campaign and formed his policies as circumstances arose. But before he died, he had established certain broad policies that guided his successors. He moved toward creating a style of rulership that cast him in the role of divine autocrat. Seeing that Greeks alone could not rule his vast empire, Alexander began to employ the talents of the conquered peoples. Persians were placed in some army and administrative posts. But from the beginning of his career, he had insisted that the Greeks would remain politically, economically, and culturally supreme within his empire. High positions in the army and the civil administration were reserved for them.

Alexander's death left most of his policies far from fulfilled, and it has often been said that his death was timely for the benefit of his fame, since his reputation might have suffered had he lived to face the task of holding his empire together. The Greek masters sat uneasily atop their

This Roman copy of an original bust of Alexander the Great (perhaps done by the fourth-century sculptor Lycippus) attempts to convey the strength of a great hero of the ancient world. *Photo: The Granger Collection*

vast domain. Greek culture was not firmly planted in the conquered territory, although many Greeks had migrated to the new cities built by Alexander. Furthermore, Alexander left no heir capable of capitalizing on the magic of his name. Aside from his conquests his positive achievements were few. His influence on the course of history lay chiefly in his legend: what later generations believed he was trying to do. At least in part, that legend portrayed Alexander as a philosopher-king determined to bring peace, harmony, and prosperity to a vast empire by Hellenizing its inhabitants. The struggle to

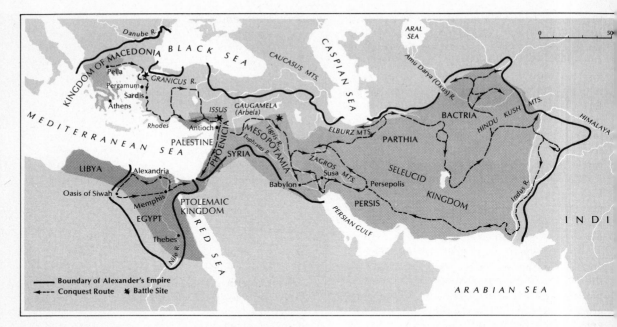

ALEXANDER'S EMPIRE 336–323 B.C.

achieve that goal shaped much of the history of his empire and of a large part of the Mediterranean world for several centuries after his death.

2. HELLENISTIC POLITICAL LIFE, 323–31 B.C.

Alexander's conquests established a legacy that shaped the political history of the vast territory comprising his empire for three centuries after his death. But that history is difficult to tell. More than one approach is possible, but no single approach quite portrays the whole story.

We can recount Hellenistic political history from the point of view of Alexander's legend: a dream of political unity, peace, and harmony. Alexander's successors tried to follow this program, especially in the early years after his death; throughout the Hellenistic period men dreamed of reconstructing the ecumenical empire. From this perspective, the Hellenistic Age was a story of failure. Hardly was the great con-

queror dead when the struggle began to divide his empire. Out of the struggle emerged a hodgepodge of political entities of various sizes, strengths, and forms of government. These "successor states" were almost constantly at war; peace and harmony seldom prevailed. Ultimately, Rome was the chief beneficiary of the strife, incorporating into her expanding empire the best parts of Alexander's domains—Macedonia, the entire Aegean area, Asia Minor, Syria, Palestine, Egypt—and taking up the dream of creating a peaceful, harmonious world order.

Or we might approach Hellenistic history by viewing the fate of Alexander's program of establishing a small minority of Greeks and Macedonians as political masters of his vast territory. Again there was partial failure. Large segments escaped Greek control. During the third century B.C. the region lying east of the Tigris-Euphrates Valley was taken over by non-Greeks, who established kingdoms of considerable importance to the future, including Bactria and Parthia. Along the southern Black Sea coast small but virile kingdoms—Pontus, Bithynia, Cappadocia —were formed by local rulers. Despite these losses, the conquering masters did retain power in a large part of the Near East, especially in Egypt, Syria, Palestine, and the southern shore of Asia Minor. And their power was solidly established; they met little resistance from the native populations. It is true that the ruling elite did to some degree adapt their ways to the political traditions of their subjects, particularly in Egypt. Still, the ability of a relatively few outsiders to hold political power over highly civilized peoples with ancient political traditions of their own was a significant achievement.

Still another approach to Hellenistic history— and the one usually taken—is to concentrate on the most prominent states that emerged from the partition of Alexander's empire. Immediately after Alexander's sudden death, a council of his generals decided to maintain a united empire under a single monarch. They elected Alexander's incompetent half-brother as king, with the understanding that should the child which Alexander's widow, the Persian princess Roxanne, was carrying be male, he would share the throne—which is what happened. But this pair could provide no direction for the shaky empire, and the generals were soon engaged in a struggle for control, and each took what he could get. The process of partition was not very rational and the exact boundaries of the emerging states were confused, but by about 275 B.C. there were three major kingdoms. In Egypt Ptolemy had established himself as successor to the ancient pharaohs and had laid claim to territories in Palestine and Syria. Another general, Antigonus, claimed the old kingdom of Macedon plus control over the Greek city-states still theoretically bound to Macedon in the league established by Philip in 338 B.C. Seleucus staked out a third kingdom embracing all the lands from Asia Minor to India; this conglomeration was most nearly similar to Alexander's empire.

Only the briefest summary of the complex histories of these kingdoms can be undertaken here. Macedonian political history centered

around the efforts of a succession of kings to maintain control over the Greek city-states and to hold back barbarians constantly pressing on the northern frontiers of the kingdom. These burdens were great for the monarchs, since Macedon was a poor land whose manpower had been badly depleted by the eastern conquests. Shortly before 200 B.C. some of the Greek city-states appealed to Rome for help against Macedon. In the ensuing wars, Roman armies overran and annexed both Macedon and Greece.

The Ptolemaic kingdom was the most stable of the Hellenistic states. The ruling dynasty inherited a homogeneous population and a rich land, established an autocratic regime such as the Egyptians had long known, and exploited the agricultural and commercial potential of Egypt with intelligence and skill. Internal stability and wealth permitted the Ptolemies to play an active role in foreign affairs; they concentrated chiefly on extending their sway in Syria, which involved them in almost constant struggle with the Seleucid kingdom. Not until the second century B.C. did Ptolemaic power begin to decline. In the face of growing internal unrest, the rulers turned to Rome for support. Eventually (in 31 B.C.), Rome annexed Ptolemaic Egypt to her empire.

The history of the Seleucid kingdom is most difficult to tell. Its huge size and mixed populace provided little basis for unity or stability. The burden of its rulers was to supply a common bond, and the task was too great. Rather quickly they lost the territories they claimed east of Mesopotamia. Their hold on Asia Minor was always tenuous and ultimately was compromised by the emergence of petty kingdoms in the northern and western portions, of which Pergamum was the most significant. Most of the royal energy was devoted to creating a viable state embracing Syria and Mesopotamia. The Ptolemies constantly challenged the Seleucids for control of Syria. The kings also had to contend with native uprisings: for example, the Maccabean revolt among the Jews in 167 B.C. resulted in independence for that long captive people until they were again subjugated by the Romans a century later. Ultimately, the Seleucid kingdom was squeezed to death by Parthian pressure from the east and Roman pressure from the west. The last Seleucid king was overthrown in 64 B.C. by the Romans, called into Asia Minor by the petty kingdoms bent on protecting their independence against Seleucid claims.

Numerous smaller realms shared the political scene with these three large kingdoms during the Hellenistic period. Chief among them were several Greek city-states which continued their independent existences and had their own histories. Their internal affairs remained a vital concern, as did their efforts to hold off Macedonian power and their rivalries with other city-states. A noteworthy development in Greek history in this period was the establishment of effective leagues as a means of holding off Macedonian might. The two chief ones were the Aetolian League in central Greece and the Achaean League in the Peloponnesus, both of which demonstrated willingness on the part of some city-states to compromise total autonomy in the interests of common effort. Among the small states of the era, the most successful were the kingdom of Pergamum in western Asia Minor and the Republic of Rhodes, both of which fared well by capitalizing on the commercial activity of the Hellenistic Age.

The mere listing of the chief states suggests another approach to Hellenistic political history: the conduct of interstate relations, an activity that took on an intensity and sophistication new to men. Great and small states developed a battery of techniques designed to gain advantage over others: military force, diplomacy, psychological warfare, internal subversion, economic penetration. In a general way, the Hellenistic world moved toward a balance of power that safeguarded the status quo rather effectively until a major outside power such as Rome moved onto the scene.

Finally, the political history of the Hellenistic Age can be approached from an institutional point of view. The Hellenistic world developed certain common patterns of political thought. The very idea of empire itself was important, especially as so dramatically fleshed out by Alexander. The Near Eastern world was, of course, familiar with this political concept as a result of

the efforts of the Amorites, the Egyptians, the Hittites, the Assyrians, and the Persians. But it was new to the Greeks, given their enchantment with the microcosmic world of the *polis*. The experiences of the Hellenistic Age put into the Greek vocabulary and mentality the vision of a great world state where men of many kinds shared a common citizenship and a common destiny. Nowhere was this ideal given more eloquent expression than in the political ideology of the Stoics, who were among the chief philosophical products of the age. And the concept of empire shaped by Greeks in the Hellenistic Age had a powerful impact on Rome.

The chief development in political institutions during the Hellenistic period, however, was the Greek acceptance of the concept of monarchical government. The Greeks had been schooled to think that a *polis* governed by the collective will of equal citizens (or at least the best of them) was the only civilized form of government. In the fourth century, as is obvious in Plato's *Republic*, that idea began to be challenged by a concept of government in which only a hero, a philosopher-king, a superman could provide just and harmonious government. The success of monarchs like Philip and Alexander served as practical demonstrations of the validity of this idea. During the Hellenistic period, monarchy became the standard form of government among the Greek rulers of the Near East. In most Hellenistic kingdoms the king's power was personal: It derived from his feats at arms, his intelligence, his will, and his favor with the gods. By virtue of his abilities, he could bestow blessings on his subjects. No constitution limited his power. No entrenched nobility acted to check him. No law other than what he decreed set limits to his authority. Only his ability defined the range of his power. Obviously, this kind of monarchy was shaped by the traditions of the ancient Near East, but it reflected a quality of its own, especially to the extent that it was personal and derived from human ability. In this sense, it bore the stamp of ancient Greece.

To exercise his vast powers effectively, the king of each Hellenistic kingdom developed a well-organized central government featuring a strong army, an elaborate bureaucracy, and an efficient taxation system. Greeks held the chief offices in these systems. The old structures of local government were usually left largely intact, except that again Greeks held the key positions of power. These Greeks tended to congregate in cities—some ancient and many newly founded. Into their new abodes the Greeks brought many political institutions and practices from their homeland. As a consequence, assemblies, councils, popular courts, and elected officials were established to give the Greek communities in the Near East considerable local autonomy. However, their ethnic identity and sense of elitism created strong bonds between them and the monarchs and generally assured their loyal support of strong royal government.

While centralized, absolutist monarchy gained the upper hand over most of the Hellenistic world, the older city-state polity persisted with considerable vitality in Greece and western Asia Minor. Many of the old Greek *poleis* remained completely autonomous during much of the Hellenistic Age. The accustomed forms of city-state government continued—democracies, oligarchies, tyrannies. The city-state world even demonstrated the power to innovate, as illustrated by the Aetolian and Achaean leagues, both of which were better organized and more effective than earlier Greek confederations. But if the *polis* lived on, it was overshadowed in every way by monarchy. In war, in beautification of cities, in patronage of the arts, in wealth, in security, Athens and Sparta could not match the Seleucid or the Ptolemaic kingdoms.

For all its confusion, the Hellenistic period was of great importance politically. The Greeks demonstrated an ability to turn their considerable talents to the creation of units larger than the city-state. They put their own stamp on monarchy, yet were willing to utilize the political experience of conquered peoples to refine the art of government. They experimented with establishing local autonomy in a larger framework and with techniques to control relations among states. The whole complex of Hellenistic government prepared the ground for the Romans, who did so much to perpetuate the Greek political experience and to make many of its features applicable to a world far larger than the Aegean basin.

3. HELLENISTIC PROSPERITY

Greek rule in the Hellenistic world resulted in vigorous economic growth, so that one of the highlights of the period was great prosperity. Alexander's conquest might well be compared to Columbus' discovery in the sense that it opened up for Greek exploitation a vast territory endowed with vast riches. The Greeks migrated from their native cities in large numbers and applied themselves with vigor to the exploitation of these new lands. As they broke away from their native *poleis,* many discarded the old attitudes that had placed a higher value on political and cultural life than on economic enterprise and became skilled entrepreneurs. All over the Near East they found a native population accustomed to economic domination by a narrow ruling group and were therefore able to seize economic control without much resistance. In many areas of the Hellenistic world well-organized agriculture, skilled industry, and well-developed trading systems already existed, again supplying openings for Greek enterprise. The energetic Greeks missed few of these opportunities.

Agriculture continued to be the basic source of wealth. The new Greek masters did not fundamentally change the established systems, but they did promote greater efficiency and productivity. Greek entrepreneurs, including the kings, sponsored land clearance, directed new irrigation projects, encouraged crop rotation and fertilization, introduced new crops and better breeds of livestock, and organized production more effectively. One senses here an application of the rational spirit of the Greeks at a very mundane level.

But it was the growth of trade and industry that fueled Hellenistic prosperity. Extensive capital came into Greek hands as a result of their seizure of the treasury of the Persian king and of the wealth controlled by the rich all over the Near East. The Greeks put this capital to work in large-scale trading and industrial ventures, centered chiefly in the great seaboard cities of the eastern Mediterranean but extending outward to the entire Mediterranean world and across southern Asia to India and even China. The

Hellenistic kings led in this activity by creating state monopolies for the exchange and production of many items. They also helped trade by clearing the seas of pirates, keeping roads safe, building canals and harbors, improving marketing facilities in their cities, establishing sound money systems, and abolishing artificial political barriers to trade. The horizons of commerce were considerably extended by geographical exploration which expanded Greek contacts eastward to India and out of the western Mediterranean to the coasts of Africa, Western Europe, and Britain. Commercial interchange contributed a great deal to create the unified world of which Alexander's admirers dreamed.

Hellenistic prosperity, however, benefited only a few—princes, civil servants, landowners, great merchants, and priests. The mass of the population on the farms and in the cities still labored for small gain. The Greeks who spread over the Near East were usually predominant in the favored upper classes, the natives generally economically oppressed. As the Hellenistic era progressed, this gap between rich and poor caused increasing social conflict. Moreover, the prosperity was not evenly distributed geographically. The chief centers of wealth were in a belt stretching from Asia Minor to Egypt. Here were the great cities, like Alexandria and Antioch, the best farms, the chief trade routes, the most skilled workers, and the most capital. Greece herself suffered a constant impoverishment during the Hellenistic Age as economic leadership moved eastward and southward. This situation bred deep hostility and boded ill for the long-run stability of Hellenistic society.

The increasing maldistribution of wealth constituted a serious failure on the part of the Greek masters. In many of the ancient Greek city-states, intelligent leadership had directed economic and social development toward the improvement of the lot of the deprived, a policy that had strengthened the whole fabric of society. But the Greek rulers and entrepreneurs of the Hellenistic Age chose to be exploiters. Perhaps this new posture was a natural product of their position as overlords rather than sharers of power with fellow citizens. Perhaps too it was the inevitable consequence of their migration

from the ancient *poleis*, a process that transformed them from aristocratic political animals into entrepreneurial economic animals.

4. HELLENISTIC LITERATURE AND ART

The three centuries following Alexander's death marked an important era in cultural history. The Greeks who fought in Alexander's armies and who migrated to populate his new cities were convinced that they had conquered "barbarians" who must be civilized, that is, Hellenized. As a consequence, they made a major effort to impose their culture on the Near East, with the result that Greek literary, artistic, philosophical, and scientific concepts spread over the entire Near East to establish the basis of cultural life. Large segments of the conquered peoples accepted the Greek way as the measure of cultural life. But at the same time, the culturally dominant Greeks found themselves separated from the intimate, tightly knit city-state environment that had originally nourished their culture. They were now widely dispersed in a huge, impersonal world where their destinies were determined by the dictates of semi-divine monarchs and complicated economic forces. In such a milieu, some aspects of their old culture appeared to have little relevance. Moreover, the Greeks soon found that the "barbarian" Egyptians, Syrians, Mesopotamians, Persians, and Indians possessed knowledge, techniques, and ideas that were both new and attractive to the conquerors. The result of this expansion of Hellenic culture into a new setting was an outburst of activity in literature, art, philosophy, and science which transformed the old modes of thought and expression in ways that broadened and enriched the classical Greek culture that had reached its peak in the fifth century B.C.

The literary output of the Hellenistic Age was massive. The outpouring was due in part to the patronage of wealthy monarchs, officials, and private individuals and in part to the increased demand for literature by a growing reading public. Greek became the common tongue of the Hellenistic world of government, commerce, and learning; the Old Testament was translated into Greek (the Septuagint) in Alexandria in the third

and second centuries B.C. for the use of Jews living there. While the writers of the Hellenistic
Age were prolific, they were not especially inventive. They imitated the epic and lyric poems,
the tragedies and comedies, and the histories of
classical Greece. Most, especially the poets, were
chiefly concerned with style. They often re-
worked old subject matter in an attempt to
achieve stylistic perfection. As a consequence,
later ages found Hellenistic literature of little interest, and almost none of it has survived. It did,
however, serve as a model for the Romans in developing their literary styles in Latin.

The Hellenistic Age also produced a multitude
of scholars who spent their lives reconstructing
earlier Greek literary masterpieces, writing extensive commentaries on their meaning, analyz-
ing their grammar, and defining their stylistic
features. This patient labor played an important
role in establishing and preserving the texts of
the Greek classics. Scholarly activity tended to
concentrate in a few great cities, of which Alexandria in Egypt and Pergamum were the most
important and Athens the most prestigious.
Supported by royal patronage, scholars at Alexandria and Pergamum collected great libraries.
The scholarly establishment provided endless
grist for an education system that was expanding in the Hellenistic Age and becoming increasingly literary and formal. Education played a
major role in preparing the Greek ruling elite to
discharge its duties and to sustain the cultural
brand that was its mark of superiority.

The artists of the Hellenistic period were no
less active than the literary men. Again classical
Greek models exerted a powerful influence,
completely overshadowing the artistic traditions
of the Near East. Architecture enjoyed a great
boom because of the numerous new cities built
by the Greeks and filled with the traditional
buildings—temples, gymnasiums, theaters, and
centers for public business. There was a tendency to stress size and ornateness in these buildings. Most Hellenistic cities were much better
planned than the older Greek cities, with emphasis on wide streets, adequate water supplies,
commercial conveniences, and parks. As a result,
Alexandria and the like were more impressive
than Athens.

This statue of an old market woman, a second-
century Hellenistic marble found in Rome, reflects
an emotionalism and realism far removed from the
serene, idealized figures of classical Greece. *Photo:
The Metropolitan Museum of Art*

Most Hellenistic sculptures were mere copies
of the masters of fifth-century Greece. Occasionally one caught the full spirit of the classical
style, such as the famous *Winged Victory of Sa-
mothrace* or the *Aphrodite of Melos* (more commonly known as the *Venus de Milo*). But some

works took on important new features. In place of the classic quest to create idealized perfection, Hellenistic sculptors tended toward realism. They came down into the streets for their subjects instead of ascending to the abode of the gods. Children, old people, common laborers, and barbarians occupied their attention, and they gave vent to emotions, seeking to portray action and violence, passion, sorrow, and suffering.

5. PHILOSOPHY AND SCIENCE

The major contributions of the Hellenistic Age were in the fields of science and philosophy. Often thinkers in this era moved beyond their predecessors, a development that seldom occurred in the field of literature and art.

The moment was especially ripe for scientific advance. The Greek philosophers of the sixth, fifth, and fourth centuries had made brilliant hypotheses about the natural world. Some of them, especially Hippocrates and Aristotle, had introduced the idea that the world could best be understood by observing it and classifying the results rationally. Many educated men shared a sense of the importance of this approach; Alexander, for example, had unusual natural specimens collected during his military ventures into the distant East. His conquest put the Greeks in touch with a huge body of data compiled over many centuries by learned men in the ancient Near East. The general use of Greek as the language of learning permitted scientific advances to spread widely. Royal patronage, especially by the Ptolemies, who built a great library and museum at Alexandria, helped to create an interest in science and to provide the necessary facilities. In this favorable climate the quest for knowledge about the natural world was actively pursued.

The new geography, of great interest in the Hellenistic period, was summed up by Eratosthenes (ca. 275–200 B.C.), who worked at Alexandria. He calculated the circumference of the earth as 24,662 miles, about 200 less than the actual figure. On the basis of his study of tides, he insisted that the Atlantic and Indian oceans were joined and that India could be reached by boat around Africa. He made maps using lines of longitude and latitude and divided the earth into zones still used by geographers. Seleucus (second century B.C.), along with others, studied the tides and came close to relating them to the gravitational force of the moon.

Astronomy likewise attracted attention. The two greatest names were Aristarchus (ca. 310–230 B.C.) and Hipparchus (ca. 185–120 B.C.). Aristarchus insisted that the earth revolved around the sun. Hipparchus denied this, and his opinion carried the day. He compiled an extensive atlas of the stars and from observation of their movement arrived at an extremely accurate calculation of the solar year. Both these great astronomers tried to calculate the size of the sun and its distance from the earth, but with little success.

Much was also done to advance mathematics. Euclid (323–285 B.C.) compiled a textbook of geometry that remained standard until the twentieth century. Archimedes (287–212 B.C.) calculated the value of pi (the ratio between the circumference and the diameter of a circle). He also devised a system for expressing large numbers, solved the problem of the relative volumes of a cylinder and sphere, and laid the foundations for calculus. Trigonometry was perfected by Hipparchus, and a fundamental work on conic sections was done by Apollonius of Perga (third century).

Scientific medicine was of great interest to the scholars of this period. Following the lead of Hippocrates, Hellenistic physicians made important progress in anatomy and physiology. Among the chief accomplishments of these men were the discovery of the nerves and the exploration of the function of arteries and the brain. Surgery advanced considerably; so did the use of medicines.

Comparatively little work was done in physics, chemistry, zoology, and botany. Archimedes, however, discovered the laws governing floating bodies and developed the theory of the lever; and Theophrastus (ca. 372–287 B.C.) wrote an important descriptive work on botany that summarized most of the knowledge of plants in his day.

Most of the important work of Hellenistic scientists had been completed by the end of the second century B.C. Thereafter, interest shifted to magic, astrology, and empty repetition of past accomplishments. The Hellenistic Greeks, like their predecessors in classical Greece, were limited in their scientific progress by lack of proper instruments. And there was still no widespread interest in the practical application of scientific ideas, although a few scientists did distinguish themselves as inventors. Archimedes, for instance, invented the windlass, the double pulley, the endless screw, and several devices for defending his native city, Syracuse, against Roman attack.

The last significant development in ancient science was the compilation of great scientific encyclopedias. Among these works were those of Ptolemy (ca. A.D. 85–160) in astronomy and geography, Strabo (ca. 63 B.C.–A.D. 21) in geography, and Galen (A.D. 130–201) in medicine. The bulk of the material in these manuals was derived from the labors of Hellenistic scientists, so that each is a monument to their accomplishments. These encyclopedias served as guides until the beginning of the great scientific revolution in early modern times; little was added in the nearly two millennia separating the Hellenistic scientists from Galileo and Copernicus.

For vigor and creativity, Hellenistic science was rivaled by Hellenistic philosophy. The old philosophical interests lived on, as evidenced by the continued activity of Plato's Academy and Aristotle's Lyceum in Athens. However, the older Hellenic quest for absolute truth about the cosmic order gave way to concern with problems of human conduct, ethical principles, and above all the human soul—the individual and his personal destiny. This trend was already evident among the Sophists of the fifth century B.C. In the Hellenistic Age it was given new impetus by the Greeks projected into a cosmopolitan world where men were on their own among strangers of many kinds. Left with only his own resources, man needed self-knowledge and reassurance to allay his anxieties.

The search for individual identity and guidance produced several schools of thought. Some caught popular fancy or aroused popular ire for their eccentricity and excess. One such group was the Skeptics, who made a principle of doubting everything and argued that men should live with no concern for truth or values. The Cynics were more spectacular; they advocated that society should abandon all its civilized conventions and wealth to return to nature. In search of converts, they took to the streets in filthy rags to deliver diatribes against the "establishment."

More profound and influential was the teaching of Epicurus (ca. 341–270 B.C.), who taught at Athens. He built his ethical concepts on a strictly materialistic basis. He argued that the universe consisted of atoms, which by chance formed themselves into beings and things. The gods, if they existed, had nothing to do with this process and therefore need be of no concern to men. Given such a cosmos, men should occupy themselves only with happiness and pleasure. Epicurus argued that mere physical pleasure is not the path to happiness but rather those things that bring a peaceful, undisturbed mind. He pleaded with his disciples to withdraw into themselves and avoid excessive wealth, politics, superstition, and too great contact with the world. This philosphy was welcome to many educated men who saw little use struggling in a world where great kings and great wealth determined most things. Although some turned Epicurus' teachings into an excuse for seeking purely physical pleasure, most Epicureans were admirable men, learned and refined, obedient to public authority, calm, and long-suffering.

Even more influential in shaping the moral atmosphere of the Hellenistic Age were the Stoics, whose founder, Zeno (336–264 B.C.), taught in Athens while Epicurus was there. Stoicism was based on Zeno's conviction that the universe is ruled by a Divine Reason, which for many Stoics was a great god who had ordained a perfect world; harmony and order would result if the laws of nature were adhered to by all creatures. Man's moral duty was thus clear. He must use his reason to attune himself and his actions to the unchanging laws of nature. He must bear all misfortune with patience, since everything that happens has been ordained by an all-knowing Providence. And he must bear his good fortune without pride, since he is not responsible for it.

The Stoic was schooled to adjust himself to circumstances; his life was a pilgrimage in which he disciplined himself to accept whatever came.

6. HELLENISTIC RELIGION

In at least one realm of life, the Greek way suffered an eclipse: religion. The old civic religion of the Greeks had already been weakened by the blows suffered by the city-states in the fifth and fourth centuries and by the assaults of the philosophers. The old gods and the communal rites in their honor ceased to have meaning to the Greeks who migrated into the Near East. From Alexander's time on, there was an attempt to encourage the worship of kings, but it took no root.

Permeating the Near East were powerful religious forces rooted deep in the past. These forces had evolved into definable cults that we shall call collectively *mystery religions*. With the passing of time, they simply overpowered Greek civic religion and drew increasing numbers of Greeks into their orbits. Many mystery cults flourished in the Near East in the Hellenistic Age: Isis worship, Mithraism, the Earth Mother cult; and the Greeks still had their own Dionysus worship. Whatever their origin, all shared certain fundamental ideas that clashed sharply with the communally oriented, humanistic cults of the *polis*. They centered around the worship of a savior whose death and resurrection provided salvation for each individual. Thus they appealed to men of all classes and nations. The mystery religions involved elaborate, emotional ritual practices and stressed the moral conduct of each believer. In the cosmopolitan atmosphere of the Hellenistic world, ideas from various mystery religions constantly mingled; this syncretism pointed toward the growth of a common faith shared especially by common men throughout the Hellenistic world. Here was the seedbed for two new religions soon to arise in the Near East—Christianity and Islam.

The mystery cults powerfully influenced several aspects of thought and expression. Science and philosophy were put to the service of these religions. Astronomy was transformed into astrology, the "scientists" studying the stars to know the future rather than to find new information, while the philosophers' efforts to understand the universe became an attempt to achieve contact with the powerful deities of the mystery cults. In this sense the peoples of the Near East conquered the Greeks during the Hellenistic Age.

This "religionizing" of thought had brought Greek culture and its Hellenistic continuation full circle: A culture born out of religion was now being absorbed back into religion. A real possibility existed that some of the finest achievements of the Greeks would be swallowed up and twisted out of shape in their losing encounter with Near Eastern religious ideas. This trend was checked at least temporarily by the emergence of Rome as a new champion of Greek civilization. Under Roman auspices Greek culture enjoyed a renaissance and increased its geographical sway considerably.

Suggested Reading

Political History

*Max Cary, *A History of the Greek World from 323 to 146 B.C.* (2nd ed. rev., Barnes and Noble). A standard survey; excellent for political history.

*F. E. Peters, *The Harvest of Hellenism: A History of the Near East from Alexander the Great to the Triumph of Christianity* (Touchstone Book). A balanced, judicious treatment of all aspects of Hellenistic history.

*C. Bradford Welles, *Alexander and the Hellenistic World* (University of Toronto Press). Especially good in this up-to-date survey are the chapters on social and economic conditions.

*W. W. Tarn, *Alexander the Great.* 2 vols. (1948; vol. I has been published as a paperback by Beacon).

*A. R. Burn, *Alexander the Great and the Hellenistic World* (Collier).

Peter Green, *Alexander the Great* (1970).

Robin Lane Fox, *Alexander the Great* (1974). Any of these four biographies will help you to understand an intriguing man; the last two are especially good.

Hellenistic Cultural Life

*W. W. Tarn and G. T. Griffth, *Hellenistic Civilization* (3rd ed., Meridian).

*John Ferguson, *The Heritage of Hellenism* (Harcourt Brace Jovanovich). Either of these works will provide an excellent description of the major features of Hellenistic cultural life.

*George Sarton, *A History of Science: Hellenistic Science and Culture in the Last Three Centuries B.C.* (Norton). A monumental treatment filled with detailed discussions of Hellenistic science.

*O. Neugebauer, *The Exact Sciences in Antiquity* (2nd ed., Dover). Provides a brief treatment of Hellenistic science.

*N. W. DeWitt, *Epicurus and His Philosophy* (Meridian).

Edwyn Bevan, *Stoics and Sceptics* (1913). These two volumes, neither of which is easy to read, will summarize Hellenistic achievements in philosophy.

Sources

*Arrian, *The Life of Alexander the Great,* trans. A. de Selincourt (Penguin). A colorful biography by a second-century A.D. author who used materials written in the time of Alexander, but since lost.

W. J. Oates, ed., *The Stoic and Epicurean Philosophers* (1940). A collection of nearly all the writings of the Stoic and Epicurean writers of the Hellenistic period.

*F. C. Grant, *Hellenistic Religion: The Age of Syncreticism* (Liberal Arts). A collection of ancient writings that will help to understand the nature of the major religious movements of the Hellenistic Age.

8

THE RISE OF ROME TO DOMINATION OF THE MEDITERRANEAN WORLD

The powerful impulses toward the establishment of a common culture in the Mediterranean basin, loosed first by the Greek city-states and then by the Hellenistic kingdoms, were picked up toward the end of the third century B.C. by a new power emerging from the West: Rome. The rise of the Romans marked the first appearance of a western Mediterranean people in a decisive role in determining the course of history. It is a story that deserves special consideration because the Romans were equipped with unique talents that allowed them not only to sustain the Hellenic and Hellenistic accomplishments but also to advance civilized life to new levels.

1. THE EARLY ITALIANS

The city of Rome provided the catalytic force that organized the peoples of the western Mediterranean world for their role in history. But the Romans relied on the Italic population for the human resources needed to achieve greatness. The formation of the Italian population was a complex process, involving many different peoples. At a very ancient date Italy was inhabited by paleolithic hunting communities. Neolithic farming culture eventually replaced paleolithic culture, perhaps introduced by newcomers from Africa. By the third millennium B.C. the peninsula was fairly heavily populated with hardy farmers, whose offspring constituted the basic

human stock on which Rome's greatness would be built. Beginning about 2000 B.C. Italy, like many other areas of the Mediterranean Basin, experienced successive waves of Indo-European invaders. While these newcomers fused with the neolithic population, they did bring with them superior technical skills, including the use of metals, and effective military and political skills, which allowed them to impose their authority on the natives. Their language, expressed in several local dialects, prevailed over most of Italy; from one of these dialects classical Latin eventually emerged.

While the level of life in Italy generally advanced across the second millennium B.C., it still lagged behind that of the eastern Mediterranean. Beginning about 800 B.C. the backward western Mediterranean world, including Italy, was powerfully stimulated by the intrusion of more advanced easterners—especially the Phoenicians, the Greeks, and the Etruscans. The Phoenician impact was slight in Italy but decisive in North Africa, where it gave rise to the powerful commercial city of Carthage, whose history was to be linked with that of the Romans for many centuries. As we have seen, the Greeks established numerous city-states in Sicily and southern Italy, each of which replicated the main features of Greek civilization, and whence flowed powerful cultural forces affecting the entire Italian peninsula.

It was the Etruscans, however, who had the

most immediate and direct influence on Italy and especially on Rome. This people is still an enigma to historians, in large part because their language has not yet been deciphered. They probably came from Asia Minor during the eighth century B.C. and established a series of cities along the western coast of Italy north of the Tiber River, a region still called Etruria after its ancient inhabitants. These cities remained politically independent of one another, but were bound together by strong economic, religious, and cultural ties. Within a short time Etruscan influence began to expand, so that between 650 and 500 B.C. they ruled supreme over western Italy from the Po Valley to Naples. After 500 B.C. their power declined as a result of native resistance and Greek and Carthaginian rivalry. During their era of power they transmitted a wide range of technical skills, economic practices, political techniques, religious ideas, and cultural models that prepared the peoples of Italy for a major historical role. Their most precocious pupils were some villagers living along the Tiber.

2. ROME TO 509 B.C.

The colorful and enduring legend recounted by the Roman historian Livy of the founding of Rome in 753 B.C. by Romulus and Remus will never cease to stir the imagination. But it hardly fits the facts. What was eventually to become the "head of the world" was founded by backward herder-farmers from a poor area known as Latium. Seeking protection for themselves and pasture for their flocks, these Latins began about 750 B.C. to build tiny villages on a cluster of seven hills lying along the south bank of the Tiber about fifteen miles upstream from its mouth. Although this site was to prove of great importance in the future because of its command of a crucial ford across the Tiber, the early settlements on the seven hills did not seem destined to greatness. Their population grew slowly, and each of the several villages retained its own lands and its own tribal political institutions. The villages shared some common religious bonds, but alone they seemed incapable of advancing toward any kind of common effort that

would assure a larger place for them, even in the affairs of Latium.

Shortly after 600 B.C., the several villages were rather suddenly transformed into a single city-state. What brought about this decisive event is not clear, but it was probably the consequence of their seizure by Etruscan warlords who imposed political unity on the villages. A single government under a king was established. The king was advised by a council of elders, called the Senate, composed of men of wealth who drew their authority from their headship of families. There was also an assembly of freemen who were grouped into thirty units called *curiae*, but it was severely limited in its power and did little more than approve the decisions of the king and the Senate. The city-state populace was divided into two distinct classes, *patricians* and *plebeians*, with the former exercising a predominant influence over society. Many plebeians were closely tied to patrician families as *clients*, an institution under which a noble *patron* protected a plebeian and assisted him materially, and the client in return performed various services, including following political directions.

Etruscan techniques, especially in trade and industry, were adopted by the fledgling Roman city-state, greatly strengthening its primitive economy. An alphabet was derived from Etruscan models, resulting in the rapid development of written Latin. Etruscan architecture and decoration served as models for the temples and public buildings in the burgeoning city. Primitive Latin religious practices took on more sophisticated patterns reflecting Etruscan usages. Rome was rapidly becoming the center of an advanced culture and a significant power in Latium.

Despite their debt to the Etruscans, the Romans chafed under their domination. Shortly before 500 B.C. Etruscan power began to be contested by her dependent subjects everywhere in western Italy, while Greeks and Carthaginians vied with Etruscan forces in the larger setting of the western Mediterranean. The challenge was too much for the Etruscans. In Rome the patricians took the lead in a revolution that dethroned the Etruscan king and established in his place two *consuls* elected annually from pa-

This portrayal of a Roman patrician bearing busts of his ancestors conveys the sobriety, seriousness, and respect for family that characterized the aristocratic citizens who acted through the Senate to lead the Roman Republic to ascendancy in the Mediterranean world. *Photo: Alinari/EPA, Inc.*

trician ranks to wield the *imperium,* that is, the highest authority of the state. This revolution marked the beginning of the Roman Republic, an episode long celebrated by the Romans as the greatest event in their history.

3. THE EARLY REPUBLIC, 590–265 B.C.

The two and a half centuries following the founding of the republic put the Romans to a severe test. From 509 to about 340 B.C. the Romans were chiefly occupied defending themselves in Latium, especially against neighboring peoples. Immediately after the revolt against the Etruscans, the other cities of Latium forced Rome to accept a position as their equal in the Latin League. This league fought a long succession of wars to hold back the Etruscans and the tough mountain peoples of central Italy. About 400 B.C. a new menace emerged—Celtic invaders from Gaul, who captured and sacked Rome in 390. Out of this desperate struggle for survival, Rome slowly emerged as the dominant force in Latium; her success bred fear in the Latin League and caused several of its members to rise against Rome in 340. The rebels were subdued within two years, and the league was dissolved, leaving Rome in control of Latium.

From this base, she turned her attention to the troublesome mountaineers. In a series of campaigns known as the Samnite Wars, stretching from 326 to 290 B.C., the Romans systematically crushed these tribes and incorporated their territory into her expanding state. In the meantime, Roman influence was expanding northward at the expense of the Etruscans and the Gauls. In fighting these various peoples simultaneously, the Romans showed considerable diplomatic skill and succeeded in keeping their foes isolated from one another. Hardly had the Samnite Wars ended when Rome was drawn into the strife-torn world of the Greek city-states in southern Italy. A series of victories in that area ended in 265 B.C. with the Romans in complete control. All Italy south of the Po Valley was hers, constituting the base for a new—although still unproved—world power.

Many factors combined to bring the tiny city on the Tiber these victories. But two were crucial: Rome's enlightened treatment of her victims and her ability to adjust her internal political system to retain and deepen the loyalty of her citizens.

The victorious Romans spurned the usual methods of brutal subjugation and exploitation of conquered peoples. Rather, they applied a variety of solutions, usually dictated by the practical demands of the situation, to bring their victims under their direction under terms that allowed conquered peoples to identify their well-being with Roman success. To some peoples, especially those in Latium, Rome extended outright citizenship. Others, especially those already organized as city-states, were made partial citizens without rights to participate in Roman public life but with rights to trade and intermarry. These cities continued to govern themselves in most matters, but their half-Roman citizens owed financial and military obligations to Rome. Still other communities were made allies of Rome, each group signing a formal treaty which left it considerable local independence but which deprived it of control over foreign affairs and imposed on it the obligation to provide men and money for Rome's wars. These arrangements for partial citizenship and alliances were based on the assumption that the subject peoples would eventually earn full citizenship when they demonstrated their loyalty and their capability to participate fully in Roman political and social life. Rome moved to hasten the process by planting numerous colonies of her citizens at various places in Italy. This complex set of arrangements meant that by 265 B.C. Rome ruled over a loose confederation of Italians, most of whom enjoyed a considerable degree of independence, but all of whom were tied to Rome by virtue of an obligation to serve in her armies and of a promise to achieve full citizenship. This system, which made Rome's yoke relatively light, soon paid off richly in her favor.

The intelligent program for conquered people was matched by a constant modification of the Roman constitution which promoted allegiance and loyalty among the citizens. When the Romans threw off Etruscan rule in 509 B.C., power fell to a narrow patrician aristocracy which controlled the elective offices, the Senate, and the assembly of the *curiae*. During the following two and a half centuries there ensued what is referred to as the "struggle of the orders." The patrician oligarchy came under constant pressure from the plebeians and grudgingly surrendered its monopoly over political life by conceding a larger share of power to the plebeians. Plebeian gains were won gradually, but they came in vital areas. Their role in the army was expanded. New assemblies emerged permitting a plebeian voice in passing laws, electing magistrates, and vetoing arbitrary decisions. One by one elective offices were opened to plebeians. Ancient legal customs were codified to guard citizens from unfair decisions by patrician judges. New legislation was enacted to protect debtors, permit intermarriage between patricians and plebeians, curb patrician monopoly on the control of public land, and encourage colonizing ventures, all promoting the economic interests of the plebeians. The cumulative results of the "struggle of the orders" can best be seen by examining the constitution of the republic in 265 B.C.

Theoretically, Rome was governed in 265 by the decisions of the total citizen body acting through the assemblies, of which two were especially important. The Assembly of Centuries was based on a grouping of the citizenry into 193 military units called *centuries*. Each citizen was assigned to one according to his wealth, reflecting the fact that the Roman army was dependent on citizens capable of arming themselves at their own expense. Because the army was largely composed of cavalry units and heavily armored foot soldiers, the majority of the centuries were composed of citizens wealthy enough to afford expensive equipment. A smaller number of centuries were assigned support functions in the army, and their ranks were filled by citizens of modest means. Since each century cast a single vote in the Assembly of Centuries, that body was dominated by men of wealth, who constituted a numerical minority of the total citizenry. However, all citizens did participate through that body in such vital functions as approving all laws and electing all officials. The other important assembly was the Assembly of Tribes. It originated as a plebeian body constituted to advise special plebeian officials, called *tribunes*, who were granted the power to veto the acts of regularly elected magistrates when those laws threatened plebeians' interests. The Assembly of Tribes was based on territorial units called *tribes*, of which there were eventually thirty-five. Male

ITALY 265 B.C.

citizens were enrolled in the tribes on a basis of place of residency, greatly reducing the importance of wealth and social status in the assembly's deliberations. Eventually, the Assembly of Tribes gained the power to enact laws, called *plebiscites*, binding on the entire state; thus it became the chief instrument for the expression of the popular will.

The decisions of the citizenry enacted in the assemblies were executed by an elected magistracy, collegiate in form: With minor exceptions, every office was occupied by a board of at least two members of equal rank, each of whom had the power to veto the acts of his colleagues. The highest executive authority in the state — the *imperium* — was exercised by two consuls who were charged with the management of all civil and military affairs. Below them were the *praetors*, elected primarily to administer justice, but under special circumstances capable of exercising the *imperium*. The *quaestors* handled the financial matters of the state. The *aediles* managed the policing of the city, the repair of streets and public buildings, the city's food supply, and the conduct of religious ceremonies. Priestly colleges were elected to carry out worship of the civic gods. All these officials were elected for one-year terms. *Censors* were elected every five years to classify the citizens for military service and to judge the moral fitness of citizens for public functions. In times of grave crisis, a *dictator* could be elected for a term of six months with unlimited powers to rule the state. According to law, any citizen was eligible for election to these offices, but since there was no pay for service and electioneering was expensive, few men of humble means aspired to high office and even fewer gained it.

Especially potent in the republican system of government was the Senate, a body of about three hundred men who served for life. New members were recruited almost exclusively from the ranks of ex-magistrates. Election to the consulship and praetorship automatically qualified a man for the Senate. Theoretically, the Senate was an advisory body, counseling the magistrates and the assemblies in all public matters. But its decisions were almost invariably accepted by the magistrates and the assemblies because of the prestige and experience of the senators.

Although ostensibly a democracy by 265 B.C., the Roman Republic was dominated by a small, wealthy, landed aristocracy, still largely hereditary. This tightly knit group acted consciously to control the machinery of government. From its ranks came most of the elected magistrates, who passed from these offices into the Senate. That body, with its extensive role in decision making, was the bastion of aristocratic control. The patricians carefully managed the election process and skillfully manipulated the assemblies, relying heavily on the institution of clientage as a means of controlling the votes of the plebeians. The chief threat to the political power of the patrician families came from able, enterprising plebeians who managed to gain wealth by exploiting the opportunities arising from Roman expansion. These "new men" had their appetite for power whetted by the opportunity for broader political participation created during the "struggle of the orders." The patricians met their challenge chiefly by absorbing the new men into their ranks, usually through carefully managed marriage alliances. This process tended to shift the basis for aristocratic status from birth to wealth, but it in no way weakened aristocratic control over political life.

Most Romans were content to entrust the fate of the city to the aristocrats, satisfied that means were at hand to curb them if they abused their power. The history of Rome from 509 to 265 B.C. justified that confidence. The aristocrats led her to mastery over Italy. They were not guilty of prolonged periods of abuse of power, and they were usually responsive to popular demands for change. They also proved capable of pursuing a consistent policy to a successful conclusion, especially in the vital areas of war and diplomacy. Seldom did Rome suffer from the indecision that hampered so many of the more popularly controlled Greek city-states.

4. OVERSEAS EXPANSION: THE PUNIC WARS, 264–201 B.C.

Rome's success in conquering most of Italy set the stage for a new role for her in a vastly larger world. Perhaps without her people yet knowing it, Rome had by 265 B.C. become a major power in the Mediterranean world. During the next century and a half, her history was to a large degree shaped by her expanding involvement in that complex world. That involvement resulted in a succession of victories that made her the dominant power in the Mediterranean world, the mistress of a vast empire created almost willy-nilly as a consequence of coping effectively with a succession of situations arising in that troubled world.

Rome's first encounter with a major Mediterranean power pitted her against the African city of Carthage. Originally a Phoenician colony, Carthage had established her independence after the Phoenicians were conquered by the Assyrians in the eighth century B.C. In the succeeding centuries, Carthage created a thriving commercial empire that was based on several colonies located at strategic places around the western Mediterranean and on a powerful fleet that controlled the sea routes through the Mediterranean. Prior to 265 B.C. Carthage's main rivals for commercial supremacy in the Mediterranean were the Greek city-states, especially those established in Sicily and southern Italy as a consequence of Greek colonization. The Carthaginians proved to be a formidable foe for the Greeks; by the third century B.C. Carthage's wealth and power had grown to the point where she could contend with anyone threatening her commerce and her sea power.

Rome and Carthage had interacted with each other almost from the beginning of the Roman republic in 509 B.C. Generally, their relationships had been friendly, resulting in a succession of treaties that recognized Carthaginian dominance of the commerce of the western Mediterranean while conceding Rome's control over Italy. Almost by accident the two powers stumbled into conflict over Sicily. In 265 B.C. the Sicilian city of Messana, seeking to escape domination by the powerful Greek city of Syracuse, appealed to both Carthage and Rome for help. Since Carthage controlled the western part of Sicily as a key link in her commercial power, she moved quickly to support Messana as a means of preventing Syracuse from expanding Greek power in that crucial area. After some hesitation, the Romans also decided to intervene, perhaps finally persuaded by fears that Carthaginian control of Messana would lead to troublesome intervention by a major power in the affairs of Rome's recently conquered and still restless allies in southern Italy. Her decision meant war with Carthage.

The First Punic War (264–241 B.C.) was a struggle for Sicily. Although the Romans initially won some land engagements, they soon realized that they would need a navy to dislodge the Carth-

aginians from their seaport strongholds in western Sicily. With exemplary resolve and help from their Greek allies, they soon achieved that end and began to challenge the Carthaginians successfully for control of the waters around Sicily. These victories made the Romans so confident that in 256 B.C. they undertook a major expedition against Carthage in Africa, but this venture ended in a disaster that prolonged the war for many years. Rome returned to her efforts to dislodge the enemy from the fortress cities in Sicily. Although she suffered a series of naval disasters in this effort, she doggedly built fleet after fleet and sustained the pressure until Carthage sued for peace in 241 B.C. By the treaty ending the war, Rome gained Sicily and a sizable monetary payment to cover her war expenses.

But the issue between the two powers was far from settled. In the years following the peace of 241 B.C., the Carthaginians turned their attention to rebuilding their strength, seriously threatened by the loss of Sicily and the Roman challenge to their sea power. Under the leadership of Hamilcar Barca, Carthage undertook to create an enlarged land empire in Spain as a new base for her power. Hamilcar successfully subdued the native Spanish population, recruited and trained a potent army of Spaniards, and collected a huge war chest. After his death in 229 B.C., his policy was carried on first by his son-in-law and later by his son, Hannibal. The efforts of the Barcas restored Carthage's power to the point where she could again challenge Rome, a goal always cherished by this gifted family. In the meantime, the Romans were too involved with other issues to pay much attention to the recovery of Carthage. Rome organized a provincial government to control into the rich land of the Po Valley at the Corsica and Sardinia, which she treacherously seized from Carthage immediately following the peace ending the First Punic War. Her forces became deeply involved in extending Roman control into the rich land of the Po Valley at the expense of Gauls already settled there. Her naval forces undertook to curb the pirates who plagued sea traffic and raided the coasts around the Adriatic Sea. Only gradually did the Romans turn their attention to the rising power of Carthage in Spain. Their efforts to intervene there soon led to a new war, provoked in 218 B.C. by Hannibal's attack on a Spanish city which Rome claimed as an ally.

The Second Punic War (218–201 B.C.) was certainly Rome's sternest military test, due in large part to the genius of Hannibal. His strategy centered on bringing a major military force into Italy in order to deprive Rome of the manpower provided by her Italian allies, whom Hannibal presumed would be glad to rid themselves of the Roman yoke. With characteristic daring he surprised the Romans by leading his army from Spain across southern Gaul and the Alps into northern Italy. On three different occasions between 218 and 216 B.C. the Romans challenged him with large armies, only to be crushed each time. The last and the most disastrous of these battles, at Cannae, convinced the Romans that they could not match Hannibal in open battle. They adopted a policy of harassing his army, otherwise leaving him free to do as he pleased. Until 203 B.C. — a total of fifteen years — Hannibal maintained an army in Italy, spreading destruction up and down the peninsula; this was a remarkable feat in view of the fact that he received almost no reinforcements or supplies from Carthage or Spain. But he failed to achieve what he counted on to defeat Rome: He never persuaded a decisive number of Rome's Italian allies to desert.

While holding Hannibal at bay in Italy, Rome resolutely undertook the long struggle to crush Carthage. She fought on many fronts, and actually won the war outside Italy. Large armies sent to Spain slowly crushed Carthaginian power and cut off Hannibal's reinforcements. Another Roman force was dispatched to Sicily to choke off a rebellion of Greek city-states led by Syracuse in support of Carthage. Roman naval forces patrolled the western Mediterranean and the Adriatic, preventing Hannibal from getting help from Carthage or from her ally, the kingdom of Macedon. She encouraged African peoples to attack Carthaginian territories. Her counteroffensive culminated in 205 B.C., when a large army under Scipio Africanus was sent to Africa. In him, Rome had found a military talent equal to that of Hannibal. He attacked Carthage, and

Hannibal was recalled from Italy in 203 B.C. to save the city. But even he could no longer stem the tide: He met Scipio in a battle in 202 B.C. at Zama and suffered a complete defeat.

After Zama, Carthage sued for peace. She was forced to surrender Spain to Rome, to destroy her navy, to accept a heavy fine to be paid over the next fifty years, and to agree never again to wage war outside Africa and within Africa only with Rome's permission. Part of her African territory was turned over to Numidia, a state Rome hoped would balance Carthaginian power in Africa. Carthage was reduced to a minor power; victorious Rome was mistress of the western Mediterranean.

5. OVERSEAS EXPANSION: DOMINATION OVER THE EAST, 200–133 B.C.

The peace of 201 B.C. left Rome with many problems: new provinces to organize, a ravaged Italy to repair, war weariness, rebellious subjects to subdue. But these matters had to go unattended, for her new role as a world power drew her toward the turbulent eastern Mediterranean. By 200 B.C., the uneasy balance of power in the Hellenistic world was breaking down, chiefly as a result of two factors. First, Egypt grew weak under the rule of the Ptolemies. Second, a pair of ambitious kings, Philip V in Macedon and Antiochus III of the Seleucid Empire, sought to capitalize on Egypt's weakness by seizing her territory and subduing the other independent states in the Near East. Each dreamed of reconstituting Alexander's empire. Their aggressive policies frightened their intended victims into a frantic search for help. They turned to the "rising cloud in the West."

In 201 B.C. Pergamum and Rhodes appealed to Rome for help against Philip V, who had invaded Asia Minor. The war-weary Roman populace, speaking in assembly, refused to become involved, but the Senate was more bellicose. Many Roman leaders feared Philip of Macedon, who had been an ally of Hannibal in the Second Punic War. At the same time, they were moved by a sense that Rome's growing might could be used to her profit. Finally, some aristocrats, including the illustrious Scipio Africanus, had

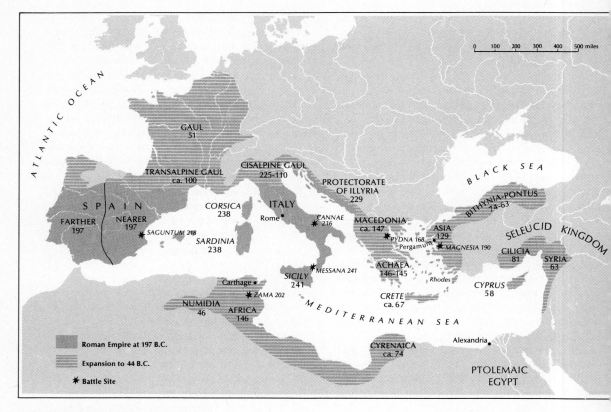

THE ROMAN EMPIRE 265–44 B.C.

become ardent admirers of Greek civilization; they were convinced that they had an obligation to save it from the barbarous Macedonians. Senatorial power asserted itself, and Rome declared war on Philip V in 200 B.C. Although her military performance was not brilliant, Rome managed to defeat him in three years. He was required to evacuate all of Greece and to confine his activities to his own kingdom. Rome then proceeded to restore peace in Greece, chiefly by bending every effort to reaffirm the autonomy of each city-state. She finally withdrew without having imposed any overlordship on the Greeks.

But Roman involvement in the East was hardly over. In 192 B.C. Antiochus III, who had sat by innocently while his fellow aggressor, Philip V, was beaten, invaded the Greek peninsula at the urging of some of the city-states

displeased with Rome's settlement. Rome again sent her troops east, and Antiochus fared no better than had Philip V. Roman legions drove him into Asia Minor, where a crushing defeat was inflicted on his army in 189 B.C. Once again, Rome tried to establish order. Antiochus was required to keep out of Asia Minor. His navy was destroyed, and a staggering fine was imposed. Rome turned over large territories in Asia Minor to Pergamum and Rhodes, sanctioning them as Roman-backed peacekeepers. Most of the Greek cities were again restored to independence, although those who had aided Antiochus were fined and forced to surrender some territories to Greek cities loyal to Rome. Again the victors annexed no lands for themselves.

With both Macedon and the Seleucid state reduced to secondary importance, peace in the

East seemed guaranteed. However, the trouble had only started. With the destruction of the old balance of power, warfare among the petty states became chronic, as did calls for Rome's attention. Even the Greeks, whom she had "saved," proved treacherous, quarrelsome, and unreliable. Plainly, a new order was needed in the Near East. Driven by a mixture of idealism, fear, and increasing greed, the Romans accepted the only possible solution—Roman rule in the East.

The first evidence of the new policy came in 171–167 B.C., when Macedon provoked another war with the collaboration of a number of Greek city-states. Rome easily crushed this alliance. She now virtually took over Macedon, leaving her only nominal independence. A few years later a minor disturbance in Macedon resulted in the annexation of the whole kingdom as a Roman province under a Roman governor. Persistent trouble in Greece resulted in stern reprisals, culminating in 146 B.C., with the complete destruction of Corinth as an example to the Greeks. By that date Rome had managed to force pro-Roman governments on most Greek cities. Now she entrusted the governor of Macedon with supervising their behavior, thus ending their freedom.

Rome's allies in Asia Minor had proved equally unreliable and troublesome. Such harsh measures had to be taken against them that the most important states, Rhodes and Pergamum, were virtually ruined. Finally, in 133 B.C., Rome took over Pergamum as a province. Once established in Asia Minor, a rich world beckoned Rome. And there was no one to stay her hand: The Seleucid kingdom and Egypt were in precipitate decline; it was only a matter of time before they would become parts of the Roman Empire.

While concentrating her attention chiefly on the East between 200 and 133 B.C., Rome continued to solidify her power in the West. The occupation of Spain and its organization into two provinces was begun. Northern Italy between the Alps and the Apennines, called Cisalpine Gaul, was reconquered and reorganized in the wake of the rebellions there during the Second Punic War. Although no longer a serious threat, Carthage continued to haunt Rome as a potential enemy. With politicians shouting "Carthage must be destroyed" as a solution to every problem, it was only a matter of time until Rome vented her fear and vengeance on her old foe. The final blow came in 149 B.C., when Rome again declared war on Carthage for no apparent reason. In 146 B.C., Carthage was captured after a heroic defense, destroyed completely, and the site sown with salt. Her territory was annexed as a Roman province.

The passing of her most formidable foe was a fitting symbol of Rome's position in the Mediterranean world as the second century B.C. neared its close. But her success posed questions: What would it profit Rome to conquer so large a world? How would she use her new power and authority?

Suggested Reading

Overview of Roman History

*Chester G. Starr, The Ancient Romans (Oxford).

Donald R. Dudley, The Romans (1970).

Thomas W. Africa, The Immense Majesty. A History of Rome and the Roman Empire (1974). Three well-written surveys of Roman history; the last is fuller than the others.

Early Italy and Rome

*Massimo Pallottino, The Etruscans (Penguin).

*E. H. Richardson, The Etruscans: Their Art and Civilization (Phoenix). Either of these works will provide a good picture of Etruscan history and culture.

R. M. Ogilvie, Early Rome and the Etruscans (1976). Clarifies the ways in which early Roman history was influenced by the Etruscans.

Raymond Bloch, Origins of Rome (1960). Presents a clear picture of the confused history of the early Romans.

The Republic to 265 B.C.

*H. H. Scullard, History of the Roman World from 753

B.C. to 146 B.C. (3rd ed., Barnes and Noble). The best detailed history of the development of the republic.

Leon Homo, *Roman Political Institutions from City to State* (1929). Provides a clear description of the political institutions of the republic and their evolution.

*R. M. Errington, *The Dawn of Empire. Rome's Rise to World Power* (Cornell).

*E. Badian, *Roman Imperialism in the Late Republic* (2nd ed., Cornell). Two outstanding treatments of Rome's expansion and the forces that motivated it.

B. H. Warmington, *Carthage* (2nd rev. ed., 1969). A superb treatment of the history of Rome's greatest enemy.

T. A. Dorey and D. R. Dudley, *Rome Against Carthage* (1971). A full account of this great struggle.

Gavin R. de Beer, *Hannibal* (1969).

H. H. Scullard, *Scipio Africanus: Soldier and Politician* (1970).

Sources

*Livy, *Early History of Rome*, trans. A. de Selincourt (Penguin).

*Livy, *War with Hannibal*, trans. A. de Selincourt (Penguin). These two works, representing selections from Livy's *History of Rome*, will provide an excellent introduction to how the Romans interpreted their own past.

Polybius, *The Histories*, trans, Mortimer Chambers and abridged E. Badian (1966). A thoughtful account by a Greek on Rome's rise to world power.

9

THE FAILURE OF THE ROMAN REPUBLIC, 133-31 B.C.

Rome's long succession of wars leading to domination of the Mediterranean area generated profound problems that inevitably had to be faced. Prior to 133 B.C., the problems had been neglected by a populace increasingly intoxicated with military success and power; the century following was dominated by a succession of crises emerging from them. Before that century had passed, the republic was in ruins.

1. THE BURDENS OF A WORLD POWER

Certain of the problems emerging prior to the period 133–31 B.C. were especially dangerous to the Roman Republic.

First, Rome's military success left her with a long frontier exposed to hostile foreigners and with a variety of conquered subjects to govern. Her citizen army was ill-suited and badly organized for the tedious burden of defending the distant frontiers. Moreover, the system developed to govern the conquered peoples was largely improvised. The Romans were inclined to view conquered non-Italians simply as subjects to be exploited. Provincial administration gave absolute military and civil power to governors who were seldom held accountable for their conduct. The residents of each province were subject to heavy tribute, the collection of which was entrusted to tax farmers (called *publicans*) who paid the Roman government what it expected from the provinces and then proceeded to extort all

they could from the provincials. No serious effort was made to establish a provincial civil service responsible to the Roman government to impose order and justice. Almost from the beginning, the provincials were exploited and abused with impunity.

Second, Rome's allies in Italy, who had fought loyally and suffered much in the wars of conquest, were ill-rewarded for their efforts. The prospect of citizenship implicit in Rome's earlier arrangements with them grew increasingly remote, and the allies became proportionately restless and rebellious.

Third, Rome's economy was subjected to major strains and transformations. The traditional backbone of the Italian economy was the small, independent farm which raised grain primarily for the owner-family and the local city market. This style of farming became increasingly unprofitable, chiefly as a result of the competition of cheaper grain imported as tribute from more productive lands in the provinces. Moreover, many small farms were devastated by the wars in Italy and depopulated to fill the incessant demand for soldiers. Also, enterprising Romans with capital began creating large estates (*latifundia*) by buying the land of impoverished small farmers and by establishing control over public lands. The new agricultural units concentrated on the production of cash crops such as grapes, olives, and livestock; increasingly the labor supply on the *latifundia* was provided by gangs of slaves, most of whom were victims of Rome's wars of conquest. Huge influxes of wealth from pillage, war indemnities, and tribute extracted from conquered peoples provided the capital for investments not only in agriculture but also in trade and manufacturing activities extending around the entire Mediterranean world. The simple economic order of the early republican period was clearly a thing of the past.

These fundamental economic changes created a fourth set of problems of a social nature. Impoverished small farmers flocked to Rome, where they became a rootless and restless proletariat, endowed with the rights of citizenship but deprived of an opportunity for gainful employment in a city that increasingly lived from tribute and slave labor. This city "mob" was forced to depend on the state or on rich patrons for its livelihood; its members "earned" their living by selling their votes and political support. The "new" Rome also produced an increasing number of business entrepreneurs who grew rich as contractors for army supplies, provincial tax collectors, bankers, and organizers of trading enterprises. The members of this class, called *equites*, began to agitate for a share of political power and for social recognition.

Finally, Rome's citizens were profoundly unsettled by new ideological factors impinging on their lives. Large segments of aristocratic society were deeply affected by the sophisticated concepts and styles of Hellenistic culture, which became irresistible from the third century onward. The lower classes were intrigued by the emotional, individualistic mystery religions from the East. The wealth that flowed into Rome from conquest bred a taste for comfort and luxury and a lust for more of both. Incessant military involvement engendered a disturbing tolerance for violence and corruption. Repeated military victories bred lack of restraint and arrogance not unusual among imperial peoples. These currents made men less willing to abide by the moral standards and rustic simplicity characteristic of the early republic.

In many ways, these vast forces of change spelled progress for Rome and Italy—greater wealth, greater sophistication, greater opportunities. But their impact called for adjustments that could only be effected by innovative political action. Here the Romans failed. During the long and difficult era of conquest, the Roman government remained essentially what it had been in 265 B.C. The narrow aristocracy dominating the government steadily increased its power. Most citizens, little understanding the complicated issues of war and diplomacy, willingly allowed the patricians to decide Rome's fate. By 133 B.C., the aristocrats had become so accustomed to unquestioned authority that they thought only in terms of their own interests. The conservative, narrowly based government, designed to rule a small city-state, was faced with the problems of a world empire. The fuse was set for an upheaval. When it came, it was so violent that the republican form of government was destroyed.

2. THE PARTIES AT WAR, 133–79 B.C.

The first phase in the ordeal of the republic was a violent party struggle for control of the government. On one side was the old ruling oligarchy, calling themselves the *optimates*—the best—and standing for the established order. Opposed was a shifting alliance of the poor and middle classes, the *populares*, usually led by strong leaders from the patrician ranks. These leaders were often men moved by a genuine urge to reform in order to safeguard the state, but they were also driven by an urge for personal power denied them by the "establishment."

The initial engagement in the power struggle occurred between 133 and 121 B.C. The champions of the *populares* were the brothers Tiberius and Gaius Gracchus. Aristocratic (Scipio Africanus was their grandfather), well educated, and politically conscious, the Gracchi were deeply troubled by the decline of Rome's free farmers and the plight of the proletariat. Elected tribune in 133 B.C., Tiberius proposed that public land, much of it controlled illegally by powerful aristocrats, be redistributed in small parcels for the use of the landless populace of Rome. Plutarch's remark that "no milder or gentler program was ever devised in the face of such injustice and greed" found no backers among the ruling clique, which used its powers to induce another tribune to veto the proposal. Tiberius then persuaded the Assembly of Tribes to oust the offensive tribune and pass his law. When he tried to apply the new law, Tiberius was constantly thwarted by the Senate. Rather than accept the will of the people, the senatorial party resorted to violence and murdered Tiberius on the pretext that he was trying to be a dictator when he sought reelection as tribune.

Ten years later, Gaius Gracchus took up the same cause, adding more radical proposals. Elected tribune for 123 B.C., he persuaded the Assembly of Tribes to pass new land laws, to provide cheap grain for the massses, to establish colonies for the resettlement of impoverished Romans, and to extend political privileges to the Italian allies. His legislation also granted extensive privileges in tax collection to the nonnoble *equites*, whose support he sought. But ultimately he failed to hold together the alliance of poor farmers, *equites*, and city proletariat, and lost his bid for election as tribune for 122 B.C. The senatorial opposition again succeeded in provoking violence and, on the pretext that the state was in danger, proceeded to kill Gaius and 3,000 of his followers.

Although the careers of the Gracchi ended tragically, their leadership had reminded the populace of its potential power, raised the issue of reform, and bequeathed a series of "causes" to the future. The Senate was deaf to the demands of the people and blind to the problems of the republic; its only concern was protecting its monopoly on power.

The death of Gaius Gracchus left the *populares* leaderless for a decade. Then a new popular hero arose to turn popular fury against the Senate. The man of the hour was a peasant's son, Marius (ca. 155–86 B.C.), who had held minor offices and who had served in the army in a badly managed and unsuccessful war in Africa against Jugurtha, a contender for the Numidian throne. In 108 B.C. Marius ran for consul, building his campaign around an attack on the Senate; although bitterly opposed by the patricians on the grounds that he was a man of no position or family connection, he was elected to serve for the year 107 B.C. He persuaded the Assembly of Tribes to vote him command of the army in Africa, and once in

office, he took a bold and fateful step: He recruited an army of volunteers to fight under his command. His control of this personal army virtually put him beyond the reach of the Senate, which could no longer safely rely on assassination as a convenient way of disposing of threats to its power.

Marius quickly justified the trust placed in him by crushing Jugurtha in 105 B.C. He was ably assisted by a young nobleman named Sulla, soon to play a major role in Rome. So great was Marius' reputation that he was reelected consul during the years 104–101 B.C. to fight Germanic tribes threatening the Roman position in northern Italy. Again he was successful, and so he was elected consul for the sixth time for the year 100 B.C. as the leader of a powerful faction proposing broad reforms that contained most of the elements of the Gracchan program as well as provision for the rewarding of Marius' soldiers. But Marius proved inept as a political leader. Before his term ended, his party collapsed and he lost most of his great prestige. The *optimates* returned to power, having learned what even an unskilled politicain could do to control Rome when backed by an army.

The next decade was relatively quiet, perhaps because moderate elements in the Senate made some effort to resolve critical problems. Two issues defied their efforts, however, and provided the fuel for the next crisis. One was the situation of the Roman allies in Italy, who had long been pressing for citizenship but were repeatedly frustrated by opposition from most elements in Rome. In 90 B.C. their disillusionment finally generated a great rebellion that threatened Rome's survival. She responded by granting citizenship to the Italians, a momentous act that ended the days of the simple city-state. In order to meet the military threat posed by the rebels, the Senate then entrusted Sulla (138–78 B.C.) with an army; by 87 B.C., he had dispersed the rebels, demonstrated his considerable abilities, and greatly enhanced his influence.

Almost simultaneously Rome was faced with another crisis caused by a second long-standing problem: the corruption-ridden, oppressive system of provincial administration that was breeding discontent throughout her empire. In 88 B.C.

Mithradates, king of the small state of Pontus in Asia Minor, played on that discontent to launch a war of liberation in Asia Minor and Greece. Despite the critical situation, there was virtual civil war in Rome over the question of who would command the desperately needed army. The Senate favored Sulla; the *populares* clamored for Marius. Sulla finally resolved the issue by marching the army he had commanded in the campaign against the Italians into Rome and securing the command in Asia by force, a procedure that was neither constitutional nor customary, but effective.

Sulla defeated Mithradates and his allies, forced the king to return to his old kingdom, and reestablished Roman dominance in the eastern provinces. But he made no final settlement of affairs in the East; his eyes were on Rome. Immediately after his departure, the *populares* under Marius had forced their way back into power and imposed a reign of terror on the Senate. They ruled supreme until 83 B.C., when Sulla and his army finally reappeared in Italy, well fortified with booty seized in the East. His battle-tested soldiers easily routed the Marians, whose leader had died in 86 B.C., and assured Sulla complete mastery over the city and all of Italy.

Once in control, Sulla had himself proclaimed dictator. He undertook a program aimed at restoring direction of the republic to the Senate. He sought to eliminate *populares* leadership by launching a brutal proscription that led to the execution of thousands of Romans who had been associated with the Marian faction. The powers of the tribunes and the Assembly of Tribes were severely limited, and the Senate was enlarged and the new seats given over to *equites*. Sulla took steps to regularize the election procedures for the magistracies, improve the working of justice, and reorganize provincial administration. Having restored the ancient constitution with the Senate in charge, Sulla retired from public life in 79 B.C. to pursue his intellectual interests and enjoy the great wealth he had accumulated. He obviously hoped that the Senate could find means of resolving Rome's problems now that it was free of rabble-rousers.

Although it might seem that Sulla's restoration of the Senate left the situation just where it had been in 133 B.C., his retirement actually ended an era. The Senate was in power in 79 B.C. not because of its own virtues, prestige, or accomplishments but because a successful military leader decreed so. It was clear that bold individuals, properly armed, might topple it as easily as Sulla had restored it. The long, bitter, indecisive clash between the *optimates* and the *populares* favored the emergence of such individuals by encouraging disregard for the law and reliance on force. The republican form of government had suffered a mortal blow.

3. THE ERA OF STRONG MEN, 79–44 B.C.

New opportunities for "strong men" were quick in coming, for the Senate proved itself completely unworthy of Sulla's confidence. Between 79 and 70 B.C. it was faced in rapid succession by a revolt in Italy led by a disaffected Roman consul, a revolt in Spain provoked by a Roman governor, a slave revolt in Italy led by Spartacus, a mounting threat from pirates to peace on the seas and to the grain supply on which the Roman populace depended, and a new war with Mithradates of Pontus. The Senate sought to meet these crises by entrusting extraordinary powers to ambitious individuals little respectful of the old order. A protegé of Sulla's, Pompey (106–48 B.C.), was given command of forces to deal with the Italian revolt and then the Spanish insurrection; he did his job well and thus emerged as a key figure. The slave revolt was handled by Marcus Licinius Crassus (ca. 115–53 B.C.), a rich and unscrupulous capitalist who aspired to political greatness. These two ascending political stars were elected consuls for the year 70 B.C. largely because both were supported by loyal armies.

During their co-consulship, Pompey and Crassus negated most of Sulla's legislation by enactments that won the applause of the remnants of the *populares* and raised suspicions among the senators. But neither was satisfied. Pompey was the first to move toward more decisive power. By manipulation he persuaded the people and the Senate to vote him two important military commands: In 67 B.C. he was granted powers to clear the Mediterranean of

These two men, Pompey (left) and Julius Caesar (right), virtually controlled the destiny of the Roman Republic and the Mediterranean world between 79 and 44 B.C. Their busts reflect the talent of Roman sculptors in portraiture. *Photos: Pompey, Culver Pictures; Julius Caesar, Alinari/EPA, Inc.*

pirates, which he did in a matter of months. And in 66 B.C. he was given even greater power to deal with Mithradates, who since 74 B.C. had again been defying Rome in the East. Pompey very shortly eliminated him, and then, while in the East, did some things for which he had no authority: He conquered new territories around the Eastern end of the Mediterranean, organized new provinces, cleaned up the administration of the old provinces, and put friends in key spots. By 63 B.C. he was virtually the ruler of the East.

Pompey's success, reminiscent of Sulla's rise to power, caused constant concern in Rome and drove other aspiring politicians to a series of maneuvers to check him. Crassus emerged as a major figure. He found a skilled ally in young Julius Caesar (100–44 B.C.), who demonstrated remarkable talents as a political manipulator. Crassus and Caesar promoted various laws to attract popular support and spent huge sums in an attempt to get the people of Rome to vote them armies and authority such as Pompey possessed. The Senate resisted their maneuvers. A major obstacle was Cicero (106–43 B.C.), a talented, ambitious lawyer who skillfully worked his way to the consulship in 63 B.C. and who advocated an alliance between Pompey and the Senate as the solution to Rome's problems. His finest hour came when he foiled a conspiracy by Catiline, a frustrated power seeker and sometime agent of Crassus. Cicero proclaimed that he had saved

THE ROMAN EMPIRE A.D. 14

the republic by exposing Catiline, much to the annoyance of Pompey.

All these political gyrations resolved nothing, for Pompey was still the key figure. But contrary to expectation, on returning to Italy in 62 B.C., Pompey disbanded his army and asked only that the Senate reward his veterans and legalize his settlement in the East.

Relieved of the prospect of another military dictator, the Senate proceeded to act in a way that drove Pompey, Crassus, and Caesar into a political alliance. It refused to reward Pompey's veterans or ratify his Eastern settlement. It took action to restrict the powers of provincial tax farmers, a step that threatened one of the main sources of Crassus' immense wealth. It placed every possible obstacle in the way of the election of Caesar to the consulship. Equally frustrated, the three joined in an informal agreement, the

First Triumvirate, designed to ensure that each obtained what he wished. Assured of the support of Pompey and Crassus, Caesar won the consulship for the year 59 B.C. Once in office, he took steps to satisfy his fellow triumvirs.

Having finished his term as consul, Caesar went to Gaul as proconsul—his reward from the alliance with Pompey and Crassus. There he remained from 58 to 49 B.C., during which time he conquered Gaul and added it to the empire. The triumvirate held together uneasily through these years, due in large part to Caesar's efforts. The marriage of his daughter, Julia, to Pompey gave him a personal tie with one member of the triumvirate, and his long-standing friendship with Crassus also helped to sustain the alliance. But Crassus was killed in 53 B.C. in a futile bid for glory in the form of a war against the Parthians. A showdown between Caesar and Pompey then became inevitable. The climax came at the end of Caesar's proconsulship in Gaul, when he sought to run again for the consulship for 48 B.C. Desirous of getting him out of office so that he could be prosecuted, the Senate blocked this move and called on Pompey to defend the state. Caesar decided to rebel. In 49 B.C. he led his legions across the Rubicon River separating Gaul from Italy and plunged Rome into civil war.

Caesar's seasoned veterans made short work of Pompey's much larger forces, smashing them first in Italy, then in Spain, and finally in the Greek peninsula. Pompey fled to Egypt, where he was murdered and his head sent to Caesar, who then used this crime against a Roman citizen as an excuse to intervene in Egyptian politics, where a struggle for control of the crown was in progress. Caesar decided to support the claims of Cleopatra against her brother-husband, Ptolemy XII. He was perhaps prompted by the fact that he had become her lover, but he may well have had another motive. Egypt was the last important Hellenistic kingdom still not under Roman control. By putting the young princess on the throne, he perhaps hoped to tap the country's fabulous riches. Thus he dallied in Egypt until Cleopatra was in control as queen. During 47 and 46 B.C. Caesar continued his march through the empire—Asia, Africa, Spain —hunting down Pompey's allies. When he returned to Rome in 45 B.C., he was undisputed master of the Roman world.

Caesar's first move upon his return to Rome was to concentrate political power in his own hands. He had himself simultaneously elected dictator, consul, tribune, high priest, and censor. The other magistracies were filled with men of his choice, and the Senate was packed with his appointees. With such power he was virtually a king in the style of Hellenistic monarchs; indeed, some of his contemporaries insisted that it was his intention to establish a monarchy.

Yet Caesar did not gather such vast powers to himself merely for personal gratification. He intended to use them to solve the major problems that had so long plagued the Roman world. He reduced the number of people in Rome dependent on the dole by mounting extensive public works projects and by sending Romans to the provinces as colonists. He provided a police force for the city, thereby ending mob violence. Measures were taken to aid the Italian farmers, and more orderly institutions of local government were established in many towns throughout Italy. New regulations curbed provincial tax collectors and governors, and ended many of their abuses.

Perhaps Ceasar had plans for addressing the most critical problem of his age—the need to reshape the entire structure of government to meet the responsibilities Rome had assumed as ruler of the Mediterranean world. If so, he was not given time. A hard core of conservative senators, probably sensing that Caesar was a threat to the continuation of the old republican order, was obsessed with the idea of stopping him. Helpless to achieve their goal legally, these would-be guardians of the "right" order had him killed in 44 B.C.

4. THE STRUGGLE FOR SUCCESSION, 44–31 B.C.

Murder proved no way of stopping the disintegration of the republic. The conspirators who assassinated Caesar had mistakenly supposed that his passing would somehow result in the restoration of the old republic. The real question was how to find a successor for Caesar's mantle. Fourteen years of civil war were necessary to produce a new master.

Two candidates quickly emerged as the main contenders for control of Rome. One was Mark Antony (ca. 83–30 B.C.), who had served Caesar as a military commander and who was an experienced politician. The other was an eighteen-year-old named Octavian, whom Caesar had adopted as his son and legal heir. More concerned with Antony, the Senate at first favored Octavian; Cicero was especially important in supporting his cause. But Octavian, soon aware that he was being used as a pawn, entered into a liaison with Antony and another general, Lepidus, dedicated to restoring order and punishing Caesar's murderers. This Second Triumvirate was given virtually absolute legal powers to last five years. Within a year, most of the senatorial party, including Cicero, had been eliminated by a brutal proscription and by a successful military campaign against the armies raised by Caesar's assassins.

After 42 B.C., Antony and Octavian continued the pose of ruling Rome jointly. Actually each was preparing to eliminate the other, although the final reckoning was delayed for ten years. Antony spent these years in the East, where he fell into the clutches of Cleopatra. In 33 B.C., he went so far as to marry her and give his approval to an ambitious program to establish Egyptian hegemony over the East and to install her children by Caesar and himself as rulers of Roman lands. It was enough that Antony already had a Roman wife—no less a person than Octavian's sister; to surrender Roman lands to an Eastern queen made him a traitor as well. Antony's efforts to bolster his declining prestige had little effect; in fact, the most serious such effort, a campaign against the Parthians in 36 B.C., ended in humiliating defeat.

Octavian made infinitely better use of his time. While establishing a solid hold on the Western provinces, he conducted a powerful propaganda campaign picturing Antony as a madman, a traitor, and the victim of a crafty Eastern harlot. Finally, in 32 B.C. he refused to continue his joint rule with Antony and declared war on Cleopatra. The decisive engagement was fought at Actium in Greece in 31 B.C. Octavian's fleet won an easy victory. The victor pursued his enemies back to Egypt, where Cleopatra made one final attempt to entice a Roman to support her. When Octavian would have none of her favors, she committed suicide, as Antony had already done. This left Octavian undisputed ruler of Rome, his sword having raised him to a position comparable to Caesar's in 46 B.C.

5. CONSEQUENCES OF THE CIVIL WARS

Octavian's victory at Actium ended a century of civil war whose impact on Roman society had been revolutionary in the profoundest sense of the word. The turmoil had caused a social upheaval that especially affected the staunchest supporters of the old order. Proscriptions and confiscation of property virtually destroyed the old aristocracy. The bids of ambitious politicians for popular support undermined the morale of the city masses, who turned from respect for the old institutions to hope for material reward. It was a golden opportunity for ambitious, ruthless, yet able men, even of low birth, to gain wealth and political power. These men, willing to accept new ideas as long as their prestige was recognized, were the greatest beneficiaries of the wars.

Compounding this social upheaval, Romans grew weary of war and murder and political intrigue and became increasingly interested in anything that would give them peace and security. A wave of pessimism and hopelessness spread during this period. People turned to pleasure seeking, to new religions, and to foreign philosophies in search of something to live by in the midst of daily violence. Under such circumstances, fewer men were willing to fight for the old order. New ideas found an increasing audience. Moreover, the wars broadened the vision of many Romans, who found the old, narrow Roman patriotism senseless in view of the world within which Rome now operated and of the millions of provincials upon whom her politicians often depended for power. These broaderminded men could hardly be expected to fight to preserve a way of life confined to the city-state.

The period from 133 to 31 B.C. proved still another thing: The traditional system of government simply could not cope with existing problems. Annually elected officials, a Senate of aristocrats, and popular assemblies attended by small numbers of people living in and around Rome failed on numerous occasions to deal with such problems as defending Rome's extensive frontiers, maintaining peace among millions of subjects, and keeping order in the city. Even the most conservative saw that the old government was outmoded and must be replaced if Rome was to survive as mistress of the Mediterranean. The wars showed just as clearly that only capable individuals possessing extensive powers could cope effectively with Rome's political problems. In spite of their disrespect for the law and their heavyhanded methods, a Marius, a Sulla, a Pompey, and a Caesar achieved something positive in this wild century, whereas all others failed.

These fundamental changes in the midst of frenzied, brutal struggles for power justify our saying that a revolution had occurred by 31 B.C. The republican form of government was replaced by a system under which one man guided political life in a vast empire stretching around the Mediterranean. What was now needed was a leader to give this new reality a formal shape.

Suggested Reading

Political Developments

*H. H. Scullard, *From the Gracchi to Nero: A History of Rome from 133 B.C. to A.D. 68* (4th ed., University Paperback). The best detailed history of the fall of the republic.

R. E. Smith, *The Failure of the Roman Republic* (1955).

*Ronald Syme, *The Roman Revolution* (Oxford).

F. R. Cowell, *Cicero and the Roman Republic* (1948).

*L. R. Taylor, *Party Politics in the Age of Caesar* (University of California Paperbacks). These four books all present highly significant but different interpretations of the causes of the failure of the Roman Republic; Syme's work is especially provocative.

Economic and Social Developments

Tenney Frank, *An Economic History of Rome* (2nd ed. rev., 1927). The early chapters of this work provide a good picture of the economic stresses affecting the Roman Republic.

W. W. Fowler, *Social Life at Rome in the Age of Cicero* (1909). A well-rounded picture of Roman society at the end of the republic, drawing heavily on Cicero's letters.

*P. A. Brunt, *Social Conflicts in the Roman Republic* (Norton). A good analysis of the social tensions that helped to change the late republic.

Biographies

Charles Oman, *Seven Statesmen of the Later Republic* (1902). Excellent short sketches of the Gracchi, Marius, Sulla, Pompey, Crassus, and Cato the Younger.

G. P. Baker, *Sulla the Fortunate: The Dictator* (1927).

Alvin H. Berstein, *Tiberius Sempronius Gracchus. Tradition and Apostasy* (1978).

John Leach, *Pompey the Great* (1978).

David Stockton, *Cicero: A Political Biography* (1971).

Matthias Gelzer, *Caesar: Politician and Statesman* (1968).

Michael Grant, *Cleopatra* (1972).

Sources

*The Fall of the Roman Republic, trans. Rex Warner (Penguin). A convenient selection of biographies from Plutarch's *Lives* depicting some of the leading figures of the late republican period.

*Cicero, *Selected Works*, trans. M. Grant (Penguin). This work will introduce the reader to a leading statesman of the period and a keen observer of the conditions of the times.

*Caesar, *The Conquest of Gaul*, trans. S. A. Handford (Penguin).

*Caesar, *Civil War*, trans. J. F. Mitchell (Penguin). This and the preceding work will provide an insight into the mentality of the greatest figure of the age.

10

THE ROMAN EMPIRE, 31 B.C.–A.D. 180

During the first and second centuries A.D. the Romans made their most notable contribution to civilization by fashioning a system of government, known as the Roman Empire, that brought peace and prosperity to the entire Mediterranean basin. Its success was so impressive that many would agree with the eighteenth-century historian Edward Gibbon who wrote that, if he had to choose a time when the human condition was happiest, he would without hesitation select the period between A.D. 96–180.

1. THE FOUNDATIONS OF THE IMPERIAL ORDER, 31 B.C.–A.D. 14

The victor at Actium was the architect of the Roman Empire and one of history's greatest statesmen. When Mark Antony and Cleopatra committed suicide after their defeat, Octavian was supreme by virtue of conquest. It was clear, however, that open military dictatorship or monarchy in any form was offensive to the Senate and people of Rome, who for five hundred years had determined their own destiny through a set of institutions that constituted the Roman Republic. But the past century had also taught that the only hope for the management of the vast, problem-ridden Roman Empire was the concentration of power in the hands of one man.

Octavian's solution, worked out cautiously

during his forty-five-year rule, was masterful. It permitted him to rule the Roman world while retaining the outward forms of the republic. The process began in 27 B.C., when Octavian dramatically surrendered all the powers he then held. Theoretically, the republic was restored; power again rested with the Senate, the elected magistrates, and the assemblies. Impressed by this noble gesture, fearful of a recurrence of civil war, and skillfully guided by Octavian, the Senate and people hastened to vote him the power of tribune for life, the authority of the consuls, command over the armies, proconsular authority over most of the provinces, and the highest priestly office. To these powers the grateful citizenry added several honors: first senator; *augustus* ("most revered one"); *imperator* ("victorious general"); and "father of his country." Some even hinted that he was divine. This array of powers and honors so elevated his authority that he was the *princeps*, the first citizen of Rome in every respect, who without a hint of illegality could do whatever was necessary to rule her. Historians have come to refer to his regime as the *principate* to reflect its unique blend of republican and monarchical ingredients.

Armed with these great powers, Augustus, as he came to be known by virtue of the title that elevated him to a revered, semi-divine position, turned to reconstructing the social order of Rome. A major concern was the demoralized condition of the citizen body, that relatively small group of Italians who now had no choice but to rule the vast empire. Adhering to the ancient Roman conviction that a class-structured society was healthiest and most effective, Augustus tried to redefine the old class divisions, assigning specific functions and responsibilities to each. Rigid standards of birth, wealth, and conduct were set up for senatorial ranking, resulting in a considerable reduction of those who qualified for this rank in society. To this elite was assigned a large share in governmental affairs. They were to hold the chief elective offices in the state, to advise the *princeps*, to serve as governors of specific provinces, and to fill high military and civil posts in the provinces. The equestrian order (*equites*), made up chiefly of rich traders and industrialists, was entrusted with secondary but critical positions in the army, the tax system, and the judicial system; here was the core of a bureaucracy made up of men of talent willing to perform the routine functions of government in the service of the *princeps*. For the plebeians, Augustus hoped to provide order and security. He concentrated on supplying cheap grain, police supervision, and entertainment for Rome's huge population and economic security for the farmers of Italy. The plebeians were expected to play a political role by exercising their powers as voters and to serve as volunteers in the armed forces. Their response was not always what Augustus expected, especially in elections; in fact, the populace seemed to prefer benevolent mastery to responsible collaboration.

To improve the morale and the patriotism of the citizen body, Augustus encouraged a revival of the ancient Roman religion; patronized writers, who turned out masses of propaganda exalting Rome's past greatness and present blessings; and arranged for numerous laws aimed at checking what he considered softening vices—luxury, sexual irregularities, divorce, childless marriages, gambling, and drinking. He also spent immense sums beautifying Rome and providing public services in the hope that its citizens would feel a resurgence of pride in the capital.

Augustus undertook a complete overhaul of the military establishment. The foundation was laid for a professional army by the formation of

This majestic statue of Augustus, created during his reign, was intended to idealize and exalt the man who had restored peace to the Roman world after the troubled times of the late republic. *Photo: Alinari/EPA, Inc.*

twenty-five legions recruited from the Roman citizen body for long terms of service. Each legion was complemented by an auxiliary unit composed of noncitizens recruited in the provinces. The total force numbered approximately 300,000 men. Careful discipline, regular pay, and adequate pensions were provided. An elaborate support apparatus of roads, supply depots, and military posts was established. The bulk of this newly constituted army was stationed along Rome's extensive frontier; only the Praetorian Guard, a picked contingent of about 9,000 men, was garrisoned in Italy to serve as the bodyguard for the *princeps*. The chief function of the army was defensive. With the exception of some serious campaigning against the Germans on the northern frontier aimed at fixing a defensible border, Augustus gave up the idea of offensive warfare and expansion. He began the process of fixing a clear boundary between the Roman and non-Roman worlds. The army's job was to hold that frontier and to strike down elements within the empire who tried to escape Roman domination.

Having provided for peace and defense in the provinces, Augustus attempted to improve the system of provincial governance. Using his proconsular powers, he began to develop a regular provincial administration that he himself carefully supervised. He selected legates to represent him in each province under his direct control, paying them adequate salaries in order to reduce their inclination to build personal fortunes by exploiting the provincial subjects. Augustus sent each province a *procurator*, usually an equestrian, to collect taxes and render account to the *princeps*. Under the careful eye of Augustus this set of administrative and financial officials almost immediately brought order to the provinces. The notorious corruption, oppression, and violence of the late republican period disappeared, to be replaced by the Roman peace. Equally important was Augustus' willingness to entrust a wide range of local affairs to members of local aristocracies, who were usually eager to support his aims in order to gain for their communities more equitable treatment than had existed in previous times.

The complex responsibilities of maintaining the army and administering the provinces generated the need for a central administrative machinery manned by professional civil servants. To an amazing degree, Augustus himself and a circle of confidants directed the far-flung operations of the principate. Slowly, however, there emerged a corps of helpers, composed to a large degree of freedmen who had no political attachments and who owed everything to the *princeps*. This addition to the political order was important: The expertise and loyalty of its members tended to place the crucial operations of government in their hands and to make the political

services of the senators and the citizen population less crucial.

Although one cannot argue that Augustus had a precise economic policy, the restoration of peace and order produced considerable prosperity. Encouraged by a political regime that provided a sound coinage, developed roads, suppressed piracy and brigandage, and imposed an equitable tax burden, agriculture, trade, and industry demonstrated new vitality.

The one remaining problem was for Augustus to ensure the empire a prosperous, stable future. Only the Senate and people could legally transmit his powers. Augustus began early to try to ensure his succession. He attempted to combine two distinct ideas. First, he hoped to establish the hereditary principle so that the second *princeps* would enjoy the prestige of descent from Julius Caesar and Augustus. Second, he wanted his successor to have gained the practical experience needed to guide the vast empire. Augustus had no sons. His only daughter, Julia, was three times married to potential heirs. Augustus outlived two of them and her two elder sons. Finally, he chose as his heir his adopted son, Tiberius, who became Julia's third husband and after A.D. 4 was granted ever-greater powers by Augustus. When the *princeps* died in A.D. 14, Tiberius was ready to assume full authority.

This brief summary hardly does justice to Augustus' career, whose constructive achievements seem almost a miracle. In part he succeeded because he was not a doctrinaire idealist seeking to create a utopian state; he was a patient, realistic, cautious, hardworking statesman to whom good fortune gave many years to work on his program. He kept certain key ideas central in his political activities: the need to concentrate power in his own hands, the need to end force as the determining factor in reaching political decisions, the need to honor the ancient political ideals of the Roman citizenry, the need to set positive goals for all elements of a widely diverse population. By working toward these ends, he fashioned a new political order. As it took shape, it elicited from the vital element in the Roman world — the people of Italy — a resurgence of their ancient virtues: patriotism, devotion to public service, loyalty, sobriety. And it persuaded millions of noncitizens that their well-being depended on direction of their affairs by the Romans. It was this elusive capability for moving men to do what had to be done much more than what he did that best describes the greatness of Augustus.

2. SOLIDIFYING THE AUGUSTAN PRINCIPATE, A.D. 14–96

Between Augustus' death and the end of the first century A.D., the Augustan system was tested by severe pressures and by strong opposition. Outwardly this era was marked by the very thing that Augustus wished to avoid: a clash between the *princeps* and the Senate. This encounter bred fear, uneasiness, and turmoil, especially in the city of Rome.

One of the factors contributing to the tension was the difficulty of finding a *princeps* possessed of the talents needed to run a vast, complex empire while respecting the authority that the Augustan system had entrusted to the Senate and the people. Augustus had bequeathed a succession system that sought to assure that men of ability and experience from his own family would hold power. This system bred intrigue and violence, only to produce rulers of limited abilities who earned incessant opposition from the Senate. The first four rulers of this era, called the Julio-Claudians, were all related to Augustus. Tiberius (A.D. 14–37) was an able man but also cold, suspicious, and disillusioned; his distrust of everyone provoked him to brutal assaults on those whom he suspected of undermining his power. Caligula (A.D. 37–41) was simply a madman whose reckless conduct earned him an assassin's knife. Claudius (A.D. 41–54) was a timid, physically unattractive, scholarly man, ill at ease in Roman high society and constantly victimized by ill-chosen wives and advisers. Worst of all was Nero (A.D. 54–68). Cruel, vain, wasteful, he kept Rome in turmoil in his attempts to satisfy his own desires. He was eventually ousted from office, avoiding assassination by killing himself, but only after he had killed his mother and two wives, disposed of numerous senators, persecuted Christians, made a fool of himself posing as an artist, and emptied the treasury in order to indulge his personal whims.

After Nero's death the army sought to control the choice of the *princeps;* that effort produced a year of civil strife reminiscent of the last days of the republic. Finally a general named Vespasian (A.D. 69–79) seized control of the office. Once in power, he instituted a hereditary system of succession which permitted his sons, Titus (A.D. 79–81) and Domitian (A.D. 81–96), to assume power without difficulty. This family, called the Flavians, were men of considerable ability, but they had little respect for the Senate and thus were constantly charged with being tyrants and obstructed in their efforts to rule effectively.

The unhealthy turmoil resulting from the quality of rulers produced by the Augustan succession system was further complicated by the imprecise definition of the powers to be exercised by the *princeps* and by the Senate and the people. For the most part, the Julio-Claudian and Flavian rulers tried to respect the authority Augustus had entrusted to the Senate and the people. But these vestiges of the revered republican order proved ill-equipped to handle most problems facing the government. When a *princeps* acted to meet pressing issues, he was often accused of usurpation of power and faced with intrigues that threatened to disrupt the operation of the state. The rulers reacted to this unthinking obstructionism by curbing criticism with a heavy hand and by introducing political actions that simply disregarded the alleged rights of the Senate and the people. Such behavior only heightened the misunderstanding and hatred surrounding public affairs. At times, at least in the city of Rome, it appeared that civil strife would again erupt because of the misunderstanding and distrust between the successors of Augustus and the champions of republican liberty, mostly concentrated in the Senate.

In reality, these quarrels that loom so large in the records of the first century A.D. were of minor significance compared to more substantial developments occurring in the Mediterranean world. Several of the rulers—especially Tiberius, Claudius, and Vespasian—were able statesmen who worked patiently and effectively to increase the power of the *princeps* and to perfect its exercise for constructive ends. They were worthy successors of Augustus, faithful to his broad policy. But their successes slowly eroded the remaining power of the Senate and people who in large part caused this decline by consistently failing to act effectively and intelligently. The place of these ancient institutions was taken by an organized bureaucracy whose expertise and devotion to public welfare permitted the rulers to carry out intelligent policies beneficial to the entire empire. The rulers ably defended the frontiers and on occasion extended them, as, for example, when Claudius conquered Britain. The provinces were well administered, and their inhabitants grew to respect the imperial regime. Several rulers extended citizenship to many provincials. Vast public works were undertaken in Rome, in Italy, and in the provinces, and trade, industry, and agriculture were given every possible encouragement. To the majority of men of the Roman world — and increasingly even to the senators — one conclusion was inescapable: that rule by a powerful *princeps* meant order and justice, prosperity, and security. These were precious gifts, well worth the sacrifice of power to the increasingly autocratic emperors.

3. THE EMPIRE AT ITS PEAK: THE "GOOD EMPERORS," A.D. 96–180

With the death of Domitian in A.D. 96, opposition to the principate virtually disappeared, and for roughly the next century, the empire enjoyed a golden age. From the Atlantic to the Euphrates, from Central Europe well into Africa, the *pax romana* became a reality. It was an era characterized by excellent and benevolent rulers, just and efficient administration, internal peace, material prosperity, and stout defense of the frontiers.

Seldom has any era produced rulers more highly praised than the five who ruled from A.D. 96 to 180. Nerva (A.D. 96–98) was an elderly man when selected by the Senate to succeed the much hated Domitian. Before he died he selected as his heir a native of Spain, Trajan (A.D. 98–117), who won the admiration of the whole Roman world by his respect for the Roman aristocracy, his brilliant military exploits, and his sound, honest administration. Hadrian (A.D. 117–138)

was a cultured humanitarian who spent most of his reign traveling throughout the empire promoting the cause of peace and material well-being. Antoninus (A.D. 138–161), by the excellence of his character and intellect, earned the title of "Pius" from the Senate. The crowning glory of the era was Marcus Aurelius (A.D. 161–180), a noted Stoic philosopher who brought a deep sense of duty, willingness to work, and nobility of purpose to the Roman political scene.

The program followed by these "good emperors," as later generations called them, was consistent. Rather early in his reign each took special care to select a successor, adopting a man of ability as a son and slowly increasing his power so that at the death of the old emperor, he was powerfully placed and widely experienced. All these rulers were tactful and respectful toward the senators, who, given most of the high offices and continually consulted, became staunch supporters of the principate, even though their independent power was extremely limited. The "good emperors" steadily developed the imperial bureaucracy. They slowly created a unified body of law for the whole empire. The interests of the provinces were promoted. Citizenship was granted to an ever-larger number of provincials, and humanitarian projects for the aid of the downtrodden in the empire were repeatedly inaugurated. All these rulers allowed local groups extensive freedom as long as that freedom did not threaten the peace. Since the services of the imperial government were costly, the "good emperors" worked tirelessly to establish a sound financial system that would provide adequate income for worthwhile expenditures. All these efforts by the emperors slowly bound the people of the empire — numbering perhaps 70 million — into a commonwealth guided from Rome.

But there was one uncontrollable factor — the frontier. Rome's army, now about 350,000 men, was spread too thinly along it for safety. Trajan tried to safeguard the frontier from the Germans and the Parthians by conquering Dacia and the Tigris-Euphrates Valley. Hadrian reversed this aggressive policy and trusted to strong defense and diplomacy. But by the time of Marcus Aurelius, the problem had still not been solved, and

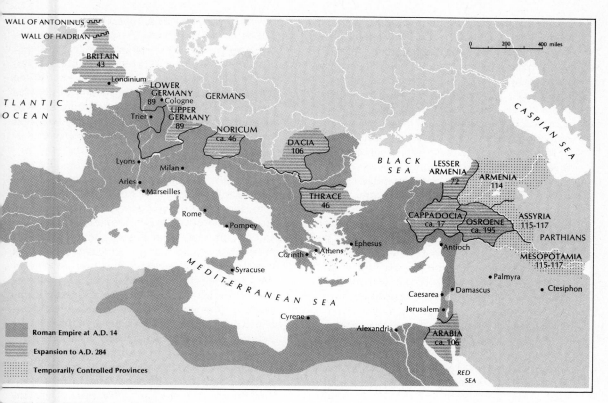

WALL OF ANTONINUS
WALL OF HADRIAN
BRITAIN 43
• Londinium
LOWER GERMANY 89 • Cologne
GERMANS
UPPER GERMANY 89
• Trier
NORICUM ca. 46
DACIA 106
CASPIAN SEA
• Lyons
• Milan
BLACK SEA
LESSER ARMENIA 72
ARMENIA 114
• Arles
• Marseilles
THRACE 46
CAPPADOCIA ca. 17
OSROENE ca. 195
ASSYRIA 115-117
PARTHIANS
• Rome
• Pompey
Corinth • Athens • Ephesus
• Antioch
MESOPOTAMIA 115-117
ATLANTIC OCEAN
• Syracuse
MEDITERRANEAN SEA
• Palmyra
• Ctesiphon
Caesarea • Damascus
Jerusalem •
• Cyrene
Alexandria •
ARABIA ca. 106
RED SEA

Roman Empire at A.D. 14
Expansion to A.D. 284
Temporarily Controlled Provinces

E ROMAN EMPIRE A.D. 14–284

this peace-loving philosopher was forced to spend much of his reign fighting the Germans. When he died, in A.D. 180, a tenuous peace that was cause for grave concern prevailed along the extensive frontier.

4. IMPERIAL GOVERNMENT IN THE SECOND CENTURY

In its mature form in the second century A.D., the principate was a marvelously effective and enlightened system of government that deserves at least a brief description. Throughout this period the Senate and the Roman people in theory still had final authority in the state. In fact, a large part of the ancient republican machinery of the government continued to operate. This kept Roman citizens solidly in touch with a sacred and meaningful tradition. Yet it had little to do with the realities of political life. These venerable organizations had but one function, to give legitimacy to the authority of the real wielder of power, the *princeps*.

The *princeps*, or *emperor* (derived from the title *imperator*, the honor voted by soldiers to their victorious general), had assumed a virtual monopoly of executive, legislative, and judicial powers, legally voted each at the beginning of his reign. His key powers were command over all military forces, control of all revenues, and control of legislation. Each also had a huge personal fortune to be spent as he pleased. Each held various honorary titles that exalted him above all others, and most emperors were believed to be especially blessed by the gods, if not actually divine.

Aside from their immense personal prestige, the emperors exercised their vast powers through two agencies: the bureaucracy and the army. The bureaucracy was divided into great departments, each headed by an experienced, able official. Below him, the top levels were manned by senators and equestrians, while the lower ranks were filled with educated plebeians or freedmen. Italians and provincials alike were accepted in the civil service, making it a cosmopolitan body.

The army had changed little since Augustus' time. The bulk of the soldiery was recruited for twenty-five-year terms from the citizen population of Italy, although by the second century more provincials were being drawn into the legions. Every effort was made to get good commanders and provide adequate training, pay, and pensions. The soldiers not only played a vital role in defending the empire, but served as transmitters of Roman culture to backward peoples living along the frontiers and to the barbarians beyond.

The support of these two agencies imposed a tremendous financial burden on the state. Salaries for the civil servants and pay, pensions, and provisions for the soldiers made imperative a large, regular income. Added to these expenses were the costs of public services supplied by the government—roads, public buildings, food for the poor of the cities, police forces, and so forth. The emperors of the first and second centuries A.D. succeeded in meeting these financial demands by developing an elaborate but fair tax system. No small part of the tax burden was borne by the provincials as their contribution to the support of their protectors.

The emperors maintained and expanded Augustus' effective provincial administration. By A.D. 180 the empire was divided into roughly forty provinces, a few still under the authority of the Senate but most under the *princeps*. A governor was assigned to each with wide powers to keep order, administer justice, and protect Rome's interests, and a *procurator* continued to collect taxes.

The second-century emperors followed Augustus' principle of allowing as much local freedom as possible, and throughout the empire city-states were encouraged to regulate their own affairs. Each city-state and its surrounding territory was ruled by a body of local aristocrats (called *curiales*) who made up a local senate. These senates elected local magistrates, collected local taxes, assumed responsibility for policing and beautifying the city, held courts, and did the many other things necessary for sound government. There can be little doubt that the Romans were inspired to this policy by the model of the Greeks. Where city-states did not already exist—especially in the Western provinces—the Romans founded as many as possible. The second century was truly the culminating age of city-state polity. It must not be thought, however, that the imperial government was totally aloof from local affairs. The emperors themselves and the provincial governors sometimes intervened in local affairs and regulated matters contrary to local wishes. Once Rome did intervene, the cities had little hope of resisting.

It is beyond question that by the second century A.D. Rome possessed the essentials of autocratic government. However, government was not despotic; seldom have rulers with such great power ruled so benevolently or humanely. The emperors were strongly motivated by rather well-defined ideas of what constituted good government and the duty of a ruler. They believed that power entailed duty, that power existed so that humanity could be served—a political philosophy based largely on Stoic ideas but also on the theories of men like Plato and on the political practices of men like Alexander the Great. The emperors were also bound by the deep Roman respect for law. The task of an emperor was to operate within the framework of the law, limiting and shaping his powers to fit it. A strong idealism thus drove emperors and their servants: Good government to these men was the first need for civilized life.

5. LIFE IN THE EMPIRE

An elaborate, orderly, powerful government brought peace and stability in which certain patterns of social and economic life flourished. For the majority of the people in the empire, farming was still the fundamental means of livelihood, and the level of agricultural prosperity was high in the second century, for the great cities and the army created a large and steady demand. Especially flourishing were the *latifundia*, nourished by the thriving trade that was the key to imperial prosperity. The reduction of artificial trade barriers, the sound money system, the good roads, and the well-policed seas encouraged the movement of goods to every corner of the empire. The Mediterranean became a busy roadway linking its bordering lands in a common economic system. The traders of the Roman world carried on their activities not only within the confines of the vast empire, but also with India and China. Although a large part of commercial activity involved the exchange of agricultural products, there was a considerable movement of manufactured goods, especially from the East, where skilled artisans produced a variety of high-quality items much in demand throughout the empire. Industrial production made remarkable progress in the previously backward West, especially in Gaul, Spain, and Africa. These complex international patterns of agriculture, trade, and industry tended to reduce the economic importance and self-sufficiency of Italy, which augured trouble in the future. For the present, probably the level of prosperity of the entire Mediterranean world was greater than it had ever been.

The social system, centered on an urban pattern of life, regained its stability. Rome, of course, was the hub of the entire empire, but many other cities—especially the great Eastern centers like Alexandria, Antioch, Corinth, Ephesus, and Athens—were worthy rivals. In them life was dominated by an aristocracy made up of wealthy landowners, successful traders, and high state officials who used their wealth and prestige to ensure themselves a full share of the comforts of life. And although they sometimes indulged their desires to vulgar excess and were always keenly and arrogantly conscious of their status, these aristocrats, moved by civic pride, poured considerable amounts of talent and wealth into the promotion of the welfare of the cities. Furthermore, the aristocracy was never a closed one; members of the lower classes could enter it by attaining wealth or winning favor with the imperial government.

Below the aristocrats was an array of city dwellers: shopkeepers, skilled artisans, minor officials, hired laborers, servants, slaves, and throngs of idle poor. Some elements of this populace fared fairly well economically and socially, but for many, life was poverty and misery, passed in slums and often dependent upon the state or a rich aristocrat for bare essentials. Still, the city had its compensations: its pageants, its public games, its splendid buildings, its religious ceremonies, its constant excitement.

Those who received the least benefit from the *pax romana* were the peasants who spent their lives tilling the soil. Isolated from the cities, they seldom felt the impact of the forces that gave

This relief shows an everyday scene in a Roman household. Food is being prepared and baked in the oven at right. The panel, now in the Musée de Trier, dates from the third century. *Photo: Alinari/ EPA, Inc.*

Roman society its vitality. The major trends in agricultural life encouraged the growth of large estates, a process that increasingly reduced the small independent farmers to dependency on powerful absentee landlords as tenants. These dependent agricultural workers, called *coloni*, were gradually burdened with the greater tax share as well. In effect, the peasantry supported the other classes in Roman society with very little recompense and less hope for a better life.

Slavery played a prominent role in Roman imperial society. In the cities slaves worked in the households of the rich and in the workshops and stalls of artisans and merchants. Nearly every agricultural establishment had slave laborers; some of the large estates depended almost totally on them. So did the mines and the great ceramics factories. Needless to say, the lot of slaves was a hard one and their treatment often brutal, especially where great gangs of them were utilized. There is some evidence, however, that their condition tended to improve. Many were given freedom by masters who in some cases seem to have been moved by moral scruples. Some slaves managed to purchase their freedom and enjoy considerable prosperity practicing trades they had learned as slaves. Numerous funerary inscriptions render praise to slaves for their loyalty and industry, and other literary sources suggest that masters and slaves often associated amicably. Imperial legislation extended several rights to slaves and sought to assure them humane treatment. Despite these signs of a more enlightened view toward slavery, the institution

demeaned labor and justified the idleness of many freemen.

One of the chief social consequences of the Roman imperial order was the degree to which barriers of every kind tumbled to create a cosmopolitan Mediterranean society. The distinction between Roman and non-Roman faded as provincials gained citizenship and wealth. The gulf between national and ethnic groups disappeared as a consequence of the free movement of peoples and the common institutions serving every part of the empire. Religions, philosophies, art forms, and ideas fused in an atmosphere of toleration. Under Roman rule, the Mediterranean basin tended to become one world racially, religiously, culturally, and economically. The Romans provided the synthesizing agency and the chief bond of unity in the form of the imperial government, one of the most humane and beneficent political systems every devised.

Even a brief description of the Roman world in the second century will elicit admiration for its peace, order, prosperity, and unity. That admiration is warranted, but it must be tempered by certain reservations. The empire had its poverty, its injustices, its oppression, its violence its greed. The callous disregard shown by the proud, self-satisfied ruling aristocracy for these conditions; the immense power concentrated in the imperial government without any checks; the signs of vulgarization, sterile imitations, and barbarization in the emerging cultural synthesis; the dangerous weaknesses in the economy—all these signs belied the Roman pride and faith that their world was destined to last to eternity.

Suggested Reading

Political History
*Harold Mattingly, *Roman Imperial Society* (Norton).
*Michael Grant, *The World of Rome* (Mentor).
*J. P. V. D. Balsdon, *Rome: The Story of an Empire* (McGraw). Any of these three works will provide a good general assessment of Roman imperial history.

*E. T. Salmon, *History of the Roman World from 30 B.C. to A.D. 138* (6th ed., Barnes and Noble). A detailed history of the period, especially good on political history.
*F. E. Adcock, *Roman Political Ideas and Practices* (Ann Arbor). Helpful in understanding the nature of

Roman imperial political institutions and the ideas that inspired them.

Mason Hammond, *The Augustan Principate in Theory and Practice* (rev. ed., 1968), and *The Antonine Monarchy* (1959). Although somewhat demanding, these two volumes provide the best description of the imperial government and its operation.

Economic and Social History

*Jerome Carcopino, *Daily Life in Ancient Rome*, trans. E. O. Lorimer (Yale).

J. P. V. D. Balsdon, *Life and Leisure in Ancient Rome* (1969).

Samuel Dill, *Roman Society from Nero to Marcus Aurelius* (2nd ed., 1926). These three works contain a wealth of interesting material on how the Romans lived.

Ramsay Macmullen, *Roman Social Relations, 50 B.C. to A.D. 284* (1974). An effective attempt to describe the feelings prompting the behavior of the major social groups in the Roman Empire.

M. I. Rostovtzeff, *Social and Economic History of the Roman World*, 2 vols. (2nd ed., 1957). A classic treatment.

Biography

*A. H. M. Jones, *Augustus* (Norton).

Stewart Perowne, *Hadrian* (1960).

A. S. L. Farquharson, *Marcus Aurelius* (1951).

Michael Grant, *Nero* (1970).

Sources

Complete Works of Tacitus, ed. Moses Hadas (Modern Library). Tacitus' *Annals* and *Histories*, both in this edition, provide a lively picture of the first century A.D., written by a conservative not always pleased with the conduct of the emperors.

*Suetonius, *The Twelve Caesars*, trans. Robert Graves (Penguin). A gossipy, personalized sketch of each emperor from Julius Caesar to Domitian.

Fifty Letters of Pliny, ed. A. N. Sherwin-White (2nd ed., Oxford). Presents an excellent picture of the activities of a Roman governor in the times of Trajan.

11
ROMAN CULTURE

As the Romans were perfecting an imperial government that served the entire Mediterranean world, their intellectual and artistic talents developed and reached maturity. Rome played a dual role in the cultural history of the Western world. In certain fields, especially in art, philosophy, and scientific thought, the Romans were not primarily creators; they borrowed from and adapted the Greek tradition, and then disseminated the synthesis among their subjects, especially those in the Western part of the empire. However, the Romans were not entirely imitators. They made major contributions in literature, architecture, engineering, and law — contributions ensuring them an important place in cultural history.

1. THE PREPARATION

Before 250 B.C. the Romans displayed little interest in literary and artistic pursuits. Although acquainted with higher culture as a result of their contacts with the Etruscans and the Greeks, they remained a simple people occupied with politics, war, and earning a living. However, their experiences in these pursuits provided them with an orientation that influenced their approach to thought and expression throughout most of their history.

The basic Roman outlook on life formed in these early centuries was shaped by four major forces — family life, agriculture, warfare, and re-ligion. The family structure was dominantly patriarchal. Fathers impressed on other members of the tightly knit families a sense of discipline, obedience, and respect for authority and tradition. Farm life made the early Romans a practical, realistic people, content to live simply and frugally. Constant warfare in defense of hearth and city deepened the sense of duty owed to the larger community and strengthened discipline.

Religion had the most profound effect on early Roman life. Existence was permeated by a sense that everything was determined by unseen but powerful forces. The Romans held these spirits in high respect, which instilled in them a deep piety. At this early date, the chief objects of this piety were household and agricultural deities: Janus, the protective god of the doorway of each household; Vesta, the goddess of the hearth; the *lares* and *penates,* spirits guarding the productive powers of the family and its lands and flocks. The city had its protectors too, a family of gods headed by Jupiter and his wife Juno. Eventually this divine circle protecting the expanding city became the object of a special mythology accounting for the behavior of each of its members, a mythology borrowed in large part from the Greeks. The conciliation of these family and civic gods was one of every Roman's burdens. The approach to the god was highly formal and unemotional. From very early times the Romans developed set patterns for offering sacrifices and prayers to their many gods; these were matched by equally well-defined expectations of what the gods would return to favor families and the city. Close observance of these customary rituals became a fixed part of responsible citizenship; any deviation threatened to earn the wrath of the gods and misfortunes for men and women. Responsibility for proper worship rested with heads of families and with priests elected to represent the city-state community before the civic gods.

Home, farm, battlefield, and altar combined to establish the basic Roman outlook and character. They made the typical Roman a sensible, unemotional, hardworking, disciplined, practical person. The Romans admired sobriety, industry, piety, and responsibility. They saw little value in originality, creativity, and individuality — all potentially dangerous to a stable society that rewarded hard work, devotion to duty, and practicality. These traits engrained in Roman society during its early history played a major role in shaping Rome's cultural history.

2. THE HELLENISTIC TIDAL WAVE

Roman expansion, beginning with her conquest of the Greek cities of southern Italy in the first half of the third century and continuing until she became dominant in the Mediterranean world at the end of the second century B.C., thrust the Romans into a cultural environment that revolutionized their cultural outlook. As a result of their contacts with Magna Graecia, their successes in wars in the East, and the influx of Greek slaves into Italy, the Romans became aware of the cultural heritage of the Greek world, particularly in its Hellenistic phase. They were so impressed that they were literally conquered by the culture of the peoples whom they were conquering politically. This experience was crucial in determining the role the Romans would play in the total stream of Western cultural history.

One of the consequences of this experience was the adoption of a new education system. Previously, the young Roman had been educated at home by his father in family customs, the principles of Roman law, farming, civic duties, and religion. Now that system was replaced

by the Hellenistic model. In every respectable Roman household educated Greek slaves were employed to teach young men to read Greek, introduce them to Greek literature and philosophy, and develop in them the skills needed to express their own ideas. Grammar and rhetoric became the touchstones of the new education system and long remained the instruments through which the young were brought into civilized society.

Their fascination with Greek culture soon spurred the Romans to imitation. Epic poems, comedies, tragedies, histories, and even philosophical tracts were produced in Latin. Most early Roman authors borrowed heavily from Greek subject matter and copied slavishly Greek literary styles. But in the process they enriched the Latin language to the point where it became a vehicle for independent expression.

In art, the Romans were even more deeply impressed by Greek models. During the wars in the East huge numbers of art pieces were pilfered to decorate Roman villas. Those who could not steal what they wanted hired Eastern artists to turn out copies. Greek styles of architecture were applied to civic buildings and private dwellings. In the process Rome became a city that not only resembled Hellenistic cities but could rival them as a center of artistic activity.

Even the masses in Rome felt the impact of Greek influences, but they were touched chiefly through religion. The wars of conquest left many people intellectually and emotionally lost. The formal religion of Rome offered little satisfaction. The Eastern religions did. New gods and rituals taken from the Greek civic religions were added to public religion in Rome, but even these additions did not satisfy many. From Eastern slaves they learned about more exciting Hellenistic mystery religions like the worship of Dionysus or Cybele or Isis. These emotional, personal cults increasingly challenged the traditional religion for the allegiance of the Italian population.

Some Romans fought this cultural revolution. Typical of the conservatives was Cato the Elder, a second-century statesman who spent his life preaching against the Greek way. He argued that Rome was being ruined by the loss of her ancient virtues. But he was fighting a lost cause.

Rome was destined by circumstance and choice to be heir to the magnificent Greek cultural patrimony.

During the first century B.C. Roman writers, artists, and thinkers began to put their own stamp on what they had borrowed. This burst of creativity resulted in Rome's "golden age" culturally; the Augustan age marked its high point. After a brief slackening in the first century A.D., there followed a second period of considerable activity during the era of the "good emperors," often called the "silver age" of Roman culture. During these three centuries from about 100 B.C. to A.D. 180, the Romans added enough to what they had borrowed from the Greeks to permit us to call the product "Greco-Roman culture."

3. LITERATURE

The most impressive and easily appreciated reflection of the Roman cultural genius is found in literature. The chief masterpieces were produced between about 100 B.C. and A.D. 150, but behind the mature works lay a long period of the formation of Latin as a superb instrument of expression. The early Latin writers were deeply indebted to Greek models for both style and content, but as the Roman genius developed, authors demonstrated certain unique talents. Roman writers poured into their works a depth of personal conviction, a powerful sense of realism, and a passion for instructing and uplifting readers.

Outstanding among all Roman writers is Vergil (70–19 B.C.). Born in rural Italy, he grew to manhood during the last years of the civil wars. Eventually he attracted the attention of Augustus, whose patronage permitted him to devote the last years of his life to writing. Although much of his great talent was poured out in the service of the new Augustan order, it would be erroneous to overemphasize Vergil's role as a propagandist; he wrote out of deep conviction and enthusiasm. His *Georgics* express a strong feeling for nature and for what involvement in pastoral life can mean — especially to those corrupted by the violence and greed surrounding the last days of the republic. Vergil's masterpiece was an epic poem, the *Aeneid*, which glorifies

Rome and shows that her rise to mastery of the world was divinely ordered. The plot centers on the adventures of a Trojan hero, Aeneas, who after the fall of Troy was ordered by the gods to establish in Italy a new city destined to rule the world. The noble Aeneas — an ideal Roman — undergoes a series of supreme tests but obeys the divine order. Never was the Roman ideal of the dedicated patriot portrayed with more force and spiritual intensity.

Two other poets, Catullus and Horace, illustrate another side of the Roman character. Catullus (ca. 85–54 B.C.) was a product of high society in the late republican period. His life was lived amid a dissolute, pleasure-seeking crowd of young nobles. Among his many adventures was a love affair with a noble lady who was already married and who eventually jilted him. The experience inspired him to pour forth powerful lyric poetry. Horace (65–8 B.C.), also a lyric poet, enjoyed the patronage of Augustus and was second in influence only to Vergil, whose intimate friend he was. His best work, the *Odes*, represents his personal reactions to hundreds of situations he met in his lifetime. Although he lacked the fire of Catullus, Horace spoke to a wider circle, his poems reflecting the reactions of an educated, humane Roman to life as a whole — a great spirit looking at the world about him with sanity, intelligence, and wit. He was and remains the ideal of a civilized man.

Lucretius (ca. 95–55 B.C.) demonstrated still another aspect of Roman poetic genius: moral seriousness. A contemporary of Catullus, he was profoundly moved by events of the civil war era. He found his personal salvation in Epicurean philosophy, which he undertook to explain in a long poem called *On the Nature of Things*. With almost missionary zeal Lucretius put poetry to the service of instruction. He made a noble plea to educated Romans to seek in philosophy the bases of moral regeneration and personal fulfillment. Seldom has a poet shown greater moral earnestness, idealism, and dignity.

Among the lesser poets were Ovid (43 B.C.–A.D. 17), who entertained Augustan high society with his *Art of Love*, a frivolous but amusing poem on the art of seduction, and his *Metamorphoses*, an entertaining, lively rendering of

Greek mythological stories into Latin; and Martial (ca. A.D. 38–102) and Juvenal (ca. A.D. 55–140), both of whom revealed the shortcomings of Roman society in their brilliant satires.

Cicero (106–43 B.C.) was the most famous prose writer in Roman history. Although an active lawyer, magistrate, and statesman, he produced a wide variety of writing, of which his speeches form a large part; he made argumentation an art. In addition, Cicero wrote two important essays on political theory, *Republic* and *Laws*, defending Roman republican institutions but pleading for the establishment of a first citizen to guide the state. He also wrote several philosophical tracts that made abstract Greek thought understandable to Roman readers. His numerous *Letters* supply a brilliant picture of Roman politics and society in the first century B.C. This eloquent, learned Roman made Latin prose capable of expressing any idea.

The earliest historical writing in Latin was influenced by Hellenistic models, but the Romans again discovered their own talent. The most influential Roman historian was Livy (59 B.C.–A.D. 17), another of those inspired to creative activity under the Augustan regime. His masterpiece, the immense *History of the Roman Republic*, covers the period 753 B.C. to A.D. 9. Although a large part of the work has been lost, it is clear from what is left that Livy believed Rome had a great historical mission and that he wished to instruct his readers on the subject. Livy was not a scientific historian, interested only in the truth; his work was a conglomeration of truth and fiction put together to teach a lesson. Nonetheless, it presented with great dramatic impact the men and events that made Rome great over seven centuries.

Less monumental but equally artistic was Tacitus (ca. A.D. 55–117), who wrote about Roman history after Augustus. His *Histories* and *Annals* covered large portions of the period A.D. 14–96. Although Tacitus was a man of senatorial and republican sentiments, prejudiced against the successors of Augustus, he wrote with brilliance and deep moral sense. Another of his works, *Germania*, gives important information about the barbarians, who were soon to play a larger part in Roman life. Suetonius (ca. A.D. 75–150) vividly portrayed the Roman emperors from Caesar to Domitian in his *Lives of the Twelve Caesars*. The works of Greek writers swelled the body of excellent histories. One of the greatest was Polybius, who lived in Rome from 167 to 151 B.C. as a hostage. He became an intimate of the pro-Hellenic Scipionic circle, and, greatly impressed by the Romans, produced a superb work chronicling Rome's rise to world power. Plutarch (ca. A.D. 46–120) provided a brilliant series of biographies of Greek and Roman men in his *Parallel Lives*. Several Romans produced personal memoirs that were of the nature of histories. Probably the best examples were Julius Caesar's *Commentaries on the Gallic Wars* and Marcus Aurelius' *Meditations*.

During the era when Greek ideas and art forms were first sweeping over the Roman world, attempts were made to imitate the magnificent Greek dramatic art. The most outstanding Roman dramatists were Plautus (third century B.C.) and Terence (second). But drama failed to take root among the Romans. Moreover, only occasionally did a fiction writer grace the literary scene. These gaps in the scope of Roman genres suggest that the creation of highly imaginative literature was foreign to the Romans, who had to be tied to reality—to history, to current moral problems, to personal experience.

This review of Roman literature, touching on only a handful of the best writers, should leave no doubt that Rome stands independent in the history of literature, for her writers handled great subjects in a powerful style, and countless generations in Western Europe in the centuries following Rome's fall were to be introduced to a civilized view of life by reading them.

4. ART

Rome's most impressive and distinctive artistic field was architecture. Greek models predominated, but the Romans added important elements to what they borrowed. They developed concrete as a building material and used it to form the basic structure of most large buildings. They also perfected and put to new uses the arch and the dome, which had been developed earlier in the Near East. These technical advances per-

The Pont du Gard, built across the River Gard to bring water to the Gallo-Roman city of Nîmes, is an impressive monument to Roman engineering skill. The structure rises 160 feet above the river bed and is about 900 feet in length; each of the large arches is about 80 feet across at its base. Roman architects and engineers have seldom been matched in the application of the arch to utilitarian ends. *Photo: Editorial Photocolor Archives, Inc.*

mitted the Romans to construct larger buildings and to depart from the horizontal lines that characterized Greek architecture.

The Romans achieved their best results in secular public buildings; they were not, like the Greeks, great temple builders. However, they did effect significant modifications of style in temple-building. The Pantheon, built in Rome in the second century A.D., is the greatest round temple ever built. Its domed roof, made of stone, is 142 feet in diameter and is supported by massive concrete walls. A rectangular porch, its roof supported by Greek columns, leads into the rotunda, supplying a pleasing mixture of Greek and Roman architectural ideas.

Much more distinctly Roman were public buildings: the baths, amphitheaters, aqueducts, bridges, meeting halls (basilicas), and palaces that from the first century B.C. onward increasingly graced Rome and were widely imitated in provincial cities over the entire empire. Some of these structures, such as the huge and magnificent sports center built in Rome (the Colosseum) to accommodate the throngs that loved violent games pitting men against each other and against animals in mortal combat, still strike the observer as awesome in terms of size and structural complexity. The Roman basilicas, built in great numbers in cities all over the empire, are especially significant in architectural history because they served as models for early Christian churches and for most Christian architecture for centuries after the fall of Rome. The basilica was essentially a long hall flanked by side aisles. The walls of the main hall were built higher than the side aisles, allowing windows to be cut in them. The structures show skillful use of the arch; in the Basilica of Maxentius (early fourth century A.D.), a concrete roof was put over a main aisle 80 feet wide. Roman baths, which consisted of a great central court surrounded by numerous smaller rooms, featured arched vaults and passageways. All these buildings are especially impressive because of their size and the technical mastery demonstrated in their construction.

Roman sculpture showed less independence from Greek models than did architecture. Although almost every form of sculpture was produced in great quantity everywhere in the empire, the best work done by the Romans was in realistic portraiture and reliefs treating historical incidents. Even statues of emperors were extremely lifelike, accentuating the dignity and manliness of their subjects but avoiding excessive idealization. The historical scenes carved on triumphal arches or the walls of public buildings are almost photographic. What little we know of Roman painting, used chiefly to decorate buildings, reflects this same sense of realism.

5. PHILOSOPHY, SCIENCE, AND RELIGION

Roman philosophers were chiefly engaged in digesting and explaining those portions of the Greek philosophical tradition that seemed applicable to Roman problems, especially to politics and ethics. They carried on the trend already established in the Hellenistic period of concentrating on the application of philosophical principles rather than on speculation. Rome's greatest accomplishment was, therefore, the transmission of part of the Greek philosophical tradition to areas where it was unknown, especially Western Europe.

Four figures represent the main currents in Roman philosophy. Cicero was eclectic, borrowing from many Greek schools of thought and working out a set of ideas he felt were fitted to Roman society in the first century B.C. Lucretius was a disciple of Epicurus who made a powerful plea for intelligent Romans to abandon the superstitions of traditional religion. He argued that a life of learning and withdrawal from the world was the true source of pleasure. Not all Epicureans, however, followed Lucretius' path; many used Epicurean materialism as an excuse for a life of sensual pleasure.

But many intelligent and sensitive Romans found greater attraction in the more sober and serious philosophy of Stoicism, which was the prevailing philosophical force of the first two centuries of the Christian era. Its two most articulate spokesmen were Seneca (ca. 4 B.C.–A.D. 65) and Marcus Aurelius (A.D. 121–180), whose *Meditations* provides a good reflection of Stoic ideas. By arguing for the need for one state and one law, the Stoics also helped to justify the Roman imperial government.

The Romans did not distinguish themselves in pure science. Their interests were practical and nontheoretical, quite in contrast with the bold speculativeness of Greek thought. The Romans "practiced" science by translating Greek concepts into Latin. Perhaps the most significant advance in science in the Roman period resulted from the efforts of scholars, such as Pliny the Elder (ca A.D. 23–79), Galen (A.D. 131–201), and Ptolemy (ca. A.D. 121–151), to compile great encyclopedias of scientific information derived chiefly from Greek and Hellenistic sources. Through their compilations a considerable part of Greek science was eventually transmitted to Western Europe.

In putting existing scientific knowledge to practical use, however, the Romans were expert. Rome's engineers were unequaled in antiquity; her roads, aqueducts, and bridges have withstood the ages. The technical skills developed by engineers and artisans formed a precious heritage perhaps as important to the West as was the literary, artistic, and philosophical tradition transmitted by Rome.

While the educated upper class of the Roman

world absorbed Greek philosophy and science and adjusted its values accordingly, the basic outlook of the great bulk of society was powerfully affected by religion. Roman religious life was greatly enriched during the era 100 B.C.–A.D. 180 by the spread of the emotional Hellenistic mystery religions throughout the empire. The ideas and practices associated with these cults tended to concentrate attention on personal problems and life after death. Their popularity weakened the appeal of the older Roman family and civic religions which once had played a powerful role in shaping Roman thought.

6. LAW

Perhaps Rome's most enduring cultural monument was her law. Although the evolution of Roman law was not confined to the period between 100 B.C. and A.D. 180, certain developments in this era decided its final character.

The Romans, unable to conceive of a state without a legal basis, had been concerned with law from the beginning of their history. In this respect they were not unique; other ancient peoples, such as the Hebrews, the Mesopotamians, and the Greeks, thought similarly. Roman law was unique in that it continued to grow century after century. Custom was constantly modified by the legislation of the assemblies in the republican period. Even more important, the chief judicial official of the republic, the *praetor*, was allowed to pronounce his interpretation of the law at the beginning of his term. This practice produced a vast but somewhat confused body of judge-made law that needed constant reinterpretation but did serve to keep the law in contact with daily life. Moreover, republican Rome began to develop a kind of international law (*lex gentium*) to apply to noncitizen subjects. It was built on ideas derived from the laws of subject peoples, on Roman legal principles and practices, and on the common-sense decisions of judges who had to dispose of cases involving noncitizens.

In the period 100 B.C.–A.D. 180, efforts were made to codify all Roman law into a single, systematic body. This was prompted by many forces. The imperial government, moving toward a unified administration, saw in a unified code a means of exercising authority more uniformly and effectively. The general trend toward removing the distinctions between Romans and non-Romans was also influential. The extensive legislation by the emperors tended to create uniformity. Stoic philosophy, with its emphasis on a universal law of nature, prompted men to think in terms of a consistent body of law for all society. These forces produced a series of notable legal authorities who devoted their lives to the codification of the law, usually with the wholehearted support of the rulers. Their writings became the basis of legal education, so that most lawyers and public administrators adopted a similar view.

The great jurists sought to relate human laws to natural principles, thus providing the legal system a theoretical basis outside human whim. They sought to make the law consistent but flexible. By the end of the second century A.D., the Roman jurists had by no means completed the standardization of Roman law; that would be done only in the sixth century by the emperor Justinian. But they had established its basic principles. Although law could be derived from many sources, it must be related to the universal order of things, that is, to the natural law. It must be supple enough to bend to changing conditions, yet firmly enough based on principle to avoid manipulation by unscrupulous men. It must serve the needs of all men and not a narrow segment of the population. These principles have survived until the present as the highest ideals of all legal systems.

7. THE ROMANS AS SPREADERS OF CULTURE

One final achievement that must be credited to the Romans is perhaps more important than anything else in their cultural history. The Romans developed a special talent for spreading their culture to backward peoples. From the first century B.C. onward, large areas in the Western part of the empire were rapidly transformed into images of Rome. This transformation was of inestimable importance for the future of Western Europe.

Roman soldiers, officials, and merchants, moving freely about the whole empire, were agents of civilization. The government founded towns in far-flung areas of the empire and encouraged Romans to live there and establish schools in them. The study of grammar and rhetoric, literature, and philosophy spread a common store of ideas and set of tastes to the far corners of the empire. Latin and Greek, the administrative languages of the empire, soon became widely known, providing large numbers of people direct access to the Greco-Roman literary tradition. Emperors built roads, aqueducts, temples, and public buildings throughout the provinces, prompting their residents to imitation. The freedom given to scholars, religious missionaries, philosophers, and artists encouraged them to seek out the culturally backward. Rome opened her doors to men with artistic and intellectual talents from all corners of the empire, thus turning all eyes toward a common cultural center and providing a channel for the spread of culture.

Myriad marks of Roman culture remain. The French and Spanish tongues are direct descendants of the Latin learned in the first and second centuries. When the modern traveler comes across an elaborate bath in the city of Bath in western England or a great amphitheater in France or a Roman bridge at one of a dozen places, he is encountering evidence of the extent of the Romanization of the Western provinces. Luckily for their subjects, the Romans did not adopt the Greek attitude of looking down on foreigners. Instead, the Romans gave their best to all, and in the process spread civilization over a large area of the world previously caught in barbarism.

Suggested Reading

General Surveys

*Edith Hamilton, *The Roman Way* (Norton). A stimulating treatment, slightly distorted by a tendency to compare the Romans unfavorably with the Greeks.

*D. R. Dudley, *Civilization of Rome* (Mentor). A good brief treatment.

Pierre Grimal, *The Civilization of Rome*, trans. W. S. Maquinness (1963). The best evaluation of the accomplishments of the Romans.

Religion

H. J. Rose, *Ancient Roman Religion* (1948).

*R. M. Ogilvie, *The Romans and Their Gods in the Age of Augustus* (Norton).

J. Ferguson, *The Religions of the Roman Empire* (1970). Three good descriptions of Roman religious ideas and practices; Rose's book is the briefest, but it is somewhat oversimplified.

Literature and Thought

H. I. Marrou, *History of Education in Antiquity* (1956). A fine survey, relating Roman literary production to the education process.

*M. Hadas, *History of Latin Literature* (Columbia). A well-organized treatment of the development of Latin literature.

M. L. W. Laistner, *The Greater Roman Historians* (1947). A perceptive evaluation of the major Roman historians and their place in intellectual history.

F. H. Sandbach, *The Stoics* (1975). A clear description of the basic ideas of Stoicism.

Art

*M. Wheeler, *Roman Art and Architecture* (Oxford).

H. Kähler, *The Art of Rome and Her Empire*, trans. J. R. Foster (1965).

Ranuccio Bianchi-Bandinelli, *Rome, the Centre of Power: Roman Art to A.D. 200*, trans. Peter Green (1970). Any of these splendid works will provide a good introduction to all forms of Roman art.

*F. E. Brown, *Roman Architecture* (Braziller). A superlative treatment.

A. Maiuri, *Roman Painting* (1953). A sound description on a matter about which our knowledge is limited.

*L. DeCamp, *The Ancient Engineers* (Ballantine). Although this volume surveys the development of engineering for the entire ancient period, it does full justice to the accomplishments of the Romans.

Law

Fritz Schulz, *History of Roman Legal Science* (1946). Perhaps the best treatment of the development of Roman law.

J. A. Crook, *Law and Life of Rome* (1967). An attempt to relate evolving Roman law to the various conditions of life in Roman society.

Sources

Kevin Guinagh and Alfred P. Darjahn, *Latin Literature in Translation* (2nd ed., 1952). This anthology provides an excellent sampling of Latin literature. It may encourage the reading of some Latin authors in their entirety. Aside from the works of Livy, Polybius, Tacitus, Suetonius, Cicero, and Caesar cited in previous chapters, the following are particularly recommended:

*Vergil, *Aeneid*, trans. L. R. Lind (Indiana).

*Horace, *Odes and Epodes*, trans. J. P. Clancy (Phoenix).

*Lucretius, *On the Nature of the Universe*, trans. R. E. Latham (Penguin).

*Ovid, *The Metamorphoses*, trans. Rolfe Humphries (Indiana).

**Stoic Philosophy of Seneca: Essays and Letters*, trans. M. Hadas (Norton).

*Marcus Aurelius, *Meditations*, trans. Maxwell Staniforth (Penguin).

Retrospect

Few epochs in all history witnessed greater achievement than that extending from the time when the Greeks emerged from their dark age about 800 B.C. to the generation that saw the Roman imperial order reach its full maturity about A.D. 180—the epoch from Homer to Marcus Aurelius. With these achievements fresh in mind, we might well ask why this epoch was so fruitful. The answer is at once simple and profound: Greco-Roman civilization made man and his well-being its central concern. Its motto was spoken by Protagoras: "Man is the measure of all things." Socrates formulated its one commandment: "Know thyself."

We cannot help being impressed at how much the Greco-Roman world discovered about man and how great were the energies unleashed by that self-knowledge. At grave risk of oversimplification, we might single out a few of these discoveries as being the foundation stones of Greco-Roman civilization, its value-giving, directive forces. First was the rationality of man. Second was the ordered universe that provided the setting for his activities. Third was rational man's capacity for positive good. Fourth was the capability of man to transcend whatever he was at any instant through knowledge and good action. Last was the political nature of man, which gave him no alternative except to join other men to realize his potential to know, to be good, and to outreach his present condition.

Yet this majestic achievement was somehow flawed, even in the minds of its creators. For one thing, the Greeks and the Romans were never completely convinced that their own vision of man was true. They suspected that in him lurked an elusive element of the demonic and that beyond him existed forces he was powerless to control. Their nagging doubts left open profound and disturbing questions: Was it really sufficient to know oneself? Was it possible? Would such knowledge always produce the good?

Moreover, the kind of society that emerged from the centuries-long effort to create a world fit for reasonable, good, enlightened men had some features that were disturbing. The confidence that political action could achieve perfection had given the state—the Greek *polis*, the Hellenistic monarchies, the Roman Republic, the Roman Empire—a dangerous dominance over men at the expense of other dimensions of their existence. The majestic assumptions about man's rationality and capacity for good had given undue power in society to those who managed to acquire the symbols of rationality and good: an education, offices, wealth, and manners. These aristocrats, seldom quite in the Homeric mold, tended to be oblivious to those who had not been enlightened or blessed with power and prestige. The politicized and intellectualized flavor of classical civilization bred in those who wielded power and participated in the mainstream of cultural life a disdain for other kinds of activity—especially labor—and for other kinds of human behavior—especially that emerging from man's emotional nature. The rationalizing of human conduct and of nature bred an intellectual posture that saw things in terms of absolute, fixed forms and found it extremely difficult to accept or to initiate change.

These insights might well have persuaded men living in the second-century Roman Empire of what now seems fairly evident: Classical men had learned much about human nature and that knowledge had liberated man so that a whole new range of talents was unleashed to enliven and beautify the world, but they had not seen man's whole nature. The civilization they constructed thus had inherent limitations arising from their restricted and distorted view of humanity. Perhaps the end product of the classical world is symbolized by a man who revealed his soul to posterity at the very end of the period—the emperor Marcus Aurelius. Marcus Aurelius was the embodiment of classical man: reasonable, good, serious, politically aware, sensitive to others. As ruler over a marvelous political system, he appeared (by classical standards) to have the power to achieve whatever the good of humanity demanded. Yet in his *Meditations* he emerges as the victim of a cruel joke—a man caught up in a mechanical universe running on forever without change, a man who knew and understood but found nothing to do, a man so good that the nature of evil eluded him, a perfect citizen who was destined to the unappetizing business of fending off stupid barbarians. What was there to do but to resign oneself? One suspects that a kind of bloodless, cold, unemotional resignation in the face of what reason and goodness cannot encompass is what classical civilization finally meant. Something of this attitude is apparent in a Greek statue or in the lines spoken by the chorus in some Greek tragedies. For all its accomplishments, the classical world had still not learned enough about man.

But whatever its limitations, classical civilization had changed the course of history. No nation, no people, no civilization of the future could escape its influence—especially not those inhabitants of Europe who first felt the force of civilized life by being drawn into the Greco-Roman world.

III

The Fall of Greco-Roman Civilization
A.D. 180-500

During the second century A.D. Greco-Roman civilization had established unchallenged sway over the Mediterranean basin and extended its influence inland from the sea to three continents—Europe, Asia, and Africa. A vast community had been created within which a bewildering variety of peoples was bound together by powerful forces. The political genius of the Romans, embodied in the imperial system of government, furnished the most potent bond of community. Almost as important were the widely shared cultural concepts that created a common system of values. Derived primarily from the Greeks and finding expression in a remarkable literature, art, philosophy, and learning, this cultural force of unity had been adopted by the Hellenistic world and then spread through the entire Mediterranean world by the Romans. The shared political system and cultural values were powerfully reinforced by a common economy that linked together the many parts of the Mediterranean world in an interdependent material existence. The simultaneous operation of these unifying forces produced one of the most magnificent eras in all human history.

However, no human order, however strong it appears, is perfect, and no community of men, however confident they are of their talents, is safe from change and its tensions. As the second century A.D. drew to an end, serious stresses and strains emerged within the splendid Mediterranean community the Romans had put together. The long process leading to the formation of that community was reversed, and forces of disintegration became dominant. Although Greco-Roman civilization was endowed with great reserves of strength, they were not enough. Within a relatively short time a vast transformation occurred in the Mediterranean basin. Greco-Roman civilization was irreparably weakened, eaten away by incurable sicknesses within its body and torn apart by the assaults of barbarians from outside. The disintegration of that civilization has always held a fascination for students of the past, ultimately prompting them to ask why it is that man's greatest achievement—a mature civilization—cannot be made to last. Intriguing as the question might be, however, the fact is that the end of classical civilization left the vast population of the Mediterranean world with no alternative but to set out again to construct new and viable patterns of life.

An era of change and decline of the Roman Empire began with dramatic suddenness during the century following the death of Marcus Aurelius in A.D. 180. In vivid contrast to the *pax romana* of the second century, this period was characterized by almost incessant civil war that deeply disturbed the internal order of the empire and increased its vulnerability to outside attack. Amid the political crisis, basic economic and social maladjustments surfaced to add to the stress. And intellectual and spiritual confusion sapped the capabilities of society to respond to the growing problems. In retrospect it is clear that the foundations of Greco-Roman civilization were being eaten away and that a desperate sickness was engulfing the Mediterranean world.

1. THE POLITICAL CRISIS, A.D. 180–284

The peaceful, humane regime of the "good emperors" suffered an astonishing reversal after Marcus Aurelius, who turned his back on the adoptive system of succession in favor of bestowing the imperial office on his son. Unfortunately, Commodus (A.D. 180–192), the son sired by the philosopher-king, was incapable of managing the one office that could sustain the *pax romana*. His misrule generated a brutal struggle among segments of the army for control of the imperial office. The ultimate victor was Sep-

12

THE DECLINE OF THE EMPIRE AND THE RISE OF CHRISTIANITY

timius Severus (A.D. 193–211), an African by origin whose career was totally identified with the army.

The Severi controlled the imperial office until A.D. 235. Their leadership sustained the empire in a generally healthy condition. However, their basic policy planted a time bomb. Following the advice of Septimius to pamper the troops and forget the rest of the population, the Severi brought the army to the center of political power. They encouraged the soldiery, now predominantly noncitizens, to think in terms of material rewards as the price for service to the state: increased pay, pensions, citizenship, and career opportunities in the bureaucracy. The immediate result of Severan favoritism toward the army was an era of civil war lasting from A.D. 235 to 284. The anarchy was caused by rebellious army units seeking to elevate their generals to the purple in expectation of new favors. In that troubled half-century no fewer than nineteen emperors were officially crowned; at least as many more generals provoked their troops to rebellion in unsuccessful efforts to seize the throne. The resultant civil wars took a terrible toll of life and property; almost as costly were the demands placed on society by the temporary victors in these struggles in order to reward the soldiers who had put them in power. The *pax romana* had turned to ashes.

Behind the warring, a fundamental change was occurring in the political structure of the empire. The "barrack emperors" were a different breed of men from the earlier rulers: By birth products of the frontier provinces and by experience inclined toward total command, they were insensitive to the problems of civil administration and to the needs of the civilian population and had little understanding of the fundamental Augustan principle of sharing power with the aristocracies of Rome and the imperial cities. Their major policy concern was with military well-being. Increasingly, administrative posts were filled from the army at the expense of the Italian aristocracy. The emperors moved inexorably toward more thorough regimentation of civilian society and economic productivity to serve military ends. They imposed a heavier and heavier tax burden on the citizenry to support the demands of the army and the enlarged bureaucracy that was required to enact the emperors' expanding role. They intruded ever more decisively into the political affairs of the previously independent city-states, forcing local aristocracies (*curiales*) to siphon money and manpower away from local interests to serve the ends of the central government. They ceased to respect the privileged role of the Italians in imperial affairs, a policy that culminated in A.D. 212 with Caracalla's extending citizenship to all freemen in the empire. Gradually, the autocratic rulers constructed around their office and persons an aura of religious sanctity. The *princeps*, a first citizen on the model of Augustus or Trajan or Hadrian, was becoming a *dominus*, an absolute lord over the total population of the empire — increasingly viewed as mere subjects.

Despite the sickening brutality and violence of this era — contrasting so sharply with the peace and order of the preceding age — the militarization of society was a realistic response to some crucial problems. The empire was facing a threat to its very existence from two of its ancient foes, the Persians and the Germans. In Persia a new dynasty, the Sassanians, greatly intensified their challenge to the Romans for mastery of Asia. Simultaneously, the threat from the Germans along the long European frontier reached crisis proportions, due in large part to developments within the Germanic world causing the numerous small tribes of an earlier age to coalesce into larger groups far more difficult for the Romans to manipulate and restrain. The logical response to the repeated assaults of these formidable foes was a more rigorously organized society striving to involve the total population and all of the resources of the empire in an effort to defend civilized society.

Yet the path to autocracy was filled with grave dangers to the established constitution. The seizure of the imperial office by military leaders narrowed considerably the political vision of the government. The concentration of power in the hands of the central government ruined local governments, long the real backbone of the empire, and entrusted the conduct of public affairs to a ruthless bureaucracy open to every form of corruption. The militarization of society reduced the freedom of every group. On balance, the transformation of the Roman imperial government into a military autocracy was destructive of the existing order. Greco-Roman civilization had begun to disintegrate at its most crucial point — the political system.

2. ECONOMIC, SOCIAL, AND CULTURAL DISLOCATIONS

The dislocations of the established order were not confined to political affairs. The third cen-

tury was marked by decreased economic production. Most serious was a decline in agricultural output. In part, this was a result of war-bred destruction, which led to the abandonment of lands in many places, especially along the frontiers, where farms were turned over to barbarian settlers who were not expert farmers. But the major causes were deeper. There appears to have been a shortage of agricultural labor, probably due to a population decline in the entire Mediterranean world. Agricultural technology did not advance, so that nothing was done to offset the inevitable soil depletion and erosion that ultimately affects any established agricultural system. The increasing prevalence of *latifundia* was depressive, chiefly because these estates were increasingly supplied with labor by dependent *coloni*.

Trade and industry suffered an even greater depression. Again, the political chaos was a contributing factor. The brigandage, banditry, and piracy that accompanied the civil wars seriously interfered with the movement of goods. The reckless fiscal policy of the emperors of the third century inflicted terrible financial burdens on traders and artisans. A regular policy of debasing the currency as a means of getting money to reward the army caused inflation and removed a basic requirement for vigorous trade — a sound system of exchange. Heavy taxation bore especially hard on the trading class, whose wealth could be easily seized. State regimentation of the economy limited opportunities for new commercial and industrial ventures. And as in agriculture, basic changes in imperial trading and manufacturing patterns now took a toll. Regions such as Gaul and Spain that once needed to import products from the advanced East were gaining self-sufficiency; as a result, the volume of trade declined. The end of Roman geographical expansion offered no new "backward" lands to generate new trade. New capital was scarce because the directive elements in the Roman world preferred to invest wealth in land or in nonproductive city beautification and luxurious living. New talent was likewise wanting; politics and war were always the more respectable careers for citizens. Finally, the aristocratic cast of society precluded any serious thought of generating commercial and industrial growth by elevating the standard of living of the lower-class members of society.

The whole texture of society was changing significantly by the third century. The military autocrats ruthlessly eliminated the aristocrats of Rome and Italy from their ancient places in the central administration and in the army. In cities throughout the empire, local aristocracies were crushed by the burden of taxation and deprived of their control over local affairs by increasing hordes of bureaucrats representing the central authority. Had the lower classes benefited from the decline of the aristocracy, the loss might not have been so serious. But the urban lower classes were increasingly regimented and their social position debased. Artisans and laborers in the cities were forced into compulsory associations (*collegia*) through which their wages and production were tightly controlled in the interests of the state. The peasantry, increasingly driven toward hereditary tenancy, were becoming virtual slaves. These trends in society obviously reduced the benefits of membership in the great Roman community.

Meanwhile, two elements in Roman society drew advantage from the changing order: great landlords and soldiers. The owners of large estates tightened their control on agricultural production and the labor force. The state, interested chiefly in securing revenue and produce from the land, gave the landowners greater freedom to exploit the peasantry and pass on to them the burden of taxation. As their control over the *coloni* increased, the great estateholders moved inexorably toward independence and the satisfaction of their local self-interest, a process that gravely threatened the unity of the Mediterranean community. At the same time, a soldier of ability could work his way to a high position in society, perhaps to the imperial throne. Even the lower ranks of the army enjoyed all kinds of favors not open to other citizens. This elevation of the military element in society had evil effects. On an ever-increasing scale, soldiers were recruited from the most primitive areas of the empire or from among barbarians willing to serve Rome. These people, little acquainted with Roman ideas and institutions, now moved to the

This detail, from a commemorative column built in the second century to celebrate the emperor Tiberius' victory over the barbarians in Dacia, shows Roman soldiers defending their position against an attack. Such attacks, repeated on all of the borders of the empire from the second century on, eventually broke through the frontier and hastened the fall of the empire. *Photo: Alinari/EPA, Inc.*

leadership of society. The result was a barbarizing of Roman life.

Even more serious was the inability of the Roman world to generate intellectual and spiritual energies to combat the political, economic, and social problems. The third century was one of the least productive periods of the whole classical era. Writers, artists, and thinkers merely imitated the past without any zest or creative power. They seemed to have lost faith in the humanistic, rationalistic values of the Greco-Roman tradition; man and his vaunted powers at last seemed inadequate to the realities of a troubled world.

In fact, the troubled society of the third century was seeking refuge and meaning in another realm — religion. The third century was alive with powerful religious currents which together seriously threatened the classical world view.

The Oriental mystery faiths, with their personal deities, their promises of eternal salvation, and their emotional rituals, won increasing numbers of adherents at all levels of society. The ancient civic deities of Greece and Rome drew intensified support as well. There was a vast resurgence of interest in astrology and magic. Even philosophy was permeated by a religious, mystical element, as demonstrated by the great vogue of Neoplatonism in the third century, especially after its tenets were systematized by the Egyptian-born Plotinus (A.D. 205–270). Although immensely complex in the form delineated by Plotinus, Neoplatonism basically denied the importance of the material world, characterizing it as unreal and evil-ridden, and asked its adherents to surrender to a contemplative life that would lead them step by step to an ecstatic mystical union with the eternal, nonmaterial Reality. In its essence Neoplatonism symbolized the whole spiritual thrust of the age — the search for salvation from a meaningless world through mystical contact with the divine. In this quest many traditional Greco-Roman values, including confidence in human reason, seemed irrelevant.

3. THE BEGINNINGS OF CHRISTIANITY

One particular spiritual movement made an especially significant impact on this age: the religion called Christianity. It requires special attention because it was destined to reshape history.

Christianity at its beginning certainly did not seem destined to be a revolutionary force. It began as a splinter movement among the Jews, who had already earned a reputation as adherents of unique religious ideas and as threats to any established order. Christianity arose in a Jewish world that was charged with tension born out of repeated frustrations of the effort to recover lost national independence and out of expectations that eventually God's promise of supremacy for his Chosen People would be fulfilled. Since the destruction of the Hebrew kingdom in 586 B.C. by the Chaldeans, the Jews had dreamed of the day when their political freedom would be restored. The Persians had allowed them to rebuild the Temple in Jerusalem and to sustain a religious community, but that was not sufficient to those who cherished the memory of David and Solomon and who were exhorted by the prophets to stand apart in the world. The Maccabean Revolt in 165 B.C. against the Hellenistic Seleucid kingdom had brought the Jews close to independence, but hope vanished when Rome took over Palestine in 63 B.C. The Romans were generous in conceding religious privileges to the Jews but were suspicious and repressive in the face of any threat of Jewish independence.

The frustration of their national aspiration had by the first century B.C. bred serious division within the Jewish community. Most Jews accepted the idea proclaimed by earlier prophets that a God-sent Messiah would deliver them from their oppressors. And they all sought to abide by the Judaic law as it was interpreted by a special group of learned men called *scribes*. But they disagreed on how to act in the immediate historic setting. The Sadducees, chiefly upper-class Jews, favored compromise with the Romans in the interests of peace and religious freedom so that the Jews could continue to live as a religious community according to Judaic law. The Pharisees, enjoying strong popular backing, were violently opposed to the intrusion of foreign ideas and customs into Jewish life. Smaller groups of radicals opted for more drastic solutions. The Zealots were willing to take up arms against the Romans. The Essenes sought to break through the letter of Hebraic law to spiritual purity and to realize their ideals by withdrawal from the Jewish community into an ascetic life. Added to these groups were innumerable individual prophets, such as John the Baptist, crying out that deliverance was at hand. Of considerable importance were the Jews of the Diaspora — those dispersed by accident or choice to all corners of the Mediterranean world during the centuries prior to Roman rule — who had been strongly influenced by Greco-Roman ideas and tended to incorporate these into their religious views. In many cities they had earned deep respect from the non-Jewish population for their piety and moral earnestness.

Into this complex and highly charged scene came Jesus, born probably in 4 B.C. as the Augustan order was taking shape. When he reached maturity, he went forth among the Jews preaching a message that was grounded in the Judaic tradition but had an appealing freshness. He proclaimed that God's promised kingdom was at hand and that men must immediately prepare for it by repentance and spiritual regeneration based on repudiation of the world and on love for God and men. He did not ask his followers to abandon their Jewish heritage but insisted that they must transcend simple observance of the law and performance of the traditional rituals by opening their hearts to God's grace. To those who repented and accepted his message, he promised eternal salvation. His message attracted an enthusiastic following — but it also earned enemies. His attack on the formalism of Jewish religion and the materialism of religious leaders turned "the scribes and the Pharisees" against him. To them, he was a threat to the whole fabric of historic Judaism. Many of his early followers lost much of their enthusiasm when he made it clear that his mission was not to create or rule an earthly kingdom and that he would not take up the sword to liberate the Jews. This combination of hostility and reduced support ended with his crucifixation in ca. A.D. 29 by the Romans in the interest of maintaining peace in the Jewish community.

Jesus' death triggered a crucial development. A group of his stoutest disciples was convinced that he had arisen from the dead, proving that he was the Christ ("the anointed"), the Messiah, the savior sacrificed in accordance with divine plan to ensure the salvation of all mankind. This belief set the little band apart from the whole world; in the words of Paul, "We preach Christ crucified, a stumbling block to Jews and folly to the Gentiles . . ." (I Cor. 1:23). A new religion had been born.

4. THE SPREAD OF CHRISTIANITY

The first Christian community in Jerusalem was vigorous, its members observing the Judaic law while also holding to Jesus' precepts. Soon their ideas spread to other cities, where they attracted the attention of Diaspora Jews and of non-Jews (called Gentiles by the Jews) attracted by the religious message of Jesus. Before long, many were asking to join the new community and were being received. This development posed a grave question for the foundling movement: whether or not new converts were to be held to strict observance of Judaic law and practices. There were those in the primitive Christian community who took a conservative position, but others, typified by Peter, leader of the disciples, increasingly insisted on universalizing Christianity so that it would be acceptable to Jew and Gentile alike.

The major figure in the mission to the Gentiles was Paul. A Jew born at Tarsus, where he was trained in a stern Pharisee tradition but also gained considerable exposure to Greco-Roman thought, Paul was initially a persecutor of Christians. But then he was dramatically converted to Christianity. Convinced that he had been marked by the Lord "to carry his name before the Gentiles, and kings, and children of Israel" (Acts 9:15), he began a long career of preaching that took him to Asia Minor, Greece, and eventually Rome. His message emphasized those precepts of Jesus that had universal application — the redemption effected by the Son of God; the need for moral regeneration through faith and love of God and man; salvation as a reward for belief in the Christ; purity of moral life. By the time of his martyrdom in Rome (perhaps about A.D. 67), the thrust toward making Christianity a universal religion had become dominant, and Christianity and Judaism had moved irreparably apart.

Once launched in the Pauline direction, Christianity steadily spread over most parts of the Roman world. During at least the first century after Jesus' death, a series of dedicated missionary preachers working under all kinds of conditions were the chief agents of expansion. They concentrated their efforts in the major cities of the empire, so that Christianity developed chiefly as an urban religion. Often these missionary preachers began their activities in the synagogues of the city. Their efforts usually

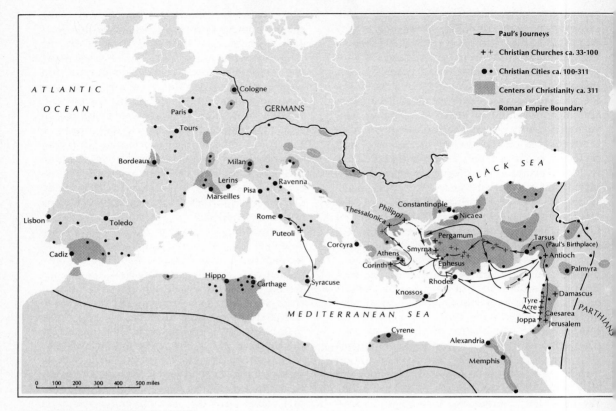

The following labels appear on the map:

Legend:
← Paul's Journeys
+ + Christian Churches ca. 33-100
● ● Christian Cities ca. 100-311
Centers of Christianity ca. 311
— Roman Empire Boundary

ATLANTIC OCEAN
GERMANS
Cologne
Paris
Tours
Bordeaux
Milan
Lerins
Pisa
Marseilles
Ravenna
BLACK SEA
Lisbon
Toledo
Rome
Puteoli
Corcyra
Cadiz
Thessalonica
Philippi
Constantinople
Nicaea
Pergamum
Tarsus (Paul's Birthplace)
Antioch
Palmyra
Athens
Smyrna
Corinth
Ephesus
Hippo
Carthage
Syracuse
Rhodes
Knossos
Damascus
Tyre
Acre
Caesarea
Joppa
Jerusalem
PARTHIANS
MEDITERRANEAN SEA
Cyrene
Alexandria
Memphis

0 100 200 300 400 500 miles

THE SPREAD OF CHRISTIANITY

won a small group of adherents who became self-sustaining "churches." The members of these cells then took up the burden of spreading the faith, working diligently in the local communities to increase the flock. By the end of the third century, vigorous and expanding Christian communities existed everywhere in the empire. The heaviest Christian population was in the cities of Egypt, Syria, Palestine, Asia Minor, Greece, and Italy. By A.D. 285, although Christians certainly formed only a small minority of the total population, they had become a potent factor in the Roman world, one far exceeding what might have been expected in view of their early struggles.

The progress of Christianity was not, however, painless and automatic. One obstacle was provided by the Roman government, which viewed the Christians with suspicion and from time to time persecuted them because of their refusal to worship the state gods. This stand made it impossible for them to fulfill many of their civic responsibilities, including army service, and caused the state to view them as lacking in patriotism. Usually the persecutions were local and temporary, although in the third century more serious attempts were made to exterminate Christianity.

The Christians also met opposition of a less official but more menacing nature from various elements of the Roman populace. Among the masses of people there spread a battery of vile rumors about strange beliefs and immoral, bestial practices, rumors fed by the Christian refusal to participate in public religious rites and by their private, semisecret services. Roman intellectuals scorned Christianity, holding up for ridicule its simplistic, illogical concepts. The leaders of the state religion and of the Jewish synagogues constantly charged the Christians with false beliefs and debased practices. These foes of the new religion became especially dangerous during the third-century troubles, when the accusation was often made that false worshipers in society's midst made the gods angry. On occasion, the government itself intervened to protect Christians from violence.

The Christians made difficulties for themselves as well. From the very beginning, there were divisions in their ranks on what constituted right belief and proper usage. The early communities disagreed on the nature of the relationship between Christianity and Judaism. The proper moral posture for a Christian was often a subject for debate, especially because some insisted on a puritanical denial of the world and its pleasures. By the second century and increasingly in the third, Christians disagreed violently on certain fundamental doctrines, thus generating what may be called the first heresies. These conflicts inevitably set Christian against Christian and diverted the faithful from proselytizing.

5. REASONS FOR CHRISTIANITY'S RISE

Yet Christianity grew. Its success was due to many factors, not the least of which were favorable conditions in the Roman Empire. The empire was so knit together that the movement of ideas was easy. Despite isolated cases of persecution, an atmosphere of tolerance generally prevailed. The growing power of centralized government and the decline of city-states weakened civic religions and caused people to seek individual spiritual satisfaction, while the chaos of the third century made the need for personal fulfillment even more urgent. The emergence of a single state uniting many peoples into one society made a religion that would apply to all men regardless of origin or class seem natural.

A fundamental source of Christian strength lay in its appeal as a religion. No matter how far in other directions we push the search for an explanation of its expansion, it is always evident that Christianity won converts primarily because its teachings answered their deepest religious needs. Such ideas as the existence of one

almighty, loving, merciful God; his sacrifice of his son to redeem men; eternal salvation based on individual worth; damnation for sinners; and universal brotherhood supplied a powerful answer to those seeking to know about God's ways toward men. The humanity of Jesus, who had lived on earth not long before, gave an intimacy to Christianity that other religions lacked. Moreover, Christian teachings were dramatically and simply presented in the New Testament, which began to take form immediately after Jesus' death.

Another reason for success was the organization that took shape during the first three centuries of Christian history. The first Christian communities consisted of a few converts lost in the non-Christian population of the cities of the Roman world. These people met together regularly to pray and sing, to share a common meal commemorating the last supper of Christ, and to be instructed. Leaders emerged in these cells; eventually, these leaders were given titles: *episcopus* (bishop), *presbyter* (priest), and *elder*. With the passage of time problems emerged that called for firmer organization: larger numbers of Christians, persecutions, increasing wealth, disagreement over what constituted right beliefs and practice. Authority over all the affairs of the Christian community in each city began to settle on the bishop. Around this office there developed a powerful ideological justification, called the concept of *apostolic succession*. This theory argued that by virtue of being ordained to the episcopal office, every bishop was a successor to the original apostles and heir to the spiritual authority which Jesus bestowed on those apostles to proclaim the faith. In many large cities the Christian population became so numerous that one church would not suffice to serve them. Additional churches were created with a priest in charge. However, the bishop retained final authority over these new establishments, assuring the organizational solidarity of the Christian community on a citywide basis. This organizational evolution resulted in tightly knit, self-governing local units that reflected a basic entity in the ancient world — the city-state.

While many "churches" were being fashioned from city to city, the Christians never lost sight of their universal brotherhood, rooted in their belief in the one God who had given his son to assure salvation for all his children. From this resulted efforts to forge bonds of unity that would make possible one "church." Jesus' disciples and the early missionaries like Paul tried to keep in touch with as many Christian communities as possible by means of extensive travel and letter writing. By the second century bishops met together on a regional basis in *councils* to discuss common problems and decide on common solutions that each could apply in his own church. Certain bishops from great cities like Jerusalem, Antioch, Alexandria, and Rome exerted considerable influence over lesser bishops in the regions surrounding these centers. By the end of the third century there were Christians concerned with vesting ultimate authority over all Christians in the hands of one of these great bishops. A prime candidate was the bishop of Rome, who gained great prestige from the fact that Rome was the capital of the world but also from an important doctrine, the *Petrine theory*, that had begun to take shape. According to this doctrine, Jesus had granted Peter a special place as his vicar on earth; Peter had chosen Rome as the seat of that power; and later bishops of Rome exercised the same authority. By A.D. 285, Peter's successors, designated as *popes* (derived from the late Latin word for "father"), were turning this claim to spiritual supremacy into active leadership in defining doctrine and prescribing discipline for Christian communities over much of the Roman Empire. And many of these communities were seeking the pope's guidance, especially in doctrinal matters; some accepted his decisions as law. A kind of second Roman Empire was being born, subdivided into well-governed local units and headed by a spiritual "emperor."

Christianity also increased its appeal, especially to the sophisticated upper classes, by developing a systematic, reasoned statement of its fundamental beliefs. This articulation of its doctrine in literary form marked a rather dramatic departure from primitive Christianity. Jesus had preached in Aramaic to an audience that was largely apart from the mainstream of Greco-Roman intellectual and literary life. The early

leaders of the new religion were quite open in their rejection of pagan culture, and thus established an anti-intellectual bias in the Christian community. However, this posture did not survive long. As soon as the Christians began to convert Gentiles, they had to employ the Greek and Latin languages and the modes of thought and expression prevailing in the Roman Empire. By the second century and more pronouncedly in the third, two particular forces spurred the Christians toward intellectualization: the need to answer the accusations of non-Christian intellectuals that the new religion was irrational, and the problem of resolving differences within the Christian ranks on the meaning of basic doctrines. The "apologists" answering the critics and the theologians defining the exact meaning of the faith borrowed heavily from Greco-Roman philosophy, especially the Platonic tradition. The most influential figures in this movement wedding Christian thought and Greco-Roman culture were two scholars from Alexandria, Clement (ca. 150–216) and Origen (ca. 185–254). Their efforts increasingly persuaded Christians that classical learning had been a preparation for the true revelation and was therefore useful in illuminating the meaning of God's word. The absorption of classical learning by Christianity had begun, to the great advantage of Christianity.

For those who were not capable of absorbing the lofty ideas of the theologians, Christianity developed a ritual that could compete on equal terms in a society accustomed to splendid religious pageants, highly emotional practices of worship, and the nonreligious spectacles provided in the circuses. To a large extent this involved adapting existing customs to Christian uses. Churches were built and decorated with art inspired by Christian beliefs. Services were conducted by a clergy in rich attire. The common meal became the center of a ritual that emphasized Christ's sacrifice (the beginning of the Mass). Prayer and music became more elaborate, and ceremonies were instituted for such events as baptism, marriage, and burial. Holidays commemorating the highlights of Jesus' life and the death of early martyrs were celebrated. Although modern men sometimes scoff at this aspect of religious life, splendid public ritual doubtless increased Christianity's appeal, especially to the vast majority of people, for whom religion was a matter more of feeling than of thought.

The Christian movement also developed a strong social consciousness. Jesus in his teachings and his life repeatedly exemplified the need for charity and kindness in dealing with others. This idea received expression in Christian practice almost from the beginning. Christians poured out their resources to help the sick, the poor, criminals, slaves, orphans, widows, and other unfortunates in society. In spite of their belief that happiness came in the hereafter, the early Christians did not close their eyes to earthly affairs.

The advance of Christianity was an amazing chapter in history. Historians have long debated whether the success of Christianity contributed to the decline of the Roman Empire. There is still no clear answer. In many ways, the Christian was a good Roman. He performed his duties as long as he was not required to deny his god. He paid his taxes and obeyed the emperor. He tried his best to help the unfortunate members of his community. He read books on Christian theology that contained huge portions of Greco-Roman philosophy. He worshiped in a fashion that bore a strong resemblance to non-Christian worship. At least the Christian was not an open rebel, bent on pulling down the established order.

In more important other ways, he was not a good Roman. He served a god who would tolerate no rivals, including Roman emperors who claimed divinity. Believing that his god disapproved of the ways of non-Christian men, he tended to avoid involvement in worldly affairs. His strong sense of sin led him to regard the world, including the Roman Empire, as hardly worth saving. His belief in the omnipotence of God and in human frailty caused him to distrust human reason and man's ability to build a paradise on earth. He thus found little that appealed to him in the basic premise of Greco-Roman civilization: the conviction that enlightened human activity could create a perfect society on earth. The Christian was a devoted, disciplined member of an organization existing independently of the Roman state. Through art, litera-

This bas-relief shows two major figures of the early Christian Church, the apostles Peter and Paul. *Photo: Alinari/EPA, Inc.*

ture, and religious services, the Church kept constantly before him a series of symbols and arguments that made him feel his separateness and his uniqueness. Every Christian convert meant one less Roman citizen in the fullest sense of the word.

What has just been said about Christianity applies to a lesser degree to the other Eastern religions of the third century. The followers of Mithra, Isis, the Unconquerable Sun, and Dionysus all found new ends to serve and gave all their energies in that service. These new religions ate away at the heart of the worldly, politically oriented thinking of Greco-Roman civilization. When men began serving these deities to gain an eternal reward, they lost interest in serving the emperor for worldly prizes.

As the third century drew to a close, Rome and all she stood for seemed destined for quick destruction. Political chaos, external assaults, economic decline, social turmoil, and desertion to foreign religions all coincided to strain the imperial structure to its limit. There was little sign of eventual recovery, for seldom had Roman leadership seemed less inspired and more selfish and brutal.

Suggested Reading

Overview of the Period A.D. 180–500

*Peter Brown, *The World of Late Antiquity, A.D. 150–750* (Harcourt Brace Jovanovich).

*A. H. M. Jones, *The Decline of the Ancient World* (Longmans). This and the preceding work are brilliant brief treatments of the decline of the Roman Empire.

Joseph Vogt, *The Decline of Rome,* trans. J. Sondheimer (1967). The best detailed analysis of the conditions that produced Rome's decline.

*C. G. Starr, *Civilization and the Caesars* (Norton). An excellent discussion of the intellectual revolution accompanying the fall of Rome.

*Donald Kagan, *Decline and Fall of the Roman Empire: Why Did It Collapse?* (Heath).

*Mortimer Chambers, *The Fall of Rome: Can It Be Explained?* (Holt). These two collections offer a variety of explanations by modern scholars of the fall of Rome.

S. Mazzarino, *The End of the Ancient World,* trans. G. Holmes (1966).

*R. M. Haywood, *The Myth of Rome's Fall* (1958). This and the preceding work provide excellent summaries of the many approaches to the collapse of the Roman world.

Third-Century Crisis

H. D. M. Parker, *History of the Roman World from A.D. 138 to 337* (2nd ed., 1958). A detailed political history.

*Franz Cumont, *Oriental Religions in Roman Paganism* (Dover). An excellent treatment of the volatile religious situation in the empire.

Rise of Christianity

Michael Grant, *The Jews in the Roman World* (1973).

*Emil Schurer, *A History of the Jewish People in the Time of Jesus* (Schocken). This and the preceding title provide a balanced treatment of a subject important in the history of early Christianity.

*Henry Chadwick, *The Early Christian Church* (Penguin).

R. A. Markus, *Christianity in the Roman World* (1974).

Robert M. Grant, *Augustus to Constantine: The Thrust of the Christian Movement in the Roman World* (1970). Either this or the preceding two titles will provide good brief accounts of the emergence of Christianity in the Roman world.

J. Daniélou and H. I. Marrou, *The First Six Hundred Years* (The Christian Centuries, Vol. I), trans. V. Cronin (1964). A longer work by two world-renowned authorities who incorporate the latest scholarship in their survey.

*W. H. Frend, *Martyrdom and Persecution in the Early Church* (Anchor). A splendid treatment of the relationship between the Roman state and the early Christians.

J. Daniélou, *The Origins of Latin Christianity* (A History of Early Christian Doctrine before the Council of Nicaea, Vol. 3), trans. David Smith and John Austin Baker (1977).

*Jaroslav Pelikan, *The Christian Tradition: A History of the Development of Doctrine.* Vol. I: *The Emergence of the Catholic Tradition (100–600)* (Phoenix). Although these two works are a formidable challenge, they provide magnificent treatments of an important aspect of Christian development.

*E. R. Dodds, *Pagan and Christian in the Age of Anxiety* (Norton).

*C. N. Cochrane, *Christianity and Classical Culture* (Galaxy). These two works treat with great insight the relationships and interactions of Christianity and classical culture.

J. A. Jungmann, *The Early Liturgy to the Time of Gregory the Great* (1959). Traces the development of Christian practices of worship from the beginning down to about A.D. 600.

J. G. Davies, *Daily Life in the Early Church* (1952). Provides fascinating glimpses of the simpler aspects of early Christian society.

Sources

New Testament. The best source of information on the primitive Church.

*Eusebius, *History of the Church from Christ to Constantine,* trans. G. A. Williamson (Augsburg). An early Christian version of the history of the primitive Church by a fourth-century author.

Early Christian Fathers, trans. C. C. Richardson (Macmillan). A collection presenting selections from the writings of early Christian thinkers.

13

THE DESTRUCTION OF THE ROMAN EMPIRE, 284-500

In A.D. 285 a general named Diocletian seized the imperial throne by force. In itself this was a repetition of what had happened during the preceding century; however, the accession of Diocletian heralded a new period. He and his most important successor, Constantine, undertook a thorough reform of the empire in an attempt to check its steady decline. Their work gave it a reprieve but did not eliminate the basic forces that were eating away the vital centers of Greco-Roman civilization. By the end of the fourth century, the empire was unable to resist the onslaught of the barbarian Germans, who during the next century smashed the empire and brought to an end a whole civilization.

1. THE REFORMS OF DIOCLETIAN AND CONSTANTINE

The way for Diocletian was paved during the years from about 260 to 284, when a series of rulers began the process of curbing the civil wars and pacifying the empire. A Dalmatian by birth and a soldier by experience, Diocletian fitted the pattern of so many previous emperors. He did have, however, considerable political talent and a clear insight into the basic problems facing the Roman world. He acted with decisiveness to restore order, stability, and prosperity to the empire.

Disturbed by the chaos resulting from the rivalry within the army for control of succession to the imperial throne and by the impossible burden imposed on a single ruler by the mounting problems of the empire, Diocletian evolved a new arrangement affecting the imperial office aimed at assuring orderly succession and shared responsibility. To himself and another he gave the title *augustus* and established for each a subordinate designated as a *caesar*. When an augustus died, his caesar would succeed to his office and immediately appoint another caesar. In theory the four co-rulers shared the imperium; in practice the burden of administering the empire was divided. It was partitioned into four parts, called *prefectures*; each augustus and caesar assumed full power to govern one of these units with Diocletian providing overall direction.

More significant was Diocletian's effort to solidify the absolute authority of the four co-rulers. He made no pretense of consulting with the Senate and the people. His pronouncements were presented as law. To create a new image, he adopted Near Eastern practices to lend a sacred character to the imperial office: He withdrew himself from public view as much as possible and established an elaborate court ritual designed to associate the ruler with divine powers in the exercise of his authority. The traditional *princeps*, first citizen, had disappeared in favor of a charismatic *dominus*, lord, whose will must be obeyed without question.

Diocletian also took practical measures to give

the co-rulers of the empire effective means of exercising the power their exalted office claimed. At each of the four courts, the bureaucracy was enlarged and the powers of its main officials were expanded to embrace more complete control over all affairs within each prefecture. To assure that the imperial will was applied effectively, the number of provinces was increased and large numbers of imperial officials were installed in each to watch over the interests of the central government on the local level. An intermediary level of administration was interposed between the provinces and the imperial court in each prefecture by the grouping of provinces into administrative units called *dioceses;* there were twelve *dioceses,* each having its own bureaucratic apparatus responsible to the augustus or caesar. This elaborate bureaucratic hierarchy gave the central government the ability to act directly and uniformly in local affairs and all but ended any meaningful role for the once active local city-state governments.

Much of Diocletian's political reorganization was inspired by his concern with the military establishment upon which the state was so dependent. The expansion and centralization of the bureaucracy were in part aimed at removing the army from the political arena where its role had been so destructive during the third century. No less important was the need to increase the military effectiveness of the army in the face of the external menace. To this end Diocletian took steps to strengthen and regularize the permanent frontier forces, whose units were settled along the frontier and assigned the task of holding back intruders. To supplement this traditional element of the army, Diocletian created a new force of mobile troops, strong in cavalry, with an ability to move quickly to contain crises arising when the settled frontier garrisons were unable to cope with attacks from external foes. This reorganization increased the size of the army considerably and raised monumental problems of recruitment and support.

The expansion of the bureaucracy and the army placed a massive new financial burden on the imperial government. Diocletian tried to meet this challenge by a major reorganization of the tax system. A survey of the empire was undertaken to identify units of land and human heads upon which a uniform set of taxes could be levied. At the same time, the central government began to impose upon the key productive elements of society a system of requisition which extracted from them crucial services and products needed by the state to sustain the courts, the armies, and the bureaucrats. To enforce this taxation and requisition system, Diocletian was forced to issue edicts freezing peasants, bureaucrats, artisans, traders, soldiers, and many others in their occupations. A kind of hereditary caste system was being shaped which required each Roman citizen to live his life for one purpose—service to the state. As a further measure to stabilize the economy and control the terrible inflation that had plagued society throughout the third century, Diocletian sought to fix prices on a wide range of commodities and services directly related to the operation of the bureaucracy and the army.

Diocletian's expanding autocracy sought to focus men's minds on the state through the restoration of religious unity. His reign was marked by a major effort to rally the populace around a worship of the old deities, whose agent the divine emperor was. This policy brought him into conflict with the increasingly numerous and confident Christians who steadfastly refused to make obeisance to these gods or the state that honored them. Their position was intolerable within Diocletian's frame of reference, and a series of punitive decrees in 303 and 304 made death the penalty for defiance. His assault on the Christians was the most serious threat they ever faced from the Roman government. They were to survive and triumph, but Diocletian's persecution symbolized the degree to which religion had come to be viewed as the sustaining force of the new autocratic regime.

In 305 the aged and ill Diocletian abdicated his power. Although contemporaries, particularly Christians, judged him harshly, his strong measures had proved effective. A well-organized administrative machine restored internal order; a strong army shored up the fragile frontier defenses; and an almighty emperor stood as surety to a troubled society. Diocletian had established the pattern of government that was to prevail for the entire empire for nearly two centuries and for some parts of it much longer.

Only one of Diocletian's reforms was a signal failure—his elaborate succession system. His abdication resulted in another series of civil wars reminiscent of the civil wars of the third century. They finally ended when one of the contenders, Constantine, established control over the entire empire by military force. Constantine was a worthy successor to Diocletian and carried on most of his policies. He strengthened the armies, tightened bureaucratic controls, further improved the financial machinery, and took more power into his own hands. Through his efforts the absolutist, bureaucratic, militaristic state envisaged by Diocletian—a dominate—was made a reality.

Constantine added important elements to the new order. Most significant was a new religious policy officially proclaimed in 313, when he and his co-emperor issued the Edict of Milan, granting religious toleration to all in the empire. The edict meant the end of the terrible persecution of Christians that had begun in 303–304 as well as legal recognition of Christianity. Behind the decree was an event of immense psychological importance: the conversion of Constantine himself. During the decisive battle of his career, in 311, he had had a vision that promised him victory if he would display the cross as his insignia. He did this and smashed his enemy. Although in fact he was not baptized until just before his death in 337, after the Edict of Milan Constantine gave every indication that he was intent on promoting Christian causes. He poured out money to build churches. He drew clergymen into the councils of state as advisers and extended a variety of special privileges to them. His legislation increasingly reflected Christian teachings in matters such as slavery and marriage. True, he did not openly attack other religions, but he treated them in a way that little encouraged them. Every sign pointed in one direction: that Christianity was the favored religion and that the empire was becoming a Christian state. Contemporary Christians hailed Constantine's conversion as a triumphant fulfillment of God's promise; their enthusiasm laid

This colossal head of Constantine, commissioned by the emperor himself and now standing in the courtyard of the Palazzo dei Conservatòrio in Rome, succeeds in conveying the majesty and power of the emperor. But it also indicates a departure from the traditional realism in portraiture for symbolism and etherialization. *Photo: Robert Emmett Bright/Rapho/ Photo Researchers, Inc.*

the basis for his enduring status as a great man in history. Perhaps his motives were not totally religious. Constantine certainly stood to gain politically by seeking the support of a considerable number of his subjects who had proved their mettle by withstanding Diocletian's persecutions. If he could win their allegiance and support by becoming the servant of their god and could turn the empire and the emperor into agencies seeking to realize what the Christians believed their god willed for humanity, then perhaps he could begin to count on a solid nucleus of supporters around which to build a unified empire obedient to an emperor who was God's chief servant. This was not a cynical manipulation of religion. Constantine was a man of his age, powerfully drawn to religion and especially to Christianity, not the least as a result of the influence exercised over him by his Christian mother, Helen. He was indeed the first Christian emperor both by conviction and in practice. The significance of his conversion lies in his yoking of the Roman Empire to the service of the world view of the Christian community in the interests of strengthening the empire and the Christians. His action was a momentous event in world history.

Equally momentous was Constantine's decision to build a new capital at the ancient city of Byzantium (which he renamed Constantinople). This action not only created a rival to "old" Rome but also shifted the center of imperial power to the East. The great change was no mere autocratic whim. Rome had been declining in importance in imperial affairs. As early as the second century, men of non-Roman origin had been elevated to the imperial throne, and their local attachments diminished Rome's aura. Also, during the third century the problems of defending the frontiers revealed that Rome was badly located strategically. Diocletian's reorganization of the empire into four prefectures led to the emergence of new centers of political authority. Diocletian established his own headquarters at Nicomedia in Asia Minor, while his co-rulers established their courts in Milan, Sirmium in the Balkans, and Trier in the Rhineland area, choices dictated primarily by military considerations.

In 324, the year that he won the final battle for supremacy, Constantine began construction of his new capital; it was dedicated in 330. He chose the site in part for very practical reasons. It was admirably situated for defense by land and sea. From it the imperial forces had easy access to the most vulnerable and hard-pressed frontiers — the Danube region and the Eastern provinces. The new city was close to the great centers of wealth in the East, whence came the chief resources of the imperial government. And it was situated where Christian strength was greatest, a matter of considerable importance to an emperor identifying himself with a religious minority. Aside from these practical aims, Constantine wished to be free from the restrictive traditions of republicanism and paganism that were entrenched in old Rome as threats to his autocracy and new religious policy.

The full impact of the founding of Constantinople was not immediately obvious. Rome still remained an important city upon which Constantine showered favors, not the least of which was a great Christian church built in honor of St. Peter on Vatican Hill at a site where the bones of the first pope were believed to be buried. Yet the relocation did have a powerful psychological impact on contemporaries. To many who cherished ancient values, it seemed that Constantine had turned the world around, allowing the East to surpass the West, the Greek to predominate over the Latin. And in the near future, when outsiders threatened to conquer both East and West, the rulers in Constantinople chose to defend "new" Rome and let "old" Rome and the West fall victim to the barbarians.

2. THE LULL BEFORE THE STORM

The vast reorganization of imperial forces carried out by Diocletian and Constantine appeared to have saved the empire: The era from Constantine's death in 337 to the end of the reign of Theodosius (379–395) was one of relative calm and order. There was a fairly regular hereditary succession of emperors, with little civil strife. Agriculture, trade, and industry seemed to hold their own, albeit under rigid state control. Society, carefully manipulated, appeared even content. The Roman political genius seemed again to have saved the civilized world, as in the days of Augustus.

Yet the old sicknesses persisted. There was no real economic recovery; in fact, the absolutist, militarized, bureaucratic state consumed wealth on a scale that depressed the economy and impoverished the empire's population. The burden of supporting the state destroyed the local aristocracies and oppressed the peasantry. Civic responsibility eroded, making it ever more difficult to muster support for the state. The decline of civic spirit took an especially heavy toll in the army, where increasingly the imperial government had to depend on barbarian Germans to fill the ranks where Roman citizens had once served. Whether this barbarian army could be trusted became a more pressing issue because the menace of outsiders along the frontiers did not disappear. While the cost of sustaining the state increased, the quality of the government deteriorated as a consequence of corruption and inefficiency emerging in a bureaucracy no longer responsible to anyone except the emperors whom they served. The imperial policy of favoring Christianity alienated those who still placed trust in the pagan religious tradition. Pagan resentment surfaced during the reign of Julian (360–363), called the "Apostate" by the Christians because he repudiated Christianity and sought to replace it with a restored pagan "church." His effort failed, but it kept alive a fundamental schism in imperial society and thought.

The Julian reaction points up the fact that Christianity did not fulfill the role Constantine expected of it in unifying the state and arousing patriotic fervor. Christianity did continue its triumphant march to dominance, culminating when Theodosius made it the state religion and outlawed all others, but during the fourth century the movement was rent with internal disagreements that promoted disorders. Even during the reign of Constantine, the Christians divided into two warring factions, the Arians and the Orthodox, over the question of the Trinity: The Arians made God the Son subordinate to God the Father, denying the absolute divinity of Christ; the Orthodox insisted that the Son was co-equal with the Father and that the two persons, plus the Holy Spirit, formed a unity. An attempt to settle this quarrel was made at the Council of Nicea in 325. Churchmen from all over the empire met under the auspices of Constantine and agreed on the Nicene Creed, which accepted the Orthodox definition of the nature of Christ. However, the quarrel continued to rage for a century, involving the imperial government as did other "heresies" that divided the Christian community and the empire. Then too, the Constantinian subordination of the Christian Church to the imperial government generated active resistance to imperial domination of Christian life, providing still another source of contention and struggle. In a larger sense, Christianity failed to supply the

vitalizing force in the "new" empire; it was a movement with its own ends and strengths, not easily bent to other purposes.

All these signs of deteriorating imperial strength and internal friction were extremely ominous, for a crisis was in the making as the fourth century drew to a close. Its source lay in Central Europe, an area beyond the control of the imperial regime, and involved the Germanic barbarians, whose pressure on Rome's defenses had been constant throughout the fourth century. About 370 a wild horde of Asiatic nomads, the Huns, suddenly swept out of the East across southern Russia. When they approached the Black Sea area, they encountered two settled Germanic nations, the Ostrogoths and the Visigoths. The former were quickly overpowered. The terror-stricken Visigoths begged permission to migrate across the Danube into Roman territory in the Balkans. Their request was granted. The Visigoths were allowed to keep their own king and were promised lands in return for military service. When the imperial government failed to provide for their needs, the Visigoths revolted. The emperor Valens marched against them but suffered a smashing defeat at Adrianople in 378. Rome now had a barbarian nation within her boundaries, a nation that she could neither control nor destroy.

3. THE BARBARIAN GERMANS

What and who were these people known as Germans? They have always been designated as "barbarians," a term that is proper if used to characterize the simplicity of their institutions and culture compared with those of the Roman world. The basic Germanic political institution was the *tribe*, composed of a number of *clans* and headed by a *tribal chief*. Kinship bonds were especially powerful, and therefore heads of clans played a vital role in shaping the chief's decisions. Freemen in the clans had a political voice through an *assembly*. The tribal government concerned itself mainly with war and worship, the clans deciding most other matters on the basis of a powerfully entrenched system of customary law. The Germans were primarily hunters and herders, although by the third century A.D., they were beginning to turn to agriculture. In religion, the Germans were polytheistic; they worshiped especially the forces of nature. There was no written language; what literature they had, mostly stories about the deeds of gods and heroes, was transmitted orally.

But the Germans were not a "backward" people. By the fourth century their society was changing in significant ways. Small tribal groups were being unified into *nations* ruled over by elected kings enjoying considerable powers, which made it easier for a single ruler to mount heavy attacks on the Roman frontier and more difficult for the Romans to play small group against small group. Within Germanic society there was also developing a unique institution — the war band (*comitatus*) — composed of tested warriors united by pledges made under oath to follow a military chief. These warriors became a kind of aristocracy, practicing war as a way of life and gaining tremendous proficiency in fighting. Also, Germanic society was moving rapidly toward a more advanced agricultural economy, but tillable land was short in the heavy forests of Central Europe. As a consequence, many nations and tribes moved south toward the rich lands of the Roman world. Moreover, agricultural economy was transforming society by creating an aristocracy of landowners and bringing elements of the population into economic dependence on them. These changing conditions made Germanic society dynamic, open to foreign influences, mobile, adaptable.

Between Germans and Romans there was no deep-seated hatred at the moment of their decisive encounter. The Germans were admirers of Greco-Roman civilization, desiring nothing more than to settle within the empire and to become "civilized" so as to enjoy its fruits — especially its material wealth. The Romans on their side respected the Germans for their splendid physical features, their fighting prowess, and their alleged moral excellence. From at least the time of Augustus they had permitted the Germans to cross the frontier as long as their movement could be controlled. Large numbers had entered the empire as soldiers and farmers and had quickly become Romanized; many rose to high places in Roman society. Influences from

the Roman world also sifted across the frontiers into the Germanic. For example, during the fourth century many Goths were converted to Christianity by Ulfilas, himself a Goth educated in Constantinople. Ulfilas provided a Gothic version of the Bible for his converts, a feat that required the creation of a written language.

It would seem that the barbarian Germans were thus moving peacefully into the mainstream of Greco-Roman civilization and might in the long run have been completely transformed, as some were before A.D. 400. However, the Romans had to be able to prevent too great a flood of Germans from pouring into the empire at once and to dominate those who did enter. Was the Visigothic victory at Adrianople in 378 a sign that Rome had lost that ability? If so, the very existence of the empire would be at stake.

4. THE BARBARIAN INVASIONS AND THE FALL OF THE EMPIRE

The crisis caused by the Visigothic victory was faced by the last great emperor of the united empire, Theodosius. He kept the Visigoths in check by establishing them as *foederati* (allies), assigning them lands in return for their supplying troops for the Roman army. He ensured that they abided by the arrangement and succeeded in confining them to the Balkan area. At the same time he worked valiantly to sustain internal order and to safeguard the frontiers.

His passing in 395 spelled the beginning of the end of the uneasy calm lying over the empire since the time of Diocletian and Constantine. Theodosius bequeathed his office to two sons, who were assigned the Western and Eastern sections of the empire respectively. Neither had much ability, and both allowed the direction of affairs to fall into the hands of powerful generals, most of whom were Germanic in origin and whose power rested primarily on the loyalty of their Germanic troops. This situation set off a series of power struggles in which the generals sought to manipulate imperial policy for their own advantage.

Its directive force caught up in ceaseless intrigue, the empire lost control over the Germanic

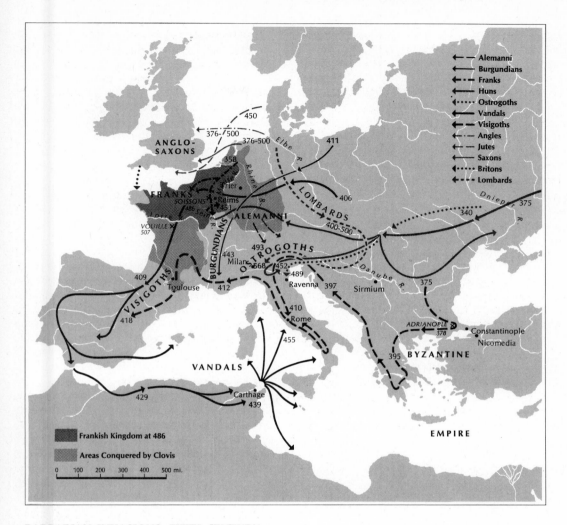

BARBARIAN INVASIONS, FIFTH CENTURY

hordes pressing in on it. As the fifth century opened, the Visigoths, led by a capable king named Alaric, were playing a dangerous game of selling their services alternately to the emperors in the West and the East. Eventually they turned against the West, having been promised by the emperor in Constantinople whatever new lands they conquered. Their attacks on Italy necessitated the recall of troops from the British, Rhine, and Danube frontiers, but to no avail. In 410 they captured and sacked Rome—the first time in eight centuries that the city had suffered such a fate. In the meantime, other Germans poured across the undefended frontiers into the heart of the empire.

The invaders were primarily interested in finding lands, not in destroying Roman government and society. The effect of their assault was, however, the dismemberment of the Western part of the empire. Wherever the Germans settled, their kings and warrior nobles became the real rulers, although they often maintained the fiction that they were allies of the Roman government. As a consequence, during the fifth century a series of Germanic kingdoms were founded on Roman soil to replace the unified imperial government. Angles, Saxons, and Jutes wiped out Roman outposts in Britain and established several petty kingdoms. The Vandals crossed Gaul into Spain; from there, their one great king, Gaiseric, led them into North Africa, where a formidable Vandal kingdom arose. It soon developed enough sea power to allow the Vandals to pillage Rome in 455. After a brief sojourn in Italy, the Visigoths settled in southern Gaul. The Burgundians created a kingdom in southeastern Gaul straddling the Rhone Valley. Late in the fifth century the Franks, led by Clovis, a ruthless, able king, seized most of Gaul as their base of power, drove the Visigoths into Spain, and overran the Burgundian kingdom. Italy fell victim to the Germans when the Ostrogoths captured it in 493 and established their king, Theodoric, as ruler. The ferocious Huns under Attila created a huge kingdom north of the Danube from which they harassed the East and then invaded the West in 451–452. Attila's Western invasion was repulsed by a coalition of Roman and German forces. Germanic tribes repeatedly ravaged the territory south of the Danube during the fifth century and hurled themselves at the Eastern provinces. Unable to bypass Constantinople, they were denied the conquest of the East. Despite this failure, the history of the fifth century really belonged to the Germans; they had won the West.

The magnitude of the Germanic victory is revealed by the slow dissolution of the imperial government in the West. Some of the generals serving the weak emperors fought valiantly to check the invasions and negotiated desperately to turn German against German. Each Germanic nation was usually persuaded to sign a treaty with the Roman government to accept *foederatus* status and nominal Roman overlordship. In fact, however, Rome's allies became independent in the areas assigned to them. The Roman bureaucracy broke down, imperial income dwindled, and the authority of the successors of Augustus disappeared. By 476 the political realities in the West were officially recognized. A German general, Odoacer, deposed the last Western emperor and turned the insignia of imperial office over to the emperor in Constantinople with the advice that there was no longer need for a ruler in the West. In theory, this reunited the empire under the sole authority of the emperor in Constantinople; in practice, the Eastern emperor had virtually no control over the West. The West belonged to the Germans by right of conquest.

5. THE FRUITS OF INVASION

The Germanic invasions of the fifth century affected every aspect of life in the empire, especially the Western part, in a way that spelled the end of Greco-Roman civilization.

The most obvious and important by-product of the invasions was the destruction of imperial government in the West. Gone were the mighty emperors, their courts, their law, their public projects, their armies, their bureaucrats. And the new masters of the West, the Germanic kings and their warriors, were not fitted to take their place. Political chaos settled over the West.

Economically, the invasion was followed by increasing impoverishment. The new overlords were primarily interested in land, and reversion to an agricultural economy was rapid. Cities suffered an especially disastrous decline, some of them shrinking to a fraction of their old population and most of them being stripped of their functions as cultural, administrative, and economic centers. Their decline meant the end of the urban aristocracies that had sustained Greco-Roman civilization in the West. While some of the powerful Roman landlords lost everything to victorious German warriors, most succeeded in retaining and even enlarging their holdings. Peasants were glad to serve great landowners in return for whatever protection the landowners, be they German or Roman, could offer; as a consequence, the ranks of the dependent peasantry swelled everywhere in the West. Most of the large estates sought self-sufficiency, with the result that the Western empire broke up into thousands of tiny self-contained economic units that had less and less interchange with each other. Trade was drastically reduced, and manufacturing centered more and more in the isolated large estates. All these developments drove standards of living inexorably down toward subsistence level.

The German rulers tried to absorb Roman civilization by learning Latin, patronizing artists and writers, and adopting Roman dress and manners. But the new leaders could do no better than imitate, and all too often their basic barbarism broke through the thin veneer of civilized life. Educated Romans in Italy, Gaul, Spain, and Africa continued to read their classics, study philosophy, send their children to schools, and even write. But their efforts were to no point; no longer was there an opportunity for the cultivated man to serve the government. The cities, long the centers of civilized life, were dead. The agricultural population, increasingly isolated and barbarized, was too provincial to uphold the artistic and intellectual traditions of the old order. The content and spirit of those traditions related to few of the real issues of the new day, and thus were cut off from the vital interaction between the world of learning and art and the world of practical life.

Finally, the Germanic invasions had created a division between East and West. The new political order in the West was markedly different from the imperial regime still surviving in the East. The simple agricultural economy developing in the West set that world apart from the more stable and sophisticated East, undisturbed by the terrors of the invasion period. The Mediterranean community was ruptured; that fact alone was fatal to Greco-Roman civilization.

We must, however, be cautious in assigning the Germanic invasions too great a significance. Destruction of life and property was not excessive, and in most cases the Germans and Romans settled down peacefully side by side. The conquerors were not numerous enough to affect the ethnic composition of the population or the language. The disintegration of the imperial government, economic decline, cultural stagnation, and division of the Mediterranean world had begun before the Germans invaded the empire en masse. What the invasions did was to accelerate these trends and make them irreversible.

6. CHRISTIANITY IN THE LATE EMPIRE

In the face of events bringing virtual ruin to the structure of late imperial society, Christianity showed great resilience and emerged from the ordeal stronger than ever. In some ways this is surprising, given that the fourth century, a glorious period in Christian history, closely identified the Church with imperial society. Great numbers of converts were made from all levels of society, and Christian leaders advanced to prominent positions in it. The wealth of the Christian establishment increased tremendously. The Church as a visible organization had taken its place as a prominent feature of Greco-Roman society. The fourth-century Roman government gave powerful support to these developments so that the triumphant Church had become to a considerable degree dependent on the rulers. All these successes meant that by 400 the Roman Empire had truly become a Christian Roman Empire, a fact recognized by Theodosius when he legally designated Christianity the state religion.

However, success brought new and serious problems. The avalanche of converts, no longer faced with the terrible possibility that baptism might spell martyrdom, diluted the spiritual fervor of pre-Constantinian Christianity. Discipline within the growing Christian ranks became more difficult. Wealth and power turned the heads of Christian leaders toward dubious ends; a hostile Christian could even describe a late fourth-century bishop of Rome as a "ladies' ear tickler." The influx of pagan ideas and practices with the many inadequately instructed and spiritually lax converts threatened to obliterate Christian practices of worship and doctrines, while generating heresies that divided Christian from Christian. Perhaps the gravest danger facing Christians was control of the Church by emperors faithful to the Constantinian view of the Christian establishment as an instrument to use in the interests of the state. In brief, the advance of Christianity to a central position threatened to deprive the movement of its uniqueness, its zeal, and its sense of mission.

The Christian community of the fourth cen-

The sixth-century church of S. Apollinare in Ravenna is a basilica, an adaptation of a Roman architectural style. The central hall (nave) is supported by columns, and its small, high windows are cut above the roof of the side aisles. *Photo: G. E. Kidder Smith*

tury proved capable of meeting these challenges, of "reforming" itself to meet the realities of the time. One response was the strengthening of the powers of the clergy, especially the bishops, over individual churches. These powers were used to define Christian behavior and modes of worship more vigorously and to compel Christians to obey the rapidly evolving Christian "law." A major beneficiary of this development was the bishop of Rome, on whom the fourth-century emperors showered wealth and relied to formulate dogma they hoped to impose on the whole empire as a means of combating the divisive heresies of the age. The popes responded by asserting their authority more positively.

During the fourth century Christianity was also able to recapture its spiritual vision. This was the feat of a new breed of men who called themselves "athletes of Christ"—the *monks*. *Monasticism* was born in the late third and early fourth centuries in the deserts of Egypt, to which pious men fled to seek perfection through prayer and mortification of the flesh, inspired by Jesus' command to leave all worldly things behind and sacrifice themselves for him. The spiritual heroics of the desert fathers, exemplified by Anthony, electrified the Christian world. Soon the individual hermits began to gather into communities, or monasteries, and accept rules, or codes of spiritual exercises for achieving perfection. By 400, monasticism had spread over much of the Roman world and created a new model of the ideal Christian.

In the face of state efforts to control religious life, many fourth-century prelates began to articulate statements that sought to define the limits of imperial authority and religious freedom. Some even argued that Christian society was more important than secular and therefore must be supreme. As the concept of the independence of the Church took shape, it spurred the problem of where ultimate authority in the Church lay. More and more Christians agreed that the bishop of Rome, Peter's successor, was the spiritual leader of the Christian world.

Perhaps the most significant success of the Christian community was its assumption of cultural leadership in the Roman world through an outburst of creative energy. Church building provided one of the chief outlets for the talents of architects, sculptors, and painters, who developed new modes of conveying the Christian message by appropriating the classical artistic tradition for Christian purposes. Some of the most inspired poetry of the age flowed from the pens of Christians. But the jewel of the period was the theological writing of a remarkable group of intellectuals called the *church fathers,* especially the Greeks Athanasius, Basil, Gregory of Nyssa, and Gregory Nazianzus. The fruit of their labors was a massive body of literature destined to provide intellectual guidelines for centuries to come. Beginning with a deep faith, they borrowed boldly and creatively from the content and methods of Greco-Roman philosophy to build a consistent, logical, articulate statement of Christian belief. In the process they literally redefined human values and reoriented the end of human existence toward the service of God. They effected an intellectual revolution which overpowered the Greco-Roman world view.

A description of one of their number especially important in Western thought will illustrate the role of the church fathers. He was Augustine (354–430), bishop of Hippo, in North Africa, two of whose works are especially significant. His *Confessions* recounts the spiritual pilgrimage of an educated Roman through most of the philosophical systems and religions of the ancient world to Christianity. The work not only argues the failure of Greco-Roman philosophy and religion but presents faith as the only adequate response to life. Even more influential was his *City of God,* written to answer pagan charges that the Visigothic sack of Rome in 410 succeeded because the gods were angry at the Romans for becoming Christians. Augustine sought to demonstrate that this catastrophe was only a step in the unfolding of God's plan for the universe. God, he said, had ordained two cities, that of God and that of men. The true City of God exists only in the other world; membership will be awarded to men who serve the true faith on earth. In this world is the sinful City of Men, of which the Roman Empire was a part. The coming of Christ had established an earthly embodiment of the City of God in the form of the Christian Church. Rome must now pass away so that men could give their allegiance to the more perfect society. Not despair, but joy should greet the fall of Rome, since that event was a preordained step toward a better world planned by the will of God. Almost immediately, Augustine's interpretation of the cosmos and of history replaced the several world views offered by classical philosophers.

Others worked in more practical ways that supplemented Augustine's intellectual effort. For example, Ambrose (ca. 340–397), bishop of Milan, set forth the basic principles of Christian morality persuasively. Jerome employed his learning to produce a Latin translation of the Bible called the Vulgate, which ensured that Latin would survive as the language of the Church and as a link to classical civilization.

Armed with this vitality, the Church survived the ordeal of the Germanic invasions and the fall of the imperial government amazingly well and emerged the most potent force in society, especially in the West. In many parts of the West, bishops replaced imperial officials as keepers of order, administrators of justice, and caretakers of the unfortunate. Pope Leo I (440–461), for example, served as the virtual governor of Rome and as a forceful diplomat defending the city against the attacks of the Vandals and the Huns. By 500 most of the Germans had been converted to Christianity, and their kings had begun to lend their support to the Church and lean on it for assistance in their efforts to rule. As the focus of life shifted toward rural centers, the Church followed and made considerable progress in incorporating a heretofore neglected peasantry into Christian society. As cultural life collapsed, the monasteries provided havens for study. By 500, the Church loomed as a pillar of order, stability, and strength. At least in the West, it had fallen heir to the leadership of society.

Suggested Reading

Political, Economic, and Social Developments

The general history of the period covered in this chapter is treated in the works of Jones, Vogt, and Parker, cited in Chapter 12. The following works examine more specialized aspects of the period:

Peter Brown, *The Making of Later Antiquity* (1978).

*Jacob Burchkhardt, *The Age of Constantine the Great* (Anchor).

J. H. Holland, *Constantine the Great* (1971).

Ramsay MacMullen, *Constantine* (1969). Three excellent biographies of a pivotal figure; the Burchkhardt study is a classic.

*A. H. M. Jones, *Constantine and the Conversion of Europe* (Collier).

A. Alföldi, *The Conversion of Constantine and Pagan Rome* (1948).

N. H. Baynes, *Constantine the Great and the Christian Church* (1930). This and the preceding three titles treat the crucial matter of the conversion of Constantine from a variety of perspectives.

*John W. Eadie, ed., *The Conversion of Constantine* (Holt, Rinehart and Winston). A collection of materials reflecting ancient and modern interpretations of the significance of Constantine's conversion.

Church History

The major developments in church history are traced in the works of Chadwick, Davies, Grant, Markus, and Daniélou and Marrou, cited in Chapter 12. The following works treat particular matters important in the period:

H. von Campenhausen, *The Fathers of the Greek Church,* trans. S. Godman (1959), and *The Fathers of the Latin Church,* trans. M. Hoffmann (1964). Clear, accurate summaries of the efforts and of the achievements of Christian thinkers during the patristic age.

D. J. Chitty, *The Desert a City* (1966). A colorful presentation of the origins of monasticism.

*Peter Brown, *Augustine of Hippo: A Biography* (University of California). A model biography of a key figure.

F. Dvornik, *Early Christian and Byzantine Political Philosophy* (1966). A good introduction to the issues of church-state relationships in the third and fourth centuries.

The Germans

*Francis Owen, *The Germanic People* (Collier).

E. A. Thompson, *The Early Germans* (1965). This and the preceding title give a balanced picture of the nature of Germanic society prior to the invasions.

E. A. Thompson, *A History of Attila and the Huns* (1948). A good study of a fascinating product of the age and his work.

Lucien Musset, *The Germanic Invasions. The Making of Europe,* trans. Edward and Columba James (1975). A balanced treatment of a disputed subject.

Sources

*Tacitus, *On Britain and Germany,* trans. H. Mattingly (Penguin). A view of the Germans from the perspective of a second-century Roman historian.

*Augustine, *Confessions,* trans. E. B. Pusey (Collier).

*Augustine, *City of God,* trans. M. Dodds, 2 vols. (Hafner). These two works will provide an excellent introduction to the seminal ideas of the patristic age.

Sidonius Appollinaris, *Letters,* trans. O. M. Dalton, 2 vols. (1915). Provides a revealing picture of conditions in the West in the era of the Germanic invasions.

Athanasius, *The Life of St. Anthony,* trans. R. T. Meyer (1950). This biography will help to capture the spirit of early monasticism.

Retrospect

At some risk of raising objections on a much disputed question, we can assign the end of Greco-Roman civilization to the years between the deposition of the last Roman emperor in the West (A.D. 476) and the capture of Italy by the Ostrogoths (A.D. 493). The Romans had created a magnificent political order that had brought peace, well-being, and concord to some 50 million people. Why had it not lasted? Within that community an enlightened, sophisticated, esthetically pleasing culture had spread to supply men with a sense of direction, a set of values, and occasion for pleasure. Why was it not sufficient? Any answer to these questions is apt to convince the reader that he has been witness to a great tragedy—almost Greek in character—to be lamented still as it was by some men of the time.

But was the collapse of classical civilization a tragedy? We might conclude that Greco-Roman civilization had become a prison for the human spirit by the third and fourth centuries. Autocratic government, regimented economy, and militarized society may have brought peace and order and security, but the price was heavy. The traditional cultural values seemed to be empty forms from which flowed no inspiration capable of breeding new thought or fresh expression.

The emergence of the Germanic barbarians as a potent force in society may from one perspective have been destructive, but from another, their presence infused society with an element of vitality. Here were fresh doers, learners, experimenters. The rapid rise of Christianity accentuated modes of thought and morality that seemed to lack the sophistication of the concepts governing classical civilization. Again, however, Christianity represented a fresh breeze in the Greco-Roman prison, a new vision of man and his destiny that provided a sense of direction and a reason for acting. The barbarians and the Christians held the key to the future. The promise of man did not die with Greco-Roman civilization.

Moreover, to speak of the fall of that civilization is to utter only a partial truth. When the Roman Empire collapsed, it left behind monuments that would serve as guides to its heirs — a magnificent literature, a great art, model forms of government, a legal system, economic institutions and techniques, moral precepts, philosophical ideals, scientific knowledge, and countless other achievements. In a sense, Greece and Rome did not really die. Little that has happened in the Western world since 476 or 493 can be understood outside its Greco-Roman background. We are all children of the classical world.

IV

The Early Middle Ages
500-1000
Struggle Toward a New Order

The fall of the Roman Empire ended the unity that had long joined together the peoples living around the fringes of the Mediterranean Sea. During the centuries that followed Rome's fall, three new cultural communities emerged, each absorbing part of the Roman world and each extending beyond its boundaries into "new" territory. One of these communities was the Byzantine cultural world with its center in Constantinople, its heartland in Asia Minor and the Greek peninsula, and its frontier in Slavic Europe. The second was the Moslem or Islamic cultural world, originating in the Arabian Desert but ultimately establishing its heartland in the belt of land stretching from Mesopotamia around the Fertile Crescent to Egypt—those very lands where higher civilization first emerged more than 4,000 years earlier. Its frontiers extended eastward to India and westward across North Africa to Spain. The third new civilization was created by the Germanic invaders of the Roman Empire. Gaul and Italy formed its center, but its influence eventually reached into modern Germany, Great Britain, Scandinavia, Spain, and the western portions of the Slavic world.

The basic features of these three civilizations were fashioned during the years extending from 500 to 1000. This was an era that has often been dismissed as a "dark age." This appellation was invented by modern historians who have chosen to give undue attention to the confusion, the false starts, and the human misery that marked the birth pangs of these three new cultures. Such a view must not hide the fact that seminal forces were at work in this period generating new institutions and ideas in each society, forces so powerful that still to this day they set apart from each other the peoples who inhabit the areas embraced by these three culture worlds.

The dynamism of this age came from various sources. In all three societies powerful vestiges of Greco-Roman civilization persisted to shape the essential features of the new civilizations. In two of them—the Moslem and the Western European worlds—new peoples supplied a leavening agent. But perhaps it was religion that furnished the chief animating force in this period. Two new universal religions dominated its history and provided the matrix within which old cultural values and new peoples interacted. Christianity finally achieved full power after a somewhat painful period of gestation and became the motor force in the Byzantine Empire and in Germanic Western Europe. Islam, bursting suddenly on the world and becoming established almost immediately as a dominant force by its warlike Arab adherents, affected the destiny of a vast area reaching across southern Asia and North Africa from the Indus Valley to the Atlantic. A meaningful comprehension of the period consequently demands careful attention to the role of religion as a dynamic, creative force in shaping the character of civilizations.

Two of the new civilizations—Byzantine and Moslem—had their centers in the eastern territories of the old Roman Empire. These lands, comprising the most affluent and the most culturally sophisticated part of the Roman Empire, provided a richer seed bed for development than did the Germanic West. As a consequence, Byzantine and Moslem cultures were more precocious and more vigorous in their youth than was the Germanic West. Since their very success in these formative centuries moved them into their own special place in history, separate from the mainstream of Western civilization, we can only give them limited attention—a choice that is unwarranted in terms of their achievements but necessary in terms of the focus selected for our study.

1. BYZANTINE CIVILIZATION: ORIGINS AND HISTORY, 395–1100

From one perspective the "fall" of the Roman Empire involved a choice on the part of the late Roman imperial regime. Its leaders simply surrendered the western part of the Roman Empire to the Germans and retreated to the richer, more populous eastern territories which could be defended against the Germans. This choice permitted the emperors who ruled in the East after the death of Theodosius in 395 to sustain the basic features of the late Roman imperial society and

14

HEIRS TO THE ROMAN EMPIRE: THE BYZANTINE AND MOSLEM EMPIRES

to claim that the Roman Empire lived on. After the deposition of the last western emperor in 476, the rulers in Constantinople claimed suzerainty over the entire ancient empire, including the newly founded Germanic states in the West. In fact, these claims were a fiction. Within the surviving Roman Empire, now constrained to the East, there emerged signs of transformation that pointed toward a new civilization differing markedly from the old classical civilization. This new society is called "Byzantine" to distinguish it from its Greco-Roman predecessor. The watershed between the two worlds can perhaps be placed in the reign of the Emperor Justinian (527–565), often called the last Roman and the first Byzantine emperor.

Justinian's claim to be called the last Roman stems from the central focus of his policy: a major effort to restore the unity of the old empire. To this end, he set out to reestablish imperial authority over the western provinces held by the Germans, a task that involved him in war for the greater part of his reign. Although his effort was brilliant, his success was partial. The best his armies could do was to recapture North Africa from the Vandals, Italy from the Ostrogoths, and a small strip of southeastern Spain from the Visigoths. Gaul, most of Spain, England, and the Danube provinces remained in German hands beyond his reach. More significantly, the price for these limited conquests was

great, for Justinian's western policy left the eastern frontiers exposed to the Sassanian Persians. By the end of his reign, it was clear that imperial resources must be concentrated in the East if areas crucial to the survival of the empire were to be held. The Germanic West would have to be abandoned.

The forces that worked to concentrate the attention of the surviving remnant of the Roman Empire on the East also promoted the development of a system of government unique to the age. Justinian worked actively to perfect the system of absolute monarchy originated by Diocletian and Constantine. An important part of this effort led him to commission a corps of legal experts to organize the complex strands of Roman law into a single code. While this great monument of legal science, known as the *Corpus juris civilis,* was destined to influence considerably the development of law in the future, it served Justinian's age to legitimatize a highly centralized, absolutist government that became a unique feature of the Byzantine world.

Justinian's reign was also marked by important religious developments. Following the trend already established by Constantine and his successors, Justinian claimed a major role as leader of religious life. Particularly troublesome in his time were several violent disputes over dogmatic issues. The emperor sought repeatedly to settle these quarrels by imperial edicts which he

These nearly contemporary representations of Emperor Justinian and Empress Theodora, executed as mosaics in the church of San Vitale in Ravenna ca. 574, convey a sense of the majesty that surrounded the imperial office. *Photos: Justinian, The Granger Collection; Theodora, Scala/EPA, Inc.*

hoped would restore religious unity but which had the effect of implanting the idea of a Byzantine church whose organization and doctrines were dependent on the authority of the autocratic, semi-sacred emperor and whose membership coincided with the boundaries of the Byzantine Empire.

Justinian's reign also witnessed the birth of a distinctive Byzantine culture. That culture was oriented particularly toward the assimilation of the ancient Hellenic component of classical culture with Christian ideology. Into that basic mix were incorporated cultural influences from the Near East, especially from Persia. The great symbol of this new culture was the magnificent church of Santa Sophia built by Justinian in Constantinople.

Byzantine political history from the reign of Justinian until the First Crusade (1095) was dominated by one theme: the constant military and diplomatic struggles of the Byzantine state to fend off a succession of attacks from aggressive outsiders, especially from the east and north. These assaults reduced the Byzantine state in size and caused modifications in its internal structure that accentuated its uniqueness among its neighbors.

Hardly was Justinian dead when the first blow was struck. In 568 the Lombards, a Germanic nation, invaded Italy and seized a considerable portion of the peninsula, leaving only Venice, a corridor of land from Rome to Ravenna, and southern Italy under Byzantine control. Little could be done to stop this assault because the Byzantine Empire was facing a greater menace elsewhere. Late in the sixth century the Sassanids mounted their greatest offensive in the East, seizing Syria, Palestine, and Egypt and advancing through Asia Minor to Constantinople. At the same time the Avars, an Asiatic people who established a state composed largely of Slavs north of the Danube, moved into the Balkans and toward Constantinople. For a moment in the first years of the seventh century it appeared that the empire would perish in the Persian-Avar pincer. But a savior appeared in the person of Heraclius (610–641), who regrouped Byzantine resources and flung back the enemies in a war of liberation that permanently weakened both.

The dynasty of Heraclius soon had to face an even greater challenge in the form of the rampant Arabs, whose rise to power we shall trace later. Within little more than a half century in the middle of the seventh century they wrested Syria, Palestine, Egypt, and North Africa from Byzantine control. By the early 700s they occupied most of Asia Minor, and in 717–718 they placed Constantinople under siege. Again a savior appeared: Leo III the Isaurian (717–741), who rescued the capital and succeeded eventually in liberating Asia Minor. However, the eastern provinces were permanently lost and the Byzantine Empire was reduced to its basic shape: a state comprising Asia Minor and the Greek peninsula.

Despite Leo III's remarkable victories, the power of the Isaurian dynasty was soon weakened, chiefly as a consequence of internal quarrels caused by its religious policy (see the next section). Meanwhile, the Franks seriously undermined the Byzantine position in Italy, and in 800 the Frankish ruler Charlemagne assumed — with the blessing of the bishop of Rome — the title of emperor, a direct challenge to the universalist claims of the emperors in Constantinople.

In the ninth century the Byzantine Empire was again threatened, this time by the emergence of the Bulgar state in the Balkans. And again the threat of foreign invaders produced a series of strong rulers, the Macedonian dynasty (867–1057), who not only threw back the Bulgars but under the greatest Macedonian, Basil II the Bulgar Slayer (976–1025), destroyed their state and extended Byzantine influence far into the Slavic world of central Europe and Russia. Under the Macedonian dynasty Byzantine power was also greatly increased in the East at the expense of the Moslem world.

By the eleventh century the Byzantine state began to suffer decline due in part to internal trouble and in part to new assaults from the east by the Seljuk Turks, from the west by the Italian city-states, and by the Normans located in southern Italy. To save the empire this time, the emperors appealed to the West, an act that was instrumental in launching the crusades and marked a fateful day in Byzantine history. The empire that had for many centuries withstood repeated attacks by relying on its own internal resources now began to move down a fatal path of dependence on outsiders for defense.

2. BYZANTINE POLITICAL, ECONOMIC, RELIGIOUS, AND CULTURAL LIFE

The ability of the Byzantine Empire to resist these blows stemmed chiefly from the strength of its government, its vast economic resources, and the devotion of its people.

The Byzantine government was an absolute monarchy whose emperor lived amid splendor and ritual that rivaled those of the great rulers of the ancient Near East. He commanded a horde of civil servants, to each of whom was assigned a specialized function, a rank, and a salary. The empire was divided into a number of districts, called *themes,* where officials representing the emperor recruited troops, collected taxes, maintained order, judged cases, and enforced the emperor's edicts. His power was buttressed by a well-organized army and navy, an efficient system of taxation, and a responsive ecclesiastical establishment. Of crucial importance was the army. During the crises brought on by Persian and then Arab attacks from the East, the government abandoned the long tradition of relying on barbarian soldiers and developed an army recruited from the small farmers of Asia Minor, to whom were awarded plots of land in return for military service. Commands were entrusted to aristocrats from the same area. For centuries these tough, loyal soldiers stood heroically against repeated attacks on the Byzantine state.

Agriculture formed the backbone of the Byzantine economy. Large estates, farmed by tenants, existed throughout the empire, but the chief strength rested with small landowners. The state took a vital interest in keeping agricultural production high so that taxes could be collected from the farmers, whether large or small, landowner or tenant. Aside from agriculture, the empire enjoyed tremendous commercial activity, and for many centuries Constantinople was the world's chief trading and industrial center. All trade and industry were rigidly controlled by the state. Wages, prices, and profits were carefully fixed. Artisans and merchants were compelled to remain in their trades and hand them on to their sons. The imperial government itself monopolized many lucrative businesses.

A strong government and a prosperous economy do not, however, fully explain the vitality of the Byzantine Empire. Byzantine life was strongly affected by Christianity, which helped to shape nearly every institution and activity. Perhaps most important, it provided the prime bond linking the populace to the imperial regime and thus supplied the basis for the remarkable loyalty of the imperial subjects. In many important ways, Christians of the Byzantine Empire were like Christians anywhere in basic belief and practice. However, with the passage of time, Byzantine Christianity underwent developments that gave rise to what is now called the Greek Orthodox Church.

The Greek Orthodox were always more completely allied and subjected to the state than Christians in the West. The emperor was accepted as the divinely ordained director of both spiritual and secular life. As a result of this *caesaropapism,* he appointed clergymen, defined dogma, settled theological disputes, imposed discipline on both clergy and laity, and used the wealth of the Church to serve the state. Byzantine religious life was also distinguished by its intense interest in questions of dogma. Quarrels over problems such as the nature of Christ and

his relationship to God aroused strong feelings in everyone from the most learned monk to the lowliest artisan and peasant and led to serious political crises on more than one occasion. Greek Orthodoxy placed a tremendous emphasis on rituals, and attempts were sometimes made to curb this tendency. The chief such effort was the iconoclastic struggle that raged from 725 until 843. This quarrel began when Emperor Leo III, backed by part of the clergy, attempted to remove all visual representations (icons) of the deity from the churches and rites, insisting that Christians were worshiping the statues instead of God and thus were guilty of idolatry. But these iconoclasts (icon breakers) ultimately failed, and in 843 the icons were restored. From then on, an elaborate ritualism characterized religious life in the Byzantine Empire. A prominent place was also given to mysticism and emotionalism — religious experiences in which believers were convinced that they could reach and commune directly with God. Monasteries were the chief centers of this type of religious expression, and monks exercised a powerful influence over every aspect of Byzantine life.

These unique characteristics of the emerging Byzantine establishment, reinforced by equally unique developments shaping Christian life in the Germanic West, led not surprisingly to a growing division in the Christian world. In part, these differences centered in dogma and ritual, but especially divisive was the ever more bitter quarrel over whether the pope in Rome was superior to or co-equal with the patriarch of Constantinople. By the end of the fourth century, the patriarchs were claiming an equal voice with the bishops of Rome in pronouncing the final word on matters of faith. This claim was stoutly maintained in succeeding centuries, usually with the support of the emperors. The slow drift toward separation on this issue culminated in 1054, when pope and patriarch excommunicated each other and created a schism that to this day has proved irreparable.

The schism between Rome and Constantinople was accentuated by the success of the Greek Orthodox in missionary affairs. From almost the beginning of Byzantine history, Greek missionaries, backed by the imperial government, began to penetrate the vast world of Central and Eastern Europe, eventually converting most of the Slavs in the Balkan peninsula and Russia. Byzantine religious practices, political ideas, and social concepts spread among them. A large portion of the Slavic world was therefore oriented toward Byzantium at a crucial point in the development of Slavic institutions and culture and thus was set apart permanently from Western Europe. The Iron Curtain was not entirely a creation of the twentieth century.

The Byzantine Empire gradually developed its own cultural life, oriented toward the preservation of the classical Greek tradition and its adaptation to the Christian world view. Within a short time after Justinian's death the use of Latin virtually ceased in the Byzantine world. An education system based on the study of classical Greek literature provided the chief avenue of contact with the past. It produced a large number of men, both laymen and ecclesiastics, who were conversant with the literary, scientific, and philosophical masterpieces of ancient Greece and the Hellenistic world. This educated group, often associated with the imperial court, the prime patron of cultural life, also collected copies of the classics, commented on them, and wrote in imitation of them. Their efforts ensured the survival of the Greek classics and their widespread dissemination. As early as the ninth century Moslem scholars began to utilize Byzantine sources to gain access to the classical past, and the cultural renaissance of fourteenth- and fifteenth-century Western Europe depended almost entirely on the Byzantine world to renew its knowledge of ancient Greek culture. The allpervasive influence of Greek models, however, tended to make Byzantine literature and thought imitative. Probably the most creative figures in Byzantine intellectual circles were the theologians, whose incessant quarrels over dogma produced a huge volume of writing in which philosophical concepts from the classical tradition were applied to Christian teachings. Byzantine historians, influenced by the models of Herodotus, Thucydides, and Polybius, also produced excellent works. Their skill is illustrated by the work of Michael Psellus (1018–1079), a high official in the imperial regime who chroni-

cled the exploits of the Macedonian emperors, and Anna Comnenus (1083–1148), the daughter of Emperor Alexius I, whose *Alexiad* colorfully describes the career of her illustrious father. Byzantine poets expressed themselves most originally in hymns, some of which can still be heard in Greek Orthodox liturgy.

Byzantine art demonstrated greater distinctiveness; it is perhaps the best mirror of the spirit of the culture. Architecture was the preeminent art. In its basic features, it represents a skillful fusion of Hellenistic and ancient Near Eastern traditions. The style was formed during the fourth and fifth centuries in Egypt, Syria, and Asia Minor and then was elevated to official status by Justinian's building program in sixth-century Constantinople. The great church of Santa Sophia was based on a floor plan derived from the Greco-Roman rectangular basilica upon which was imposed a great central dome after the Persian manner. The glory of this combination lies in the vast internal spaciousness it permits. The dome of Santa Sophia is more than 100 feet across and rises about 180 feet above the floor of the church. Although it rests on four great arches springing from four massive pillars that form the central square of the nave, the dome indeed seems "to hang by a golden chain from heaven," as a contemporary put it. Justinian, upon viewing the completed church, exclaimed: "I have outdone you, O Solomon." The architectural style represented by Santa Sophia was widely imitated, and in the course of time a variation gained considerable popularity: a ground plan based on the Greek cross with its four equal arms, each crowned by a dome, as is the space where the arms cross. The famous church of St. Mark in Venice is an example of this five-domed structure. Byzantine architects also built huge and splendid palaces, most of which have unfortunately disappeared.

Byzantine architecture, for all its technical ingenuity is incomplete without its decor. The churches and palaces were immense frames for sumptuous decoration. Santa Sophia's interior, for instance, blazed with precious metals, mosaics, paintings, jewels, and fine stone. The techniques and themes of church decoration were especially influenced by Near Eastern traditions.

Byzantine mosaics and frescoes, the best examples of which have survived in the churches built in Ravenna in the sixth century, centered primarily on portraying the great chapters of the Christian epic. Byzantine artists made an immense contribution to the development and enrichment of Christian iconography. Their work was never basically concerned with a realistic portrayal of the world; rather they sought to use human, natural, and abstract forms to evoke spiritual understanding. Color, created by glowing combinations of stones, metals, jewels, and paints, played a crucial role in enhancing the impact of every artistic creation.

Byzantine artists did not concentrate all their talents on religious themes; they were noted also as skillful jewelers, goldsmiths, silversmiths, manuscript illuminators, and workers in almost all the other minor arts. In every medium, the same features predominated — the fusion of Greco-Roman and Oriental motifs and styles, the love of elaborate decoration and color, and the preoccupation with symbolism.

3. MOSLEM CIVILIZATION: ORIGIN AND EXPANSION

No less vital was the second civilization that emerged in the East. This was the Moslem civilization, originally the creation of the nomadic inhabitants of the Arabian Desert. Although in the ancient past peoples from this desolate area had powerfully influenced the course of history (the Akkadians, the Assyrians, the Hebrews), no one living about 600 would have guessed that they were soon again to play a major role. Badly divided into numerous competing tribes led by *sheiks,* the desert dwellers, called Bedouins, lived a poverty-stricken nomadic life dependent chiefly upon pasturage of animals. Influences from the more advanced civilizations of the Byzantine and Sassanid empires had penetrated the Arab world, especially the cities which served as trading centers along the caravan routes that traversed the desert. The most important was Mecca, a flourishing and cosmopolitan trading and religious center where many Bedouin tribes came annually to worship at a famous temple called the Kaaba. But these outside influences barely touched the lives of the nonliterate, economically backward, politically divided desert dwellers; they seemed unlikely candidates for a major role in history.

Yet in little more than one generation, this is the role they played. The catalyst was a religious prophet, Muhammad, who galvanized the Arab world into unity and jolted it out of its isolation. Muhammad was born in Mecca about 570. Orphaned in his youth, he was brought up by an uncle as a trader. Eventually, he entered the service of a rich widow whom he married, thereby ensuring himself a respectable and leisured career in Mecca. As a trader, Muhammad appears to have traveled abroad and to have been in contact with foreign merchants who came through Mecca. But there is reason to suspect that the decisive aspects of his life were shaped less by these extraneous conditions than by his own introspective, brooding, ascetic spirit, which caused him to spend much of his time in prayer and meditation, often in the solitude of the desert.

When Muhammad was about forty, he suddenly claimed that God — *Allah* in Arabic — had spoken directly to him and named him his prophet. Thereafter he dedicated himself to convincing others that Allah had shown him the way to righteousness and truth.

What did Allah reveal to his prophet? The answer to this question lies in the *Koran,* the sacred book of Islam, which was compiled shortly after the prophet's death by his associates as a record of what he had proclaimed as Allah's message. Muhammad said that there is but one god, Allah; his followers must reject their worship of many gods for monotheism. Allah revealed himself bit by bit down through the ages, the Jewish prophets and Jesus all being accepted as his spokesmen. However, Muhammad was the last and greatest prophet, superseding all others, and Muhammadanism was destined to conquer the world. Allah requires complete submission to his will; the religion is thus called *Islam,* which means "submission to God." Every true adherent of Islam, called a *Moslem,* must regulate his life so as to abide completely by the will of Allah as revealed to the prophet. Those who believe in Allah and submit to his law will gain a happy life after death, while the nonbelievers and the disobedient will be damned. It is obvious that many of these fundamental teachings were closely akin to beliefs long held by Jews, Christians, and Zoroastrians, a fact that has led to the charge that **Muhammad** was little more than a borrower of the religious ideas of others. Whatever the truth may be in this matter, it neglects the essential fact: that the prophet brought to the Arab world a religious vision which was not only new to the Arabs but which also gave them the historic mission of spreading the true religion revealed in God's final revelation.

To these simple articles of faith Muhammad added a list of duties required of all believers. All must pray five times daily while facing Mecca, give of their wealth to support the poor, fast during one month of each year, and, if possible, make a pilgrimage to Mecca once in a lifetime. Muhammad also laid down strict rules regulating diet and marriage, prohibiting drinking and gambling, and demanding honesty, fair play, and respect for others. This code of conduct, strongly reminiscent of that defined for the Jews in the Bible, injected a strong ethical vein into the new religion. Each man was personally responsible to Allah; there was no church, no clergymen, no sacraments to assist in gaining Allah's favor.

For several years, the preaching of the new prophet netted only a few hundred converts. In fact, Muhammad won many more enemies than followers. By 622 these foes forced him to flee to Yathrib (later renamed Medina, which means "city of the prophet"), north of Mecca. This flight, called the *Hegira,* marked a turning point in the history of the new religion. Feeling spurned and convinced that the will of Allah had been defied by the Meccans, Muhammad began to shape a religious-political community dedicated to punishing sinners and spreading the true religion by force of arms. He molded his converts, including many Arab nomads from Medina and its vicinity, into an armed political following, held together by the commands of the prophet. By 630 his following was strong enough to recapture Mecca, a feat that persuaded many Arab tribes to join the prophet. During his last years Muhammad also turned his forces against other Arab tribes to compel them to join his community. When he died in 632, he was the leader of a large following of Arabs willing to obey Allah and his prophet.

Muhammad's success in drawing together the Arab world was impressive enough, but even more astonishing developments were to come. Almost immediately the new "nation" burst out of Arabia and began a series of military conquests that affected most of the civilized world. Between 632 and 656, the Arabs destroyed the Persian Empire; wrested the prize provinces of Syria, Palestine, Egypt, and extensive areas of North Africa from the Byzantine Empire; were probing India; and were challenging Byzantine sea power for control of the Mediterranean. After a brief interlude to settle internal problems over Moslem leadership, the advance resumed. All of North Africa was conquered, and Arab forces pushed into the Indus Valley and the outer reaches of China. An offensive was mounted in Asia Minor that moved closer and closer to Constantinople. Before 700 the Arabs were in virtual control of the Mediterranean. In 711 they crossed from Africa into Europe and quickly overran the Visigothic kingdom in Spain. From there they began to raid Gaul to threaten the Frankish kingdom. But the drive was weakening: In 717–718 Arab forces were defeated at Constantinople by Leo III and soon after were driven out of Asia Minor. In 732 — exactly a century after Muhammad's death — the Frankish leader Charles Martel defeated them at Tours in Gaul and halted their further advance in Europe.

The conquest of this vast empire within a century represents one of the great military feats in all history. Several factors played a part in this expansion. For one thing, the Arabs' opponents were weak. The Sassanid Empire was exhausted from its long struggle with the Byzantines. Religious disaffection among the Christians in the eastern Byzantine provinces caused the residents of these areas to welcome the Arabs as liberators from the religious tyranny of the emperors at Constantinople. The conquerors interfered little with local affairs, including established religions, and thus made their overlordship easy to accept. They demonstrated great military prowess; their long training as desert warriors

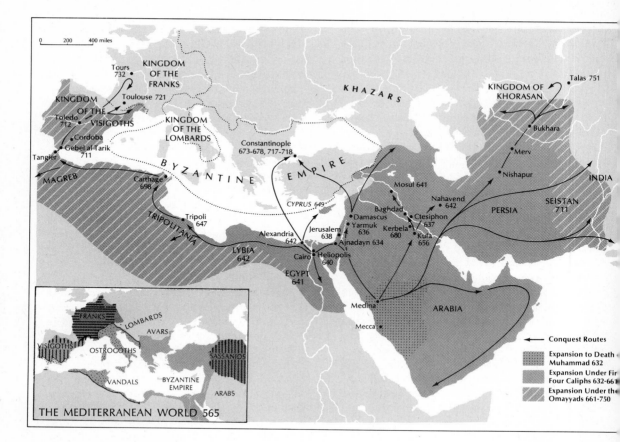

THE MEDITERRANEAN WORLD 565

THE EXPANSION OF ISLAM

had paid off. Their enthusiasm for their cause was certainly also a factor. Muhammad had said, "Fight and fear not; the gates of Paradise are under the shade of the swords." Their wars were thus holy wars, and the Arabs fought in that spirit.

4. MOSLEM POLITICAL, ECONOMIC, AND CULTURAL PATTERNS

The rapid expansion of the Arabs of course had a profound effect on the Mediterranean world, for nearly a third of the old Roman Empire had been absorbed by the new power. Despite their limited experience, the Arabs managed to establish a new political order to direct the destiny of the vast empire they had won. After Muhammad's

death down to 661, his close associates picked one from among them to serve as *caliph*, or successor, to interpret and apply the law as revealed by the prophet. This function gave the caliph vast authority over the political and religious activities of the Moslems. With the passing of Muhammad's personal associates as a source of leadership, a struggle developed for the caliphate; in 661 a military leader seized control and made the office of caliph hereditary. The dynasty he founded, known as the Omayyads, held power until 750. Its legitimacy was challenged from the beginning by Muhammad's son-in-law, Ali, and his son, Hussein, who claimed authority to interpret the prophet's word on the basis of their kinship with him. Their claims resulted in their assassinations. But the followers of these martyrs formed a powerful and dedicated dissident religious-political faction called the Shiites, which still plays a major role in the Moslem world. The Omayyad center of power was located at Damascus in Syria. The leaders of the dynasty were determined imperialists; they insisted that Islam was the special religion of the Arabs and that the Arab mission was to conquer the world in the name of Allah. But they also realized that the task of ruling what the armies conquered demanded well-developed political institutions. Markedly influenced by Byzantine models, the Omayyads created a centralized court, a bureaucracy, an efficient tax system, and a strong army and navy.

In 750 the Omayyads were overthrown (except in Spain), and the caliphate fell into the hands of the Abbasids, who ruled until 1258. The new dynasty was much more cosmopolitan and held that all Moslems, whether Arab or non-Arab, were equal. The Abbasids' rise to power thus marked the end of Arab domination of the Moslem world. The Abbasids shifted their capital from Damascus to Bagdad on the Tigris River, close to the heart of the old Persian Empire. In this new atmosphere the militancy that the Arabs represented was greatly diminished, and the energies of the Moslem world were turned inward to develop the potential of the vast empire.

The Abbasids enjoyed a period of great political power, especially in the late eighth and early ninth centuries; the dynasty's most magnificent caliph was Harun al-Rashid (786–809), immortalized in the *Arabian Nights*. But the Moslem Empire lacked permanent political stability, perhaps chiefly because of its immense size and diverse population. By the end of the ninth century, Abbasid power began to decline. Rival caliphs were established in Spain, North Africa, Syria, and India and quickly began to compete with each other for a dominant position in the Moslem world. Seeking to protect itself against these rivals, the Abbasid family increasingly placed its trust in Seljuk Turkish mercenary soldiers, barbarians from Central Asia who by 1055 had made the Abbasids their puppets. By that time, Moslem political unity had vanished forever.

The expansion of the Arabs promoted a significant economic revival. The key to this was a network of trade routes stretching from Spain to India and China. Cordoba in Spain, Damascus, Bagdad, and Alexandria, whose merchants and artisans were seldom restricted by Moslem governments, became centers of production. The wealth of the Moslem world at this time exceeded even that of the Byzantine Empire and far outstripped that of Western Europe, which was still dependent upon a backward agricultural economy.

However, religious and cultural developments established the main features of Islamic civilization. The religion of Muhammad demonstrated an amazing power to win converts, usually without force, since Arab conquerors seldom insisted that their subjects accept the new religion. They only imposed a special tax on their non-Moslem subjects for the privilege of retaining their old religion and excluded them from government positions. As the years passed, however, most devotees of other religions—Christians, Jews, Zoroastrians, and Hindus—were converted. Important non-Moslem communities always remained, but they had little influence on the mainstream of life.

Islam itself tended to grow more complex from the ninth century onward as a result of the efforts of theologians and lawyers, who developed a rich body of literature in the form of commentaries on the Koran and on other pronouncements attributed to Muhammad. Their work resulted in an orthodox faith rather far removed from that first proclaimed by the prophet; its adherents were called Sunnite Moslems and constituted the vast majority in the Islamic world. But there were dissenters and heretics, the chief of which were the Shiites, who insisted that the true faith was preserved by Muhammad's blood descendants. Despite these rifts, Islam provided the prime basis for unity in the Moslem world. The religious ties that hold the followers of Allah together have had a major influence on world affairs to this day.

Moslem expansion also brought about a tremendous cultural revival and joined together in a single society nearly all the world's chief cultural traditions: Greco-Roman, Persian, Mesopotamian, Egyptian, Germanic, Jewish, Indian, and Arabic. The semibarbaric Arab conquerors took these diverse traditions and molded out of them a new culture with its own distinct characteristics. The religious convictions of the Moslems again supplied the unifying force. Since Muhammad had forbidden the translation of the Koran into any other language, all Moslems had to learn Arabic; and since the Koran contained the final truth, it was necessary to reconcile the knowledge of older cultures with Moslem religious teachings. The response to these challenges was a brilliant outburst of scholarship that rightly allowed the Moslems to claim to be the cultural heirs of the ages.

Many historians would agree that the greatest Moslem achievements were in philosophy and science. Moslem philosophers devoted their efforts chiefly to reconciling Greek philosophy with the teachings of the Koran. At the same time, they wrestled with the contradictions inherent in the Greek tradition, especially those separating Platonic and Aristotelian thought. Their efforts are closely akin to those of the scholastic philosophers of medieval Western Europe (see Chapter 22). In fact, the speculations of the greatest Moslem thinkers, Avicenna (980–1037) and the Spanish Ibn Rushd (1126–1198), known in the West as Averroës, exercised a direct influence on Western scholasticism.

In science, the Moslem achievements were spectacular. Their efforts as collectors put at their disposal a huge body of scientific information from Greek, Indian, Persian, Mesopotamian, and Egyptian sources — more than scientists had possessed anywhere in the world until modern times. To this they added their own contributions, all of which were made widely available to a large circle of educated people because they were written in Arabic.

In mathematics, the Indian numerical system was adopted and the use of the zero was added to create the Arabic system of numbers which is used almost universally today. A Moslem, al Khwarizmi (ca. 780–850), combined Greek and Indian concepts to create algebra. Astronomy advanced tremendously with the joining of Greek views, such as Ptolemy's, to Persian and Mesopotamian. The works of medical writers

like al Razi (865–925) and the philosopher Avicenna represent compilations from numerous sources. Moslem doctors studied diseases, dissected bodies, and experimented with drugs, thereby adding tremendously to the existing body of medical knowledge. Geographers and physicists followed the same course.

Moslem literature also demonstrated great vigor and variety. Its poetry, familiar to western readers chiefly through the works of Omar Khayyám, is marked by brilliant imagery and highly complex technical skill in the use of the Arabic language. Perhaps the most characteristic feature of Moslem literature was the ability of writers to recast subject matter borrowed from various non-Arabic sources into masterpieces skillfully attuned to the spirit of Moslem religion and the values of Moslem society. Nothing illustrates this better than the *Arabian Nights*, in which the fascinating adventures of Sinbad the Sailor and the amazing feats of Aladdin are stories gleaned from the literary traditions of many non-Moslem peoples but which are given a unique coloration by the genius of Arabic authors, who retell them in a mode reflecting the spirit and the tastes of their own culture.

Like most of Islam's culture, its art reflects a creative synthesis of many traditions. Architectural talents were devoted chiefly to the building of mosques and palaces. The mosques, primarily places for individual prayer rather than community worship, are simple structures whose inner space is often divided by rows of graceful columns creating aisles covered by arches. As a rule, the mosques are covered by domes similar to those of Byzantine churches, above which rise graceful towers (minarets) from which the call to prayer is issued. Before each mosque is an open court containing a purification fountain and surrounded by a covered passageway. The greatest mosques, such as those at Damascus and Cor-

This view of the interior of the magnificent mosque built at Cordoba, Spain, in the eighth century illustrates key features of Moslem architecture, especially in the skillful use of arches and pillars to create spaces for private worship and in the employment of geometric decorative designs. *Photo: Georg Gerster/Rapho/Photo Researchers, Inc.*

doba, are beautiful structures marked by delicacy and grace. Surviving palaces, such as the Alcazar at Seville and the Alhambra at Granada, reflect the same architectural style as mosques but are much more elaborate.

Most Moslem buildings are rather bare on the outside but brilliantly decorated inside, especially with paintings and mosaics in splendid colors. Since the use of human and animal forms was discouraged lest the faithful be tempted to compromise their monotheism by worshiping a graven image, decorative arts accentuated floral designs and geometric patterns (arabesques). Exquisite artistry also manifested itself in the crafts; Moslem fabrics, tapestries, carpets, leather work, metalwork, weapons, and jewelry were the most prized articles in the medieval world.

Moslem civilization reached its apogee in the ninth and tenth centuries. Thereafter it began to suffer a variety of internal dislocations which sapped its energies and permitted outsiders to take advantage of it. We shall return to these problems in another connection. Despite the afflictions that beset Moslem society, the immense achievements of the preceding centuries ensured its civilization a permanent place in the history of human accomplishment.

5. WESTERN EUROPE AND HER EASTERN NEIGHBORS

The brilliance and vitality of the Byzantine and Moslem civilizations received little competition from the Germanic-Roman portion of the old Roman Empire, which lagged far behind them until the twelfth century. Outwardly, considerable hostility marked the relationship between the West and its more mature Eastern neighbors. During most of the early Middle Ages, both worlds posed threats to the West, although the Moslem danger was far the greater. Religious and linguistic differences promoted discord. Western Christians, who looked on the Moslems as heathens, believed any story of atrocity told about them and distrusted the Byzantines almost as much.

Yet over the gulf passed influences that played a crucial role in shaping the culture emerging in Western Europe. From both Byzantines and Moslems, the West derived an extensive body of technical knowledge, especially for manufacturing and trade, as well as almost all the luxury items that added to its refinement of life during the Middle Ages. Western Europe inherited Roman law from the Byzantine Empire in the form of Justinian's code. The first distinctive architectural style to develop in the West in the Middle Ages, the Romanesque, derived from Byzantine models, as did the sculpture and painting styles used to decorate Romanesque churches. Throughout the Middle Ages and into the Renaissance, Western scholars learned about the splendid culture of ancient Greece from those who played a vital role in preserving it in Constantinople. Moslems passed their large body of philosophical and scientific knowledge to Christians encountered in Spain. This knowledge was the chief leaven in the resurgence of culture in twelfth- and thirteenth-century Western Europe. Finally, European literature received a priceless heritage in the Moslem love poetry.

In short, during these centuries no aspect of Western European civilization escaped the subtle influence of the East. It is a debt often forgotten today, when the West has so far materially outstripped the Near East.

Suggested Reading

Overview
*R. E. Sullivan, *Heirs to the Roman Empire* (Cornell).
*H. St. L. B. Moss, *Birth of the Middle Ages, 395–814* (Galaxy).

*A. R. Lewis, *Emerging Medieval Europe, A.D. 400–1000* (Knopf). This and the two preceding titles will provide useful orientations to the major features of the age covered in this section.

Byzantine Civilization

*Steven Runciman, *Byzantine Civilization* (Meridian). A good introduction.

Georg Ostrogorsky, *History of the Byzantine State,* trans. J. Hussey (rev. ed., 1969).

D. Obelensky, *The Byzantine Commonwealth; Eastern Europe, 500–1453* (1971). Two very good, detailed histories of the Byzantine Empire. Obelensky's work gives special stress to Byzantine-Slavic relations.

*R. Jenkins, *Byzantium, The Imperial Centuries, 610–1071* (Vintage). A detailed survey of the period covered in this chapter.

*John W. Barker, *Justinian and the Later Roman Empire* (Wisconsin). A stimulating treatment of a key figure in Byzantine history.

F. Dvornik, *The Slavs: Their Early History and Civilization* (1956).

A. P. Vlasto, *The Entry of the Slavs into Christendom* (1970). This and the preceding title will provide a learned and sympathetic consideration of an oft-forgotten people.

R. M. French, *The Eastern Orthodox Church* (1951). A thorough but dull treatment of an important institution.

*D. T. Rice, *Art in the Byzantine Era* (Oxford). A splendid treatment.

Tamara Talbot Rice, *Everyday Life in Byzantium* (1967). Provides a good feel for ordinary affairs in the Byzantine world.

Moslem Civilization

*P. K. Hitti, *History of the Arabs: From the Earliest Times to the Present* (10th ed., St. Martins). A standard narrative account.

*J. J. Saunders, *A History of Medieval Islam* (Routledge and Kegan Paul).

W. Montgomery Watt, *The Majesty That Was Islam* (1974). Good treatments in detail of medieval Islamic history.

*Maurice Lombard, *The Golden Age of Islam,* trans. Joan Spenser (Elsevier). An excellent survey of economic history in the Moslem world from the seventh through the eleventh centuries.

*H. A. R. Gibb, *Mohammedanism: An Historical Survey* (Oxford).

*A. Guillaume, *Islam* (2nd ed., Penguin). Two clearly presented descriptions of the basic features of Islamic beliefs and practices.

*Tor Andrae, *Mohammed, The Man and His Faith* (Harper Torchbook).

*Maxime Rodinson, *Mohammed* (Vintage). Two judicious and sympathetic biographies of one of the world's great figures.

Gustave E. von Grunebaum, *Medieval Islam: A Study in Cultural Orientation* (2nd ed., 1953).

W. Montgomery Watt, *The Formative Period of Islamic Thought* (1973). Either this or the preceding work will provide a full introduction to the most important intellectual developments in the Moslem world.

*D. T. Rice, *Islamic Art* (Oxford). A perceptive survey.

East and West in the Middle Ages

Spiros Vryonis, *Byzantium and Europe* (1967).

*Karl Bosl et al., *Eastern and Western Europe in the Middle Ages* (Harcourt Brace Jovanovich).

*P. K. Hitti, *Islam and the West: An Historical Cultural Survey* (Anvil).

W. Montgomery Watt, *The Influence of Islam on Medieval Europe* (1972). These four works are rich in information clarifying the debt that the West owes the East as a result of interactions in the medieval period.

Sources

*Procopius, *Secret History,* trans. Richard Atwater (Penguin). A gossipy, scandal-filled picture of the court of Justinian.

The Koran, trans. N. J. Dawood (Penguin). The best source for an understanding of the Islamic religion.

15

HEIRS TO THE ROMAN EMPIRE: THE GERMANIC WEST, 500-750

The third heir to the Roman Empire, the Germanic society in the West, fared much less well than did the Byzantine and Moslem worlds in the immediate postclassical period. In simplest terms, the Western Europeans suffered through an age of instability and disorder. Only slowly and painfully did they begin to create a shaky basis for a new order. By 750 the first dim outlines of that new order were becoming evident in the form of new institutions and ideas that were destined to be crucial for the future of Western Europe.

1. POLITICAL DEVELOPMENT

To a large extent the chaos in the Germanic West was a product of political instability stemming from two interrelated factors. First, during the fifth century the conquering Germans had divided the once unified imperial territory of the West into several independent kingdoms: Visigothic, Ostrogothic, Vandal, Burgundian, Frankish, and Anglo-Saxon. The boundaries of these kingdoms were ill-defined and fluid, resulting in a constant shifting of boundaries and even the elimination of some of these states between 500 and 750. Second, all of these states were badly governed internally, resulting in a chronic state of violence and disorder everywhere in the West. Only slowly and painfully did this double source of political instability begin to be corrected.

One major political development of the period between 500 and 750 was the rearrangement of the fragile boundaries of the several Germanic kingdoms. Decisive in this respect was the role of the Franks. Until just before 500 the Franks were relatively insignificant allies (*foederati*) of the Roman government, occupying a small territory in extreme northern Gaul and serving as protectors of the lower Rhine frontier. Their first great king, Clovis (481–511), transformed his people into a crushing military force which he and his immediate successors led to conquer Gaul by 550. In the process, they destroyed the Burgundian kingdom, drove the Visigoths out of Gaul into Spain, and pushed into areas east of the Rhine not previously part of the Roman Empire. Clovis' conversion to orthodox Christianity greatly aided his advance, for the other major Germanic nations were Arian Christians and thus viewed as heretics by the orthodox Roman population of Gaul, while the orthodox Franks were accepted as "liberators." Frankish conquests shaped a large kingdom that embraced peoples with both Roman and German backgrounds, and out of this mixture emerged many of Western Europe's fundamental political, economic, and social institutions.

Justinian's attempted reconquest of the West in the middle of the sixth century was likewise a decisive step in shaping the new map of Europe. His armies destroyed the Vandal kingdom in North Africa and the Ostrogothic state in Italy.

The Lombards invaded Italy in 568 and established a kingdom embracing a good part of northern Italy, but the Byzantines retained their hold on several areas, notably around Venice, Ravenna, Rome, and in southern Italy.

Still another major change in the political map of Western Europe resulted from the spectacular expansion of the Moslems. Their relentless drive westward across North Africa destroyed Byzantine power there, established Moslem control over the Mediterranean seaways, and in 711 wiped out the Visigothic kingdom in Spain, where, except for a few tiny Christian states in the extreme north, the Moslems were to remain supreme for centuries.

On a somewhat less dramatic scale, the political map of the West was being shaped in important ways in other areas. In England the several Anglo-Saxon kingdoms remained independent, often competing entities, but they were slowly discovering common grounds that pointed toward eventual unification. In central Europe large numbers of Slavs moved westward and southward into lands vacated by the Germans when they migrated into the Roman Empire and began to develop their own political identity. In the Scandinavian world, new political groupings were taking shape that would in the not-too-distant future permit the peoples of the North to play a major role in Western European history.

Thus, by 750 the political map of the West had assumed a configuration of basic significance to the future. While only three Germanic peoples survived as separate kingdoms, that is, the Lombards, the Franks, and the Anglo-Saxons, they controlled the heartland of Western Europe — central and northern Italy, Gaul, western Germany, and England. On the south these Germans faced the Byzantine Empire, entrenched in southern Italy and Sicily, and the Moslems, controlling Spain, North Africa, and the Mediterranean Sea. To the east and north were the Slavs and the Scandinavians, peoples still less advanced than the Germanic masters of the heartland but nonetheless constant threats to the fragile order that had replaced the *pax Romana*.

While the political boundaries of Western Europe were being so painfully reshaped, constant experimentation went on within each Germanic state as leaders searched for a workable system of government. Although the efforts of each of the Germanic kingdoms existing in 500 to develop a viable form of government contributed something to the basic pattern of political life in the West, only two systems ultimately prevailed: that of the Anglo-Saxons and that of the Franks. We shall return to the Anglo-Saxons later (see Chapter 16); here we shall concentrate on the Frankish system of government to illustrate the major aspects of the new political order emerging in the West.

When the Franks began to establish their power in Gaul, they — like most other Germans — sought to create a government based on a strong monarchy. Clovis, the first of the Merovingian dynasty, which ruled the Franks until 751, claimed for himself the roles of supreme lawgiver, final judge, sole commander of the armies, and religious director of his subjects, whether Frankish or Roman. He was obviously influenced by Roman concepts, for earlier Germanic kingship had been much more limited. To execute these vast powers, Clovis and his immediate successors borrowed heavily from Roman precedents. They created a central court of officials, many of whom bore old Roman titles and were assigned comparable duties; and they retained the old Roman territorial divisions of Gaul as the units of local administration. Each district, now called a *county*, was governed by a *count*, appointed by and responsible to the king.

However, the history of the Merovingian dynasty is one of steady decline from the exalted position claimed by Clovis, a decline so drastic that the last Merovingians were dubbed "do-nothing" kings. Many factors explain this failure. The Merovingians could not divest themselves of an ingrained habit of using force to gain their ends, so that they appeared to many as bloodthirsty tyrants. They had a very limited sense of public service and so little managerial ability that their administrative machinery degenerated into virtually a household officialdom serving only to meet the king's personal needs. They persisted in the ancient Germanic custom of treating the state as private property for their male heirs to divide at the end of each reign. By the early eighth century, Clovis' kingdom had split into three distinct subkingdoms as a consequence of repeated division, and the weakening of royal authority allowed other groups to break away. The Merovingians never managed to command sufficient financing to conduct good government. They followed another Germanic practice of allowing each man to be judged by the law under which he was born, be it Frankish, Roman, Burgundian, Visigothic or whatever, thereby creating more division among a populace already set apart by differences in custom, language, religious practice, and cultural level. All these royal failures were accentuated by the fact that powerful elements in Frankish society, including the royal family itself, persisted in the Germanic tradition of the feud, entire families taking up arms to avenge wrongs done by other families against their members. In the face of this ingrained lawlessness, weak kings were unable to perform even the basic governmental function of maintaining order in the kingdom.

Yet the Merovingian political experience, for all its failures, did establish a limited form of monarchy as an important and necessary political institution. Able kings could exercise positive powers as leaders of armies, lawgivers, protectors of the Church, and dispensers of justice. Furthermore, the royal family served as a visible symbol of unity for a diverse group of people thrown together by conquest. Monarchy was taking shape as a visible embodiment of public life at a moment when poor communications, economic fragmentation, and cultural differences created tremendous obstacles to the formation of viable political groupings.

Severely limited in their efforts to create an effective centralized government, the Merovingians were eventually forced to share their power with the great landowners, both lay and ecclesiastical. The emergence of the landed nobility as possessors of political power was one of the major developments of the era. It stemmed chiefly from the inability of the kings to sustain an effective taxation system and a professional bureaucracy. When they needed an army or civil servants, they had to depend on subjects who could and would serve the royal government at their own expense. Only the great landowners

could afford such service, and in return they exacted from the kings grants of land and the right to govern their private estates as they saw fit. Inexorably, a system of private government evolved with the great nobles controlling affairs in their localities and interposing themselves between the central government and the populace. The kings devoted increasing attention to their relationships with the nobility, seeking to purchase their support and limit their independence. The growing power of the nobles was a source of incessant strife in the Merovingian state, for the demarcation between royal authority and noble privilege was imprecise.

This trend was accentuated by the widespread tendency for the weak in society to seek out the protection of the strong. At all levels of society, individuals of their own free will pledged under oath to serve another in return for protection and material support, a process known as *commendation*. These arrangements meant that strong men in society, chiefly the great landowners, built up private followings of *vassals* over whom they exercised considerable governing powers. Here were the roots of the feudal system. The practice created private jurisdictions that spread political power widely through the noble ranks of society and that fragmented the state into many separate entities.

Thus by 750 the political picture in the Germanic West was a somber one. Only slowly — and accompanied by constant warfare — were the boundaries of the chief powers being defined. Within the several states, royal power had been severely circumscribed, chiefly as a result of the inadequacies of the rulers. Powerful landowners were exerting tremendous political influence at a local level, often irresponsibly. The shape of this new order was a poor substitute for Rome's splendid government and certainly much less effective than the political systems operating in the Byzantine and Moslem empires. But its full potential for orderly existence had not yet been exploited.

2. ECONOMIC AND SOCIAL LIFE

The economic and social conditions prevailing in the Germanic West between 500 and 750 reflect the same backwardness and depression characteristic of political developments.

The most notable development of the period was the progressive strangulation of commerce and the industrial life associated with it. As we have seen, trade and industry were already moribund in the West by the fourth century. In the period of the Germanic invasions (the fifth and sixth centuries), this decline accelerated, especially in the frontier zones of the empire. Moreover, the Germans were little interested in trade, and when they assumed political power they did little to sustain it. Near the Mediterranean, especially in southern Gaul, Spain, Italy, and North Africa, commerce did not suffer so much, and contacts with the richer East were maintained. There was perhaps even a slight quickening of trade after the middle of the sixth century as a result of the political stability brought by Justinian's reconquests and the establishment of the Frankish kingdom. But this modest revival did not persist. Toward the end of the seventh and the beginning of the eighth centuries, trade again contracted, perhaps because of the seizure of control of the Mediterranean by the Moslems or because of more restrictive economic policies introduced by the Byzantine Empire. By 750 there was little circulation of goods in the West, the flow of money was small, city life had deteriorated badly, and the skilled artisan class had virtually vanished or had retreated to the large agricultural estates to produce for strictly local consumption.

Economic life had become almost totally agricultural. Possession of land provided not only the key to survival but also the measure of a man's status in society. Agricultural organization tended toward large, self-sufficient estates, called *villas*, a trend that carried over from the later empire's great *latifundia*. Many of the Roman *latifundia* survived the invasions, especially in the areas near the Mediterranean. Where Germanic settlement was heaviest, the Roman estates often disappeared and were replaced by villages inhabited by free landowners. But by the eighth century village establishments were being supplanted by villas which proved to be more economically efficient and politically viable in a disordered age.

The early medieval villa was a farming unit of several hundred acres owned by a noble or by the Church. The owner usually reserved part of this land for his own support. His basic concern was for a labor force to work the land and to turn its produce into articles he needed. There were still slaves, but a surer labor supply was provided by tenants. Between 500 and 750 increasing numbers of peasants were legally bound to the great estates, given a piece of land from which to derive their own living, and required to work the lord's land and render him dues in return for their tenancy. This pattern of exploitation laid the groundwork for the medieval manor and for serfdom, basic institutions in the future development of Western European civilization.

The villa system is not one that elicits praise; yet in the context of the early Middle Ages, it proved a vital institution. In a time of declining population it allowed an effective concentration of labor. In an age of political chaos it enabled men to cooperate fruitfully under effective direction. It provided stability for the peasantry by tying them to a piece of land. Even before 700 its potential for economic growth was manifested by the clearance of new lands around some villas, reversing the centuries-long trend toward decreased cultivation.

The social structure in the West also changed to meet new conditions. The direction of change was toward a simpler system than had been characteristic of the Roman world. The distinction between Germans and Romans gradually disappeared. Urban social groups, so vital in the Roman Empire, vanished. The main thrust of social development was toward the creation of a new aristocracy composed of men who proved capable of acquiring land, seizing political power, and grouping dependents around themselves. The new aristocrat was a self-made man, usually crude, aggressive, and lacking in refinement; he was more likely the descendant of the Germanic warrior than the Greco-Roman nobleman. Accompanying the emergence of this new aristocracy was that of a large lower class, chiefly peasants, who were legally tied to the great estates and dependent on a powerful overlord. All but a few freemen, both German and Roman, were swallowed up into this class of the semi-free. Liberty had dubious benefits in an age of political chaos and economic difficulty; protection by a strong man and the security of a piece of land were far more precious.

3. THE CHURCH

Western society needed more than the reshaping of its political, economic, and social structure, for the passing of Greco-Roman civilization posed a threat to moral, spiritual, and cultural standards. To the Church fell the struggle against the barbarism that threatened to engulf Western Europe. It was especially fitted for this task because it had survived the fall of Rome better than had any other institution, carrying over into the new age an appealing, satisfying religious message plus large elements of Greco-Roman culture that found their way into its organization, theology, liturgy, and moral code.

But the Church itself faced great adversity in the West between 500 and 750. It lost the beneficial support of the Roman government. Under the influence of recently Christianized German rulers, it broke into sections that coincided with the boundaries of the Germanic states, which threatened its unity. Moreover, by 750 differences in theology, ritual, and organization had already separated the Greek and Latin churches, and as the Christian world divided its energies, the assaults of Moslems and Slavs rolled back its frontiers.

Even more dangerous than fragmentation of the Christian community was the decay of the quality of religious life. In part this was a product of the changing character of Christian leadership. The general political and economic disarray of the age placed a premium on securing large landholdings and numerous dependents as a means of exercising authority. As men of considerable influence, ecclesiastical officials, especially bishops, entered into this quest for security, often at the cost of neglecting their pastoral duties. Insofar as they succeeded in making their offices the focus of power and wealth, they generated an unholy competition for these offices, with the result that the strong and the worldly usually won over the pious. Bishoprics

and abbacies became prizes that kings offered to their loyal followers and that self-seeking nobles appropriated to themselves for the profit that could be extracted. Under these pressures ecclesiastical leadership became increasingly worldly. Discipline among the lower clergy suffered badly as a consequence of lack of spiritual concerns among ecclesiastical superiors. The typical priest who dealt directly with the people was unlettered, ignorant of the rudiments of the doctrine, unfamiliar with the liturgy, and lax in moral life. Even when a bishop was inclined to assert his spiritual leadership over the lower clergy, his efforts were increasingly impeded by the growing numbers of private churches founded by laymen on their own estates as private possessions over which their patrons had total control.

Religious life in general reflected its inferior leadership. Recently converted pagans mixed their old religious ideas with Christianity to create bizarre beliefs and practices. Most Christians had but a vague understanding of such ideas as the Incarnation, the Redemption, and the rewards of the good life; their daily life was dominated by efforts to avoid Satan's hordes, who had to be defeated by magic and the intervention of the saints. Church writers of the period complained bitterly about sexual promiscuity, violence, thieving, and general unruliness among Christians. People were in need of instruction and discpline, neither of which was forthcoming from the degraded clergy.

Few of these grave difficulties had been corrected by 750, but some forces of revitalization had begun to appear, chiefly from within the Church itself. As these forces began to affect the troubled Christian world, they gave the Christian establishment in the West its own unique character that set it apart from Christian communities elsewhere.

A major source of religious vitality during this period was the Church's ability to win new converts. We have already noted that most of the Germanic invaders accepted Christianity as soon as they entered the Roman Empire. Just after the fall of the Empire in the West, Clovis and his Franks were converted, thus bringing into the Christian camp the Germanic nation destined to dominate the West. Backed by the Franks, missionaries in the sixth and seventh centuries slowly pushed the Christian frontier eastward from the Rhine. About the same time, the Anglo-Saxons were converted by missionaries converging on England from Rome and from Ireland, which had been converted in the fourth century. In the first half of the eighth century, English and Irish missionaries crossed to the Continent to win new converts on the northern and eastern frontiers of the Frankish kingdom. While the Christian frontier was being pushed outward, the less spectacular task of converting the rural population of the West went forward. As new converts were won, the Church organization was extended to serve their needs. New bishoprics, monasteries, rural churches, and private chapels appeared. By 750 this missionary effort had enfolded most people in the West—Romans and Germans, nobles and peasants, rich and poor—into a common body: the Church.

A second positive achievement of the Church was its growing participation in activities that were not strictly religious. It often shouldered the burden of caring for the weak in society— widows, orphans, cripples, slaves, prisoners. It maintained the only hospitals and schools available. It injected some of its ideas of justice and mercy into the harsh law codes of the era. Each time the Church intervened in these matters, its prestige as a social agency and its influence over society increased. These activities set new standards of social welfare that were to serve as models in reawakening social consciousness in general.

Most notably, the Church proved able to attack the weaknesses within its own body—corruptness and worldliness among the clergy, moral laxness, ignorance, and lack of discipline. Two agencies proved especially important in this corrective work: the Roman papacy and the Benedictine monastic establishment.

The progress of the papacy between 500 and 750 resulted in part from the strong position established by earlier successors of St. Peter, who benefited from the Petrine theory to establish wide acceptance as guardians of true doctrine and right Christian practice. The collapse of the Roman imperial government in the West and the shift of the imperial court to Constantinople that resulted from the barbarian invasions deprived the bishops of Rome of the beneficent and prestige-building support of the emperors. But there were compensations. The popes became the virtual rulers of the city of Rome, as was so dramatically evidenced by the role of Pope Leo I (440– 461) in protecting the Eternal City from the attacks of the Huns and the Vandals. Coupled with the spiritual prestige already enjoyed by the popes, this prominence in the political realm prompted the popes to broaden their vision. This expanding sense of papal authority was reflected by Pope Gelasius I (492–496) in his formulation of the *theory of the two swords*. He argued that religious and secular power represented two separate realms of authority, each established by God to achieve different aspects of the divine plan and each independent in its own sphere. This bold doctrine created a broadened ideological basis for expanding papal powers and for independence from secular authority.

However, the political turmoil that resulted from the collapse of imperial power in the West severely tested the ability of the popes to exert the authority they claimed. When the Arian Ostrogoths established control over Italy in 493, their great king Theodoric was little inclined to respect the popes who had long condemned all Arians as heretics. When Justinian destroyed Ostrogothic power, he reincorporated Rome into the Byzantine Empire and treated its bishop as just another imperial bishop who deserved even less respect than did the chief ecclesiastical official of his own capital, the patriarch of Constantinople. After the Arian Lombards seized most of northern Italy in 568, the popes were compelled to accept Byzantine protection and overlordship lest Rome be swallowed up by the Lombards and the papacy made victims of barbarian domination. Finally, papal influence over most of the West was disrupted and diminished as the newly established Germanic kings manipulated religious affairs in their realms to serve their political ends.

The recovery of the papacy was charted by the first great Western churchman of the Middle Ages, Pope Gregory I the Great (590–604). De-

In this German miniature, Benedict supervises the building of a monastery. *Photo: Bayerische Staatsbibliothek, Munich*

scended from a noble Roman family and educated for a political career, Gregory rejected worldly affairs to become a monk. Eventually, he left monastic life to serve as a papal diplomat in Constantinople and then to accept the papal office. Coupling deep religious fervor with hardheaded business sense, Gregory I pursued the policy of making the pope politically and economically independent while at the same time asserting the authority of the papal office as the fountainhead of spiritual life in the Christian world.

Convinced that the papacy must command material resources to survive in the troubled Italian scene, Gregory took an active part in the management of papal property in Italy, collecting everything due him, goading his agents into farming better, and acquiring new lands. He used this income to establish full control over the city of Rome without too much consideration for the authority of the legal ruler of the city, the emperor in Constantinople. His expanding independence permitted him to play one side against the other in the incessant struggles between the Lombards and the Byzantines, a course that again enhanced papal prominence. But Gregory was not simply a wily politician and administrator; he never forgot his spiritual responsibilities. During his busy pontificate he found time to write important books on theology and pastoral administration. His powerful sermons, widely circulated in the West, revived the art of preaching. He improved the liturgy. He sought to bestir princes and clergymen to reform their lives. Perhaps his most spectacular achievement was his sponsorship of the conversion of England, which allowed him to organize the new church there under papal guidance. All of this meant that those in the West who would listen found a fresh source of spiritual guidance in the face of the needs of the era.

Gregory's successors continued his policies. As a consequence, papal political independence, economic strength, and spiritual influence continued to increase. A new force of unity and discipline was emerging, although by 750 it had not yet achieved dominance in the Christian West.

The papacy was buttressed by a vigorous troop of workers produced in the monasteries of the West. Monasticism had been imported from the East as early as the fourth century and had received an enthusiastic reception, so that there were many thriving monastic centers in the West by the fifth century. None was more vital than that in Ireland, where the severe ascetic practices of the East took deep hold. The Irish monasteries became vigorous centers of learning and incubators for a powerful missionary movement that during the sixth and early seventh centuries took Irish monks to England and the Continent armed not only with great piety but also with considerable learning. But on the whole, early Western monasticism, perhaps too imitative of the East, failed to sustain its initial vigor. The West needed its own style of monastic life, and another great churchman appeared to answer that need.

Benedict of Nursia (480–543) stands alongside Gregory the Great as a leader capable of responding to the needs of his time. He too was an aristocratic Italian who abandoned his worldly career to become a hermit, but his rigid practices and holiness attracted so much attention that he was forced to create a monastery for his followers at Monte Cassino, a village between Rome and Naples. There he put into practice the rule he had devised to govern the community of monks. The rule was so sensible and well fitted to the needs of the period that by 750, the Benedictine monastic system had spread all over the West and had begun to play an important role in revitalizing the whole Christian world.

The *Benedictine rule* contained several basic principles that explain its success. It established the idea that a community of men could serve God better than a single individual. Such a community must, however, be made up of rigorously selected members. After a long testing period, each new member was required to take vows promising to renounce all personal wealth, to remain chaste, to obey his superiors, and to remain permanently in the community he entered. The rule entrusted absolute authority to an *abbot*, a sensible move in view of the desperate need for discipline in the Church. Probably the most important part of the rule was its provision for an orderly daily routine, consisting of three kinds of activity. First, all monks were required to join together in prayer eight times each day. Second, each monk was to perform some form of labor involving from four to eight hours each day: cooking, field work, handicraft work, clerical work, or whatever else was needed to provide for the self-sufficient operation of the community. Finally, all were required to study books that would enhance their spiritual state. Although the obligations imposed by the rule on a monk were not light, they were moderate and balanced compared to the excessive asceticism demanded by other earlier and contemporary styles of monastic life.

Benedict's rule won widespread favor in many parts of Western Europe (and was eventually adopted for women's religious communities), in no small part because of the powerful endorsement given it by Pope Gregory I. By 750 "schools for the service of God," as Benedict called his monasteries, had become the predominant form of monastic life. Their service to society was immense: Monks carved new estates out of Europe's wilderness and made them into the best-managed economic institutions in the West. From them backward peoples learned all kinds of technical skills. They taught bewildered Christians the basic tenets of the faith and the proper performance of Church rituals. Their devotion, charity, and purity of life inspired others to reform. They bore the brunt of mission work. They were preservers and transmitters of culture. In a time of uncertainty, these "athletes of Christ" were a small but stable bulwark against barbarism and important shapers of society.

4. THOUGHT AND ART

The chaotic and depressed conditions of the age were little conducive to creative thought and expression. Yet these centuries saw developments decisive in determining the cultural future of Western Europe and directing its cultural energies into unique paths.

In the realm of literature and learning, the chief accomplishment was the preservation of classical and patristic Latin literature (the use of Greek had virtually ended in the West). In the sixth century this activity was carried on by both secular society and the Church. Aristocrats of Roman descent in Italy, Gaul, and Spain struggled to maintain the old municipal schools where their sons could learn the traditional Latin rhetoric and grammar and continued to read classical Latin authors. Germanic courts, especially that of the Ostrogoth Theodoric in Italy, actively patronized literature and learning. One of the intellectual luminaries of that court, Boethius, set out to translate the works of Aristotle and Plato into Latin. His famous *Consolation of Philosophy*, written while he was in prison awaiting execution for alleged treason, was a moving defense of learning and rational thought filled with the classical spirit. Another of Theodoric's servants, Cassiodorus, left the court to found a monastery which became famous for its library of classical works, setting an important precedent for the role of monasteries in the preservation of learning.

Before the end of the sixth century, secular society ceased to play this role, and the burden of preservation fell to the Church and primarily to the monasteries. Faithful to Benedict's injunction to serve God by study, the Benedictine monks established schools to teach their neophytes to read and write, copied classical authors and church fathers, compiled textbooks in Latin grammar and rhetoric, and wrote simple commentaries on the old texts to make them understandable. The monastic concerns tended to be narrow, governed by a passion to know God, to understand his word, and to pray well. Thus the monks were selective in their endeavors as preservers. And they felt no compunction about turning the classical heritage to Christian purposes, sometimes distorting classical thought almost beyond recognition. Nonetheless, they did save much of classical Latin literature and patristic writing.

A few creative figures, almost all churchmen, managed to transcend merely preservative activities to produce literary works with unique qualities. One of these was Boethius; another was a Visigothic bishop, Isidore of Seville, who compiled the *Etymologies,* an encyclopedia of information (and misinformation) about nature that encouraged interest in science and organized knowledge. Pope Gregory the Great's important works set forth basic theological concepts in direct, simple terms more suited to the age than the sophisticated presentations of the great fathers from whom he borrowed most of his ideas. A Frankish bishop, Gregory of Tours (ca. 538–594), in his *History of the Franks* demonstrated a real ability to compile and organize historical material. The most outstanding intellectual figure of the age was an English monk named Bede (673–735), whose theological, historical, and biographical writings set high standards of style. His *Ecclesiastical History of the English People* is one of the best pieces of historical writing of the entire Middle Ages.

During this period, the lay world in the main sank into illiteracy. One work that might suggest their patterns of thought has survived this period—the magnificent Anglo-Saxon epic *Beowulf,* which put into writing a story of heroism that had circulated widely in oral form. The illiteracy of the laity did create one situation of immense cultural significance in Western European history: the language of learning, literature, and religion became different from the *vernacular,* the language that men spoke. This condition was destined for centuries to make learning and letters the property of an elite, chiefly churchmen, and to necessitate the mastery of a foreign tongue in order to join that elite. And it was destined to keep learning and letters somewhat remote from many of the realities of life.

The art of this period reflects a mixture of old and new. As in every realm of life, Greco-Roman forms persisted in architecture, sculpture, and painting. Many of the churches built in the West followed the basilica plan characteristic of Roman structures. Byzantine architectural forms, given definite shape by Justinian's building program, exerted a strong influence in sixth-century Italy and persisted there to affect building styles in other areas of the West. In sculpture and painting, classical and Byzantine influences tended to merge, so that pictorial art increasingly emphasized symbolic representation of religious motifs. The Germans and Celts added an important ingredient: a distinctive decorative style utilizing animal and geometric forms to create fantastic abstract designs. The vigor of this youthful art is evidenced in the designs created to illustrate handwritten manuscripts, so well exemplified by the Irish Book of Durrow (late seventh century), the English Lindisfarne Gospels (eighth century), and the Irish Book of Kells (early ninth century). On the whole, the art of this period reflected considerable freedom from fixed canons and unusual combinations of merging artistic traditions. Artistic expression tended toward abstraction, symbolization, and a search for religious values at the expense of earthly concerns.

By the middle of the eighth century the Western world had by no means emerged from the time of troubles that followed the fall of Rome. Habits of violence, ignorance, poverty, and moral decadence had been ingrained into men's lives and were to affect the conduct of Westerners for many centuries. However, out of the experiences of this period had emerged innovative institutions and patterns of life: monarchy, a new nobility, a stabilized peasantry, an involved Church, the papacy, Benedictine and Celtic monasticism, a treasury of Greco-Roman learning and literature, a new art style. The potential of these forms had not been realized, but their existence ensured the survival of civilized life in the West and compensated to some degree for what had been lost by the fall of Greco-Roman civilization.

Suggested Reading

Political, Social, and Economic History
*J. M. Wallace-Haddrill, *The Barbarian West: The Early Middle Ages* (Harper Torchbook). An excellent general survey of the period.
D. T. Rice, ed., *The Dark Age — The Making of European Civilization* (1965). A beautifully illustrated book in which several experts point up the contributions of diverse peoples to the new order emerging in the West.
J. M. Wallace-Haddrill, *Early Germanic Kingship in England and on the Continent* (1971). Helps greatly in understanding the unique nature of monarchy as it developed in the West.
*Henri Pirenne, *Mohammed and Charlemagne* (Barnes and Noble). A seminal study advancing the thesis that Merovingian history was a continuation of Roman civilization and that only the Islamic invasions brought a break with the classical world.
Samuel Dill, *Roman Society in Gaul in the Merovingian Age* (1926).
Robert Latouche, *The Birth of the Western Economy,* trans. E. M. Wilkinson (2nd ed., 1962).
*Georges Duby, *The Early Growth of the European Economy. Warriors and Peasants from the Seventh to the Twelfth Century,* trans. Howard B. Clarke (Cornell).
Renée Doehaerd, *The Early Middle Ages: Economy and Society* (1978). These four titles each present an excellent picture of the economic and social conditions prevailing in the West in the period.

Church History
H. Daniel-Rops, *The Church in the Dark Ages,* trans. A. Butler (1959). A good survey of the major developments affecting the Church in the West during this period.

P. Batiffol, *Saint Gregory the Great* (1929). Provides a full and fair treatment of the role of Gregory I.
Jean Décarreaux, *Monks and Civilization,* trans. C. Haldane (1964). A broad survey of monastic development in the early Middle Ages with special emphasis on the role played by the monks in shaping the new society.
Justin McCann, *St. Benedict* (1937). An excellent introduction to the origins of the Benedictine monastic movement.
Ludwig Bieler, *Ireland: Harbinger of the Middle Ages* (1963). A brilliant assessment of the nature and role of Irish monasticism.

Cultural History
*M. L. W. Laistner, *Thought and Letters in Western Europe, A.D. 500–900* (Cornell). The standard survey of early medieval cultural history, stressing especially classical survivals.
*Pierre Riché, *Education and Culture in the Barbarian West,* trans. John J. Contreni (South Carolina). A pioneering work which shows the unique aspects of early medieval cultural life.
Jean Leclercq, *Love of Learning and Desire for God: A Study of Monastic Culture,* trans. C. Misrahi (1961). A provocative interpretation of early medieval culture, emphasizing its monastic orientation.

Sources
*Boethius, *Consolation of Philosophy,* trans. V. E. Watts (Penguin). Illustrates the powerful attraction of classical civilization to a sixth-century scholar.
Gregory the Great, *Pastoral Care,* trans. H. Davis (*Ancient Christian Writers,* No. 11, 1965).
———, *Dialogues,* trans. O. J. Zimmerman (*Fathers of the Church,* Vol. 39, 1959).

————, *Selected Epistles* (*A Select Library of Nicene and Post-Nicene Fathers of the Christian Church*, 2nd Series, Vols. XII–XIII, 1956). A sampling from these works by Gregory I will provide a good introduction to intellectual concerns in the West in the early Middle Ages.

Rule of Monasteries, trans. L. J. Boyle (1949). St. Benedict's rule.

Gregory of Tours, *History of the Franks,* trans. O. M. Dalton, 2 vols. (1927). A dramatic account of Frankish history by a bishop who was involved in it.

*Bede, *The History of the English Church and People,* trans. L. Sherley-Price (Penguin). One of the outstanding literary works of the period by an Anglo-Saxon monk and scholar.

Beowulf, trans. D. Wright (Penguin). A work reflecting the values of the lay nobility of the early Middle Ages.

Lives of the Saints, trans. J. F. Webb (Penguin). A representative collection of one of the most popular literary forms of the early Middle Ages.

16

THE FIRST REVIVAL OF EUROPE: THE CAROLINGIAN AGE, 750-900

By 750, the new institutions and viewpoints forming in the Germanic West had borne only modest fruit. Then, rather suddenly and spectacularly, it enjoyed a revival which was brief in duration—hardly more than a century—but of great historical significance. The revival was the handiwork of a narrow segment of society: on the Continent, a new Frankish royal family, the Carolingians; in England, the kings of Wessex; and in both, other dynamic elements in society, especially clergymen and aristocrats, who clustered around these Germanic ruling houses. Their efforts were promoted and given direction by important changes in the relationships between the West and its neighbors—Byzantium, Islam, the still pagan Slav and Scandinavian worlds. Although the dreams of this narrow elite were by no means realized, their work had two particularly important results: It made the West visible in the larger world as a coherent unit possessing its own institutions and strengths. And it gave to the West an internal awareness of its civilization. The activities of these men created the first "Europe."

1. THE RISE OF THE CAROLINGIANS

The central figures in Western Europe's first revival were the Carolingians. At first they were only one of the ambitious landowning families that joined other nobles in undermining the authority of the weakening Merovingians. In the middle of the seventh century, the Carolingians gained hereditary control of one of the key offices in the Merovingian political system, the office of *mayor of the palace* for their home region, the subkingdom of Austrasia. This position gave its holder considerable control over court activities and royal lands, an opportunity that the Carolingians used to increase family wealth and build up a muscular circle of dependents. As their power increased, they shifted their ambitions toward establishing their control over the Merovingian courts in the subkingdoms of Neustria and Burgundy. Their decisive moment came in 687, when Pepin of Herstal defeated the rival mayor of Neustria and claimed mayoralty of the entire Frankish kingdom.

Pepin of Herstal's victory was exploited to the fullest by his successors as mayors of the palace, Charles Martel (714–741) and Pepin the Short (741–751), who became the most powerful men in Western Europe, far overshadowing the Merovingian kings whom they served. Both defended the frontiers against hostile invaders, and Charles Martel gained undying fame by defeating the invading Moslem army at Tours in 732. Both tried to improve the royal administration so that justice might be rendered, taxes collected, and the weak protected. Both labored to check the disintegration of the Frankish realm into independent regional entities and to recapture for the crown lands that had been usurped by lay and ecclesiastical nobles or given away foolishly by the weak Merovingians. Both generously supported missionary work, sought to reform the clergy, and encouraged the improvement of the quality of religious life throughout the kingdom.

Although Charles and Pepin were still only servants of the "do-nothing" Merovingian kings, it became clear as the years passed that the real power lay in the hands of the mayors of the palace. Finally, Pepin took steps to transfer the Frankish crown to his own family. Fearing that a forcible deposition of the Merovingians would arouse hostility among the Franks, who held a deep respect for the sacred blood of their ancient royal house, Pepin sought the sanction of a higher authority. His choice was a momentous one: He sent an envoy to ask Pope Zachary if it were not right that one who really exercised power should wear the crown. When Zachary approved, Pepin deposed the Merovingian king and had himself elected king of the Franks. The Franks' acceptance of the new dynasty on papal authority was a mark of how great the prestige of the papacy had grown. When Pepin was crowned as King Pepin I in 751, a papal legate was present to anoint him.

Papal sanction of the dynastic change was dictated in considerable part by new and desperate problems facing the bishops of Rome. Since the days of Justinian, Rome had been part of the Byzantine holdings in Italy, and the popes had relied—if sometimes contentiously—on the Byzantine emperors for protection. During the first half of the eighth century, however, the Moslem onslaught left Constantinople increasingly unable to defend its position in Italy. Moreover, the iconoclastic policy adopted by Emperor Leo III was viewed as heretical by the papacy and caused the popes to repudiate the emperors as defenders of the orthodox faith. The decline of Byzantium's power in Italy encouraged her longtime rivals, the Lombards, to take the offensive. But Lombard expansion threatened to engulf Rome and deprive the papacy of its nearly independent control over the city tolerated by the Byzantine government and of its extensive property in Italy. The popes needed a new defender. Who better than the rising Carolingians?

In 753–754 Pope Stephen II made a journey to the Frankish court to secure a protector. After long negotiation, an agreement, called the Donation of Pepin, was reached. Pepin promised to ensure papal control over specified Byzantine territories in Italy, some of which the Lombards now held. Stephen may have persuaded Pepin of the legality of disposing of lands that belonged to others by confronting him with a document known as the Donation of Constantine, a forgery which alleged that back in the fourth century Emperor Constantine, out of gratitude for having been cured of leprosy, had granted to Pope Sylvester complete control over the Western Empire, especially Rome and Italy. In return for Pepin's grant, Stephen not only reanointed Pepin as king of the Franks but bestowed on him the somewhat vague title of "patricius of the Romans," signifying his role as protector of the papacy and of the papal state. Pepin then made two campaigns into Italy and forced the Lombards to surrender some of the territories claimed by the papacy.

The alliance of the Franks and the papacy was truly a landmark. The Frankish kings now ruled by the grace of God bestowed through the papacy. They had assumed the responsibility of safeguarding their realm against all enemies of Christianity and of encouraging their subjects to become more perfect Christians. They had placed themselves under the guidance of the pope, who claimed the power to lead the Christian world. At the same time the papacy had lifted itself to a new position of authority and had established its own political area, the Papal States, within which it could operate in freedom.

2. THE REIGN OF CHARLEMAGNE (768–814)

The preparations made by Charles Martel and Pepin I were brilliantly exploited by Charlemagne (reigned 768–814), who emerges as the first great Western European secular ruler. To his contemporaries he possessed many qualities of greatness: imposing physical stature, courage, generosity, joy for life, intelligence, devotion to family and friends, and deep piety. His actions made him a hero to them.

The energetic, talented Charlemagne was

above all a successful war lord. His first notable success came in 774, when he defeated the Lombard king of Italy and annexed all the peninsula except the Byzantine territories in the south and the Papal States, over which he was already protector. Even earlier, Charlemagne had attacked the Saxons who lived on the northeastern frontier of the Frankish kingdom. He finally subdued them after thirty years of struggle, a victory that marked the incorporation of the last major remnant of pagan, barbarian Germans into the Christian, civilized West. His armies also drove down the Danube into the land of the Avars and the Slavs, annexing another large territory. His attack on Moslem Spain resulted initially in his famous defeat at Roncesvalles, but persistent pressure in that direction led to the creation of the militarized border district, the Spanish March, south of the Pyrenees. The stubborn inhabitants of Brittany were beaten into submission. Beyond the new frontiers established by direct conquest, and especially in Central Europe and southern Italy, Charlemagne employed a skillful combination of diplomacy and force to create a large number of tributary peoples who were willing to respect Frankish territory. This aggressive policy permitted Charlemagne to rule over the largest state in the West since the fall of Rome. In all his wars Charlemagne managed to create the impression that he was not merely serving his own greed, but rather overpowering barbarians, pagans, and infidels to save his Christian subjects from grave danger. Popes, poets, and nobles hailed him as "the strong right arm of God."

Charlemagne aimed to set up good government as well as to conquer and made significant innovations in the system his family had taken over from the Merovingians. He supported himself and his large court chiefly by the careful use of royal lands and the booty won in battle. The king's commands, usually arrived at by consultation with the court circle, were executed locally by counts and dukes whom he appointed and rigorously supervised through special officials, called *missi,* sent out from the court to prevent local officials from exploiting their offices for private advantage. He issued a constant stream of royal orders (called *capitularies*) touching on all phases of life to guide his officials in the discharge of their responsibilities. He made wide use of commendation to bind not only royal officials but most of the great nobles to him as vassals obligated by oath to serve him loyally. Often he rewarded his vassals with grants of land to be enjoyed as long as they served him faithfully. The growing dependence of the king on feudal usages was especially evident in the military establishment. The eighth century witnessed the emergence of the heavily armored mounted warrior as the chief instrument of warfare. The limited resources of the royal government made it impossible for the king to bear the heavy expenses involved in outfitting and maintaining large armies of mounted warriors. From the time of Charles Martel the rulers relied increasingly on great landowners to perform military service at their own expense; in return, the Carolingians granted them benefices from which the revenues necessary to provide military service could be derived. Charlemagne's military successes were, in no small measure, the fruit of his perfection and careful control of this system.

Charlemagne's efforts to rule well were animated by a much more elevated sense of the public well-being than had been present in the earlier Frankish state. He felt a deep responsibility for instituting a regime of order and justice that would serve all his subjects. In large part his concept of the role of a ruler was grounded in Christian ideals of right order and justice. Many of these concepts about the nature of the state and the good society lived on long after Charlemagne to provide the basic guidelines for political action; his role in exemplifying these ideals was one of his major contributions to the Western world.

Among other things Charlemagne's new political vision, coupled with his deep personal piety, caused him to concentrate great energy on reforming religious life in his realm. He was convinced that his divinely sanctioned royal office imposed on him the responsibility to sustain the Church in its mission of saving souls. He encouraged the spread of Christianity by supporting missionaries and even by using force to compel reluctant pagans to receive baptism, as

THE EMPIRE OF CHARLEMAGNE

was the case with the stubborn Saxons. He legislated constantly to strengthen church organization, protect church property, impose higher moral and educational standards on the clergy, establish uniform doctrines and rituals, and eliminate pagan superstitions. Such zeal to improve the quality of religious life led to constant royal intervention in every aspect of religious activity, to the point where it seemed that Charlemagne was both king and priest. In formulating and enacting his religious program, Charlemagne relied heavily on guidance from the papacy, so that his effort marked a decisive step in imposing a Roman stamp on the religious life of

Western Europe; in this sense he was a major architect of the Roman Catholic Church. His dependence on the pope greatly enhanced papal prestige throughout the West; at the same time his constant involvement in religious life severely limited the independence of the Church.

All of these achievements pointed toward the culminating event in Charlemagne's career: his elevation to the emperorship. The stage was set for this event by serious disturbances in Rome in 799 which led to charges of misconduct against Pope Leo III (795–816) and his forced flight to Charlemagne's court. As part of his effort to settle the difficulty in his role as protector of the Romans, Charlemagne went to Rome in late 800 and acted directly to exonerate the pope and restore him to full authority. Then on Christmas Day, 800, while the king was attending mass in St. Peter's Basilica, the pope placed a crown on his head and the clergy and people hailed the king of the Franks as "Augustus, crowned by God, the great and peace-bringing Emperor of the Romans."

Historians still argue about who instigated this event and what it signified. Some have argued that Leo III was responsible, acting boldly to reassert his supremacy over the secular ruler who had just rescued the pope from a demeaning experience by bestowing on Charlemagne an exalted office that only the pope could give. Others refuse to believe that the astute Frank could have been so easily maneuvered by a pope whose position was so tenuous. Despite the fact that Charlemagne's biographer, Einhard, wrote that the king was surprised and did not want the new title, these historians argue that such a title reflected much better than did his old title the role the great king had come to play by virtue of his success as conqueror, ruler of diverse peoples, lawgiver, and protector of the Christian world and its sacred center, Rome. Why, they ask, may it not have occurred to Charlemagne that he deserved the highest title then known, especially in view of the widely shared opinion in the West that the emperors in the East had failed to protect Christendom and safeguard the orthodox faith? There is strong evidence to suggest that some of Charlemagne's ecclesiastical advisers may have inspired the coronation.

Many of them were talking about a new Christian empire required to fulfill God's plan to join all Christians into a single earthly commonwealth under a Christian prince who would serve as the new David and the new Constantine to assure the enactment of God's will. Who could better fill this vision, deeply influenced by Old Testament models and St. Augustine's *City of God,* than the heroic and saintly Frank? Without knowing for certain, perhaps we can suggest that the initiative for renewing the empire in the West was shared by the pope, Charlemagne, and his advisers as a means of realizing different aspirations and that they collaborated in staging the momentous scene that unfolded on Christmas Day, 800.

Historians likewise cannot agree on what Charlemagne's elevation to the emperorship meant. In fact, it probably meant different things to different people. The Byzantine rulers saw it as an outrageous usurpation of a title long held in the new Rome. If not in the short run, at least in the long run the popes viewed the event as the precedent for their right to designate the ruler of the Christian world, a right that carried with it the power to judge his conduct. For an important circle of churchmen close to Charlemagne, the event was a signal to renew the effort to create a totally Christian commonwealth dedicated to the service of God. This inspiration made them a powerful force in political life in the Carolingian world after 800. There is good evidence to suggest that the coronation mystified and confused many of Charlemagne's Frankish followers, especially those who saw his greatness in his military prowess, which resulted in rewards for those who served him well as companions in war.

What Charlemagne thought of his new title is an enigma. He ruled fourteen years as emperor. Some of his actions during these years suggest that he took the title seriously. He conducted a skillful military and diplomatic drive that compelled the Byzantine emperor to recognize him as emperor. He took up more vigorously than ever the cause of religious reform in his realm, suggesting a responsiveness to the Augustinian political idealism of those advisers who had encouraged the revival of empire. On the other

This representation of Charlemagne is from a twelfth century reliquary (a piece of art created to contain the relics of a saint) now in Aachen, the great ruler's chief place of residence. It idealizes Charlemagne as a noble ruler and, especially, as a protector of the Church, a symbol of which he holds in his right hand. *Photo: EPA, Inc.*

hand, Charlemagne would have little to do with the trappings of his new office; he continued to act like a Frank and to insist that he was still king of the Franks. Contrary to all that the imperial title implied about the unity of his realm, he made plans to divide his empire in order to provide a "kingdom" for each of his three sons; such a division was avoided only because a single son, Louis, outlived Charlemagne. In 813 Charlemagne himself crowned Louis as emperor without any involvement of the papacy. This act suggests that Charlemagne viewed the imperial title as a personal honor that he had earned by virtue of his great achievements and that he could dispose of as he pleased. Whatever the case, the event of 800, which translated an ancient title rich in political symbolism into a Germanic context, was of great significance in creating a Western European political consciousness. Insofar as he had set the stage for this event through his prodigious and wide-ranging activi-

ties, Charlemagne was indeed a maker of Western Europe.

3. THE CAROLINGIAN RENAISSANCE

Perhaps the most lasting achievement of the indefatigable Charlemagne was the cultural renaissance that distinguished his age, a revival brought about chiefly through his personal efforts. The motivation behind his cultural policy was pragmatic: He was convinced that the quality of religious and political life could be improved only by the development of better-educated leaders, especially churchmen. Practical though it was, this was a radical idea in a barbaric society that had almost forgotten that there might be a connection between learning and the quality of life.

His chief instrument to this end was a palace school which he began to form in the 780s and 790s but which took on special vigor after he built a church and palace at Aachen about 800 and made that city the center of his political activities. This school attracted the best minds from all over Europe, so that it became a focal point where diverse cultural trends mingled and matured.

In one sense, the palace school served as a locus for study, writing, and reflection on intellectual issues, generating sufficient creative activity to prompt some of its members to call it the "new Athens." Charlemagne himself was an active participant in these activities. But a more important function was the development of a sound education program. Under the guidance of the Englishman Alcuin, a product of the cultural environment that had produced Bede a century earlier, the school's teachers labored primarily to create the tools and methods of instruction for a proper grounding in the true religion. They sought authentic versions of Scripture, missals, laws, patristic texts, classical authors, church regulations, even Germanic legends—all those precious sources that would guide men to what the Carolingians often spoke of as "the norms of righteousness" which should define and govern Christian life. The court scholars sponsored the compilation of improved textbooks of Latin grammar and spelling and the search for models of good expression in classical authors. The workshops where this copying took place, called *scriptoria,* turned out sufficient copies of these basic works to stock many libraries. The Carolingian copyists developed a beautiful script called *Carolingian minuscule,* which provided the base for all modern scripts and typefaces.

As the tools of education were forged, Charlemagne employed his authority to universalize their use. He insisted that monasteries and bishoprics organize schools and adopt the books and methods developed at the palace school. His efforts led to a significant expansion of education and a greatly increased concern for the quality of teaching in the monastic and episcopal schools. After Charlemagne's death, the palace school declined and cultural leadership passed to these new centers, especially the monastic schools, which sustained the Carolingian renaissance through much of the ninth century.

Although the major energies of the court schoolmen were consumed in gathering and mastering the models of good thought, style, and language, some of them and their contemporaries produced distinguished original works. Einhard's biography of Charlemagne was excellent. Alcuin compiled several important textbooks of grammar and logic and was a lively letter-writer. An Italian, Paul the Deacon, pro-

duced a well-organized *History of the Lombards.* Theodulf, a Spaniard, wrote excellent poetry. A succession of theologians prepared impressive commentaries on Scripture and compiled doctrinal tracts pieced together from materials derived from Scriptural and patristic sources. Perhaps the most original mind of the age and the most competent Western theologian since Gregory the Great an Irishman, John Scotus Erigena, who lived in the Frankish kingdom from 850 to 875. Although the bulk of the work of these and lesser lights was derivative and timid in the face of new ideas, it was infused with an esthetic sense reflecting a genuine appreciation of classical literature. Thus one may speak of a Carolingian humanism mingling with deeply ingrained Christian values.

The Carolingian revival of the arts also grew out of religious concerns. Several fine churches were built, the most splendid of which was Charlemagne's at Aachen. Considerable effort was made to decorate them with mosaics and frescoes. In many ways the best Carolingian art was in miniatures: illuminated manuscripts, ivory carvings for altar adornment, metalwork, jewelry. All Carolingian art mixed diverse traditions: classical, Byzantine, Germanic, Celtic. Again, the men of this age appropriated past styles and formed them into new shapes.

4. THE DISINTEGRATION OF THE CAROLINGIAN EMPIRE

Charlemagne's political empire did not persist long. He did not succeed in developing political institutions capable of surviving him. Especially dangerous was his widespread use of feudal practices in an effort to assure the loyalty and to gain the services of the great nobles. To buy their services he had been forced to grant large blocks of land to them and to concede *immunities* which gave the nobles authority to exercise governing powers over these lands. Charlemagne tried to keep these men faithful to him by having them swear allegiance to him as his vassals, but this arrangement could work for the emperor's benefit only if he were forceful enough to compel his widely scattered vassals to perform the services owed the ruler as their lord. This was a

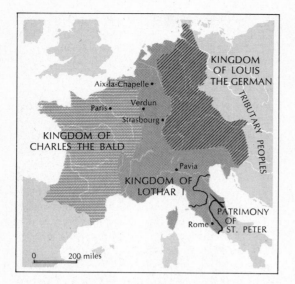

PARTITION OF THE CAROLINGIAN EMPIRE 843

tremendous burden; failure would allow the nobles to escape royal control still in possession of the lands granted to them to secure their loyalty and services. Charlemagne's successors could not manage and paid a disastrous price.

Moreover, Charlemagne's empire was never wholly unified. Germans, Romans, and Slavs were still divided by differences in language and cultural background. The Church, upon which Charlemagne relied so heavily to inspire and guide his subjects to obey and to serve, was actually a doubtful ally. Its leaders in Rome and in the great bishoprics and monasteries scattered over the empire were uneasy about his interference in Church affairs. While aspiring to the same end that he did—an earthly society dedicated to the service of God—many churchmen preferred to lead society themselves rather than bend before a layman. Their independence was a harbinger of bitter conflicts between church and state later in the Middle Ages.

The empire was also threatened by powerful external foes. On the south were the aggressive Moslems, especially strong in sea power, against which the Franks had little defense. On the east the Slavs, under the pressure of new invaders from Asia, the Magyars, pushed relentlessly

westward. Finally, the Vikings or Norsemen (Danes, Swedes, and Norwegians) threatened on the north. The Vikings, virtually strangers to Western Europe in the early ninth century, quickly became the greatest danger.

The Vikings were still barbarians and heathens. They had long dwelt along the wild coasts of Scandinavia, surviving chiefly by fishing and piracy. Politically, strong clans played a dominant role, although by 800 loose kingdoms were in the process of formation. In the ninth century, the Vikings began to expand. Traveling by sea in small groups, they spread over an immense area, touching Ireland, England, the whole Atlantic coast of Europe, the southern shores of the North and Baltic seas, Russia, Iceland, Greenland, and perhaps North America. Wherever they went, they pillaged the land and hauled off vast quantities of loot. In the late ninth and tenth centuries some of them began to settle permanently in the lands they had been raiding, especially in England, Ireland, France, and Russia, and piracy gave way to trade. The Vikings slowly accepted the religion and culture of Western Europeans, but too late to spare the Carolingian Empire. Charlemagne's successors had to face the full fury of the destructive attacks and found no effective defense against the dreaded raiding parties.

Compounding these external problems, the Carolingian state suffered from inadequate leadership throughout much of the ninth century. Charlemagne's son Louis (814–840) was an indecisive ruler. His strongest impulse was to pursue the universalist ideals embraced by the Carolingian political ideology. This inclination carried him toward a close alliance with powerful churchmen, whose gratitude earned Louis the title "Pious," but who were not averse to bending imperial policy to suit their ends. Equally powerful elements in Frankish society resisted the realization of the imperial idea with its implication of strong central government, and Louis on occasion surrendered to their pressures. The major problem of his reign centered around what provision he would make for his sons. He was torn between safeguarding the unity of the empire by designating a single successor and observing the ancient Frankish cus-

This representation of Viking ships filled with fierce warriors illustrates the terror that was struck in those who witnessed such vessels approaching their undefended shores. One senses that the artist had witnessed such a scene. *Photo: Culver Pictures*

tom of dividing his empire among his heirs. His efforts to compromise these conflicting ideas led his sons to revolt.

Before his death Louis did provide a "kingdom" for each of the three surviving sons and granted to his eldest, Lothair, the title of emperor with a vague authority over the others. Almost immediately the younger sons declared war on Lothair, and in 843 forced him to sign the Treaty of Verdun. This document legalized the division of the empire into three parts: the kingdom of the West Franks 'roughly modern France); the kingdom of the East Franks (roughly modern Germany); and the kingdom of Lotharingia, a narrow band lying between the west and east kingdoms and stretching from the North

Sea to Italy. Further divisions of Lotharingia later in the ninth century led to the creation of three other kingdoms: Italy, Burgundy, and Provence.

After 843, Carolingian unity was fatally compromised. The energies of the Carolingian rulers were absorbed in petty wars aimed at snatching territory from one another; these senseless struggles left little time for problems of religion, justice, internal order, and defense against the mounting attacks of outsiders. The later kings continued the practice of buying support by granting new lands to nobles and conceding political powers to them. This constant diminution of the royal estates and power eventually left the Carolingian rulers powerless to curb the nobility.

High churchmen usually supported the later Carolingian kings and were rewarded by rich royal endowments, but in the long run ecclesiastical support worked against the interests of the

Carolingian family. The Church became bolder and bolder in its claims to supremacy over the state. By the middle of the ninth century, the pope was openly claiming superior authority over all Christians — including kings. Pope Nicholas I (858–867) actually tried to exercise these claims by interfering in the private lives of the kings, while at the same time carrying on extensive diplomatic negotiations in an attempt to halt the civil wars raging everywhere, legislating for the whole Church, and taking the lead in spreading Christianity.

By 900 the Carolingian dynasty was thoroughly discredited and the empire divided beyond repair. Invaders pillaged Western Europe almost at will. Landed nobles tightened their holds on their small principalities and compelled the lower classes to submit to their petty domination. Even the Church, the last bastion of unity, suffered fragmentation. The dream of Charlemagne and his advisers to make Western Europe a single political unit had foundered.

These obvious failures must not hide the deeper significance of the Carolingian Empire. Germanic rulers — represented by Charlemagne — developed a deepened awareness of a responsibility other than conquering lands for their own private profit. In the centuries following his death, Charlemagne provided the model for the good Christian ruler. Certain Carolingian techniques of government, especially the practice of creating lord-vassal ties to define the relationship between ruler and ruled, long served as the basis for political life in the successor states that emerged from the breakup of the Carolingian Empire. Under its Carolingian champions, the Western Church succeeded in imposing a considerable degree of doctrinal and liturgical uniformity throughout the West and gained important ground in creating an independent state in Italy. The papal role in sanctifying the Carolingians first as kings of the Franks and then as emperors established a significant precedent for the fundamental medieval idea that the state must have the blessing of the Church. The revival of the idea of empire dramatically reaffirmed the tie between Western Europe and classical Rome. The renewed interest in Roman civilization reflected in the Carolingian renaissance cemented the tie with the classical past, to which Western Europeans would turn repeatedly for models by which to enrich their lives. The true significance of the era must thus be sought in the world of ideas: It was a period when some Western Europeans tried to define what they wanted politically, socially, religiously, and culturally. Although few of their ends were attained in their time, much of later medieval history consists of working out the details of ideas developed in the Carolingian period.

5. EARLY MEDIEVAL ENGLAND

While the Carolingians were shaping much of Western Europe, the small Anglo-Saxon kingdoms of England were undergoing an important transformation. After a long period of fruitless warfare, these kingdoms began to coalesce, chiefly as a result of two outside forces — Christianity and the Viking menace.

England had been Christianized in Roman times, but the Anglo-Saxon invaders wiped out Christianity in the territories they occupied. Late in the sixth century missionaries penetrated England from both Rome and Ireland and within a century reestablished Christianity as a common religion in the different kingdoms. For a brief period in the seventh century, Roman and Irish missionaries clashed bitterly for the right to dominate England. Rome won, assuring uniformity of organization, ritual, and doctrine and putting the English in touch with the mainstream of continental religious life.

The threat of the Vikings was a more important unifying force. No area suffered more from their pillaging, especially during the first half of the ninth century, and some Vikings settled permanently in a large northeast territory known as the *Danelaw*. Several of the old Anglo-Saxon kingdoms were swallowed up by the invaders.

The kingdom of Wessex became the center of resistance and eventually of counterattack against the Vikings. The reign of Alfred the Great (871–899) was the decisive period. He not only stopped Viking expansion, but also laid the groundwork for the reconquest of the Danelaw. His leadership served to revitalize the Church and the dormant English intellectual life, and both accomplishments helped stir up the English against foreigners. During the tenth century Alfred's heirs rewon the Danelaw, pushing the English frontier to about the present boundary between England and Scotland. All the conquered territory and its peoples, including the Danes, were made subjects of a single king, who was no longer king of Wessex but king of England.

The unification of England necessitated a single government system. This system, based on institutions introduced by the Anglo-Saxons in the early fifth century, assumed its final shape by 1000. A king, claiming to be supreme judge, leader of the army, head of the Church, and lawgiver, ruled over the land. Actually, royal power was limited, since the king lacked effective means of exercising his authority. He supported himself and his court chiefly from the income derived from royal estates. Only on rare occasions could he levy a direct tax on his subjects — for instance, several kings collected the Danegeld, levied first in 991 to buy off Viking raiders. Although he could theoretically summon all freemen to serve in the army (called the *fyrd*), the king depended heavily on his noble companions, whose support was won by grants of land. He was advised by the *Witan,* an assembly of great nobles and churchmen that in a general way was held to represent all freemen, on matters of great importance such as waging war or enacting new laws. However, a strong king could act without its approval. The whole complex of institutions surrounding him — household officials, fyrd, armed retainers, and Witan — made the central government important but certainly not strong enough to control political life in all England.

Much more significant was the system of local government that had long been evolving. England was divided into *shires,* of which there were about forty in the tenth century. The king was represented in each by three officials — the *earl,* the *sheriff,* and the *bishop.* The earl had the most rank and prestige, but the sheriff usually conducted most of the royal business. A court was held in each shire twice a year, and all freemen were expected to attend. The king's orders were proclaimed and all civil and criminal cases were handled at this court, where any freeman could bring a complaint. The law administered was customary law, dating from far back in Anglo-Saxon history and known by the local landowners who sat in the court. Each shire was subdivided into *hundreds,* where courts presided over by a royal official met monthly for minor cases. The agricultural villages also had their own courts, usually conducted by great landowners. As a rule, Church business was handled in the shire and hundred courts. This network of local institutions, tied to the central government through royal officials but largely self-sufficient, provided an element of orderly political life in England that was sometimes lacking on the Continent.

Suggested Reading

The Carolingian World
The general works by Sullivan, Moss, Lewis, and Wallace-Haddrill, cited in Chapters 14 and 15, will be helpful in establishing the broad outlines of Carolingian history.

Louis Halphen, *Charlemagne and the Carolingian Empire* (1977). The best survey of political history.

*Jacques Boussard, *The Civilization of Charlemagne* (McGraw).

H. Fictenau, *The Carolingian Empire: The Age of Charlemagne,* trans. Peter Munz (1957).

Friedrich Heer, *Charlemagne and His World* (1975).

*R. E. Sullivan, *Aix-la-Chapelle in the Age of Charlemagne* (Oklahoma). This and the preceding three works provide interesting interpretations of the nature of Carolingian society, emphasizing especially the role played by Charlemagne in shaping the main features of that society.

Pierre Riché, *Daily Life in the World of Charlemagne,* trans. Jo Ann McNamara (1978).

*Peter Munz, *Life in the Age of Charlemagne* (Capricorn). These two works provide fascinating pictures of life in Carolingian times. These can be supplemented by the economic histories cited in Chapter 15, especially Duby and Doehaerd.

Richard Winston, *Charlemagne* (1954). A well-written biography.

Robert Folz, *The Coronation of Charlemagne: 25 December 800* (1974). A judicious explanation of an event about which historians disagree.

R. E. Sullivan, ed., *The Coronation of Charlemagne: What Did It Signify?* (1961). Presents the conflicting views of several authorities concerning the nature and meaning of the coronation.

Rosamond McKitterick, *The Frankish Church and the Carolingian Reform, 789–895* (1977). An excellent survey of a matter that occupied much of the attention of the Carolingian rulers and churchmen.

Eleanor S. Duckett, *Alcuin, Friend of Charlemagne* (1951), and *Carolingian Portraits: A Study in the Ninth Century* (1962). These two works provide valuable insights into the nature of the Carolingian renaissance. Details of that renaissance are provided by the study of Laistner, cited in Chapter 15.

*Roger Hinks, *Carolingian Art* (Ann Arbor).

J. Hubert et al., *The Carolingian Renaissance* (1970). These two works provide excellent studies of artistic life.

Vikings

*Johannes Bronsted, *The Vikings* (Penguin).

Peter G. Foote and David M. Wilson, *The Viking Achievement: A Survey of the Society and Culture of Early Medieval Scandinavia* (1970). Two excellent descriptions of the major features of Viking civilization; the latter work is perhaps the better.

Anglo-Saxon England

*D. Whitelock, *Beginnings of English Society: Anglo-Saxon Period* (Penguin).

*P. Hunter Blair, *Introduction to Anglo-Saxon England* (Cambridge). Two concise, well-organized, clearly written surveys of Anglo-Saxon England.

*E. S. Duckett, *Alfred the Great: The King and His England* (Phoenix). A good account of the accomplishments of a great king.

Alf J. Mapp, Jr., *The Golden Dragon: Alfred the Great and His Times* (1974) An excellent biography of an English hero.

Sources

The Letters of St. Boniface, trans. E. Emerton (1940). These letters written by an Anglo-Saxon missionary on the Continent throw a great deal of light on conditions in the Frankish world in the first half of the eighth century.

*Einhard, *Life of Charlemagne,* trans. S. E. Turner (Ann Arbor). The essential work by a contemporary of the great emperor.

Son of Charlemagne: A Contemporary Biography of Louis the Pious, trans. A. Cabaniss (1961).

*S. C. Easton and H. Wieruszowski, eds., *The Era of Charlemagne* (Anvil). A selection of documents representative of Carolingian life, accompanied by perceptive commentaries.

D. Whitelock, ed., *English Historical Documents, c. 500–1042* (1952). A collection similar to the preceding one, illustrative of English society in the Anglo-Saxon period.

17

THE FEUDAL AND MANORIAL SYSTEMS

The idealistic dreams that moved a few men to struggle toward a unified Christian Europe in the Carolingian age were blasted by the events of the last half of the ninth century. Amid the wreckage, two institutions emerged to provide a workable base for society: *feudalism* and *manorialism*. Both were products of forces that had been germinating in political, social, and economic life since the fall of the Roman Empire. By the late ninth and tenth centuries, they emerged as the focal organisms of Western European society.

1. ORIGINS AND NATURE OF FEUDALISM

By about 900 feudalism was becoming the dominant form of political organization over much of the territory once embraced in the Carolingian Empire. This institution grew out of the merging of two ancient practices: personal dependence and a system of shared rights in land tenure. The first was rooted in the Germanic *comitatus* and the Roman clientage system and the second in the Roman tenancy system on the *latifundia*. The confusion and chaos in Western Europe after the Germanic invasions caused these usages to become widespread by the seventh and eighth centuries. In search of a strong protector, many men were happy to engage in a commendation agreement. Likewise, those in search of a livelihood or a way to enlarge their holdings were willing to accept the use of another's land in return for service. Many small landholders were even willing to surrender ownership of their land to a more powerful man on condition that he grant it back to them as a *benefice* for their use in return for service. The greatest landowners, especially the Church, were eager to free themselves of the obligation of exploiting their extensive holdings by granting benefices to those willing to accept the use of the land in return for some service to the grantor.

As we have noted, the strongest Carolingians vigorously applied these usages as a means of expanding their power, thereby giving them greater universality and more precise legal definition. They required the great men of the realm, especially public officials, to become their vassals and rewarded them with benefices, now called *fiefs,* in return for a variety of services, the chief of which was military. In many cases they also granted their vassals *immunities* which conceded to them extensive governing powers over their fiefs. Vassalage and benefice came to be interconnected to the point where personal dependence almost always involved an interchange of land, specifically defined obligations, and political rights.

The eclipse of central government after about 850 amid the mounting fury of Saracen (Moslem), Magyar, and Viking raids forced society to depend more and more on these systems for some political stability. Military security was

This view of the medieval fortress at Carcassonne in southern France dramatically illustrates the kind of security that its possessor could offer to those who were his vassals. And it likewise suggests how defiant that same possessor and his followers could be in the face of those who claimed authority over them. *Photo: Bernard G. Silberstein/Rapho Photo Researchers, Inc.*

most essential, and the emerging feudal system was especially suited to this end. A resourceful lord and his warrior vassals were the only effective force capable of defending a locality against the quick-hitting raiders. All who could sought vassalage under a strong lord; every powerful figure tried to find new vassals to swell his military following. To ensure that such arrangements would persist, vassalage and fiefs were made hereditary. As these local centers of power developed, those who controlled them assumed the political functions formerly exercised by kings. Sometimes the kings granted these powers, but just as often the local potentates simply usurped them. By the beginning of the tenth century, considerable areas of Europe, especially the northern parts of the old Carolingian Empire, were fragmented into hundreds of small private jurisdictions ruled by persons whose relationships were controlled wholly by their private agreements — by feudal contracts. Public authority was too weak and too remote to be effective.

One important point must be added. Long before the beginning of the tenth century, the bulk of the peasant population had already become associated in a condition of dependency with self-sufficient agricultural estates — the villas or, as they came to be called, *manors*. Their dependency was a condition that bound them to serve a possessor of land in the performance of menial services in return for use of a tenancy sufficient to the needs of a family. As a consequence, the peasants were not, properly speaking, participants in the feudal order. Feudalism involved freemen capable of performing the honorable services of fighting and governing and of managing the fiefs that were granted them. It was therefore a sociopolitical system embracing a small class of aristocrats. These same feudal lords and vassals ruled over the peasant population through a set of institutions collectively called *manorialism*.

2. THE FEUDAL CONTRACT

The political bonds involved in the feudal system were defined by the feudal contract. The ritual that evolved to witness such a contract provides a convenient key to the nature of these bonds. One man knelt before another, placed his hands between the other's, and declared himself willing to become his "man." By this voluntary act between two freemen, called *homage*, the first became a vassal and the second a lord. The lord lifted up his new "man" and kissed him, signifying that he accepted him as a vassal. The vassal then swore an oath of *fealty*, binding himself in the sight of God to live up to his obligations. The lord then gave him some object like a banner, a clod of dirt, or a ring. This was called *investiture*. It symbolized the granting of a fief, usually a piece of land, by the lord to the vassal. By the three acts of homage, fealty, and investiture, two individuals bound themselves together in a way that gave to each important rights and imposed on each duties that controlled his political and social activities to a large degree.

The relationship between lord and vassal was intended to last until one party died, unless either broke the contract by some illegal act. By the time the feudal system had reached its full development in the tenth century, the whole arrangement had become hereditary. When a lord died, his eldest son took his place, receiving homage and fealty from his father's vassals and investing them with their fiefs. When a vassal died, his

In this illustration from a manuscript one vassal is rendering homage to the king of Asturias (in Spain) while three others await their turn to perform an act which would oblige them to serve their lord, the king, who in turn was obligated to protect them. The noble standing has probably already done homage and awaits investiture with a fief. *Archive of the Crown of Aragon, Barcelona. Photo: MAS*

lord accepted his son as a vassal and permitted him to retain the fief of his father. Under these arrangements, lord-vassal relationships continued for generations in the same families, adding considerable stability to the entire system.

The exact obligations of each party were defined by local custom—which came to serve as feudal law. Custom varied greatly from place to place in Europe. Generally, however, the lord obligated himself to protect his vassal and give him justice—to use his army to defend a vassal against attack and to maintain a court where the vassal could appear and receive a hearing for any grievances he might have. Put briefly, the feudal contract imposed on the lord the grave responsibility of running a small-scale government for his vassals.

The vassal had equally important obligations. He was expected to conduct himself honorably and loyally toward his lord so as to bring no disgrace upon him—an obligation that generated a special life style in the feudal world. More specifically, he owed his lord four basic obligations: First, there was *military service*, which required the vassal to serve at his own expense as an armed knight for forty days a year. Second, the vassal had to give *counsel* by attending the lord's court and performing other political duties. Third, the vassal was obliged to give *aids* in the form of money payments in certain specific situations (for the ransom of his lord, the knighting of the lord's eldest son, and the marriage dowry of his eldest daughter). Finally, the vassal had to extend *hospitality* to the lord when he and his entourage visited the fief that the vassal had received. In addition, the vassal was obliged to respect certain privileges, called *feudal incidents*, pertaining to the lord by virtue of the fact that he had a vital interest in the fief he had granted to the vassal. The vassal had to maintain the fief in good condition. His heir had to pay an inheritance tax, called a *relief*, when he succeeded to it. The lord had the right of *wardship* over a vassal's minor heir and had to approve the marriage of his daughter, since her husband might someday become heir to the fief. Finally, the vassal was obliged to recognize that if he died without heirs, the fief reverted to the lord (the right of *escheat*).

How were these feudal contracts (which were seldom written down) enforced? When a contract is made in our society, the state stands above the parties as the enforcing agency. In the tenth century there was no effective higher authority; enforcement, too, had to be settled by lords and vassals. The chief instrument was the lord's court, in which the customs that governed feudal contracts in the given area were applied as law. A vassal accused of infidelity to his contract was judged by his "peers"—other vassals—and punished as custom dictated. To this same court every vassal had a right to bring complaints against his lord; again, the vassal's peers judged whether he had redress. Despite this machinery, force was always the final recourse. A lord could call on his other vassals to march against an unfaithful vassal, and a wronged vassal could appeal to his fellow vassals to join him in revolt against an unjust lord. Such wars were numerous in the feudal age.

It would be wrong, however, to picture lords and vassals as seeking any opportunity to start a brawl. In a society that knew no other workable political system, lords were anxious to keep their vassals and gain their services, and vassals were equally anxious to enjoy the protection of a lord. Thus it was to their mutual advantage to live up to the terms of the contract. Then too, in an age when men took religion seriously, there was a good deal of reluctance to break an oath sealed in the presence of God.

3. FEUDALISM AND THE STATE

In theory, feudalism was not necessarily contradictory to the functioning of a large monarchical state. The king was the supreme lord and theoretical owner of all the land in his kingdom. He could at his pleasure accept the vassalage of some of his subjects and grant them fiefs for which they owed him the services previously described. The great vassals of a king could then subdivide their holdings into smaller fiefs and grant them to other men willing to become vassals. This *subinfeudation* could continue until fiefs had been created that were only large enough to permit a single vassal to support himself and fulfill his obligations. In theory, a vast hierarchy was constructed, with the king at the top and with each rank beneath owing allegiance and services to an authority above (see diagram, page 211).

In practice, the feudal system did not work that smoothly. First, if the king or any other lord granted away too much of his land, he had no

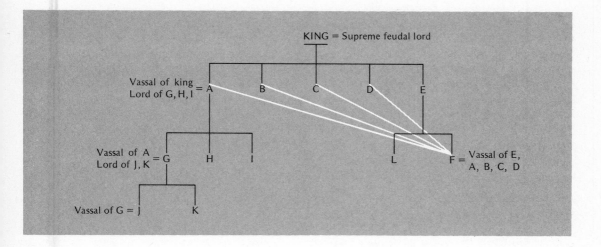

means at his disposal to compel his vassals to render him the services they owed and thus was powerless to enforce his authority over them. Second, subinfeudation created contradictory loyalties which disturbed the hierarchy. There was nothing to keep a vassal of one lord from becoming the vassal of and accepting a fief from another. To illustrate, let us return to the diagram. Man F, dissatisfied with his status as a simple vassal of E, also does homage to A, B, C, and D in return for fiefs from each one, owing services for each of these fiefs. Suppose A and D go to war. Whom should F serve, since he owes military service to each? Or suppose that by all his deals F acquires control over more land than any of his lords—A, B, C, D, or E. Obviously, he would be in a position to defy them and turn the feudal hierarchy upside down. Subinfeudation, by creating conflicting allegiances, made it impossible for feudalism to operate effectively for the control of a large state. As feudal institutions matured, attempts were made to counteract the fragmentation of authority resulting from subinfeudation by developing *liege homage,* a system whereby a lord required not only his own vassals but also their vassals and subvassals to pledge prime allegiance to him. But this practice developed too late to prevent the atomization of power in early feudal society.

Thus, in the areas where feudalism developed first and spread most widely—the kingdoms of the West Franks (France), Burgundy (Arles), and Italy—it seriously weakened royal power in the tenth and eleventh centuries. The kings granted numerous fiefs to vassals who proceeded to turn them into a confusing array of virtually independent duchies, counties, viscounties, marches, and other principalities. Most royal vassals subinfeudated their fiefs, and many of them were unable to control their vassals, who created their own smaller versions of independent political entities. As feudalism spread outward across Europe from its center of origin, it generally tended to fragment large kingdoms and to weaken central government by creating small jurisdictions, each with its own complex network of lord-vassal ties, its own feudal laws, and its own instruments of government. Aside from France, its disintegrative impact was felt most keenly in Germany, central Europe, and, to a lesser degree, Spain and Scandinavia. The major exception was England, where feudalism was imported by a continental conqueror who applied it skillfully to increase royal power.

However, the generally adverse impact of feudalism on larger political entities must not be overemphasized. In many parts of Europe, feudalism provided the means by which local potentates were able to build political structures that were highly effective in providing local protection and order. These principalities eventually became the building blocks for reconstructing larger kingdoms. Moreover, the feudal structure always reserved for kings a variety of rights which they could use to establish their place atop the feudal hierarchy as effective rulers of feudal kingdoms. As we shall see (Chapters 19 and 20), Western Europe witnessed a remarkable political reconsolidation when kings began to exploit the feudal order as a means of expanding royal power over extensive states.

4. THE FEUDAL NOBILITY

The emergence of the feudal system brought with it the crystallization of Western Europe's nobility as a distinct class. As we have seen, that class was long in the making; its ancestors included the old Roman nobility, the Germanic warriors, the Merovingian landholder politicians, the Carolingian royal vassals. The maturing of feudalism drew these strains together into a class of specialists in warfare and government with a definite role to play in maintaining society. As it took shape, this class developed a style of life impregnated with the usages of feudalism that made it a distinctive, exclusive group almost inaccessible to the rest of Europe's population. Like its fiefs, its place became hereditary, making it self-perpetuating.

In the ninth and tenth centuries that way of life was rough and crude. No better picture of it can be found than in the epic poems written to celebrate it, especially the *Song of Roland* or *The Cid*. The great virtues of the feudal noble were loyalty, bravery, faithfulness, and generosity. Above all, he had prowess: His life centered in a career of fighting for his lord, his lands, his serfs — and his God. From his youth, he learned his craft as an apprentice in the service of one who already knew the art. The culmination of his education was his knighting, an elaborate ceremony surrounded by religious symbolism which ended with his investment with the tools of war. These made him a noble. Of course, he had to sustain himself as a warrior, so that the management of his ancestral lands constituted a part of his education. And he had a political function stemming from his position as the vassal of another and probably as a lord over still

others. Therefore, his education had economic and political dimensions.

His style of life was in general crude, which stemmed in part from the economic limitations of society but also from the fact that the feudal world was a man's world. The typical noble residence was a wooden fortress designed for defense rather than comfort. The routine of life featured pursuits typical of soldiering: heavy eating, drinking, gambling, hunting, dancing, wenching, the mock warfare of the tournament, and often real warfare. Usually nobles were illiterate, "reading" by listening to tales of war sung by bards and to the simple preaching of the priests. Marriage was arranged with an eye toward gaining new lands, new vassals, or new political opportunities; seldom was it marred by considerations of sentiment. But the family was another matter, for a household rich in strong sons and nubile daughters possessed a great asset in this world of war, land acquisition, and personal relationships. The nobles were religious in a simple, unintellectual way: They trusted God to take care of them if they were brave and faithful and generous. Their way of expressing their faith was active, impelling them to do something visible to show their piety — build a church, give land to a monastery, go on a pilgrimage, or fight for God.

Under the impact of improving economic conditions, greater order, and new spiritual impulses, the feudal nobility moved toward greater gentility and refinement, and ultimately developed an elaborate code of conduct known as *chivalry* (see Chapter 18). But even in its harsh, crude form, the ethos of the feudal noble constituted a vital factor in Western European history. It nourished a sense of responsibility for the security of society. It engendered independence of action and prowess. All these qualities developed leaders with potential for constructive activity on a scale wider than the fief or petty principality.

5. FEUDALISM AND THE CHURCH

Feudalism had a drastic effect on another vital institution in Western society: the Church. Under the guidance of the great Carolingian rulers of the eighth and early ninth centuries, the Church had enjoyed a tremendous upsurge in power and influence, owing to better organization, reform of the clergy, and standardization of ritual and doctrine. The coming of feudalism undid most of this work and pushed the Church into one of most trying periods.

The difficulties of the Church in feudal society stemmed chiefly from its position as a great landholder. Much of its land had been acquired in the form of grants from kings and other powerful laymen, who expected the bishops and abbots so favored to render services as did any other vassals. Once having acquired large fiefs, these officials acted as did other feudal landholders: They granted their lands out as fiefs, and thus became lords in their own right. And as lords, they had to concern themselves with protecting their vassals, holding courts, and guarding their interests in general. The consequences were disastrous for the spiritual well-being of Western Europe. Ruling Church officials became preoccupied with secular matters at the expense of their religious duties. Laymen refused to invest any bishop or abbot with a fief unless he had the qualities of a good vassal. In effect, this meant that laymen controlled elections to high offices. The top level of the Church organization thus came to be filled with good fighters and good administrators who had little interest in religious problems. They neglected discipline, education, charity, and moral conduct. The lower clergy sank into ignorance. Religious life in lay society suffered an assortment of evils worse than in any other age in Christian history. Even the pope, who was the head of the Church, did not escape. During the tenth century the papal office was filled with men chosen by powerful feudal lords in central Italy.

One must be somewhat cautious, however, in decrying the abysmal condition of the Church in the feudal age. For its feudalization drew it into intimate contact with the basic institutions and elements of society. This prepared it for an even more decisive role than it had previously enjoyed and gave it a relevance to reality such as it had seldom before had. Perhaps it would not be wrong to say that for the first time since its beginnings Christianity had become fully engaged in the world and was finally in a position where it could move the world by bestirring itself.

6. THE MANORIAL SYSTEM

The feudal nobility was supported by the peasantry, comprising the great bulk of the population and living in a world apart in terms of legal status and social position. By the tenth century, peasant life in most parts of Western Europe was bound up in the manorial system that had taken shape slowly over several earlier centuries. The manor was an economic unit organized to produce everything needed by its noble possessor, called the *seigneur* or lord of the manor, and its peasants. It was also a political and social unit providing for the governance of the peasants living there.

The typical manor was an estate of considerable proportions, its exact size being determined by the requirements of self-sufficiency. A workable manor had to have arable land for raising crops, meadowland for hay and pasture, woodland for fuel and building material, and a natural water supply. Some feudal nobles possessed only enough land to constitute one such unit, while others held a fief large enough to incorporate several. One-third to one-half of the manor's tillable soil was reserved as a *demesne* for the seigneur's support. The rest was divided into small tenancies allotted to the peasants for their own support. The untillable land, like meadows, pastures, and woods, was exploited in common. Under the widely used *open-field system,* the tillable land was divided into large, unfenced plots that were exploited as units. Each open field was subdivided into strips. The lord reserved a third to a half of these strips in each large field to himself and assigned others to each tenant. In this way everyone got a share of good and bad land.

Farming techniques were crude. Most labor was done by hand, since few peasants could afford to feed oxen, long the chief beast of burden. Teams of oxen for heavy jobs like plowing and hauling were communally owned. Most labor was also performed as a common effort. To protect the fertility of the soil, part of the land was

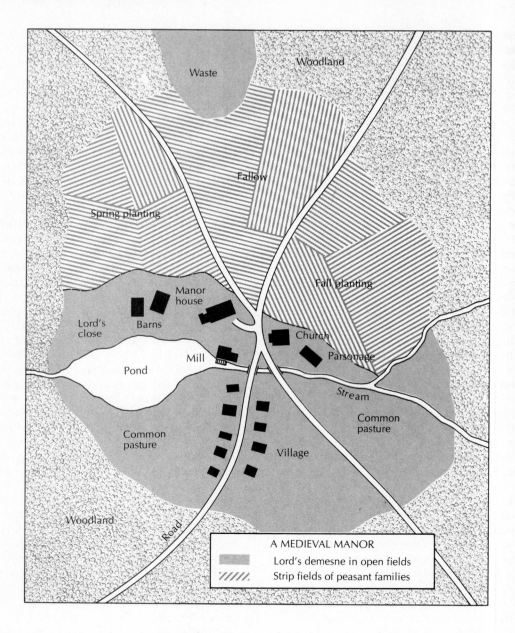

A MEDIEVAL MANOR

Lord's demesne in open fields

Strip fields of peasant families

left idle each year. Until about 900 a *two-field system* of rotation was widely used; then the more efficient *three-field system* began to spread. The arable land of each manor was divided into three open fields, seigneurs and tenants having strips in each. Every year and in rotation, one field lay fallow, a second was planted with wheat in the fall, and a third with barley or rye in the spring. In spite of this system, yields were small with the result that famines were common. Most peasants raised vegetables on the small plots surrounding their huts; these gardens were often very productive because they were fertilized with human and animal waste. Pigs and goats were especially popular because they could live off the woods and wasteland.

Most manufactured goods had to be made on a manor since there was little trade. Although specialized artisans such as blacksmiths, carpenters, and masons sometimes plied their trades there, the peasants were generally required to make and repair needed equipment, buildings, and furnishings. Women, including noble ladies, made clothing, preserved food, concocted medicine, and practiced a dozen other skills.

The center of a manor was a village containing a manor house, peasant huts, a church, granaries, a mill, a bakery, and the like. This village was more than a collection of buildings; it was a community containing a government and a social system. Its governor was the seigneur, typically a member of the feudal order, who had the power to judge, punish, and exact what he wished from his peasant-subjects. Only rarely did an outside force—the king, the seigneur's feudal overlord, the Church—succeed in intruding into the manorial jurisdiction. If the seigneur lived on his manor, he usually exercised his power in person. If he lived elsewhere, as many great nobles who possessed numerous manors did, he entrusted management to *stewards* and *bailiffs,* usually recruited from the ranks of the peasantry. Each manor had its own governmental institutions—a court, a law, a police force. The law, consisting of a vast body of custom defining every aspect of the relationship among those living on the manor, was of crucial importance in regulating manorial life.

The peasant population of a typical manor was divided into complex legal groupings, the exact status of each group being defined in terms of the obligations its members owed to the lord. On some manors, there were slaves who were simply the property of the lord; there were also freemen who rented land and returned payments in money and produce for its use but were otherwise free to do what they wished. The ordinary peasant was a *serf* or *villein* who was bound to the soil and obligated to provide services to the lord at his will, the most important being labor. Serfs almost always held a tenancy from which they could not be dispossessed, making their status a secure one. On some manors, there

were peasants who had no tenancy but simply possessed a hut and garden; these *cottàrs* often owed some kind of service to the lord and sometimes worked for hire, either for the lord or for other peasants. These legal distinctions tended to become meaningless as a result of economic and political conditions on the manors: Because slavery was not economically feasible, most slaves merged into the class of serfs; because the freeman's liberty meant little in a world of limited choices, many of them preferred the security of serfdom.

More important to the peasant than his precise legal status were the obligations he owed his seigneur. These obligations, defined by manorial custom, varied greatly over Europe, but everywhere certain dues were imposed on the peasants. The chief was labor service. On most manors the serfs owed *week work,* which required each to spend three days a week tilling the demesne of the seigneur. In addition, serfs owed *boon days,* extra days of work during the planting and harvesting seasons. Finally, there was the *corvée* requiring special labor services to maintain the roads, buildings, and fortifications of the manor. The time left to the serf was devoted to tilling his own land. All peasants rendered payments in kind to the seigneur from the meager return from their tenancies; this *taille* amounted to a primitive taxation system. And they had to pay *tithes* to the Church; very often these payments found their way into the hands of the seigneur. On most manors, the peasants were obliged to pay *banalities* for the use of the mills, ovens, and wine presses over which the seigneur maintained a monopoly—perhaps because he alone could afford to build these facilities. The seigneur collected a death tax (*heriot*). A serf whose daughter married outside the manor also paid a tax (*formariage* or *merchet*). There were, of course, fees and fines to be paid by peasants involved in litigation in the manorial court.

It is obvious that the manor provided the seigneur with considerable opportunities to enrich himself from the peasants. There were, however, limits on his exploitation, as the manor was wholly dependent on them for one prime ingredient of the manorial economy—labor. There was no substitute for human labor and no source for it except manor dwellers. The lord had to act with some justice and benevolence toward his laborers if he hoped to get efficient and constant work from them. The manorial system also supplied considerable security for the peasant. The little surplus that the collectivity could amass was a hedge against the frequent crop failures and plagues that might have meant death to a peasant on his own. The Church was ever-present on the manors, offering its particular kind of solace in the face of life's hardships. In the manorial village, the peasant found an array of pleasures—beer drinking, gaming, singing, dancing—all capable of easing a life of bare subsistence.

Feudalism and manorialism do not usually receive a sympathetic evaluation; the political,

social, and economic bases of most other civilized societies seem far superior and considerably more effective. Despite their limitations, however, the operation in the backward society in which they developed was crucial. Each worked to create small associations of men that established stability in an unstable, undisciplined world. Each integrated groups of people from various levels of society and with various talents. These simple collectivities soon demonstrated an immense potential for development. It is not just coincidence that Western European society began a spectacular period of growth *after* feudalism and manorialism had emerged. They constitute the foundation stones the infant Western European society had been struggling to find since the collapse of Greco-Roman civilization.

Suggested Reading

Feudalism

*Carl Stephenson, *Mediaeval Feudalism* (Cornell). A simple, straightforward description.

*F. L. Ganshof. *Feudalism*, trans. P. Grierson (Harper Torchbook). A work stressing the legal aspects of feudalism.

*Marc Bloch, *Feudal Society*, 2 vols. (Phoenix). The classic treatment of the subject, approaching feudal institutions from a sociological perspective.

John Critchley, *Feudalism* (1978). A good recent study that compares European feudalism to similar institutions in other societies.

*John Beeler, *Warfare in Feudal Europe, 730–1200* (Cornell).

J. F. Verbruggen, *The Art of Warfare in Western Europe during the Middle Ages (From the Eighth Century to 1340)*, trans. S. Willard and C. M. Southern (1977). Two fine studies of an institution important to the feudal order.

Joseph and Frances Gies, *Life in a Medieval Castle* (1974). Provides a good sense of medieval aristocratic life.

Manorialism

N. Neilson, *Medieval Agrarian Economy* (1936). An excellent, brief description of the manorial system.

*Georges Duby, *Rural Economy and Country Life in the*

Medieval West, trans. Cynthia Postan (South Carolina). This detailed study based on the most recent research is undoubtedly the best work on the nature and evolution of the medieval agricultural system.

*Marc Bloch, *French Rural History: An Essay on Its Basic Characteristics*, trans. Janet Sondheimer (California). A work that tries to describe the historical roots of the manorial system in France and to trace its evolution.

*H. S. Bennett, *Life on an English Manor* (Cambridge). An engaging picture of manorial life, stressing peasant conditions.

*Eileen Power, *Medieval People* (10th rev. ed., Barnes and Noble). Delightfully describes typical representatives of medieval social groups; her portrait of a medieval peasant is especially effective.

Sources

*David Herlihy, ed., *The History of Feudalism* (Humanities). A highly informative collection of legal, literary, and narrative sources, illustrating the nature of feudal institutions and practices.

The Song of Roland, trans. F. B. Luquiens (Macmillan).

The Poem of the Cid, trans. L. B. Simpson (University of California). Aside from their literary value, these two medieval epic poems reveal a great deal about the mentality of the feudal nobility.

Retrospect

In a letter written in 593 or 594, Pope Gregory I called his contemporaries' attention to the strife, suffering, destruction, and injustice seen everywhere. "See what has befallen Rome, once mistress of the world," he mourned. "What is there now, I ask, of delight in this world?"

In a way, Gregory supplied the key to the history of the early Middle Ages. Most of what had characterized Greco-Roman civilization had been lost, and society was poorer. One can easily write—as many have—the history of the early Middle Ages in terms of the destruction of classical civilization; from this perspective the era is indeed a dark age.

However, between A.D. 500 and 1000 much happened to replace what had been lost. Three new civilizations—Byzantine, Moslem, and Western European—had been shaped within the confines of the classical world. Each retained precious elements of the old order. Each developed new institutions and ideas to suit its needs and situation. An inventory of what men had fashioned in these difficult centuries gives ample evidence that these "dark" years deserve a decisive place in the continuum of history. By 1000 there were still "things of delight" in the world.

The emergence of three new civilizations was not the only transformation that occurred in the early Middle Ages. In addition to the creative forces at work within each, a new dynamism had developed in the form of interactions among these civilizations. The Greco-Roman world had tended to absorb existing cultures into a unified pattern that stood counterposed to the barbarian world. By 1000 lines of interaction and points of tension existed among civilized societies rather than between the civilized and uncivilized orbits. This was a forceful determinant in the course of future historical development.

The period just reviewed belonged to the East; Byzantium and Islam far surpassed Western Europe in every respect. This little appreciated fact demands attention, for the accomplishments of the Byzantine and Moslem worlds in these centuries gave their peoples a proud sense of contribution to the creation of civilized life that other other societies later forgot. None benefited more from the achievements of these leaders than the struggling Western Europeans, whose future glory would have been different had it not been for what they absorbed from the East.

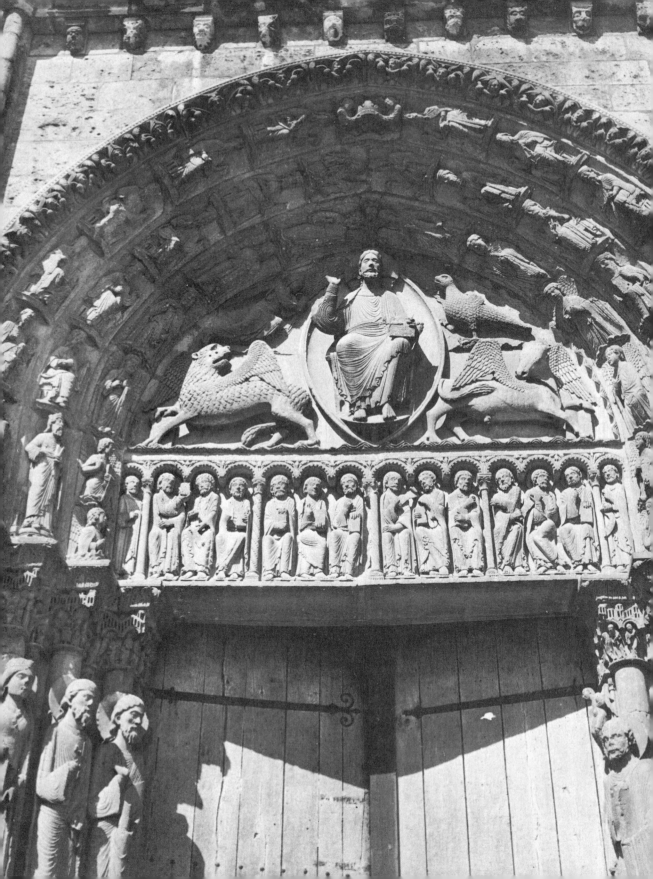

V

The High Middle Ages
1000~1300
The Revival of Europe

An eleventh-century chronicler named Ralph Glaber tells us that many Europeans were convinced that, in accordance with ancient prophecy, the world would come to an end at the end of the first millennium of Christian history, that is, in the year 1000. But, wrote Ralph, when that fateful year passed without the appearance of the Antichrist, "it was as if the very world had shaken itself and cast off its old age." Everywhere, he said, men rivaled each other to build better churches and were filled with new ardor for the faith. This bit of medieval legend, whatever its validity in summing up the actual state of mind of Western Europeans in the late tenth century, provides a fitting introduction to this section. In actual fact, Western Europe did enjoy a sudden revival beginning about 1000 and continuing with unabated vigor until about 1300. This era is often referred to as the High Middle Ages. It is the period in which medieval Western European society reached its full maturity.

As our account of these effervescent, creative centuries unfolds, it should become increasingly clear that the revival of Western European civilization was rooted in certain basic institutions that had been forged during the preceding era: feudalism, manorialism, the Church, the precious treasure of learning stored up by Carolingian scholars. Although primitive in many ways, these institutions and ideas provided basic patterns of organization, social control, thought, and belief which permitted men to apply their energies and intelligences constructively. They were suddenly capable of producing new wealth. They found themselves able to construct larger political entities and to form new class relationships. Their spiritual, intellectual, and esthetic capabilities were expanded so that a wide range of cultural achievements was possible. They found themselves

able to turn outward from their be-
leaguered world to make a major impression on wide areas of the world
heretofore little known to them. In
short, the High Middle Ages was an
era of creative activity that made
Western European civilization a factor
of major significance in the world. The
long centuries of painful experimentation that marked the Early Middle Ages had clearly ended.

Throughout the Early Middle Ages a major de-
terrent to growth of any kind was the severely
limited level of material resources available to
Western European society. Between 1000 and
1300 that situation was dramatically changed by
a remarkable economic revival accompanied by
major adjustments of the social order. These
changes had their source at the base of society;
their agents were modest manorial seigneurs,
toiling peasants, peddler merchants, and simple
artisans. The more spectacular accomplishments
of the High Middle Ages in politics, religion,
and culture owed a great debt to these simple
members of society who showed remarkable talents in finding ways to increase the wealth of
Western European society.

1. POPULATION GROWTH

The forces that generate economic growth in any
society are so complex that they defy clear description; so it was in Western Europe in the
tenth century. However, one contributing factor
is evident: The population expanded rapidly between about 900 and 1350. This demographic
change, reversing a trend that had prevailed
since late Roman times, resulted in a doubling of
the population of Western Europe during that
period; one generally accepted authority has estimated that the population grew from about 30

18

ECONOMIC AND SOCIAL REVIVAL

million in 1000 to about 60 million in 1300. While the growth was general in Europe (and in fact all across Asia to the Far East), the heaviest growth was concentrated in certain areas: northern France, the Low Countries, the Rhine basin, and northern Italy.

The causes of this worldwide growth are obscure. There is some evidence that Eurasia was relatively free of killer diseases, especially bubonic plague; the destructive aspects of warfare were curbed; and more food was available. Conditions of relative stability and security may have encouraged population growth. The expanding population both put enormous pressures on the agricultural system for great productivity and provided new hands which could be turned to new economic enterprises.

2. AGRICULTURAL EXPANSION

The catalytic force that triggered economic growth between 1000 and 1300 was expansion of agricultural productivity. By the tenth century the manorial system had developed to the point where it contained a potent reservoir of forces capable of generating economic growth: managerial ability, trained manpower, and technical skills. For reasons not entirely clear—although the pressure of growing population was probably crucial—these latent forces were unleashed.

The result was a considerable expansion of agricultural production which, in turn, stimulated new ventures in trade and industry.

The agricultural expansion involved four interrelated developments. First, more land was put under cultivation as a result of an immense amount of land clearance and peasant resettlement. Much of this land clearance simply involved pushing out the boundaries of existing manors, which in the Early Middle Ages stood as cultivated islands in vast stretches of forest, to put newly cleared land to the plow. But many European cultivators, often encouraged by enterprising landlords, moved great distances to settle on the frontiers of Western Europe. The chief areas of colonization were on the German frontier east of the Elbe River and in Spanish lands being wrested from Moslem control. It appears that the cultivated acreage in Western Europe doubled or trebled between 1000 and 1300.

Second, technological advances greatly increased the efficiency of the labor force, especially by supplying new sources of power. More efficient wheeled plows were perfected. New harnesses, including the shoulder collar, were developed which allowed wider use of the speedier, more efficient horse as a draft animal. Water- and windmills were greatly improved, and complicated power trains (particularly those involving the principle of the crank) were developed to allow the power these mills produced to be applied to such tasks as grinding grain. Human labor freed by these devices was put to more productive uses.

Third, agricultural production was increased by improved methods of tillage and animal husbandry. Irrigation systems were developed in some parts of Western Europe. Agricultural specialization, as in the vineyards of Burgundy and the great sheep-raising granges in England, was made possible by increasing opportunities for exchange that we shall describe later. Greater attention was given to fertilization. The three-field system of tillage spread, which protected the fertility of the soil, promoted efficient use of labor and equipment, and permitted a greater variety of crops to be grown. Better seeds were developed in many parts of Europe to take advantage of local soil and weather conditions. And there were improvements in animal breeds producing better animals and more animal products, such as meat and wool.

Finally, production was expanded as a consequence of what we might call agricultural entrepreneurship. Planning and the adaptation of ancient customs freed labor to clear new lands around existing manors, to apply new tools and techniques, and to dispose profitably of any excess production. Bold foresight resettled groups of peasants on distant lands, and new modes of operation sustained these settlements. Innovative thinking developed new seeds, bred new animals, and launched specialized production. Entrepreneurship, exercised in small and undramatic ways, perhaps provides the key to the greatest agricultural revolution in world history between the neolithic discovery of agriculture and the advent of modern mechanized farming.

3. REVIVAL OF TRADE AND MANUFACTURING

The expansion of agricultural production after 1000 stimulated an economic development of equal magnitude and importance: the revival of trade and manufacturing. Trade had never entirely vanished from the Western European scene, but it had declined steadily from late Roman times. During the late tenth and early eleventh centuries, a revival began that continued until the mid-fourteenth century. During this era, commerce became the catalytic force in European economy. Among the factors contributing to the commercial revival were population growth, agricultural expansion, greater political order, outside stimuli, and Western European political, military, and religious expansion. But to these must be added the labors of men whose activities are for the most part unknown to us.

In considerable part, the Europeans' commercial expansion was a story of their ability to break into the flourishing Byzantine and Moslem trading complexes and to gain control of a share of them. Western Europe had always remained in contact with the Eastern trade centers, primarily through Byzantine outposts in Venice and southern Italy. In the tenth century this activity began to quicken. The Venetians took the leading role, steadily enlarging their contacts by sea with Constantinople and bringing an ever-increasing volume of goods to the West. In the eleventh century Pisa's and Genoa's navies loosened Moslem control over the western Mediterranean, and their merchants established trade relations with the Moslems in Spain and North Africa. The successes of the early crusading movement (see Chapter 21) allowed the Italian cities to establish important footholds in eastern Mediterranean Moslem cities in the twelfth century, and the conquest of Constantinople in 1204 during the Fourth Crusade gave the Venetians virtual control over Byzantine trade. By the thirteenth century the efforts of Italian merchants were reinforced by those from coastal cities in France and Spain; collectively they had become the dominant force in Mediterranean trade. The lifeblood of this international trade was luxury items, especially spices and fine cloth. At first these goods were paid for by European gold, but gradually the Europeans developed products that found a market in the East.

Meanwhile, another window to the East was opened on the northern fringes of the Continent by Viking pirates whose raiding ventures opened a path through the Baltic Sea and along the rivers of Russia to the Black Sea and Constantinople. Traders from many areas of north-

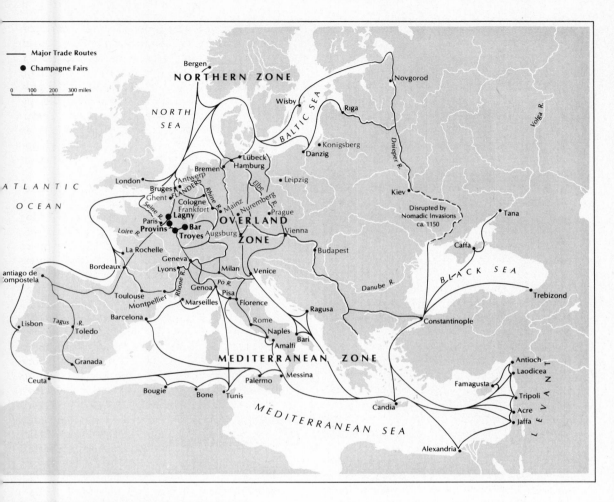

Major Trade Routes

● **Champagne Fairs**

0 100 200 300 miles

NORTHERN ZONE

Bergen

NORTH SEA

Novgorod

Wisby

BALTIC SEA

Riga

Konigsberg

Danzig

Leipzig

Dnieper R.

Volga R.

Lübeck
Hamburg

Bremen

London

Antwerp
Bruges
FLANDERS
Ghent
Cologne
Frankfort
Paris
Lagny
Provins ● Bar
Troyes ● Augsburg
OVERLAND ZONE

Rhine R.
Mainz
Nuremberg
Prague
Vienna
Elbe R.

Kiev

Disrupted by
Nomadic Invasions
ca. 1150

Tana

ATLANTIC OCEAN

Seine R.
Loire R.

La Rochelle

Geneva
Lyons

Bordeaux

Santiago de
Compostela

Rhone R.

Milan
Po R.
Genoa
Pisa
Florence
Venice

Budapest

Danube R.

Caffa

BLACK SEA

Trebizond

Toulouse
Montpellier
Marseilles

Barcelona

Rome

Naples
Amalfi
Bari

Ragusa

Constantinople

Lisbon
Tagus R.
Toledo

Granada

Ceuta

Bougie

Bone
Tunis

Palermo
Messina

MEDITERRANEAN ZONE

Candia

MEDITERRANEAN SEA

Antioch
Laodicea
Famagusta
Tripoli
Acre
Jaffa
LEVANT

Alexandria

**TRADE ROUTES, TWELFTH AND THIRTEENTH
CENTURIES**

ern Europe eventually followed the Vikings
along this route to carry a variety of goods to and
from the lands bordering the North and Baltic
seas and Constantinople. The focal point of this
northern trading complex came to be Flanders
and the cities of northern Germany and to a
lesser degree English ports.

By no means so spectacular as the expansion
of international trade but probably more important was a steady growth of trade within Europe.
Its fundamental impetuses were two: the demand of Europe's aristocracy for luxury items

and the needs of manors and towns for the
necessities of life.

The aggressive Italian and Flemish merchants
took the lead in distributing luxury items from
the East across the face of Western Europe. As
early as the eleventh century, Italian merchants
began moving out of northern Italy into the
Rhone and Rhine valleys and onward into
France and Germany. Flemish traders penetrated
England by the Thames and France and Germany by the Rhine, Scheldt, and Meuse valleys.
From these prime arteries an ever-widening

In this scene the bishop of Paris is giving his blessing to various merchants who are waiting for the opening of the fair held annually just outside Paris near the monastery of St. Denis. Such fairs provided a major setting for the exchange of goods from far and near. The presence of a figure so important as the bishop of Paris suggests that these fairs were viewed as a vital part of life. *Bibliothèque nationale, Paris, ms. lat. 962, f. 264. Photo: Bulloz*

network of overland and river routes spread out in all directions. During the twelfth century, the great meeting place of international traders were the fairs of Champagne in France. Here merchants from all Europe came to display their wares to other merchants who in turn carried their purchases to local markets and prize customers. By the thirteenth century the fairs were increasingly giving way to permanent markets established in cities.

Complementing the traffic in luxury items was an ever-growing exchange of goods between formerly self-sufficient manors and the growing towns. Local trade in such items as salt, wine, and metals had always existed, and from the eleventh century onward, it broadened to provide the growing towns with foodstuffs and raw materials and to carry manufactured products of the towns back to the villages. In terms of volume and of the number of people involved, the town-country exchange undoubtedly constituted the larger component of medieval trade.

The expansion of commercial activity in Western Europe promoted the growth of manufacturing. By the twelfth century the towns began to offer opportunities for skilled artisans to make a single product for sale to their fellow townsmen and rural buyers or to merchants who distributed them wherever there was a demand. This kind of manufacturing long remained a vital element of the town economy and put a vast quantity of commonplace goods into trade. Some high-quality items found an international market. By the thirteenth century some areas of Europe, particularly Flanders and northern Italy, had developed more complex manufacturing organizations involving merchant entrepreneurs who "put out" raw materials into the households of hired laborers. This "putting out" system, or "cottage" industry, was especially applied to wool processing, which became international in scope: Raw wool was produced in England and processed into fine cloth in Flanders and northern Italy.

There is no way of ascertaining what the revival of trade and manufacturing meant to the Western European economy in quantitative terms. It is probably safe to venture that by the thirteenth century, Western Europe surpassed the classical world in trade and industry. Agriculture was certainly still the most important element in the total economy, but the added wealth created by exchange and expert craftsmanship had decisive importance.

4. ECONOMIC CONSEQUENCES OF INCREASED PRODUCTION

The new level of prosperity generated by the increased agricultural, commercial, and industrial productivity in Western Europe manifested itself in a hundred ways: better homes, bigger churches, more elaborate dress, greater quantities and varieties of food, more art and literature, more leisure. By 1300 the specter of constant poverty and starvation had vanished for most Europeans. But aside from the general increase in wealth, greater productivity had more specific results.

First, economic growth caused the revitalization of city life. Towns had never disappeared from Western Europe. But between the fall of Greco-Roman civilization and about 1000, they became for the most part ecclesiastical, administrative, or defense centers, sparsely populated and economically dependent on agriculture. Between 1000 and 1300, ancient towns grew dramatically in area and population, and new towns appeared in many places. Whereas in 1000 most towns had only a few thousand inhabitants at most, by 1300 there were cities of considerable population: Milan had 200,000 people; Venice, Florence, and Genoa all had at least 100,000; Paris boasted 80,000; and London had some 50,000. By that date perhaps 10 percent of Europe's population lived in urban centers. More significantly, the great bulk of the residents earned their livelihood from trade and manufacturing, thus turning the "new" towns into completely different institutions from the old. The urbanization of Western Europe had begun, never to stop to the present.

In terms of physical growth, most important towns of the era were simply enlargements of older episcopal, monastic, administrative, or military centers. Merchants and then artisans were attracted to these centers for many reasons: security, favor shown them by ruling authorities, access to rivers and roads, availability of buyers. Often they settled haphazardly outside the walls of the old center, their shops, stalls, and households creating a *suburb* (Latin, "under the city"). As commercial activity increased, the walls were extended to enclose the suburbs. Often the suburban marketplace became the focus of urban life. New towns were often established at locations favorable to commerce, and their physical growth resembled that of the old centers.

A second consequence of economic expansion was the growth of a money economy. Money had always circulated in Western Europe, but minimally until the eleventh century. Thereafter its use rapidly expanded to meet the needs of trade. The money economy soon spread to agriculture, where payment in kind had long prevailed as the basis of exchange. Its impact was revolutionary. A whole new form of wealth emerged to challenge the monopoly held by land. Old economic relationships were dissolved and replaced by new. The exploitation of money shaped a new set of economic values.

A third major effect of economic growth was the transformation of manorialism. The market for surplus food provided by the towns gave landlords and peasants money incomes, in return for which they could embellish their lives with products from the town markets. This new potential for profit changed the emphasis on the manors from self-sufficiency to surplus production. And under this pressure, the traditional manorial system began to dissolve.

The dissolution proceeded in two broad directions. In many areas of Western Europe, especially in the twelfth century, landlords began to break their demesnes into tenancies and rent them to peasants for cash. And they commuted the labor obligations of their serfs and the dues owed them in kind to money payments. Serfs could afford to buy off their obligations because the town market offered them a chance to sell produce and save a little money; they were especially favored because the whole era was inflationary. But many landlords, particularly in the thirteenth century, moved in the opposite direction, expanding their demesne and managing its cultivation themselves for profit. A most profitable course was to concentrate on a specialized crop for sale. Lords who did this often displaced peasants from their ancient tenancies, imposed more rigid labor obligations on them, and forced them to work for wages. In either case, the old manorial system dissolved over much of Western Europe. In place of the self-contained manors emerged a variety of forms of agricultural exploitation where the concern for profit dominated, an end that could only be achieved by linking the countryside to the towns, their markets, and their money.

The fourth economic change is no surprise: the rise of the profit motive. No longer were men content with self-sufficiency; they worked and planned in order to gain more worldly goods. Western Europeans began to perfect means to achieve this end. High-profit overseas trading ventures were often financed by a non-merchant investor under a contract (called a *commenda*) that provided for sharing the profits after the merchant returned and disposed of the goods. We have already described how landlords manipulated their lands for profit. Lending money for profit (called *usury* by the Church and condemned as a sin) was widespread by the thirteenth century. These are only a few of the multitude of practices that heralded a new economic spirit. A protocapitalist economy was developing.

Finally, Western Europeans had achieved such economic growth by 1300 that they had seized economic leadership in the vast area surrounding the Mediterranean—a leadership that would eventually be extended to the whole world. No longer did Byzantium and Islam stand in the relationship of advanced economic centers to a backward West. As we shall see later, international political factors helped promote the advance of the Europeans, but it is equally obvious that their enterprise and their methods played a vital role in establishing their economic leadership. It is ironic that their rapid rise was in large part due to their ability to intrude into the richer economies of the East and exploit them for the benefit of the West.

5. SOCIAL CHANGE: THE BOURGEOISIE

The far-reaching economic transformation of the era from 1000 to 1300 had a significant impact on the simple social order that characterized the feudal-manorial world of the tenth century. The most important social development was the emergence of a new class, the *bourgeoisie.* Those engaged in commerce and living in towns found themselves in a society that had no place for them: no legal status, no understanding of their needs, no respect for them. One challenge facing them was to compel the fuedal-manorial-ecclesiastical world to recognize and accept them and their activities. Another was to devise rules and techniques for conducting their activities in an orderly, efficient fashion.

As soon as men began to devote full time to commerce and manufacturing, they felt a basic need for personal freedom. Their livelihood depended on freedom to move about in a world that fixed men to fiefs and manors, to dispose of their property at will in a world where property was bound up in an intricate network of obligations, to apply their talent and labor to whatever opportunity arose in a world where long-sanctioned customs dictated how men spent their time and efforts. And so the merchants and the artisans of the towns struggled for personal freedom and were successful in achieving it. Their methods were various: purchase; force; grants won from kings, feudal lords, and bishops; flight. By 1300 simply living in a town meant personal freedom. This freedom constituted a prime legal mark of the new class: Its members were freemen, legally distinct from both aristocrats and serfs.

But personal freedom, although vital, was not sufficient. The merchants and artisans could not operate adequately under the institutions of government and laws of the feudal world. To meet their political and legal needs, the inhabitants of a town often banded together and sought to gain political privileges. Usually the object of their corporate action was a *charter* granted by a king, a feudal lord, or a bishop. Often the charter was not to be had for the asking, but acquiring one grew easier when the power wielders began to appreciate the advantages of having thriving towns in their domains. The typical charter usually recognized the citizen body of the town as a *corporation* that could act and be treated legally as a person. It almost always granted personal freedom to the residents of the town and called for dues in money instead of personal service. Finally, most charters granted the townsmen permission to institute their own local government. In a few cases, especially in Italy, towns gained complete political freedom; such towns, called *communes,* were the exception. More commonly, the townsmen had only the right to regulate local affairs while respecting some higher authority in matters not strictly local.

In shaping political institutions, the townsmen experimented considerably. In most towns there was some degree of popular participation in political life, authority being vested in an elected council. In a typical commune the council usually possessed complete power to legislate, conduct courts, levy taxes, expend money for civic purposes, and negotiate with outside powers. Its only responsibility was to the citizens of the town. Many towns chose a chief administrative official — *mayor, burgomaster, podesta* — who functioned under the supervision of the council. Judicial affairs were entrusted to specially trained judges. Towns with only limited political freedom often had to respect the authority of a royal official or a representative of a feudal lord who exercised many powers in judicial and financial matters. Whatever the form of government, the towns quickly created an elaborate new body of law regulating civic affairs. As a consequence, the bourgeoisie lived in an entirely different legal setting from that of nobles, clergy, and serfs.

A grave problem facing the bourgeoisie was the regulation of economic activity among merchants and artisans, a problem for which the rest of society had no solution. The usual answer was the establishment of *guilds* within each town. The merchants usually formed a merchant guild while the artisans formed several craft guilds, one for each trade. The merchant guild existed primarily to protect the interests of merchants from outsiders and to restrain the members from taking unfair advantage of one another. Each guild enacted specific rules governing prices to be charged, trading practices to be observed, and the conditions under which trade could be conducted. The craft guilds similarly imposed regulations on their members concerning prices, quality of goods, conditions of labor, and quantity of production. They also controlled the conditions for entering a trade, a power which gave them a vital role in education. Boys began their careers as *apprentices* to a master, working from two to seven years under his guidance and living in his household. The apprentice then became a *journeyman* who worked for hire until he had saved sufficient money and developed adequate skill to open his own shop and become a *master.* Before he acquired that rank, he had to submit his workmanship to a rigid examination by the guild. Along with their regulative functions, merchant and craft guilds had purely social functions. Each usually had its own guild-hall, where banquets, pageants, and religious affairs were conducted for the entertainment and edification of the members. Each guild also aided its members when sickness or death struck a family.

New business methods also developed rapidly in the towns. The use of money became typical of the town economy. Sound systems of coinage were developed, especially among the Italian towns, whose coins were used over much of Europe until royal governments finally developed national currency systems. Banks appeared and lent money for interest, supplied bills of exchange to merchants who did not want to carry large sums with them, and provided places of deposit. Although the Church strenuously opposed usury and tried to keep it a function confined to Jewish moneylenders, its struggle was not successful. By the thirteenth century several rich Italian merchant families and the great crusading orders, especially the Templars, conducted large-scale lending ventures. Gradually, the Church modified its position, conceding that great risk justified compensation and that a borrower who did not pay his debt promptly ought to be penalized. Indeed, churchmen were among the best customers of Italian bankers. Insurance was developed to protect merchants against almost any risk. Wholesaling became a regular practice. Bookkeeping systems were devised. In brief, a modern businessman would have been much at home among his medieval predecessors.

For all its success in carving a place for itself in medieval society, the bourgeoisie was still by 1300 not very exalted. The nobility looked down on the new class as uncultured and boorish, an attitude that often caused the bourgeoisie to spend their riches aping the habits of the nobles. The Church officially disapproved of many bourgeois activities as violations of Christian morality. The peasants were suspicious of the sharp practices of the townsmen; the "city slicker" is no recent invention of the rural mind. Still, the bourgeoisie was solidly established in law and was in fact a dynamic factor in the social order. It is worth noting that neither the Byzan-

tine nor the Moslem world produced a comparable class, although trade, manufacturing, and city life in these societies were older and no less vigorous. Perhaps the reason was that the state was too powerful in those societies. In the final analysis, the rise of the bourgeoisie in Western Europe was a consequence of successful private initiative carried out by men who operated in a society where there was considerable room for free action.

6. SOCIAL CHANGE: THE FEUDAL ARISTOCRACY AND THE PEASANTRY

The other, more traditional classes were also powerfully affected by these new forces. From the late eleventh century on, the nobility increasingly refined its pattern of life as greater wealth afforded it more luxury and leisure. The warrior's code stressing loyalty, bravery, generosity, and military prowess expanded into *chivalry*—a code of behavior brilliantly celebrated in the literature of the troubadors and the writers of romances. Chivalry placed a higher premium on courtly manners than on battlefield prowess. Women became the center of attention as objects of devotion, loyalty, and sentimental attachment. Even the warrior impulse was transmuted—at least in theory—to a quest for some ideal for which to fight, such as the spread of the true faith or the protection of the weak.

While the noble's life was becoming more complex and refined, economic and political changes were reducing his real power. The evolving money economy created a new kind of wealth that challenged the monopoly of land-based riches. The nobleman's quest for a share of this money wealth led many aristocrats to bargain away their total mastery over the manorial structure in return for cash-paying tenancies. In an era of inflation, rents lost their value in the long run, so that many nobles were in dire economic straits by the thirteenth century. The development of stronger central governments in many parts of Western Europe reduced the nobleman's role in warfare and government and made the lord-vassal relationship and its attendant mutual obligations less important. The weakening of the lord-vassal nexus tended to narrow the typical aristocrat's interest to people of his own class. By the thirteenth century a nobility of refinement and privilege had evolved out of a class which in the tenth and eleventh centuries was made up of specialists in warfare and governance.

The peasantry was also affected socially by the currents of change. During the twelfth and thirteenth centuries, there was large-scale freeing of serfs, especially in France, England, Flanders, Italy, and western Germany. Some peasants purchased their freedom; some gained it in return for colonizing new lands, and others by leaving the manors for the city. A more important cause was the willingness of landlords to surrender their rights to a serf's produce and services for money payments. In much of the West the serf was thus becoming a tenant farmer, enjoying whatever benefits freedom brought, but also losing the paternalistic protection the manorial lord had often extended. In a general way, the tenants prospered, chiefly due to the inflation which raised prices for their produce faster than their rents. However, the economic improvement of the peasant's lot did not elevate his social status; he was still at the bottom of the social scale, perhaps even farther removed from the top than ever because of the increasing complexity and refinement of aristocratic life.

Without question, then, the landlords, peasants, merchants, and artisans had combined their productive efforts to enrich Western Europe between 1000 and 1300. And their diverse economic activities generated not only new wealth but also a battery of economic skills and techniques capable of promoting still more growth. These centuries laid the economic groundwork for the world supremacy of Western Europe. Meanwhile, the social order had shifted into more complex patterns which allowed greater flexibility and adaptability.

Suggested Reading

Overview of the Period 1000–1300

Christopher Brooke, *Europe in the Central Middle Ages, 962–1154* (1964).

John H. Mundy, *Europe in the High Middle Ages* (1973). This and the preceding title provide coverage in depth of the major aspects of development in the period covered in this section.

*R. W. Southern, *The Making of the Middle Ages* (Yale). A brilliant essay, concentrating on certain "silent" changes affecting society.

*Friedrich Heer, *The Medieval World, 1000–1350* (Mentor). A work that touches most aspects of life in the medieval period in an attempt to prove that Western Europe passed from an "open" to a "closed" society in this era.

R. S. Lopez, *The Birth of Europe* (1967). A masterful interpretation which is more meaningful if the reader has some knowledge of the history of the period.

Economic History

*R. H. Bautier, *The Economic Development of Medieval Europe* (Harcourt Brace Jovanovich).

*N. J. G. Pounds, *An Economic History of Medieval Europe* (Longmans). Two excellent general surveys incorporating the best of modern scholarship.

*Georges Duby, *Rural Economy and Country Life in the Medieval West* (South Carolina). The best comprehensive treatment of agricultural life in the era.

*R. S. Lopez, *The Commercial Revolution of the Middle Ages, 950–1350* (Cambridge). A sprightly description of commercial development by a great authority.

E. Ashtor, *A Social and Economic History of the Near East in the Middle Ages* (1976). A good introduction to an aspect of economic history that was vital to the development of the West.

*Lynn White, Jr., *Medieval Technology and Social Change* (Galaxy).

*Jean Gimpel, *The Medieval Machine: The Industrial Revolution of the Middle Ages* (Penguin). This and the preceding study are helpful in appreciating how innovative medieval peoples were in technology.

Social History

*C. Brooke, *The Structure of Medieval Society* (McGraw).

Charles T. Wood, *The Age of Chivalry: Manners and Morals, 1000–1450* (1970).

*Sidney Painter, *Mediaeval Society* (Cornell).

P. Boissonnade, *Life and Work in Medieval Europe: The Evolution of the Medieval Economy from the Fifth to the Fifteenth Century* (1927). This and the preceding three titles attempt to paint in broad terms the chief characteristics of the medieval social order. The works of Brooke and Painter provide the most straightforward descriptions of the social order.

*Henri Pirenne, *Medieval Cities* (Princeton).

*Fritz Rorig, *The Medieval Town* (California). While awaiting a truly comprehensive synthesis on medieval cities, these two works offer the best picture of the character of medieval urban development.

S. Baldwin, *Business in the Middle Ages* (1937). A brief but excellent summary of the conduct of business in the Middle Ages.

Richard Barber, *The Knight and Chivalry* (1970). An intriguing attempt to reconcile the ideals and realities of the world of chivalry and of the aristocracy of the period.

*U. T. Holmes, *Daily Life in the Twelfth Century* (Wisconsin). An intimate picture of life in Paris as seen by a university student.

Sources

*H. L. Adelson, *Medieval Commerce* (Anvil).

*R. S. Lopez and I. W. Raymond, ed., *Medieval Trade in the Mediterranean World* (Norton). This and the preceding work provide a variety of documents illustrative of the world of commerce in this period.

*J. H. Mundy and Peter Riesenberg, *The Medieval Town* (Anvil). Original sources illustrative of town life in this period.

19

POLITICAL REVIVAL: THE HOLY ROMAN EMPIRE

While Western Europe's lesser men and women were producing new wealth at an astonishing rate and rearranging their social relationships into dynamic new patterns, its kings were successfully building political structures capable of providing a positive directive force in society. Their efforts resulted in a level of political order in the West that had not existed since the fall of the Roman Empire. No less important, the major political entities created in this period between 1000 and 1300 marked the origins of states that have persisted until the present. The political revival was general in Western Europe, but its fundamental patterns were established chiefly in Europe's heartland—Germany, Italy, France, and England. We shall concentrate on them to exemplify the basic characteristics of Western Europe's political revival during the High Middle Ages.

1. GENERAL POLITICAL PROBLEMS AND SOLUTIONS

As we have repeatedly noted, Western Europe's major political problem since the fall of the Roman Empire centered in establishing an effective centralized authority that could organize, control, and direct to common ends the activities of a considerable number of people living within a territory of any significant size. Such efforts in the Early Middle Ages had culminated in the tenth century in the feudal-manorial order, which promoted political fragmentation and

marked the triumph of localism. That order posed the essential political problem of the High Middle Ages—how to overcome extreme localism.

The solution rested with the monarchs of the tenth century. Although woefully feeble, they represented an ancient institution everywhere accepted as necessary to right order. An important aura of authority deeply rooted in tradition surrounded the institution of monarchy in the tenth century. There were memories of earlier Germanic "nations"—Franks, Lombards, Saxons —each sustained by legends of hero-kings and by traditions of power enshrined in law and custom. More vivid was the Carolingian ideal of a universal Christian ruler whose authority had roots in the ancient Roman Empire and in a Christian religious ideology that gave the monarch a key role in the drama of salvation. More immediately important was the fact that tenth-century kings stood at the apex of the feudal hierarchy, which invested them with theoretical rights to command the loyalty, obedience, and service of their vassals. The political history of the High Middle Ages is basically a story of the struggles of kings to assert their rights as supreme feudal lords and to turn feudal usages into monarchical institutions, which would allow them to control large political entities. While they never eschewed any benefits they could derive from more ancient religious and legal precedents supportive of royal power, the kings built their new regimes primarily on a feudal basis; they were first of all feudal monarchs.

2. THE FOUNDING OF THE HOLY ROMAN EMPIRE

The earliest and most impressive effort at political reconstruction during the period 1000 to 1300 involved the Holy Roman Empire. This state resulted from the combination of two kingdoms established by the divisions of the Carolingian Empire. The most important was the kingdom of the East Franks, or Germany, defined by the Treaty of Verdun in 843. A generation later, further divisions of the Carolingian state created the kingdom of Italy. Until the early years of the tenth century, royal power steadily declined in both, and the kingdoms tended to break into smaller principalities. In Germany, the counts and dukes who had once served as representatives of Carolingian royal authority usurped royal power to create virtually independent domains, the chief of which were Saxony, Bavaria, Franconia, Swabia, and Lorraine. In 911 the dukes deposed the Carolingian dynasty and elected one of themselves, Conrad, duke of Franconia, as king. A comparable process but much more violent and confused was occurring in Italy, where the kingdom was torn to bits by local potentates. To complicate the situation, in the late ninth and early tenth centuries Germany was attacked by the Vikings and the Magyars, while Italy felt the lash of the Magyars and the Saracens. Since the only hope of resisting these marauders lay in well-organized local defenses, royal authority and centralized government were further weakened.

In Germany the path toward disintegration and localism was suddenly reversed by a royal dynasty emerging from the duchy of Saxony. When Conrad I died in 918, Henry, duke of Saxony, was elected king. Although Henry I (919–936) concentrated his attention chiefly on the governance of Saxony, his leadership created a solid base of power for his son, Otto the Great (936–973), who made Germany the chief political power in Europe and created the Holy Roman Empire.

Otto I was a man of great vigor and skill whose political concepts were strongly influenced by Carolingian ideas. His most pressing task was to curb the forces that were fragmenting his kingdom. This policy pitted him against the great dukes, and only after years of struggle was royal authority successfully imposed on them. In the course of the struggle he uprooted some of the old ducal families and replaced them with more docile vassals, often his own relatives. Otto's efforts to defend his kingdom were rewarded in 955 at the great Battle of Lechfeld, where the royal armies smashed the Magyar horde so completely that it never again seriously threatened Germany. Not content to trust the safety of his realm to one military victory, he launched a policy of military expansion, colonization, and missionary activity into the Slavic world, a "drive to the East" that continued for centuries.

Otto chose to base his political power on an intimate alliance with the clergy, convinced that clergymen were more loyal to the idea of monarchy than lay nobles. He made large grants of land on what amounted to a feudal basis, creating ecclesiastical fiefs in every corner of Germany, in return for the military and political services he required to sustain his royal authority. To make this policy work, Otto had to be certain of the capabilities and loyalty of the men who filled high ecclesiastical offices and received as fiefs the lands attached to these offices. He therefore assumed the power to designate the clergymen who were to receive royal lands and to serve the king. In effect, through *lay investiture,* the ecclesiastical establishment became an arm of the monarchy much as it had under the strong Carolingian kings.

Successful in uniting and defending his kingdom and served well by his ecclesiastical vassals, Otto became the strongest king in Western Europe. His success bred new ambitions. We have already noted his efforts to expand his kingdom to the East. No less attractive was Italy. By the mid-tenth century many Italians were looking for an outsider capable of doing what their feeble kings could not do: curb internal disorder and defend them from outside attacks. Among them were the popes, long captives of local Roman aristocrats and mindful of what powerful outsiders — the Carolingians — had done to guarantee their independence. Otto was drawn toward Italy not only by ambition but also by political realities. Some of his most powerful subjects, particularly the dukes of Bavaria, were fishing in these troubled waters in search of a base of power from which to defy him. In 951 he made his first venture into Italy and assumed the title of "king of Italy." Troubles at home delayed a definitive settlement in Italy, but he returned in 961 to solidify his hold over his new kingdom. In 962 he seized the city of Rome and persuaded Pope John XII to crown him emperor, the title once held by the Carolingians. This move led to conflict with the Byzantine Empire, which controlled southern Italy, but eventually a settlement was reached which resulted in Byzantine recognition of Otto as emperor and in a marriage alliance between Otto's son and a Byzantine princess. In the meantime, Otto forced quarrelsome Italian nobles to accept his overlordship. Powerful churchmen became his vassals and were vested with authority as his agents in controlling affairs in Italy. Especially significant was Otto's policy toward the papacy. When John XII refused to accept a subservient position toward the newly crowned emperor, Otto deposed him, dictated the election of a more pliant successor, and imposed a rule that no pope would be elected in the future without the consent of the emperor. This opened an era of German domination of the papacy and of the entire religious establishment in the empire.

This renewed Western empire—usually called the Holy Roman Empire—made the emperor at least in theory the head of all Christian princes in the West. Otto of course was actual master only of Germany and Italy, and his huge, multinational empire left his heirs a terrible burden. But for the moment, the ruler of Germany was the greatest political figure in Western Europe.

3. OTTO'S SUCCESSORS AND THE GATHERING OPPOSITION

From Otto I's death in 973 until 1056, a succession of five emperors continued and expanded his policies with considerable success. In Germany the independent spirit of the old duchies was greatly reduced. The Church was skillfully

This tenth century ivory plaque shows Emperor Otto I offering a model of the cathedral church of Magdeburg to Christ who is seated in majesty. It reflects not only the conviction that the emperor controlled the Church but also that he was the intercessor between Christ and the faithful Christians on earth. *Photo: The Metropolitan Museum of Art, Gift of George Blumenthal, 1941*

manipulated to keep it a willing servant of the rulers. Its contribution to the administration of the realm was supplemented by the development of a corps of secular administrators (called *ministeriales*) recruited from the nonnoble class and completely devoted to royal service. The emperors kept a firm hold on Italy, acting there chiefly through the powerful bishops. Strong pressures continued to be applied in the East, so successfully that by 1056 Poland, Bohemia, and Magyar Hungary all recognized imperial overlordship. On the western frontiers, German influence was extended into a significant remnant of the Carolingian Empire, the kingdom of Burgundy.

The Holy Roman Empire remained the most important state in Western Europe, but as it grew, the authority of the emperors inevitably bred opposition. Perhaps most ominous was the growing strength of the German aristocrats who were busy extending their landholdings, consolidating their hold on the peasantry, and building their own alliances with the Church by founding monasteries which they controlled. This strength could potentially be turned against the emperors, whose administrative machinery was not yet sufficiently developed to exert sustained direct control over the aristocrats and who lacked the rights over them permitted by the feudal system, which had not yet made extensive inroads into Germany. The royal office was particularly vulnerable in the face of the nobility because it was elective; despite their efforts the tenth- and eleventh-century rulers had not been able to set aside the ancient Germanic elective principle in favor of hereditary succession, a failure that would soon cost them dearly.

Italy was also a source of growing opposition. The nobles remained resentful of imperial authority. More serious was a new force emerging in Italy: the commercial cities. Waxing richer and stronger from their exploitation of growing opportunities in trade, they sought an independence that could be gained only at the expense of imperial power.

The strength and aggressiveness of the Holy Roman Empire also bred resistance from outsiders. The French in the West and the Slavic kingdoms in the East were hostile and suspicious. Particularly significant was the emergence of a powerful Norman state in southern Italy and Sicily (see Chapter 21), whose ambitious, aggressive leaders by 1050 looked to the north as an area of expansion; and this led them to a confrontation with the Holy Roman emperors.

Finally and most important was a vast reform movement in religious life, which in its ideological aspects challenged the long-prevailing concept that the emperor was the divinely ordained leader of Christian society and in its practical aspects was directed against the feudalization of the Church. Its origins lay in the tenth-century monastic world, especially the Cluniac movement in France (see Chapter 22), one of whose basic principles was that monastic communities should be free from lay control over their property and personnel, for spiritual purity could not be achieved unless monks were separated from all secular influences on their lives. By the mid-eleventh century, powerful spiritual currents were surging through European society in support of liberty for the Church, spiritual purity in the clergy, and more intense piety among laymen. Ironically, among the most ardent supporters of religious reform was the saintly emperor Henry III (1039–1056), who was seemingly unaware of its implications for his power.

Ultimately, the reform movement found its leadership in Rome. The turning point came when Henry III installed a dedicated reformer, Leo IX (1049–1054), as pope. Under Leo's leadership, the reforming spirit took over the papal court. Its driving force was a monk named Hildebrand, later to be pope as Gregory VII, who gave the movement a more radical, political orientation. He saw the Church as an earthly corporate body which had the responsibility to work out God's will — the salvation of man — and which must become a visible community with its own head, its own law, its own resources, and its own liberty. All Christians, even the greatest princes, must be directed by the pope to the proper execution of their responsibilities in the drama of salvation. Herein lay the radical element of the reform ideology: It denied the role of secular rulers as divinely ordained directors of Christian life.

Beginning with Leo IX, the papacy turned its new ideology into a practical reform program that impinged directly on the existing political and ecclesiastical establishments. Popes began to legislate against the immorality and corruption afflicting the clergy, especially *simony* (buying and selling Church offices) and violation of clerical celibacy. They began to build a centralized administrative machinery to enforce these rules over all Europe. In 1059 a papal decree provided that henceforth popes would be chosen by the College of Cardinals, a body of key officials centered in Rome who assisted the pope in directing the Church administration. The emperor was deprived of any voice in papal elections except to approve what the cardinals decided. Seeking to strengthen its position, the papacy in 1059 formed an alliance with the Normans in southern Italy and Sicily to ensure itself protection from a source other than the emperor.

This aggressive policy naturally generated resistance in many quarters. Immoral clergymen squirmed at talk of reform. Many sincere bishops and abbots, long accustomed to independence, resented Rome's growing interference in local religious affairs. Laymen were uneasy at the prospect of losing the right to appoint Church officials and thus control over its extensive lands. If the popes were successful, the whole feudal order was endangered. Especially vulnerable was the Holy Roman emperor, who relied on a subservient Church as a chief source of power. This formidable opposition might well have blighted the reform movement had it not been for Gregory VII. A strong, willful man of great political ability and courage, he was not afraid to act to achieve what he believed right. Once elected pope in 1073, he moved resolutely to carry through legislation against corrupt clergymen, and he began to remove bishops whom he judged unfit for high office. In 1075 he decreed that *lay investiture* — that is, the practice of control by laymen of the election and installation of ecclesiastical officials — was illegal. Henceforth, church officials would be chosen and installed by the Church itself, as was ancient custom. This act opened the investiture struggle and put the papacy on a collision course with most of the secular rulers of Western Europe.

4. THE INVESTITURE STRUGGLE

During the critical period when the papacy was repudiating the traditional relationship between secular rulers and the Church, the imperial forces were temporarily crippled. Henry III died in 1056, leaving as his successor the child Henry IV, who did not reach his majority until 1065. When he did finally assume full power, Henry showed repeatedly that he fully intended to follow the policies that had made his predecessors strong. Among other things, he proceeded to appoint men of his choice to episcopal office, despite papal attacks on lay investiture.

The break that was sure to come developed in 1075 in connection with a vacant episcopal see in Milan. Since control of this city was vital to imperial power in Italy, Henry IV acted decisively to impose his candidate. Late in 1075, Gregory sent Henry a letter ordering him to do penance for violating Church law and threatening him with excommunication and loss of his office. With the backing of most of the German bishops, Henry replied by declaring that "the false monk" Hildebrand was not even pope, since his election had been improper. Whereupon in 1076 Gregory excommunicated the emperor, suspended him from public office, and invited the Germans to elect a new king. A considerable number of German nobles and bishops leaped at this opportunity to weaken the king. They commanded Henry to appear before a meeting to be held in Germany in the near future with the pope in attendance. If he could not clear himself of excommunication before this meeting, he would be deposed.

Henry IV faced a crucial issue. The specific question of lay investiture was no longer so critical as was the broader implication that the pope could claim to judge the emperor unworthy of his office and bring about his deposition. Henry had to offset this claim if he were to save his regime. His next action was tactically brilliant. He set out to intercept Gregory before the pope could reach Germany to preside over the projected meeting. In January 1077, he found Gregory at Canossa in northern Italy. In the garb of a penitent, he begged the pope's forgiveness. Although Gregory realized that to grant this would free a strengthened Henry to continue the imperial policy, he could not abdicate his role as priest. Henry was absolved. The pope had won a moral victory by forcing the most powerful ruler in Europe to admit that he had a superior, but his action deeply disappointed his supporters in Germany and weakened the cause against Henry.

Henry moved at once to deal with his most dangerous immediate foes, the German nobility, who persisted in their plans to depose him. The king, however, skillfully and speedily beat down their resistance and set aside the king they had elected in his place. He then turned to Italy, captured Rome, forced Gregory VII into exile, elevated a supporter to the papal throne, and had himself crowned emperor in 1084. By 1085 it appeared that the empire was saved.

But the victory was a hollow one; the papal challenge had unleashed too many enemies. Henry was unable to hold Rome against the papal allies, led by the Normans, and the papal office was returned to strong and independent hands, especially those of Urban II (1088–1099). In Germany, the nobles kept up their resistance and slowly undermined royal power. Although Henry defended his power valiantly, by the end of his reign he was a virtual fugitive from the rebellious nobles, including his own son.

Henry IV's three successors, who ruled until 1152, could not stem the tide against monarchical power. Imperial political power in Italy nearly disappeared, usurped by independent towns, nobles, and the papacy. The imperial crown tended to become a pawn of warring noble factions, election going to the prince who seemed least likely to exert effective power. Imperial resources were dissipated or usurped, and the administrative machinery broke down. In 1122 Emperor Henry V made peace with the Church over the specific issue of lay investiture by signing the Concordat of Worms, which provided that election to ecclesiastical offices be made by the Church, while the lands and secular powers associated with the office be invested by the ruler. This compromise settlement gave the emperor an effective veto over elections by allowing him to withhold the property of the office. But it also deprived the monarchy of absolute control over its major support.

Although the investiture issue had been set to rest, the struggle involved had created a crucial problem from the German monarch's point of view: In Germany (and to a lesser extent in Italy) it encouraged the rapid spread of feudalism. Interminable civil wars drove the weak to seek the protection of the strong and the strong to strengthen their hand by marshaling as many followers and as much territory as possible. The desperate emperors often conceded lands and rights in an effort to buy the support of nobles. The emergence of a feudalized Germany left the monarchy out of the picture, for the emperors had traditionally claimed authority on a basis other than feudal rights. By 1152 the German monarchy that had been so successful in the tenth and eleventh centuries had lost touch with the new society that had emerged during the investiture struggle. A kingdom that had escaped feudalization in the tenth century had now acquired a feudal structure, and the monarchy had limited means of coping with it.

5. THE HOHENSTAUFENS

Despite the destructive impact of the investiture struggle, the Holy Roman Empire survived. At mid-twelfth century a new dynasty, the Hohenstaufens, took up the task of rebuilding the imperial government. The first notable Hohenstaufen was Frederick Barbarossa (1152–1190). Elected king with a remarkable show of unanimity among the most powerful princes and the chief churchmen, Frederick I began from a position of strength, and he set resolutely about establishing a basis for royal power that would fit the new political world in which he lived. In essence, his policy aimed at turning feudalism to royal advantage in order to build a system of government based on secular rather than theocratic principles, principles that Frederick derived in considerable part from the Roman law then enjoying a revival in Western Europe.

His first task was to establish order. He made broad concessions to a few great nobles and allowed them to curb their troublesome vassals, the lesser nobles. The chief beneficiary of this policy was the leader of the traditionally anti-Hohenstaufen faction, Henry of Saxony, who with royal approval became the master of Saxony and Bavaria. But Frederick was careful to define his regalian rights clearly and to insist that his great vassals respect them. To enforce these rights, he gave special attention to increasing his royal domain, much of which was concentrated in Swabia (the Hohenstaufen homeland) and in the Kingdom of Burgundy, which was annexed to Frederick's realm in 1156 as a result of his marriage to its heiress. A corps of nonfeudal civil servants was developed to administer this domain. He continued the old imperial policy of turning the German Church to royal support, a policy that entailed royal control of ecclesiastical elections.

The Investiture Struggle: A Medieval Revolution?

An American medievalist has written that the investiture struggle was one of four "world revolutions" that shaped the Western world. This may seem a little exaggerated in view of the many momentous revolutions occurring later in Western Europe. However, medievalists do in general agree that the investiture struggle was crucial in the course of the history of Western Europe.

One school of investigators sees the struggle as a revolt against a deeply imbedded system governing church property and offices. When the Germans established their mastery over the Western Roman Empire, they brought with them a concept that everything connected with a piece of property belonged to the proprietor. As a consequence, they viewed churches built on lands they occupied as private property and could not conceive of them as belonging to a corporate entity, the Church, as had been the case under Roman law. It was but a simple step from this concept to treating offices associated with churches—priestly, episcopal, abbatial, and even papal—as properties to be disposed of by the possessor as he saw fit. This led to proprietors' controlling appointments to ecclesiastical offices and buying and selling them. Thus emerged the feudal Church, a creation based on Germanic concepts of property. The investiture struggle was in essence an attempt to liberate church property and offices from private ownership and to vest them in corporate hands. The revolutionary implications are obvious: the shifting of vast wealth and thus power from secular to clerical hands and the possibilities of independence open to the corporate Church.

Another and not unrelated view emphasizing the revolutionary nature of the investiture struggle centers on its political implications. Many generations of historians have viewed the clash as an event that condemned Germany and Italy to centuries of internal political chaos and backwardness. They argue that during the period 962–1075 the Holy Roman Empire, representing a limited revival of the Carolingian Empire, had become the strongest, best-organized political unit in Western Europe. Its basic strength derived from a close and mutually beneficial union between church and state. Pope Gregory VII's program worked to detach the German and Italian clergy from the relationship with the emperor with the ultimate consequence of destroying the constitutional basis of the Holy Roman Empire and opening the way for secular nobles to establish independence from the emperor.

Other historians view the investiture struggle more radically—as an effort by an ecclesiastical faction led by Gregory VII to apply a revolutionary sociopolitical ideology. For centuries, Western Europeans had accepted the basic idea that the welfare of Christian society depended upon the actions of divinely ordained rulers whose elevation to office gave them God's blessing to subordinate and direct all society, including the clergy, toward salvation. The royal office combined the functions of both *rex* and *sacerdos*, king and priest, to the end that the divine will be accomplished. The Gregorian party challenged this conception of right order. Its members insisted it was God's will that the priests should direct society, including its secular rulers, toward its ultimate destiny. The true Christian community—the Church—was a society of the baptized guided by priests whose office gave them the divine grace and wisdom to instruct the faithful according to God's plan. The kings were only agents of the priests, obligated to do the priestly bidding so that right order would be maintained.

Several scholars see the investiture struggle as a revolution less in itself than in its consequences—the fact that it led to a radical change in the governance of the Church. The papacy turned its energies toward defining precisely its powers over the clergy and laity and developing techniques for asserting its claims. The outcome was the papal monarchy and the centralized Church that reached maturity in the thirteenth century and has since remained an important ingredient in Western European society.

Still another group of scholars sees the investiture struggle primarily as a revolutionary shift of the monastic idea that the true path to spiritual improvement involved withdrawal from the world to the holy precincts of a monastery. The investiture struggle directed holy men—exemplified by Gregory VII—to move out of the cloister into the wicked world in order to attack evil and to persuade sinful kings, nobles, bishops, priests, and ordinary men to "convert" to the true Christian life. The investiture problem and its attendant abuses reversed the centuries-long tradition idealizing flight from the world and replaced it with an activist ethos of involvement in worldly affairs.

Whether these issues constitute the "stuff" of real revolution will depend on one's judgment of what is decisive in human affairs. However, when a particular episode in history entails control of property, the constitution of a powerful political entity, the nature of right order in society, the character of ecclesiastical government, and how man acts to change society, then surely revolutionary issues are at stake. One test might be to watch for the extent to which these issues dominated historical development after the investiture struggle.

Although Frederick's early relations with the papacy were friendly, permitting him to be crowned emperor in 1155, he made it clear that he had no intention of admitting papal supremacy or of allowing the papacy to restrict what he considered to be his rights over the Church. Moreover, he laid down a new set of rules to govern the relationship between the emperor and the rich Italian towns. Henceforth, the emperor would reclaim the regalian rights which the towns had usurped. They were to pay regular taxes, accept imperial officials as their rulers, and permit the emperor to coin money and regulate commerce. At one stroke, the freedoms the Italian cities had been fashioning during the previous century were to be severely limited.

Once Frederick had made clear his policy with respect to the papacy and the towns, the storm broke. For most of his reign he was forced to fight an imposing array of enemies that became known as the Guelf faction. The Guelf struggle against the Hohenstaufen forces (often called the Ghibellines) was led by Pope Alexander III (1159–1181), a true heir to Gregory VII. Frederick tried repeatedly to replace Alexander with a pope favorable to imperial interests, but with no success. The towns of northern Italy provided the backbone of Guelf strength, especially after they joined hands with papal blessing to form the Lombard League. In 1176 at the Battle of Legnano, this League inflicted a crushing defeat on Frederick's army that greatly impeded his efforts to assert his authority over the towns. The Guelfs could usually count on the support of the Norman kingdom of Sicily in resisting Hohenstaufen power. Finally, there was a strong Guelf following among the German nobility and clergy opposed to strong monarchy.

Frederick managed in the long run to withstand this powerful coalition, chiefly by compromising some of his ambitions. In 1177 he gave up his attempt to establish a German pope and recognized Alexander III. In 1183, at the Peace of Constance, the Italian towns came to terms, recognizing Frederick's overlordship in return for certain specific rights, such as choosing their own officials and levying their own taxes. In 1186 he arranged for the marriage of his son Henry to the heiress of the Norman kingdom of Sicily, detoothing one of his most persistent foes. Frederick's sensible compromises had not gained him full control of Italy or subdued the papacy, but his authority was still extensive there and his position as emperor intact. His long-standing policy of trying to live with a few great princes in Germany did not prove wholly successful. Eventually, he had to smash the chief Guelf prince, Henry of Saxony. Thereafter, he decided to break up the large principalities and grant the territory to many lesser nobles. This step relieved the immediate danger but in the long run, by further promoting feudalization, proved fatal to royal power.

Frederick Barbarossa's illustrious career ended in 1190 when he drowned while leading the Third Crusade. His son, Henry VI (1190–1197), began as if he would sustain his father's work, fighting a successful war to incorporate into the empire the kingdom of Sicily, which he claimed by virtue of his marriage to the heiress of that realm. But then instead of concerning himself with maintaining effective control over the restless German nobility, he became enmeshed in a series of schemes to extend his power over the Mediterranean to the Holy Land, France, and Spain. As his schemes unfolded, the foes of strong central rule began to join hands. Only a premature death in 1197 relieved him from paying the full price for too great ambition.

For the next two decades the fate of the Holy Roman Empire was determined by the most powerful of all the medieval popes, Innocent III (1198–1216). In 1198 he assumed guardianship over Henry VI's three-year-old heir, Frederick, and in that role took virtual control over the kingdom of Sicily. His concern was to prevent a single Hohenstaufen from ruling Germany and Sicily, a policy that would allow him to restore papal power in central Italy. In Germany a faction of the nobles remained loyal to the Hohenstaufens, and elected Philip of Swabia as king. Innocent immediately promoted the claims of a Guelf candidate, Otto of Brunswick. This led to a civil war that lasted until 1212 and virtually ruined Germany. Papal diplomacy encouraged the northern Italian towns and the nobles of central Italy to throw off imperial control. The work of Frederick Barbarossa seemed completely ruined; the Holy Roman Empire had become a pawn of the papacy.

In 1212, with the aid of the king of France, Innocent engineered the election of his ward to the kingship of Germany and eventually to the Holy Roman emperorship. Frederick II paid for papal support by making sweeping concessions that returned control of the German Church to the papacy and fortified papal independence in Italy. But he proved no docile servant of the pope. He took up the battle to build a strong Holy Roman Empire with a political skill, ruthless ambition, and personal qualities that made him one of the most intriguing figures in all medieval history. His enemies—and they were many—branded him irreligious, immoral, dishonest, cruel, and Antichrist, while his admirers saw him as a new man driven by a secular spirit quite distinct from that of his era.

Frederick II took a new view toward the Holy Roman Empire. He was little interested in Germany as the base for imperial power; Italy was the focus of his political concern. After becoming ruler of Germany, he remained there only until 1220. He spent these years surrendering royal power. He was as generous to the great feudal princes as to the papacy: He made their fiefs hereditary, gave full rights of government over the fiefs, and even turned over to them the strong position the early Hohenstaufens had established in the towns.

As he progressively disengaged himself from Germany, Frederick turned his energies to building his homeland, Sicily, into a centralized, bureaucratic state where royal power resembled the Byzantine. From this base he sought to extend his control of all of Italy. But this program reopened ancient hostilities. For nearly thirty years a series of able popes backed by the cities battled Frederick II, who fought skillfully and with great flair but lacked the resources to win. Papal prestige was too extensive in Europe for him to form an effective antipapal alliance. He drew almost no help from the Germans who were too busy enjoying the privileges he had extended them to render help. Frederick II died in 1250 far from realizing his ambitions; in fact, his policy had irreparably damaged any realistic base for imperial authority.

Amid bickering and foreign intervention, the German nobles did not agree on a new king until 1273, when they elected Rudolph of Hapsburg, qualified chiefly by his lack of strength. In the interval 1250 to 1273, known as the Interregnum, the last vestiges of effective imperial power were destroyed. Germany had finally broken to pieces politically. Meanwhile a French prince, Charles of Anjou, accepting a papal invitation, assumed the crown of the kingdom of Sicily in 1266. In the rest of the peninsula each city, each noble, each churchman went an independent way, respecting no higher authority and feeling no attachment to Italy. The Slavic kingdoms that had so long been under strong German influence were also free. One of the cherished dreams of medieval men—of a Christian empire in which men who held one faith would enjoy one ruler and one law—had failed.

Suggested Reading

The Holy Roman Empire

*Geoffrey Barraclough, *The Origins of Modern Germany* (Capricorn). The best treatment of the subject in English.

Karl Hampe, *Germany under the Salian and Hohenstaufen Emperors,* trans. R. Bennett (1973).

Josef Fleckenstein, *Early Medieval Germany* (1978). This and the preceding title treat German history in this period in considerable detail.

J. K. Hyde, *Society and Politics in Medieval Italy: The Evolution of Civil Life, 1000–1350* (1973). A good introduction to the history of the Italian cities during this period.

R. Folz, *The Concept of Empire in Western Europe from the Fifth to the Fourteenth Century*, trans. Sheila A. Ogilvie (1969). This work will clarify the ideological concepts undergirding the efforts to create a universal Christian empire in the Middle Ages.

*R. W. Herzstein, ed., *The Holy Roman Empire in the Middle Ages: Universal State or German Catastrophe?* (Heath). A selection of modern authorities presenting different interpretations of the nature and fate of the medieval Holy Roman Empire.

The Investiture Struggle

G. Tellenbach, *Church, State, and Christian Society at the Time of the Investiture Struggle* (1959). A balanced and comprehensive treatment of the ideological issues involved in the investiture struggle.

*Schafer Williams, ed., *The Gregorian Epoch, Reformation, Revolution, Reaction?* (Heath). A collection of essays by modern authorities treating the nature of the investiture struggle.

Walter Ullmann, *The Growth of Papal Government in the Middle Ages* (2nd ed., 1962). A controversial but provocative analysis of the papal position in the struggle with the Empire.

Biographies

Peter Munz, *Frederick Barbarossa: A Study in Medieval Politics* (1969).

Thomas C. Van Cleve, *The Emperor Frederick II of Hohenstaufen: Immutator Mundi* (1972).

A. J. Macdonald, *Hildebrand: A Life of Gregory VII* (1932).

Sources

The Correspondence of Gregory VII, trans. E. Emerton (Norton). Presents an excellent picture of Gregory's ideas and his efforts to apply them to the reform of Christian society.

Imperial Lives and Letters of the Eleventh Century, trans. T. Mommsen and K. Morrison (1962). A collection of documents that illuminates the imperial position in the struggles of the eleventh century.

*Boyd J. Hill, *Medieval Monarchy in Action: The German Empire from Henry I to Henry IV* (Allen Unwin). The collection of documents appended to this description of the reigns of the first German emperors is invaluable in illustrating the nature of the imperial system of government.

*Otto of Freising, *Deeds of Frederick Barbarossa*, trans. C. C. Mierow and R. Emory (Norton). An account of Frederick I's reign by a contemporary bishop.

20

POLITICAL REVIVAL: ENGLAND AND FRANCE

While the German rulers struggled valiantly but in vain to create a strong state embracing Germany and Italy, political change progressed less dramatically but more effectively in England and France. The rulers of each, chiefly by exploiting feudal rights, slowly built their power to the point where they exercised extensive control over their states, largely because they had created effective institutions of royal government. Strong central government developed in England earlier than in France, but the powers of the French monarchy were ultimately greater — so great, in fact, that France had become the dominant political power in Europe by the end of the thirteenth century.

1. ENGLAND: THE NORMAN CONQUEST

As we have seen (Chapter 16), a well-established system of government had evolved in Anglo-Saxon England, reaching its apogee in the tenth century: an effective central government, strong local institutions, a legal system based on customary law, and a military and financial organization that permitted a king like Alfred the Great to defend his people against the Vikings and to impose his authority on most of the country. The kings exercised considerable power directly over their subjects, most of whom were freemen, at a time when royal power was being replaced by the feudal system in many areas on the Continent.

During the eleventh century, Anglo-Saxon monarchy began to show signs of losing its vitality. The rulers' chief local officials, the earls and sheriffs, steadily secured rights of private government. The kings began to grant royal lands to *thegns* who pledged military service in return but often failed to render it. Many freemen were forced to become dependents of the powerful nobles as either vassals or serfs. New Scandinavian inroads undermined royal prestige and encouraged local independence. Canute, a Dane, even took the English crown (1016–1035). He dreamed of drawing England into a vast northern maritime empire, but his plans were foiled by his early death and by ineffective successors.

After this interlude of foreign rule, the old Anglo-Saxon royal line was restored with Edward the Confessor (1042–1066) as king. His reign was characterized by a rapid deterioration of royal power to the special advantage of the great earls, of whom Godwin of Wessex was the most powerful. When Edward died without heirs, the Witan elected as king Harold, Godwin's son, who was immediately faced with an invasion led by Harald Hardrada, king of Norway, who coveted the English throne. Into this mounting crisis entered William, duke of Normandy. This ambitious chief of a powerful feudal principality and leader of an aggressive nobility laid claim to the English crown on the basis of his distant kinship with Edward. Harald and William chose almost the same moment to assert their claims, forcing a settlement on the battlefield in 1066. King Harold crushed the invading Scandinavians only to meet disaster a short time later, in October, at the Battle of Hastings, where William's Norman knights overpowered the Anglo-Saxon forces and made it possible for their leader to assume the English crown as William I (1066–1087).

William made it clear at his coronation that he would observe Anglo-Saxon customs and exercise all the rights belonging to the Anglo-Saxon kings. This gave his office a far broader theoretical base and a far more extensive claim on his subjects than was the case with contemporary continental kings, where feudalism had eroded royal power. To provide the means to exert these rights and powers William took a momentous step: He introduced feudalism into England. William claimed all her land by right of conquest. He set aside about one-sixth of it as the royal domain and granted out most of the rest as fiefs to his Norman followers. In return, they became his vassals, owing him services, chiefly military, in proportion to the size of the fiefs. Most of his direct vassals (called *tenants-in-chief* or *barons*) subinfeudated their lands and acquired their own vassals. William, however, insisted that all subvassals owed first allegiance to the king, thereby establishing a meaningful feudal hierarchy with the king at the head. Through these steps, he not only secured a valuable royal domain but also the military service of about 5,000 knights, enough to ensure his mastery of England, as well as the obedience of her powerful men. In short, the feudal system allowed him to impose a new ruling elite on England in a fashion that gave him as king control over it.

As successor to the Anglo-Saxon kings and chief lord of the feudal hierarchy, William had the authority and resources to lay the groundwork for a strong central government. The Anglo-Saxon Witan was replaced by a feudal body called the *curia regis,* at whose meetings the king's lay and ecclesiastical vassals were expected to judge cases and advise the ruler. William continued to collect the taxes owed the king from Anglo-Saxon times, the chief one being the Danegeld, originally imposed in 991 to provide ransom money to the Danes. In 1086 William's agents compiled the Domesday Book, a survey of England's wealth fief by fief which documented what men possessed and how much they owed the king. No other monarch in Europe was in a position to reach so directly into the affairs of his subjects.

William was careful to retain the local units of administration he had inherited, the Anglo-Saxon shires and hundreds, and to see to it that the local officials, especially sheriffs, served royal purposes. Through this system of local government the king kept in direct touch with the English populace in matters of justice, peace keeping, and taxation. The English system of local government prevented the fragmentation of authority that accompanied the feudalization of continental kingdoms.

Overlooking no possible source of power and prestige, William acted to attach the Church to his new establishment. William won the support of the reformers and the blessing of the papacy by promising at the time of the conquest to undertake the reform of the badly corrupted Anglo-Saxon Church. Once in control of England, he brought in a Norman, Lanfranc, as archbishop of Canterbury, and Lanfranc considerably improved religious life in England. William was generous in endowing the Church with property and in permitting it liberty to conduct its own courts. However, he never relinquished real control over it, especially in the choice of high ecclesiastical officials. Such a policy risked a quarrel with the Church, but he applied it successfully, which assured him of the immensely valuable support of key church officials.

The Norman conquest was thus a watershed in English history. A disintegrating monarchy was given new political vitality by injecting into its structure certain Continental feudal practices that provided the king-lord with the opportunity to make himself the real master of England. Moreover, the coming of the Normans drew England into the mainstream of Western European life by involving her people more directly in the vigorous economic, religious, and cultural forces that were revitalizing society on the Continent. Some contemporaries—and even greater numbers among later generations of Anglophiles—lamented that much was lost in the submersion of Anglo-Saxon society, but on the whole England gained from being drawn into the mainstream of Continental society. Her greatest gain was the foundation of a sound political order.

2. ENGLAND: GROWTH OF THE MONARCHY

During the next century William's successors (known as the Norman-Angevin dynasty) were energetic, capable kings who worked hard to develop royal power: the rough, brutal William II (1087–1100); the quiet, prudent, and avaricious Henry I (1100–1135); the ambitious, tempestuous Henry II (1154–1189); and the colorful, romantic ideal knight, Richard I, the Lionhearted (1189–1199). Only one difficult interlude intervened, brought about by a disputed succession in 1135. The twelfth-century kings were men with interests far transcending the governance of England. They managed to expand English influences into Wales, Scotland, and Ireland. William left them with a Continental possession in Normandy that Henry II expanded into an "empire" embracing half of France. Richard played a leading role in the Third Crusade. These activities made England a major power in twelfth-century Europe. But we must neglect these aspects of English history in order to concentrate on the successful efforts of the kings to perfect effective monarchical government.

One of the major achievements of the twelfth-century English kings, especially Henry I and Henry II, was the formation of an effective central administration, fashioned by combining and adapting features of the old Anglo-Saxon royal household and of new feudal assembly (called the *curia regis*, that is, court of the king) in which the king's tenant-in-chiefs were obliged to serve. Development moved along two complementary lines. On the one hand, the kings began to draw men from the *curia regis* to serve for prolonged periods instead of returning to their private affairs after brief meetings of this body. To this full-time core the kings gradually added increasing numbers of permanent civil servants, often of nonnoble origin. On the other hand, the

kings began to assign specialized functions to this body of permanent servants—the beginnings of departments of administration. During the twelfth century, four specialized groups took shape: the *Exchequer*, for financial administration; the *Treasury*, for guarding and dispensing royal money; the *Chancery*, for issuing royal orders and composing royal correspondence; and the *royal law courts*. So competent did this permanent body of royal servants become that Richard I was able to spend most of his reign abroad without any loss of power. It hardly need be added that its growth greatly reduced the dependence of kings on the political services of their vassals.

The kings continued to sustain and strengthen the ancient system of local government. They resisted the ever-present tendency for the sheriffs to usurp royal power for private advantage by using the agencies of the central government to maintain control over the sheriffs and to broaden their activities in support of the king. Henry II was especially effective in providing clearer definitions of the obligations of the sheriffs. Thus the old local institutions of government remained a powerful support of royal authority and a constant barrier against localism.

The kings were careful to guard the financial and military resources needed to support the growing agencies of the royal government and to restrain potential foes, especially the feudal nobles. The financial support of the government still depended heavily on the exploitation of the royal domain; the kings' agents were remarkably efficient and even ruthless in administering these estates. The royal government zealously collected every possible feudal due owed by royal vassals and all fines and fees due to the king for breaking his law or utilizing services performed by his agents. Custom duties were levied on an ever wider scale, allowing the kings to capitalize on growing trade. The royal government also devised ways of imposing direct taxes on the income and property of its subjects. The revenues from these many sources provided the twelfth-century English kings with a sounder financial base for their power than was enjoyed by any other royal government in Europe. The kings' military strength was based on the military service owed by the tenants-in-chief. To complement the feudal army, the kings maintained the ancient royal right to summon the *fyrd,* the army of all freemen in the realm. Toward the end of the twelfth century the kings began to allow those who owed them military service to make money payments, called *scutage* or shield-money, in lieu of personal service; this income was used to hire mercenary troops.

Beyond all doubt, the most important development of the twelfth century was the formation of a royal system of justice. This effort was in large part a response to the confusion of the traditional system of justice. Courts were conducted by the king, his local representatives in the shires, feudal lords, seigneurs on the manors, the Church, and the towns. In each set of courts different systems of law, different procedures, and different systems of punishment were applied by judges whose legal competence varied greatly. The kings and their legal advisers sought to diminish this confusion by perfecting a royal system of justice common to all—a step that had the added attraction of increasing royal income.

One of the chief steps taken was to increase the number of royal courts, to man them with expert judges, and to encourage them to apply a unified legal code. Henry I began the *circuit court system,* sending itinerant judges at set intervals to shires throughout England to try cases involving the king's interests. By the time of Henry II, this had become a regular practice, and by comparing notes the judges were soon able to erect a common set of principles for deciding cases. A *common law* was in the making. Henry II established the first of England's great central courts, sitting permanently at Westminster to handle many cases previously heard by the *curia regis.* Soon this body began to divide into specialized courts, like the *court of common pleas* and the *court of the king's bench.* The decisions of these central courts guided the activities of itinerant judges and contributed greatly to uniformity in the royal legal system.

As royal judicial activity increased, the kings' agents began to challenge the jurisdiction of the feudal, manorial, ecclesiastical, and town courts. In this competition the kings and their lawyer-servants showed great ingenuity. The kings expanded their authority over criminal cases by legislation that defined new crimes against the peace and ordered royal judges to punish violators. Increasing royal control over civil cases, chiefly involving property disputes, was more complicated and met with considerable opposition, especially from feudal and seigneural lords long accustomed to dealing with property disputes in their own courts. Insisting that a man should not lose his property unjustly (who would disagree?), the kings declared that a dissatisfied litigant could purchase a *writ* ordering a royal inquiry into his case. The fertile minds of the royal lawyers soon devised writs that applied to almost every conceivable kind of property dispute. In effect, purchasing a writ amounted to transferring a civil dispute from feudal or manorial courts to royal courts.

To encourage the use of royal courts, important innovations were made to ensure speedier and more efficient judicial processes: regularly scheduled court sessions, clearly fixed court fees, utilization of trained judges, uniform punishments. Most significant in this respect was the introduction of the *jury system.* For a long time English kings and their officials had been summoning groups of their subjects and requiring them to tell under oath what they knew about some matter of public interest. After 1164 Henry II applied this idea to criminal cases. Sheriffs summoned a *presentment* or *grand jury* made up of men from the area where a crime was committed. On the basis of the evidence these jurors produced, the sheriffs could proceed to bring the suspected criminals to trial. By the thirteenth century groups of men known as *petit* (little) *juries* were used to decide guilt or innocence.

The jury system quickly proved superior to traditional practices, which relied on trial by ordeal, by battle, or by compurgation to ascertain God's will in proving guilt or innocence. Trial by ordeal required one charged with an offense to submit to a physical test, such as being thrown into water or walking through fire. The outcome of the ordeal revealed the truth. For example, if the accused sank in the water, he was innocent because the water accepted him, but if he floated, he was guilty. In trial by battle, the victor won the case. Trial by compurgation required the accused to produce oath-swearers — the number being determined by the nature of the crime and the status of the accused — who would attest to the innocence of the person charged.

As the Norman-Angevin kings shaped monarchical government, they had to concern themselves with their relationships with the Church. As might be expected in an age when the Church was aggressively seeking its liberty and

Manuscript illustration showing the murder of Thomas à Becket in the cathedral at Canterbury.
Photo: The Walters Art Gallery, Baltimore

advancing its power, royal confrontations with the Church were often sharp. In general, the English kings managed the problem with considerable skill and in a way that reinforced their authority. William I set the pattern for his successors by richly endowing the Church and supporting its reforming moves, while insisting firmly on royal control of ecclesiastical offices and of a portion of the Church's wealth. During the reign of William II, the Church, led by Anselm, archbishop of Canterbury, challenged the monarchy's right to appoint church officials. This struggle was resolved by the Compromise of Bec in 1106, which allowed the Church to elect its own officials, but reserved to the king the privilege of investing these officials with their lands. A more serious struggle arose when Henry II tried to limit the jurisdiction of Church courts. Thomas à Becket, archbishop of Canterbury, defended the Church's cause so skillfully that an enraged Henry finally cried out for his murder. Thomas' martyrdom forced the king to concede considerable freedom to the Church in judicial matters. On the whole, however, the English kings exercised a powerful control over the Church, and the Church gave its support to the strengthening of monarchy. England escaped the fatal plague of the Holy Roman Empire — an eternal war with the Church.

3. ENGLAND: LIMITING ROYAL POWER

During the twelfth century the rapid, aggressive expansion of royal authority generated surprisingly little resistance. As noted, the Church was sometimes balky, but on the whole supported the kings. The feudal nobles chafed under expanding royal power, but their opposition was sporadic and ineffectual; in fact, the nobility tended to identify their interests with a strong, peaceful kingdom. During the thirteenth century, however, the kings met more formidable opposition. Nobles, churchmen, and the rising bourgeoisie joined hands to compel the kings to recognize a principle inherent in feudal monarchy: that royal power was limited by the "law" of the feudal contract. This challenge marked a major step in establishing constitutional monarchy in England.

The conflict broke into the open during the reign of John (1199–1216). Politically able, although devious and rash, John brought part of his trouble on himself by making inordinate demands on his subjects in an effort to sustain the growth of royal government. He also had the misfortune of having as his enemies two of the most formidable personalities in medieval history, King Philip Augustus of France and Pope Innocent III. Philip captured a considerable part of the French territories under English control in a war that required John to impose a heavy burden of service and taxation on his subjects in a losing cause. Then John became involved in a struggle with Innocent III over the appointment of the archbishop of Canterbury. Again he lost, being forced to acknowledge that he was a vassal of the pope holding England as a fief.

These rebuffs, coupled with a series of tyrannical acts by John, led to a rebellion in 1214 from which he extricated himself only by signing the Magna Carta in 1215. Loudly celebrated by later generations as a charter of liberty, the Magna Carta basically affirmed the privileges of nobles, churchmen, and townsmen. The king promised to refrain from intruding royal authority into certain areas, involving chiefly taxation, the administration of justice, and landholding. The charter was therefore conservative, seeking to limit the expansion of royal power. Its framers had no thought of destroying effective royal government. They insisted on the principle that a king's subjects had rights, defined by law, custom, and contract, which the king must respect. This essential concept imbedded in feudal monarchy was destined to play a vital part in the future political development of Western Europe.

John's concession in no way resolved the clash between the king and the privileged. It continued throughout the long reign of his weak, extravagant, foolish son, Henry III (1216–1272), who made problems for himself by relying on Frenchmen for advice, making outlandish concessions to the papacy, and pursuing costly but futile foreign adventures. The exasperated nobles resisted him in a variety of ways: forcing him to reissue Magna Carta, using their influence to compel him to dismiss his foreign advisers, and forming a council of nobles to reform

and supervise the operation of royal government. When these efforts failed, they resorted to a major uprising in 1264–1265 led by Simon de Montfort. The rebels won the upper hand temporarily, and de Montfort summoned the nobles, the clergy, and representatives from the towns and shires to a *Parliament* which would establish control over the monarchy. This effort was thwarted by the inability of the rebels to agree and by the actions of Henry's son, Edward, who mustered royal arms and crushed the rebels. However, brute force was hardly an answer to the issues involved in the rebellion.

The astute, capable Edward I (1272–1307) saw that few of the nobles who had opposed John and Henry III wished to end strong monarchy or destroy its institutions. In fact, during the troubled times of John and Henry III these institutions had continued to develop in complexity and effectiveness. The protest was against the misuse of royal government and the abuse of ancient rights. More significantly, Edward recognized that a *community of the realm* had begun to emerge, consisting of great barons, lesser nobles, churchmen, and townsmen, all of whom felt a common interest in the political affairs of England as a nation. This feeling led them to act together in confronting the royal government and to transcend on occasion the narrow confines of feudal contracts, ecclesiastical privileges, and town charters. The community of the realm was the product of English political history since the conquest, of two centuries during which royal power was strong enough to affect all men in a substantial way. Its emergence provided the basis for the modern English national spirit and for new political institutions through which the community of the realm could find expression.

Edward I's reign represented an attempt to strengthen the central government by taking these views into account. He first took steps to remove complaints that the nobles, clergy, and townsmen had raised about the administrative and judicial systems. Second, a series of fundamental laws was enacted defining more clearly the rights and powers of the crown and how these would be exercised. In general, this legislation further limited the power of feudal lords and the Church, while expanding that of the king and his courts, but Edward's political skill usually disarmed protests before they became dangerous.

Edward's chief means of avoiding opposition and one of the major developments in English history was the regular use of Parliament. Advisory bodies, like the Witan and the *curia regis,* had long played a part in English political life, but within a narrow framework of feudal practices. Simon de Montfort's Parliament of 1265 was a new kind of structure, joining representatives of the shires and towns to the feudal barons and churchmen to create a body claiming to direct the affairs of the realm. Edward I clearly sanctioned this precedent in his Model Parliament of 1295. He commanded that each county and town select two representatives to Parliament to take counsel with the barons and ecclesiastical lords. Such a body was soon accepted as having the power to speak for all Englishmen. Edward called Parliament to serve his own purposes, and especially to get extra money or to have some piece of legislation approved that promised to irk part of the population. For at least another century, the organization of Parliament was vague and its powers were few. Its importance lay in Edward's recognition that he had to listen to the demands of his subjects and in his willingness to promote an institution that gave them a voice in government.

Edward's death in 1307 heralded the end of one age and the beginning of another. His career, built upon the work of his predecessors, left England with a sound set of political institutions. The chaos that had threatened to engulf England before 1066 had been replaced by a solidly established monarchy whose authority was widely accepted yet limited by law and ancient custom.

4. FRANCE: ROYAL IMPOTENCE, 843–1108

Monarchical power grew at a slower pace in France than in England and without a decisive turning point comparable to the Norman conquest. In the long run, however, the medieval French kings emerged more powerful than their English counterparts. The kingdom of France was established by the Treaty of Verdun in 843,

when the sons of Louis the Pious divided the Carolingian Empire. Except for brief intervals, the Carolingians ruled this new kingdom until 987, but their power declined steadily, especially because of Viking invasions and the general ineptness of the rulers. Feudalism took root more deeply in France than anywhere else in Western Europe. The kings were still recognized in a vague way as feudal overlords of all France, but real power had settled in the hands of the great vassals who held extensive fiefs from the king, enjoyed the right to govern these lands, and seldom rendered any of the obligations they owed their lord.

In 987 the French nobles and churchmen finally ended the Carolingian dynasty by electing as their king one of the chief feudal lords in France, Hugh Capet, count of Paris. Hugh's descendants, called the Capetians, ruled France without interruption until 1328. Although the Capetians were ultimately the architects of a strong French monarchy, their success was hardly instant. Under the first four Capetians, who ruled from 987 to 1108, the kings exercised almost no power outside their own royal domain, a territory around Paris known as the Ile de France. The rest of the country remained divided into feudal principalities, some larger and richer than the royal domain.

The real political history of France during the eleventh century must be told in terms of the history of each of these principalities. The dukes, counts, and viscounts who held them made remarkable progress in establishing control over their subvassals, developing institutions that made their power effective, and amassing the military and financial resources needed to perpetuate their supremacy. These powerful royal vassals brought order to their fiefs primarily by utilizing their rights as feudal lords. In brief, they made feudalism an effective instrument for establishing sound government on a small scale. This solidification was most notable in the great fiefs of northern France, especially Normandy, Flanders, Anjou, Maine, Champagne, Burgundy, and Blois. In southern France, feudalism was slower to develop, and fiefs such as Aquitaine, Gascony, and Toulouse remained more chaotic. The kings had little role in these local developments. For the most part they were fully occupied with controlling their limited domain, keeping the throne in their family, and retaining the support of the Church. Only rarely and seldom in any decisive way did they assert their rights as feudal overlords in the fiefs controlled by their powerful vassals. But neither did they surrender these rights.

5. FRANCE: THE RESURGENCE OF ROYAL POWER, 1108–1223

The period between 1108 and 1223 saw a decisive upturn of Capetian fortunes and a notable advance in the strength of French monarchy. The first accomplishment of the twelfth-century Capetians was the establishment of effective control over the Ile de France, a goal that had already been achieved by many of the king's vassals in their fiefs. Louis VI (1108–1137) was chiefly responsible for this. He patiently set about forcing his vassals there to end their lawlessness and creating an administrative machinery capable of collecting their dues to the king. In the main, he was successful. His control of the royal domain gave him greater ability to play a significant role as feudal lord over his vassals outside the Ile de France. On occasion he acted as judge in disputes between his vassals, protected weaker ones against stronger, and influenced the succession to fiefs held from the king. Nothing illustrates this new strength better than the decision of the dying duke of Aquitaine to entrust his daughter and heiress, Eleanor, to the protection of his overlord, the king of France, Louis VI promptly married his ward to his son, thereby setting the stage for the annexation of Aquitaine to the royal domain.

Louis VI's successor, Louis VII (1137–1180), lacked the energy and clearheadedness to navigate the murky waters of French feudal politics. Thanks to the able work of his father's administrators, Louis VII did keep a firm hold on the royal domain, but his efforts elsewhere were ineffectual. He proved incapable of controlling Aquitaine, where the feudal nobility acted in complete defiance of the king's will. His participation in the Second Crusade not only won him no glory but cost him a wife and her dowry. The

gay, romantic Eleanor accompanied him and was rumored to have dallied with some of the more attractive knights of the crusading army. This scandal was too much for the pious Louis; added to it was the fact that Eleanor had produced no son to assure the survival of the Capetian dynasty. Perhaps Eleanor had had enough too; she is alleged to have said that she discovered she had married a monk instead of a king. In any case, Louis arranged to have the marriage dissolved, with consequences that were dangerous to his power.

The king's major difficulties, however, did not stem from his political and marital ineptness. During his reign the Angevin "empire" emerged as a major threat to the very survival of French monarchy. It was the handiwork of a succession of royal vassals who ruled one of the great fiefs of France, the county of Anjou. The eleventh-century counts of Anjou had been ruthless, ambitious men who had constantly expanded their holdings. By the twelfth century Anjou had become one of the most powerful principalities in France. Count Geoffrey extended the earlier gains, establishing control over Normandy and Britanny by marrying the daughter of Henry I of England, also duke of Normandy. Geoffrey died in 1151; the next year his son and heir, Henry, won the hand of Eleanor, recently repudiated by Louis VII, and acquired her duchy of Aquitaine. For all these territories Henry was a vassal of Louis VII, but obviously his resources far exceeded those of his lord. Then in 1154 this same Henry became king of England as Henry II, further increasing his power and endangering Louis VII.

The French king could do little to check Henry's empire building or his aggression against royal territory and authority. But the next Capetian, Philip II Augustus (1180–1223), met the new challenge successfully. Philip bided his time as long as Henry II lived, only doing what he could to make his vassal's burden in ruling his French territories as heavy as possible. This task was made easier by the fact that Eleanor had blessed Henry II with a brood of unruly sons, among them Richard the Lionhearted and John, who delighted in joining their mother in making trouble for their father and her husband. With the accession of Richard I, the Lion-hearted, Philip began the struggle to break Angevin power. He was finally successful against John, whose conduct alienated many Continental vassals and caused them to turn to John's feudal overlord for justice. When John refused to appear to be judged, Philip declared his fiefs confiscated and proceeded to annex Normandy, Anjou, Maine, the Touraine, and parts of northern Aquitaine to the royal domain. His control of these key territories was assured in 1214 by the Battle of Bouvines, where he and his allies, Pope Innocent III and Frederick II of Hohenstaufen, crushed the armies of John and his ally, Otto of Brunswick. As a master of a greatly enlarged royal domain, the king had emerged as the major force in France, a position dramatically different from that of the earlier Capetians.

6. FRANCE: CONSOLIDATION OF ROYAL POWER, 1180–1328

Louis VI and Philip II had established the key-stones of Capetian policy: expansion of the royal domain by the annexation of lands belonging to the king as feudal overlord and careful adminis-tration of that expanding domain. Successful pursuit of these policies characterized the reigns of the later Capetians and accounts for France's emergence as the strongest state in Europe in the thirteenth century. After Philip II's decisive vic-tory at Bouvines, the French kings added new territories to the royal domain with relative ease, exploiting every possible means to lay hold of them: marriage, purchase, confiscation, escheat. No holding was too small to escape their atten-tion and none too large to defy them. By 1328 a large part of France had been consolidated under royal control; a kingdom of France had become a reality.

In order to control their expanding territories, the later Capetians, especially Philip II, Louis IX (1226–1270), and Philip IV (1285–1314), con-stantly increased the power and activity of the royal government. In broad outlines that govern-ment resembled the twelfth-century English government, from which the Capetians bor-rowed heavily. They based their expanding

power primarily on their rights and obligations as feudal lords, relying also on concepts taken from Roman law and Christian political ideol-ogy. The thirteenth- and fourteenth-century kings increased their power chiefly by expand-ing and modifying primitive institutions bequeathed to them by the earlier Capetians. First, there was the *curia regis,* the meeting of the king's vassals to judge cases and to advise their overlord. Second was the royal household (the *hôtel*), made up of officials who cared for the per-sonal needs of the royal family and its retainers. Finally, there were the *provosts,* who managed the royal estates.

One of the chief accomplishments of Philip II, Louis IX, and Philip IV was the shaping of an ef-fective central administration out of these primi-tive institutions. Philip II increased the amount of royal business put before the *curia regis,* add-ing full-time nonfeudal administrators (mostly lawyers) to the original core of feudal vassals. The royal household began to merge with the *curia regis* to serve as a single judicial and ad-ministrative body. Paris became the fixed seat of royal government. Louis IX and Philip IV con-tinued to enlarge the activities of the *curia regis* and began to divide it into specialized depart-ments: the *conseil,* a small circle of intimate advisers of the king; the *parlement de Paris,* con-cerned chiefly with the administration of royal justice; the *chambre des comptes,* which handled financial matters; a *chancery* for producing royal orders and keeping records. By the reign of Philip IV the central administrative system had developed into a complex, sophisticated organ-ism manned by experts completely devoted to the service of the king.

As the royal domain grew, the kings were faced with the monumental task of creating a system of local government. The French kings were not so fortunate as the English in this re-spect; local government had long been monopo-lized by feudal and manorial lords. Philip II at-tacked this problem by extensive use of officials known as *baillis* (bailiffs). Usually selected from the nonnoble personnel of his court, these of-ficials were assigned to specific areas in the royal domain to hold courts, collect taxes, and keep order. Succeeding kings expanded the numbers

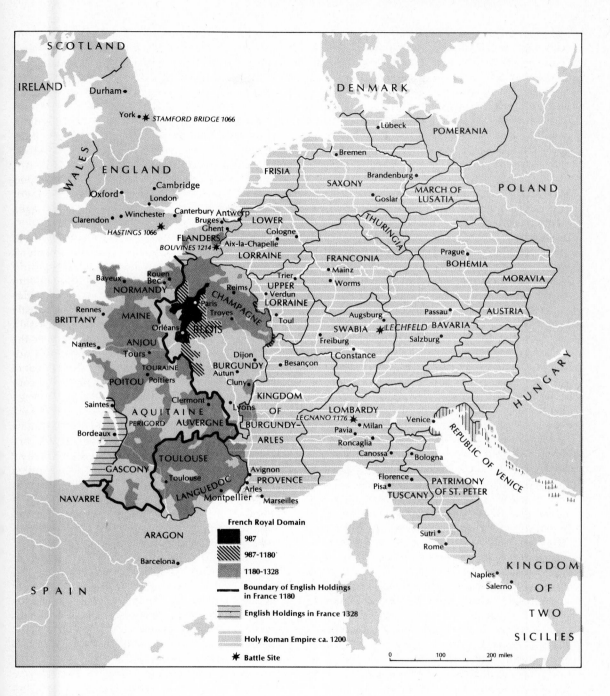

SCOTLAND

IRELAND

Durham •

York • ✳ *STAMFORD BRIDGE 1066*

WALES

ENGLAND

Oxford •   • Cambridge
           • London
Clarendon •   • Winchester Canterbury • Antwerp
              Bruges • Ghent •   LOWER
           FLANDERS •   Cologne •
HASTINGS 1066 ✳   Aix-la-Chapelle • LORRAINE
BOUVINES 1214 ✳

Bayeux •   • Rouen Bec •
NORMANDY   Reims •   CHAMPAGNE
                    Paris • BLOIS
Rennes •   MAINE   Troyes •
BRITTANY   UPPER
                 Orléans •   Verdun • LORRAINE
Nantes •   ANJOU   Toul •
         Tours •
         TOURAINE
POITOU • Poitiers   Dijon •
                 BURGUNDY   • Besançon
                 Autun •
                 Cluny •
Saintes •   Clermont • Lyons •   KINGDOM
AQUITAINE AUVERGNE   OF   *LEGNANO 1176* ✳
PERIGORD   BURGUNDY-
Bordeaux •   ARLES

GASCONY   TOULOUSE   Avignon •
NAVARRE   • Toulouse LANGUEDOC   Arles • PROVENCE
              Montpellier • • Marseilles

ARAGON

Barcelona •

SPAIN

FRISIA

DENMARK

Lübeck •   POMERANIA
Bremen •
           Brandenburg •
SAXONY   MARCH OF   POLAND
  • Goslar LUSATIA

THURINGIA

FRANCONIA   Prague •   BOHEMIA
  • Mainz
  • Worms   MORAVIA

Trier •
           Augsburg •   Passau •   AUSTRIA
SWABIA ✳ *LECHFELD* BAVARIA
Freiburg •   Salzburg •
   • Constance

HUNGARY

LOMBARDY
  • Milan
Pavia •   Venice •
Roncaglia •
Canossa • • Bologna   REPUBLIC OF VENICE

Florence •
Pisa •   PATRIMONY
TUSCANY OF ST. PETER

Sutri •
Rome •

KINGDOM
OF
TWO
SICILIES

Naples •
Salerno •

French Royal Domain

■ 987
▨ 987-1180
▨ 1180-1328

━ Boundary of English Holdings
   in France 1180

≡ English Holdings in France 1328

≡ Holy Roman Empire ca. 1200

✳ Battle Site

0   100   200 miles

MEDIEVAL ENGLAND,
FRANCE, AND
THE HOLY ROMAN EMPIRE

and the activities of the *baillis*. Louis IX established special officers called *enquêteurs* to check on the conduct of the *baillis* and report misdeeds to the central government. The *baillis,* acting in the name of the king, steadily assumed functions once monopolized by feudal nobles and churchmen. All during the thirteenth century (and far beyond) the nobility continued to perform many political functions, sharing the task of governing France with the central authority. But they were no longer at liberty to do what they pleased.

The broadening range of royal activities, especially warfare, placed a heavy financial burden on the kings. A prime source of income remained the royal lands. Feudal dues of all kinds were carefully collected. The thirteenth-century kings were usually willing to allow their vassals to discharge their service obligations by money payments. Special assessments were exacted from the towns, the Church, Jews, foreigners, and anyone else the kings could exploit. The Capetians were always short of money, but they managed to raise sufficient income to sustain a strong government.

In the early fourteenth century, the Capetians instituted another practice that strengthened their position. They began to summon representatives of the three classes (*estates*), nobles, clergymen, and townsmen, from all over their realm to advise them and approve their policies. Philip IV convoked three of these *Estates General,* which always ended in approval of what the king proposed and added tremendous weight to royal power by making it appear that the entire nation approved what the king wished to do. The Estates General was much more the tool of the monarchs than was the English Parliament, largely because the French nobles never stood as a group to resist the king and exact a share of power. Perhaps this was the fruit of the extreme feudalization in the ninth and tenth centuries that had made the French nobles particularistic and independent. Nonetheless, the development of the Estates General was important in uniting the major classes of France under a single government.

While the Capetians were expanding and consolidating their hold on France, they drew valu-

able assistance from the Church. The kings bestowed considerable wealth on the Church, helped to reform it, took its side in the investiture struggle, and respected its liberties. In return, the Church supported the claims of the Capetians to greater power and lent its wealth and talent to their government. The long, happy relationship did not end until the reign of Philip IV, who became embroiled in a bitter quarrel with Pope Boniface VIII (1294–1303) over the extent of the king's power to tax church property and to judge clergymen. When Boniface commanded Philip to obey papal orders, the king turned French public opinion against Rome, cowed the French clergy into submission, and sent his agents to Rome to capture the pope (see Chapter 25). The mighty head of the Church, so long successful in thwarting the Holy Roman emperors, had suffered a crushing defeat. The explanation is clear: By the early fourteenth century the king of France possessed a power that the pope could not dissolve by simple command.

The victory of Philip IV over Boniface VIII points to a final achievement of the Capetians: their ability to endow their office with an image that exemplified kingship at its best. Their prestige was best reflected by Louis IX, eventually made a saint by the Church. In no small part because of his actual accomplishments, he was lauded as a lover of justice for his subjects, true Christian, gallant knight, crusader, peacemaker, promoter of morality, ideal son, husband, and father—in short, the perfect prince. This aura of superiority added immensely to the authority of the Capetians, proving them as skillful in fashioning an image as in shaping political institutions.

Thus by 1300 England and France had resolved a problem that had persisted since the fall of the Roman Empire—how to create a stable, just political order. The answer was feudal monarchy. In fashioning his power, however, the feudal monarch learned to respect the rights of privileged groups—vassals, churchmen, townsmen—as partners in the tasks of government. The political systems evolved in England and France gave these kingdoms the strength, order, and stability that ensured them a central role in the future of European civilization.

Suggested Reading

England

*C. W. Hollister, *The Making of England, 55 B.C. to 1399* (Heath).

*Christopher Brooke, *From Alfred to Henry III, 871–1272* (Norton). Either of these two brief, well-written surveys will provide an excellent overview of English political development.

*D. M. Stenton, *English Society in the Early Middle Ages (1066–1307)* (4th ed., Penguin). A study that succeeds particularly well in relating social, economic, and cultural factors to political history.

*C. W. Hollister, ed., *The Impact of the Norman Conquest* (Wiley). A collection of modern views on the nature and significance of the Norman Conquest.

*G. O. Sayles, *Medieval Foundations of England* (2nd ed., Perpetua). A provocative interpretation of constitutional development which has caused a lively debate among historians.

Bryce Lyon, *A Constitutional and Legal History of Medieval England* (1960). A detailed description of the evolution of political institutions and legal structures in medieval England.

*J. C. Holt, *The Making of Magna Carta* (Virginia). A thorough analysis of this great document and its significance.

*G. L. Haskins, *The Growth of English Representative Government* (Perpetua).

*G. O. Sayles, *The King's Parliament of England* (Norton). Either this or the preceding title will provide a good introduction to an important institution; Sayles' book is simpler.

R. C. van Caenegem, *The Birth of the English Common Law* (1973). An excellent introduction to a complex subject.

France

*R. Fawtier, *The Capetian Kings of France* (St. Martin's). The best general survey in English.

Charles Petit-Dutaillis, *The Feudal Monarchy in France and England from the Tenth to the Thirteenth Century*, trans. E. D. Hunt (1964). Especially good in showing parallels in constitutional development between England and France.

John B. Henneman, ed., *The Medieval French Monarchy* (1973). A collection of essays treating various aspects of French government between ca. 900 and 1500.

Biographies

*David Douglas, *William the Conqueror: The Norman Impact Upon England* (California).

*W. L. Warren, *Henry II* (California).

*Amy Kelly, *Eleanor of Aquitaine and the Four Kings* (Harvard).

David Knowles, *Thomas Becket* (1970).

James A. Brundage, *Richard the Lion Heart: A Biography* (1974).

*W. L. Warren, *King John* (rev. ed., California).

Margaret W. Labarge, *Saint Louis: Louis IX, Most Christian King of France* (1968).

Sources

D. C. Douglas and G. W. Greenway, eds., *English Historical Documents, 1041–1189* (1953). A splendid collection of materials illustrating the working of English medieval government.

Jean de Joinville, *Life of St. Louis*, trans. René Hague (1955). An assessment by an admiring contemporary of the great French king.

21

THE MEDIEVAL EXPANSION OF EUROPE

The agricultural and commercial growth, the social readjustments, and the political solidification of Western Europe's heartland — Germany, Italy, France, England — created the potential for European expansion. The realization of that potential between 1000 and 1300 is another aspect of the revival of the West. In the three centuries after 1000, Western Europeans brought extensive territories under their sway at the expense of the Byzantines, Moslems, Slavs, and Scandinavians. The outward thrust took many forms: missionary activity, commercial penetration, colonization, conquest. The consequence was a major step toward the domination of the world by Western Europeans.

1. MISSIONARY EXPANSION

The missionary urge had been present in the Christian community in the West even during the darkest hours of the Early Middle Ages. It remained vigorous during the High Middle Ages and resulted in the conversion of many peoples. The first effort to convert the Scandinavians in the ninth century had been abortive, but it was pursued successfully after the worst of the Viking attacks had subsided. The late tenth and eleventh centuries marked the crucial era in the conversion of Denmark, Norway, and Sweden. In most cases the conversion of the kings was the decisive event. The new Christian kings received invaluable help in their

work from pious churchmen, especially from England and Germany, who devoted their careers to proselytizing the Scandinavians. Once Christianity was implanted in Scandinavia, an episcopal organization, often closely linked with Rome, developed.

Meanwhile, Christian forces also moved across the Elbe into the Slavic world, usually with German political and ecclesiastical backing. Here again, the first expansion came in the Carolingian period, but permanent successes were achieved only when the Holy Roman emperors gave their support to it. During the late tenth and eleventh centuries, the Bohemians, Poles, and Hungarians were gathered into the Roman Catholic fold, while Byzantine missionaries drew the Balkan Slavs, Bulgars, and Russians into the Greek Orthodox orbit. Over a long period Christian influences, again promoted by the Germans and often backed by force, spread along the Baltic to convert the Wends, the Prussians, the Finns, the Livonians, and the Lithuanians.

In the thirteenth century, primarily as a consequence of the crusading movement, Western missionaries ventured all the way to the Mongol Empire and China. Although their labors were ephemeral, their explorations opened vast new prospects. There were also efforts to spread Christianity among the Moslems of North Africa and the Near East, but these proved little susceptible to the Christian message.

Wherever the missionary effort succeeded—Scandinavia, Central Europe, Iceland, the Baltic area—the Church brought learning, literature, and art that often represented the first significant contact of the new converts with higher civilization. The Church was also often instrumental in shaping political and social institutions in these areas along lines similar to institutional patterns in Western Europe.

2. COLONIZATION AND COMMERCE

While some Western Europeans thrust outward with the cross, others were driven beyond Europe's boundaries primarily by economic interests. As we have discussed, one of the great accomplishments of medieval men during the era from 1000 to 1300 was the opening and colonization of an extensive agricultural frontier on the eastern fringes of Europe—in today's terms, a territory comprising northern Poland, most of East Germany, large areas of Czechoslovakia, and Austria. This Germanic "drive to the East" had the strong backing of the Holy Roman emperors, but in the main it was carried out by landowners and peasants seeking new lands to exploit. Churchmen gave the movement their support because it assured the Christianization of the occupied territories. As the German tide moved eastward, many Slavs adopted Western European political, religious, and cultural practices at the expense of their older traditions.

Likewise, between 1000 and 1300 merchants reached beyond Europe to establish the Western European presence in a much larger world (see map in Chapter 18). Italian merchants, powerfully abetted by crusading armies, wrested control of the Mediterranean seaways from the Byzantines and the Moslems, and established trading posts in Constantinople and several Moslem seaports in Syria, Egypt, and North Africa from which they penetrated inland. Northern Europeans, spearheaded by the Vikings, established settlements at Novgorod, Smolensk, and Kiev; from these emerged the Kievan principality that constituted the first effective state in Russia. Scandinavian raiders also settled Iceland and drew it into the European world. After the conquest of Constantinople in 1204 by the armies of the Fourth Crusade, Western European merchants established bridgeheads around the Black Sea which opened access to the cities of Central Asia and China. Italian traders roamed widely across the Asian world, reaping rich profits and reporting the potential of that vast area in travel accounts such as that composed in the late 1200s by the Venetian Marco Polo. A few bold Europeans were finding their way toward the waterways leading to India and the Indies, but their progress was impeded by the barrier resulting from Moslem control of Egypt, which the crusaders repeatedly but unsuccessfully attacked in the thirteenth century. Simultaneously, Western seafarers were pushing southward along Africa's west coast, drawn chiefly by the fame of the gold mines of Senegal. These many forays by adventuresome, profit-seeking merchants presaged a new age of European expansion.

3. MILITARY EXPANSION IN SPAIN AND SOUTHERN ITALY

The most spectacular form of expansion during the High Middle Ages was military conquest, which added considerable territories to the Western European world and gave temporary control over others. Europeans were impelled by a variety of motives: land hunger, quest for markets, adventure, religious zeal, fear. Military expansionism manifested itself around the whole rim of the European heartland, but the thrust was aimed primarily at Byzantium and Islam, those heirs of the classical world that had so outstripped Western Europe in the Early Middle Ages.

One of the most important focuses of expansion was Spain. When the Moors (as Moslems are called in Spanish history), conquered the Iberian Peninsula in the eighth century, they failed to subdue small pockets of Christians in the extreme northern part of the peninsula. Prior to about 1000 several petty states developed in this area—Leon, Castile, Navarre, and Barcelona. Here was generated a drive to rewin Spain—a thrust that turned into a war of liberation called the *Reconquista*. The task for the Christians was made easier by the disintegration in the early

CHRISTIAN EXPANSION IN IBERIA

eleventh century of the once powerful caliphate of Cordoba and the emergence in Moorish Spain of numerous warring principalities. Given this opportunity, the militant Christians turned their energies to a common assault on the Moors. Large numbers of Christian knights from outside Spain, especially from France, joined the fray. The kingdom of Leon-Castile (united in 1037) took the lead and drove to Toledo, capturing it in 1085. After 1085, the Christian frontier was rolled back as a result of Moslem reinforcements called in from Africa, rivalry among the Christian states, and political dissension within them. By the mid-twelfth century, the Christians renewed their offensive; this time the recently established kingdom of Aragon, which incorporated Barcelona, took the lead. A new kingdom, Portugal, emerged as a result of successful aggression in the west. By 1300 the Christians had occupied all of the peninsula except Granada.

The Reconquista created three major new kingdoms—Castile, Aragon, and Portugal. Each developed its own system of government, although all had certain basic similarities. Monarchy was the basic institution, and the kings steadily gained prestige as a result of their leadership of the Reconquista and Church support of their cause. The resources they gained from the Moors bolstered their power. Newly conquered lands gave them a chance to settle people as farmers or townsmen under conditions that allowed the king to retain his authority. These factors retarded the coming of the feudal system, but eventually, feudal practices not unlike the French did develop. Hereditary fiefs were granted to nobles in return for services, and some vassals gained a large degree of immunity from royal control. The Spanish monarchs sought to develop centralized administrations, well-organized financial systems, and effective courts. Several thirteenth-century kings of Aragon and Castile legislated extensively to define royal powers and appointed local officials, comparable to the French bailiffs, to represent them. Nobles and townsmen resisted the expansion of royal power, and in the long run compelled kings to accept limitations on their authority. In each kingdom there developed a *Cortes*, a representative body composed of nobles, clergymen, and townsmen with considerable power to limit royal decisions on a variety of matters, including taxation.

As the Spanish kingdoms developed, society in each took on many features common to the rest of Christian Western Europe. But Spanish society retained its unique features which were by-products of the merging of Christian and Moslem institutions and ideas during the long period of the Reconquista. As a result, Spain played a special role in the medieval West as the channel through which many Moslem influences flowed into the mainstream of Western European society, especially in the realms of learning, art, and technology.

Another area of European military expansion was southern Italy and Sicily. Norman nobles were the aggressors here, intruding into chaotic Byzantine territory in southern Italy and establishing dominance by the mid-eleventh century and snatching Sicily from the Moslems before 1100. In 1130 these feats were given formal recognition when the papacy sanctioned the creation of the Kingdom of Sicily, embracing southern Italy and Sicily. A strong monarchy was soon shaped, incorporating a mixture of northern European feudal, Byzantine, and Moslem practices that made the king virtually absolute, and a brilliant cultural life developed at this meeting place of three worlds. The Kingdom of Sicily passed into Hohenstaufen hands at the end of the twelfth century and reached its apogee under Frederick II (see Chapter 19). Then in 1266, as part of its struggle to thwart Hohenstaufen power, the papacy invited Charles of Anjou to take over the kingdom. French domination lasted only until 1282, when a rebellion, called the Sicilian Vespers, gave the royal house of Aragon control. These rapid changes of masters, often prompted by outside interests little concerned with the well-being of the population of the kingdom, led to a deterioration of political order in the kingdom and a blight on its vital cultural and economic life. But it remained in Western European hands, a prime example of Western military prowess and organizational ability.

4. MILITARY EXPANSION: THE CRUSADES

The most dramatic expansionist effort of the Western Europeans involved a succession of military campaigns directed toward the eastern Mediterranean world over the course of nearly two centuries. These campaigns, called the Crusades, were viewed by contemporaries as religious wars against Islam for control of the holy places where Christianity originated. However, as they progressed, their objectives became more complex and diverse.

In part, the crusading movement began because developments in the Near East offered Western Europeans opportunities and inducements. As early as the ninth century, the vast Abbasid caliphate began to break up into independent caliphates bitterly contending with one another for territory. One area where the rivalry was especially keen was in Syria and Palestine. The aggressive Fatimid caliphate based in Egypt sought to absorb this area at the expense of the Abbasids. The Byzantine Empire also had ambitions in this area, which it still claimed as part of the old Roman Empire. And so did the Italian city-states, seeking to expand their trading connections in the East. In its efforts to protect its claims and to bolster its declining strength, the Abbasid dynasty brought a vigorous new force into the picture: the Seljuk Turks. They were a people of Asiatic origin who had entered the eastern Moslem world in the tenth century, became converts to Islam, and used their military prowess to expand their influence in the political life of the eastern Moslem world. By the mid-eleventh century, the Seljuks had established their dominance over Bagdad and made the Abbasid caliphs their puppets. They then turned their energies westward in an effort to enlarge their sphere of influence. This thrust brought them into conflict with the Fatimids and the Byzantine Empire and made the eastern Mediterranean world a confusing battleground. In the midst of this confusion, local Moslem leaders established several small principalities in Syria and Palestine; they were willing to make any arrangements that would thwart the efforts of the major rivals to establish control over this crucial territory. In short, confusion and rivalry in the Moslem world created enticing targets for aggression—especially where the holy places were located.

The Byzantine Empire was also undergoing a crisis in the eleventh century. Under the Macedonian dynasty (867–1057) it had enjoyed its most glorious days, but after the death of the greatest emperor of this dynasty, Basil II (976–1025), the imperial throne was occupied by ineffectual rulers who allowed the defense system to deteriorate by failing to protect the free peasantry that constituted its backbone from increasing exploitation by the aristocracy. The Normans wrested southern Italy from imperial control and posed a growing threat to imperial control in the Balkans. The Italian city-states, especially Venice, challenged Byzantine sea power. More seriously, in 1071, Byzantine forces suffered a crushing blow at the battle of Manzikert from the Seljuk Turks, who in succeeding years conquered most of Asia Minor. This deepening crisis finally produced an effective ruler, Alexius Comnenus (1081–1118). His most pressing problem was to recover Asia Minor, a task that appeared more and more possible as a consequence of internal quarrels among the Seljuk Turks. But Alexius needed military help. To secure it, he began to appeal to the pope and the princes of Western Europe, thereby presenting Westerners with fresh opportunities and inducements to become involved in the East.

Despite the inviting situation in the East, there would have been no crusading movement without the coincidence of a variety of factors in the West. Increasing material wealth provided the means for more ambitious military undertakings, and the greater political order which curbed local warfare freed the war-loving aristocracy for foreign ventures. The growing military potency of feudal society was being demonstrated by victories on the German, Spanish, and Italian frontiers. The Italian cities were eager to advance their commercial interests in the eastern Mediterranean. The longstanding animosity toward Islam was sharpened by the wars in Spain and Italy. The wave of religious reform sweeping over Western Europe emphasized the idea that Christians must serve God by working collectively through outward, active demonstrations of their piety. This activist vision of religious responsibility appealed especially to the increasingly chivalric nobility, who began to transform their traditional warlike ethos into the idea of holy war against the infidel.

The resurgent papacy, enmeshed in the investiture struggle and nourishing dreams of a more effective leadership over a united Christendom, provided the direction that turned these forces into a specific program. The key figure was Pope Urban II (1088–1099), a man deeply imbued with the idea of papal leadership and keenly aware of the militant sentiments of the aristocracy. An appeal for help from Alexius Comnenus in 1095 opened up the prospect of channeling aid to Byzantium in its struggle against the Moslem Seljuk Turks, in return for which the pope could gain Byzantine recognition of papal supremacy over the whole Christian world and could heal the schism that in 1054 had finally ruptured rela-

tionships between Rome and Constantinople. And the combined forces of a reunited Christendom could rewin the holy places as a supreme act of piety in the service of God.

After carefully setting the stage, in 1095 Urban delivered a stirring speech at Clermont in France calling for Christian knights to join forces under leadership designated by the papacy in attacking the Moslems, defending the Christians in the East, and liberating the Holy Land.

The pope's appeal was greeted enthusiastically, especially in France, and a number of feudal potentates (but no kings) gathered separate armies, a development that augured ill for the future. Meanwhile, an undisciplined horde of peasants and artisans stirred to crusading fervor by overenthusiastic preachers proceeded to Constantinople. Before its annihilation by the Turks soon after Alexius hastily dispatched it from Constantinople, this peasants' crusade aroused hostility along its entire route because of its participants' unruly conduct. By the summer of 1096 the main armies, totaling about 15,000 knights and foot soldiers and a large contingent of hangers-on, began to move eastward by various routes, and they converged on Constantinople in the fall and winter. Protracted negotiations, necessitated by lack of coordination and rivalry among the leaders and by misunderstandings between the crusaders and the Byzantine government, finally led to an arrangement that allowed the armies to move forward. Alexius persuaded the crusading leaders to swear an oath of allegiance to him personally and to release to Byzantine control conquered territories that had previously belonged to the empire. In return, he promised to provide supplies and military support.

In the spring of 1097 the crusaders began their march across Asia Minor. One decisive battle at Dorylaeum brushed aside Turkish resistance and allowed the crusaders to pass on toward the Holy Land. Once in Syria, the armies began to split up, chiefly because their leaders were anxious to assure their private fortunes. One group left the main body to establish control over Edessa and its surrounding territory. After the key city of Antioch had been captured in June 1098, a Norman prince, Bohemond, refused to

This manuscript illustration shows the crusaders making their final assault on Jerusalem in 1099 to mark the successful end of the First Crusade. Their victory ended with the slaughter of those shown defending the city. *Photo: Snark International/EPA, Inc.*

leave it, claiming it as his by right of conquest. Not until July 1099 was Jerusalem captured by the remaining crusaders, who vented their fury by slaughtering hundreds of its inhabitants. This great victory made the First Crusade a success.

Jerusalem, Antioch, Edessa, and other key cities were now in the possession of the crusaders. Disregarding their pledge to Alexius to serve as his vassals and a papal plan to create a state subordinate to Rome, the crusaders elected Baldwin, a leading crusader who had established himself as count of Edessa, as king of the Latin Kingdom of Jerusalem in 1100. He created a series of fiefs whose holders acquired

vassals of their own, creating a typical feudal hierarchy. The king ruled this kingdom with the advice of his vassals, who met regularly at Jerusalem. A Latin patriarch of Jerusalem was installed, subordinating the Christian establishment to Rome. The native population was disturbed very little. Usually their previous local rulers continued to control them under the supervision of the Latin rulers.

The chief problem of the new kingdom was defense. The Latins seized the chief Mediterranean seaports with aid from Italian navies. They built powerful castles at strategic locations in the Holy Land. Before 1130 they established the two great crusading orders, the Knights Templar and the Knights Hospitaler, vowed to defend Christians living in and coming to the Holy Land. Nevertheless, the Christians' position was always weak, and their plight repeatedly persuaded Western Europeans over the next two

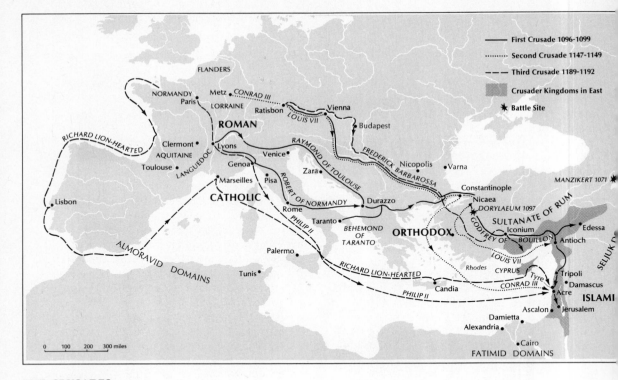

First Crusade 1096-1099
.... Second Crusade 1147-1149
- - - Third Crusade 1189-1192
Crusader Kingdoms in East
★ Battle Site

FLANDERS
NORMANDY
Paris
Metz • CONRAD III
LORRAINE
Ratisbon
Vienna
RICHARD LION-HEARTED
Clermont •
ROMAN
Budapest
LOUIS VII
AQUITAINE
Lyons
RAYMOND OF TOULOUSE
Toulouse •
LANGUEDOC
Venice •
FREDERICK BARBAROSSA
Nicopolis
• Varna
MANZIKERT 1071 ★
Genoa
Zara •
Marseilles •
Pisa
ROBERT OF NORMANDY
Constantinople
Lisbon
CATHOLIC
Rome •
Durazzo
Nicaea
DORYLAEUM 1097 ★
SULTANATE OF RUM
ALMORAVID DOMAINS
PHILIP II
Taranto
Iconium
Edessa
BEHEMOND
OF
TARANTO
ORTHODOX
GODFREY OF BOUILLON
Antioch
SELJUK D
Palermo
LOUIS VII
Rhodes
CYPRUS
Tyre •
Tripoli
Tunis •
RICHARD LION-HEARTED
Candia
CONRAD III
Acre •
Damascus
PHILIP II
ISLAMI
Ascalon •
Jerusalem
Damietta
Alexandria •
0   100   200   300 miles
• Cairo
FATIMID DOMAINS

THE CRUSADES

centuries to go crusading as a way of serving God.

The Second Crusade was prompted by the loss of Edessa in 1144 to the Turks. Papal appeals for action attracted two kings as its leaders: Conrad III, Holy Roman emperor, and Louis VII, king of France. Despite such prestigious leadership, the crusading armies were virtually destroyed by the Turks in Asia Minor. When the two rulers did arrive in the Holy Land with remnants of their forces, their misdirected military efforts aided little in the defense of the Latin kingdom.

During the years following the Second Crusade, more effective leadership began to emerge in the Moslem world surrounding the Christian holdings. These leaders sought to create a unified state stretching from Syria to Egypt to replace the many small, quarreling Moslem principalities that had existed when the crusaders first attacked the Holy Land. The most effective of these new leaders was Saladin, who joined the Moslem forces of Egypt and Syria into a powerful threat to the Latin Kingdom of Jerusalem. By 1187 he captured almost all the Christian hold-

ings except Tyre, a few isolated castles, and the northern counties. The pope called for a new crusade and received the promises of Henry II of England, Philip II of France, and Frederick Barbarossa of Germany to lead armies against Saladin. Frederick left first but was drowned en route. Henry II also died before he could begin his march; however, his successor, Richard the Lionhearted, stepped into his place. He and Philip, almost always at odds, made their way to the East by 1191. Philip, anxious to snatch away Richard's French possessions, stayed on the scene only a minimum time. The colorful English king remained for over a year. After several inconclusive engagements with Saladin, he finally agreed to a truce by which Jerusalem remained in Moslem hands and Christians were allowed to visit it. Aside from the return of a few coastal cities to Latin control, the Third Crusade did little to improve the Christian position.

The Fourth Crusade, which ultimately made a travesty of the crusading movement, was initially prompted by Pope Innocent III, who was perhaps aware of the weakening of Moslem power that followed Saladin's death in 1193. However, the pope soon lost control over the forces that were raised. To ensure transportation to the East, the crusading leaders turned to the Venetians, who invested far more in ships to transport the crusaders than the disappointingly small force was able to collect for its expenses. To resolve this problem, the Venetians and the crusading leaders agreed to support a claimant to the Byzantine throne in return for trade concessions for Venice and money and troops for the crusaders to attack Egypt. But having ensconced the Byzantine ally in the imperial office, they found him unwilling or unable to deliver on his promises. The crusaders therefore decided to take Constantinople for themselves.

Their attack was successful, and the city fell into Western hands in 1204. The crusaders immediately proclaimed a Latin Empire of Constantinople and elected a Flemish noble as emperor and a Venetian clergyman as patriarch of the Greek Orthodox Church, thus reuniting the Church for the moment. Innocent III gave his sanction to the whole arrangement. The crusading nobles began immediately to carve out rich fiefs for themselves, especially in the European sector of the Byzantine Empire. The Venetians, who assumed control over the chief port cities of the empire, were the real beneficiaries of the whole undertaking. The Latin Empire of Constantinople survived until 1261. Much of its history was a constant defense of its existence against Greek forces whose leaders kept alive a legitimate Byzantine government in Asia Minor and fought valiantly to oust the usurpers.

After the Fourth Crusade, the movement lost much of its appeal to Europeans. Innocent III organized a fifth crusade, but he died before it got under way in 1217. Its armies attacked Egypt and captured Damietta, a major Mediterranean port. The crusaders could have traded it for Jerusalem, but greed led them deeper into Egypt, where they were trapped by a Nile flood and destroyed by the Moslems.

Frederick II led the next crusade, chiefly because he wanted to secure possession of the Holy Land, to which he had a legal right by virtue of his marriage to the heiress of the Latin Kingdom of Jerusalem. Frederick's crusade was fraught with difficulties from the very beginning. Because of his refusal to accept papal direction, he was in the bad graces of the papacy when he departed for the Holy Land. Once in the East, he chose to gain his ends by diplomacy rather than by the sword. In 1229 he signed a treaty with the Moslems that restored Jerusalem to the Latins and provided for a cessation of war between Christians and Moslems. This was a great victory, but the way it had been gained outraged many in the Christian West. When Frederick occupied Jerusalem, he was under a sentence of excommunication, and the city was immediately placed under papal interdict.

After this, the turmoil among the Christians in the Latin Kingdom of Jerusalem increased, making it more vulnerable; and in 1244 the Moslems again captured the Holy City. This loss prompted Louis IX of France to organize what amounted to the last major crusade. He spent four years in the Holy Land, but his presence did little to strengthen the Christian position. In fact, his Egyptian campaign increased the danger by providing the opportunity for a strong, aggressive ruling dynasty, the Mamelukes, to establish themselves in Egypt.

The increasing pressure on the Latin Kingdom of Jerusalem was relieved temporarily in the mid-thirteenth century when Christians and Moslems allied against the Mongol threat. Early in the century a great leader, Genghis Khan, had transformed the Mongol nomads of Central Asia into a potent military force that swept over Eurasia and fashioned an empire stretching from China to Central Europe. The Mongol threat began to lessen after 1260, and the old hostilities between Moslem and Christian were renewed. In 1291 the Mamelukes took the last Christian strongholds in the Holy Land. After nearly two centuries, the Latins had finally been ousted from Syria and Palestine; from the whole crusading venture they retained only some Mediterranean islands, specifically Cyprus and Rhodes.

So ended the most overt and dramatic manifestation of medieval Western European expansionism, but its consequences endured. The crusades generated an interaction between East and West which "educated" Europeans to new ideas, products, and styles of life. The ventures extended Western Europe's commercial power. They decisively affected the histories of both the Byzantine Empire and the Moslem world, weakening the former and provoking the latter to a new aggressiveness that was to make an impact on Europe in the Late Middle Ages. Perhaps the most significant legacy of the crusading movement were the images created by Western Europeans in the Near East: the greedy, faithless, crude warrior; the crafty, grasping merchant; the ambitious, worldly churchman—all of whom would do anything to acquire land, wealth, and power. These images were not to be transformed easily.

5. WESTERN EUROPE AND THE WORLD

By 1300 there were many signs that Western Europe's outward thrust was abating. But certainly the efforts of missionaries, colonizers, merchants, and warriors had immensely changed the relationship between Western Europe and the world. First, the offensive had captured and brought under Western control considerable territory—the Iberian Peninsula,

southern Italy and Sicily, the lands between the Elbe and the Oder, much of the Baltic coast, Iceland—as well as the Mediterranean Sea and its crucial trade routes. Second, the expansion had established outposts in the great trading centers of the Near East: Constantinople and the ports of Syria, Palestine, Egypt, and North Africa. Third, Western influences had powerfully affected the development of peoples living on the periphery of the European heartland and drawn them into the Western pattern of civilization. The evolution of Poland, Bohemia, Hungary, and the Scandinavian states was largely determined by European religious patterns, literary and art styles, political practices, agricultural and commercial techniques, educational practices, and value systems. Finally, the Western Europeans exerted an important influence on great powers beyond their direct control. The histories of the Byzantine Empire and the Moslem caliphates between 1000 and 1300 cannot be told without reference to the impact of the Europeans. This was an amazing turnabout considering the impotence of the West vis-à-vis these civilizations prior to 1000.

Suggested Reading

Missionary, Commercial, and Colonial Expansion
Considerable information on commercial and colonial expansion can be found in the economic histories cited in Chapter 18, especially the works of Lopez and Duby.
K. S. Latourette, *A History of the Expansion of Christianity*, Vol. II: *The Thousand Years of Uncertainty, A.D. 500–A.D. 1500* (1938). A detailed survey treating not only the history of missionary work but assessing the impact of the new religion on the converts.

Expansion in Spain, Southern Italy, and Sicily
W. Montgomery Watt, *A History of Islamic Spain* (1967).
Anwar G. Chejne, *Muslim Spain. Its History and Culture* (1974). Either of these two titles will provide an ex-

cellent introduction to the brilliant Moslem accomplishment in Spain.
*G. Jackson, *The Making of Medieval Spain* (Harcourt Brace Jovanovich).
Joseph F. O'Callaghan, *A HIstory of Medieval Spain* (1975).
Angus Mackay, *Spain in the Middle Ages: From Frontier to Empire, 1000–1500* (1977). Any of these three titles will provide a full history of Spain's development in the medieval period.
*C. H. Haskins, *The Normans in European History* (Norton).
David C. Douglas, *The Norman Achievement, 1050–1100* (1969), and *The Norman Fate, 1100–1154* (1976).
John LePatourel, *The Norman Empire* (1976). This and the preceding two authors do a brilliant job of as-

sessing the impact of the amazing Normans on European history.

The Crusades

Jonathan Riley-Smith, *What Were the Crusades?* (1977). The author's answer to this question provides an excellent introduction to the nature of these intriguing movements.

Carl Erdmann, *The Origin of the Idea of Crusade,* trans. Marshall W. Baldwin and Walter Goffart (1978). An original work explaining why the Crusades happened; it stresses the ideological origins.

*H. E. Mayer, *The Crusades,* trans. J. Gillingham (Oxford). An excellent short account of the events of the Crusades.

*Steven Runciman, *A History of the Crusades,* 3 vols. (Harper Torchbook). A study in great detail, enhanced by many provocative interpretations.

James A. Brundage, ed., *The Crusades: Motives and Achievements* (1964). A selection of essays by various authorities dealing with the causes and consequences of the crusading movement.

Joshua Prawer, *The Crusaders' Kingdom: European Colonialism in the Middle Ages* (1972).

Jean Richard, *The Latin Kingdom of Jerusalem* (1978).

R. C. Smail, *The Crusaders: In Syria and the Holy Land* (1973).

Bon-Ami (pseud.), *Social Change in a Hostile Environment: The Crusaders' Kingdom of Jerusalem* (1969). This and the three preceding titles represent excellent attempts to portray what happened to the crusaders in their new environment.

R. J. H. Jenkins, *The Byzantine Empire on the Eve of the Crusades* (1953). A good assessment of the problems facing the Byzantine Empire as the crusading era began. This work can be supplemented by the appropriate sections of the works of Ostrogorsky and Obelensky, cited in Chapter 14.

Geoffrey Hindley, *Saladin* (1976). A good study of a major figure.

Sources

The Chronicle of the Slavs by Helmold, Priest of Bosau, trans. F. J. Tschan (1935).

The Chronicle of Henry of Livonia, trans. J. A. Brundage (1961). These two works provide a great deal of insight into the process by which Christianity spread eastward in this era.

J. A. Brundage, ed., *The Crusades: A Documentary Survey* (1962). A fine selection of contemporary accounts of crusading ventures.

William of Tyre, *History of Deeds Done Beyond the Sea,* trans. E. A. Babcock and A. C. Krey, 2 vols. (1943). A massive history of the early crusading movement by a twelfth-century Latin bishop living in the East.

Fulcher of Chartres: Chronicle of the First Crusade, trans. M. E. McGinty (1941).

The Deeds of the Franks and Other Pilgrims to Jerusalem, ed. and trans. R. Hill (1962). Two descriptions of the First Crusade by participants.

Anna Comnenus, *The Alexiad,* trans. E. A. S. Dawes (1928). A long poem by the daughter of the Emperor Alexius I which reflects the impression made on Byzantine society by the crusaders.

Ambroise, *The Crusade of Richard Lion-Heart,* trans. M. J. Hubert and J. L. LaMonte (1941). Treats the most glamorous of all the crusaders.

*Geoffrey de Villehardouin and Jean de Joinville, *Memoirs of the Crusades* (Penguin). Eye-witness accounts of the capture of Constantinople in 1204 and of the exploits of St. Louis during his crusading venture.

Arab Historians of the Crusades, trans. F. Gabrieli (1969). Views of the crusades as seen from the perspective of contemporary Moslems.

22

THE REVIVAL AND TRIUMPH OF THE CHURCH

During the High Middle Ages, potent movements were so changing religious life that with some justice their effect has been characterized as a "reformation." Two aspects of this reformation emerge as the most significant: first, the drive to strengthen the Church as an earthly community by perfecting its organization, defining its teaching, and disciplining its members; and second, the drive to probe more profoundly the spiritual meaning of the Christian message. To some at least, the closest approximation of the City of God on earth had been realized by the thirteenth century when the reformation had run its course.

1. ORIGINS OF THE REFORM MOVEMENT

Perhaps we need not seek further for the origins of the reforming movement of the High Middle Ages than the nature of Christianity itself. Throughout its history it had demonstrated a dynamic quality that dramatized men's imperfections and drove them to perfect their lives. The reforming surge from the tenth century onward was but another manifestation of the search for perfection, aimed specifically against the secularization, immorality, and spiritual insensitivity that had engulfed the feudalized Church in the ninth and tenth centuries (see Chapter 17). However, more specific factors in-

volved in the reforming movement gave it a unique form.

First was a powerful ferment within the monastic establishment. The monastic spirit emphasized denial of the world, extreme asceticism, contemplation, and mysticism. Drawing on a rich tradition of spiritual concepts related to these practices, the monastic world of the High Middle Ages generated a powerful stream of moral precepts, devotional practices, educational ideals, and emotional perceptions that flowed into and leavened the mainstream of religious life.

A second factor promoting reform was a new intellectualism surging through Western European society that emphasized bringing order out of disorder and establishing norms for human endeavors. This movement promoted religious reform by encouraging men to collect the rich traditions of the faith, to submit them to logical scrutiny in order to eliminate contradictions, and to formulate syntheses that supplied the norms of Christian behavior. The reforms born of this intellectual activity tended to affect church organization, law, doctrine, and discipline.

A third source was popular piety. Reform from this source arose from popular responses to certain simple elements of the faith: the deeds of Jesus, his suffering, the travail of the Virgin, the miracles of the saints, the anticipated pleasures of heaven and the agonies of hell. Popular reform movements often took the form of protest against the power, wealth, and misconduct of the great in society, especially the clergy; the celebration of poverty as the condition most conducive to godliness was a central idea in popular religious movements. These movements often were surrounded by social radicalism, frenzied emotionalism, apocalyptic visions, and even violence, all of which occasionally led to charges of heresy and to repression. Nonetheless, the popular conscience played its part in the ongoing search for perfection.

Wherever these reforming forces were at work, they all placed a premium on looking back into history for models and ideals. Thus the reformation of the High Middle Ages was deeply rooted in tradition—as perhaps all religious reformations are. Because of the traditionalist spirit surrounding this religious revival, one is sometimes tempted to conclude that there was nothing new in Christian life between 1000 and 1300. In one sense, this is true; every facet of religious change built on the old. But in another sense, everything was new, for the real essence of the reformation of the High Middle Ages consists of the originality with which tradition was interpreted and the vigor with which it was applied to the realities of the world.

Chronologically, the origins of the medieval reformation are traced to the new monastic community established in 910 at Cluny in east-central France. The Cluniac movement, which spread rapidly over Western Europe, represented an attempt to purify Benedictinism by restoring strict observance of the Benedictine rule and freeing monasticism from lay control. Adding to this were powerful religious stirrings in every element of the population in the late tenth and early eleventh centuries: Bishops, kings, nobles, simple priests, and peasants all manifested an urge to purify religious life and to rescue the Church from the perilous position into which it had fallen in the feudal age. By the eleventh century the movement found a dramatic focus in the papacy, and thereafter until 1300 the popes charted its major direction. But throughout the eleventh to thirteenth centuries a bewildering array of reform ideas emerged from monasteries, schools, bishoprics, and lay circles.

2. CHURCH ORGANIZATION

One major thrust of the reform movement of the High Middle Ages was toward centralization of the organization of the Church under papal control. This trend paralleled and even outstripped the concurrent efforts to centralize secular political control. Its roots reached back to a rich tradition exalting the ideal of a single community of the faithful—to Scriptural passages, to the acts of general (ecumenical) church councils, and to the efforts of a long series of popes. But prior to 1000 this idea was far from a reality; even in the West, the Christian community was made up of many churches which sometimes rendered a vague obeisance to a titular head located in Rome but in fact acted as local churchmen—and often powerful laymen—wished.

The situation began to change with the radical papal reformers who came to prominence during the last half of the eleventh century with Hildebrand, later Pope Gregory VII, as their leader. As we noted previously, the Gregorian reformers envisaged the Church as a visible earthly community pursuing a common goal, eternal salvation. This community needed its own head, its own law, its own resources, and its own liberty. On the basis of the ancient Petrine theory, the bishop of Rome was obviously the divinely commissioned head, God's earthly vicar. To him, God entrusted the two kinds of divinely ordained power, spiritual and temporal. The pope held the spiritual sword but vested the temporal in lay princes to be used to promote the quest for salvation. He retained full authority to direct the use of temporal power by any prince and to recall it if spiritual needs so dictated.

Gregory VII acted to convert this ideology into reality. His efforts led him into conflict with secular rulers on the issue of the supremacy of church over state, a struggle which went on long after his death and in which the Church made considerable progress in establishing the principle that the pope was the final arbiter in the earthly community of the faithful. The Gregorian

This mosaic from the old basilica of St. Peter in Rome conveys something of the lordly bearing of the greatest of all medieval popes, Innocent III. *Photo: The Granger Collection*

ideal also pointed toward creating a stronger, more centralized, more universal church organization under papal control. Even before Gregory's papacy, his circle established the College of Cardinals as the body empowered to elect the pope, thereby putting the office beyond lay control. Gregory launched an extensive legislative program, aimed in large part at eliminating abuses that distracted his clergy from pastoral work (simony, marriage, immorality) and practices that limited Church control over its personnel and property (lay investiture). Papal legates were sent to all parts of Europe to ferret out and correct clerical abuses and infringements on the Church's liberty. Difficult cases were referred back to Rome for settlement. Special attention was given to papal finances, with the intention of regularizing and increasing income.

Gregory VII did not live to see his program succeed. The immense task he had mapped out

met resistance from many quarters, particularly from the bishops and princes, who rightly sensed that their ancient freedoms were threatened. But Gregory's successors pursued his policy with skill and persistence, and step by step through the twelfth and thirteenth centuries an ecclesiastical monarchy was built. This centralizing trend reached a culmination during the pontificates of Innocent III (1198–1216), Honorius III (1216–1227), Gregory IX (1227–1241), and Innocent IV (1243–1254), who headed an immense organization capable of wielding power on a pan-European scale.

These popes were in control of an extensive Church bureaucracy located in Rome and called collectively the papal *curia*. This body was divided into departments dealing with finances, correspondence and records, judicial cases, and the treatment of sinners and was manned by clerical specialists who made careers of papal administration. The College of Cardinals, made up of churchmen especially selected by the pope, sat with the pope in special meetings (called *consistories*) to decide major policies, and often directed the routine administration of the curia. In many areas, clergymen designated as papal *legates* resided for extended periods to control local affairs in the name of Rome; special legates were also sent out often from Rome to perform some specific activity in the interest of the papacy. The legatine system, coupled with the curia's extensive correspondence and the numerous judicial appeals to Rome, kept the popes well informed about local conditions throughout Europe. A huge and constantly increasing income, derived from papal property, gifts, fees, assessments on the laity and the lesser clergy, and other sources, sustained this organization.

Ranked under the pope was the age-old hierarchy of archbishops, bishops, and priests. By 1300 the exact functions of each level were defined in canon law, and papal control over archbishops and bishops was extensive. Each headed a small-scale model of the papal curia, called a *cathedral chapter*, staffed by *canons* who played a significant role in the episcopal election, advised their superior, and directed the administration of his *diocese*. The bishop and canons conducted judicial proceedings, collected and dispensed considerable diocesan income, managed the bishopric's properties, and supervised the parish priests who directed the religious life of laymen.

The centralized church organization imposed a high degree of uniformity on European religious life. Christians participated in the same ceremonies, received the same sacraments, said the same prayers, and were taught the same doctrines. A single code of laws imposed a common discipline. The whole thrust of organizational centralization was toward exalting religious conformity and damning heterodoxy. A manifestation of the growing emphasis on conformity was the development in the thirteenth century of a special papal court, called the *Inquisition*, charged with searching out and punishing heretics. Armed with almost total freedom to devise its own methods of inquiry and impose severe penalties, the Inquisition became a devastating weapon against those who balked at accepting the Church's rules.

The powerful, centralized administration permitted churchmen to extend their influence far beyond religious affairs. Nothing illustrates this better than the role played by Innocent III in European political life, a story replicated by the careers of most of the thirteenth-century popes. We have already observed how he manipulated affairs to make his ward, Frederick II, Holy Roman emperor. After a long quarrel Innocent compelled Philip II of France to take back his second wife, whom he had repudiated the day after their marriage. John of England and several lesser kings were compelled or persuaded to acknowledge themselves as papal vassals. Innocent launched the Fourth Crusade and exercised considerable influence in Byzantine affairs after the capture of Constantinople, and he organized a crushing crusade against the heretical Albigensians in southern France. Innocent made no distinction between religion and politics. He used religious weapons to gain political ends and political pressure to impose his spiritual leadership. When he spoke of his right to exercise "the fullness of power," Innocent meant complete mastery over all aspects of life. And while the pope was acting on the international stage, the extensive hierarchy under his author-

ity was exerting a potent influence on European society at the local level.

3. CANON LAW AND DOCTRINE

The inspiration behind this effort at centralization was not merely a quest for power; papal leaders sought to use their authority to direct their huge flock to right behavior and right belief. As a consequence, careful attention was given to defining and standardizing church law and doctrine. By the eleventh century the Church possessed an immense body of law, much of it dating from earlier periods. Many of its provisions were contradictory, and some no longer applied. Moreover, new difficulties were constantly arising in this era of reform to demand new legal solutions. Guided by Scripture, papal decrees, the acts of church councils, the writings of the early fathers, and the example of the Code of Justinian, church lawyers worked to create a consistent and organized collection of canon law. A decisive figure in this effort was Gratian, who in 1140 published his *Decretum*, a compendium that treated canon law in a strictly logical fashion to remove contradictions and confusions. His work immediately became the guide for Church administration and discipline. Among many other things, Gratian's work defined the powers of each rank of the clergy, the jurisdiction of ecclesiastical courts, crimes against the Church and their punishments, the proper use of Church income and property, and the manner of conducting religious ceremonies. Throughout the work ran one predominant idea—the supremacy of the papacy in the governance of the Church. Extensive commentaries on Gratian's work eventually led to new codifications, usually made under papal auspices, and by the end of the thirteenth century, canon law had assumed a form and a substance that has persisted with little change to the present.

Church doctrines were even more confused than the law of the Church. There were also those who took up the challenge of defining right belief. Perhaps the decisive figure in the development of a systematic theology was a French school master, Abelard (1079–1142), who aroused considerable criticism by calling attention to the conflicting teachings of Scripture, the church fathers, and tradition on certain fundamental doctrinal questions. He insisted that human reason could resolve these differences. This method of clarifying revealed truth by the use of reason soon came to be known as *scholasticism,* and most theologians quickly adopted it. During the thirteenth century, a series of great scholastic philosophers, the chief of whom was Thomas Aquinas, worked to systematize the Church's teachings and eliminated most of the earlier confusion. In the process, they tried to weave all human knowledge into a unified body consistent with revealed truth, giving the Church a single truth to teach to all.

At the heart of the theological system elaborated during the twelfth and thirteenth centuries stood the doctrine of grace and the sacramental system. According to the theologians, God had created man in order that he might enjoy eternal salvation, human life being but a test of worthiness. His nature corrupted by original sin — the stain imposed on all by the disobedience of Adam and Eve — man was powerless to save himself; only the grace of God could effect this end. That grace was bestowed on man through the sacraments instituted by Christ as an essential part of his mission of redemption.

By the twelfth century the number of sacraments was set at seven, each of which drew its efficacy by virtue of the fact that it was administered by the Church, without whose services no Christian could expect to be saved. *Baptism,* usually administered at infancy, removed the stain of original sin. *Confirmation,* usually received during the difficult years of adolescence, infused into a Christian the Holy Ghost, strengthening his faith and fortifying him against the devil at a particularly critical moment. *Extreme unction,* administered to those in danger of death, strengthened them at the moment they must face the judgment of the Almighty and removed from their souls the stain of minor (or venial) sins. *Marriage* sanctified the wedded state and family life. *Holy orders,* or ordination, conferred on select Christians the priestly powers which permitted them to act as valid successors of Christ and the apostles in teaching the faith and administering the grace-giving sacraments, espe-

cially the eucharist and penance. The *eucharist* was the sacrament by which Christ himself was present to the faithful. Its exact nature was not defined until the Fourth Lateran Council in 1215, held under the direction of Innocent III, pronounced the doctrine of *transubstantiation:* When a priest consecrated bread and wine at mass, their substance changed miraculously into the body and blood of Christ, although their external accidents (color, shape, taste, etc.) remained the same. Partaking of this sacrament — receiving communion — infused the grace of Christ's substance into the soul. No punishment was more terrible than excommunication — being cut off from receiving the eucharist. The last sacrament was *penance,* whereby a Christian who confessed his sins to a priest and resolved not to repeat them received God's forgiveness, provided that he made some sacrifice or did some good work assigned by the priest. Since the stain of sin barred one from heaven, Christians constantly needed to resort to the confessional; the Fourth Lateran Council decreed that the faithful must confess at least once a year.

The sacramental system, offering God's saving grace to men and women at the crucial points in their earthly pilgrimage, made the Church the indispensable institution in the drama of salvation. Embroidered on it was a rich array of Church-sanctioned practices and beliefs to facilitate the winning of God's favors. There were prayers and ritual ceremonies that invoked God's help in every conceivable situation. Sacred objects, especially relics, available to almost every Christian possessed powers to draw God and men together. An army of saints filled heaven to plead the cause of humanity with God and to assist in frustrating the hordes of devils that schemed under Satan's command to corrupt men. These adjuncts to the sacramental system were enlarged and enriched during the High Middle Ages, a process that added a powerful emotional dimension to the rather awesome concepts of the sacramental system.

4. MONASTIC REFORM

While the quest for greater order proceeded within the Church, there was an accompanying search for deeper spiritual understanding, centering chiefly in the monastic world which during the High Middle Ages witnessed more intense activity than in any other age in Christian history.

The dominant monastic force during the tenth and eleventh centuries was the Cluniac movement, which sought to restore the primitive purity of the Benedictine rule as a means of rescuing monastic life from the debasement it had suffered during the feudal age. In a spiritual sense, the Cluniac movement placed heavy emphasis on the performance of an elaborate daily round of religious services as the main duty of the monks. The Cluniac liturgy was a splendid model of externalized religion, appealing especially to the feudal aristocracy and having an impact on the religious ethos of that class. Cluniac concepts of piety, clerical conduct, and ecclesiastical governance helped shape the eleventh-century attacks against lay investiture and clerical corruption. However, as the century progressed, the Cluniac Order, increasingly rich and complacent, lost its spiritual leadership to new forces which began to modify and even turn away from the Benedictine ideal of withdrawal into a holy community where selected individuals could earn salvation without fear of corruption from contact with the world. These new spiritual movements increasingly sought ways of assuring personal perfection and making monasticism a force that would reshape the world rather than run from it.

The urge for personal perfection generated attempts to return to the practice of the hermit life undertaken by the early desert fathers. The most notable exemplar of this was the Carthusian Order, established in France in the late eleventh century. Selecting the most unattractive sites for monastic houses, the order was never very popular as a result of the severity of its regimen, but it did impress upon an admiring world a model of denial of self and the world.

The new spirit circulating in the monastic world found its most appealing expression in the Cistercian Order, founded in 1098 by a Benedictine who felt that the ancient rule was not being strictly observed. It proved immensely popular, so that by 1300 there were about seven

The most solemn moment during the celebration of the Catholic mass is the Consecration, when according to Church doctrine, the wafer of bread, here held aloft by the priest, is changed into the body of Christ. *Photo: The Walters Art Gallery, Baltimore*

hundred Cistercian monasteries spread over all of Europe. The Cistercians were especially effective in establishing new houses in remote areas, which the labor of the monks quickly turned into rich agricultural establishments. As the order spread, it developed a unique organizational pattern that combined local autonomy and centralized direction. The abbot of each house directed local affairs but was required each year to attend a general meeting at the mother house at Cîteaux; these meetings decided policies affecting all houses, and a system of regular visitations was developed to see that local houses adhered to general rules. The Cistercian movement exerted powerful influences on all aspects of religious life. Owing largely to the influence of its greatest member, Bernard of Clairvaux, the order became a militant agency seeking to arouse all men to purity and piety. Bernard viewed monastic life as a preparation for action in the cause of God. He insisted that a monk fortified by physical deprivation, long prayer, and contemplation could without fear of corruption go forth into the world to fight sin and spiritual indifference. His life exemplified this idea. During his long career in the order (1113–1153), he was involved in nearly every important event in Europe. His preaching promoted the Second Crusade; he became the papacy's chief support in hunting down corrupt clergymen (he even turned his blasts against a pope or two); he was a relentless foe of any unorthodox or heretical movement; he hounded Europe's kings constantly to improve their lives and their governments; he had no peer as a popular preacher. He and other monks like him — an army of puritanical, industrious soldiers of Christ — penetrated every corner of Europe urging men to be better Christians.

Other movements of the twelfth century contributed to the deepening of religious life and the broadening of the monastic influence on society. An order called the Augustinian Canons was organized to improve the moral quality of the clerics who made up the cathedral chapters. Its rule bound the canons to poverty, prayer, and moral excellence, while allowing them to move about freely as preachers and administrators. This same century saw the founding of the great crusading orders — the Templars, the Hospitalers, and the Teutonic Knights — which played a decisive role in defending Christians in the Holy Land. The military orders also organized numerous charitable agencies to help pious crusaders in the difficult journey to the holy places.

The trend toward involvement in the world became dominant in the early thirteenth century with the establishment of the *mendicant* (begging) orders, the Dominicans and the Franciscans. Both represented a religious response to a new factor in European life, the city, and to the

blight that success and wealth visited on earlier monastic movements. The mendicants sought the answer to these challenges in a life in the world and a refusal of any wealth, either individual or corporate. Because they did not confine their members to a fixed residence, the new orders were able to extend the Church's influence in sectors of life where there was tremendous ferment — the cities, the universities, and the courts of the powerful kings.

The Dominican Order was the product of the fertile mind of a Spanish priest named Dominic (1170–1221). During a tour through southern France, where the Albigensian heresy was rampant, he became convinced that orthodoxy would prevail only if preachers learned in theology and free from all suspicion of excessive wealth mingled with the heretics. In 1215 Innocent III authorized him to organize a new order dedicated to the destruction of heresy by preaching. The rule provided for an austere life sustained by begging. Even greater stress was placed on education. Each Dominican was put through a rigorous training program aimed at making him an expert theologian. The Friars Preachers, as the order was called, quickly established themselves as one of the strongest arms of papal power, especially useful in directing the Inquisition against heretics and controlling the teaching of theology in the great universities.

The inspiration for the Franciscan Order was supplied by one of the most appealing figures in all history, Francis of Assisi (1182–1226). The son of a wealthy Italian merchant, Francis established a reputation as a playboy and jovial companion. But while still a young man he underwent a fundamental spiritual conversion that convinced him that he must imitate Christ in a most literal sense and he turned to a life of poverty, preaching, and the performance of charitable works. He was especially effective as a preacher because of his personality, which exuded joy, lightheartedness, and a sympathy for all men. To his contemporaries, he was "God's own troubadour," filled with happiness and love. Almost immediately both men and women began to follow him. They surrendered their wealth, worked or begged for a livelihood, and preached a simple message of love for all. In 1210 Francis sought from Innocent III permission to formalize his work in a religious order. Innocent hesitated, feeling that Francis' demands on his followers were too severe, and perhaps concerned lest the simple message of love and repentance would breed a crop of heretics with little regard for the elaborate machinery that the organized Church supplied for saving souls. Finally, however, he consented to Francis' request. Between then and 1226, when Francis died, the order grew rapidly, spreading to nearly every part of Western Europe and even beyond. As the order expanded, its governing rule was modified to provide an organization and a discipline more formal than the founder's simple command that his followers imitate Christ. To many devoted Franciscans this compromise represented a de-

St. Francis of Assisi, portrayed here in a painting done by Cimabue ca. 1280, was perhaps the most powerful spiritual force in the thirteenth century. His ideas on poverty and love deeply affected many of those searching for religious values in his age. *Photo: Alinari/EPA, Inc.*

nial of the Franciscan ideal; as a result the order was plagued by internal conflicts. And there were other problems. The Friars Minor met opposition from local clergymen all over Europe because of their stirring sermons, their exaltation of poverty, and their ability to attract attention. The Franciscans flourished despite this opposition. Their fresh approach to religious life was welcome, especially among the masses.

The mendicant orders were pillars of strength for the thirteenth-century Church. The Dominican Order, emphasizing education and teaching, became the refuge of scholars and preachers, who studied, systematized, and propagated Christian doctrine with a vigor seldom seen in the earlier history of the Church. The ardent disciples of Francis, preaching a message of repentance and love, provided an outlet for those dissatisfied with the rigorous, rather formal activities of the organized Church. The mendicants proved especially useful to the papacy, for they lent themselves to the containment and direction of theological speculation and popular religious ferment.

5. POPULAR RELIGIOUS MOVEMENTS

A confusing array of popular movements and heresies added an important dimension to religious life between 1000 and 1300. Probably they were in part a result of a deeper understanding of the gospel message brought about by more pious and serious priests and monks. The increasing number of articulate and educated laymen in society produced a leadership for such movements. Likewise, the social and economic pressures resulting from the growth of towns and changes in the manorial order sensitized laymen to injustices and abuses within the Church. Whatever the causes, a powerful urge developed in lay society to live in imitation of the poverty and humility of Jesus.

This new spirit produced numerous individual preachers from all levels of the lay world. Often they succeeded in establishing bands of followers who shared their wealth, engaged in works of charity, cared for the sick, and worshiped after their own style. Some of these leaders spiced their exhortations to live like Christ with passionate attacks on the clergy and the wealth of the Church, thus making anti-clericalism a regular part of popular religious movements and leading in extreme cases to overt action. For example, in the mid-twelfth century an Italian monk, Arnold of Brescia, so aroused the populace of Rome against the wealth and secular power of the papacy that he was able to drive the pope out of the city and hold it until the pope persuaded Frederick Barbarossa to depose and execute the radical troublemaker. Often programs that began innocently enough as pious efforts ended by being outlawed and suppressed at the hands of the Church and the political authorities. Intolerance toward heterodoxy and anticlericalism grew as the Church developed the organizational strength to enforce conformity. Two particular movements, the Waldensians and the Cathari (Albigensians), illustrate the nature and fate of many popular reform groups.

The Waldensians were inspired by Peter Waldo, a rich French merchant who in 1173 gave away his wealth and took up a life of poverty in imitation of Christ. His large band of followers took as their only authority the New Testament, refusing to accept the dictates of popes and bishops, who were only men and who because of their wealth were not good Christians. Practicing poverty and a strict moral life that reflected many Cistercian ideas about sobriety, temperance, honesty, and simplicity, the Waldensians went among the people, preaching and praying in vernacular languages, condemning the ordinary clergy, and refusing to admit many of the current teachings of the Church. They developed their own clergy and their own religious services. Eventually they were accused of heresy and attacked by the Church hierarchy. Some Waldensian groups, especially in France, returned to orthodoxy, but in northern Italy they survived persecution throughout the Middle Ages.

Far more radical were the Cathari, or Albigensians. Their belief originated in the Near East as early as the fourth century, probably from the mixing of Christian and Zoroastrian ideas. It spread slowly westward, finally reaching northern Italy and southern France in the tenth cen-

tury, and by 1200 it exerted an influence throughout Europe, with its major center of strength located in southern France. The Cathari believed that two powers, good and evil, battle constantly for the world and for men. Good was spiritual, while evil was materialistic. True Cathari refused to marry, holding that even reproduction was evil. They ate no meat, milk, or eggs, which are the fruits of sexual union. They owned no property and refused to shed blood. The "perfect," as they called themselves, were certain that they were saved. Allowance was made, however, for weaker men. Second-grade Cathari, called "believers," were permitted to indulge more freely, although every "believer" hoped someday to become a "perfect." Because the Church had wealth and dealt in worldly affairs, it was condemned; and the Cathari developed their own clergy, simple services, and rules of conduct. The fervor and the discipline engendered by these convictions produced communities that were remarkably resourceful in devising means to assert their political and economic dominance over the areas where they lived. Needless to say, their unique beliefs and their material successes aroused the ire of those outside their exclusive communities. Almost from the beginning the Cathari were considered heretics. Early in the thirteenth century the papacy and the French monarchy organized a ferocious crusade that virtually eradicated the movement in its major stronghold in southern France.

6. THE CONSEQUENCES OF THE MEDIEVAL REFORMATION

The religious reformation in the High Middle Ages transformed the Christian establishment in the West. It is perhaps not an exaggeration to say that a "new" Church was created. Traditional patterns of religious practice and thought were reshaped and reapplied so that they little resembled what they had been. And to them were added new elements that would have been foreign to the apostolic or patristic or Carolingian ages. In sum, the reform created the Roman Catholic Church that has survived to our day and that has only recently begun to alter its medieval configurations.

One major consequence of the medieval reformation was to furnish the Church with an organization that had the power and resources to impose upon its membership one body of belief, one code of conduct, and one set of religious practices. And not only did this organization have the capability to unify the European population, it also had the intention of imposing conformity; its whole outlook was universal and catholic. The "new" Church therefore worked at achieving conformity, so that by the thirteenth century it was chiefly responsible for providing Western European civilization with its integrating element.

A second major consequence was a revolutionary redefinition of the relation between church and state. Throughout the period 1000 and 1300, Church leaders insisted that it had an independent sphere of activity, an area of liberty into which no other authority could intrude; and indeed it stood superior to all other authorities. In the society of the High Middle Ages the Church developed immense powers to impose its influence on political, economic, social, and cultural life, and it seldom missed an opportunity to do so. In a larger historical perspective, the Church's quest for independence played a role in defining political freedom. And more significantly, it freed the state to a degree from serving religious ends, thereby opening up to it a new range of activities.

Finally, the medieval reformation articulated an immensely broader range of spiritual possibilities in Christianity. It may be true, as some have insisted, that the totality of Christian spirituality was present from the beginning, but a study of the first millennium of Christian history does not persuade one that believers realized the range of spiritual possibilities available to them. After 1000 the search for meaning in religion produced an amazing array of new spiritual insights. It can be argued that many of the most potent spiritual concepts associated with Christianity date from the High Middle Ages rather than from the apostolic or patristic ages.

Suggested Reading

General Surveys

David Knowles and D. Obolensky, *The Middle Ages* (*The Christian Centuries*, Vol. II) (1968). The most up-to-date survey of all aspects of Church history in this period.

*R. W. Southern, *Western Society and the Church in the Middle Ages* (Penguin). An intriguing overview stressing the relationships between the Church and the secular world.

*J. B. Russell, *A History of Medieval Christianity: Prophecy and Order* (AHM Pub.). A general treatment of Church history focusing on the tensions between the forces of order and of prophetic demands to restructure the world.

Organization, Law, and Doctrine

S. Baldwin, *The Organization of Mediaeval Christianity* (1929). A brief description of the main features of Church organization.

Geoffrey Barraclough, *The Medieval Papacy* (1968). A compact survey of papal history.

S. R. Packard, *Europe and the Church Under Innocent III* (1968). An excellent picture of the papal government in action at the height of papal power.

W. Ullmann, *Growth of Papal Government in the Middle Ages* (2nd ed., 1962). A provocative treatment of the ideology that inspired papal activity in the High Middle Ages.

R. C. Mortimer, *Western Canon Law* (1953). Helpful, but far from adequate on a subject that has not yet been adequately treated in English.

E. Vacandard, *The Inquisition* (1908). A good treatment from a Roman Catholic perspective.

Monastic Reform, Popular Religion, and Heresy

H. B. Workman, *Evolution of the Monastic Ideal from the Earliest Times to the Coming of the Friars* (1927). The best general survey of monastic development.

Joan Evans, *Monastic Life at Cluny* (1920).

L. Bouyer, *The Cistercian Heritage* (1958).

W. H. Hinnebusch, *The History of the Dominican Order,* Vol. I: *Origin and Growth to 1500* (1966).

J. R. H. Moorman, *A History of the Franciscan Order from Its Origin to the Year 1517* (1968). This and the preceding three titles will provide a full picture of the major characteristics of the chief new monastic movements of the High Middle Ages.

J. B. Russell, *Dissent and Reform in the Early Middle Ages* (1965). Traces the major movements of dissent to the twelfth century.

*Norman Cohn, *The Pursuit of the Millennium* (Galaxy). A brilliant study of messianic concepts and their social implications between the eleventh and the thirteenth centuries.

Walter L. Wakefield, *Heresy, Crusade and Inquisition in Southern France, 1100–1250* (1974). An excellent treatment of the Albigensian movement and its suppression.

J. B. Russell, *Witchcraft in the Middle Ages* (1972). A fascinating aspect of medieval religious life treated with seriousness.

Biographies

Helene Tillmann, *Pope Innocent III* (1978).

Paul Sabatier, *The Life of St. Francis,* trans. L. S. Houghton (1930).

W. Williams, *Saint Bernard of Clairvaux* (2nd ed., 1953).

J. Sikes, *Peter Abailard* (1965).

P. F. Mandonnet, *St. Dominic and His World* (1944).

Sources

Selected Letters of Pope Innocent III Concerning England, eds. C. R. Cheyney and W. H. Semple (1953). Provides glimpses of the operation of the papal curia in the thirteenth century.

*Brian Tierney, *The Crisis of Church and State, 1050–1300* (Spectrum). A remarkable collection of materials illustrating contemporary views on church-state relationships.

G. G. Coulton, *Five Centuries of Religion,* 4 vols. (1923–1950). A vast, badly organized collection of source materials illustrating religious life, but full of details which put the reader in touch with the real world of the High Middle Ages.

The Letters of Bernard of Clairvaux, trans. B. S. James (1953). An intimate view of one of the great figures of the age.

Saint Francis of Assisi (1963). A fascinating collection of materials reflecting the reaction of contemporaries to a great saint.

W. Wakefield and A. P. Evans, eds., *Heresies in the High Middle Ages* (1969). A fascinating introduction to the world of heterodoxy.

R. I. Moore, *The Birth of Popular Heresy* (1975). Another good collection of documents illustrating the nature of popular dissent in the Middle Ages.

23

INTELLECTUAL AND ARTISTIC ACHIEVEMENTS

The crowning achievement of Western Europeans in the High Middle Ages was the original and creative work done in thought, literature, and art. After a long apprenticeship, they came alive culturally and demonstrated a singular genius in all forms of intellectual and esthetic expression. These activities were no less important in establishing Western Europe preeminence than were the remarkable advances in politics, economics, religion, and expansion.

1. A CHRONOLOGICAL OVERVIEW

In 1000 Western European cultural life was at a low ebb. The gains of the Carolingian renaissance had not been lost, but their impact was felt primarily in the narrow world of the monasteries. The brutal realities of the ninth and tenth centuries were not conducive to vigorous cultural activity. Then, rather suddenly in the eleventh century and extending into the twelfth, there was a spectacular outburst of cultural activity. One famous American medievalist has labeled it "the twelfth-century renaissance," unabashedly claiming for it accomplishments usually attributed to the more famous Renaissance three centuries later.

Whatever we choose to call this renewal, it was a movement marked by great vigor and freshness. The impetus came from many directions: new religious ideas, economic growth, social change, political developments, and wider contacts with the outside world. The range of cultural activities broadened immensely. New educational institutions challenged the monopoly on education held by the monastic schools. Theological speculation quickened, and men began to develop an interest in the study of law and the natural sciences. Literary activity was greatly intensified and took an array of forms: Latin poetry, hymns, history, and drama; vernacular epics, lyric poetry, romances, fables. New artistic concepts found expression in the design and decoration of Romanesque churches and the beginnings of the Gothic style. The twelfth-century renaissance was a remarkably "open" cultural movement, encouraging men to experiment with a wide variety of new ideas, forms, and techniques and drawing into the world of thought, literature, and art not only more churchmen but also important segments of the lay world.

Shortly after 1150 the cultural climate began to change. The buoyant, questing spirit of the revival lost its edge, and men began to concern themselves more with synthesizing their accomplishments. This was especially true in the "sciences": theology, law, studies of the natural world. The prime objective of intellectuals was to reconcile their knowledge with Christian faith in order to produce statements of an ultimate truth. Literary activities became more stylized. In the arts, the thirteenth century was the age of the Gothic, which was a product of an attempt to

**ECCLESIASTICAL AND CULTURAL
CENTERS IN THE HIGH MIDDLE AGES**

merge all forms into a style that would reflect the great truths of the faith. This age of synthesis produced the most mature expressions of medieval culture: the theological writings of Aquinas, the poetry of Dante, exquisite Gothic cathedrals, the great romances. But it lacked the spontaneity, the freshness of the twelfth-century renaissance.

2. EDUCATION

There were two cultural spheres in medieval Western European society. The line of demarcation between them was linguistic. In one, Latin was the vehicle of expression. As the official language of the Church, Latin provided the key to the prime sources of the Christian faith: Scripture, the church fathers, the law, the liturgy. When medieval men had something important

to say, they said it in Latin. Those who used it were the "learned men," and the great majority of them were churchmen. In the other cultural world, the languages of the people, the vernacular tongues, prevailed. That sphere developed its own interests, styles, and values. In general, it did not concern itself with the subjects of the Latin world of learning—theology, philosophy, law, science, liturgy, political theory. It tended to reflect lay life, especially that of the aristocracy. The worlds of Latin learning and of vernacular culture were never isolated from one another, but they were enough separated so that ideas and concepts prevailing in each were clearly different.

Since Latin was a language that medieval men had to learn, education was vital to the learned world. In 1000 formal education in Western Europe was confined largely to monastic schools, although there were a few modest cathedral schools and, in Italy, some municipal schools. They touched a narrow segment of the population and cultivated a narrow range of interests. In the eleventh and twelfth centuries they underwent an amazing expansion, due chiefly to the demands of the Church, royal governments, and cities for more literate men capable of handling the growing complexities of administration and commerce. Cathedral and municipal schools, best suited to meet these needs, expanded at a greater rate than did monastic schools. Especially in the cathedral schools there was a marked intensification of the study of the seven liberal arts. Three of these arts (called the *trivium*) — grammar, rhetoric, and dialectic (logic) — captured the chief interest of the era. Many cathedral schools owed their fame to individual masters who specialized in one of these arts and who worked hard to expand its content and to sharpen the skills associated with it. To a large extent, the subject matter in these disciplines was provided by classical models, so that the schools became centers of a renaissance of classical studies. The other four liberal arts (the *quadrivium*) — arithmetic, geometry, astronomy, music — were not so central to the interests of society, but still their content was constantly expanded, again chiefly as a result of contacts with the classical world.

Toward the end of the twelfth century the monastic, cathedral, and municipal schools no longer met the needs of some elements of society, particularly the masters and students. The accomplishments of these institutions opened up intellectual vistas which abbots and bishops had no utilitarian interest in fostering. Moreover, during the last half of the twelfth century Western Europe was flooded by new knowledge, primarily from the ancient Greek world by way of the Moslems, which challenged existing religious beliefs. The response to these pressures was a new educational institution, the university, which in its origin represented a community of scholars seeking to create an independent setting for study. The first universities tended to concentrate on one area of learning: Salerno and Montpellier, for example, on medicine, Bologna on law, Paris on theology.

Universities were founded by the action of either students or faculty, who organized themselves into self-governing corporations, or guilds (the general Latin term for "guild" was *universitas*). At Bologna the students formed a *universitas* because they felt the need for protection against the townsmen and the masters. At Paris the teachers of the arts in the city's episcopal school broke away from the control of the bishop and founded a self-governing body, the faculty of arts, to control the educational process. Later, faculties of law, theology, and medicine were added.

The base of the university curriculum was the seven liberal arts, taught by a faculty of several masters rather than only one, as in the cathedral school. The arts program, often lasting six or eight years, usually culminated in a master of arts degree, which entitled its holder to teach. Eventually, a bachelor of arts degree was instituted, requiring four or five years of study but not entitling its holder to teach. The doctor's degree was taken in theology, law, or medicine; at Paris the theology doctorate took at least thirteen years of study. The granting of degrees was another aspect that distinguished the university from earlier institutions.

Teaching consisted chiefly of commenting on texts. Students who could afford to buy a manuscript copy of the authority under discussion made notes of the teacher's comments in the margins of the text. Those without a text tried to copy it as the master read it (thus the origin of the lecture system, since reading from a text was called *lectio*). Examinations at the end of four, six, or thirteen years tested the student's ability to expound on a text or defend a thesis.

At first most university classes were held in rented halls, while students took lodgings in private homes. During the thirteenth century, men of means began to endow establishments for housing and feeding students. Such establishments, called *colleges*, became the centers of most educational activities. The first such institution was the Sorbonne at Paris, endowed in 1258 by Robert de Sorbon, a rich courtier. Usually students and faculty were considered members of the clergy and thus were under the jurisdiction of church courts. This led to endless conflicts between townsmen (who had to tolerate students without being able to control them)

This scene portrays a teacher and scholar lecturing to a group of students at a medieval university. His bearing coupled with the reaction of his students to his wisdom suggests the continuity between the Middle Ages and the modern world. *Culver Pictures*

and the university community. Medieval students were a tough, rude lot who demanded much and were willing to use almost any means to get what they wanted; some of their exploits make the modern academician thankful for the serenity of the modern university and the seriousness of modern students.

3. THEOLOGY AND PHILOSOPHY

A major portion of the intellectual energies of medieval men of learning was absorbed in a quest for a fuller understanding of the Christian faith. Out of this quest came one of the chief

monuments of medieval culture: a body of theology and philosophy that attempted to clarify Christian doctrine and to relate all other branches of knowledge to Christian teaching.

In the eleventh century, ever-increasing attention was devoted to the question of the extent to which human reason could be useful in grasping religious truth. One of the early and influential exponents of this approach was Anselm of Bec (later archbishop of Canterbury), whose aim was to provide a logical proof of the existence of God. Rational inquiry into revealed knowledge reached a decisive point with the career of Peter Abelard (1079–1142). Even as a student, this bold thinker disturbed the intellectual leaders of his generation. His stormy career as a teacher was disrupted by a love affair with one of his young pupils, Heloise. This misadventure not only led to Abelard's emasculation by Heloise's outraged kinsmen but also condemned the victim to a life of wandering from monastery to monastery — perhaps always haunted by the memory of a true love. Despite these difficulties, Abelard sustained his intellectual activities, and certain of his ideas influenced both his contemporaries and later theologians.

Superbly skilled as a logician, Abelard began to systematize a method by which reason could be used to enlarge man's vision of God. In a famous book entitled *Sic et Non (Yes and No)* he set down numerous cases of direct conflicts between authorities on matters of faith. Obviously, only human reason could resolve these. Abelard also developed new insights into how men know. He maintained that the truth consists of concepts formed in the mind from the study of created things, such concepts being the nearest approximation to the perfect knowledge that is God. A philosopher's task is to organize in a logical fashion all that he knows so as to create a mental image of God's universe. The opposition to Abelard's rationalism, led by Bernard of Clairvaux, was strong, and some of his teachings were condemned by the Church before his death. However, his approach to theology soon became predominant, especially after Peter Lombard (1100–1160) used it in his *Sentences*, which undertook to resolve rationally differing doctrinal opinions in order to present a consistent treatment of theology as a whole.

The utility of the approach was powerfully enhanced when scholars had to face the vast body of new knowledge that became available in the West during the late twelfth and early thirteenth centuries. Numerous Greek and Moslem philosophical and scientific works were translated into Latin in Spain and Sicily, including most of Aristotle's writings; he quickly became the leading authority on logical methods and scientific learning. This new knowledge posed a serious challenge: Not only did it supply theologians and philosophers with unfamiliar information, but it also confronted them with logically demonstrated systems of truth that directly contradicted basic Christian doctrine. Their recourse lay in a systematic application of reason.

The major concerns of thirteenth-century thought, especially in the universities, centered on this task. Many scholars, collectively called the *scholastics*, labored to master the new knowledge, organize it into a rational system, and reconcile it with Christian doctrine. Differing responses were articulated, often accompanied by bitter quarrels centering on fundamental intellectual issues, especially those posed by Aristotle's philosophical system. These intellectual wars belie the often-stated notion that the Middle Ages was a time of uniformity and conformity in the world of ideas.

The initial reaction to the new knowledge was fear and suspicion so strong that the teaching of Aristotle was forbidden at Paris, but the knowledge was irresistible, and its study soon became the major intellectual fare at the universities. One group, called the Averroists after the famous Moslem thinker, whole-heartedly accepted Aristotelian rationalism, arguing that reason was capable of defining an order of truth that had its own validity irrespective of the tenets of faith. At the opposite pole was a school of thought that rejected the main elements of Aristotelianism and built a philosophical system that strongly reasserted the Platonic tradition and Augustinianism. The most notable figure in this group was a Franciscan, Bonaventura (1221–1274), a teacher at Paris and eventually head of the Franciscan Order. Bonaventura argued that reason could not discover the ultimate truth, which must come to man by a mystical illumination. The phenomena of the natural world which the senses and reason comprehend are but symbols of the reality of the divine order.

But the most representative response to the new knowledge was formulated by the succession of scholars who tried to reconcile reason and revelation. By far the most influential advocate of this approach was Thomas Aquinas (1225–1274), an Italian Dominican who spent most of his life studying and teaching at the university in Paris and producing a huge body of theological writing. His chief work, the *Summa Theologiae*, is probably the best product of medieval thought. In this and all his works Thomas begins with the assumption that God created the universe in such a way that all its parts fit together and have a single purpose. Every man has the duty to know God and his works. There are two paths to this knowledge: revelation and reason. The task of the human mind is to seek the truth by applying itself to those things that are the proper subjects for reason while accepting on faith those things that can be learned only by revelation. Thomas accepted on faith the creation, the Trinity, and the Incarnation but applied reason to such problems as the existence of God, immortality, the operation of the natural world, the nature of government, and ethics. If there is a conflict between revelation and reason, it results from faulty reasoning.

Following the rules of logic formulated by Aristotle, and relying heavily on him for knowledge on subjects proper to human reason, Thomas measured the whole realm of human knowledge item after item against the revealed truth. His method consisted of a rigorously applied series of steps: formulation of a truth, statement of all possible contrary positions, demonstration of the fallacies in these, demonstration of the logical validity of the true position. Each single truth in Thomas' system is part of an interlocking structure of thought which relates all things to a perfect truth. The final result of Aquinas' work is a synthesis of all knowledge into one vast structure glorifying God and demonstrating his power.

The Thomistic synthesis perhaps best represents the overall spirit of medieval thought: the quest to integrate existing knowledge into a single structure; new knowledge was seldom a concern. Out of this effort there emerged a bent toward closely reasoned, highly organized learning that was destined to play a major role in the future of thought in Western Europe. During the Middle Ages, however, there was an important limitation on rationalism: Reason was always controlled, disciplined, and channeled by revealed truth and was therefore not free to seek where it would. It had always to test its findings against the teachings of Christianity.

4. SCIENCE, LAW, AND POLITICAL THEORY

The scientific work of medieval scholars seems pale by the standards of our age, and indeed their accomplishments were limited. Even in the thirteenth century, when European thinkers had at their disposal the excellent scientific works of Greek and Moslem authorities, they made little effort to correct errors inherited from Scripture, mythology, and popular lore or to pursue new knowledge about the natural world. This lack of interest was largely due to the intellectual preoccupation of the age with reconciling all knowledge to revealed truth.

Occasionally, however, the medieval world did produce men with a true scientific spirit. An important group, most of them Franciscans, centered at Oxford in the thirteenth century; Robert Grosseteste (1168–1253) and his pupil Roger Bacon (ca. 1214–1294) were its most distinguished members. These men insisted on the necessity of experiments to ascertain the truth about the natural world. Bacon argued that most scholastics put too much trust in ancient authorities and himself engaged in experimentation, especially in optics. Although his work was far from outstanding, he and his fellow scientists prepared the ground for the later revolutionary explosion of scientific knowledge.

Actually, during the Middle Ages there was a steady increase in practical knowledge of medicine, mechanics, and plant and animal life, but it was merely accumulated without thought for scientific method as it is conceived of today. A typical example is alchemy. The efforts to change base metals into gold by a variety of magical practices unearthed a great deal of information on the nature of metals and how to handle them. Yet no one thought to change the direction of his work from seeking the formula for gold to looking at what might be done with some of the discoveries.

The study of law was pursued avidly during the twelfth and thirteenth centuries, especially at the University of Bologna. We have previously noted the work of the canon lawyers and in particular Gratian, who in his *Decretum* created a model compendium of canon law. A long succession of twelfth- and thirteenth-century canon lawyers continued the work of compilation and commentary grounded in a rational approach; their labors produced a highly sophisticated body of law that found widespread application in the governance of the Church. The chief concern in civil law was the Code of Justinian, which began to be studied in the eleventh century after a long period of neglect in the West. Civil lawyers spent most of their time writing commentaries (called *glosses*) on the code to try to elucidate its intention and relate its principles to existing society. Their work had a great impact on the kind of law the rising monarchies administered in their realms.

Political theorists in the High Middle Ages produced a rich harvest. They were spurred by a variety of influences: the Christian concept of the nature of the state and society (especially as articulated by Augustine), the conflict between church and state, the need to justify the powers and actions of the new monarchies, the revival of Roman law, the recovery of classical Greek and Roman works on political theory (notably Aristotle). In the eleventh and twelfth centuries, political thought tended to reassert the Augustinian idea that the state was a divinely ordained organism established to curb man's sinful nature, the ruler being God's agent for correcting men. Under the impact of classical ideas, this concept gradually changed.

Thomas Aquinas argued that the state is a manifestation of the natural law, instituted to fulfill man's nature, and is therefore necessary, good, and constructive. To function properly, it must be made up of classes, each with a specific function. Peasants and artisans must work, nobles must rule, and priests must pray and administer the sacraments. The function of the state and the ruler is to see that each does his duty and gets his reward; this is justice. A tyrannical king, a merchant who charges unfair prices, a banker who charges interest, a lazy or rebellious peasant are all guilty of injustice in that they are depriving someone in the community of his due. Aquinas placed upon the ruler the heavy responsibility of discovering the principles of natural law that God has ordained to regulate human society and applying them in a way that would produce a human community in accord with the divine order.

5. LITERATURE

The world of learning produced its own vast body of literature, chiefly in Latin, concerned with theology, law, science, and philosophy. That literature was rivaled by another body, produced to instruct and entertain a broader audience.

Much of this second kind of literature was also written in Latin, chiefly by clergymen who learned the tongue as a part of their professional preparation. Although classical influences were strong, there were fresh and innovative aspects of medieval Latin literature. The vocabulary was constantly being infused with new words and meanings, and inherited literary forms were modified considerably. Probably the best Latin literature of the High Middle Ages was lyric poetry on religious themes, often composed to serve the religious liturgy, especially as hymns. The most moving Latin poetry employed a new verse technique based on rhyme and accent rather than on long and short vowels, the classical technique. The new style also lent itself well to nonreligious themes as in the numerous student songs, called collectively Goliardic poetry, celebrating drinking, sensual love, gambling, and a variety of other worldly subjects. From 1000 to 1300 there was also a great outpouring of historical literature and biography written in Latin, some of it marked by keen observation of contemporary events, good organization, and excellent style.

But it is vernacular literature, written in the tongues that Europeans spoke in their daily lives, that represents the best of the High Middle Ages, for here we can see the original literary genius of Western Europeans coming to maturity. Most vernacular works were produced to entertain the feudal nobility. One of the earliest forms of this literature was the epic, or *chanson de geste*, a song recounting the deeds of great warriors and based on oral tradition. The great Anglo-Saxon epic *Beowulf* is largely rooted in pre-Christian Germanic society. So are the Scandinavian sagas, the *Poetic Edda* and the *Prose Edda of Snorri Sturlson*, not written down until the twelfth and thirteenth centuries but reflecting a much earlier society of violence and paganism. The chief Germanic epic, the *Nibelungenlied*, composed about 1200, likewise reflects a tradition dating back to the time of the Germanic invasions. The most representative *chansons de geste* were produced in France, the best known being the *Song of Roland,* written about 1100. Its subject is Charlemagne's expedition to Spain in 778 to attack the Moors, an expedition that ended in the defeat of the Frankish forces at Roncesvalles. However, the unknown author adorned the event and the hero, Roland, with the ideals and customs of eleventh-century feudal Europe. The writer of the *Song of the Cid,* the Spanish counterpart of the French epic, likewise embroidered on a famous knight's deeds fighting the Moors.

The epic genre was soon rivaled by a new vernacular literary form, the lyric, which during the twelfth and thirteenth centuries enjoyed a tremendous vogue among the nobility. It developed first in Provence, in southern France, from where it spread over most of Europe. Its creators, called *troubadors,* found their inspiration in love for a lady (usually married to someone else) rather than in the action-filled, male-dominated world of the *chansons de geste.* The troubador reflected a whole new set of values in the aristocratic world. His poetry, based on his personal emotions — longing for love or a sign of recognition from the beloved, suffering from a lack of it, anticipating the consummation of his love — became an instrument for self-understanding, feeling, and refinement. As the lyric style spread (lyric poets in northern France were called *trouvères* and in Germany *minnesänger),* its forms tended to become highly stylized, the concept of love more ethereal and elevated. The lyric writers (some four hundred have been identified for the twelfth and thirteenth centuries) left an indelible mark on both the feudal world and Western European literary history. They developed a new vehicle for self-identification, charting a new set of values and probing emotions quite unknown to the classical world and absolutely anathema to the early Christian view.

Before the end of the twelfth century, the epic and lyric traditions merged to produce a third type of vernacular literature, the *romance.* This was a story, combining the love theme with high adventure, written to entertain nobles. The love aspect was treated in an exaggerated manner. The adventure element centered on three broad themes: the deeds of Charlemagne, the adven-

tures of King Arthur and his knights, and the actions of Greek and Roman heroes. These basic plots were used with complete disregard for historical accuracy. A reader might find Alexander the Great fighting the Seljuk Turks, attending mass, and engaging in a tournament. Many romances were run of the mill, comparable to the bulk of modern novels and movies. A few writers, however, fashioned works with enduring appeal. Among them was Chrétien de Troyes, a twelfth-century French author whose treatment of the Arthurian material established a powerful picture of the ideal knight and of chivalric ideals. Another, the thirteenth-century German Gottfried von Strasbourg, gives a masterful revelation in *Tristan* of the meaning of love in the lives of two who were its prisoners. *Parzival,* by his countryman Wolfram von Eschenbach, is an appealing picture of a man in pursuit of an unobtainable ideal, symbolized by the Holy Grail.

While the epics, lyrics, and romances were being written, sung, and read by nobles, the middle class was producing dramas and *fabliaux.* Medieval drama had its origin as a part of church liturgy; dramatized parts of services eventually moved outside the church into the marketplace. By the thirteenth century the guilds had taken over the responsibility for producing these dramas on religious festivals. Several types were popular: mystery plays, enacting scenes from the Bible; miracle plays, treating the highlights of saints' lives; morality plays, personifying human virtues and vices. The *fabliaux* were short tales recited in public squares for the entertainment of the crowds. Whatever the subject — it could be almost anything — the *fabliaux* were always close to city life, faithfully representing everyday events in the lives of ordinary people. They were often filled with vulgar humor and satire aimed especially at priests and women. The most famous collection of *fabliaux* was the *Romance of Reynard the Fox* made up of stories in which animals symbolize people and human characteristics.

Of the many writers during the High Middle Ages one genius, Dante Alighieri (1265–1321), towers above all others. He was to literature what Thomas Aquinas was to theology. Dante was a product of Florence, actively engaging in political life in that city and eventually suffering exile. It was while in exile that he wrote in his native Tuscan language the masterpiece the *Divine Comedy*. Outwardly it is an account of Dante's journey through hell, purgatory, and heaven. Guided through the first two by Vergil and through heaven by Beatrice, he is permitted to see all things from the depths of hell to God himself. Within this framework Dante weaves a rich tapestry reflecting many aspects of medieval thought. He is a philosopher, presenting with consummate skill the medieval idea that all things in the universe are ordered by God. He is a mystic, yearning to the depths of his soul to catch a glimpse of God. He is a love poet; Beatrice, his guide in heaven, is a symbol of human love, which purifies and uplifts man. He is a scientist, incorporating many medieval ideas about the structure of the physical universe. He is an admirer of Greek and Roman classicists, although he has to condemn them to hell as non-Christians. He is a keen political observer, full of fierce partisanship. On his long journey from the gates of hell to its very pit, where Lucifer chews up three great traitors, Brutus, Cassius, and Judas, Dante discusses with Vergil nearly every kind of sin, showing a deep understanding of human nature and its weaknesses. The ascent from hell through purgatory to the very seat of God in heaven offers him equal opportunity to discourse on every aspect of virtue. Few artists have grasped human life and human aspirations more fully or written of them with greater artistry.

6. THE ARTS

The High Middle Ages marked one of the decisive epochs in the history of art. Two major styles, Romanesque and Gothic, were perfected between 1000 and 1300. A great spate of building adorned almost every town and village with impressive new structures. Most of these were churches, for the Church was the prime agency promoting artistic endeavor. Architecture was queen; the other arts were used to adorn structures.

The Romanesque and Gothic styles were the fruits of a long artistic evolution. The starting point of medieval church architecture was the Roman basilica, the rectangular meeting hall. The early Christians placed their altars in the semicircular *apse* at the rear and conducted the mass there. The *nave* provided space for the faithful participating in the sacred rites. A lateral aisle, called the *transept*, sometimes crossed the nave just in front of the apse, so that the early church took the form of a cross. Over the centuries, this basic ground plan of church architecture and the art that decorated it was considerably modified by influences from the Byzantine, Germanic, and Celtic worlds and by new creative forces emerging from daily life. During the High Middle Ages artists finally succeeded in blending these many tributaries into distinctive new styles.

Romanesque architecture first appeared in the late tenth century and flourished through most of the twelfth. Its main features are admirably illustrated by several churches still standing: Notre Dame la Grande in Poitiers, the cathedral of Saint-Sernin in Toulouse, the cathedral church of Worms, the Abbey Church of Maria Laach in Germany, and the church of Sant'Ambrogio in Milan. The Romanesque style was characterized both by technical innovations and by a new spirit. The monastic world, especially the Cluniac reformers, played a dominant role in developing and spreading this style, for their emphasis on rituals involving large numbers of monks and their concern with the veneration of relics and pilgrimages dictated churches large enough to house a number of chapels and accommodate great crowds. Architects had also long been concerned with replacing the traditional wooden roofs, which so often were destroyed by fire. The solution was a capacious church built entirely of stone. Round arches were utilized to support the stone barrel vaults thrown over the full length of the nave and side aisles to create the roof. Cross vaults were evolved to cover the area where the nave and transept crossed. Since the stone vaulting exerted a tremendous downward and outward thrust, Romanesque churches had heavy walls and a minimum number of windows. Wherever the walls were pierced for passageways, massive piers spanned by equally massive arches had to

This view of the facade of the Benedictine abbey of the Church of St. Sernin at Toulouse, France, reflects the basic features of Romanesque architecture: the fortress-like solidarity of the structure, the external simplicity, the rounded arches used to pierce the heavy walls. No one could doubt that this structure offered protection from the evils of the world. *Photo: EPA, Inc.*

The interior of a Romanesque church, as illustrated by this view of the chapel of St. Michel in Tournus, France (built between 1050 and 1125), was characterized by round-vaulted ceilings over nave and aisles, thick supporting columns and walls, and a limited number of openings to the outside. *Photo: Niepce/Rapho/Photo Researchers.*

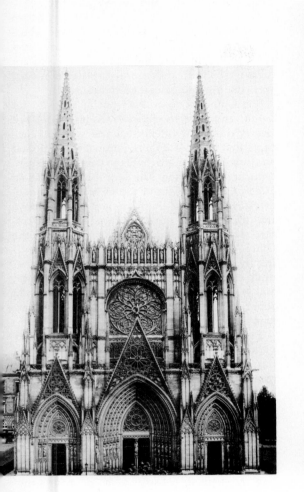

This view of the exterior of the cathedral at Amiens, France (built ca. 1220-1235), illustrates how the Gothic style piled pointed arch upon pointed arch to achieve great height and delicate grace. Note also how much artistry was spent to decorate the exterior of such structures as a way of celebrating the glory of God. The interior of the cathedral of Notre Dame in Paris, shown in the following illustration, has the same soaring quality, achieved through an intricate skeleton of slender columns and pointed arches fitted together to allow light to fill the structure and to draw one's attention upward. *Photo: EPA, Inc.*

Cathedral of Notre Dame in Paris (interior). *Photo: EPA, Inc.*

This scene shows the weighing of souls at the Last Judgment. It is part of a larger sculptural treatment of the Last Judgment above the west entrance of the Romanesque church of St. Lazare at Autun, France. The stylized, distorted figures and the grotesque personification of forces involved in the final judgment convey the mystical sense that typifies Romanesque art and give it its intense emotional quality. This scene bears comparison with a treatment of the same idea in another culture (see **page 21**). *St. Lazare, Autun; Photo: Ciccione/Photo Researchers*

be constructed. Thus the typical Romanesque church had an atmosphere of gloom and mystery that was not dispelled by the decorative paintings on piers, arches, and walls. Yet this atmosphere was due as well to the religious mentality that viewed the church as God's citadel standing against a world filled with evil forces, a sacred fortress where men could commune with the mighty God who protected them from the howling demons and the frightening forces of nature.

By the mid-twelfth century the European world was changing rapidly, and the new environment produced a new architectural style, the Gothic. It appeared first in Ile de France, the domain of the Capetians; the earliest full-scale Gothic church was the Abbey Church of St. Denis near Paris, rebuilt 1137–1144 by Abbot Suger, the adviser to kings Louis VI and Louis VII. From here the Gothic style spread over much of Europe; only Italy was little affected, for there by the thirteenth century a classical revival was creating a Renaissance architecture.

The Gothic style evolved out of a desire for height and light in churches, a desire derived largely from new intellectual and spiritual concepts that fostered a more rational view of God and saw his chief attributes in terms of reason, light, and proportion. The Gothic church was an attempt to leave behind the mystery-shrouded, awesome world of the Romanesque and move into the light and purity of paradise—the paradise Dante pictured in poetry. Among the Gothic structures that achieve this effect magnificently are Notre Dame at Paris and the cathedrals at Chartres, Rheims, Amiens, Strasbourg, and Bourges in France; at Lincoln, York, and Salisbury in England; and at Cologne in Germany.

Technically, this transformation was made possible by the pointed arch, which carried thrust downward, and the ribbed vault, used to concentrate the thrust at a few points. Architects were able to combine them to fashion tremendously tall skeletons of stone whose weight flowed to earth through a series of slender pillars. The outward thrust, greatly reduced and concentrated, could be offset by thickened columns at the outside of the building or by flying buttresses, pillars set away from the main structure and joined to it by bracing arches high above the ground. Thin walls, supporting nothing but their own weight, could be filled in between the pillars. More important, light could be let into the structure by great arched windows, often interlaced with delicate decorative stonework, piercing the lofty clerestory and the side aisles and majestic round windows at the ends of the nave and transept. The windows were often filled with many-hued stained-glass figures or scenes that suffused the interior with a breathtaking display of colored light.

Nearly every other visual art was put to work to decorate medieval churches. The exterior of a

Romanesque church was generally plain except for the façade, where the great doorways leading to the nave and side aisles provided a setting for sculpture. As illustrated by churches at Arles and Vézelay, these spaces were filled with massive, highly symbolical sculpture portraying human figures, animals, and abstract decorative patterns. A favorite subject was the Last Judgment, in which a stern Christ relegated men to heaven or hell. Within a Romanesque church there was more sculpture, chiefly decoration for the massive piers. The large, flat wall spaces were decorated with frescoes portraying scriptural scenes, particularly those that stressed the suffering of Christ and his judgment on men. The style of Romanesque sculpture and painting is a somber one that makes man small, powerless, and dependent; it grips the emotions rather than the mind.

Gothic architecture brought about changes in the other arts. The exteriors of Gothic churches provided innumerable places for decorative sculpture, giving stone carvers an opportunity to experiment with a fantastic array of decorative motifs. Statues were more realistic and humanistic, expressing more the human qualities of Jesus, the Virgin, the apostles, and the saints.

The interior of Gothic churches offered less space for painting and sculpture than did Romanesque churches; decoration was concentrated chiefly on columns and arches. Not images but light fills the Gothic church. The painted walls of the Romanesque church were replaced with stained-glass windows. Their creators drew their themes from scriptural sources, but in their renditions they reflected in amazing detail the daily activities of medieval people. The stained glass at Chartres and in the beautiful Sainte-Chapelle built by Louis IX in Paris enthrall the viewer.

Another art associated with religious activity, music, also developed significantly during the High Middle Ages. Church music consisted primarily of melodies with verses taken from Scripture (especially the psalms) or composed for liturgical events (such great hymns as *Dies Irae* and *Stabat Mater* came from the Middle Ages). *Gregorian chant* (its alleged inventor was Pope Gregory I) or *plain song* developed as early as the sixth century. At first, the singing was in unison, but over the centuries variations worked on plain song developed into contrapuntal music. The variations required a different scheme of written indications for the music, so that by the eleventh century, the musical notation system still in use today had been developed. By the thirteenth century, complex and moving contrapuntal compositions, rendered by many voices and various instruments, filled the churches with sounds almost as heavenly as the light that poured through the stained glass windows.

These Gothic figures from the south portal of the cathedral at Chartres, France, illustrate the warmth and realism of Gothic sculpture. The contrast with Romanesque sculpture (see page 286) is striking. *Photo: Jean Roubier*

The great cathedrals commanded the best artistic talent and the bulk of the wealth that medieval society had to devote to art. However, there were other lines of artistic pursuit. Many feudal castles, massive rather than elegant or comfortable, were built in the Romanesque style. In the towns, especially from the thirteenth century onward, beautiful town halls and guildhalls were constructed, putting Gothic principles to new uses. These structures were impressive signs that the Church never completely absorbed artistic energies.

7. THE UNDERLYING SPIRIT OF MEDIEVAL CULTURE

Certainly it is not easy to find a common denominator for Thomas Aquinas, Dante, the architects and sculptors who built the churches at Poitiers, Amiens, and Chartres, the troubadors, the romance writers, and the authors of *fabliaux*. The culture of the High Middle Ages was marked by variety. Medieval cultural life exhibited signs of nearly every attitude or idea present even in modern society, a fact that increasingly has led scholars to insist that modern Western European culture was born in the eleventh to thirteenth centuries.

Most medieval art and thought is permeated by a quest for truth and light beyond the world of men. This reaching out of the mind and the imagination sprang from the almost universal belief that God controlled the universe and that it was man's duty to know and worship him. The artist and the writer stood in awe of God and used their talents humbly to serve him. Medieval culture viewed as a whole, therefore, has an atmosphere of otherworldliness and of surrender to a power beyond human understanding.

Yet, intertwined with this aspiration and submission to the divine there is a warm, sympathetic feeling for humankind. Medieval men believed that man was God's finest creation. Artists and writers were never disdainful of human powers and potentialities. They took joy in presenting man as he was and wrestled constantly with the problem of understanding human nature more fully.

The medieval genius shines most brilliantly in attempts to synthesize these two outlooks. Men seldom felt that otherworldliness and secularism, spirituality and humanism were exclusive terms. Medieval thinkers and artists respected their own powers enough to believe that they could reach out toward God — by building cathedrals higher or by putting together greater *summae* of knowledge or by flights of poetic fancy. Yet they were men of great enough faith to believe that their quest would lead them to a power infinitely greater than themselves.

Suggested Reading

General Surveys

*John W. Baldwin, *The Scholastic Culture of the Middle Ages, 1000–1300* (Heath). A perceptive brief survey.

H. O. Taylor, *The Medieval Mind* (4th ed., 2 vols., 1949). The best of longer studies written by a nonspecialist with imagination and deep understanding.

*C. H. Haskins, *The Renaissance of the Twelfth Century* (Meridian).

P. Wolff, *The Cultural Awakening*, trans. A. Carter (1969).

*Christopher Brooke, *The Twelfth-Century Renaissance* (Harcourt Brace Jovanovich). This and the preceding titles cover all aspects of cultural life in the early part of the period. Haskins originally designated these developments as a "renaissance."

Education

*C. H. Haskins, *The Rise of the Universities* (Cornell).

L. J. Daly, *The Medieval University, 1200–1400* (1961). Two excellent brief surveys of the emergence of the university system.

*Jacques LeGoff, *The Intellectuals of the Middle Ages* (Harper Torchbook). An interesting sketch of an important group in the High Middle Ages.

*H. Wieruszowski, *The Medieval University: Masters, Students, Learning* (Anvil). A brief description accompanied by a fine selection of source materials illustrating the university system.

University Records and Life in the Middle Ages, trans. Lynn Thorndike (1944). Especially good for the picture it presents of student life.

Theology and Philosophy

*D. Knowles, *The Evolution of Medieval Thought* (Vintage). The best brief survey, perhaps stressing too much the continuity between classical and medieval thought.

Gordon Leff, *Medieval Thought from St. Augustine to Ockham* (1958). Another brief survey, perhaps easier to read than Knowles.

Etienne Gilson, *History of Christian Philosophy in the Middle Ages* (1955).

Jaroslav Pelikan, *The Christian Tradition: A History of the Development of Doctrine*, Vol. III: *The Growth of Medieval Theology* (1978). This and the preceding title are detailed treatments of medieval theological and philosophical developments.

*Richard McKeon, ed., *Selections from Medieval Philosophers*, 2 vols. (Scribners). A representative anthology.

*A. C. Pegis, ed., *Introduction to Saint Thomas Aquinas* (Modern Library). Provides a good introduction to the ideas and methodology of the scholastics.

James A. Weisheipl, *Friar Thomas d'Aquino. His Life, Thought, and Work* (1974). A sympathetic, clearly presented treatment.

Science, Law, Political Theory

*Richard C. Dales, *The Scientific Achievement of the Middle Ages* (Pennsylvania).

A. C. Crombie, *Medieval and Early Modern Science*, 2 vols. (2nd ed., 1959). Two good surveys of medieval science; the latter work is somewhat technical.

R. C. Mortimer, *Western Canon Law* (1953).

P. Vinogradoff, *Roman Law in Medieval Europe* (3rd ed., 1961). These two works, although not entirely satisfactory, provide insight into legal developments.

J. B. Morrall, *Political Thought in Medieval Times* (2nd ed., 1960).

Walter Ullmann, *A History of Political Thought: The Middle Ages* (1965). Two excellent brief treatments.

Ewart Lewis, *Medieval Political Ideas*, 2 vols. (1954). A fine collection of medieval writings on political theory.

Literature

W. T. Jackson, *The Literature of the Middle Ages* (1960). A convenient introduction to a vast and complex subject. It is perhaps better to read medieval literature itself than about it. The following works are especially recommended:

Beowulf, trans. David Wright (Penguin).

Nibelungenlied, trans. A. T. Hatto (Penguin).

Prose Edda of Snorri Sturlson: Tales from Norse Mythology, trans. J. I. Young (University of California).

Song of Roland, trans. F. B. Luguiens (Macmillan).

An Anthology of Medieval Lyrics, ed. A. Flores (1962).

J. A. Symonds, *Wine, Women, and Song* (1925).

Medieval Romances, ed. R. S. and L. H. Loomis (Modern Library).

Arthurian Romances by Chrétien de Troyes, trans. W. W. Comfort (Dutton).

Aucassin and Nicolette and Other Medieval Romances, ed. E. Mason (Dutton).

*Wolfram von Eschenbach, *Parzival*, trans. H. M. Mustard and C. E. Passage (Vintage).

*Gottfried von Strassburg, *Tristan*, trans. A. T. Hatto (Penguin).

Medieval Mysteries, Moralities and Interludes, ed. V. F. Hopper and G. B. Lakey (Barron).

Everyman and Medieval Miracle Plays, ed. A. C. Cawley (Dutton).

Five Comedies of Medieval France, trans. O. Mandel (Dutton).

The Comedy of Dante Alighieri, trans. D. Sayers and B. Reynolds, 3 vols. (Penguin).

The Arts

H. Focillon, *The Art of the West in the Middle Ages*, 2 vols. (1963). A great work, made more effective by excellent illustrations.

François Souchal, *Art of the Early Middle Ages* (1968).

K. J. Conant, *Carolingian and Romanesque Architecture, 800–1200* (1959).

A. Grabar and C. Nordenfalk, *Romanesque Painting* (1958). This and the preceding two titles effectively treat various aspects of Romanesque art.

*A. Martindale, *Gothic Art from the Twelfth to the Fifteenth Century* (Praeger).

*Robert Branner, *Gothic Architecture* (Braziller).

*Otto von Simson, *The Gothic Cathedral* (Princeton).

*Emile Mâle, *The Gothic Image* (Harper Torchbook). This and the preceding three titles fully characterize the nature of Gothic art.

Jean Gimpel, *The Cathedral Builders,* trans. C. F. Barnes, Jr. (1961). Describes the techniques of medieval builders.

*Henry Adams, *Mont Saint Michel and Chartres* (Anchor). A classic work that contrasts the spirit of Romanesque and Gothic.

*E. Panofsky, *Gothic Architecture and Scholasticism* (Meridian). A stimulating attempt to interrelate the intellectual and artistic worlds.

*H. Hutter, *Medieval Stained Glass* (Crown). A good introduction.

Gustav Reese, *Music in the Middle Ages* (1940). Excellent, although highly technical.

Retrospect

The events upon which attention has been focused in this section were decisive in world history, for the central development of the era from 1000 to 1300 was the rise of Western Europe. The High Middle Ages was distinguished by the remarkable expansion of the primitive society that had been so painfully and tenuously pieced together atop the ruins of classical civilization. At every level of society and in every phase of life, there was sustained, constructive activity that increased wealth, secured order, changed the social structure, expanded mental horizons, deepened understanding of human existence, and enlarged capabilities for expression. The new institutional patterns and ideas that were fashioned during this remarkable age — the youthful national states, the social structure of nobility, peasantry, and bourgeoisie, the towns, the Church, the universities, the theology and philosophy, the vernacular literature, the art styles, the commercial and agricultural practices, the laws, the technology — have all survived in their essential forms almost to the present. They are developments basic to an enlarged understanding of the later history of Western Europe.

But the era has another, equally important, dimension. While gathering strength internally, Western European society began to impinge on the outside world. The High Middle Ages was the period of the first decisive steps toward the establishment of European preeminence in the world. Those who would understand the situation today would be well served by attempting to identify the ingredients which by 1300 had given Western Europeans the capability to influence the destinies of other peoples.

In our concentration on the remarkable growth of Western European society and its outward thrust toward other civilizations, we have perhaps not given enough attention to an internal development that may well supply the key to its future history. In considering the High Middle Ages, one is constantly struck by the fact that, as Western European society matured, its institutional and ideological fabric was laced with dichotomies and contradictions. Basic to the political order was tension between strong monarchical government and the privileges and rights of feudal nobles, the Church, and townsmen. Political thought and practice was divided by the clash between the universalism represented by the Holy Roman Empire and the localism inbred in the emergent nations. Engrained in Western European civilization were the contrasting aspirations of church and state. The religious structure was riven by the thrust toward universalism represented by the papacy and the local self-determination claimed by the ancient bishoprics existing all over the West. Everywhere some men struggled to impose uniformity and conformity in religious belief and practice, while others reached out toward personal, individualistic varieties of expression. In the economic realm, commercial towns contended with agricultural villages. On the farms, the traditional forms of collective, manorial exploitation stood juxtaposed with specialized, capitalistic exploitation. In the cities, the guilds sought to impose just prices, common standards of production, and equitable division of business opportunities, while resourceful entrepreneurs tried to follow their private ends. A universal Latin culture competed with localized vernacular cultures. The revealed tenets of the faith were challenged by the dictates of human reason. The world-denying spirit of the monastic world confronted powerful secular, humanistic interests. One is almost forced to conclude that as a consequence of its historical development during the High Middle Ages, Western European civilization in a unique way was compounded of contradictory thrusts. It was like a Gothic cathedral in which height was limited by weight, light met dark, color competed with stark bareness, space was confined by structure.

Can we say perhaps that this juxtaposition of opposites that emerged from 1000 to 1300 constitutes the essence of Western European civilization? Dare we suggest that these medieval contradictions have supplied the Western world with its dynamism? Might we suspect that the history of the West after 1300 may be a story of the resolution of these contradictions: central government versus private interests, rights, and privileges; state versus church, reason versus faith; national states versus universal empire? Perhaps when the West has relieved its inner tensions by resolving these medieval issues, it will have lost its vitality.

VI

The Late Middle Ages
1300-1500

A long sweep of history is sometimes difficult to describe with a single neat phrase. Such is the Late Middle Ages, the era from 1300 to 1500. In the centuries since, historians have labeled it "the dawn of a new era," "the age of the Renaissance," "an age of transition," "the ordeal of transition," "the autumn of the Middle Ages," "the waning of the Middle Ages," "the death of medieval civilization." The descriptions all suggest that change was the keynote of these two centuries—but they also suggest that historians are not at all agreed on the direction of that change. Some emphasize new forces emerging; others stress the dissolution of old ways.

Perhaps we should let those who lived then tell us what was fundamental. Reading the literature and viewing the art of the period, we are struck by the frustration, bitterness, morbidity, and doubt gripping men's minds. Their comments on their world show they sensed that something was amiss; and with few exceptions, they seemed lacking in confidence and incapable of hope. These reactions argue that the dominant theme of the Late Middle Ages must be decline and disintegration rather than renaissance and the onset of modernity. Our description will follow that lead by suggesting that the equilibrium established in the thirteenth century between the numerous dichotomous forces in Western European civilization failed to survive. Perhaps Thomas Aquinas could reconcile revelation and reason, but his successors could not make the blend hold. The architects who built the Gothic cathedral at Amiens might balance height and weight, but their successors who tried to achieve greater height saw their cathedrals crash to earth. The Magna Carta might juxtapose royal authority and baronial right, but that settlement would not keep the peace. And so it was in most aspects of society. The fragile balance of contradictory forces that had been fashioned during the

High Middle Ages failed to last. The fourteenth and fifteenth centuries mark a period when men were acutely aware of the failure.

The tensions that began to alter what had been forged in the High Middle Ages were of the essence of civilized life in the West in the Late Middle Ages. Tension breeds deterioration — but it also generates new forces in society. They were numerous and powerful, and we must return to them in future discussions. Men living from 1300 to 1500 could not, however, sense their promise as well as we can, gifted as we are with hindsight. To those men, the age was filled with the agonies that mark the passing of the known and familiar.

Politically, the fourteenth and fifteenth centuries were filled with disorder. Such typically medieval institutions as the Holy Roman Empire, the Byzantine Empire, and the feudal monarchies of England, France, and Spain failed to cope with new political problems. Their inadequacies bred civil strife, class struggle, international war, and internal injustice everywhere in Western Europe. Behind much of this trouble lay economic and social problems arising from the growing failure of medieval agricultural and commercial institutions.

1. THE DECLINE OF THE HOLY ROMAN EMPIRE

We have previously traced the efforts made by a succession of rulers between 950 and 1250 to join Germany, Italy, and the western fringes of the Slavic world into a Holy Roman Empire and the powerful opposition, led by the papacy, these efforts generated. The death of the last great emperor, Frederick II, in 1250 marked the beginning of the end: Not only did the empire as an institution disintegrate in the Late Middle Ages; so did the political ideal that had given it a rationale — that a Christian commonwealth uniting the faithful under a single Christian prince could be created and sustained.

Frederick II's death opened a quarter century

24

POLITICAL, ECONOMIC, AND SOCIAL TENSIONS

of civil strife, marked by an interregnum caused by the inability of the German nobility to elect an emperor and exacerbated by the incessant intervention of the papacy and of France and England. During this struggle, nobles, clergy, and townsmen successfully extended their independence from central authority. In 1273, the rivalry for the crown ended with the election of Rudolph of Hapsburg (1273–1291), who confined his efforts to increasing his family holdings in the area of modern Austria. His success caused the German princes to repudiate the Hapsburgs in 1308 in favor of Luxembourg's Henry VII (1308–1313), who greatly strengthened his family's position by establishing control over Bohemia. In 1314 Louis IV (1314–1347) of Bavaria was elected out of fear that the house of Luxembourg was getting too powerful. By the attitude they reflected in the election process, the German nobles demonstrated that they would not tolerate a strong ruler; those who desired to gain the imperial office fully realized the situation.

This trend was finally given legal definition by Emperor Charles IV (1347–1378) of Luxembourg. His most important act was to promulgate the famous Golden Bull of 1356, providing that in the future the Holy Roman emperor would be elected by seven German princes designated as the *electors:* the archbishops of Cologne, Trier, and Mainz, and the princes of Saxony, Brandenburg, the Palatinate, and Bohemia.

The papacy was excluded from the election process, which was now a strictly German affair. Each of the electors was granted almost complete independence within his own territory.

After 1356 Germany progressed rapidly toward decentralization. Other princes demanded and gained the same kind of independence enjoyed by the electors, making Germany a confederation of roughly one hundred independent states. The emperor could call together the princes, churchmen, and representatives of the towns in meetings called *diets*, but he lacked any means of enforcing decisions; he had no national army, no tax system, and no court system. Within their small principalities, many princes created stable, well-organized political systems — Germany was not a lawless, ungoverned land by any means. But she did lack unity, and for this she was to pay heavily in early modern times, when she had to meet the competition of the large unified national states that emerged elsewhere in Europe.

In Italy, the trend toward decentralization after 1250 was even more pronounced. The elected emperor was in theory the ruler of Italy, and from time to time some Italians did seek to have him exert his authority (as Dante's powerful political tract, *On Monarchy*, illustrates). After the early fourteenth century, the emperors seldom even tried to exert any influence, and a welter of independent states of all sizes and descriptions emerged. Among them, a few stand forth as most important.

In southern Italy the old Norman-Hohenstaufen state was now divided into the Kingdom of Naples, ruled by a French prince, and the Kingdom of Sicily, ruled by a member of the royal family of Aragon. Their rivalry and misrule brought steady decline to this once rich area. The Papal States dominated central Italy, their independence firmly established through the efforts of the great thirteenth-century popes. However, papal overlordship was bitterly resisted by the local nobility. It was badly compromised by the long residency of the popes at Avignon (1309–1377) and by the Great Schism that followed (see Chapter 25). When the papacy was finally reestablished in Rome early in the fifteenth century, that authority was restored by a succession of popes who used all the tactics of power politics and intrigue to impose a despotic regime. These activities made them powerful, but badly tarnished their reputation as spiritual leaders throughout most of Europe.

The other "major" powers in Italy were the northern city-states of Milan, Venice, and Florence. They accomplished much between 1300 and 1500 that would eventually exert a major influence on all of Western Europe; these were the golden years of their Renaissance. The city-states were preeminently the products of commercial and industrial activity, which made them unique in the West. After the death of Frederick II, they battled one another for land, trading advantages, power, and security. Internally, they tended to move from considerable citizen participation toward one-man or oligarchical rule, a trend encouraged by the pressures of intercity warfare and class strife within each city. Milan was taken over by a despot early in the fourteenth century when the Visconti family established its power. Visconti domination, which made Milan rich and powerful, lasted until 1447, when the Sforzas replaced them. Florence resisted despotism longer, but an aggressive banking family, the Medici, established control in the city shortly after 1430. Venice always remained subject to an oligarchy of rich merchants whose methods did not differ greatly from those of the despots. The turbulent, strife-filled times promoted notable progress in the arts of war and diplomacy. The new style of politics, described brilliantly in Machiavelli's *The Prince*, tended to stress the absolute sovereignty of the state, its right to create its own moral sanctions, its superiority over its subjects. Many historians see these developments as prototypes for modern Western diplomacy and power politics.

Despite the vitality of the Italian Renaissance states, their history in the Late Middle Ages has a tragic dimension. The fragmentation of the peninsula doomed Italy to weakness in the face of the more integrated Spain and France and even the larger German principalities. When in 1494 Charles VIII of France was called into Italy by the Sforza ruler of Milan in order to gain advantage for his city, his invasion opened a long era during which the many states of Italy became pawns in European power politics.

2. THE FAILURE OF FEUDAL MONARCHY IN FRANCE, ENGLAND, AND SPAIN

After 1300 England, France, and the Iberian kingdoms encountered troubles nearly as serious as those of the Holy Roman Empire. As the fourteenth century progressed, their feudal monarchies began to show signs of instability and inadequacy. Kings were not content to share power, and nobles, clergy, and townsmen were unwilling to surrender more of their privileges. Kings lacked the power and resources to solve the major problems caused by wars and economic crises, and the vested interests were not blessed with vision great enough to face them. The result was a heightening of tension in each kingdom, a situation that led inevitably to civil wars that pitted the crown against the nobles and noble factions against each other. Under constant stress, the essential features of feudal monarchy and the concepts that animated the political order of the High Middle Ages slowly broke down.

The evolution of France and England from 1300 to 1500 must be dealt with together because the histories of the two center around a single event, the Hundred Years' War (1337–1453). This struggle was an extension of a conflict between England and France that had begun in the twelfth century and climaxed in the decisive French victory won by Philip II over John of England in 1214. The first phase of the struggle seemed to be settled by the Treaty of Paris (1259), which recognized French control over the northern part of the old Angevin Empire which Philip II had wrested from John but left England still in control of a large portion of the old duchy of Aquitaine, including Guienne and Gascony. However, that settlement only bred continued rivalry. The strong French kings Louis IX and Philip IV kept extending their influence into southern France to threaten the fief of their vassal, the king of England. English and French interests also clashed in the County of Flanders, where the English sought to resist French domination in order to protect their interests in the Flemish woollen industry, which depended on English raw wool. Also French support of the efforts of the Scots to win their independence troubled the English, especially after the Scots virtually assured that end with their victory at the battle of Bannockburn in 1314.

It was Edward III (1327–1377) who moved to settle the issue. The moment seemed ripe for the English. In 1328 the last member of the Capetian house died, and Philip of Valois, a man of little talent, succeeded to the throne as Philip VI. After taking careful steps to gather a strong army and to build a system of allies, Edward III announced in 1337 that he was claiming the throne of France on the grounds that he had a better hereditary claim than did Philip VI. The French king answered by pronouncing Edward a rebellious vassal and confiscating his continental fief.

The first phase of the Hundred Years' War lasted until 1360 and was nearly fatal to France. English ships won control of the Channel, and English armies, made up largely of nonnoble longbowmen and pikemen, cut to pieces the flower of French feudal nobility in two great battles at Crécy (1346) and Poitiers (1356). The crowning blow came at the battle of Poitiers, when John of France (1350–1364) was captured and carried off to England. Without a king, France was plunged into crisis. Charles, John's son, tried to carry on as regent, but his authority was challenged on every side. The Estates General, led by powerful Parisian merchants, under-

took extensive reforms aimed at curbing royal taxation, correcting abuses in the royal government, and putting controls on royal civil servants. A peasant revolt, called the *Jacquerie* uprising, broke out in 1358 in protest against taxes and war losses. Bands of unpaid soldiers ran wild over France, often serving nobles who sought greedily to extend their privileges. Charles finally crushed the rebellious Estates General by force, while the terrified nobles smashed the peasants. John bought his release by signing a humiliating peace with the English in 1360, giving Edward III full title to Guienne.

The next phase of the war, extending from 1364 to 1415, was marked by little decisive fighting but by tremendous internal dissension in each kingdom. France enjoyed a brief recovery under the rule of Charles V (1364–1380), who rebuilt France's military strength and increased royal income. Using these resources skillfully, he slowly weakened England's hold on Guienne. However, his work was not continued by his pitiful successor, Charles VI (1380–1422), who took the throne as a minor. His regency was dominated by his greedy uncles, of whom Philip, duke of Burgundy, was the most powerful; on reaching his majority, Charles fell under the spell of his brother Louis, duke of Orléans. Moreover, he began to suffer from spells of insanity and each required the reinstitution of a regency. The Burgundians and the Armagnacs (partisans of the duke of Orléans) competed bitterly for control of the regency and the kingdom. By the early fifteenth century their rivalry divided the nobility into two great camps that plunged France into civil chaos in an incredible display of violence, greed, and selfishness. The final proof of the political bankruptcy of the nobility came when the Burgundians and the Armagnacs each began to dicker with the English to help destroy the other.

England was hardly less troubled during these years. Edward III ruled until 1377 amid increasing trouble. To wage war against France, he needed money, and the easiest way to get it was to call Parliament. Frequent meetings resulted in the rapid development of parliamentary organization. The *House of Lords*, comprising the great feudal barons and high churchmen, separated

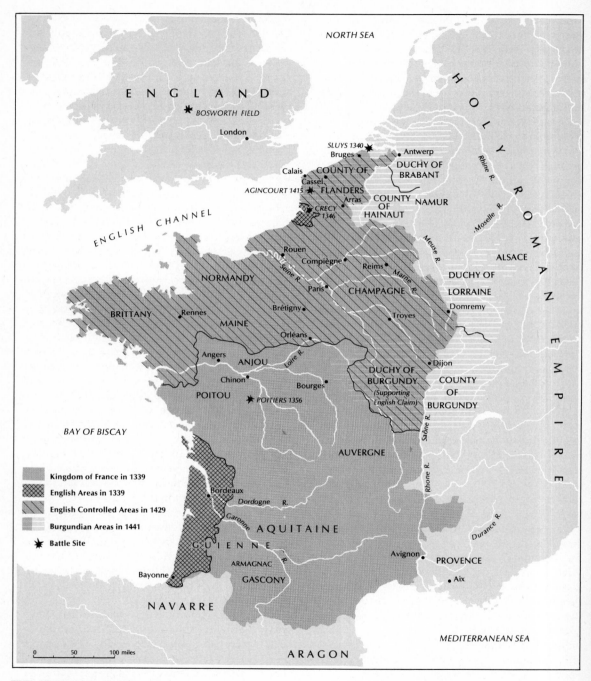

NORTH SEA

E N G L A N D

✴ BOSWORTH FIELD

London

SLUYS 1340 ✴
Bruges ● ● Antwerp
Calais ● COUNTY OF DUCHY OF
Cassel ● ● BRABANT
AGINCOURT 1415 ✴ FLANDERS COUNTY
Arras ● OF NAMUR
CRECY ● HAINAUT
1346

ENGLISH CHANNEL

Rouen ●
Compiègne ● Reims ●
NORMANDY ● Paris CHAMPAGNE
ALSACE
Seine R.
Meuse R.
Rhine R.
Moselle R.
DUCHY OF
LORRAINE
Domremy ●
Marne R.
Troyes ●

BRITTANY Rennes ● Brétigny ●
MAINE Orléans ●
Angers ● Dijon ●
ANJOU Loire R. DUCHY OF COUNTY
Chinon ● Bourges ● BURGUNDY OF
POITOU (Supporting BURGUNDY
English Claim)
✴ POITIERS 1356
Saône R.
AUVERGNE

BAY OF BISCAY

Kingdom of France in 1339
English Areas in 1339
English Controlled Areas in 1429
Burgundian Areas in 1441
✴ Battle Site

Bordeaux ●
Dordogne R.
Garonne R.
AQUITAINE
Rhône R.
Durance R.
GUIENNE
Avignon ● PROVENCE
Bayonne ● ARMAGNAC
GASCONY ● Aix

NAVARRE

MEDITERRANEAN SEA

0   50   100 miles

ARAGON

HOLY ROMAN EMPIRE

THE HUNDRED YEARS' WAR

from the *House of Commons,* made up of towns-men and of the lesser gentry representing the counties. Each house steadily increased its powers. Aside from extensive control over taxation, Parliament began to gain a voice in spending money, controlling royal officials, and initiating legislation.

The stormy reign of Edward's successor, Richard II (1377–1399), was filled with civil strife arising from dissatisfaction with royal government. A great Peasants' Revolt broke out in 1381 and had to be crushed by force. The nobles, acting in Parliament, tried hard to limit royal power, and when the autocratic Richard resisted their efforts, he was deposed by Parliament. Henry IV (1399–1413) of Lancaster was elected in his place — an event that made the monarch more than ever responsible to Parliament. However, Parliament proved neither capable of directing the kingdom nor willing to trust the king to do so. It became a forum for factional agitation aimed at dominating the king in order to secure greater privileges. Often the parliamentary struggles ended in civil strife which became endemic in English society.

Henry V (1413–1422) hastened both England and France along their troubled paths by reopening the Hundred Years' War. Desirous of distracting his nobles from efforts to curb his authority and assured that he would find support among France's warring factions, he invaded her in 1415. He crushed a French army at Agincourt in 1415 and then captured a series of key west-central cities. The Burgundians and Armagnacs tried to use the English to destroy one another, and eventually, the Burgundians allied with Henry V, permitting him to force the humiliating Treaty of Troyes on Charles VI in 1420. By its terms Henry married Charles' daughter; he or his successor was to rule France when Charles died; and until then he would act as regent for the mad Charles. Most of France north of the Loire River was in English hands.

But the English were not to enjoy their dominance for long. After both Henry V and Charles VI died in 1422, leaving the nine-month-old Henry VI as king of both nations, the French made a spectacular recovery. It was inspired by a new hard-to-define feeling of patriotism, of love for France and hatred for foreigners. The chief beneficiary was the son of Charles VI, soon to be known as Charles VII. In 1428 a simple peasant girl, Joan of Arc, came to him claiming God had revealed to her that Charles must free France from the English and assume the throne. Her pleas bestirred the dispirited Charles, long virtually a prisoner of the Armagnacs, and pumped new confidence into the French soldiers loyal to him. Joan herself was present with the army that captured Orléans in 1429, the first French victory for many years, and on the strength of it she persuaded Charles that he should brave the English danger to go to Rheims to be crowned.

From 1429 to 1453 the French won victory after victory, until the English held only the city of Calais in France. But Joan did not live to see these victories. In 1430 she was captured by Burgundian troops, turned over to the English, tried by the Church for heresy, and burned at the stake in Rouen in 1431. Yet, the maid of Lorraine lived on as a symbol to rally the French.

The reign of Charles VII saw a great revival of royal power. He was not a strong ruler, but he was served by excellent ministers who guided him wisely. A strong, well-trained army was created and paid for by the king, who thus ended his dependence on the sort of useless feudal army that had failed so badly at Crécy, Poitiers, and Agincourt. In 1439 the Estates General voted Charles the power to impose at will a direct tax, called the *taille,* on persons. Although there remained in France many powerful nobles who continued to act in their own interest, political life more and more focused on the royal government with its increasing ability to establish order and curb irresponsible behavior on the part of the princes. When Charles VII died in 1461, his son, Louis XI (1461–1483), inherited a solid base from which to rule. His accession marked the beginning of a new era.

England was in a less happy state. Strife among rival factions of nobles contending to dominate weak kings finally led to the Wars of the Roses, so called because the opposing forces adopted the white and red rose as their symbols. This struggle had its origins during the reign of Henry VI (1422–1461). Because he became king in infancy, there was a long regency. Moreover, his family, the Lancastrians, had been elevated to the throne by parliamentary action and did not have as strong a hereditary claim to the throne as did their foes, the Yorkists, who insisted that the crown belonged to them as a result of their closer kinship to Edward III. The final blow was an attack of insanity that Henry suffered after reaching his majority. Two major factions of nobles, formed around the rival Lancastrian and Yorkist claimants to the throne, locked in a deadly struggle. The basic issue was simply power and the benefits it could bring. While this civil war raged, the regular processes of orderly government were neglected. Tyranny, intrigue, murder, confiscation of property, and pursuit of private ends were the order of the day, perpetrated by nobles acting through bands of armed retainers. Henry VI and his supporters held the crown until finally defeated by Edward of York, who as Edward IV (1461–1483) tried to restore royal authority. The Lancastrians refused to accept his rule and kept the struggle going.

Edward was succeeded by his twelve-year-old son, Edward V, but within three months the young king's uncle seized the throne as Richard III. He tried vigorously to restore order in England, but he could neither dispel the view that he was a usurper nor blunt the hatred of the Lancastrians. Finally in 1485, Henry Tudor, a Lancastrian, defeated Richard in a pitched battle at Bosworth Field and assumed the throne as Henry VII. Although his claim to the crown was extremely tenuous, the nation, weary of civil disorder, was willing to follow anyone who promised to restore peace and security. The old noble factions had been decimated. Henry was therefore free to do much as he pleased. He used the opportunity to end the feudal state and create a strong central government that united the English people into a nation.

The three major Iberian kingdoms—Aragon, Castile, and Portugal—also had their difficulties during the Late Middle Ages. By 1300 the holy war against the Moslems ceased to be the significant factor in Spanish affairs, for they had been confined to the narrow territory of Granada. The Christian kingdoms then turned on one another, competing bitterly for territory. Added to these wars was the almost constant civil strife within

each kingdom that replicated the struggles in England and France. Castile was especially plagued by a long series of disputed successions that undermined royal authority. Aragon's internal order was compromised by the aggressive overseas policy pursued by her kings, especially in Italy, a policy seldom favored by the nobility, and by conflict between the landed and the commercial interests. These senseless quarrels finally began to abate when in 1469 the heiress of Castile, Isabella, married Ferdinand, the heir of Aragon. In 1479, when this couple had succeeded to both thrones, they quickly took steps to end the strife and unify their lands into a single state.

Portuguese kings did not meet such violent resistance as did the other Iberian kings, and they gained considerable internal support because of their heroic struggle to prevent Castile from absorbing Portugal. They also promoted commercial interests throughout the fifteenth century, backing Portuguese merchants who expanded southward along the African coast and found lucrative markets.

3. EASTERN EUROPE AND THE MEDITERRANEAN WORLD

While the Western European states were undergoing internal crises and engaging each other in rivalries that sapped their strength, highly significant political changes were unfolding along Europe's eastern and southeastern frontiers. These developments drastically altered the relationships that had been established between the West and these eastern areas in the High Middle Ages.

The Byzantine Empire never fully recovered from the attacks of the Seljuk Turks in the late eleventh century and the capture of Constantinople by Western Europeans in 1204 during the Fourth Crusade. After the Europeans were finally ousted in 1261 and Greek emperors again assumed power, a fatal illness seemed to afflict the empire. Civil strife slowly sapped the strength of its government. The Italian city-states, led by Venice, deprived the empire of much of its trade, and bit by bit its territory was pared away, especially by the Ottoman Turks, a

THE OTTOMAN EMPIRE AND RUSSIA TO 1505

rising Moslem power. The emperors of the fourteenth and fifteenth centuries appealed desperately to the West for help but received little, since Western Europeans were too enmeshed in their own rivalries. Finally, in 1453 Constantinople was captured by the Ottomans, ending forever the power that had so long shielded Europe.

The Ottoman victory marked the reappearance of an aggressive Moslem force threatening Western Christendom, a danger long dormant. The disintegration of the Abbasid Empire and the resulting internal rivalries had removed most of the pressure of Moslem expansion and prepared the way for the European counterattack during the Crusades. Upheavals continued to shake the Moslem world after the crusading movement had subsided; the chief cause was the intrusion of non-Moslem Asiatics. In the thirteenth century the already weak Abbasid dynasty disappeared before the avalanche of the Mongols led by Genghis Khan and his successors. When the Mongol threat began to recede by the end of the century, the Moslem portions of the Mongol Empire broke into rival principalities. One of the most powerful was that of the Ottoman Turks in Asia Minor.

The Ottoman Turks, distantly related to the Seljuks, were Asiatic nomads who had been uprooted by the Mongols and pushed westward. Permitted to settle in Asia Minor in the thirteenth century by the Seljuk Turks, the newcomers had accepted Islam and adopted many of the ways of Moslem society. Within a short time the Ottomans had established their independence. Their first great ruler was Osman, or Othman (1290–1326), whence the term "Ottoman." The new state began to expand almost immediately, and by the end of the fourteenth century the Ottomans had taken over Asia Minor and gained control of most of the Balkans as well.

Early in the fifteenth century Ottoman power was nearly destroyed by Tamerlane, a Mongol warrior who sought to reconstruct the empire of Genghis Khan. But Tamerlane's death in 1405 was followed by a sudden collapse of his empire. The Ottomans soon recovered from these defeats and returned to their attack on Byzantium and the Balkans. With Constantinople captured,

early in the sixteenth century they conquered Syria, Palestine, and Egypt, creating a state that stretched from the Danube to the Nile. As the Middle Ages ended, the Ottomans loomed as a major threat to Western Europe.

Central and Eastern Europe began to assume a modern shape in the wake of the decline of the Holy Roman and Byzantine empires. The south coast of the Baltic Sea was dominated by Germans, an expansion spearheaded by the crusading order of the Teutonic Knights who brought traders, missionaries, and agricultural colonists in their wake. Their presence filled the Slavs of Central Europe with an abiding distrust for and fear of the Germans. The Germanic threat resulted in a union of the ruling houses of Poland and Lithuania under the Lithuanian prince Jagiello, who married a Polish princess and governed both states as King Ladislas II (1386–1434). The house of Jagiello exerted considerable military pressure on the Baltic Germans and the Russian states to the east during much of the fifteenth century, but it never succeeded in creating an effective government for its huge kingdom. To the south, Hungary continued to develop, but her energies were increasingly absorbed in defending herself against the Ottoman Turks and holding back ambitious German nobles bent on taking the Hungarian throne. Until the Ottomans seized control of the Balkans at the end of the fourteenth century, a flourishing Serbian kingdom dominated that area; after its destruction, the Hungarians stood as Western Europe's outpost against the Turks.

Farther east, the Mongol *khans* (emperors) had seized much of Russia during the thirteenth century and forced the numerous conquered princes to become subordinates and collect tribute for them from the Russian populace. In the fourteenth century the princes of Moscow gained the privilege of collecting these sums from all the other Russian princes, and they used this function skillfully to begin building a strong state. Early in the fifteenth century they rejected the overlordship of the khans, whose power was rapidly deteriorating, and started a series of wars for the purpose of Muscovite expansion and liberation. Ivan III (reigned 1462–1505) finally broke the Mongol hold on Russia and compelled most Russian princes to accept his authority. After the fall of Constantinople, the Muscovites claimed they were the heirs of the Byzantine tradition and the protectors of the Greek Orthodox religion. Ivan III began calling himself *tsar*, which implied that he was the successor of the caesars. This sense of protecting an ancient heritage gave Russia a new mission that would help solidify her into a powerful nation in the future.

4. ECONOMIC AND SOCIAL TENSIONS

Responsible in part for the political difficulties were basic economic and social problems troubling most areas of Europe. In brief, the entire economic system was suffering from a series of contractions that curbed growth and promoted social disequilibrium.

Especially damaging during the fourteenth and fifteenth centuries was the leveling off of commercial expansion, long the vital factor in Western European economic growth. The incessant warfare upset established trade processes. Europe's population ceased growing, chiefly because of recurrent famines and the epidemic of bubonic plague, the Black Death, which between 1347 and 1350 wiped out nearly one-third of the population (perhaps more in the cities), and returned sporadically well into the fifteenth century. The rise of Ottoman power made it more difficult for Western Europeans to penetrate new geographical areas. The independent cities that had been the sources of medieval commercial growth lacked the manpower, the wealth, and the political strength to offset these numerous difficulties. Sustained cooperation among commercial cities for mutual benefit proved nearly impossible. The most successful effort of this kind was the Hanseatic League, which linked together about seventy cities in northern Germany, Scandinavia, and the Low Countries. But ultimately the league declined, chiefly because its members refused to sacrifice local interests. All these limitations on commerce did not mean that the fourteenth and fifteenth centuries enjoyed none of the benefits of trade; however, trade did not grow so fast as it previously had; in many areas it declined.

Industry experienced a comparable constric-

tion. The guild system, which had once promoted the growth of industry, grew increasingly restrictive. Seeking to protect their monopoly on production in each city, the guilds passed rules excluding the products of outsiders. They barred technical changes that seemed to threaten their members, and they turned away new applicants or admitted them at inferior rank. Often their pricing arrangements were unrealistic. Such practices curtailed production and discouraged expansion into new kinds of industry.

Agricultural production, the foundation of the European economy, likewise suffered a depression. Widespread warfare ravaged many lands, and there is some evidence that a climatic change hurt growing conditions in many regions. The eastern frontier was closed, limiting areas for colonization and new land clearance. Especially crucial was the impact of the Black Death, which not only decimated the rural labor force, but also sharply reduced the city market. A major consequence was the abandonment in many parts of Western Europe of land once under cultivation. Under these pressures the old

This illustration from a manuscript shows the people of the city of Tournai (Flanders) desperately at work burying the victims of the Black Death in their city. Their facial expressions suggest the crushing psychological impact of the plague.
Photo: The Granger Collection

manorial system continued to break up. Since landowners across much of Western Europe became interested in money income, they manipulated rents and imposed on their peasant tenants whatever remnants of the old manorial dues system they could. Some also resorted to enclosing their land for the production of specialized crops or livestock and using hired labor to farm it.

Economic dislocation and contraction led to considerable social tension and disturbance in the Late Middle Ages. In a general way, the social structure lost its earlier mobility. The aristocracy's status as the wealthiest segment in society was challenged by the rising capitalist entrepreneurs in commerce, industry, and finance. Its monopoly on warfare was destroyed by the nonnoble professional soldier. The nobles completely discredited themselves politically by their attempts to seize power for their own interests; then ultimately and perhaps most significantly, they turned to the monarchs to sanction and protect their privileges. With the old bases of social preeminence dissolving, the nobility of the Late Middle Ages turned increasingly to ruthless exploitation of its lands and to costly indulgence in a mode of life based on an exaggerated version of chivalry. It closed ranks and sought to control and exploit other groups who might threaten its position, as did the capitalists. Disadvantaged groups chafed under these circumstances and often resorted to violence to better their lot.

Although the virtual disappearance of serfdom improved the social position of most peasants in Western Europe, their status deteriorated in other ways. They were thrown more and more on their own economically. As tenants they could no longer appeal to a lord in times of war and famine. Royal taxes fell heavily on them, and the wars they thus paid for often ravaged their farms, especially in France, Italy, and Germany. Declining prices coincided with reduced opportunities in the troubled cities and closed frontiers. Peasants expressed their discontent by frequent and violent rebellions that often reached frightening proportions, like the *Jacquerie* uprising in France in 1358 and the Peasants' Revolt of 1381 in England. The rebels always cried out for justice and punished their oppressors savagely; but

their fervor seldom supported a positive program, and they were usually brutally crushed by kings, nobles, and clergymen acting in concert.

Equally unhappy were certain elements of the bourgeoisie, especially in Flanders and Italy. Many artisans were reduced to the ranks of laborers for hire and lost the political power they had enjoyed in the twelfth and thirteenth centuries. The rich entrepreneurs more and more dominated political life in the cities. The monopolistic guilds often excluded new artisans from the trades, leaving them with little means of livelihood. The laborers and the unemployed frequently resorted to mob violence, but with little more success than the peasants.

The social group making the greatest advance in the fourteenth and fifteenth centuries was an elite segment of the bourgeoisie engaged in capitalistic ventures, again particularly in northern Italy and Flanders although also in France, England, and parts of Germany and Spain. The success of this group is exemplified by the Medici and the Bardi in Italy, the Fuggers in southern Germany, Jacques Coeur of France, and some of the entrepreneurs associated with the Hanseatic League, which monopolized trade in the Baltic and North seas. Members of this group accrued huge fortunes in such fields as banking, moneylending, and the wool industry. They seized political control of most city governments and found increasing favor with kings. Culturally they were able to patronize the advancing cause of the humanists and to set standards of fashion. In a sense, this group now represented the bourgeoisie; others who had formerly been counted in this class — simple artisans and small shopkeepers — were emerging as a group apart, a laboring class. The new bourgeoisie was destined to play a major role in the future of the West.

More and more it became obvious that the solution to the economic and social problems of the era lay with a stronger central government. Nobles, peasants, capitalists, industrial workers — all pressed the government to impose controls on trade, industry, agriculture, and the class structure. In countries such as England and France, kings responded to this pressure and began regulating economic and social conditions on a national scale. This trend was proof of the passing of medieval society, which had been built on social stratification, economic localism, and group protection of vested interests.

By approximately 1450 the worst of the economic and social stresses of the Late Middle Ages were over, and there were signs of recovery everywhere. Aside from the return of political order accompanying the restoration of royal authority, the population had begun to grow again. The agricultural system became increasingly stable, chiefly on the basis of a system of renting that bound landlord and peasant together on a money basis. New technological advances were being made and were being applied more widely — water mills in the textile industry, better mining techniques, printing, improved shipbuilding, the compass, the astrolabe, gunpowder. New frontiers were opening by way of the seas that washed Europe's western shores. All these forces pointed toward new growth in Western Europe. It was obvious, however, that this growth would be achieved in ways different from those that prevailed in medieval Europe.

Suggested Reading

Overview of the Period 1300–1500
*Denys Hay, *Europe in the Fourteenth and Fifteenth Centuries* (Longman). A brief but provocative interpretation of the era.
*R. E. Lerner, *The Age of Adversity: The Fourteenth Century* (Cornell).
*Margaret Aston, *The Fifteenth Century: The Prospect of Europe* (Harcourt Brace Jovanovich). This and the preceding work succeed remarkably well in capturing the major trends of the age.
W. K. Ferguson, *Europe in Transition, 1300–1520* (1962). An excellent survey in detail.
*J. Huizinga, *The Waning of the Middle Ages* (Anchor). A classic study, exploring the psychological changes affecting society in a troubled time.

The Holy Roman Empire
Joachim Lauschner, *Germany in the Later Middle Ages* (1978). This work can be supplemented by the study by Barraclough cited in Chapter 19.
*D. Waley, *The Italian City-Republics* (McGraw). A fairly successful attempt to treat the complex history of the Italian city-states in the Later Middle Ages in general.

England, France, and Spain
E. Perroy, *The Hundred Years' War* (1951). A thorough treatment not only of military history but also of internal developments in France and England.
*A. R. Myers, *England in the Late Middle Ages, 1307–1536* (Penguin). An excellent survey.

*George Holmes, *The Later Middle Ages, 1272–1485* (Norton). Especially good on economic and social history.
P. S. Lewis, *Late Medieval France: The Polity* (1968). One of the few works in English on French political development.
John Holland Smith, *Joan of Arc* (1973). A balanced and well-written treatment of a much disputed subject.
Spanish history in the Late Middle Ages is well treated in the works by Jackson, O'Callaghan, and Mackay, cited in Chapter 21.

The Eastern Mediterranean and Eastern Europe
Donald M. Nicol, *The Last Centuries of Byzantium, 1261–1453* (1972).
Constance Head, *Imperial Twilight: The Palaiologus Dynasty and the Decline of Byzantium* (1977). Two well-done attempts to synthesize late Byzantine history.
*Steven Runciman, *The Fall of Constantinople, 1453* (Cambridge). A splendid portrayal of the last days of a great city and a great empire.
Halil Inalick, *The Ottoman Empire: The Classical Age, 1300–1600* (1973). The best treatment of a subject that has not always been given an objective evaluation.
J. J. Saunders, *The Story of the Mongol Conquest* (1971).
B. Spuler, *The Mongols in History* (1971). This and the preceding work provide a remarkably clear picture of the role of the Mongols in reshaping world history.
F. Dvornik, *The Making of Central Europe* (1949), and *The Slavs: Their Early History and Civilization* (1956).

Two extremely useful studies of the evolution of Slavic society and culture.

G. Vernadsky, *The Origins of Russia* (1959). A brilliant treatment.

Economic and Social History

*H. A. Mishkimin, *The Economy of Early Renaissance Europe, 1300–1460* (2nd ed., Cambridge). An excellent study in detail; more general treatments can be found in the works of Bautier and Pounds, cited in Chapter 18. More specialized aspects of late medieval economic and social history are treated in the following works.:

P. Dollinger, *The German Hansa*, trans. D. S. Ault and S. H. Steinberg (1970).

*Philip Ziegler, *The Black Death* (Harper Torchbook).

*W. M. Bowsky, ed., *The Black Death: A Turning Point in History?* (Krieger).

M. Mollat and P. Wolff, *The Popular Revolutions of the Late Middle Ages*, trans. A. L. Lytton-Sells, (1973).

Guy Fourquin, *The Anatomy of Popular Rebellion in the Middle Ages*, trans. Anne Chesters (1978).

R. L. Kilgour, *The Decline of Chivalry* (1937).

Sources

*Jean Froissart, *Chronicles*, trans. G. Brereton (Penguin). A fascinating picture of a society caught up in the Hundred Years' War.

*Chaucer, *Canterbury Tales*, trans. Nevill Coghill (Penguin). An entertaining view of English society around 1400.

*William Langland, *Piers the Ploughman*, trans. J. F. Goodridge (Penguin). A poem reflecting the bitter resentment felt by the lower classes of England against the powerful.

*R. Pernoud, ed., *Joan of Arc, by Herself and Her Witnesses* (Stein and Day). Creates a fascinating picture of a key figure in late medieval France from contemporary sources.

*Johannes Nohl, ed., *The Black Death: A Chronicle of Plague Compiled from Contemporary Sources* (Humanities).

25

THE DECLINE OF THE CHURCH

The tensions that beset Western European political, social, and economic institutions in the fourteenth and fifteenth centuries afflicted the Church even more severely. After 1300 this powerful institution, which had earlier influenced all aspects of human activity, encountered increasing difficulties in asserting its traditional leadership role. Its teachings, its system of government, and its leaders were subjected to merciless criticism and to open defiance. And the Church failed to discover new resources with which to meet these criticisms.

1. THE DECLINE OF THE PAPACY

The most dramatic challenge to the Church's authority focused on its very center of power: the papacy. This office, brought to its apogee by the talented popes of the thirteenth century, came under severe challenge during the pontificate of Boniface VIII (1294–1303). This vain, ambitious "prince of the new Pharisees," as Dante called him, was guilty of stating his claims to power in terms far beyond his ability to sustain. His failures dramatized the vulnerability of the papacy and led to increasing attacks on the office.

His first serious setback came at the hands of the powerful kings of England and France, Edward I and Philip IV. Each proposed to impose new taxes on the Church in his realm in order to war against the other. Boniface responded with a papal bull, *Clericis laicos*, maintaining that only

with papal consent could any taxes be laid upon the Church. Edward and Philip defied him and took steps to cut off all revenues from their kingdoms to Rome. Boniface had to retreat from his position, something the popes were not accustomed to doing.

Before long he was involved in a new quarrel with Philip IV, this time over the question of the proper courts for trying clergymen. Again the strong-minded pope stated his case in a way that outraged Philip. In the bull *Unam sanctam*, Boniface spoke to the issue by insisting that the French king and all men must subject themselves to the pope to be saved. Philip counterattacked violently. He turned public opinion in France against the pope by blatantly distorting the papal position and finally sent some of his henchmen to Italy to capture Boniface. Philip's agents were successful, and the pope escaped what might have been an even more painful defeat by dying. St. Peter's vicar had suffered a humiliating defeat at the hands of a secular leader whose place was to defer to papal authority.

Philip IV capitalized on his victory by arranging for the election of a Frenchman as pope. Aware that he would be unwelcome in the turbulent Papal States, the new pope took up residence at Avignon in 1309, and until 1377 this city remained the residence of the papacy. During these years of what the Italian writer Petrarch called the "Babylonian Captivity" (referring to the episode in Jewish history when God's chosen people were held captive in Babylon by the sinful Chaldeans — now equated with the French monarchy), the popes were accused, unfairly, of being pawns of the French kings. The English, who were engaged in the Hundred Years' War with the French, used the situation to reduce papal control over ecclesiastical affairs. The German emperors and princes were equally defiant. Many Christians were troubled by the fact that the pope's claim to power was based on succession to St. Peter as bishop of Rome, not Avignon. These critics were not impressed by the plea of the papacy that Rome was not safe; neither had it been for Peter nor for many earlier popes. The Babylonian Captivity caused scholars and writers to raise major questions regarding church government and to arrive at answers that challenged papal supremacy.

The Avignon popes were not idle during these years, however. Several of them succeeded in pushing papal control over church organization to its greatest height. They increased the number of offices which they could fill with their own appointees willing to pay for such honors. They collected taxes with great vigor and even discovered new sources of income. They steadily increased the number of cases that had to be appealed to papal courts and derived a huge income from this activity. They enlarged the papal bureaucracy beyond anything previously known. In terms of revenues, subordinates, and business transactions, the Avignon popes were actually more powerful than their predecessors.

However, this emphasis on organizational affairs did the papacy more harm than good in terms of prestige. Abuses of the worst kind began to plague the papal government. The increasing horde of papal bureaucrats engaged in every type of corruption, such as selling offices and accepting bribes. Many buyers of Church offices were interested only in income and never went near the office; absenteeism thus became a major problem. Bishops and abbots in all parts of Europe resented growing papal interference in local Church affairs and tried to escape papal control, often by turning to their kings, who gladly protected them — for a price. Papal taxation

aroused bitterness everywhere. Edward III of England reflected the dislike of the money-grabbing popes when he said: "The successor of the Apostles was ordered to lead the Lord's sheep to the pasture, not to fleece them." The officials of the papal *curia* spent much of this wealth on luxurious living; a symbol of their luxury was the splendid papal palace built in Avignon. The ecclesiastical life style of the city, which Petrarch called "the sewer of the world," aroused the bitter anger of many in Europe whose lot was poverty. The popes at Avignon were not entirely responsible for this situation. Corruption and moral laxness are problems any huge organization has to face. But the popes did nothing to correct them, and as a result, they were blamed for them.

The Babylonian Captivity finally ended in 1377 with the return of the pope to Rome. But this move led to the election by a part of the College of Cardinals of a second pope, who continued to live at Avignon. Thus began the Great Schism, forty years in which the Church was headed by two popes directing two administrations, two tax systems, two sets of Church courts. Everyone was at a loss to know who was the right pope. Corruption increased. Rival popes played politics furiously, each seeking to gain enough allies to oust the other. Many Europeans — and especially princes — thought in terms of obeying the pope who offered the best political deal. Few took seriously the claim of either pope to be spiritual leader of Europe; popes who competed with one another and encouraged the division of Christendom seemed little better than greedy politicians.

Before the schism was many years old, serious men began to search for a way of ending the division. Eventually, many came to believe that a general council should be called to heal the schism and reform the clergy. According to the advocates of the conciliar theory, an assembly of bishops possessed an authority superior even to the pope's. This ancient idea seemed revolutionary in the context of the Late Middle Ages and threatened the concept of papal supremacy. Four councils were held between 1409 and 1449, all stormy affairs marked by interminable negotiations. Although the Council of Pisa (1409) resulted in the installation of a third pope to complicate further the schism, the Council of Constance (1414–1418) did succeed in restoring a single pope. Thereafter, the popes generally devoted sharp attention to controlling the councils and ending this dangerous threat to papal authority — not too difficult a task, since the council membership was often split by quarrels among the clergymen representing different nations. A major tactic used by the popes to curb the claims of the conciliarists to exercise final authority over the Church was to make concessions to monarchs in return for their support of papal power. For example, the pope accepted the Pragmatic Sanction of Bourges, issued in 1438 by Charles VII of France with the backing of the French clergy; this agreement gave the French monarch extensive rights over ecclesiastical income and the clergy. Comparable agreements worked out with other rulers seriously limited papal power and hastened a trend toward the creation of "national" churches.

Probably the greatest failure of the councils was their inability to institute meaningful reform. Despite numerous attempts to enact reforming legislation, the members of the councils were never able to agree on a practical reform program. When the last council disbanded in 1449, most people had lost confidence in this means of revitalizing the Church. The greatest influence of the conciliar movement was indirect: It opened the Church's organization to question and caused many to conclude that the papacy was not necessarily sacred.

The popes of the last half of the fifteenth century concentrated on strengthening their control over the Papal States in Italy and competing in the many power struggles raging in Italy in this period. To all outward appearances each was a secular prince, scheming, bribing, and brawling to get what he desired for himself, his family, and his friends and enjoying a luxurious existence. A few led scandalous lives and several became patrons of Renaissance artists and writers who were openly advocating ideas and values that challenged Christianity. The popes ceased to enjoy the respect and veneration of

This fresco from the church of St. John Lateran in Rome shows Pope Boniface VIII proclaiming the great jubilee held in Rome in 1300. The artist, perhaps Giotto, catches something of the autocratic spirit of the proud pontiff whose efforts to assert papal authority led to deep trouble for the Church. *Photo: Alinari*

most Christians. No one would deny that the popes were powerful in terms of wealth and political resources. What they had lost was the moral authority that had been their chief source of influence in the thirteenth century, and without that authority, the papacy became a liability to the Church.

2. THE DECLINE OF THE CLERGY

Hardly less significant than the prolonged decay of papal prestige was the steady deterioration of the whole body of the clergy. Especially pronounced was the decline of monasticism. Between 1300 and 1500 not a single new order of any importance was established in Western Europe, and the older monastic institutions became increasingly corrupt. Monasteries were no longer a refuge for the spiritually dedicated or a stage from which the zealous could launch their efforts to cleanse religious life.

Except for a few purists, the most powerful orders, the Franciscans and the Dominicans, forgot their ideals of poverty and service and turned instead to the pursuit of wealth and power. Lesser orders followed suit. Strict rules on moral excellence and piety were relaxed to the point where monks and nuns openly broke their vows. Little attention was paid to the kinds of recruits entering monasteries; many were aristocratic ladies who could not find husbands, younger sons without land, and commoners who wanted to escape work. Absentee abbots thought only of garnering monastic incomes. Of course, not all monks were guilty of this laxness and this lack of religious fervor. However, the culprits, as usual, got most of the publicity. One needs to read only a little of the literature of the fourteenth and fifteenth centuries, such as some of the stories in Boccaccio's *Decameron* or Chaucer's *Canterbury Tales*, to realize that monasticism was held in low repute. Monastic life had come to signify laziness, greed, immorality, and hypocrisy.

The secular clergy, charged with the Church's everyday business, was equally plagued by corruption and moral laxness. The tone was set by the powerful officials of the papal curia, especially the cardinals, whose vast entourages, immense wealth, and talent for political machinations indeed made them "princes of the Church." Many bishops purchased their offices, paying prices that left them little choice but to wring money out of their subjects, and heavy papal taxes tempted them and lesser clergymen to undertake shady financial practices. Some held several offices at once, making it impossible for them to perform the duties of any. Absenteeism was common, many bishops and priests preferring life at Avignon or at a royal court to life in their episcopal sees or parishes. Absentee clergymen often turned their religious duties over to ignorant clerks who were incapable of guiding religious activities. Services, instruction, confessions, preaching, and counseling were slighted, leaving people with religious problems lost and unhappy.

3. OLD PRACTICES AND NEW IDEAS

The Church of the later Middle Ages was weakened also by its inability to accommodate increasingly frequent and extremely vigorous heterodox religious trends in Western European society. Chiefly as a result of the intense effort to impose uniformity on religion during the High Middle Ages, after 1300 Roman Catholic belief and religious practices fell into a rather unbending, formal pattern that became increasingly mechanical; most churchmen were content to equate piety with going through the motions of attending services, receiving the sacraments, and obeying the clergy.

Dissatisfaction with this situation was demonstrated in many ways. One of the most important was an increase in the number of mystics, that is, persons who believed they could experience and know God directly through intuitive powers. Mysticism was present throughout the Middle Ages; St. Bernard and St. Francis of Assisi were mystics. But the fourteenth and fifteenth centuries produced an especially large number. Many of the most influential were simple men and women who never wore clerical garb, like Joan of Arc. None was more prominent than Catherine of Siena (1347–1380). On the basis of visions of Christ she claimed to have experienced, as well as through her efforts to help the poor, the sick, the criminals, and the downhearted, she earned a reputation as a saint. Although she, as well as many like her, was never seriously at odds with the Church, Catherine practiced a kind of Christianity unfamiliar to contemporary officials of the cult.

The activities of the mystics led to the development of communal movements that operated almost independently of the Church. A prime example was the Brethren of the Common Life (and its female counterpart, the Sisters of the Common Life), founded by a lay preacher named Gerard Groote (1340–1384), who was one of the many spiritual heirs of the great German mystic, Meister Eckhart (1260–1327). This loosely knit movement was a product of a new kind of piety, called the *devotio moderna*, which stressed prayer, love, and direct communion with God. Devotees of the new piety joined together as brothers and sisters in communities where they shared their worldly goods, joined in common worship, confessed their sins to each other, devoted themselves to works of charity, and even produced their own devotional literature. One of the best examples of their literature, still read today as a spiritual guide, is Thomas à Kempis' *Imitation of Christ*. The many communities of Brethren seldom strayed into heresy, but their piety, their puritanical life, and their mysticism set them apart. Not surprisingly, the Brethren were often attacked for spreading dangerous ideas, and some of the most important later reformers of the Church were educated in their schools.

The fourteenth and fifteenth centuries produced a hardier crowd of radicals—usually condemned as heretics—who voiced ideas that provoked many to violent actions against the Church. Some of them were intellectual figures, such as Marsiglio of Padua, whose devastating book, *The Defender of the Peace*, appeared in 1324. Its thesis was that the Church was obligated to fulfill certain spiritual duties but was not entitled to any secular powers. Marsiglio advocated that it be deprived of its wealth and made a branch of government, subservient to the ruler. He argued that the Church as a community of all Christians should be ruled by a council representing all elements in Christian society, not by a clerical hierarchy headed by the pope.

Somewhat later, John Wycliffe (1320–1384) delivered even heavier attacks on the Church. This Oxford scholar and teacher entered the ranks of rebellion late in life, apparently moved by a growing tide of anticlericalism and antipapalism emerging in an England troubled by the Hundred Years' War and internal stresses. In his first attacks on the Church he argued that the Church had abused its right to hold property and that all church property should be confiscated by the state. Later he advocated the destruction of the whole clerical hierarchy on the ground that salvation depended not on clergymen but on the power of God; every man was his own priest. Here, of course, he was striking at a keystone of the medieval Church. Wycliffe also attacked many of the religious practices of the Church—elaborate rituals, prayers to saints, veneration of relics, pilgrimages, and the like. He even questioned the validity of the sacraments. He argued that Scripture alone must be the authority for Christian doctrine and translated the Bible into English so that all could read it.

Although Wycliffe was soon condemned as a heretic and forced to leave Oxford, his teachings attracted many followers, known as the Lollards, and for many years Lollard preachers and writers agitated for their master's ideas in England. In time, however, they came to challenge all authority, and the English kings of the fifteenth century joined the clergy in destroying the movement.

Wycliffe's ideas had their most disturbing effect not in England but in Bohemia (modern Czechoslovakia). The leading disciple there was John Huss (ca. 1373–1415), a priest who taught at the University of Prague. When his preaching of Wycliffe's precepts raised a protest from the clergy and ruling faction, most of whom were German and were passionately hated by the native population, Huss became a national hero of the Bohemians. He also was excommunicated, and he consented to journey to the Council of Constance under a promise of safe-conduct from the German emperor. But there he was imprisoned, tried, and executed as a heretic in 1415. A rebellion broke out immediately in Bohemia and raged until 1436. Crusade after crusade was preached by the papacy against the Hussites; several German armies, led by an emperor who was anxious to reclaim Bohemia, were soundly thrashed by the fanatical Bohemians. Eventually peace was restored when certain religious concessions were granted to the Hussites. However, a faction of the followers of Huss and Wycliffe, called Taborites, was not satisfied by these concessions and became practically a church apart in the last years of the Middle Ages.

Manifestations of religious ferment and frustration took many other forms during the fourteenth and fifteenth centuries. There were any number of fiery preachers proclaiming the end of the world and the coming of God's wrathful judgment. Wildly emotional cults, such as the Flagellants, who whipped one another to atone

John Huss, the Bohemian religious reformer and national hero, was burned as a heretic in 1415.
Photo: Rosgartenmuseums, Konstanz

4. THE FAILURE OF INTELLECTUAL LEADERSHIP

The Church suffered another serious blow as a consequence of fundamental shifts in the intellectual development of the Late Middle Ages. This transformation was not dramatic, but it struck a terrible blow at the Church's control over a supportive intellectual establishment. Outwardly, the life of learning continued down familiar paths. The universities remained the focal points of scholarship and teaching in theology, law, medicine, science, and the arts and provided the major attraction to most intellectuals. The scholastic method, although increasingly pedantic, reigned supreme. But the emphasis in intellectual endeavor underwent a subtle change. The majestic scholastic synthesis of the thirteenth century, exemplified by the works of Thomas Aquinas, failed to hold. It left so many questions unanswered that many thinkers not only despaired of the dream of reconciling revelation and reason but also began to attack the basic proposition that faith and reason were compatible. Synthesis gave way to analysis. As we have seen, even while the Thomistic synthesis was being hammered out, there were those who refused to accept it; the resistance intensified after 1300.

Shortly after Aquinas' death in 1274, the attack on his position quickened. The Franciscan scholar John Duns Scotus (ca. 1266–1308) argued with great force that God's freedom and power were so exalted that all attempts to describe his attributes rationally imposed untenable limits on him. In effect, Duns Scotus was saying that theology was not a proper matter for rational speculation. This trend of thought was expanded by William of Ockham (ca. 1300–1349), an English Franciscan who taught at Oxford and served in the court of Emperor Louis IV of Bavaria until the Black Death claimed his life. A powerful logician, Ockham assailed the basic rational supports upon which Thomistic theology was constructed. In his mind knowledge of such things as the existence of God and the immortality of the soul came only by intuition and mystical experience. Theology and philosophy thus became separate "sciences," incapable of reconciliation.

for the world's sins, preyed on men's religious sensibilities, especially in times of great crisis like the Black Death. Brutal massacres of the Jews in the name of Christian righteousness marred the histories of many cities. Witchcraft flourished on an unprecedented scale. Increasingly men sought assurances of salvation by purchasing indulgences, which ensured that the punishment due for sins would be removed. Never were relics more appealing and more brazenly manipulated, as illustrated by Chaucer's pardoner with his bag full of "pigs' bones." Literature, art, and sermons were preoccupied with death in particularly horrible forms.

Clearly, religious ferment in Europe was powerful and widespread. Neither the gentle mystics nor the fiery-tongued rebels, neither the adherents of the occult nor the victims of hysteria were at home in the Roman Catholic Church. People were striking out in all directions, questioning ritual, organization, and dogma. But the institution that claimed to care for men's souls either ignored the quest or ruthlessly crushed the discontent. It was failing its central mission: to meet the basic religious needs of its vast flock.

In defining the realm of reason, Ockham argued that only by sense perception of individual objects could man know; in this respect he was a philosophical *nominalist*, repudiating the long tradition that ideas constituted the ultimate reality (philosophical *realism*). Duns Scotus and William of Ockham gained powerful disciples who followed up the assault on Thomism. The crescendo of attacks shattered the thirteenth-century confidence in one all-embracing truth and with it a powerful prop of the Church.

The disarray among the scholastics encouraged thinkers to take new intellectual paths. Since reason was distinct from faith, political theorists like Marsiglio of Padua constructed new concepts of the governance of church and state which were especially destructive to theologically based justifications of the Church's power. The attack on rational theology nourished mysticism and opened the way for the radical theological concepts of Wycliffe and Huss. Many intellectuals, disillusioned by the barren exercises of late medieval scholasticism, found intellectual sustenance in classical literature and philosophy, drawing from these sources a secular, humanistic world view and value system. Most pregnant for the future was the growing interest in science. Following Ockham's argument that rational inquiry must confine itself to tangible objects, scholars, especially at the universities of Paris and Oxford, produced a considerable body of scientific knowledge and provided significant corrections to Greco-Arabic scientific generalizations. Their efforts laid the groundwork for the revolutionary discoveries of Copernicus, Galileo, and others in the sixteenth and seventeenth centuries. As intellectual life became more pluralistic, the potential for criticism of the Church increased, and the Church's ability to control intellectual activity for its benefit decreased.

5. THE PRESSURE OF NEW FORCES

While the Church decayed from within, it had to contend with powerful forces — many portending a new era in Western Europe — that challenged its leadership and depleted its following. The new, aggressive national states emerging in Western Europe harassed it, as everywhere princes, although still Catholic, sought to limit and dominate it. In England king and Parliament joined in enacting a series of laws to prevent the papacy from taxing church property and controlling ecclesiastical appointments. In France the royal government worked steadily, often with the clergy's help, to establish a "French" church, independent of the papacy and subservient to the crown. In Spain late in the fifteenth century the monarchs even undertook to reform the Church independently of the papacy. As 1500 approached, national churches were becoming a reality at the expense of the universal Church.

The middle class, accepting a capitalistic philosophy, was likewise challenging the Church's social and economic teachings. Many capitalists would have liked to see church wealth put to a different use. Most of them paid no attention to religious arguments against charging interest or on behalf of fair prices. More ominous was their value system, grounded in secularism, the goods of this world, pleasure, individualism, and practicality. These new values combined with economic interests to reduce the hold of the Church on bourgeois energies and wealth.

Finally, a new breed of thinkers, writers, and artists, sometimes called collectively *humanists*, was emerging to criticize, disregard, or repudiate many teachings and practices of the Church. The new humanism, developing first and most vigorously in Italy and then spreading to other parts of Western Europe, was oriented toward the joys and wonders of the physical world. It found its major intellectual sustenance and its esthetic values in classical models. Its setting was urban, and its patronage came chiefly from the emerging bourgeois elite. Its orientation was toward realism and naturalism. Its spirit was individualistic. It generated a critical temper not averse to challenging authority. Wherever the humanistic spirit manifested itself, it was at odds with some of the most basic positions taken by the Church. The progress of humanism thus challenged and weakened the cultural undergirding that had helped sustain the medieval Church.

The combination of internal difficulties and challenging outside forces that undermined the power of the Church in the late Middle Ages demonstrate emphatically that an epoch was ending. Admittedly, the breakup of the medieval empires, the decline of feudal institutions, the dislocation of the class structure, the failure of manorialism and the guild system—all point toward the transformation of medieval civilization. However, for centuries the Church had played the leading role in determining what men thought and how they acted. Its weakening position was the surest sign of the end of an epoch in Western European history.

Suggested Reading

Decline of the Church

A. C. Flick, *The Decline of the Medieval Church*, 2 vols. (1930). A detailed narrative account.

L. Elliot-Binns, *History of the Decline and Fall of the Medieval Papacy* (1934). A balanced, thorough account.

T. S. R. Boase, *Boniface VIII* (1933). This excellent biography highlights many of the problems that eventually brought the papacy low.

*Charles T. Wood, ed., *Philip the Fair and Boniface VIII: State vs. Papacy* (Holt, Rinehart & Winston). Presents an interesting variety of interpretations on the significance of a decisive clash between state and church in medieval society.

Yves Renouard, *The Avignon Papacy, 1305–1403*, trans. D. Berthell (1970).

G. Mollat, *The Popes at Avignon, 1305–1378*, trans. Janet Love (1963). These two treatments, the former brief and the latter more detailed, make clear the impact of the Babylonian Captivity on the papacy.

W. Ullmann, *The Origins of the Great Schism: A Study in Fourteenth Century Ecclesiastical History* (1948). A learned study that provides a careful analysis of the factors producing the Great Schism.

Brian Tierney, *Foundations of the Conciliar Theory* (1955). A careful study stressing the legal basis of conciliar ideas.

New Religious Movements

R. M. Jones, *The Flowering of Mysticism* (1939).

J. M. Clark, *The Great German Mystics: Eckhart, Tauler, and Susa* (1949).

A. Hyma, *The Christian Renaissance: A History of the Devotio Moderna*, 2nd ed. (1965). This and the preceding two titles provide rich insight into late medieval mysticism and the communal movements it produced.

G. Leff, *Heresy in the Later Middle Ages*, 2 vols. (1967). A detailed survey covering almost every movement that met the disapproval of the Church.

Malcolm Lambert, *Medieval Heresy: Popular Movements from Bogomil to Hus* (1977). An excellent synthesis.

*Norman Cohn, *The Pursuit of the Millennium* (Oxford). A brilliant description of aberrant movements which disturbed the religious scene in the Late Middle Ages.

K. B. McFarlane, *John Wycliffe and the Beginnings of English Non-Conformity* (1952). A good analysis of Wycliffe's ideas and the environment that produced this reformer.

H. Kaminsky, *A History of the Hussite Revolution* (1967). A thorough study of the Hussite movement.

M. Spinka, *John Hus: A Biography* (1968).

Cultural History

Georges Duby, *Foundations of a New Humanism, 1280–1440* (1966). A remarkable synthesis that will convince a reader that the so-called Renaissance was not an unexpected phenomenon.

Sources

*William of Ockham, *Philosophical Writings*, trans. P. Boehner (Liberal Arts Press). The master logician of the Middle Ages is difficult to manage, but he provides the best insight into the intellectual changes in progress in the Late Middle Ages.

Marsilius of Padua, *Defensor Pacis*, trans. A. Gerwith (1956).

R. C. Petry, ed., *Late Medieval Mysticism* (1957). An excellent anthology illustrating a major religious movement in the age.

*Thomas à Kempis, *Imitation of Christ*, trans. L. Sherley-Price (Penguin). A classic illustration of medieval mysticism.

M. Spinka, ed., *Advocates of Reform from Wyclif to Erasmus* (1953). A good sampling of the ideas of the most outspoken advocates of reform in the Late Middle Ages.

V. Scudder, *St. Catherine of Siena as Seen in Her Letters* (1905). A precious view of the life of a unique Christian in the Late Middle Ages.

Retrospect

By 1500 there were many signs that Western European society stood again on the threshold of a remarkable era of expansion; that date marked a moment comparable in many ways to the year 1000, when Western Europe made its first great leap forward. Yet it is understandable that most men living in 1500 were dimly, if at all, aware of the great promise before them. Like men in most ages, they were better instructed by the immediate past than by the unrealized future. That immediate past had been a troubled one. Our review of it in the preceding two chapters emphasized the multiple stresses and tensions which affected the basic patterns of civilization characteristic of the Middle Ages. Given the magnitude of these difficulties, it is not surprising that men's thoughts were colored by pessimism and despair and that their reactions to life were marked by excess and violence.

In retrospect, the causes of the troubles of the Late Middle Ages seem fairly clear. The major institutions, thought patterns, and value systems that had been created prior to 1300 as essential to medieval Western European civilization had unstable features that began to emerge after 1300. The medieval political ideal of a Christian commonwealth, institutionalizing in the Holy Roman Empire, was flawed by fundamental disagreements about the leadership of the ideal commonwealth and by deep-seated localism. The feudal monarchies were beset by conflicts between royal authority and private privilege. The universal Church, with its central leadership and uniform doctrine, liturgy, and discipline, was challenged by religious localism, new concepts of leadership, and heterodox spiritual visions. Localistic, monopolistic, self-sufficient economic organizations contended with international, profit-seeking, individualistic enterprises. Faith and reason, Latin and vernacular cultures, religious and secular values confronted each other in men's minds. In all these institutional and intellectual contradictions, each opposite side was an integral part of the medieval order. The strength of medieval civilization rested in the balancing of the two. When the balance became unsettled, then strife and turmoil and uncertainty ensued.

In a superficial way, the general situation prevailing between 1300 and 1500 might resemble that which marked the third and fourth centuries of the Christian era, when classical Greco-Roman civilization suffered its fatal decline. In both eras there was violence and tension arising primarily from flaws in the institutions and values basic to their existence. However, a little reflection will reveal that, unlike the situation in the late classical period, the difficulties facing late medieval society arose not from the total exhaustion of an established pattern of civilization, but from the deepening disparity between vital forces vying to establish the dominant tone in Western European civilization. It was not the onset of decrepitude, but the release of vital energies stored up in institutions and concepts that caused the disturbances in the Late Middle Ages. The release of these energies for new growth only awaited the decision to opt for one way or the other between the alternatives posited by medieval Western European civilization: strong central government or private interest, reason or faith, individualistic religious concepts or a universal Church.

By 1500, these contradictions had begun to be resolved. The path toward the future was emerging. Strong monarchy, reason, religious diversity, a pluralistic culture, a capitalistic economy, among other things, were gaining the upper hand. The future of Western European society lay in the development of these patterns as the essence of civilized life; a future that would be spectacular. But as it unfolded, it was never marked by a catastrophic break such as that which signaled the transition from classical to medieval Western European civilization. The wave of Europe's future had already formed in the medieval world. In fact, "modern" Europe was born in the Middle Ages, and its history is unintelligible without a knowledge of the civilizaiton of that period.

VII

The Beginning of Modern Times
Fifteenth and Sixteenth Centuries

In the previous section, we have observed the various tensions and weakening institutions that marked the decline of the medieval world during the fourteenth and fifteenth centuries; now we shall see how the institutions that we have come to call modern grew out of the decaying medieval system.

In place of the declining feudal monarchies and empires there arose the national or territorial state, which became the dominant political institution of the modern era. The first of these national states to emerge were Spain, Portugal, France, and England. From then until now, the history of the Western world has revolved around them and the other national states that were patterned after them.

Europe's medieval economy, characterized by subsistence agriculture, monopolistic guilds, and localism, gave way to capitalistic practices and institutions. The landed aristocracy who had dominated the medieval economy now found themselves challenged and threatened by a new middle class of aggressive entrepreneurs, whose ambition and vitality pushed Europeans out of their own small world into the larger one. The end result was the discovery and domination of much of the rest of the world.

The decline of the Western Christian Church in the last two centuries of the Middle Ages had important repercussions not only on religious institutions and beliefs, but also on the nonreligious thought, the literature, and the arts of the Western European world as well. Theology could no longer command the attention of most of the best minds. Increasingly, they turned to humanistic philosophy and to science—natural and political. Artists became obsessed with the beauties of the physical world. In short, there was a *renaissance* (rebirth) of secularism.

The Western Church itself split, and much of northern Europe became

Protestant. This, in turn, provoked or at least hastened a Roman Catholic revitalization or reformation. The breakup of the powerful Roman Catholic Church, which had so dominated medieval Western Europe, contributed further to the secularization of society.

Since these four great movements—the rise of national states, the rise of a capitalistic economy, the renaissance of secularism, and the Reformation (Protestant and Roman Catholic) occurred primarily during the fifteenth and sixteenth centuries, it may be useful to conceive of the fifteenth as a century of transition and the sixteenth as the first century of the modern era.

In fifteenth-century Europe, at least four royal monarchs succeeded in creating powerful national states. They did so at the expense of the feudal barons who were unable to adjust to changing conditions, and had lost their former necessary function as the main support of the monarchy. The longbow and gun powder had begun to destroy the fighting effectiveness of the mounted armored knight as early as the fourteenth century. At the same time, reviving commerce, bringing with it a moneyed economy and a prosperous middle class, undermined the economic monopoly of the landowning aristocracy. The kings made use of the new, moneyed class and with its support hired standing armies equipped with the new weapons. To legalize their growing power, the kings utilized the principles of Roman law to evade the common law upon which feudal holdings were based. (Roman law considered kings to be sovereigns in whose hands the welfare of all the people was placed.)

Another factor that facilitated the building of nation-states was the rise of a national consciousness based primarily upon language. In each of the lands that are now Spain, Portugal, France, England, Germany, and Italy, one dialect became predominant. Once established, the national vernacular became the instrument for propagating the common traditions, customs, and legends on which national pride and loyalty were built.

26

THE RISE OF NATIONAL STATES

Although other factors retarded unification in Italy and Germany until the nineteenth century, Spain, Portugal, France, and England were already well on their way to becoming powerful national states in the late fifteenth century.

1. SPAIN

The most powerful and influential of the new states at the opening of the modern era was Spain. The energy and enthusiasm that Spain displayed at this time may be attributed in part, at least, to her long and finally successful struggle against the Moors. By the middle of the thirteenth century the Moors had been driven out of the entire Iberian peninsula except for the southernmost province of Granada. Furthermore, the numerous medieval feudal holdings in what is now Spain had been consolidated into four large kingdoms—Castile, Aragon, Granada, and Navarre (south of the Pyrenees). The marriage of Ferdinand of Aragon and Isabella of Castile in 1469 united for all practical purposes the two largest kingdoms. During their reign (1474–1516)[1] Granada and Navarre were conquered. Thus, within a forty-seven-year span from 1469 to 1516 the Spanish national state was created.

---

[1] Isabella ruled Castile from 1474 to 1504, and Ferdinand ruled Aragon from 1479 to 1516.

Ferdinand and Isabella strove for political and religious unity. In order to suppress further the jealous nobility, they allied themselves with the middle class, leaning heavily upon it for financial and administrative assistance. In return, the joint sovereigns did everything in their power to advance the fortunes of the merchants. Vigorous enforcement of law and order, stabilization of the currency, building of roads and bridges, tariff protection of home industries—all served to advance the economic prosperity of Spain in general and the middle class in particular. This commercial expansion was greatly enhanced in 1492 with the discovery of the New World in the name of Spain. The ensuing profits and loot further strengthened the hands of the Spanish sovereigns by freeing them from dependence upon the Cortes (the representative bodies dominated by the nobility) for funds.

In religious affairs also Ferdinand and Isabella attained virtually complete unity for their country. Against the two non-Christian groups in their realm, the Jews and the Moslems, the "Catholic Sovereigns" waged a campaign of conversion or extermination. The Jews had long been the object of hatred and persecution in Christian Europe. In part this hatred derived from religious differences, but there was also an economic factor. Church laws against usury had given the Jews a monopoly on moneylending, which high rates of interest rendered very prof-

Habsburg Dominions
Ottoman Empire
━━━ **Boundary of the Holy Roman Empire**

ATLANTIC OCEAN

NORWAY
Bergen
Oslo
Stockholm

SCOTLAND
Edinburgh

NORTH SEA

DENMARK
Copenhagen

BALTIC SEA

SWEDEN

IRELAND
Dublin

WALES
York
ENGLAND

Danzig

Hamburg
BRANDENBURG
Berlin
Vistula

London
Canterbury
Calais (England)

DUTCH NETH.
Munster
Antwerp
Brussels
Cologne
Wittenberg
SAXONY
SILESIA
Breslau

BELG. NETH.
LUX.
Trier
Schmalkalden
BOHEMIA
Prague
MORAVIA

St. Malo
Rouen
Paris

Metz
Worms
Ratisbon
PALATINATE
Strasbourg
Augsburg
Vienna

Orléans
Bourges

BURGUNDY
FR COMTÉ
Basel
SWISS CONFEDERATION
Geneva

BAVARIA
Munich
AUSTRIA

TYROL

Angoulême
Bordeaux

FRANCE

SAVOY
Trent
Venice
Milan
Parma
VENETIAN REPUBLIC

Mohacs

Santiago

DAUPHINÉ
Avignon
Marseilles

Genoa
Florence
DALMATIA

BOS

Oporto

Bayonne
PYRENEES

PORTUGAL

Valladolid
Burgos
NAVARRE
ARAGON

SPAIN
Escorial
Madrid
Toledo

CATALONIA
Barcelona

Corsica (to Genoa)

Elba (to Florence)
Rome
PAPAL STATES

MONTENEGRO

Lisbon

Valencia
Balearic I.

Sardinia (to Aragon)

NAPLES (Aragon)
Naples

Seville
Granada
GRANADA

Cadiz

MEDITERRANEAN SEA

Palermo
Sicily (to Aragon)

Melilla (Spain)
Algiers
Tunis

Malta (Knights of St.

SULTANATE OF FEZ

SULTANATE OF ALGIERS

SULTANATE OF TUNIS

B A R B A R Y   S T A T E S

0   100   200   300 miles

itable. The envy and hatred of the Christians led to periodic outbreaks of violence. In the late fourteenth century, an outbreak of unusual severity forced many Spanish Jews to seek safety in outward conversion. But these Marranos, as the pseudoconverts were called, were the object of increasing suspicion. Finally Ferdinand and Isabella, yielding to Dominican fanatics, permitted the Inquisition to be introduced into Spain. At the mercy of this dread Church court, the Marranos were terrorized by imprisonment, torture, and loss of life and property. In 1492 the remaining Jews were ordered to leave the country. The exiles thus banished (estimated to be in the neighborhood of one hundred and fifty thousand) took much of their wealth and all their economic energy and skills with them.[2]

Shortly afterward the Moslems suffered a similar fate. Upon surrendering their last stronghold in Granada, in 1492, they had been promised religious freedom in return for submission to the political authority of the Spanish crown. However, again the "Catholic Sovereigns" yielded to the increasing pressure of religious intolerance, and in 1502 the Moslems were ordered to accept Christianity or leave Spain. Although thousands did leave, even more thousands remained and went through the farce of outward conversion. But these "converts" called Moriscos, only delayed their fate. In the two succeeding reigns they too were persecuted and expelled. A little later the Inquisition was also used to rid Spain of Protestantism. Spain, then, was unified religiously, but at an economic and intellectual cost that was to blight her future. Nevertheless, territorially consolidated and politically unified by Ferdinand and Isabella, enriched by the wealth of the New World, and inspired by the crusading zeal of a purified and triumphant religion, Spain was to be the most powerful and influential of the new national states during the first century of the modern era.

EUROPE 1526

---

[2] The Jews had earlier been expelled from England, France, and the German states.

A coin of Ferdinand and Isabella, sovereigns of Spain. Spain was the most powerful of the new national monarchies and her coins enjoyed wide circulation in Europe and predominance in the Spanish and English empires in North and South America during the sixteenth, seventeenth, and eighteenth centuries. The Spanish piece-of-eight was commonly called the "dollar," and in 1787 the dollar was adopted by the United States as its standard unit of value. *Photo: American Numismatic Society*

2. PORTUGAL

Next to Spain the most prosperous and energetic national state in the sixteenth century was Portugal. The origins of this state can be traced back to the eleventh century, when, in return for his services in the struggle against the Moors, Count Henry of Burgundy was granted a fief in the vicinity of Oporto by the king of Leon. Count Henry and his doughty successors not only asserted and achieved independence from their Spanish overlords, but by driving the Moors steadily southward, carved out for themselves the sizable state of Portugal. Meanwhile, the Portuguese dialect was developing into a national language somewhat different from Spanish.

Hemmed in by their larger Spanish neighbors on land, the Portuguese turned to the sea. In the fifteenth century adventuresome navigators such as Diaz and Vasco da Gama carried the Portuguese flag around the Cape of Good Hope to India and laid the foundation for a vast empire. As a result of the papal Line of Demarcation (1493) and the Treaty of Tordesillas (1494) with Spain, Portugal obtained a monopoly on trade with the East around the Cape. From this trade she amassed more wealth than Spain extracted from the New World. However, so many of Portugal's able merchants and administrators went out to the East to make their names and fortunes that her sparse reserves of talent were depleted at home.

Like Spain, Portugal persecuted and expelled her Jews, Moslems, and Protestants, at great cost eventually to her intellectual life and to her economy.

3. FRANCE

The reign of Louis XI (1461–1483) may be said to mark the beginning of France as a modern national state. Louis came to the throne of France eight years after the end of the Hundred Years' War with England. His predecessor had used the war emergency to obtain a permanent tax (*taille*) and a standing army for the crown. During the last phase of the war a great upsurge of French national spirit aided by the exploits of Joan of Arc made possible, at long last, the expulsion of the English invaders. Louis XI put these inherited advantages to clever use. First of all, he set out to crush the power of the feudal nobility who had taken advantage of the royal distress during the Hundred Years' War to assert their virtual independence of the crown. By craft and by direct military force he broke up the league that the insubordinate nobility formed against him and reduced the individual nobles to submission. In order to achieve this goal, Louis utilized the rising middle class. In return for its support he placed many members of this class in his councils and in key administrative posts and did what he could to foster commerce and industry. Roads, harbors, and waterways were improved. Shipbuilding, commerce, and industry were encouraged by royal subsidies and protective regulation.

Louis XI virtually completed the territorial consolidation of the French national state. He brought province after province under direct royal control, until by the end of his reign France had acquired all of its modern territory except the northwesternmost peninsula of Brittany (which was acquired by Louis' son) and a few territories along her fluid northeastern frontier. This expansive movement brought Louis XI into

This altar relief from the Capilla Real in Granada shows the surrender of the last Moorish kingdom to the Catholic sovereigns in 1492. The conquest of Granada and the expulsion of the Moors from Spain completed the territorial and religious unification of the Spanish nation—but at great cost, intellectually and economically. *Photo: Foto Mas*

conflict with Charles the Bold of Burgundy. Charles the Bold (perhaps "the Rash" would have been a more accurate title) had inherited rich and strategically located territories that included the Netherlands, the duchy of Burgundy, and the free county of Burgundy. These he hoped to consolidate into a great national state— the old Middle Kingdom of Charlemagne's grandson Lothair—between France and Germany. Had he succeeded in doing so, the course of history might have been changed significantly. However, Charles the Bold and his successor, Mary of Burgundy, were no match for the "Spider King" of France. Charles was killed battling the Swiss, and Mary was unable to prevent Louis XI from seizing the duchy of Burgundy, Picardy, and part of Flanders. (The abortive Burgundian "Middle Kingdom" has

been a battleground between France and Germany throughout much of the modern period.) Thus consolidated and enlarged, France was to play a dominant role in European affairs in the centuries that followed.

Louis XI's schemes, however, did not include the betterment of the condition of the lower classes. Having paid for his ambitious programs with heavy taxes but having received little in return, the lower classes remained disaffected and discontented.

4. ENGLAND

Modern times, so far as English history is concerned, may be said to have begun with the reign of Henry VII (1485–1509), the first of the Tudor dynasty. The political unity of the English national state had been brought about as early as 1066 by William the Conqueror (aided to a considerable degree by geography). However, the feudal system, with its decentralization of administration and society, the Hundred Years' War with France (1337–1453), and the Wars of the Roses (1455–1484) between the rival houses of Lancaster and York, had by the last quarter of the fifteenth century brought England to a state of turmoil bordering on anarchy. Henry Tudor acquired the English throne by victory on the battlefield over the Yorkish king, Richard III, who was slain. Himself a member of the Lancastrian family, Henry ended the bloody dynastic feud by marrying Elizabeth of York.

The most pressing task confronting the strong-willed new monarch was the suppression of the turbulent nobility. The great feudal barons had taken advantage of the decades of civil war and of the long rule of a weak king prior to the war to defy royal authority. They retained their own private armies and overawed the local courts. At once and with great vigor Henry VII proceeded to enforce the laws against livery and maintenance,[3] thereby destroying the illegal feudal armies. Since the regular local courts were too weak to proceed against the nobility, Henry set up his own Court of Star Chamber, which, backed by the royal army, was able to overawe the most powerful barons and bring them to justice and to submission to the crown.

In these undertakings Henry VII had the wholehearted support of the lesser gentry and the middle and lower classes, all of whom yearned for peace and order. The middle class, particularly, desired stability for the sake of its growing business activities, and it was with this class that the Tudors allied themselves. Henry selected many of his counselors and administrators from the ranks of the bourgeoisie. He made favorable commercial treaties with the Netherlands, Denmark, and even with Venice, the jealous queen of the rich Eastern Mediterranean trade. Navigation acts were passed to protect English shippers. Henry's frugality and careful collection and handling of revenues not only were good business, but freed the king of dependence upon Parliament for funds.

Henry VII, unlike Louis XI of France, attempted to protect the interests of the English peasants, who were being forced off the land by the enclosure movement. The landed nobility, taking advantage of the brisk demand for wool, were turning their farming lands into sheep runs. Thousands of dispossessed peasants roamed the countryside as beggars or drifted to the cities looking for work at any price. Laws passed to protect the peasants from dispossession proved to be largely ineffective, however, as anyone traveling through the lush green and frequently untilled English countryside can observe today.

Henry VII died in 1509, prematurely worn out by his arduous labors. But he passed along to his glamorous son, Henry VIII, a united and orderly national state and a well-filled treasury. And under his granddaughter, Elizabeth, England rose to a position of first-rate importance in European and world affairs.

5. GERMANY AND ITALY

Although Germany and Italy have played a vital role in modern European history, they did not

---

[3] So called from the practice of the peasantry wearing the lord's badge or livery, signifying membership in his private army, in return for the lord's promise to maintain (support) them in courts of justice.

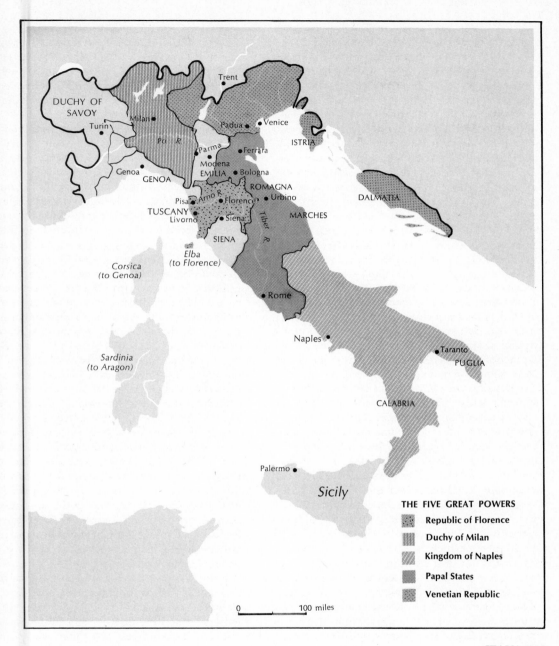

THE FIVE GREAT POWERS

- Republic of Florence
- Duchy of Milan
- Kingdom of Naples
- Papal States
- Venetian Republic

0   100 miles

ITALY 1454

achieve political unity at the opening of the modern period. That failure, although it did not prevent them from making important contributions to the arts and sciences, did create political maladjustments that account for much of

Europe's modern turmoil, particularly in the twentieth century.

During the fifteenth century, when the Spanish, Portuguese, French, and English peoples were becoming united under powerful national monarchs, the German-speaking peoples remained split up into more than three hundred virtually independent units. The only political bond between them was the impotent government of the Holy Roman Empire. This ramshackle institution—a survival of the organization set up by Charlemagne in 800 and revived by Otto the Great in 962—purported to be a restoration of the old Roman Empire, but it never was. In the Middle Ages, when the Spanish, Portuguese, French, and English sovereigns were consolidating their territories and their authority, the German emperors were frittering away their time and energy trying to bring Italy under their control. While they were away from Germany on these quixotic ventures, the local feudal barons conspired against them, consolidated their own power, and built up hereditary states of their own within the empire. Meanwhile, territory after territory slipped from under the emperor's control, until by the opening of the modern period, the Holy Roman Empire included for all practical purposes only the German-speaking states (plus Czech-speaking Bohemia).

Eventually seven of the emperor's most prominent subjects gained the right to elect him. This elective feature not only diminished the prestige of the emperor, but forced candidates to bribe the electors and bargain and promise away any chance of strengthening the imperial office. Since the emperor had no sure income, he had no military force with which to enforce his will. Even to defend the empire, he was forced to call upon his subject princes to furnish troops. The lawmaking and taxing powers lay in the hands of the Diet, which was composed of three houses: the house of electors, the house of lesser princes, and the house of representatives of the free imperial cities. The Diet had no regular time or place of meeting, and was seldom able to reach agreement on any important question. In the late fifteenth century an imperial court was set up to settle disputes between member states. However, lacking any means of enforcing its decisions, this instrument too proved ineffective.

The one factor that gave any semblance of vitality to the Holy Roman Empire was the Hapsburg family. A Hapsburg was first elected

emperor in 1273. After 1438, with only one brief exception, no one but a Hapsburg was elected until the empire finally died at the hand of Napoleon in 1806. By marriage and diplomacy, the Hapsburgs expanded their original Austrian lands until they possessed at the opening of the modern period one of the largest and richest dynastic estates in Europe. Although, therefore, the Holy Roman emperor as emperor was virtually powerless, as head of the house of Hapsburg he was one of the most influential of monarchs. Nevertheless, all efforts of the Hapsburgs to strengthen the central government of the empire foundered on the rocks of German particularism—the local interests of the jealous princes.

Italy's modern history has paralleled to a considerable degree that of Germany. At the opening of the modern period the Italian peninsula was divided into six major independent states without even the pretense of a Holy Roman Empire to unite them. The six were the Kingdom of the Two Sicilies, the Papal States, Florence (Tuscany), Venice, Milan, and Piedmont. The Kingdom of the Two Sicilies, the poorest and most backward of the Italian states, occupied the southern third of the peninsula and the large island of Sicily. During the fifteenth and sixteenth centuries it was a bone of contention over which France and Spain repeatedly fought. The Papal States occupied the central portion of the peninsula. These states were ruled by the pope not only as supreme pontiff, but also as political head. The popes based their claims to political rule over these states upon the Donation of Pepin, the father of Charlemagne, who drove out the Lombards and gave the territory to the pope in 756. Florence and Venice, republics in name, were dominated by rich banking and commercial families. Milan, another thriving center of commerce, was ruled by an autocratic duke. Piedmont, occupying the northwesternmost portion of the peninsula, was the property of the house of Savoy. This mountainous state, which eventually assumed leadership in the unification of Italy, played a relatively minor role in Italian affairs before the nineteenth century.

An important factor accounting for Italian disunity in the first centuries of the modern era was the presence of the Papal States in the strategic

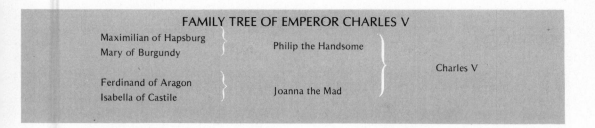

FAMILY TREE OF EMPEROR CHARLES V

Maximilian of Hapsburg
Mary of Burgundy
} Philip the Handsome
}
Ferdinand of Aragon
Isabella of Castile
} Joanna the Mad
} Charles V

center of the peninsula. Fearing the loss of their territories to a national monarch, the popes vigorously opposed all efforts to set up an Italian national state. A second factor was the long tradition of independence and the great commercial prosperity in the thirteenth, fourteenth, and fifteenth centuries of Florence, Venice, and Milan, where a spirit of local rather than national pride and loyalty prevailed. The political division and weakness of the Italians in an age of powerful national states continued to be a standing invitation to aggression against them.

6. INTERNATIONAL RIVALRIES IN THE AGE OF CHARLES V, 1516–1556

The rise of national states failed to bring peace to Europe. The national monarchs, supported by the bourgeoisie, had justified their own aggrandizement on the grounds that it was necessary to end the interminable feudal wars, and they had in fact established a large measure of internal law and order. However, the little feudal wars were followed by big national and dynastic wars. Throughout the first modern century — the sixteenth — international strife revolved around the house of Hapsburg.

During most of the first half of the century the house of Hapsburg was headed by Emperor Charles V. Charles V inherited from his parents and four grandparents an array of territories and claims that have been exceeded in history only by those of his son, Philip II. From his grandfather Maximilian he inherited the Hapsburg provinces generally spoken of as Austria, to which were added in Charles' lifetime Hungary, Bohemia, Moravia, and Silesia. As a Hapsburg, he also inherited a good claim to the imperial crown of the Holy Roman Empire. From his grandmother Mary he inherited the Burgundian lands: the free county of Burgundy (Franche Comté), the Netherlands, Luxembourg, Flanders, Artois, and claims to the duchy of Burgundy and Picardy, which had been seized by Louis XI. From his grandfather Ferdinand he received Aragon, the Kingdom of the Two Sicilies, and numerous islands in the Mediterranean. From his grandmother Isabella he received Castile and a claim to the entire Western Hemisphere based upon the papal Line of Demarcation (1493) and the Treaty of Tordesillas (1494). And from Ferdinand and Isabella jointly, he inherited Granada and Spanish Navarre.

The very size of Charles V's far-flung holdings spelled perpetual trouble. The language problem alone was appalling. To this were added differences in local customs, tastes, and eventually religion. Moreover, Charles V was sure to become involved in all the major international conflicts of Europe. Born and reared in the Netherlands, Charles got himself accepted in Spain only after serious opposition and open revolt. His efforts to strengthen the government of the Holy Roman Empire and to raise money and troops there were frustrated by the local German princes. Finally, the Lutheran revolt further split the empire and shattered completely the personal power of Charles in Germany.

Charles V found himself almost continually at war with Francis I of France. Each feared the other's power. Francis vigorously contested Charles' election as Holy Roman Emperor. They fought over conflicting territorial claims in Italy, the Burgundian lands, and along the French-Spanish border. Charles won nearly all the battles, but was never able to make his victories permanent.

The relations between Charles of Hapsburg and England were limited to a personal family quarrel. When Henry VIII sought an annulment of his marriage to Catherine of Aragon, the aunt of Charles V, Charles used his influence with the pope to block the proceedings, thus touching off a chain of events that ended with the separation of England from the Roman Catholic Church. It was under Charles' son, Philip II, that conflict between Spain and England was brought to a climax.

Among Charles V's more constructive achievements was his marriage to Isabella of Portugal, which brought about a brief union of Spain and Portugal under Philip II, and his repulse of the Ottoman Turks. The Ottoman Turks had migrated to Asia Minor from Central Asia in the thirteenth century, converted to Islam, and by the beginning of the sixteenth century had built an empire that extended from Egypt to the Danube. Under Sulieman the Magnificent (1520–1566), their ablest ruler, they crushed the Hungarians at Mohacs (1526), swept across Hungary, and in 1529 laid siege to Vienna, the capital city of Hapsburg Austria. At the same time they conquered all of North Africa as far west as Morocco, and their fleets dominated the Mediterranean. It was feared that all Western Christendom might fall to the Moslems. At this point, Charles V rallied the forces of the empire and the Hapsburg provinces and drove the Turks back into Hungary. His captains also administered some defeats to the Moslem Barbary pirates in the Western Mediterranean.

In 1555 Charles V began to divide his holdings between his son, Philip II, and his brother, Ferdinand. To Philip he gave the Burgundian provinces and Spain, with her appanages in Italy, the Mediterranean, and the New World. To Ferdinand he gave the Austrian provinces and suc-cessfully promoted his candidacy to the crown of the Holy Roman Empire. Henceforth there were two branches of the Hapsburg dynasty—Austrian and Spanish—both of which would long continue to play important roles in European and world history.

7. SUMMARY—THE POLITICAL MAP OF EUROPE IN 1555

At the beginning of the modern period, then, four powerful national monarchies, those of Spain, Portugal, France, and England, dominated Europe. Germany and Italy were divided into many small states. The German states and Slavic Czech-speaking Bohemia were in the Holy Roman Empire. The Netherlands, owned by the Hapsburgs, was a part of the empire. Switzerland, nominally in the empire, was in reality an independent confederation of semiautonomous cantons. Elsewhere in Europe, Scotland was still independent, and England's control over Ireland was only tenuous. Denmark owned Norway and was in temporary union with Sweden. Poland, including Lithuania, occupied a large stretch of territory east of Germany, but her anemic government made her impotent at home and abroad. Russia, under Ivan III, had just freed herself from Tartar overlordship and as yet counted for little in European or world affairs. The Balkan peninsula and most of Hungary were part of the Ottoman Empire. The four new national states which represented the political wave that the rest of Europe and most of the world would eventually follow had been firmly established. But their new internal strength brought not a more peaceful international order, but war on a larger scale, as symbolized by the continental scope of the operations of Charles V.

Suggested Reading

General — The Modern Era
R. Palmer and J. Colton, *A History of the Modern World*. Probably the best.

Beginning of Modern Times
*E. P. Cheyney, *The Dawn of the New Era* (Torch). The first volume of the excellent Rise of Modern Europe series.

The New National Monarchies
R. Altamira, *History of Spain from the Beginning to the Present Day* (1930). Best brief survey.

C. E. Nowell, *History of Portugal* (1953). Best in English.

P. Champion, *Louis XI* (1929). Good biography of the "Spider King."

*C. Read, *The Tudors: Personalities and Practical Politics of the Sixteenth Century* (Norton). By a leading specialist.

Germany and Italy
*K. Brandi, *The Emperor Charles V: The Growth and Destiny of a Man and of a World Empire* (Humanities). Best biography of the central political figure of Germany and Europe at the opening of the modern era.

G. Trevelyan, *A Short History of the Italian People from the Barbarian Invasions to the Attainment of Unity* (1920). Brief; well written.

Sources
Comines, *The History of Comines*, trans. Thomas Danett (1897). An eyewitness account of the struggle between Louis XI and Charles the Bold.

Historical Fiction
*Charles Reade, *The Cloister and the Hearth* (Washington Square). About the unwed parents of Erasmus. Vivid pen pictures of life in the fifteenth century.

27

A NEW ECONOMY AND THE EXPANSION OF EUROPE

The rise of the modern national state was closely associated with the rise of a modern capitalistic economy. The royal monarchs who created the national states made great use of the rising middle class in overcoming the feudal aristocracy. The strength of this middle class lay in its capitalistic wealth. The term *capitalism*, stripped to its barest essentials, may be defined as a system of putting money to work to make more money. It involves, among other things, private property, the profit motive, a substantial amount of free enterprise and individual initiative, the hiring of labor, and the lending of money for interest.

1. ROOTS AND BEGINNINGS OF MODERN CAPITALISM

Although we are likely to think of capitalism as a typically modern system of economy, it reached a fairly high development in ancient Greece and Rome. The reader will recall from earlier chapters that trading, banking, and production of certain wares on a capitalistic basis thrived in and among the Greek city-states, particularly in the Hellenistic age. Capitalism developed to a higher degree in the Roman world. For many centuries all roads and all ship lanes in the Western world led to Rome and were protected by Rome. Interest rates came down, and the standard of living went up.

However, the reader will also recall that, with the breakdown of the Roman Empire, capitalistic practices virtually disappeared. Early medieval economy, like early medieval government, was decentralized. Each manorial estate produced almost all its own needs. Agriculture was collectivist or cooperative. Commerce was a mere trickle of luxuries for the rich, and necessities such as iron, implements, and salt. The Church insisted upon the "fair price" rather than competitive pricing, and since it also forbade the lending of money for interest (usury), only the Jews, who were not bound by these dictates, practiced what small-scale lending of money there was.

During the course of the Middle Ages commercial activities and capitalistic practices began to revive. A slight increase may be observed as early as the eleventh century, and by the thirteenth century a pronounced recovery was under way. The Crusades contributed significantly to this revival. The huge movement of men and supplies from Western Europe to the Holy Land enriched the merchants and shippers of Venice and other Italian cities. Some of these set up permanent trading posts in the Near East and introduced the luxuries of the materially more advanced Moslem and Byzantine worlds to Western Europe. The Fourth Crusade, which the Venetians diverted to the looting of Constantinople, was particularly fruitful for rising Western capitalism. The Venetians seized not only a great hoard of gold and silver in the stricken Eastern imperial capital, but also almost half the territory of the Byzantine Empire itself. This wealth flowed into the stream of Western European commerce.

Foremost among the centers of this newly revived commerce and capitalism were the city-states of northern Italy, such as Venice, Genoa, Florence, and Milan. Venice was the queen of the Mediterranean in the thirteenth, fourteenth, and fifteenth centuries. After she had succeeded in crushing the sea power of her chief rival, Genoa, in the fourteenth century, Venice enjoyed a virtual monopoly over the lucrative trade with the East. At the peak of her prosperity, her merchant marine numbered some thirty thousand sailors. Milan was the starting point of the overland traffic across the Alps to northern Europe. In the late fourteenth century she gained control of the port city of Genoa. Florence manufactured large quantities of fine woolen textiles on a capitalistic basis, and in the fourteenth and fifteenth centuries was the banking capital of the Western world. The Medici family alone possessed at one time some two hundred branch banks scattered throughout Western and Central Europe.

In northern Europe, the Hanseatic League, composed of some eighty German Baltic and North Sea cities, enjoyed a brisk trade in such commodities as fish, furs, grain, and timber. In southern Germany and the Rhine Valley, numerous trading centers such as Augsburg, Nuremberg, and Cologne sprang up along the overland route between Italy and northern Europe. Finally, the Netherlands, Paris, and London shared in this early period of revived commercialism.

By the end of the fifteenth century, however, the further growth of European commerce was threatened by a number of obstacles that little feudal fiefs and independent cities were not able to overcome. One was the expense of the trade routes between Europe and the East, which were partly overland, especially after Moslem middlemen had taken their share of the profits. Another was the inadequacy of the gold and silver supply to serve as a satisfactory medium of exchange. A third was the restrictive practices of the guilds.

This woodcut, A.D. 1500, illustrates Venice at the peak of her power. During the thirteenth, fourteenth, and fifteenth centuries Venice was the queen of the Mediterranean. After she had succeeded in crushing the naval power of her chief rival, Genoa, in the fourteenth century, she enjoyed a virtual monopoly on the trade between Western Europe and the East. Her merchant marine numbered some thirty thousand sailors. Built on a group of islands, and possessing the world's strongest navy, she was practically impregnable. *Photo: The Granger Collection*

These obstacles provided worthy challenges for the four new national monarchies.

2. THE AGE OF DISCOVERY

In the late fifteenth and early sixteenth centuries, European mariners made a series of daring voyages in which they discovered not only the

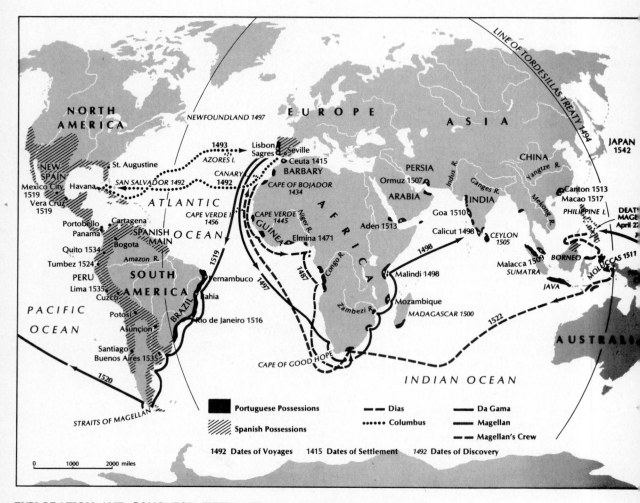

EXPLORATION AND CONQUEST, FIFTEENTH AND SIXTEENTH CENTURIES

New World, but also new and much better routes to the East. These voyages were promoted by the governments and people of the four nation-states along the Atlantic coast. Their principal motive was a desire to by-pass the Venetians, the Moslems, and the land barriers that separated them from the riches of the East. But there was also a powerful outward impetus in the spirit of inquiry and adventure kindled by the Renaissance interest in the secular world, and in the Christian missionary zeal that had always been a spur to expansion.

The first to begin in the fifteenth century were the Portuguese. Pushing steadily down the coast of West Africa they rounded in 1488 the Cape of Good Hope. In 1498 Vasco da Gama, in what was probably the greatest voyage in the history of navigation, reached India, the object of the quest. Vasco da Gama was out of sight of land 93 days—three times as long as Columbus on his voyage to the New World. That the Portuguese knew what they were up to is proved by the fact that Vasco da Gama's return cargo sold for sixty times the cost of the expedition. These glad tidings sent a host of Portuguese adventurers hurrying to the East Indies, where they carved out a huge commercial and political empire.[1] One of these adventurers, Cabral, swinging too far westward, touched the eastern bulge of South America, thus laying the basis for Portugal's claim to Brazil. With the discovery of an all-water route to the East, the commerce of the Italian city-states began to wither. So did that along the overland route from Italy across Germany.

Meanwhile, Spain was sending her mariners westward, for by the late fifteenth century most educated people in Western Europe assumed that the earth was round, although they greatly underestimated its size. It was therefore believed by many navigators that the East Indies could be reached by sailing west. The first European to attempt it was Christopher Columbus. (Nothing had come of the tenth-century voyages to Greenland and northern America of the roving Norsemen, Eric the Red and Leif Ericson.) Columbus was born in Genoa but moved to Portugal. When, however, Portugal failed to support his proposed westward voyage, he turned to Queen Isabella of Castile, who gave him the necessary backing. His three ships touched a West Indian island on October 12, 1492. Thinking that the West Indies were islands off the east coast of Asia, Columbus made three further voyages in the hope of by-passing these barriers and sailing on to his real goal, the East Indies. Instead he was turned back by the South and Central American mainlands and died disappointed, not having realized the magnitude of his discovery.

But others soon realized it, and in the first half of the sixteenth century, Spanish expeditions to the New World multiplied. As previously noted, the pope in 1493 had drawn a line of demarcation dividing the non-Christian world between Spain and Portugal. This line was somewhat altered in favor of Portugal the following year by the Treaty of Tordesillas. Since all of North and South America except the eastern part of Brazil and most of Greenland fell to Spain, the Spanish

sailors continued to move westward. Ponce de Leon, de Soto, and Coronado explored the southern part of what is now the United States. Balboa crossed the Isthmus of Panama and looked out upon the Pacific Ocean. In 1519 Magellan set out around the world by way of the

This illustration is from a letter of Columbus to the treasurer of the King of Spain, published in Basel a year after his first voyage. Here the Spaniards are offering the Indians gifts as they approach the island. Pictures such as this excited the wonder and greed of many Europeans. *Photo: NYPL Picture Collection*

---

[1] For conditions in southern Asia at the time of the European intrusion see pp. 427–431.

Straits of Magellan. Although he himself was killed in the Philippines, one of his ships in 1522 completed the circuit. Also in 1519, Cortez began the conquest of the Aztec Empire in Mexico. In 1531–1532 Pizarro conquered the Inca Indians in Peru.

The other two national states, England and France, were relatively inactive in discovery and exploration during the fifteenth and early sixteenth centuries. The English crown did, however, sponsor voyages to northern North America by the Italian mariner John Cabot in 1497–1498. These voyages became the basis for England's claims to North America, where she later built a great empire. The French government sponsored Jacques Cartier, who in 1535 sailed up the St. Lawrence to what is now Montreal and claimed Canada for France. Nonetheless, it was not until the seventeenth century that Spain and Portugal were replaced as the world's leading imperial and commercial powers.

3. THE FOUNDING OF THE SPANISH NEW WORLD EMPIRE

Although most of the Western Hemisphere at the beginning of the sixteenth century was sparsely inhabited by primitive and often savage Indian tribes, the Spaniards did find two rich and colorful civilizations: those of the Aztecs in Mexico and the Incas in Peru.

The American aborigines are clearly members of the Mongoloid branch of the human family. They are generally believed to have come from Asia across the Bering Strait, perhaps as long as forty thousand years ago.

The first of these primitive tribes to build a highly civilized society were the Mayas. They are believed to have come into what is now Guatemala and the Yucatán peninsula of southeast Mexico from the northwest about 1000 B.C. Their civilization reached its height between A.D. 400 and 600. It was a city-state civilization resembling that of ancient Greece approximately a thousand years earlier. Their writing, most of which has been lost, was a combination of pictures and ideographs. Their best art was brightly colored pottery, gems, gold and silver ware, and sculpture. Probably their most remarkable cre-

ations were a system of mathematics based on the decimal (actually vigesimal) system and a calendar based upon astronomy, both of which were in advance of those used in contemporary Europe. Their massively walled stone cities were connected by elaborately paved roads. These cities, however, were continually at war with one another, and in the twelfth century the less-civilized but better-organized Toltecs conquered the Mayan city-states much as Philip of Macedon conquered the Greeks.

In the fourteenth century the warlike Aztecs came down from the north and founded a city on an island in Lake Tezcoco—the present Mexico City. From this base they conquered and organized a military empire or confederacy comprising most of what is now southern Mexico. The Aztecs were the Romans of the New World, and like the Romans they acquired most of their culture from the earlier civilization (Mayas). Theirs was the gift of military and political organization. They developed an elaborate, though stern, system of justice. Their religion was important and highly organized. Several thousand priests, both regular and secular, tended the impressive temple and supervised education and morals. The numerous gods, taken mostly from the Mayas, were headed by the terrible war god, whose unquenchable thirst for blood demanded human sacrifice, usually prisoners of war. And yet the rank and file Aztecs were gentle lovers of poetry and art. A flourishing commerce, agriculture, and mining added to the wealth obtained by conquest.

An even more colorful civilization was that of the Incas on the Andean Plateau of South America. In the eleventh century the Inca Indians began to extend their sway over their neighbors until their empire covered an area 1500 miles long and 300 miles wide—including present-day Ecuador, Peru, and parts of Bolivia and Chile. An elaborate system of roads and communications tied this vast and lofty empire together. Incan society was a combination of benevolent despotism and socialism. The all-powerful Inca (ruler) was treated as a god. However, he had a body of advisers and administrators, chosen from the upper classes. All land and all production were owned and directed by the state. The regimented lower classes did all the work under close supervision and shared from the common stores. A high degree of specialization was practiced. Agriculture was well advanced, and huge terracing and irrigation projects had been developed to overcome the difficulties of the Andean terrain. Religious worship, particularly of the sun god, was a beautiful and important feature of national life. Although Incan writing was backward, its art was well advanced. Outstanding were pottery, architecture, textiles, and gold and silver ornamental objects.

The beautiful native American civilizations were no match for the marauding Europeans with their modern military hardware. Cortez with a band of some six hundred soldiers and eighteen horses overcame the Aztecs by a combination of treachery and superior weapons. He took advantage of the Aztec belief that the Spaniards were ancient gods whose return had long been expected. Once inside the capital city, the Spaniards were too strong to be expelled. They slaughtered and looted the poorly armed Aztecs without mercy. Even more spectacular was the conquest of the Incas. Pizarro enticed the Incan emperor into a conference. At a given signal Pizarro's small but well-armed band of Spanish soldiers fell upon the splendidly dressed but primitively armed Incan troops and slew them by the thousands. Not a Spaniard lost his life. Pizarro promised to free the Incan chieftain in return for a ransom of gold objects sufficient to fill a room seventeen by twenty-two feet to a height of nine feet, plus a larger amount of silver. This ransom was collected and paid, but Pizarro, who never really intended to free the emperor, had him put to death anyway. When this gold and silver, an estimated ten million dollars' worth, reached Spain, the money shortage in Europe was relieved.

Throughout the sixteenth century Spaniards flocked to the New World. By 1607, when the first permanent English colony was founded in North America, a quarter of a million Spaniards had settled in the vast Spanish Empire stretching from what is now Arizona to Cape Horn. A number of distinguished missions and cathedrals had been erected, and several thriving universities had been founded. The native civili-

zations had been almost wholly destroyed and replaced by the Christian civilization of Spain. Meanwhile, the Portuguese, in addition to reaping a golden harvest from their commerce with the East, were duplicating the Spanish feats on a smaller scale in Brazil.

4. THE COMMERCIAL REVOLUTION

The discovery of the New World and of all-water routes to the Far East resulted in an expansion of European commerce on such a scale that the term *commercial revolution* may accurately be used to describe it. As the main routes shifted from the Mediterranean to the Atlantic, the stranded Italian and German cities decayed, and new commercial centers to the west began to flourish. Contrary to one's expectations, Spain, surfeited with gold and silver from Mexico and Peru, never developed a thriving commercial capitalism. And although Lisbon became the first great terminus of goods pouring in from the East, the Portuguese, like the Spanish, were so preoccupied with their vast overseas empire that they neglected the marketing opportunities in Europe itself.

These lucrative opportunities were first seized by the Dutch. Enterprising Dutch merchants purchased the goods in Lisbon, shipped them to the Netherlands, and sold them at a nice profit throughout northern and Western Europe. In the sixteenth century Antwerp, with its excellent harbor and location, was the leading commercial center in Europe. In the seventeenth century, following the sack of Antwerp in 1585 by Spanish troops, Amsterdam and London led the commercial world. The Dutch even took advantage of their newly won independence from Spain and of Portugal's temporary conquest by Spain in 1580 to seize the best part of Portugal's Eastern Empire, the area of present-day Indonesia.

Another phase of the commercial revolution was the advent of more bounteous supplies of commodities. Spices, coffee, tea, sugar, dyes, tropical fruits, fine textiles, tapestries, and precious stones, long known but in scarce supply and too expensive for all but the very rich, now came into Europe in ever-increasing volume. From the New World came potatoes, corn, to-

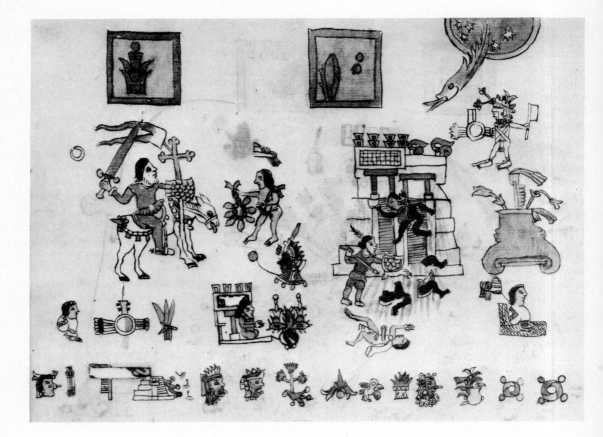

Although there are many Spanish records of their arrival and explorations in the New World, this Aztec manuscript (ca. 1519–1522) is one of the few surviving Indian versions of the coming of the Europeans. This illustration shows Cortez arriving in Mexico. *Photo: La Biblioteca Apostolica Vaticanna, Rome*

bacco, and chocolate (all of which were previously unknown in Europe), new dyes and medicines, gold and silver.

A different kind of new product — black slaves — also helped to swell the rising stream of commerce. This most nefarious traffic of modern times was first begun in the later fifteenth century by the men of Portugal's Prince Henry the Navigator. It was later taken over by the Spaniards to supply labor for their empire in the New World. When the Spaniards discovered that the native Indians were poor slave laborers, they turned to tropical Africa. Thousands of Negroes were bought from local chieftains and crowded into the holds of ships. Many of them died during the crossings, but the survivors were sold like cattle for a high price in the New World markets. So heavy was this immensely profitable traffic that the racial and social complex of the New World society was drastically altered.

New types of business organizations were developed to accommodate the expanding volume of commerce. *Chartered companies* were organized to by-pass the medieval guilds, which were unable or unwilling to meet the new demands. The most efficient type of chartered company proved to be the joint stock company. The members of a joint stock company pooled their resources, hired or elected their management, and shared in the profits in proportion to the amount of stock owned. In this way permanence was achieved by selling or buying the stock of changing personnel. Moreover, unlimited amounts of capital could be raised by selling stock. This type of business organization has never been improved upon for large-scale efficiency, as present-day joint stock companies such as General Motors, Exxon, and AT & T demonstrate.

Two of the earliest joint stock companies were the British East India Company, founded in 1600, and the Dutch East India Company, founded two years later. The British company was given not only a trading monopoly over British India, but political control as well. The Dutch company was given a monopoly over all Dutch trade east of the Cape of Good Hope. Annual profits of 300 percent were not uncommon for these giant companies. The annual profits of the Dutch East India Company never fell below 12 percent over a period of two hundred years.

Although there was some expansion of industrial capitalistic activity in this period, it was relatively slight until means had been found to overcome or evade the obstruction of the monopolistic craft guilds. Wherever the production of goods was done on a capitalistic basis, the domestic or "putting out" system was generally used. Entrepreneurs would purchase the raw materials and distribute them to craftsmen, who would do the piecework in their cottages. Then the entrepreneur would collect the finished products, pay the cottagers for their work, and market the goods at a profit. While this system had certain advantages, it limited the volume of production. Until the coming of the machine and the factory system in the late eighteenth and early nineteenth centuries, therefore, large-scale capitalism was to remain commercial rather than industrial.

Banking expanded in proportion to commerce. In the sixteenth century the Fugger family of Augsburg occupied the place in the financial world that the Medicis of Florence had held in the fifteenth. Jacob (the Rich) Fugger loaned Charles V the money with which he bribed his way to the emperorship of the Holy Roman Em-

pire. He also loaned the Archbishop of Mainz the money with which he purchased his archbishopric; and it was the selling of indulgences by this archbishop in order to repay the loan that was one of the sparks which touched off the Protestant Reformation. In the seventeenth century the Bank of Amsterdam and the Bank of England were founded on a seminational basis. Both of these banks were really private joint stock companies, but in return for certain monopolies, such as the handling of government funds and the issuance of currency, they were obliged to accept a degree of government regulation. Banks of this size were able to mobilize sums of money and credit sufficient not only to launch and control large-scale commercial ventures, but to influence government and religion as well.

5. A NEW COMMERCIAL POLICY—MERCANTILISM

Governments attempted to exercise some control over economic developments. From the beginning of the Age of Discovery in the late fifteenth century until the end of the eighteenth century, all the governments of Western Europe except the Dutch Netherlands pursued a policy that has come to be called *mercantilism*. Mercantilism was, in essence, economic nationalism. While the monarchs of the new national states were consolidating their political power, they were also attempting to unify and centralize their national economies. Efforts were made to standardize national currencies and weights and measurements. Internal commerce was encouraged by improving communications and reducing or removing internal tariff barriers. These efforts, however, were only partially successful. More attention was paid to the aggrandizement of each nation's economy at the expense of its neighbors. The basic assumption of mercantilist theory was that gold and silver are the true measure of national prosperity and power. Gold and silver, the mercantilists believed, in addition to being convenient mediums of exchange, could purchase anything—consumer goods, armies, navies, and administrative personnel. Spain's good luck in Mexico and Peru and her sixteenth-century brilliance and influence undoubtedly strengthened this view.

Spain alone was fortunate enough to come upon the gold and silver directly. All the other states had to devise more roundabout means of acquiring the precious metals. The favorite device was to seek a *favorable balance of trade*. The importation of expensive manufactured goods was discouraged by high tariffs, whereas the exportation of manufactures was encouraged, if need be, by subsidies. The reverse was true of inexpensive raw materials. The national aim was to buy low and sell high. Colonies were sought as sources of raw materials and markets for manufactured goods. But the colonies were not to be permitted to compete with the manufacturers and shippers of the mother country. Navies were advocated for the protection of the colonies. Sometimes the mercantilists closely regulated a nation's manufactures with a view to maintaining a reputation abroad for high quality. This phase of mercantilism reached its highest development in France in the seventeenth century under Louis XIV's economic minister, Colbert. It was not until the latter part of the eighteenth century that the British economist Adam Smith and the French physiocrats began to undermine public faith in the validity of mercantilist principles and to prepare the way for an era of *laissez faire*, or free trade.

6. POLITICAL AND SOCIAL CONSEQUENCES

The immediate political consequence of the rise of modern capitalistic economy in Western Europe was the strengthening of royal absolutism. The monarchs made use of the merchants and bankers in order to increase their own power at the expense of the rival nobility. More money was now available for the royal treasury and the royal army. The middle classes, of course, shared the benefits of their alliance with the royal monarchs. Many members of the bourgeoisie were appointed to key positions in the royal administrations. With their increased wealth came increased social and political influence. The strongholds of their influence were the towns and cities whose growth paralleled the expansion of commerce. Western European society was becoming more urban—yet another change from the medieval pattern.

As the power of the national monarchs and the middle classes grew, the position of the nobility declined. Their wealth and power were based upon land, and now money was more important. A severe inflation brought on by the great influx of gold and silver into Europe further hurt the nobility in relation to the moneyed bourgeoisie. Not overnight, but slowly and with occasional setbacks over the decades and centuries, the nobility of Western Europe were displaced by the middle classes in political and social influence. Only in England and the Netherlands did they avoid disaster by openly engaging in business operations.

The ascendance of the middle class did not bring an immediate improvement in the condition of the lower classes. Indeed, the *nouveaux riches* often proved to be harsher taskmasters than the older aristocracy, who had had time to learn that power brings responsibility. The urban wage earners, no longer protected by the guilds, were especially hard hit by the inflation. In France and England some peasants who had converted their feudal dues to money payments profited, but most of the peasants in Western Europe and all of those in Central and Eastern Europe suffered from the inflation and the general loss of feudal security. The distressed landlords were likely to pass their hardships along to the peasantry. Peasant revolts were common throughout Europe in the sixteenth century. However, the rise of the middle class and the disappearance of feudal class lines produced a more fluid social structure and made possible the future growth of democracy. Money is more easily acquired by the commoner than is blue blood or title.

7. EUROPEAN DOMINATION OF THE GLOBE

Europe's Age of Discovery and the rise of modern capitalistic economy were momentous also for the rest of the world. Much of the Western

Hemisphere, southern Asia, and the coastal areas of Africa were quickly brought under European domination. This amazing expansion continued until by the end of the nineteenth century practically the entire world was dominated by Europe and European civilization. Spanish, Portuguese, English, French, and Dutch colonists, followed later by the nationals of all the other European countries, flocked to the New World, taking their Western Christian culture with them. The brilliant Aztec and Incan civilizations of Mexico and Peru were destroyed. The more primitive tribes of American Indians were exterminated, absorbed, or confined to reservations. The Moslem, Hindu, Buddhist, and Confucian civilizations of Asia and Africa were virtually enslaved by the aggressive European imperialists. Modern European history is therefore world history, and the details of European expansion (and eventual contraction) constitute a considerable portion of the history of Western civilization in the modern era.

Thus we see Europe's static, agricultural, collectivist, "fair price" economy transformed into a dynamic, urban, competitive, profit-motivated economy. The rise of capitalism not only changed the nature of European society; it also provided much of the explosive force that enabled tiny Europe to dominate most of the rest of the world.

Suggested Reading

General
H. Heaton, *Economic History of Europe* (1948). Excellent survey.

The Age of Discovery
*C. E. Nowell, *The Great Discoveries and the First Colonial Empires* (Cornell).
S. E. Morison, *Admiral of the Ocean Sea*, 2 vols. (1942). Masterful life of Columbus.
*S. E. Morison, *Christopher Columbus, Mariner* (Mentor). Useful brief account.

Overseas Empires
*W. H. Prescott, *The Conquest of Mexico* (Modern Library). A classic.
*W. H. Prescott, *The Conquest of Peru* (Dolphin). Even better.

*F. Parkman, *Montcalm and Wolfe* (Collier). The best of Parkman's numerous excellent volumes on the French in North America.

The Commercial Revolution
*L. B. Packard, *The Commercial Revolution 1400–1776* (Berkshire). Excellent brief account.

Sources
*R. Hakluyt, *Principal Navigation, Voyages, Traffiques and Discoveries of the English Nation* (Everyman). Colorful contemporary account.

Historical Fiction
*Thomas B. Costain, *The Moneyman* (Permabooks). The story of Jacques Coeur, France's leading merchant and financier of the fifteenth century.

28

THE RENAISSANCE: ITALY

The term *renaissance* means rebirth, and in the development of Western civilization it designates particularly the rebirth of a secular civilization that was inspired in large measure by the civilizations of ancient Greece and Rome. However, *rebirth* implies too sharp a change with the immediate past. Secular interests had never completely died out, even at the peak of the Church's prestige in the Middle Ages; and the revival of secular interests was a gradual process. Furthermore, the Renaissance was not merely a return to pre-Christian culture; new elements that had not existed previously were added. It would be better to regard the Renaissance as an intensification of the secular spirit in Western European thought, literature, and art during the fourteenth, fifteenth, and sixteenth centuries. The key word here is *secular*, meaning that which pertains to this physical world as contrasted with the religious emphasis on the spiritual. The Renaissance began in Italy, where many physical reminders of the glory that was Greece and the grandeur that was Rome had remained.

1. GENERAL NATURE

Probably the most basic of the secular attitudes that characterized the Renaissance was humanism — the focusing of interest on man rather than God. In a period dominated by humanistic concepts, the arts, the sciences, and all forms of intellectual and practical activity tend to be directed toward man. The emphasis on theology, concerned with the nature of God, changes to one on a philosophy centered on the nature and condition of man. During the Renaissance man, not God, was enthroned as lord of the universe. In this respect, Renaissance thought was like that of pagan Greece and Rome and unlike that of the Christian-dominated Middle Ages. The medieval Christian theologians distrusted the flesh as an enemy of the spirit, and human wisdom as a frail thing unable to perceive divine truth by rational processes unless guided by Christian inspiration. But men of the Renaissance, like their Greek and Roman kinsmen, glorified the human form as a thing of beauty and the human intellect as capable of discovering all truth worth knowing.

Humanism extols not only mankind in general but also individual man. Individualism, therefore, was another important facet of the secular spirit of the Renaissance. In this respect, the difference between the medieval and the Renaissance spirit was primarily one of degree. Probably no influence in history has done more than Christianity to elevate the dignity of the individual soul and the individual personality. Christianity taught that even when a sparrow falls God sees and is concerned. How much more then is he concerned for every man, made by him in his own image and for his own glory. But the medieval churchmen feared pride as the deadliest of all the sins. Therefore, they taught that the individual ego must be carefully held in check. Medieval monasticism went so far as to attempt to suppress the individual ego altogether and submerge it in the group. In practice, then, medieval Christianity, like medieval economy, tended to be collectivist. Church artists and writers usually did not sign their names to their work, which was supposed to contribute only to the greater glory of God. Renaissance individualism, like that of Rome, was of the lusty variety. One could hardly imagine a Machiavelli or a Boccaccio hiding his identity. This kind of individualism also gave rise, as in ancient Rome, to excessive men. No more egotistical individual can be found in history than Benvenuto Cellini, liar, thief, murderer, rapist, and one of the most gifted artists of the Renaissance era.

That a Cellini should be not only tolerated but also honored by his contemporaries may be further explained by the fact that he represented another cardinal principle of the Renaissance ideal—versatility. We are reminded of Pericles' all-round man of Athens of the fifth century B.C. and of the broadly educated Roman patrician. The educated man of the Middle Ages was usually a specialist—a theologian or a church artist or administrator. But the most renowned Renaissance schoolmasters taught many subjects in addition to the traditional formal ones—dancing, fencing, poetry, and vernacular languages, to mention a few. Many of the Renaissance universities secularized and broadened the old theology-oriented seven liberal arts and made much greater use of pagan classical literature and philosophy in the curriculum. One of the most popular books in Europe in the sixteenth century was Castiglione's *Book of the Courtier*. The ideal courtier, said Castiglione, is not only a gentleman and a scholar, but also a man of action—a soldier and an athlete. Probably the best illustration of versatility in any age is Leonardo da Vinci. This revered Renaissance figure, one of the most celebrated painters of all time, was also an able sculptor, architect, mathematician, philosopher, inventor, botanist, anatomist, geologist, and engineer.

Finally, the secular Renaissance civilization was urban—again like that of ancient Greece and Rome, but unlike that of the Middle Ages, which was rural. Renaissance writers and artists were more often than not sustained by rich merchants and bankers, first in the revived commercial cities of Italy and later in those of northern Europe.

2. LITERATURE

These secular characteristics of the Renaissance spirit are richly illustrated by the Italian literature of the fourteenth century. The best of that literature was produced by the Tuscan Triumvirate—so called because it consisted of three men who lived in Florence in the old Etruscan province of Tuscany. The first was Dante Alighieri (1265–1321). In an earlier section (see Chapter 23) we discussed Dante as the greatest of the late medieval writers. His masterpiece, the *Divine Comedy*, is so full of medieval Christian lore and theology that it has been called a *Summa Theologiae* in poetry. Nevertheless, there is so much of the secular spirit in the *Divine Comedy* and in Dante's other writings that he belongs also to the Renaissance. In the "Inferno" of the *Divine Comedy*, Dante paints vivid, sensuous word pictures that smack of this world rather than the next. The blazing fires and sulfurous fumes of hell, the cries of lament and curses of the damned come alive in our imagination. Furthermore, the author venerates such pagan classical writers as Vergil and Cicero to a much greater degree than had the medievalists (although a number of medieval writers had tried to make Vergil a Christian).

Dante's other major writings are entirely secular. His love lyrics, written in his native Tuscan vernacular and addressed to Beatrice, are among the most beautiful in any language. In fact, Dante's writings greatly enriched the Florentine dialect and raised it eventually to the status of the national language of Italy.

Dante was also versatile; he was a man of public affairs as well as of letters. An active participant in the turbulent politics of Renaissance Italy, he was exiled from his native Florence when his faction lost out. Dante even went so far as to fill hell in the *Divine Comedy* with his political enemies. His political treatise, *On Monarchy*, argues for a united Italy under the leadership of the Holy Roman Emperor.

Petrarch (1304–1374), the second of the Tuscan Triumvirate, like Dante wrote beautiful love lyrics in the Tuscan vernacular. His exquisite odes and sonnets were poured out for Laura, a noble lady whom he saw at mass and loved from afar. He goes on rapturously about Laura's bosom, arms, face, and feet with most unmedieval abandon. The sonnet is Petrarch's own invention.

Boccaccio (1313–1375) did for Italian prose what Dante and Petrarch did for Italian poetry. In his *Decameron*, a collection of one hundred tales or novelettes, Boccaccio makes no pretense of using Christian restraint. He relates bawdy romances with skill and grace, condoning and even glorifying the seamy side of human nature. Here we have open revolt against the medieval ideal.

3. HUMANISM

Toward the end of the fourteenth century, the original Italian Renaissance literature was stifled by the rise of humanism. Italian humanism was a movement consisting of two rather distinct phases. One was the passionate quest for Greek and Latin literary manuscripts; the other was the development of a many-sided secular philosophy of life.

The search for classical literary manuscripts conflicted with the creation of original Italian literature by siphoning off the interest and energy of the writers. This conflict is illustrated by Petrarch, who rather early in life ceased writing what he called his "worthless" lyrics in order to discover lost classical manuscripts and to copy their style. He did succeed in bringing to light many priceless classical literary gems, but his epic *Africa* (relating the exploits of Scipio Africanus), written in Latin after the style of Vergil's *Aeneid,* lacks spontaneity and is all but forgotten.

Petrarch interested Boccaccio in the recovery of Greek and Latin manuscripts, and the search soon became a fad. Popes, princes, rich merchants, and bankers subsidized the humanists, so called because the pagan Greek and Latin literature dealt with human rather than divine affairs. (Studies concerned with classical literature and language, art, philosophy, and history came to be called the humanities.) In the fifteenth century, Italy was busy with professional humanists

hunting, copying, translating, and editing ancient manuscripts.

Meanwhile, the content of the classical masterpieces was influencing the growth of a secular philosophy of life. This phase of humanism had many facets, such as the rise of the concept of the nonmoral state, the revolt in private and social behavior against Christian moral restraints, and the development of a critical or scientific attitude. Machiavelli, in his celebrated *The Prince,* suggested that Christian morals have no place in government. Since men are self-seeking animals, the prince (or ruler or governing officials), to be effective, must be both amoral and ruthless. The prince must assume that his own lieutenants, like all rival princes, are conspiring for his crown. Therefore, his own chief subjects must be set against each other and maneuvered into impotence. Foreign rivals must be deceived and treacherously attacked at the most favorable moment before they can do the same. While Machiavelli was trying to remedy the deplorable reality of a divided Italy overrun and pillaged by more powerful foreign enemies, he also reflected the thinking of a man-centered, secular age. Few books have had more influence on, or been more descriptive of, modern political thought and practice.

The humanistic revolt against Christian restraints on private behavior is illustrated by the fabulous career of Benvenuto Cellini. This gifted Florentine — some say the greatest gold- and silversmith of all time — boasts loudly in his *Autobiography* of his lies, thefts, illicit loves, even of rape and murder. Admittedly Benvenuto Cellini is an extreme case, but the fact that such a character should have been honored in early sixteenth-century society indicates the degree to which Italian Renaissance society had departed from the medieval Christian ideal.

Another facet of the humanistic or secular view of life was the development of an analytic or scientific attitude. When Lorenzo Valla proved by linguistics that the Donation of Constantine was a forgery, the scholarly and secularminded pope raised no objections, although this was one of the documents upon which the papacy had based its claims to temporal power in the West. In fact, Pope Nicholas V made Valla his

"The Flight into Egypt" by Giotto. In the fourteenth century Giotto began to break medieval artistic traditions by humanizing his figures and introducing perspective and naturalistic backgrounds. This trend led to the glorification of the human body by the great Renaissance painters of the fifteenth and sixteenth centuries. In this fresco the subject matter is religious but its treatment is secular. *Photo: Alinari/EPA, Inc.*

secretary. By making this discovery, Valla established himself as the father of modern critical historical scholarship.

4. ART

The renaissance of secularism is vividly illustrated in the Italian visual arts of the fourteenth, fifteenth, and sixteenth centuries. Medieval art in Europe had been closely allied with the Church. Painters deliberately penalized human flesh in order that the spirit might shine forth unimpeded. The figures, nearly always saints, were stiff, haggard, flat, and elongated. The physical world too was blanked out with solid gold backgrounds. The styles were stereotyped.

In the early fourteenth century Giotto, a contemporary of Dante, began to break this medieval mold of artistic custom by humanizing his figures and painting functional landscape backgrounds. Although his magnificent frescoes in the church of St. Francis at Assisi depicting the life of St. Francis were still rather flat, with diffused lighting, this did not make them less decorative—an artistic principle known to ancient Egyptian artists. True, Giotto's subject matter was almost entirely religious, but his treatment of it was such that the secular spirit made definite advances at the expense of the sacred. In the early fifteenth century, Masaccio greatly developed the trend begun by Giotto a century earlier. He increased the illusion of depth by introducing atmospheric perspective and by further developing linear perspective. He also introduced the principle of the known light source, which thereafter replaced diffused light in painting. His nude human forms were further rounded and humanized. His landscape backgrounds were realistic and detailed. With Masaccio, the transition from medieval to Renaissance painting was completed and the stage set for such towering geniuses of the Italian High Renaissance as Leonardo da Vinci, Michelangelo, Raphael, and Titian.

It would be difficult to find a more representative figure of the Italian Renaissance than Leonardo da Vinci (1452–1519). All the colorful facets of the secular spirit are richly illustrated by the career and work of this versatile genius. As a painter, he is probably unsurpassed in any age. Leonardo was an illegitimate child, as were a number of the famous figures of the Renaissance. He was born near Florence and began his career there, but some of his most productive years were spent in the employ of the duke of Milan. He finally followed King Francis I to France, where he died. Like most Renaissance artists, Leonardo dealt primarily with religious subject matter, but, also like the others, his treatment of it was invariably secular and human. In his *Virgin of the Rocks*, for instance, Leonardo creates with exquisite grace and beauty the Virgin Mary and the Christ child. The Virgin, however, is the loveliest of women, and the Christ child is a plump and playful baby boy. The characters are human, not divine. The background is a strange rock formation, naturalistic

enough to reveal a keen interest in this material earth, and yet arrestingly abnormal. The plant forms in the background are actually identifiable. Leonardo's *The Last Supper* depicts the reactions of the twelve disciples to Christ's words, "One of you shall betray Me." This celebrated fresco, exhibiting the artist's complete mastery of technique and draftsmanship, is essentially a study in human psychology—a subject in which Leonardo showed a special interest. The famous *Mona Lisa* is not religious in subject matter; it is the portrait of a real woman. The mysterious half-smile—the mouth smiles but the eyes do not—so captivates the viewer that he is likely to overlook other features of the picture, including the hands, which are said to be the most sensitive ever painted. In the *Mona Lisa*, Leonardo, who appears to have been little interested in women in real life, is believed to be probing the universal human nature of womanhood.

Michelangelo (1475–1564) is second only to Leonardo da Vinci as a versatile Italian High Renaissance genius. Since Michelangelo was primarily a sculptor, his painting is sometimes called "painted sculpture." His favorite subject was the virile, muscular male nude. Although a Florentine, much of his life was spent in Rome, where he labored in the service of the popes. His greatest painting—some say the greatest single painting of all time—was the ceiling fresco in the Vatican Sistine Chapel. The hundreds of individual figures, representing nine scenes from the book of Genesis, marvelously blend together into one harmonious whole. A subdued, blond cast adds to the religious atmosphere of the work. And yet the figures are all vibrant human beings. Later Michelangelo painted the *Last Judgment* as an altarpiece for the same chapel. The Christ in this picture is actually a terrifying, pagan giant, hardly the Jesus of Nazareth of the New Testament and the Christian Church.

Some critics believe Raphael (1483–1520) to be the greatest painter of all time; others say that he merely synthesized the original work of others. The output during his brief life was enormous. His favorite subjects were religious, but his Madonnas were feminine, gracious women and his Christ childs pudgy and mischievous. His best-known paintings, the *Sistine Madonna* and

With Leonardo da Vinci (1452–1519), Renaissance painting reached its peak. In the "Virgin of the Rocks," the Virgin is a beautiful woman, and the Christ child is a playful, cuddly little boy. The rock formation is authentic, and the plants are identifiable specimens. *Photo: Archives Photographiques, Paris*

Masaccio, early in the fifteenth century, developed still further the trend toward secularism and naturalism begun a century earlier by Giotto. His "Expulsion of Adam and Eve from the Garden of Eden" depicts a religious subject in a very secular manner. The background is realistic and detailed. The nude figures are rounded and humanized. Masaccio set the stage for the great geniuses of the Italian High Renaissance. *Photo: Alinari/Scala EPA, Inc.*

the *Madonna of the Chair*, both in oil, well illustrate this secular treatment of a sacred theme. Many of his vivid portraits are of lay princes and tycoons. His monumental fresco *The School of Athens* reveals the veneration that Renaissance man felt for the pagan glory of Greece.

The fourth of the great painters of the Italian High Renaissance was Titian (1477–1576). A citizen of Venice, the most prosperous commercial city of the fifteenth and early sixteenth centuries, Titian reflected the secular spirit of the Renaissance to an even greater degree than his three renowned contemporaries. Although a considerable portion of his painting was of religious subjects, his focus was nearly always the pomp and pageantry of the Church rather than its teachings. But a large part of his subject matter

Raphael and his students produced an enormous number of paintings. So great was the demand for this painter's work that Raphael would often sketch in the outline and allow his students to finish the painting. His "Sistine Madonna" illustrates the typical Renaissance characteristic of treating a religious theme in a secular manner. Raphael's madonnas were bland, feminine, gracious women, and his Christ childs were very human, pudgy boys. *Photo: Alinari/EPA, Inc.*

The genius of Michelangelo, master sculptor of the Renaissance, is exemplified in this work, "The Dying Slave," now in the Louvre, which glorifies both the human form and the human spirit. Michelangelo believed that the most beautiful object in nature was the male nude. *Photo: Courtesy Michigan State University*

The largest Christian church in the world, St. Peter's Basilica in Rome, was built in the sixteenth and seventeenth centuries at enormous cost. The secular-minded Renaissance architects of St. Peter's were influenced by the styles of pagan Greece and Rome.
Photo: Anderson/Art Reference Bureau

was purely secular. The wealth and brilliance of Venice, overflowing with cargoes of luxurious fabrics, tapestries, and gems from the East, provided a challenging array of sensuous and colorful material for the artist to depict. And in the use of color, particularly vivid yellows, reds, and blues, Titian had no peer. He always painted the hair of his women a reddish-gold hue that has come to be called titian. His portraits of some of the great lay personages of the sixteenth century, such as Francis I of France, Emperor Charles V, and Philip II of Spain, are masterful character studies. With Titian, the break with medieval painting, begun by Giotto and Masaccio and widened by Leonardo, Michelangelo, Raphael, and many other great Italian painters too numerous to mention here, was completed.

In sculpture, the artist without peer in any age is Michelangelo. It is true that he had Roman copies of the sculpture of Hellenic Greek masters such as Praxiteles and Scopas to guide and inspire him. But the gifted Florentine was no mere copier. The Greek masterpieces, for all their beauty and grace, were idealized types—half gods, half men. Michelangelo and his lesser-known immediate predecessors and contemporaries added a typically Renaissance characteristic to sculpture: individuality. The statues of the Italian Renaissance are not only human beings, but human individuals. Even Michelangelo's *Pietà*, which represents the mother of Jesus holding the dead body of her son as she looks down piteously, is a study in human emotions. The helplessness and hopelessness of the huge, all-engulfing mother displays the pagan resignation at the finality of death—not the Christian hope of resurrection and eternal life. His *Moses* portrays the fierce and rugged strength of man, not God. Moses' beard, as crude as icicles beneath a water tank in the month of January, displays the sculptor's ability deliberately to distort for effect. The three-dimensional medium of marble enabled Michelangelo to exploit to the full his favorite subject, the masculine nude. Numerous statues of David are used to convey not only the virile muscular power, but also the agile grace of the male animal. His *Dying Slave* is a sublime portrayal of both the human form and the human spirit struggling to free themselves from bondage. Some critics think that the great sculptor's finest genius is displayed in the companion statues of two members of the Medici family—Lorenzo, the contemplative type, and Giuliano, the man of action. In these two pieces the master craftsman and artist exhibits every technique of sculpture. The work of Michelangelo is probably our best example of the Renaissance glorification of man as lord and master of the universe.

The subject of Renaissance sculpture cannot be dismissed without brief mention of the work of Benvenuto Cellini. His work in gold and silver was of an exquisite delicacy that has never been equaled. His most famous larger work is the bronze statue of Perseus holding up the Gorgon's head. In this amazing conglomeration of unrealities, Cellini showed complete disregard of all accepted traditions and standards, yet with happy results. Such bold and original pioneering was typical of the self-confident, secular nature of the Renaissance mind.

Renaissance architecture, like Renaissance sculpture, drew heavily from Greek and Roman sources. From Greece by way of Rome came columns (now merely decorative) and horizontal lines; from Rome came the dome, the arches, and the massiveness that characterized Renaissance buildings. All of these features (except massiveness) represented a revolt against the Gothic architecture of the later Middle Ages, although the Gothic style had never gained much of a foothold in Italy. The two greatest monuments of Italian Renaissance architecture are the dome of the cathedral in Florence and St. Peter's basilica in Rome. St. Peter's cannot be called a cathedral, since it has never been the seat of a bishop. The Florentine cathedral is essentially Tuscan Gothic. Its ornate rectangular façade and bell tower reflect Byzantine and Islamic influences. But its most distinguishing feature is its gigantic octagonal dome, designed and constructed by Brunelleschi in the early fifteenth century. This symbol of the grandeur of ancient Rome served as a model for such later great domes as St. Peter's in Rome, St. Paul's in London, and the Capitol building in Washington. But the most grandiose achievement of Renaissance architecture is St. Peter's. This magnificent structure was to the Renaissance era what the Pyramids, the Parthenon, the Colosseum, and the Gothic cathedrals were to their respective epochs. It was built during the sixteenth and early seventeenth centuries at a cost that shook all Western Europe religiously and politically. Its numerous architects drew primarily upon pagan Greek and Roman sources for their inspiration. Even seventeenth-century baroque features eventually entered into its design. Raphael served for a time as chief architect, and Michelangelo designed the dome. One has to step inside St. Peter's to appreciate the breathtaking grandeur of this awesome structure. Its lofty proportions and gigantic pillars, its brilliant paintings and sculptures, its gold, marble, and mosaic decorations all glorify the material things of this world rather than the spiritual aspects of this world and the next. Built by the popes of the Western Church, St. Peter's is really a temple dedicated to the sensuous beauty, earthly pride, and confidence in man that characterized the secular spirit of the Renaissance.

Music was another field of art in which many original contributions were made during the Renaissance period, particularly the sixteenth century. Although most of these developments occurred in northern Europe, especially the Netherlands, Italy was the scene of some of great importance. Instrumental music became popular, and great improvements were made in the instruments. The harpsichord and the violin family of instruments came into existence. Musical techniques such as major and minor modes, counterpoint (the blending of two contrasting melodies), and polyphony (the interweaving of several melodic lines) rapidly developed. The most illustrious musician of the sixteenth century was Palestrina, chief musician to the pope, and probably the greatest master of polyphonic music of all time. Although most of the music of the Renaissance still centered about the Church, it was now more sensuous and versatile. More-

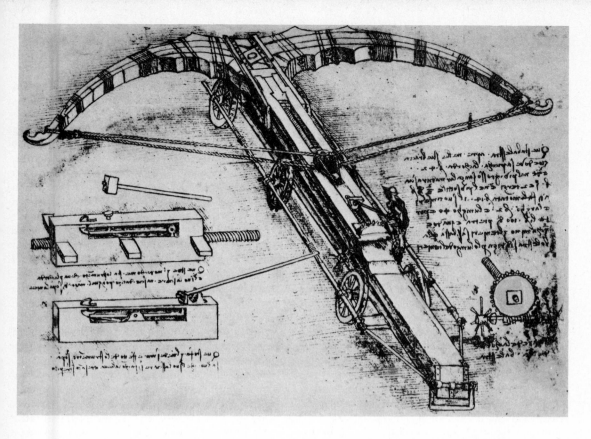

over, new and entirely secular forms appeared. The madrigal, popular throughout Europe in the late sixteenth century, was a musical rendition of stanzas of secular lyrical poetry. Renaissance musicians laid the foundations for modern classical music in all its major forms—concerto, symphony, sonata, oratorio, opera.

5. SCIENCE

It was almost inevitable that a renewed interest in the physical world, combined with optimism and confidence in the wisdom and self-sufficiency of man, should have resulted in scientific inquiry. Although the flowering of natural science did not occur until the seventeenth and eighteenth centuries, that blossoming sprang from the seedbed of the Renaissance. Leonardo da Vinci, for example, made accurate observations and pondered deeply on such subjects as geology, anatomy, botany, and applied mechanics. His inventions, drawings, and scientific predictions are impressive even today.

In 1543 two of history's most original and provocative scientific works—Copernicus' *Concern-*

This drawing from one of Leonardo da Vinci's notebooks shows a giant crossbow that could be operated mechanically. Leonardo wrote backwards; one must use a mirror to read his notes. Leonardo exemplifies the Renaissance ideal of versatility. Although he is known chiefly as a painter, this illustration depicts his interest in science and technology. *Photo: The Bettmann Archive*

ing the Revolutions of Celestial Orbs and Vesalius' *Concerning the Structure of the Human Body*— were published. Both were in large measure products of the free atmosphere of the University of Padua. Copernicus was a Pole, and Vesalius was a Fleming. Both were attracted by the intellectual climate of Renaissance Italy, and both attacked long-accepted theories. Copernicus challenged the geocentric theory of Ptolemy (A.D. second century) that the earth is the center of the universe in favor of the heliocentric theory, according to which the sun is the center of the solar system, the earth being only one of many planets revolving around it. Vesalius assaulted the theories of Galen (also second century) concerning the structure of the human body, particularly the heart. Both books raised a storm of opposition, and both were popularly rejected. However, after a century of controversy, Copernicus was to become the father of modern astronomy, Vesalius the father of modern anatomy and physiology. This spirit of scientific inquiry completely supplanted medieval scholasticism. More important, the beginnings made by Leonardo, Copernicus, and Vesalius were to bring forth in the seventeenth century and after, an incredible expansion of scientific knowledge.

6. DECLINE

The Italian Renaissance slowly changed and then declined, as the center of Renaissance activity shifted from Italy to northern Europe. This shift closely paralleled that of commerce from the Mediterranean to the Atlantic. When Venice, Florence, and Milan were the most prosperous commercial and banking centers in Europe, they were at the same time the most vigorous seats of Renaissance culture. As their economy stagnated with the shifting of the trade routes to the West, their cultural vigor likewise declined, although Italian art, heavily patronized by the Church, kept its momentum for several generations longer. Literature had declined by the end of the

fourteenth century, and humanism by the end of the fifteenth; by the end of the sixteenth century, art too had lost its vigor.

Another factor that undoubtedly contributed to the decline of the Italian Renaissance was the revival of interest in religion, a result of the Protestant and Roman Catholic reformations. Italian humanism which was more secular and pagan than Northern humanism, was particularly hard hit by the religious revival. It must be remembered also that the Renaissance was in large measure of, by, and for the elite only. The Italian humanists were particularly contemptuous of the masses. Other causes of the decline of the Italian Renaissance are obscure. One frequently reads that the invasion of Italy by the French, Spanish, and German armies and the general military and political instability of the period constituted important factors in the decline. This proposition, however, is difficult to prove. The ancient Greeks and modern Germans—to cite two parallel cases—produced their greatest cultural achievements while they were split up into many political units, and often under adverse conditions such as foreign invasion or civil war. The causes of the decline of brilliant civilizations and epochs remain a challenge to the student of history.

Suggested Reading

General
*M. P. Gilmore, *The World of Humanism, 1453–1517* (Torch). The best single-volume survey.
*W. K. Ferguson, *The Renaissance* (Berkshire). Brief summary by a leading authority.
*J. Burckhardt, *The Civilization of the Renaissance in Italy,* 2 vols. (Torch). A classic that has influenced all subsequent studies of the subject.

Literature, Humanism, Science
J. B. Fletcher, *The Literature of the Italian Renaissance* (1934). Scholarly.
*F. Chabod, *Machiavelli and the Renaissance* (Torch).
*A. Wolf, *A History of Science, Technology, and Philosophy in the Sixteenth and Seventeenth Centuries* (Torch).

The Arts
*H. Wölfflin, *The Art of the Italian Renaissance* (Schocken).
*K. Clark, *Leonardo da Vinci* (Penguin). By a well-known critic.

Sources
*P. Taylor, *The Notebooks of Leonardo da Vinci: A New Selection* (Mentor). Well illustrated.
*B. Castiglione, *The Book of the Courtier* (Anchor). Contemporary textbook for gentlemanly behavior.
*B. Cellini, *Autobiography* (Bantam). The artist's own account of an adventuresome life.

Historical Fiction
*Irving Stone, *The Agony and the Ecstasy* (New American Library). Novel about the life of Michelangelo. Based upon excellent historical research.

29

THE RENAISSANCE: THE NORTH

The Northern Renaissance was in large measure an importation from Italy. Northern European scholars such as Chaucer visited Italy as early as the fourteenth century. By the late fifteenth century, such inspirational journeys to Italy were commonplace. The development of the secular spirit in northern Europe was also furthered by the shifting of trade routes from the Mediterranean to the Atlantic.

1. GENERAL NATURE

Not only was the Northern Renaissance later than the Italian Renaissance, but it was also somewhat different in nature. Painting, sculpture, and architecture played a much less prominent role; humanistic philosophy and literature, on the other hand, were relatively more important. Northern humanism itself, though an importation from Italy, was markedly different in nature. Whereas Italian humanism very frequently represented an open revolt of pagan secularism against Christian ideals, Northern humanism sought, for the most part, to humanize Christianity and thereby to reconcile the sacred and the secular.

2. NORTHERN HUMANISM

The trend to secularism as a basic attitude toward life began in earnest in northern Europe in the late fifteenth century. One of the first evan-gelists of the new man-centered faith was Johann Reuchlin, a German scholar. After a sojourn in Italy during which he became imbued with the ideas of the Italian humanists, Reuchlin undertook to introduce the new classical learning into Germany. Specifically, he sought to broaden and enrich the university curriculum by establishing the study of the "un-Christian" Hebrew and Greek languages and literature. The Church and university interests vested in the medieval order of things attempted to thwart him, invoking the Inquisition to try him on grounds of heresy. Reuchlin fought back courageously and enlisted a large and enthusiastic following. Eventually the pope condemned him to silence. However, the victory really lay with Reuchlin and his humanist supporters. The tactics and self-centered motives of the churchmen and scholastic pedagogues disgusted most of the genuine scholars and students of the day, and during the first few decades of the sixteenth century the new humanistic curriculum became established in all the major universities of Germany.

Meanwhile, in England a group of Oxford professors was accomplishing with less opposition what Reuchlin had fought for in Germany. John Colet was the most prominent member of this group. He, too, visited Renaissance Italy. In true Northern humanistic fashion he gave a rationalistic slant to his preaching and teaching of the Scriptures at Oxford. Probably the greatest of

Colet's contributions to the new learning was the founding of St. Paul's grammar school in London, with a curriculum devoted largely to the pagan classics. To guarantee its secular orientation, he chose as trustees a guild of London merchants. St. Paul's soon became a model for many other such schools throughout England.

The most famous of the early sixteenth-century English humanists was Sir Thomas More, Lord Chancellor of the Realm. More's *Utopia*, like Plato's *Republic,* blueprinted an earthly, not a heavenly, paradise. In picturing his ideal commonwealth, More indicted the social, religious, and political evils of his own time. Utopia was a socialistic society in which private property and profits were unknown. Much attention was given to public health and education. The economy was planned and cooperative. War was outlawed except in self-defense. Religious free-

dom was granted to all but atheists. Although More eventually was to accept death by beheading rather than to recognize Henry VIII as head of the English Church in place of the pope, his ideal society was entirely secular. Man through his own wisdom would create his own perfect world here on earth.

Towering above all the other Northern humanists was Desiderius Erasmus (1466–1536), the intellectual dictator of the sixteenth century. In his efforts to humanize Christianity itself, the "Prince of the Humanists" presented the fundamental issue of Western civilization: Are the basic faith, ideals, and standards of Western civilization human or divine? Erasmus was born in Rotterdam in the Netherlands, the illegitimate son of a priest. Reared as an orphan, he was educated in a school run by the Brethren of the Common Life, a pietistic order of laymen that taught the Greek and Latin classics and emphasized simple inner piety rather than ritual and formal creed. (It is interesting and probably significant that Martin Luther, the great contemporary and adversary of Erasmus, also attended a school of the Brethren of the Common Life.) At the age of twenty-one Erasmus entered an Augustinian monastery (again like Luther) and was eventually ordained. Instead of serving as a priest, however, he spent every possible moment studying his beloved classics — a pursuit he was to continue at the Sorbonne and for the rest of his life.

Erasmus' vast erudition combined with his great personal charm made him a much-sought-after man. His first book was *Adages,* a collection of wise sayings of the Greeks and Romans together with his own comments. It was an immediate success, and other books soon followed. His greatest work was the *Praise of Folly,* in which he ridiculed with subtle humor and delightful satire the ignorance, superstition, credu-

The "Prince of the Humanists," Erasmus, is shown in this fine portrait by the Northern Renaissance painter Hans Holbein. Erasmus' attempt to humanize the Christian religion was the beginning of one of the most important and enduring controversies of modern times. *Photo: Archives Photographiques, Paris*

lity, and current practices of his day, particularly those connected with the Church. The folly which he praised was man's very human light-heartedness, his sense of humor. Wherever Erasmus went—France, England, Italy, Switzerland, Germany, the Netherlands—he was received with admiration and awe. No man so advanced the cause of Northern humanism by popularizing the study of the pagan Greek and Latin classics.

In addition to popularizing the new humanistic learning north of the Alps, Erasmus is significant in history for at least two other reasons—his influence on religious and social reform, and his efforts to humanize and intellectualize Christianity. He was at his best when laughing to scorn the abuses and superstitious practices of the Roman Catholic Church. The taking of money from the poor and ignorant masses by wealthy and corrupt churchmen, veneration of relics, and unquestioning belief in the miraculous were in the eyes of Erasmus beneath the contempt of enlightened men. But he was clever enough to sheathe his barbs with humor, thus making them more subtle and effective. Erasmus, however, was no Protestant. When Martin Luther first began his attacks on the Roman Catholic Church, Erasmus thought that he was merely seeking to correct glaring abuses and hailed him as a fellow spirit. But when Erasmus discovered that the German reformer was primarily interested in doctrinal reform and that the Protestants were as dogmatic as the Roman Catholics (actually more so in the early sixteenth century), Erasmus would have nothing more to do with him. The great humanist found it more comfortable to remain in the Roman Catholic Church. The two men ended hurling epithets at each other. Nevertheless, Erasmus' incessant attacks on the abuses in organized Christianity undoubtedly encouraged both the Protestant and the Roman Catholic reformations.

Erasmus' efforts to humanize Christianity, however, are far more significant historically than his campaign to eradicate religious and social abuses. Since the fall of the Roman Empire the great common denominator of Western civilization has been the Christian religion. The vast majority of the members of Western society have

subscribed to even if they have not lived up to its creeds, ideals, and moral standards. Furthermore, the vitality of these creeds, ideals, and moral standards has derived, in large measure, from the belief that they are of divine origin and sanction. Indeed, it is difficult to conceive of Western civilization as it has developed thus far without this basic faith at its center. This is why Erasmus' questioning of the divine origin and nature of the Christian religion—his efforts to humanize it—is of such deep significance. Although the "Prince of the Humanists" never did specifically say so, the implication running through his writings is that Jesus was a human being—the greatest, best, and most charming man who ever lived, the man we should all try to emulate, but nevertheless man, not God. Erasmus would by-pass formal creed, dogma, ritual, organization, and seek the "historical" Christ. Now, all this is quite appealing to the rationalistic humanist, but it is not quite so simple as it first appears. The historical Christ is a most elusive figure. As a matter of fact, the only documentation we have for Christ is in the New Testament, and if we apply to it the same standards of critical analysis used for other historical documents, its evidence is by no means conclusive. And yet the secondary evidence—the word of mouth and written tradition—is overwhelming. Few historians today would deny the existence of Jesus of Nazareth. However, all we have to go on for the "historical Christ" is the New Testament and the early tradition, and the Christ of both these sources is not the Christ of Erasmus. He is a miracle-working Christ who claimed to be the son and image of God, to have the gift of eternal salvation, who "spake as no other man ever spake." Far simpler to reject Christ as did many of the Italian humanists than to humanize him. Erasmus' attempt was not only the ultimate in the renaissance of secularism, but the beginning of a controversy that has endured until today.

3. THE NATIONAL RENAISSANCE LITERATURES

The national literatures that flourished during this period differed greatly from the literature of the Middle Ages, which in the main (with note-worthy exceptions) centered around religious subjects and was international in viewpoint. Al-though the literature of the Northern Renais-sance owed a great deal to the Italian literature of the fourteenth century, it reached its prime much later—in the sixteenth and early seven-teenth centuries. The most important literary de-velopments in this era were in England, France, and Spain.

English Renaissance literature began with Chaucer (1340–1400), who traveled to Italy, be-came acquainted with Boccaccio, and brought back to England the spirit and much of the tech-nique of the early Italian Renaissance writers. His *Canterbury Tales* are almost an English *Decameron* in charming verse. Salty and very earthy characters from all walks of life parade past us on the way to Canterbury, their human frailties and sins of the flesh forgiven them by the author. Only hypocritical churchmen get the censure of the English Boccaccio, and even they with a light and subtle touch. As in Italy, how-ever, the century following Chaucer was rather barren in a literary sense; it was not until the mid-sixteenth century, the time of Queen Eliza-beth I, that his plantings suddenly burst forth in full flower.

The reign of Elizabeth I (1558–1603) was a period of great energy and optimism in England. To the rediscovery of the achievements of an-cient Greece and Rome were added the discov-ery of the New World, and of new routes to the riches of the Far East. English seamen such as Drake, Gilbert, and Howard first plundered the Spanish treasure ships, and then crushed the "Invincible Armada" of the world's chief mili-tary power, making England mistress of the seas for the next three centuries. English explorers boldly laid the foundations for a future empire in the East and in the West. England's commerce increased, and the standard of living for the mid-dle and upper classes rose sharply. The Queen herself knew how to stimulate national pride revolving around her own person. England be-came "a nest of singing birds" such as the world has never seen or heard. Edmund Spenser's *Faerie Queen* glorified the versatile man of the Italian humanists, particularly the ideal set forth

by Castiglione in his *Book of the Courtier*. Chris-topher Marlowe in his brief life wrote man-cen-tered plays of such caliber that some critics think he would have achieved the stature of Shake-speare had he lived. His *Tamburlaine the Great* and *Edward II* treat of the worldly drama of royal ambition. The central figure in *The Jew of Malta*, a forerunner of Shylock, is a product of the revived commercial capitalism. *Doctor Faustus* dramatizes the theme, later immortal-ized by Goethe, of the intellectual who in true Renaissance fashion sold his soul to the devil in return for earthly knowledge and pleasure.

Mightiest of all the artists of the English Re-naissance was, of course, William Shakespeare (1564–1616). Shakespeare was born in the same year that Michelangelo died, a fact that ought to remind us that many of the same circumstances that stimulated the Italian artists of the sixteenth century to design St. Peter's and paint the *Sistine Madonna* spurred the English artists to write the *Faerie Queen* and *Hamlet*. So little is known of Shakespeare's life that there is still controversy over whether or not he is actually the author of the poems and plays we attribute to him. Shake-speare wrote some of the world's most beautiful lyrical poetry. His most important work, how-ever, was in the field of drama. Here he was heavily indebted to his contemporary, Chris-topher Marlowe, as well as to the ancient Greek and Roman dramatists. Marlowe developed the blank verse form which Shakespeare perfected. In plays such as *Hamlet, Macbeth, Othello, King Lear, Merchant of Venice, As You Like It, Henry IV, Romeo and Juliet*, and *Julius Caesar*, Shakespeare displayed a mastery of every known technique of the dramatic art.

More important for the student of history, he exemplified and dramatized every facet of the secular spirit of the Renaissance. Secular man is Shakespeare's subject matter. Rugged, distinc-tive human personalities are the heroes and villains of his plays. No human emotion, aspira-tion, or psychological conflict escapes his eye. On the whole, Shakespeare, unlike the Greek dramatists, makes man the master of his own fate. In addition to making man the center of his universe, Shakespeare illustrates the Renais-sance spirit and times in other ways. Admiration for pagan Greece and Rome, a keen interest in new-found lands, the first stirrings of modern natural science, the commercial revolution and social problems arising from the emergence of the capitalistic middle class, the rise of national monarchy and a national patriotic spirit—all enter into the fabric of the plays. In spite of the fact that both the Protestant and the Roman Catholic reformations loomed large in the affairs of England and the rest of Western Europe just before and during Shakespeare's time, he showed little interest in matters of religion. In this respect, too, he was a true child of the Renaissance.

One of Shakespeare's most important contemporaries was Sir Francis Bacon. Though not Shakespeare's peer as an artist, Bacon was nonetheless an intellectual giant. His father, Sir Nicholas Bacon, was one of the chief administrators and advisers of Queen Elizabeth, and Francis spent much of his life seeking political fortune. Finally he succeeded, becoming Lord Chancellor of England, only to be convicted of dishonesty, stripped of his powers, and for a time imprisoned. That his reputation and his own self-esteem could survive such misfortune is indicative of the moral relativism of the Renaissance era. Bacon's intellectual interests were broad, and his knowledge encyclopedic. His *History of the Reign of Henry VII* is still an important source. His *Novum Organum* is one of the first important treatises on modern natural science. Bacon preached the absolute necessity of accurate and unbiased observation in acquiring scientific truth. His major contribution to Renaissance literature is his *Essays*, which he continued to polish and refine as long as he lived. The final result is fifty-eight gems of pithy, salty, practical, and very human wisdom.

The last of the giants of Elizabethan literature was Ben Jonson. This robust personality, a familiar figure in the bohemian taverns of London, could serve as a trooper in the English army and also write "Drink to me only with thine eyes." Jonson was first a connoisseur of classical literature. With exquisite plays reminiscent of the Greek dramatists, he attempted unsuccessfully to reverse the trend toward cheap popularization and sensationalism that had characterized the English stage after the death of Shakespeare. Jonson's death in 1637 marked the end of the most glorious epoch in the history of the world's literature—England's greatest contribution to the Renaissance and the Renaissance spirit.

The two chief figures in French Renaissance literature were François Rabelais and Michel de Montaigne, both of whom lived in the sixteenth century. Rabelais was a renegade priest, a bored physician, and a loving student of the classics. Although he stumbled quite by accident and late in life upon his gift for writing, he turned out to be one of the greatest creative geniuses in the history of literature. His masterpieces are *Pantagruel* and *Gargantua*. They are fantasies about two completely unrestrained giants who wallow and revel unashamedly in all the sensuous and sensual pleasures known to man. These works are an open assault upon Christian moral standards and restraints. The wit is coarse and lewd, and sympathetic toward the frailties of human nature. Rabelais' rich imagery, his marvelous gift of expression, and his graceful artistry combine to make him one of the founding fathers of modern French prose. He shares that honor with his contemporary, John Calvin, whose lucid and incisive Protestant writings Rabelais hated no less than the works of the Roman Catholic theologians and the scholastic philosophers.

Montaigne was a prodigy born of a wealthy family. Like Rabelais, he was an ardent lover of the classics. This, together with the fact that his mother was Jewish and his father Roman Catholic, probably accounts for his skepticism in matters of religion. The result of his life of study and reflection was his *Essays*. Montaigne was a skeptic. To arrive at reliable truth, he believed, one must rid himself of all religious prejudice. He was a moral and spiritual relativist, rejecting all absolutes. Unlike his successors of the eighteenth-century Enlightenment, he distrusted the authority of human reason. Unable to replace the authority of Christian dogma with any other firm conviction, Montaigne was nearly always negative in his conclusions. But he immensely enjoyed this game of intellectual hide-and-seek. In fact, Montaigne believed that the chief purpose of life is pleasure—not the "eat, drink, and be merry" pleasure of Rabelais, but urbane, sophisticated, restrained, intellectual pleasure. The influence of Montaigne has been enormous — obviously upon essayists from Bacon to Emerson and later, but also upon the development of modern rationalism in general.

Standing out above all others in Spanish Renaissance literature are Miguel de Cervantes and Lope de Vega. Cervantes was a contemporary of Shakespeare, the two dying within a few days of each other in 1616. Cervantes' early life, like Shakespeare's, is obscure. In time he became a soldier of fortune, fought heroically and was wounded in the great naval battle of Lepanto with the Turks, suffered a five-year imprisonment in Algeria, and finally served as a quartermaster for Spain's Invincible Armada. In poverty-stricken later life he settled down to write *Don Quixote*, called by some critics the greatest novel ever written. This masterpiece of Spanish literature relates with urbane grace and humor the adventures of a slightly addled knight who filled his noble head too full of the lore of chivalry, and of his groom, Sancho Panza. Sancho, a squat plebeian on a donkey, and Don Quixote, an emaciated knight on a tall, lean horse, go about Spain from one delightfully charming adventure to another. It is altogether necessary to read a few pages, almost any few pages, of this rollicking fantasy to appreciate the genius of Cervantes. Since all types and classes of people in all parts of Spain are lucidly portrayed, *Don Quixote* is a valuable historical source for descriptions of life in sixteenth-century Spain. But Cervantes does not stop with sixteenth-century Spain; he probes the depths of human nature. All of us are Don Quixotes — at least all of us who are not Sancho Panzas. Cervantes' more immediate purpose was to laugh out of existence what was left of medieval chivalry. He therefore did to feudal society what Erasmus and Rabelais were trying to do to medieval Christianity, and in much the same manner.

Lope de Vega, a contemporary of Ben Jonson, wrote a fabulous number of works in practically every known genre. His plays alone exceed in number those of any other writer, whether we accept the writer's own claim to twenty-two hundred or recognize only the seven-hundred-odd plays that can be accounted for today. Secular man, pictured in every conceivable dramatic situation, is the hero of the great Spanish playwright. Lope de Vega was an ardent Spanish nationalist; he sailed with the Invincible Armada. Like the Elizabethans and other Northern Renaissance writers, he thought that his country and the sixteenth and early seventeenth centuries were an exciting place and time to live.

Thus the writers of the Northern Renaissance had much in common. Their chief interests were contemporary man and the exciting, rapidly expanding material world around them. Their chief inspiration was the pagan classics of Greece and Rome. They were on the whole nationalistic, and wrote in the new national vernaculars. Although the Protestant and Roman Catholic reformations were tearing Western European society apart during the sixteenth and early seventeenth centuries, the men of letters were in the main either apathetic or, as in the case of Rabelais and Montaigne, hostile to theology in general and to Christianity in particular.

4. NORTHERN RENAISSANCE ART

Northern Renaissance art did not equal either the northern literature or the Italian art after which it was largely patterned. It was, however, noteworthy. The best Renaissance painters outside Italy were the Flemings (Belgians) and the Germans. The Van Eyck brothers, Hubert and Jan, lived in Ghent in the Flemish Netherlands in the early fifteenth century. Like Masaccio, their Italian contemporary, they brought to near completion the transition from medieval to Renaissance painting. Their greatest joint work is *Adoration of the Lamb*. Not the least of their contributions to painting was the development of oil as a medium. It was from them that Leonardo da Vinci learned to work in this medium, which he perfected in such masterworks as the *Mona Lisa* and the *Virgin of the Rocks*.

In sixteenth-century Germany, Albert Dürer of Nuremberg and Hans Holbein the Younger of Augsburg were the leading painters. Dürer was primarily a master craftsman of delicate and graceful line. Probably for this reason, his woodcuts and engravings are better than his paint-

The Van Eyck brothers, Hubert and Jan, of Ghent in the Netherlands, were early fifteenth century contemporaries of Masaccio. Among their contributions to the craft of painting was their introduction of the use of oil as a medium, which Leonardo da Vinci and the other great masters of the Italian High Renaissance carried to perfection. This painting, "The Virgin and Chancellor Rolin" by Jan Van Eyck, illustrates the clear, naturalistic perspective, the precision of line and detail, and the secular treatment of a religious theme that were characteristic of Northern Renaissance paintings. *Photo: Scala/EPA, Inc.*

ings, and in these media he is without peer in any age. Holbein was a skillful sketcher and woodcutter, but he made his greatest contributions in the field of portrait painting. He painted several portraits of Erasmus and illustrated Erasmus' *Praise of Folly* with pen-and-ink drawings. Many of his most productive years were spent in England in the employ of Henry VIII. Among his greatest portraits are those of Henry VIII, Edward VI, Mary Tudor, and Sir Thomas More. Both Dürer and Holbein were interested primarily in the contemporary things and people of the material world around them.

Renaissance artists did not produce many architectural monuments outside Italy, probably because commercial capitalism had not yet developed sufficiently in northern Europe to finance this more costly type of undertaking. The largest Renaissance structure outside Italy is the vast Escorial near Madrid, which Philip II of Spain built as a royal palace and mausoleum. Its rugged massiveness, rectangular shape, and horizontal lines typify the Renaissance style. Some of the best examples of Northern Renaissance architecture are the Renaissance wing of the Louvre in Paris, which is the world's largest and probably greatest art gallery, and some of the largest chateaux along France's Loire River. This

architecture was essentially derivative; the French Renaissance chateaux were really fortresses being played with.

The Netherlands were the music capital of the Western world during the Renaissance period. It was from the Flemings that the Italian Renaissance musicians, including Palestrina, derived much of their knowledge and inspiration (see p. 348).

5. PRINTING WITH MOVABLE TYPE

A major Renaissance contribution to the world of intellect and literature was the invention of printing with movable type. In ancient and medieval times manuscripts were written and copied in longhand on parchment or papyrus, a slow and costly process that greatly retarded the dissemination of knowledge. In the fourteenth century printing from carved wooden blocks came to Western Europe from China by way of the Moslem world and Spain. This process too was tedious, costly, and limited. Also from China came paper, made of various fibers, silk, cotton, or flax. Paper was a great improvement over parchment or papyrus for purposes of mass production. (Even the art of printing by movable type itself was a Chinese [Korean] invention, although this is not believed to have influenced its invention in the Western world.)

Johannes Gutenberg set up the first practical printing press using movable type in Europe at Mainz in western Germany. The Gutenberg forty-two-line Bible printed ca. 1456 is the earliest known book to be printed by the new process. The invention was an immediate success and spread quickly to all the other countries of Western Europe. It is estimated that by the end of the fifteenth century more than twenty-

This woodcut of the Four Horsemen from his Apocalypse series (ca. 1497–1498) shows Albert Dürer's skill as a master of delicate, graceful line. Note the artist's signature at center bottom. This Northern Renaissance artist exhibited a skill in his engraving and woodcutting that matched the painting genius of his Italian contemporaries, Leonardo and Michelangelo. *Photo: Marburg/Art Reference Bureau.*

An illuminated page from the Gutenberg Bible, after a facsimile. This forty-two-line Bible, printed by Johannes Gutenberg ca. 1456, is the earliest known book printed by movable type in the Western world. The craftsmanship exhibited by this illustration is remarkable. Gutenberg's invention launched a revolution in communications. *Photo: Rare Book Division, New York Public Library, Astor, Lennox and Tilden Foundations.*

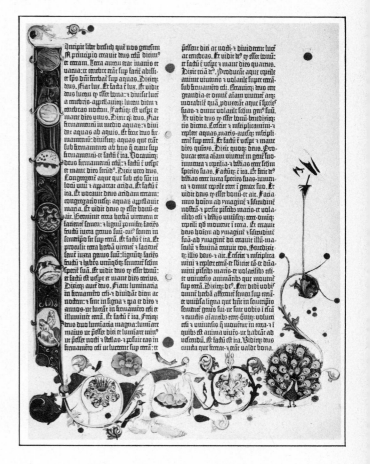

five thousand separate editions and nearly ten million individual books had been printed. To appreciate the significance of the new invention in making knowledge available to the masses, the reader need only reflect for a few moments on the probable cost of this book if it were copied in longhand on parchment or printed from seven hundred hand-carved wooden blocks at present-day wages. As a result of Gutenberg's invention and later improvements few people in the Western world today can excuse their ignorance of good literature on the grounds that it is unavailable.

6. SIGNIFICANCE OF THE RENAISSANCE IN HISTORY

In retrospect, then, it is apparent that the Renaissance was a transition from the God-centered civilization of the Middle Ages to the man-centered, secular civilization of the modern period. In some measure it was a rebirth of the classical civilization of pagan Greece and Rome, but it was not merely that. There was much in the Renaissance that was fresh and original. The rediscovery of the brilliant culture of antiquity and the rising secular spirit with its confidence in man, versatility, egotism, materialism, and individuality combined to produce some of the most beautiful art and literature the world has ever known. In addition, the foundations were laid for the later rise of science. The Renaissance was also a serious challenge to Christianity, directly in Italy and somewhat indirectly in northern Europe. That it did not destroy or palsy Christianity as a dynamic force in Western civilization is due in some measure to the Protestant and Roman Catholic reformations, which revitalized Christianity. To these great movements, which paralleled the Renaissance in its later stages and which were in part provoked by it, we must now turn.

Suggested Reading

General
See items at end of previous chapter.
*J. H. Randall, *The Making of the Modern Mind* (Columbia). Widely used study. Science is the hero, Christianity the villain.

Northern Humanism
E. H. Harbison, *The Christian Scholar in the Age of the Reformation* (1956). By a leading scholar in the field.
*J. Huizinga, *Erasmus and the Age of the Reformation* (Torch). Probably best single volume on Erasmus.

Literature
*H. O. Taylor, *Thought and Expression in the Sixteenth Century* (Collier). Now in five handy volumes, the most appropriate of which for this chapter are *The English Mind* and *The French Mind*.

Art and Painting
O. Benesch, *The Art of the Renaissance in Northern Europe: Its Relation to the Contemporary Spiritual and Intellectual Movements* (1945).
P. Butler, *The Origin of Printing in Europe* (1940).

Sources
*Erasmus, *The Praise of Folly* (Ann Arbor).
*T. More, *Utopia* (Appleton).
*F. Rabelais, *Gargantua and Pantagruel* (Penguin).
*M. de Montaigne, *Autobiography* (Vintage).
*M. de Cervantes, *Don Quixote* (Modern Library).
*G. T. Matthews (ed.), *News and Rumor in Renaissance Europe* (Capricorn). A collection of reports of the agents of the Fugger bankers from all over Western Europe.

30

THE PROTESTANT REFORMATION

The Protestant and Roman Catholic reformations, which split Western Europe into two hostile religious camps, virtually completed the destruction of the medieval synthesis, for this synthesis had centered on the Church. (Russia and the Balkans with their Orthodox Church had never been a part of this synthesis.) The Protestant Reformation had strong political, economic, and intellectual overtones; nevertheless, it was primarily a religious movement. Western Europeans of the sixteenth century were intensely interested in religion (even the humanists, relatively few in number, were interested in changing the traditional Christian religion). The Church was still at the very center of their lives, and most of the unlettered masses knew a good deal about matters of doctrine and ritual. The leaders of both the Protestant and the Roman Catholic reformations were certainly men whose lives were dedicated to religion.

1. BACKGROUND

In the Late Middle Ages there developed within the ranks of the Roman Catholic Church a growing dissatisfaction with some of its fundamental doctrines (see pp. 310–312). Some had come to believe that the Roman Catholic Church had departed so far from the spirit and practices of the apostles and early fathers that it could no longer be considered God's appointed custodian of the Christian religion. They began to define *The Church* to mean the sum total of all those who put their faith in Christ, not any one specific institution.[1] The Scriptures alone, not the decisions and traditions of an organized church, became for these reformers the sole authoritative source for Christian dogma. Their growing conception of the Christian religion as a direct relationship between man and God tended to lessen the importance of the professional clergy and the sacraments of the Roman Catholic Church. They spoke of the priesthood of all believers. These ideas the reformers believed to be in harmony with those of St. Augustine and the early Church, as well as with those to be found in the Scriptures. They clashed sharply, however, with the beliefs and practices of the Roman Catholic hierarchy of the Late Middle Ages. This doc-

---

[1] The reformers disputed the Petrine doctrine upon which the popes based much of their claim to headship over the Christian Church. The popes claimed that, as bishops of Rome, they inherited the authority of St. Peter, the first bishop of Rome, whom Christ designated to head his Church. ("... thou art Peter and upon this rock I will build my church ...," Matthew, 16:18.) The reformers maintained that in the original Greek the word for Peter is *petros*, meaning an individual stone, and that the word for rock is *petra*, meaning a large body of stone. Therefore, they assert, Christ did not mean to say that he would found his Church upon Peter, but upon the faith that Christ was the son of the living God, which Peter had just affirmed.

by one man of more offices than he could adequately serve (pluralism)—all were subjects of loud and growing complaint. Many of the higher clergy, even the popes, became infected with the secular spirit of the Renaissance. Often they displayed greater interest in humanistic pleasures and pursuits than in feeding their flocks. Eventually the Church hierarchy came to realize the seriousness of these abuses and took drastic steps to remedy them, but not until much of Western Christendom had left the Roman fold.

Politically the rise of national states and of local loyalty to them clashed with the international character of the Church. The national monarchs became increasingly jealous of the pope's claims over their subjects, and in many cases supported native Protestant leaders and movements.

Economic motivation undoubtedly played a significant part. Church taxes drained away to Rome much wealth from the local economy. The rich tax-exempt lands of the Church all over Western Europe excited a great deal of envy. The Church's opposition to usury and its close alliance with the landed aristocracy antagonized the rising capitalistic classes.

Finally, the intellectual activities of the humanists weakened the hold of the Church on many minds. Erasmus and other humanists heaped ridicule on what they considered to be the superstitious beliefs of the Church. Their scholarly translations and critical textual studies exposed errors in the sacred documents upon which the Church based its claims. It must not be assumed, however, that the Protestants were more humanistic than the Roman Catholics. As a matter of fact, the sixteenth-century humanists found the Protestant leaders even more dogmatic and uncongenial than the Roman Catholic hierarchy. However, the humanists unwittingly

trinal split within the ranks of organized Western Christendom was the most fundamental of all the causes of the Reformation.

Other factors, however, contributed to the break within the Roman Catholic Church. Quite apart from matters of doctrine, many abuses had arisen in the Church during the fourteenth and fifteenth centuries when the Church was torn by the Babylonian Captivity, the Great Schism, and the struggles between the popes and the councils (see pp. 307–309). Ignorance and worldliness of the clergy, the sale of Church offices and services (simony), the favoring of relatives for lucrative Church offices (nepotism), the holding helped to bring about the Reformation by weakening the position of the Church.

As early as the fourteenth century such reformers as John Wycliffe in England and John Huss in Bohemia had voiced their protests against the Church. By the opening of the sixteenth century the religious, political, economic, and intellectual opposition to the Church had reached explosive proportions. All that was needed for revolt was a dynamic personality to lead it and an incident to set it off.

2. LUTHERANISM

The Protestant Reformation was composed of four major distinct but related movements— Lutheranism, Calvinism, Anglicanism, and Anabaptism. From these four main stems have sprung the hundreds of Protestant denominations that exist today. The Lutheran revolt was first in point of time.

Martin Luther (1483–1546) was the son of an ambitious ex-peasant miner of central Germany. At a boarding school run by the pietistic Brethren of the Common Life he, like his contemporary Erasmus, was introduced to a type of Christianity that emphasized simple piety rather than dogma and ritual. Later at Erfurt University he received a traditional liberal arts education. He was an excellent student. However, upon the completion of his undergraduate course and just as he was ready to begin study of the law, he suddenly renounced the world and entered an Augustinian monastery. This decision was no passing whim. As a child, Luther had been much concerned over the fate of his soul, and throughout his university days, his religious yearning had increased.

But the young friar found no satisfaction in the monastic life of the sixteenth-century Church. He scourged himself, donned beggar's garb, and went out among his former fellow students with sunken cheeks and gleaming, feverish eyes. It was not until, on the advice of a perceptive supervisor of his monastic order, he began to read the writings of St. Augustine and St. Paul that Brother Martin found the answer to his lifelong quest. On reading in Paul's Letter to the Romans (1:17) "the just shall live by faith,"

he concluded that here was the true means of salvation—not good works, sacraments, and rituals, but simple faith in Christ. Over a period of years he developed a theology based on this fundamental concept. Gradually he regained his old radiance and energy.

In the meantime Luther had become a member of the faculty of the newly founded University of Wittenberg in Saxony, where he was to remain for the rest of his life. For several years he taught philosophy and theology, quite unaware that his belief in salvation by faith alone was in fundamental conflict with the dogma of his church. Students flocked from afar to listen to him.

One day a friar named John Tetzel came into the vicinity of Wittenberg selling indulgences. According to the doctrine of indulgences, which had grown up in the Late Middle Ages, Christ and the saints, by their good works while on earth, had accumulated in heaven a treasury of excess merit which the pope could apply to the credit of penitent sinners, thereby shortening for them or their loved ones their stay in purgatory. By the opening of the sixteenth century the dispensing of this extra-sacramental means of grace had become hardly more than a money-making venture. Huge sums, taken from the credulous all over Europe, were brought to Rome for the construction of St. Peter's or for other costly papal projects.

On October 31, 1517, Martin Luther posted on the church door in Wittenberg ninety-five theses or propositions concerning the doctrine of indulgences, which he proposed to be debated publicly. It did not occur to him that this event would mark the beginning of an upheaval to subside only after nearly half of Western Christendom had broken away from the Roman Catholic Church. He was astonished and at first dismayed to find himself suddenly the national hero of all the various disgruntled elements throughout Germany. When, however, two years later in a public debate at Leipzig Luther finally realized that his position was hopelessly at odds with that of the Church, he lost no time in making the break clean. He published a series of pamphlets in which he violently denounced the pope and his organization, and called upon the German princes to seize the property of the Church and make themselves the heads of the Christian Church in Germany.

A papal bull of excommunication (which Luther publicly burned) soon followed. A few months later Emperor Charles V called the troublesome monk to appear before the Diet of the Holy Roman Empire at Worms (1521). There Luther boldly refused to recant and was outlawed by the highest civil authority in Germany. Although Luther remained under this death sentence with a price on his head for the rest of his life, he was protected by his prince, the elector of Saxony, and by German public opinion.

Martin Luther often referred to himself as "a peasant, the son of a peasant." This was not exactly true. His father, though of peasant stock, was an ambitious miner who moved into the ranks of the bourgeoisie. Luther's heavy features, so ably depicted here by Cranach, belie the brilliant mind and personal force of one of the great leaders and movers of history. *Photo: Culver Pictures*

By this time all Germany was in religious and social turmoil. Nearly everyone with a grievance of any kind was looking to Luther for leadership. Religious zealots, many of them calling themselves Anabaptists, began preaching individualistic and more radical doctrines in his name, and he found it necessary to repudiate them. Taking a somewhat more conservative stand, he decided that only those features of the Roman Catholic Church that were opposed to the Scriptures ought to be rejected. In the early stages of the conflict Erasmus and many other humanists thought they saw in Luther a kindred spirit, but this alliance was short-lived. Erasmus soon found Luther to be as dogmatic and uncompromising in matters of doctrine as the Roman Catholic theologians, if not more so. Erasmus was primarily interested in matters of the intellect, and Luther in those of religious faith. Erasmus found it more convenient and comfortable to remain in the Roman Church, which he had done so much to discredit. He and Luther ended their days hurling recriminations at each other.

Luther also found it necessary to break with a group of rebellious peasants in south Germany. The condition of the peasants was bad and growing worse. The landed aristocracy, themselves losing ground to the rising middle classes, were depriving their peasants of long-established manorial rights such as free use of meadows and woodlands. In 1524 widespread disturbances broke out in southwestern Germany. The next year the peasants published a list of moderate demands; when these were refused, the peasants rebelled in the name of Luther, whom they believed to be against all oppressive authority. Luther, although sympathetic, pleaded with them to refrain from violence. This the peasants refused to do, and when they went on a bloody rampage, killing and burning in Luther's name, he repudiated them and called on the civil authorities to suppress the revolt by force. The alarmed authorities did so with a vengeance.

In the end both sides blamed Luther for the revolt and its painful results. South Germany has remained a Roman Catholic stronghold to this day. Luther was in favor of peaceful social reform, but he believed that successful reform depended upon a change of heart. In short, the first Protestant leader found it necessary quite early in the revolt to make it clear that Protestant Christianity was neither a humanistic philosophy nor a materialistic social reform movement, nor yet a free-for-all for everyone to believe and preach anything he chose.

Luther's new religion, as he eventually formulated it, made the Scriptures the sole authoritative source of Christian dogma. That all might have access to the Bible, he translated it into German.[2] He conceived of the Church as the whole body of believers in Christ, not the Roman Catholic Church or any other specific organization. He abolished the hierarchy of pope, cardinals, and bishops, and reduced the importance of the clergy in general, proclaiming the priesthood of all believers. He made the various secular rulers the heads of the Christian Church in their territories. He abolished monasteries and the celibacy of the clergy. Luther himself married an ex-nun. The ritual of worship was made much simpler. Of the seven sacraments of the Roman Catholic Church, Luther kept only the two he found mentioned as sacraments in the Bible: baptism and the eucharist. He rejected the Roman Catholic doctrine known as transubstantiation.[3] Luther interpreted the Scriptural passages that refer to the Holy Eucharist, or Lord's Supper, to mean that during the administration of the sacrament Christ's body somehow enters into the bread and the wine, but the bread and wine remain. He denied the Roman Catholic belief that a sacrifice is involved.

The Emperor Charles V was greatly distressed by this religious revolution, which further divided his scattered and chaotic empire. Although determined to suppress the Protestants,

he was too busy with his wars against the French and the Turks to make much headway. Nine years of indecisive fighting between the Roman Catholics under Charles V and the Protestants ended in 1555 with the compromise Peace of Augsburg. Each of the more than three hundred German princes was left free to choose between Lutheranism and Roman Catholicism; his subjects were to abide by his choice. Luther himself died in 1546, just before the fighting began. Lutheranism triumphed in the northern half of Germany and soon spread to Denmark, Norway, Sweden, and most of the Baltic provinces (now Latvia, Estonia, and Finland), which were then under Swedish control. In addition, Lutheranism heavily influenced all later Protestant movements.

3. CALVINISM

Calvin shares with Luther the position of first importance in the founding of Protestant Christianity. Born in France in 1509, John Calvin was twenty-six years younger than Luther. He was the son of a lawyer who was secretary to the bishop of Noyon in Picardy. Young Calvin had a radiant personality that made for warm friendships. Long association with aristocratic friends probably accounts for his elegant manners. His father sent him first to the University of Paris for a thorough grounding in the humanities and theology, and then to the best law schools in France, where Calvin ruined his health by overwork. Upon finishing his legal training, he entered upon a humanistic literary career and quickly showed signs of becoming a second Erasmus. Suddenly at the age of twenty-four, he was converted to Protestant Christianity, probably as a result of reading Luther.

The zealous young reformer soon aroused the ire of Roman Catholic authorities in France and of the French government, and was forced to flee for his life. Calvin then spent the next two years in hiding writing the first edition of *The Institutes of the Christian Religion*. Published in Basel, Switzerland, when Calvin was only twenty-six years of age, this theological treatise was to become the most influential writing in the his-

---

[2] Luther's translation was in such excellent German that it had great influence on the standardization of the modern literary German language.

[3] The New Catholic Dictionary defines transubstantiation as "the marvellous and singular changing of the entire substance of the bread into the entire substance of the Body of Christ and of the entire substance of the wine into His Blood."

This portrait of Calvin as a young man by an unknown painter reveals his intellectual keenness and his elegant bearing. Calvin was an uncompromising zealot for the Protestant faith. His enemies thought him a kill-joy and a tyrant—a "Protestant pope." His friends and followers considered him the most gentle and inspiring of men. *Photo: Société du Musée Historique de la Réformation, Genéve*

tory of Protestantism. Its precise and forceful logic reveals not only the fine legal training of the author, but also one of the most powerful intellects in history. Its lucid and facile style had much the same influence on the formulation of modern literary French that Luther's translation of the Bible had on German. It immediately made Calvin an important name in literary and theological circles.

Probably Calvin's most significant contribution to Christian theology is his sublime concept of the majesty of God. To the author of the *Institutes*, the Divine Creator is so majestic and awe-inspiring and man so insignificant by comparison that salvation by election, or *predestination*, as it is more often called, seems to follow logically. According to Calvin, God in the beginning planned the whole universe to the end of time, For unfathomable reasons of his own, God selected those human beings who would be saved and those who would be damned. He planted in the minds of the elect a saving faith in Christ and an insatiable desire to live the Christian life and to bring about the Kingdom of God on earth. In no other way could man acquire this faith and this desire. Calvin based this doctrine upon the Scriptures (particularly the writings of St. Paul), which he considered to be the sole authoritative source for Christian theology. St. Augustine, the most influential of the early Church fathers, and Luther also believed in salvation by election, but neither they nor anyone else had ever spelled out the doctrine so precisely.

Shortly after the publication of the *Institutes*, Calvin went to Geneva. That city, like most of the rest of Switzerland, was in the throes of religious and political revolt brought on partly by the influence of Luther and the native Swiss reformer, Ulrich Zwingli (1484–1531). The Protestant leaders in Geneva immediately recognized in Calvin a natural leader and with difficulty persuaded the gifted but modest young man to remain there and make Geneva a model city of God on earth. Calvin, by sheer force of personality and intellect, soon rose to a position of virtual dictatorship over the city. He brought the town council, which was remarkably democratic and representative for the sixteenth century, under the dominance of a consistory composed of Protestant pastors and laymen. In other words, Geneva became a theocracy. Under Calvin's leadership, the town council and the consistory set up a strict system of blue laws. Churchgoing was compulsory. Dancing, card-playing, theater-going, drinking, gambling, and swearing—all were forbidden. Enforcement was vigorous, and penalties severe, even for the sixteenth century. The most famous penalty was the burning of Michael Servetus, an eccentric amateur scientist and theologian whom the Roman Catholic Church had already condemned to death for heresy.[4] Servetus escaped his Catho-

---

[4] The most serious of Servetus' heretical views was his denial of the Trinity, which cast doubt on the divinity of Christ.

lic persecutors and came to Geneva for the purpose of destroying Calvin and his works. Calvin had warned him to stay away on pain of death; when Servetus arrived, he was seized, tried, convicted, and burned at the stake.

A strong minority in Geneva had no use for Calvin, his theology, or his blue laws. To them Calvin was a kill-joy, a bigot, and a tyrant, a verdict that has found its way into many textbooks. The majority of the Genevans, on the other hand, practically worshiped their leader; they considered him the most brilliant, inspiring, sympathetic, kindly, and gentle of men. Protestant Christians came from many countries to sit at the feet of Calvin and to study at the University of Geneva, which he founded. John Knox, who came from Scotland to study under Calvin, called the Genevan theocracy "the most perfect school of life that was ever on earth since the days of the apostles."

Calvinist ritual was even simpler than that of the Lutherans. The worship service consisted of preaching, praying, and psalm-singing. Like Luther, Calvin retained only two of the seven sacraments — baptism and the Holy Eucharist, or Lord's Supper. But to Calvin, Christ was present only in spirit in the bread and wine, and only for the elect. Calvin patterned his system of church government after that of the very earliest church as described in the Bible (Acts of the Apostles). The local churches were governed by laymen called *elders* who were elected by the congregations. A measure of unity in faith and practices was maintained by means of a hierarchy of representative assemblies.

Calvinism became dominant in most of Switzerland (Swiss Reformed), the Dutch Netherlands (Dutch Reformed), Scotland (Presbyterian), and the German Palatinate. It also had a strong minority following in England (the Puritans), and a smaller but vigorous following in France (the Huguenots), Bohemia, Hungary, and Poland. The Calvinists played an important part in the founding of the United States, particularly the Puritans in New England, the Dutch Reformed in New York, and the Scotch-Irish Presbyterians along the frontiers of all the original states. Such well-known denominations in present-day America as the Congregationalists, the Presbyterians, and the Baptists are Calvinist in

origin. The Calvinists were the most zealous and evangelical of all the major early Protestant groups. In later years they made a strong appeal to the rising middle classes. Wherever they were found, they were a powerful influence for the growth of democracy and for public education.

4. ANGLICANISM

The occasion, though not the cause, of the beginning of the Reformation in England was the desire of Henry VIII (1509–1547) for a male heir. Catherine of Aragon, to whom he had been married for eighteen years, had given him only a daughter, Mary. When it became apparent that Catherine would have no more children, Henry decided to ask the pope to annul the marriage. The pope, however, was in no position to grant the annulment. Catherine was the aunt of the Emperor Charles V, whose troops were at that very moment in control of the city of Rome. When Henry finally realized the pope was not going to accommodate him, he took matters into his own hands. At his bidding a subservient Parliament passed the Act of Supremacy, making the king of England, not the pope, head of the Church in England. Later the monasteries, strongholds of papal influence, were dissolved. Meanwhile, Thomas Cranmer, whom Henry made archbishop of Canterbury, had arranged the annulment, and Henry had married Anne Boleyn. (He was to marry six times in all.) Henry was, of course, excommunicated by the pope.

But Henry VIII was no Protestant. In the days before the annulment controversy the pope had given him the title "Defender of the Faith" for his anti-Lutheran writings. Now he had Parliament pass the Six Articles reaffirming the Catholic position on all controversial doctrinal points except that of papal supremacy. Protestants, on the one hand, and Roman Catholics who refused to acknowledge the headship of Henry VIII in place of the pope, were persecuted with equal severity. Death was the penalty for both.

It was during the reign of Henry VIII's young son, Edward VI (1547–1553), that the Anglican Church first became Protestant. Archbishop Cranmer drew up a *Book of Common Prayer* and Forty-two Articles of faith that were definitely Calvinist in flavor. Edward VI was succeeded by his elder sister, Mary (1553–1558), who was the daugher of Catherine of Aragon and a devout Roman Catholic. Mary's ambition was to restore her kingdom to the Roman Catholic fold. Her first step was to marry her cousin, Philip II of Spain, the most powerful champion of resurgent Roman Catholicism in all Europe. Next she asked and received papal forgiveness for her wayward people. Finally, "Bloody Mary" burned at the stake some three hundred Protestants, including Archbishop Cranmer. But Mary's marriage to a man soon to be king of England's most dangerous rival and her persecutions were extremely unpopular in England; in the long run her policies hurt rather than helped the Roman Catholic cause there.

Elizabeth I (1558–1603), the Protestant daughter of Anne Boleyn, followed Mary on the English throne. This high-spirited, cynical, and politically minded queen found theology tiresome. Her chief interest was to find a satisfactory compromise that would unify her people. During the course of her long reign the Anglican Church became definitely, but conservatively, Protestant. Cranmer's *Book of Common Prayer* was readopted with slight alterations. The Forty-two Articles were changed to the Thirty-nine. Some of the more controversial doctrinal points that seemed to prevent the various Protestant sects from uniting were reworded. Although celibacy of the clergy was abandoned, the episcopal system (government of the church by bishops) was retained. A rather elaborate ritual was adopted. Two of the sacraments, baptism and the eucharist, were retained.

Although the great majority of the English people appeared to have accepted Elizabeth's compromise settlement, two groups remained dissatisfied. An extreme Calvinist element sought to "purify" the Anglican Church of all remaining traces of Roman Catholicism. These Puritans were to increase in strength until under Oliver Cromwell's leadership in the next century they gained temporary control of the country. The Roman Catholic minority, on the other hand, lost steadily in numbers. The support that some Roman Catholics gave to Philip II's attempt to conquer England and to the effort of Mary, Queen of Scots (a Roman Catholic) to overthrow

Elizabeth (see Chapter 31) tainted all of them with the suspicion of treason and played into Elizabeth's hands. By the end of her reign, England was one of the Protestant countries of Europe.

5. THE ANABAPTISTS

Some reformers believed that Luther, Calvin, and the Anglican leaders had not gone far enough. They would break more sharply with all the existing institutions of the early sixteenth century — political, economic, and social as well as religious. Hence the term *radical* is often applied to them. Since these "radicals" were highly individualistic in their approach to religion, it is difficult to generalize about the many sects with their widely differing views and points of emphasis. One of the most commonly held beliefs was their opposition to infant baptism. The true Christian, they believed, was one who was "born again" and baptized as an adult according to Scripture. Those who had been baptized as infants must be rebaptized. Anabaptism means *re*baptism. The Anabaptists believed that the true church of Christ on earth is a gathered church composed only of born-again Christians (in contrast with the territorial or state churches of the Roman Catholics, Lutherans, Calvinists, and Anglicans which of necessity contain many who are not genuine Christians). The Anabaptists attempted to live lives of uncompromising holiness as dictated by the Bible or by the Holy Spirit speaking directly to each individual. All human institutions are evil. These sects refused to recognize or participate in civil government, take oaths of allegiance, recognize titles, or serve in armed forces. Some practiced a shared or communistic economy. Most of them were poor. They were feared and cruelly persecuted, of course, by all organized secular society, and by Roman Catholics, Lutherans, Calvinists, and Anglicans alike.

A few of the early Anabaptist leaders were violent activists, such as Thomas Müntzer, who inflamed the peasant rebels of southwest Germany, and John of Leyden, who set up a violent dictatorship in Münster in northwest Germany. This bizarre "heavenly Jerusalem" held out for

What Is the Meaning of the Protestant Reformation?

Most historians agree that the breakup of the all-powerful medieval Church was probably the most significant factor in bringing the Middle Ages to an end and that the Reformation was, therefore, of major importance in the rise of modern Western civilization. But there the agreement ends. Was the Protestant Reformation spiritual, as its leaders firmly believed, or was it something else — intellectual, political, economic? As the modern Western world has become more and more secular, so have interpretations of the Reformation.

The historians of the Enlightenment of the eighteenth century tended to think of the Protestant Reformation as the religious aspect of the Renaissance. They liked to believe that the early Protestants were seeking intellectual freedom and individualism in their search for theological truth. Whatever might be said about the trend of Protestantism in later centuries, this interpretation of early Protestantism, with the possible exception of certain minor sects, is certainly based upon faulty information. It did not take Erasmus very long to discover that the early Protestant leaders were more dogmatic and less compatible with his humanistic approach to Christianity than was the Roman Catholic hierarchy.

From the mid-nineteenth century to the present day, many historians have thought of the Protestant Reformation in political terms. They have viewed the various religious movements of the sixteenth century as adjuncts of nationalism. They believe it to be significant that the Protestant Reformation began in Germany, where there was no strong central government to protect the German people from exploitation by the Italian papacy. Luther strongly and openly appealed to German nationalism against Rome, and there can be little doubt that his nationalistic appeal gained many followers. By contrast, the strong rulers of France and Spain were able to extract such concessions from the pope as to create what amounted to a Gallican Church and Spanish Catholic Church, while successfully withstanding the Protestant challenge. The various Calvinistic churches were generally set up along national lines, such as the Swiss, Dutch, German, and Scottish Reformed churches. And of course the Anglican Church was a national church. All this was in striking contrast to the medieval Church, which had encompassed all of Western and Central Europe.

Another popular twentieth-century interpretation has been that of the Freudian psychologists, who have used the theories of Freud to analyze the personalities of the early Protestant leaders, particularly Luther. The founder of this school of historical interpretation is Eric Erickson, who strives mightily in his *Young Man Luther* (1958) to prove that Luther's revolutionary theology as well as his actions were the result of his adolescent striving for identity against a domineering father. Erickson's numerous followers have attempted to employ the same technique to explain the ideas and actions of many other historical figures and to aid the understanding of history in general.

Most popular of the secular interpretations of the Protestant Reformation from the late nineteenth century to the present has been the economic interpretation. Those who emphasize this line of thought point out the hunger for the rich lands held by the Roman Church, the resentment over the tax exemption of these lands and over the draining away of money to Rome, and the opposition of the commercial class to the Church's ban on usury. From this viewpoint, Protestantism seemed to promise an end to all these "abuses." The ultimate in economic approaches to explaining the Reformation is that of the Marxists, who regard all religion as the "opiate of the people"—a trick of the "haves" to keep the "have nots" quiet and obedient.

A widely accepted economic interpretation of the Reformation is that of Max Weber, a German sociologist who was strongly influenced by Karl Marx. The Weber thesis was first published in 1904–1905 in two articles entitled "The Protestant Ethic and the Spirit of Capitalism." Weber believed that Protestantism, particularly Calvinism, contributed heavily to the rise of capitalism, and that the early Protestants were economically motivated. Protestants, for instance, removed the ban on usury, making possible unlimited profits. The doctrine of salvation by election encouraged its believers to work hard, each in his appointed calling, for the glory of God and for the assurance that he is one of the elect. This hard work, coupled with the asceticism Calvin preached, resulted in growing surpluses which were reinvested in capitalistic enterprises. Weber also offers as evidence the capitalistic successes of the Calvinistic Dutch and Swiss and the Puritans of England and New England. Weber's thesis has won the support of thousands of readers.

His critics, however, have demonstrated his surprising unfamiliarity with the actual writings of the early Protestants. Calvin devoted only 50 out of some 30,000 pages of his published writings to economic matters; Luther devoted about twice as many pages to this topic out of a similar total. Both Calvin and Luther repeatedly warned against the danger of riches and admonished lenders not to take advantage of the poor and distressed. Nowhere did they consider prosperity as a sign of election. The voluminous writings of the seventeenth-century English Puritans continue in a similar vein. Critics of Weber point out that capitalism is much older than Calvinism, and wonder why Weber did not cite the early modern commercial prosperity of Roman Catholic northern Italy, southern and western Germany, or the Belgian Netherlands, or the lack of capitalistic activity in Calvinistic Scotland. Weber's most influential disciple was R. H. Tawney, a British economic historian active in Labour party politics. His *Religion and the Rise of Capitalism*, published in 1926, reveals a great deal more knowledge of history than does Weber, and more subtlety and sophistication, but adheres essentially to the Weber thesis.

It would appear that writers and readers of history tend to impute their own motives to the makers of history—to read the prevailing spirit of their own times into the spirit of earlier epochs. This is particularly true in the field of religious history, where it is impossible to know the hearts of the proclaimers of the various faiths. Historians very frequently reveal their own times more than the times of the period about which they write.

more than a year against besieging Lutheran and Roman Catholic armies. The leaders were then tortured to death and their bodies hung in iron baskets from a church tower for three hundred and fifty years. But the great majority of the Anabaptist leaders were pious and gentle—in fact, pacifists. Conrad Grebel, the first prominent Anabaptist leader, was a humanist from an upper class family of Zurich, Switzerland. Probably the most successful and influential of all the Anabaptist leaders was the convert Menno Simons, a gentle former Roman Catholic priest from the Dutch Netherlands. His followers, the Mennonites, spread throughout much of Western Europe and later the United States. Also in the Anabaptist tradition was the Society of Friends, commonly known as Quakers. Founded by George Fox in England in the mid-seventeenth century, this pietistic and pacifistic sect has spread to many parts of the world. It has furnished two presidents of the United States.

6. SUMMARY

By the end of the third quarter of the sixteenth century, then, Protestantism had triumphed in the northern half of the Germanies, in Scandinavia, in most of the Baltic provinces, in most of Switzerland, in the Dutch Netherlands, Scotland, and England. In addition, it had gained a strong minority following in France, Poland, Bohemia, and Hungary. And, no matter how much the various Protestant denominations might disagree among themselves on minor details, they presented a solid front against the Roman Catholics. All Protestants rejected papal supremacy, the divine sanction of the Roman Church, the celibacy and indelible character of the priesthood, monasticism, and such other characteristic Roman Catholic doctrines as purgatory, transubstantiation, invocation of saints, and veneration of relics. These doctrinal differences between the Protestants and the Roman Catholics were fundamental, and no middle ground for a compromise was ever found. Nor was the Roman Church, notwithstanding its strong comeback, ever able to reconquer the territories in which the Protestants had gained a definite majority. The Reformation split Western Christendom into two sharply defined and hostile camps. In place of the two major divisions into which Christianity had been separated since the early Middle Ages (Eastern Orthodox and Roman Catholic), there were now three.

Suggested Reading

General

*G. R. Elton, *Reformation Europe, 1517–1559* (Torch). Probably the best single volume on the Reformation. Does not include the English Reformation.

H. J. Grimm, *The Reformation Era*, 2nd ed. (1973). Sound and readable.

Lutheranism

*R. H. Bainton, *Here I Stand: A Life of Martin Luther* (Mentor). Combines excellent scholarship with a journalistic style.

Calvinism

*W. Walker, *John Calvin, the Organizer of Reformed Protestantism* (Schocken). Probably still the best single-volume biography of Calvin.

*J. T. McNeil, *The History and Character of Calvinism* (Oxford). By a leading authority.

Anglicanism

*A. G. Dickens, *The English Reformation* (Schocken). Best survey.

*J. J. Scarisbrick, *Henry VIII* (University of California). Best biography.

*J. E. Neale, *Queen Elizabeth I* (Anchor). By a leading authority.

The Anabaptists

F. H. Littell, *The Anabaptist View of the Church* (1952). An excellent brief account.

Sources

*R. H. Bainton, *The Age of the Reformation* (Anvil). A handy selection of excerpts from the writings of important Reformation figures.

*H. E. Bettenson, *Documents of the Christian Church* (Oxford). Another useful selection.

31

THE ROMAN CATHOLIC REFORMATION

The loss of almost half of Western Christendom by the Roman Catholic Church and the threatened loss of the rest touched off a reform movement within the Church. By the middle of the sixteenth century the Roman Catholic reform movement was well under way. The Church was revitalized, and a counteroffensive was launched against the Protestants—one that not only prevented their further encroachment on the Roman Catholic domain, but pushed them back a bit.

1. THE RISE OF A REFORM MOVEMENT

Long before the revolt of Luther and Calvin, there had been a demand for reform by many loyal Roman Catholics. In Spain, around the turn of the sixteenth century, Cardinal Ximenes had forestalled a possible protest movement by enforcing strict discipline upon the clergy and waging bitter warfare against heresy. However, in the rest of Western Christendom, the secular interests of the Renaissance popes and prelates and the popes' fears that a reform council might again challenge the absolute authority of the Holy See prevented effective action. Now, with area after area becoming Protestant, countermeasures of a rather drastic nature became imperative. There were two schools of thought concerning the proper course of action. One, led by the liberal Cardinal Contarini of Venice, advocated compromise and conciliation. Contarini eventually went so far as to meet with Melanchthon, a close friend of Luther and an important figure in the Lutheran revolt, in earnest

quest of an acceptable compromise. They were unsuccessful; the two religions appeared to be incompatible. The other school of thought was led by the conservative Cardinal Caraffa of Naples. Caraffa believed that many corrupt practices in the Church needed to be reformed, but that no compromise whatever should be made in the dogma. He believed that the Protestants were heretics and could reunite with the Roman Catholic Church only by recanting and submitting to the pope. This is the school of thought that triumphed, and Caraffa became Pope Paul IV. The upshot of this line of thinking was the calling of a Church council at Trent, an imperial city in northern Italy.

2. THE COUNCIL OF TRENT

The Council of Trent, which was in session off and on for eighteen years from 1545 to 1563, was probably the most important council in the history of the Roman Catholic Church. The popes skillfully controlled its membership and voting procedure. The ultimate decisions of the council were in two categories: dogmatic and reformatory. In matters of faith or dogma, all the traditional doctrines of the Church were reaffirmed and redefined, especially controversial ones such as the sacraments, transubstantiation, auricular confession, celibacy of the clergy, monasticism, purgatory, invocation of the saints, veneration of relics, and indulgences. The dogmatic canons and decrees of the council concluded: "Anathema to [accursed be] all heretics! Anathema! Anathema! Anathema!" The council also took stern measures to stop corrupt practices. Simony, nepotism, pluralism, and immorality and ignorance among the clergy were condemned. Schools for the education of the clergy were called for. Bishops were admonished to exercise closer supervision and discipline over the lower clergy. To implement its canons and decrees, the council endorsed the Inquisition, which had recently been set up in Rome to combat heresy, and inaugurated the Index of Forbidden Books to prevent the reading of heretical literature except by authorized persons. Both instruments were placed under papal control and supervision. The Index, periodically revised, proved to be particularly effective. Thus the Roman Catholic Church at last spoke out, selected its weapons, and girded itself for more effective battle against the Protestants. At its service were the militant new Jesuit order and the greatest military power of the sixteenth century, Philip II's Spain.

3. THE SOCIETY OF JESUS

The founder of the Society of Jesus, Ignatius Loyola (1491–1556), was a member of the Spanish lesser nobility, and until early middle life was an obscure and ignorant soldier. In a battle with the French his leg was crushed by a cannon ball. Without benefit of anesthetic, he had it set and, when it grew crooked, twice broken and reset. He remained a cripple for the rest of his life. During the months of agony and convalescence Loyola read lives of the Christian saints and underwent a deep spiritual conversion. He determined to devote his tremendous energies and latent talents to the service of the Roman Catholic Church — to become a soldier of Christ, the Virgin Mary, and the pope. Since his first efforts only revealed his ignorance and got him into trouble with the clerical authorities, he set off for the University of Paris to begin his education. Loyola was, however, not a scholar or theologian, but a man of action. He soon began to attract a band of followers, with whom he organized the Society of Jesus.

The Jesuit Order, as the Society of Jesus is commonly known, was founded along military lines. A general, elected for life and residing in Rome, issues orders that are transmitted through a hierarchy of officials to the rank and file. Absolute and unquestioning obedience is the first requirement. Loyola admonished his followers, ". . . if she [the Church] shall have defined anything to be black which to our eyes appears to be white, we ought in like manner to pronounce it to be black." Members are urged to cut all earthly ties, even with family and friends, that might divide their loyalties or impede their wholehearted devotion to the work of the order. Applicants for membership are carefully screened. Only those of superior intelligence, sound health, and attractive appearance are chosen. Then follows a two-year testing time, a sort of officer-training school, during which the novices are severely tried and examined for signs of weakness of will or purpose. Those who survive are next given a long and rigorous education as scholastics in preparation for their specialized work. When found to be ready, they are admitted to full-fledged membership as coadjutors. They may now serve as priests, teachers, medics, diplomats, or in almost any other capacity suitable to their talents and training. Whatever their work, it is "all for the greater glory of

Ignatius Loyola, founder of the Society of Jesus, was not a scholar or theologian of the stamp of Luther and Calvin, but he was easily their equal as an organizer and leader. The Jesuit Society halted the advance of Protestantism in a number of areas of Europe. *Photo: Culver Pictures*

God," which to the Jesuit means for all practical purposes the Roman Catholic Church. After years of service a few of the most outstanding are admitted to the highest circle. These select few take, in addition to the three Benedictine vows of poverty, chastity, and obedience, a fourth vow of special obedience to the pope. It is from this inner circle that all the high officers of the order are chosen.

For the spiritual guidance and inspiration of the members of the Society, Loyola wrote the *Spiritual Exercises*. Revealing the author's deep understanding of psychology, the *Exercises* guide the member through a solid month of concentrated meditation, a week each on the horrors of sin, the life of Christ to Palm Sunday, his suffering and crucifixion, and his resurrection and ascension. This remarkable work has proved to be a powerful stimulant in time of flagging zeal.

Loyola's high standards, far from deterring applicants, served as a challenge and an attraction. The Society of Jesus grew rapidly. As priests, the Jesuits were nearly always the best trained, the most popular, and the most influential. As teachers, they were usually more highly educated, devoted, and attractive than their competitors. They have always been keenly aware of the power of education, especially for the very young. "Give me the child, and I care not who has the man." The Jesuits soon got control of all education in most Roman Catholic countries.

These dedicated soldiers of Christ also made the best missionaries. In North and South America the dauntless Jesuits went among the Indians, risked and in many cases lost their lives, learned the languages of the natives, lived with them, and converted most of them to Roman Catholic Christianity. In the Far East, Francis Xavier, second only to Loyola himself in Jesuit history, converted tens of thousands.

Not the least important of Jesuit activities was that of gaining the confidence of kings, princes, and other high political personages, and thereby influencing state policy. This militantly zealous order was a powerful stimulant to the wavering cause of Roman Catholicism. In Italy, Spain, Portugal, and Ireland, where Protestantism had only a weak foothold, the Jesuits stamped it out altogether. In France and Belgium they helped to turn the tide against the Protestants. In southern Germany, Poland, and the Austrian Hapsburg lands, all of which seemed to be on the point of going Protestant, the Jesuits reversed the trend and made those lands the strongholds of Roman Catholicism they are today.

4. THE CRUSADE OF CATHOLIC SPAIN

Also at the service of the Roman Catholic Church in its counteroffensive against the Protestants was the world's greatest military power of the sixteenth century — the Spain of Philip II. Emperor Charles V had bequeathed the greater part of his vast empire to his son Philip II (1556–1598). In addition to Spain, Philip's inheritance included the Netherlands, Franche-Comté, Milan, the Kingdom of the Two Sicilies, Sardinia, the Balearic Islands, holdings along the west coast of Africa, and the Western Hemisphere. When in 1580 Philip conquered Portugal in the name of his Portuguese mother and became master (at least in name) of Portugal's huge Eastern empire, he exercised legal rule over more of the earth's surface than any other man in history.[1] Philip II, unlike his father, was a native Spaniard. The gold and silver now flowing in a steady stream from the New World and the lucrative commerce of the East Indies and of the busy Netherlands he utilized in the interests of Spain. The Spanish infantry were the best foot soldiers of the sixteenth century. Philip II was a firm believer in the divine rights of monarchy. Ignoring the Cortes and the local rights of Aragon and tending personally to the myriad details of government, the meticulous and stubborn Philip brought Spain under his sway to an extent that Ferdinand and Isabella and Charles V had never been able to do. Little wonder that the king of Spain was the most feared man in Western Christendom.

More important even than Spain in the mind of Philip II, however, was the Roman Catholic Church. He conceived it to be his chief mission in life to use the great wealth and power of Spain to restore the dominion of the Roman Church over all of Western Christendom. In the Nether-

---

[1] Sixty years later Portugal regained her independence.

lands, in England, and in France, Philip II threw the might of Spain on the side of the Roman Catholics in their counteroffensive against the Protestants.

Philip II, unlike his father, Charles V, was considered by the Netherlanders to be an unsympathetic foreigner who taxed their prosperous commerce and industry for the benefit of Spain. The absolutist monarch and his Spanish administrators also overrode the traditional political privileges of the nobles and the cities in the Netherlands. Nonetheless, religion was the foremost cause of dissension. By mid-sixteenth century, nearly half the people in the Netherlands had become Protestant. Most were Calvinists, but a considerable number were Anabaptists. Philip II, who would tolerate no heresy in his empire, took stern measures to stamp out Protestantism. The Inquisition was used to enforce the laws against heresy. In 1566, bands of outraged Protestants began to deface Roman Catholic churches. Philip thereupon dispatched 10,000 Spanish soldiers to reduce the Netherlands to submission. A six-year reign of terror followed, in which thousands were put to death.

Far from being cowed, however, the Netherlanders resisted fiercely. They found a brilliant leader in William of Orange, or William the Silent, as he came to be known. They took to the sea, playing havoc with Spanish commerce and communications. When, in 1580, Philip conquered and annexed Portugal, the hardy Dutch "Sea Beggars" seized the richest parts of the Portuguese Empire in the East Indies. The Spanish infantry quickly overran the ten southern (Belgian) provinces, but against the seven northern (Dutch) provinces, made up largely of islands and peninsulas and skillfully defended by the Dutch fleet, Spain's armies could make little headway. Most of the Protestants soon fled north from the Spanish-occupied southern provinces. Likewise, most of the Roman Catholics fled south from the Protestant-dominated north. In 1579 the ten Roman Catholic southern provinces (now Belgium) fearful of the growing power of the Protestant northern provinces, submitted to the Spanish yoke. The seven northern provinces, however, banded together in the Union of Utrecht and continued the struggle for independence. When in 1584 William the Silent was as-

Philip II was the most feared monarch in the Western world during the second half of the sixteenth century. As ruler of Spain he devoted the resources of the world's most extensive empire to the extinction of Protestantism and the restoration of the Roman Catholic Church to its position of exclusive power in Western Christendom. *Photo: Alinari/Scala EPA, Inc.*

sassinated by a hireling of Philip II, other able leaders arose to take his place. Finally in 1609, eleven years after Philip's own death, Spain agreed to a twelve-year truce, and in 1648 Spain recognized the complete independence of the Dutch Netherlands, as the seven northern provinces are commonly called. In the seventeenth century the little Dutch republic led the world in commerce, in banking, and in painting and was second to none in science and philosophy.

Thus Philip II's crusade in the Netherlands was only partly successful. He saved the southern provinces for Spain for another century, and for the Roman Catholic Church, but the Dutch provinces, the richest in his empire, were lost both to Spain and to the Church.

Most grandiose of all Philip II's crusading efforts was his attempt to restore wayward England to the Roman Catholic fold. His first move was to marry England's Roman Catholic queen, Mary Tudor. This was done in 1554, two years before he began his own rule over the Spanish Empire. However, Mary's marriage to the king of a feared and hated rival power and her persecution of English Protestants only increased her own unpopularity and that of the Roman Catholic cause in England. Moreover, the marriage failed to produce an heir. When Mary died in 1558, Philip sought to continue his influence in England by trying to marry her successor, Elizabeth. But Elizabeth, a Protestant and a high-spirited English patriot, refused. Instead, she aided the Dutch Protestant rebels and encouraged English sea dogs to plunder Spain's treasure ships sailing from her New World colonies — indeed, to plunder the colonies themselves.

Eventually Philip II undertook to conquer England by direct military action. In 1588 his "Invincible" Armada sailed forth — 130 ships, many of them great galleons. Aboard was a formidable Spanish army. The Armada was to go first to the Netherlands and pick up additional Spanish veterans. In the English Channel it met the somewhat larger English fleet, composed mostly of smaller but swifter and more heavily armed ships. The Spaniards fought well until finally their formation was broken by English fire ships sent into their midst. Once scattered, the Spanish ships were no match for the English fleet. Storms added to the catastrophe. Only about half the ships ever reached Spain by way of northern Scotland, whither they had fled. It was at this point that England began to wrest control of the seas from Spain. Philip II had not only failed to exterminate Protestantism in England, but the Roman Catholic cause there was now tainted with treason, and Protestantism was stronger than ever.

Philip found it more profitable to crusade against the Moslem Turks than against the Protestants. In fact, one of the few clear-cut successes of his career was the great naval victory over the Turks at Lepanto. Under the urging of the pope, Venice, Genoa, and Spain amassed a fleet of more than two hundred vessels under the command of Philip's illegitimate half brother, Don Juan. In 1571 this fleet caught and annihilated the somewhat larger Turkish fleet off Lepanto on the coast of Greece. Lepanto greatly diminished the Turkish menace to Christendom by sea.

5. THE RELIGIOUS WARS IN FRANCE

In France and Germany the Roman Catholic counteroffensive against Protestantism resulted in bitter religious wars in the late sixteenth and early seventeenth centuries. Crusading Spain participated in these wars, but here her role was relatively minor and indecisive. In France, Calvinism had made slow but steady progress during the reigns of Francis I (1515–1547) and Henry II (1547–1559) in spite of vigorous persecution by those Roman Catholic monarchs. By 1559 the Huguenots, as the French Calvinists were called, numbered possibly a tenth of the total population. However, since their ranks included many of the prosperous bourgeoisie and some of the greatest noble families of France, their influence was far greater than their numbers would indicate. Enmity between the Huguenots and the Roman Catholics, which had smoldered under the strong rule of Francis I and of Henry II, broke into open and consuming flame under Henry II's three weakling sons, who ruled in succession from 1559 to 1589. All three were dominated by their unscrupulous and ambitious mother, Catherine de Médicis. This situation invited political as well as religious faction and intrigue, and in the civil wars that followed politics and religion were intertwined.

The leadership of the Roman Catholic faction was assumed by the powerful Guise family; that of the Protestants by the influential Bourbon family, who were related to the royal line. The first eight years of fighting were ended in 1570 by an uneasy truce. However, Catherine de Médicis, fearful of the growing influence of the Huguenots, decided to exterminate them all. She was, of course, supported and urged on by the Guises. At a given signal at midnight, August 24, 1572 (St. Bartholomew's Day), the Roman Catholics in Paris fell to slaughtering the Protestants. The massacre soon spread to the provinces and went on for weeks. Thousands of Huguenots were slain. When news of the Massacre of St. Bartholomew reached Madrid, Philip II, who seldom smiled, smiled.

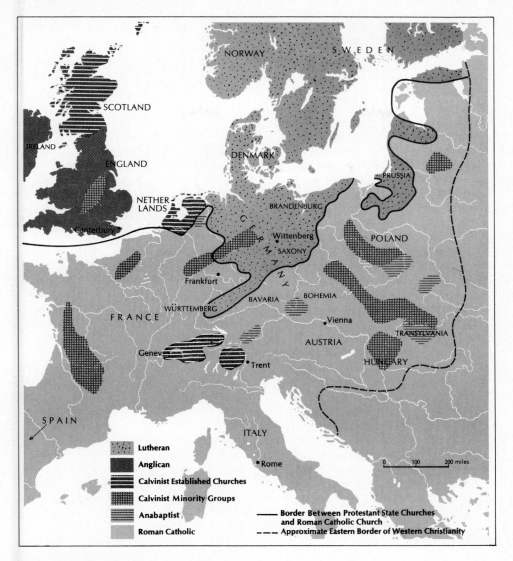

RELIGIOUS MAP OF EUROPE, CA. 1560

The ablest of the Huguenot leaders, young Henry (Bourbon) of Navarre, escaped and rallied the remaining Protestant forces for the war that was now renewed in earnest. The wealth and energy of the numerous bourgeois and noble members of the Huguenot faction, plus the brilliance of their dashing young leader, offset the superior numbers of the Roman Catholics. Eventually Henry III, the third son of Catherine de Médicis to rule France, organized a moderate Roman Catholic faction to stand between the uncompromising Guise faction and the Protestants. The struggle now became a three-cornered "War

of the Three Henrys" (Henry, duke of Guise, Henry of Navarre, and Henry III, king of France). Philip II of Spain threw his support to Henry, duke of Guise. Henry III, now regarding Henry, duke of Guise, as the greater menace to his own royal authority, had him assassinated in 1588. The next year an agent of the Guises assassinated Henry III. This left Protestant Henry of Navarre, by right of succession, King Henry IV of France. However, it was only when he abjured Protestantism four years later and went through the formality of becoming a Roman Catholic that the great majority of his subjects, who were

Roman Catholics, allowed him to enter Paris and be legally crowned. "Paris is worth a Mass," he is alleged to have remarked. Five years later (1598) he issued his famous Edict of Nantes (see p. 387), which by granting toleration to the Protestant minority, ended religious strife in France for nearly a century.[2] Once again the crusade of Philip II had stalled.

---

[2] The Huguenots rose up in a brief rebellion (1627–1629) against Cardinal Richelieu when he removed their military and political privileges (see p. 387).

6. THE THIRTY YEARS' WAR IN GERMANY

The Peace of Augsburg (1555), which had brought to a close the first armed conflict in Germany between the Roman Catholics and the Lutherans, proved to be only an uneasy truce. Since the signing of the treaty, which recognized only Roman Catholics and Lutherans, the Calvinists had made strong headway in several states of the Holy Roman Empire and demanded equal recognition. Furthermore, lands of the Roman Catho-

This print shows Magdeburg, where in 1631 one of the battles of the Thirty Years' War was fought. The last and the bloodiest of the religious wars that accompanied the Roman Catholic Reformation, the Thirty Years' War, devastated much of Germany and exhausted its participants. *Photo: NYPL Picture Collection*

Thirty Years' War (1618–1648). In this war the religious issue was complicated and often confused by political and dynastic issues. The individual princes of the empire were struggling to maintain or even increase their independence of the emperor. The Hapsburg dynasty, both Austrian and Spanish, threatened to become so powerful that the apprehensive Bourbons of France entered the war against them. The upshot was that eventually the Roman Catholics, the Holy Roman Emperor, and the Hapsburg dynasty (the emperor was an Austrian Hapsburg) formed one faction against which were arrayed the Protestants, most of the individual princes of the empire, and the Bourbons.

The long-brewing Thirty Years' War began in 1618 when a group of Bohemian noblemen, mostly Calvinists and fearful of losing both their religious and their political rights, declared their Hapsburg ruler deposed and chose the Calvinist elector of the Palatinate as their king. The Hapsburg Holy Roman Emperor, aided by the Roman Catholic League and by Hapsburg and Roman Catholic Spain, took the field and easily crushed both Bohemia and the Palatinate. Hundreds of Calvinist Bohemian noblemen were executed and their property confiscated. Protestantism was outlawed in Bohemia. The Calvinist Palatinate was annexed to Roman Catholic Bavaria. This quick and crushing victory by Roman Catholic and imperial forces frightened not only the Protestant princes of northern Germany, but also the Protestant neighboring states.

In 1625 Lutheran King Christian IV of Denmark, who held numerous bishoprics in Germany that had been illegally secularized, entered the war against the Roman Catholic and imperial forces. Christian IV was aided by English subsidies and numerous German Protestant princes. At this critical juncture a brilliant soldier of fortune, Albrecht von Wallenstein, offered his services to the emperor. This military genius raised

lic Church were constantly being secularized in Protestant areas in violation of the treaty. On the other hand, the Roman Catholics, becoming more aggressive as a result of the clarification of their position by the Council of Trent and the activities of the militant Jesuits, talked of exterminating Protestantism in the Holy Roman Empire and recovering all their lost lands and souls. The Protestants in alarm formed a defensive league. The Roman Catholics countered by forming a league of their own.

The increasing tension finally erupted into the

SHETLAND I.

NORWAY

SWEDEN

ORKNEY I.

• Bergen

• Stockholm

SCOTLAND

KINGDOM OF
DENMARK AND NORWAY

• Edinburgh

NORTH SEA

DENMARK

BALTIC SEA

IRELAND

• Copenhagen

• Dublin

ENGLAND
(COMMONWEALTH
1649–1660
UNITED KINGDOM
1707)

SCHLESWIG

SWEDISH
POMERANIA

BRANDENBURG-PRUSSIA

• Danzig

UNITED
PROVINCES

HOLSTEIN

POMERELIA

ATLANTIC OCEAN

London •

• Hamburg
• Bremen

HANOVER

BRANDENBURG
Berlin •

GREAT
POLAND

Vistula

LIT
POL

Wa

ENGLISH CHANNEL

Amsterdam •
Ryswick •

SPANISH
NETH.

• Brussels

MINOR
GERMAN
STATES

Leipzig •

SAXONY

SILESIA

BOHEMIA

MORAVIA

Paris •

Verdun

LORRAINE

FRANCE

Toul

FRANCHE
COMTE

ALSACE

BAVARIA
Augsburg •

AUSTRIA
Vienna •

KINGDOM OF HUNGARY

Bu

HUNGA

SWISS
CANTONS

SAVOY

PIEDMONT

REP. OF VENICE

SLAVONIA

Milan •

Venice •

PYRENEES

CATALONIA

Marseilles •

Parma •

Zara •

BOSNIA

MONTENEGRO

SE

TUSCANY

PAPAL
STATES

ADRIATIC SEA

PORTUGAL
(TO SPAIN
1580–1640)

CASTILE

Madrid •

ARAGON

CORSICA
(Genoa)

Rome •

Lisbon •

SPAIN

BALEARIC I.

MINORCA

MAJORCA

SARDINIA

Naples •

NAPLES

Bari •

KINGDOM OF THE
TWO SICILIES

IONIA
(Venic

GIBRALTAR
• Ceuta (Spain)

Tangier
(Portugal)

MEDITERRANEAN

Palermo •

• Oran (Spain)

Algiers •

SICILY

SEA

FEZ AND MOROCCO

ALGERIA

Tunis •

TUNISIA

MALTA (Spain)

B A R B A R Y   S T A T E S

Austrian Hapsburgs

Spanish Monarchy

Swedish Dominions

Brandenburg-Prussia

——— Boundary of the Holy Roman Empire

0   100   200   300 miles

RUSSIA

• Moscow

RIA

THUANIA

• Minsk

A N D

Kiev •

LIA

niester R.

YEDISAN

LDAVIA

BESSARABIA   CRIMEA

CHIA

DOBRUJA

BLACK SEA

anube R.

BULGARIA

O M A N

• Constantinople

E M P I R E

N

• Smyrna

RHODES
(Turkish)

CYPRUS
(Turkish)

TE
ice)

a volunteer army of 50,000 adventurers of various nationalities whose only motivation was hope of plunder. Wallenstein's army, together with the regular imperial and Roman Catholic forces, defeated Christian IV and drove him out of Germany. The Danish king was deprived of nearly all his German holdings. Upon the conclusion of this phase of the war in 1629, the victorious emperor issued the Edict of Restitution, restoring to the Roman Catholic Church all the lands illegally secularized since the Peace of Augsburg—more than a hundred tracts, large and small.

The whole Protestant world was now genuinely alarmed at the resurgent power of the Roman Catholics. The German princes were faced with the loss of their powers to the Holy Roman Emperor. The French Bourbons were concerned about the rapidly growing strength of the Hapsburgs. At this juncture another Protestant champion stepped forward—Gustavus Adolphus of Sweden. This Lutheran "Lion of the North" was a military leader of great ability. Furthermore, he was well backed by French gold. Gustavus Adolphus led his army victoriously through the Germanies, gaining allies among the Protestant princes as he went. The Hapsburg emperor hastily recalled the ambitious Wallenstein, whom he had dismissed upon the conclusion of the Danish phase of the war. Two of the ablest military commanders of early modern times now faced each other. In the battle of Lützen (1632) Wallenstein was defeated, but Gustavus Adolphus had been killed and the victory was far from decisive. Fortunately for the Protestants, Wallenstein was dismissed and two years later was assassinated. Since Sweden had failed to turn the tide of the war, the Bourbon King of France in 1635 threw the full weight of his military might directly into the fray. For thirteen more years the war dragged on until all participants were exhausted. The Treaty of Westphalia in 1648 finally brought the struggle to a close.

In general, thanks largely to the intervention of France, the Roman Catholics, the Holy Roman

EUROPE 1648

Emperor, and the Hapsburgs suffered a setback. Not only were the Roman Catholics thwarted in their efforts to exterminate Protestantism in Germany, but the Calvinists now gained equal status with the Lutherans and Roman Catholics in the Holy Roman Empire. The Edict of Restitution was nullified. The Holy Roman Empire practically fell apart. According to the terms of the Treaty of Westphalia, each of the more than three hundred individual princes could now make his own treaties. Three of the most important princes, the rulers of Brandenburg, Bavaria, and Saxony, made sizable additions to their territories. Sweden gained strategic territories along the German Baltic and North Sea coasts. France gained the important bishoprics and fortress cities of Metz, Toul, and Verdun, and the province of Alsace except for the free city of Strasbourg. These former imperial territories gave both Sweden and France a vote in the Diet of the Holy Roman Empire and a say in German affairs. The complete independence of Switzerland and the Dutch Netherlands was officially recognized. The Austrian Hapsburgs retained their hereditary possessions but lost prestige as emperors of a disintegrating Holy Roman Empire. Also, their relative position declined as that of France rose. The Spanish Hapsburgs fared worse. After eleven more years of fighting with France they yielded a strip of the southern Netherlands and another strip along the Spanish border to France. Spain's days of greatness were finished.

The immediate effect of the Thirty Years' War on Germany was disastrous. For three decades hostile German and foreign armies had tramped back and forth across Germany, killing, raping, and looting the defenseless inhabitants. In the wake of Wallenstein's army of 50,000, for instance, swarmed 150,000 camp followers bent on plunder. To the usual horrors of war was added religious fanaticism. Many years would be required for Germany to recover from these wounds.

The Thirty Years' War was the last and the bloodiest of the religious wars that accompanied the Roman Catholic Reformation. Although there would still be much religious strife and controversy, the religious map of Europe henceforth would change very little. In a real sense, then, 1648 marked the end of the era of the Protestant and Roman Catholic reformations. The Roman Catholic Church, by closing ranks, setting its house in order, and availing itself of the militant Jesuit Society, had checked the further spread of Protestantism in Europe, but had been able to win back relatively little that had been lost. Western Christendom was now definitely split into two irreconcilable camps—Roman Catholic and Protestant. After 1648, political rather than religious affairs would occupy center stage in the Western world.

Suggested Reading

General
*G. R. Elton, *Reformation Europe, 1517–1559* (Torch). Has excellent chapters on the Roman Catholic Reformation.

Index and Inquisition
R. Burke, *What Is the Index?* (1952). Gives the Roman Catholic position on censorship.
*J. Plaidy, *The Spanish Inquisition, Its Rise, Growth, and End* (Citadel). Good survey.

The Jesuits
H. Boehmer, *The Jesuits*, trans. P. Strodach (1928). Standard survey.
P. Dudon, *St. Ignatius of Loyola* (1949). The best biography by a scholarly, objective Jesuit priest.

The Crusade of Philip II
*R. T. Davies, *The Golden Century of Spain* (Torch). Good survey.
*P. Geyl, *The Revolt of the Netherlands* (Barnes & Noble). Downplays the religious view.

*G. Mattingly, *The Armada* (Sentry). Brilliantly shows the impact of the Armada's failure on all of Europe.

Thirty Years' War
*C. V. Wedgwood, *The Thirty Years' War* (Anchor). The best single volume on the subject. Tries a bit too hard to minimize the war's destructiveness.

Sources
J. Waterworth, *History of the Council of Trent* (1948). Contains the canons and decrees of the council.
*E. M. Burns, *The Counter Reformation* (Anvil). Contains many interesting documents.

Retrospect

During the fifteenth and sixteenth centuries, medieval civilization did not abruptly end and modern civilization begin. As a matter of fact, lords and ladies still exist in Western Europe; people still revel in the symbols and pageantry of chivalry; agriculture is still a necessary part of Western economy; and the Christian religion still holds the allegiance of millions. Nevertheless, the world of 1600 was very definitely not the world of 1400.

During these two centuries, the first four modern national states had come into being, shattering once and for all the theoretical political unity of Western Europe under the Holy Roman Empire and ending the actual independence of thousands of feudal fiefs by bringing them under the authority of the national monarchs.

The revival of commerce and the development of capitalist practices and institutions ended the monopoly of medieval Europe's agricultural economy and of the land-owning class, the nobility. The nobility now faced competition for influence from the new middle class—from merchants, bankers, lawyers. It is true that the bourgeoisie sought most of all to enter the ranks of the nobility, and did so whenever possible, and that the nobility held the upper hand politically and socially for two or three more centuries. But by 1600 class lines had become more fluid. European civilization was becoming more urban. Furthermore, much of the rest of the world had come under European economic and political domination.

Even in the fourteenth century, a secular trend in Western European literature and art could be observed. This turning (or returning) from the sacred, God-centered ideals of the Middle Ages to the secular, man-centered interests of the modern world accelerated during the fifteenth and sixteenth centuries. Western Europeans had become more self-centered, proud, versatile, and materialistic. These humanistic Renaissance qualities produced, as in ancient Greece and Rome, some of the world's greatest literature and art. They also laid the basis for an era of natural science.

Finally, by 1600 the Christian Church, which in 1400 still monopolized religious life and strongly influenced the intellectual, political, and economic life of Western Europe, was split asunder. This may have been the most important of all the developments that brought the medieval system to an end and ushered in the modern era, for nothing so characterized medieval civilization as the dominance of the Church. By 1600 the Western Christian world had become fragmented. On the other hand, the Protestant and Catholic Reformations revived interest in and allegiance to the Christian religion at a time when Western man appeared to be turning his attention to secularism, nationalism, and capitalistic enterprises. Although Christianity had lost its position of dominance, it continued as a major force in the modern world.

But what of the immediate future? Now that organized Christianity was split asunder and millions of Western Europeans were weary of doctrinal disputes and bloody wars that had accompanied the Protestant and Roman Catholic Reformations, what would occupy center stage of the drama of Western civilization that for so long had been held by the Christian Church? It appeared in the middle of the seventeenth century that the immediate future lay with the royal monarchs of the rising national states. Already by 1648 they had asserted themselves decisively in he religious affairs of Europe.

VIII

The Age of Royal Absolutism

Seventeenth and Eighteenth Centuries

As we have seen, the kings of Spain, Portugal, France, and England gained the ascendancy over the feudal nobility in the late fifteenth century and welded the first four national states around their own persons. In the sixteenth century, Spain and Portugal were at the peak of their power and affluence. They acquired vast and lucrative colonial empires in the West and in the East. During the reigns of Charles V and Philip II, Spain was the dominant military power in Europe. After Philip's death in 1598, however, Spain's decline was as rapid as had been her rise a century earlier. Although her huge empire in the New World was still intact and although her greatest outpouring of literature and art was yet to come, her military and political power and influence were spent. Portugal's decline was equally precipitous. When in 1580 she was annexed to Spain, the Dutch, then fighting the Spanish for their independence, took advantage of Portugal's misfortune to seize the richest part of her Eastern empire. Although Portugal regained her independence in 1640, she never recovered her sixteenth-century wealth and influence.

The decline of Spain and Portugal left France in a favorable position to dominate Western Europe. Henry IV, the first of the Bourbon line of kings, who ascended the throne in 1589, brought the three decades of religious and political turmoil in France to an end. The Bourbon kings set out to make themselves supreme in France, and France supreme in Europe. In England royal absolutism had reached its peak during the sixteenth century under the vigorous Tudor dynasty. By the opening of the next century, Parliament was ready to challenge the royal authority—and the kings were the politically inept Stuarts. Meanwhile, the French, the English, and the Dutch were preparing to replace the Iberian nations as the leading commercial and colonial empire builders.

In Central and Eastern Europe two vigorous new dynasties—the Hohenzollerns of Prussia and the Romanovs of Russia—began to assert themselves. Their natural enemies were the Austrian Hapsburgs, the Ottoman Turks, the Poles, and the Swedes.

European history in the seventeenth and eighteenth centuries, therefore, is predominantly political, in contrast to that of the sixteenth century, which was in large part centered on religious strife. For the most part, this political history revolved around the various royal monarchs.

France was the dominant nation in Europe throughout most of the seventeenth and eighteenth centuries. Under Louis XIV royal absolutism not only reached its peak in France but also served as a model that all other monarchs sought to emulate. The well-lighted stage across which the "Sun King" strode was set for him by three able predecessors—Henry IV, Richelieu, and Mazarin.

1. THE RISE OF FRANCE UNDER HENRY IV, RICHELIEU, AND MAZARIN

When Henry IV became king of France in 1589, his country was torn from several decades of bitter religious war. Respect for law and order had broken down. The feudal nobility had in many cases reasserted its own authority. The finances of the central government were in chaos. Roads and bridges were in disrepair. French prestige abroad was at a low ebb; even the city of Paris was garrisoned by the Spanish troops of Philip II.

Henry of Navarre, the first of the Bourbon dynasty to rule France, set out to change all this. The new king, in his prime at the age of thirty-six, was debonair and witty, courageous, generous, optimistic, and democratic in his social life. His slogan, "A chicken in the pot of every peasant for Sunday dinner," was more than an idle phrase; it is little wonder that *Henri Quatre* became the most popular monarch in French history. The romantic Henry had in the Duke of

32

THE DOMINANCE OF FRANCE: THE AGE OF LOUIS XIV

Sully an able, methodical administrator to serve and steady him. The most urgent task was to restore the authority of the central government. This he set out to do by vigorously suppressing brigandage and enforcing the law. The lesser nobility was brought to heel directly and quickly. The powerful nobility was dealt with more gingerly, but by the end of Henry's reign real headway had been made toward reducing the nobles to obedience to the central government.

Henry and Sully launched a comprehensive program of economic reconstruction. Agriculture and commerce benefited from the increased security of life and property, from the repair of roads, bridges, and harbors, and from the freeing of internal and external commerce of many obstructions and tariff barriers. Marshes were drained for farming. Better breeding methods were introduced. The peasants' livestock and implements were protected against seizure for debt or taxes. New industries producing glass, porcelain, lace, tapestries, and fine leather and textiles were subsidized and protected by the state. Silk culture, which brought vast wealth to France, was introduced. The building of France's overseas empire began in 1608 when Champlain founded Quebec, the first French colony in the New World.

When Henry IV came to the throne, only about one-fourth of the heavy taxes, from which the clergy and the nobility were largely exempted, ever reached the national treasury. The rest went into the pockets of corrupt officials and tax farm-

ers, that is, the collectors who bid a fixed sum for the privilege of collecting the taxes and were permitted to keep anything over and above the contracted amount. Sully was unable to change this vicious system, but by means of careful bookkeeping, efficient administration of expenditures, and elimination of corruption, he was able to show a surplus for the first time in many years.

Another major achievement of Henry's reign was the granting of religious toleration to the Huguenot minority. Although Henry abjured Protestantism in order to gain acceptance as king of an overwhelmingly Roman Catholic nation, the sympathy and probably the faith of this former leader of the Huguenots remained with the Calvinist minority. The Edict of Nantes, which Henry IV issued in 1598, granted not only complete freedom of conscience and limited public worship to the Huguenots, but also civil and political equality. Moreover, they were given military control of some two hundred fortified cities and towns as a guarantee against future oppression. The Edict of Nantes stands as a monument in the bloody and endless struggle for religious freedom — one of the most precious possessions of civilized man. It antedates the work of Roger Williams in Rhode Island by thirty-eight years.

Having laid the foundations for royal supremacy, economic health, and religious toleration, Henry IV in the last years of his reign devoted an increasing amount of attention to foreign affairs.

He talked vaguely from time to time about a sort of league of nations for perpetual peace, but nothing came of it. His specific goal was to make France first secure and then supreme in Europe by weakening the power of the Spanish and Austrian Hapsburgs. In 1610 he readied his armies for a campaign, but just as he was preparing to join them he was assassinated by a fanatical Roman Catholic who doubted his orthodoxy.

After fourteen years of retrogression under Henry IV's Italian wife, Marie de Médicis, and their young and inept son Louis XIII, Cardinal Richelieu gained active control over the government of France. Although technically a mere servant of the fickle Louis XIII, the masterful cardinal made himself so indispensable that for eighteen years (1624–1642) he held firm control over French affairs. Handsome, arrogant, and calculating, Richelieu was a true Machiavellian. His twofold policy, from which he never veered, was that of his predecessor, Henry IV — to make the royal power supreme in France and France supreme in Europe.

Believing the high nobility and the Huguenots to be the chief threats to royal absolutism, Richelieu crushed them both. With the royal army at his disposal, he boldly destroyed the castles of the nobles who remained defiant, disbanded their private armies, and hanged a number of the most recalcitrant. The special military and political privileges that the Huguenots enjoyed under the Edict of Nantes were considered by Richelieu to be intolerable, giving them the status of a state within a state. After a bloody two-year struggle, he stripped the Huguenots of these privileges, although he left their religious and civil liberties intact.

In order to by-pass all local political influence, which in some provinces was still strong, the dynamic minister divided France into some thirty administrative districts called *généralités*, each of which was placed under the control of an *intendant*,[1] who was an agent of the crown. So absolute was the power of the *intendants* over local af-

fairs, even of the most minute nature, that they came to be called the "thirty tyrants of France." They were chosen from the ranks of the bourgeoisie and were shifted around frequently lest they become too sympathetic with the people over whom they ruled. The royal will was thus extended to every part of France.

Although Richelieu was a cardinal in the Roman Catholic Church, he did not hesitate to plunge France into the Thirty Years' War in Germany on the side of the Protestants. His purpose, of course, was to weaken the Hapsburgs, chief rivals of the French Bourbons for European supremacy. As a result of Richelieu's intervention, Protestantism in Germany may have been saved from extermination, but the Hapsburgs were humiliated. When Richelieu died in 1642, he had gone far toward bringing to fruition Henry IV's policies of royal supremacy in France and French supremacy in Europe. Richelieu, however, did not share Henry IV's concern for the common people. Their lot became harder under the imperious and ruthless cardinal, at whose death they rejoiced.

Richelieu was succeeded by his protégé, Cardinal Mazarin. Louis XIII's death in 1643, one year after that of his great minister, left the throne to Louis XIV, a child of five. Mazarin played the same role in the early reign of Louis XIV that Richelieu had played during most of the reign of Louis XIII. From the death of Richelieu in 1642 until his own death in 1661, Mazarin vigorously pursued the policies of his predecessor. The Thirty Years' War was brought to a successful conclusion. All who challenged the crown's absolute authority were crushed.

Although the policies were the same, the methods of carrying them out were quite different. Whereas Richelieu was bold and forthright in dealing with even his most formidable enemies, the Italian-born Mazarin was treacherous, deceitful, and devious. The most noteworthy events during his administration were two uprisings, known as *Frondes*, against his tyranny. The Frondes were revolts of the disgruntled nobility, supported by various other rebellious elements, against the ever-increasing authority of the central government. At times it looked as if the rebels might succeed, but the

---

[1] The *intendants* existed before Richelieu's time, but he greatly increased their power and functions.

crafty Mazarin was too much for them. The failure of the Frondes marked the last overt resistance to royal absolutism in France until the French Revolution in 1789. When Cardinal Mazarin died in 1661, he passed along to young Louis XIV a royal power that was at last absolute and a national state that was easily the first power of Europe.

2. LOUIS XIV AND HIS GOVERNMENT

Louis XIV was twenty-three years of age when, in 1661, he stepped forth as the principal actor on the world's gaudiest stage. Young Louis was well fitted for the part. He had a sound body and a regal bearing. His lack of brilliance and of deep learning were more than offset by a large store of common sense, a sharp memory, a sense of responsibility, and a capacity for hard, tedious work. From his Spanish mother, from Mazarin, and from his tutors he had gained the conviction that he was God's appointed vicegerent for France. In Bishop Bossuet he had the most famous of all theorists and exponents of royal absolutism. Bossuet in numerous writings argued that absolute monarchy is the normal, the most efficient, and the divinely ordained form of government. Furthermore, the royal monarch, the image of God and directly inspired by God, is above human reproach and accountable to God alone. These ideas were the culmination of the thinking of James I of England a half century earlier (see the next chapter). As acted out by Louis, they gained and held the ascendancy throughout the continent of Europe (and far beyond it) during the late seventeenth and most of the eighteenth centuries.

Absolute though he might consider himself (the words, "*L' état, c'est moi*" ["I am the state"] are often attributed to him), Louis could not possibly perform all the functions of government personally. Actually, the great bulk of the decisions and details of government were handled by a series of councils and bureaus, and administered locally by the *intendants*. The functions of the chief councils, such as those of state, finances, dispatches, and the privy council, appear on paper to have been overlapping and ill-defined. As supervised by the industrious Louis

"Cardinal Richelieu," by Champaigne. The imperious and ruthless Richelieu played a major role in making the royal power supreme in France and France the supreme power in Europe. *Photo: Scala/ Florence/EPA, Inc.*

XIV, however, the administrative machinery worked smoothly and efficiently. In fact, it was the envy of his fellow monarchs and probably constituted his most constructive achievement. There was no semblance of popular participation in government. The role of the people was to serve and obey; in return, they enjoyed reflected glory and received such benefits as the monarch might be willing and able to bestow upon them. The Estates-General was not called once during the seventy-two years of Louis XIV's reign or the fifty-nine-year rule of his successor.

The Palace of Versailles. This chateau, built by Louis XIV in the late seventeenth century, was designed to be a palace fit for the greatest of all the absolute monarchs. The palace is so huge that no single view of the whole can show the elaborate detail of the baroque style of architecture in which it was built. This frontal view of the center section reveals some detail. *Photo: The Bettmann Archive*

3. THE KING AND HIS COURT: VERSAILLES

In line with Louis XIV's concept of divine right absolutism, he believed that he should have a palace worthy of God's chief vicegerent on earth. Hating tumultuous Paris, congested and crowded with vulgar tradesmen, he selected Versailles, 11 miles southwest of the city, to be the new seat of government. There as many as thirty-five thousand workmen toiled for thirty years, turning the marshes and sandy wastes into the world's most splendid court. The cost was so staggering that Louis destroyed the records. The greatest artists in the land were employed in the creation of the palace and the grounds. The most costly marbles, glass, tapestries, paintings, and inlaid woods were used in profusion in the ornate baroque style of the period. Hundreds of acres of gardens, parks, walks, canals, and artificial lakes were laid out with mathematical precision. Playing fountains and marble statues formalized the landscape.

Around his court Louis XIV gathered the great nobles of France. Henry IV, Richelieu, and Mazarin had broken their power; Louis XIV turned them into court butterflies. The inevitable jostling for the king's attention, which was the one source of preferment, and the conflicting claims of so much titled rank necessitated the drawing up of an elaborate code of etiquette. The king was dressed and undressed, bathed, and fed by the highest noblemen in the land—all in strict ritual. The household personnel consisted of ten thousand soldiers in brilliant uniforms and four thousand civilians. Nor was the pageant of Versailles mere glitter alone. Louis XIV subsidized or gathered around himself the leading French artists and literary figures. Mansard the architect and Lebrun the painter were the chief designer and decorator, respectively, of the palace. Corneille, Racine, Moliére, La Fontaine, La Rochefoucauld, Saint-Simon, and Madame de Sévigné made Louis XIV's reign the golden age of French literature. (See Chapter 36.)

But there was a reverse side to the coin. Versailles was a showplace, not a comfortable home for the king. It was cold, drafty, and inconvenient. The balls, parades, hunts, and social ritual were not sufficient to absorb the energy of the vivacious and ambitious nobility of France. The court seethed with gossip, scandal, and intrigue. Nor did the hard-toiling, heavily taxed French masses, who were supposed to enjoy the reflected glory of the monarch, always appreciate such extravagant glamor. Indeed, there were increasing expressions of discontent.

4. COLBERT AND THE FRENCH ECONOMY

Louis XIV was fortunate to have at his command during the first half of his reign a prodigious financial manager. Jean Baptiste Colbert was an inordinately ambitious social climber who realized that, because of his bourgeois origin, his only means of advancement was through indispensable service to the king. An engine of efficiency, he toiled endlessly, supervising the countless details of the French economy.

Colbert's first and probably his most difficult task was to balance the national budget, which had become badly unbalanced under Richelieu and Mazarin. The careful accounting of receipts and expenditures that Sully had inaugurated three quarters of a century earlier was resumed. Some of the debts that the government had contracted at exorbitant rates of interest were canceled; on others the rates were reduced. Dishonest tax collectors were dismissed and punished.

With Colbert, mercantilism reached its peak. French industries were protected by prohibitive tariffs, while exports and new industries were subsidized. Raw materials, however, were strictly husbanded. Imperial and commercial activities in India and North America were vigorously promoted. It was at this time that Marquette, Joliet, and La Salle explored the Great Lakes and the Mississippi Valley for France. To protect this growing empire and the commerce with it, a large navy was built. But Colbert did not stop with these traditional mercantilist practices. In order to gain a world-wide reputation for the uniformly high quality of French products, all manufacturing was subjected to the most minute regulation and supervision. So many threads of such and such quality and color must go into every inch of this textile and that lace. A veritable army of inspectors enforced the regulations. This extreme phase of mercantilism, the economic adjunct to royal absolutism, has come to be called Colbertism. It achieved its immediate end so far as quality and reputation were concerned, but it stifled initiative and retarded future industrial development. That Colbert was able to balance the budget and achieve general economic prosperity in the face of Louis XIV's lavish expenditures, including the building of Versailles, was a remarkable feat. It is well, however, that Colbert died in 1683, for Louis' wars of aggression eventually wrecked most of the great minister's work. With the exception of the Netherlands, practically all of Europe copied Colbert's policies and techniques during the latter part of the seventeenth and most of the eighteenth centuries.

5. ABSOLUTISM AND RELIGION

It was virtually inevitable that Louis XIV's concepts of divine right monarchy would have religious repercussions. First of all, they ran counter to the claims of the pope. All his life Louis considered himself to be devoutly loyal to the Roman Catholic faith, as were the majority of his subjects. But when it came to matters of church administration Louis was not willing to have his royal authority limited, even by Rome. Numerous conflicts between king and pope led to the calling of a great council of the French clergy in 1682. This council, under the domination of Bishop Bossuet, faithful servant of Louis XIV and famed exponent of the theory of royal absolutism, drew up a statement of Gallican Liberties, special privileges or freedoms of the French church from Roman domination. These were in essence: (1) A church council is superior to the pope. (2) The pope's jurisdiction is supreme only in matters of faith and morals, and his rulings even here are applicable in France only after they have been accepted by the French clergy. (3) The traditional customs and practices of the French church shall be respected. The Gallican Liberties brought the French church to a position close to that of the English church under Henry VIII. They might even have led to eventual separation from Rome had not Louis XIV in later life fallen increasingly under the influence of the Jesuits and his pious mistress, Madame de Maintenon, who were able to rekindle his loyalty to the pope.

Louis' absolutism also ran afoul of the Jansenists, so called because they were followers of a Belgian bishop, Cornelius Jansen. This group represented a Puritan movement within the Roman Catholic Church. The Jansenists had no intention of breaking away from the Church, to which they considered themselves entirely loyal. It was their wish to return to the teachings and practices of the Church in the days of St. Augustine. They emphasized predestination, inner piety, and the ascetic life. A number of intellectuals and people of means were attracted to their ranks, including the dramatist Racine and the mathematician and philosopher Blaise Pascal. At Port Royal near Versailles a group of prominent Jansenists practiced a communal life and established an excellent school that attracted much favorable attention. It was probably fear for the reputation of their own schools that aroused the jealousy of the Jesuits, militant watchdogs over Roman Catholic orthodoxy and papal supremacy. After a long and bitter controversy, the pope was persuaded to declare Jansenism heretical, though no bill of particulars was ever presented. Eventually the Jesuits also aroused against the Jansenists the animosity of Louis XIV, who could tolerate no deviation from his own views even in matters of religion. He outlawed the sect and destroyed its buildings. But he was unable to destroy Jansenism itself, which has continued to exist to the present time.

The chief religious victims of Louis XIV's absolutism were the Huguenots. Ever since Richelieu had removed the military and political privileges they had enjoyed under the Edict of Nantes, the Huguenots had lived quietly as good French citizens, clinging unobtrusively to their Protestant faith. Although the Huguenots numbered not more than one-tenth of the total population of France, many of them were industrious, prosperous, and educated members of the middle class. The Jesuits had little difficulty kindling the ire of Louis XIV against these heretical subjects who had the audacity to consider the king's religion not good enough for themselves. The Huguenots were subjected to one of the cruelest persecutions in the bloody history of religious intolerance. Barbarous regular army troops were quartered in Huguenot homes and instructed to live licentiously. Students familiar only with twentieth-century civilian armies will need to reflect a little to realize the significance of this move. Whole Huguenot communities would abjure their faith at the approach of the troops. Finally, in 1685 the Edict of Nantes was revoked and the Protestant religion outlawed. Although Huguenots were forbidden to emigrate, many—probably a quarter million—succeeded in doing so, taking much of their wealth and all their economic knowledge and skills with them. Not only were these industrious citizens, the backbone of French commercial and industrial life, lost to France, but they greatly strengthened some of France's rivals and enemies, such as England, the Dutch Netherlands, and Brandenburg, who welcomed them. Forbidden to enter the underpopulated French colonies, many Huguenots helped to people the English colonies in America.

6. LOUIS XIV'S WARS OF AGGRESSION

The Sun King was not content to rule the world's most powerful nation. France was not big enough to satisfy his vanity, ever inflated by the constant flattery of his courtiers. He coveted a wider domain. Louis' immediate and expressed goal was to extend his rule to France's natural frontiers. Since the French boundaries were already delimited by mountains and sea on every side but the northeast, it was in that direction that Louis looked for expansion. He claimed that only the Rhine River would provide France with an adequate natural strategic boundary on that side. This was, of course, pure fiction. River valleys unite rather than separate people; nor have rivers ever proved to be effective military barriers. A glance at the map (p. 394) will quickly reveal that an advance to the Rhine would involve France in war with most of Europe. Between the French frontier and the Rhine lay the Spanish Netherlands, much of the Dutch Netherlands, imperial territory belonging to the Austrian Hapsburgs, and many German states. England, too, would be threatened, and the balance of power upset. But Louis felt himself equal to the task of defeating these powers.

Louis' war minister, Louvois, is often considered the father of modern militarism. Louvois organized France's huge military establishment on a scientific and businesslike basis, replete with supply depots and hospitals. He introduced strict discipline, uniforms, and marching drill. Louis had other distinguished military aides. Vauban was one of the great designers of fortifications and of siege operations. It was a common saying that a city defended by Vauban was safe and that a city besieged by Vauban was doomed. Condé was an able and dashing military leader, and Turenne a masterly planner of campaigns and battles.

During the last four decades of his seventy-two-year reign Louis XIV fought four wars of aggression. In 1667 he unceremoniously sent French armies in to conquer the Spanish (Belgian) Netherlands. Spanish power had declined rapidly since the sixteenth century, and Louis' armies captured one fortress city after another. The Dutch, however, took alarm and formed an alliance with England and Sweden to check the French menace. This array of power in addition to Spain caused Louis to accept a peace that granted him only a slice of the Spanish Netherlands.

The frustrated Grand Monarch determined to punish the upstart prosperous Dutch. He sent huge French armies into the Netherlands. The cause of the Dutch seemed hopeless, and in desperation they opened their dikes. Large portions of their land were flooded, but the French were held at bay. Meanwhile, the power of France frightened Spain, the Holy Roman Emperor, Brandenburg, and several small German states into joining the Dutch in alliance. Louis XIV won many victories over the allies, but when the English Parliament forced Charles II to break his agreement with the French king and join the alliance against him, Louis XIV decided to make peace. Again hapless Spain was the loser, giving up to France the long-coveted Franche-Comté (free county of Burgundy) and another strip of the Spanish Netherlands.

At the end of the Dutch War (1678) Louis XIV stood at the peak of his power. He had defeated all the greatest military powers on the Western European continent and had gained valuable territories. But the tide was about to turn.

Turenne was killed near the end of the Dutch War, and the aged Condé retired at the end of the war. No comparable generals were found to replace them. Colbert's hard-won surplus and balanced budget were now things of the past, and France's economy was suffering. All Europe had become alarmed by the French aggression. Louis XIV, however, was not statesman enough to perceive the realities of the present. His ever-growing appetite for power was hardly whetted.

No sooner had the Dutch War ended than Louis began trumping up claims to various territories in Alsace and Lorraine and sending in his armed forces to occupy them. The result was another defensive alliance against Louis composed of the Dutch Netherlands, Spain, Sweden, the Holy Roman Emperor, and a number of small German states. The heart of the alliance was William of Orange, stadholder of Holland, and when the redoubtable Dutchman became King William III of England after the Glorious Revolution of 1688, England, too, was brought into alliance against Louis. The alliance was called the League of Augsburg. After nine years of fruitless struggle, Louis accepted a peace giving him only the city of Strasbourg.

But the Sun King, still blinded by pride and greed, was not about to give up. He persuaded the last monarch of the Hapsburg line in Spain just before he died in 1700 to choose one of Louis' grandsons as king. The prospect of Spain and the Spanish Empire joined to the already inordinately powerful French monarchy frightened the other powers of Western Europe into once more forming an alliance against France. This alliance, known as the Grand Alliance, was also engineered by William III; it consisted of England, the Dutch Netherlands, Austria, Brandenburg, several small German states, Savoy, and Portugal. The ensuing War of the Spanish Succession lasted eleven years (1702–1713) and surpassed all previous wars in modern times in destructiveness. The allies, led by the brilliant duke of Marlborough (John Churchill, a direct forebear of Winston Churchill), administered to the French and Spanish armies a series of severe defeats. In 1713 Louis XIV, beaten and exhausted, was forced to accept the Treaty of Utrecht. Although Louis' grandson was permitted to re-

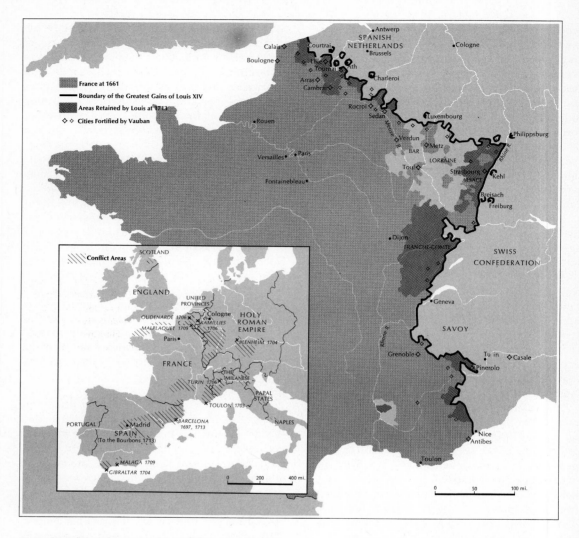

THE GROWTH OF FRANCE UNDER LOUIS XIV

tain the Spanish throne, France yielded New-
foundland, Nova Scotia, and Hudson Bay to
Great Britain.[2] Spain gave up Gibraltar and Mi-
norca to Great Britain, and ceded the Belgian
Netherlands, Naples, Sardinia, and Milan to
Austria. The duke of Savoy received the title of

king and the Spanish island of Sicily (which he
later exchanged with Austria for Sardinia). The
Hohenzollern margrave of Brandenburg was
granted the title "king in Prussia," and henceforth his state was called Prussia. Thus the
houses of Savoy and Hohenzollern, which later
were to create the Italian and the German nations, respectively, added greatly to their prestige. France was somewhat humbled. She was
beginning to lose ground overseas to Great Bri-

---

[2] The term *Great Britain* replaced the term *England* in
1707 when England and Scotland were united.

tain, and in Europe she had been halted short of the Rhine. But she was still the most powerful single nation in Europe.

Louis XIV lived only two years after the signing of the Treaty of Utrecht. He had long outlived his popularity. As the body of the grandest of all the absolute monarchs was drawn through the streets of Paris, some of his abused people cursed in the taverns as the coffin passed. A faint scent of revolution was already in the air.

Suggested Reading

General
*G. N. Clark, *The Seventeenth Century* (Galaxy). Good brief survey, emphasizing cultural aspects.
*J. B. Wolf, *Emergence of the Great Powers, 1685–1715* (Torch). Scholarly volume in Rise of Modern Europe series.

Rise of France Under Henry IV, Richelieu, and Mazarin
P. F. Willert, *Henry of Navarre* (1902). Still the best biography of Henry IV.
*C. V. Wedgwood, *Richelieu and the French Monarchy* (Collier). Brief but sound.

Louis XIV and His Court
*W. H. Lewis, *The Splendid Century* (Anchor). Very well written.
*J. B. Wolf, *Louis XIV* (Norton). Supersedes all other biographies of Louis XIV.

Religious Affairs
A. J. Grant, *The Huguenots* (1934). Brief and readable.

Sources
*L. R. Saint-Simon, *The Memoirs of the Duc de Saint-Simon* (Macmillan). A disgruntled courtier's detailed eyewitness account of Versailles under Louis XIV.
Marie de Sévigné, *Letters from Madame la Marquise de Sévigné*, ed. and trans. Violet Hammersley (1956). Charmingly written eyewitness account of life at Versailles.

Historical Fiction
*Alexandre Dumas, *The Three Musketeers* (Penguin). Famous novel depicting French life at the time of Richelieu.
Francis Steegmuller, *The Grand Mademoiselle* (1956). Novel about the richest woman in Europe and cousin of Louis XIV. Based upon excellent historical research.

33

THE CHALLENGE TO ABSOLUTISM: ENGLAND AND THE DUTCH NETHERLANDS

While royal absolutism was being perfected in France, England and the Dutch Netherlands were restricting the power of their kings (England) and nobles (the Netherlands). In these maritime nations, the numerous and prosperous commercial bourgeoisie played an important role in strengthening the rule of law and in establishing the principle of individual rights and liberties. These achievements strongly influenced later struggles against absolutism in many parts of the world.

1. ENGLAND: TUDOR AND EARLY STUART ABSOLUTISM

Absolutism reached its pinnacle in England during the Tudor period (1485–1603). We have already reviewed the methods practiced by Henry VII, Henry VIII, and Elizabeth I to control the political, economic, and religious destiny of their tight little island (see Chapter 26). Their success demanded great political skill, chiefly because they were heirs to a medieval tradition of limitation on royal power institutionalized in Parliament and the common law. The great Tudor monarchs carefully avoided assaulting these institutions openly. Instead they worked with infinite patience to consult with Parliament on controversial issues, to control its membership, and to respect the decisions of the courts. They were successful in large part because their ideas on the good of England happily coincided with the

basic interests of their subjects. Internal peace, prosperity, religious reform, success in foreign wars — no matter how achieved — were all popular.

However, as the Tudor period neared its end, there were increasing signs of tension and discontent. Many parliamentary leaders were increasingly restless with the way they were being manipulated. There was increasing dissatisfaction with the Tudor religious settlement, especially among the growing number of Puritans who believed that the Anglican establishment needed further reformation. Powerful economic interests, especially the country gentry and the burgeoning commercial classes, were eager to assert greater control over royal policy in order to promote their particular interests by removing ancient feudal restraints on agriculture and internal trade and by promoting a more aggressive position in foreign trade. Finally, the lessening of the Spanish threat after 1588 decreased dependence on the crown as the protector of the realm. A major change was in the making in England as the seventeenth century opened.

Despite the mounting problems, "Good Queen Bess" died a beloved ruler. But she left no immediate heirs, and the crown fell to a cousin, James Stuart, king of Scotland. James I (1603–1625) was a convinced absolutist, believing that God had set him on the throne to do as he pleased. But he was woefully ignorant of the hard work and the compromises required to make absolutism a reality in England. This combination of rigid ideology and political ineptitude soon led to a polarization of political forces in England.

James I began his reign by alienating the Puritans, who had great hope for sympathetic treatment because the new king had been ruler of Presbyterian Scotland. In fact, James was an avowed Anglican who met Puritan demands by threatening to harry them out of the land if they did not conform to the Church of England. He increased both Puritan and patriotic concerns by failing to support the Protestant forces in the Thirty Years' War and by making peace with Spain—moves that seemed to compromise the entire Protestant cause and England's national interests. As a practitioner of autocracy, James was a failure. He surrounded himself with incompetent and corrupt royal administrators. He repeatedly dismissed Parliament because of its refusal to grant his incessant requests for money and its bitter criticisms of his policies, his conduct, and his advisers. Without grants of funds from Parliament, James tried to utilize other means of raising funds which the courts declared contrary to custom and thus illegal. His response was to dismiss the stubborn judges, further confirming the growing belief that he had no respect for the constitution or the law.

As time passed, the mounting discontent found its focus in Parliament, especially in the House of Commons, a body theoretically representing all Englishmen but actually dominated by well-to-do country gentry, lawyers, and businessmen. On the whole, these were patriotic, God-fearing, conservative men who had no idea of triggering a revolution. But they were also men of political experience, intent on sharing with the king the governance of England because they believed the constitution gave them this right. James could not accept the outrageous idea that his power must be shared. As a consequence, his reign was marked by repeated confrontations between crown and Parliament, each increasingly marked by the issue of control over religious, administrative, financial, and foreign policy.

Under James' successor, Charles I (1625–1649),

the conflict developed into civil war. Charles was no less stubborn than James in refusing to bend before Parliament and the courts in their efforts to control his demands for taxes and the actions of his detested advisers. His heavy-handed resistance continued to alienate his subjects. The situation was made worse by a blundering foreign policy that resulted in costly wars but no victories. The sharpening antagonisms finally led the leaders of Parliament to confront the king with the Petition of Right (1628). This bold document demanded that the king desist from various illegal acts: imposing martial law in peacetime, taxing arbitrarily, imprisoning citizens without trial, and quartering soldiers with private citizens. It clearly posited a fundamental constitutional principle upon which Parliament was ready to stand: that even the king must be bound by the law. Desperate for money, Charles initially yielded to this challenge to his absolutist position. But when Parliament, in its next session in 1629, insisted that the king respect the Petition, he dismissed it over the bitter protests of its leaders.

For eleven years, Charles ruled without Parliament. To do so, he was forced to resort to financial and legal measures that constantly expanded the opposition to his tyranny. Ultimately, it was his religious policy that forced him once again to confront his enemies on their ground—in Parliament. Under the guidance of William Laud, archbishop of Canterbury, the royal government mounted a concerted effort to force a rigid Anglicanism on the entire realm. Not only was this policy so detestable to the Puritans that many of them fled to the New World in the name of religious liberty, but also it alarmed many Anglicans because it seemed to point England once again toward Roman Catholicism. It was the Scotch Presbyterians who refused to bend and thus precipitated a crisis. In 1639, they revolted and forced the king to summon Parliament in 1640 in order to raise money to resist their threat to the kingdom.

The first Parliament of 1640, called the Short Parliament, was dismissed after three weeks because it again challenged royal authority. But the Scots continued to press and Charles was forced to capitulate. He summoned the so-called

Long Parliament, which proceeded to legislate the end of Stuart absolutism. It forced Charles to sacrifice his chief ministers, including Laud. It abolished the hated extraordinary courts, including the Star Chamber and the Court of High Commission, which had long been tools of the crown to dodge the common law. An act was passed requiring a meeting of Parliament every three years and curbing the power of the king to dismiss Parliament. Severe limitations were placed on the king's power to tax without parliamentary approval. To all of this Charles acceded, chiefly because he needed money to fight the Scots.

Up to this point, Parliament had succeeded brilliantly in legislating what amounted to a bloodless revolution. But having established the upper hand, the parliamentary force began to falter in terms of how to use its power. This indecisiveness provided an opportunity for extremists to push their cause. They not only became more radical in their assaults on monarchy but also moved to end Anglicanism "root and branch" in favor of some form of Puritanism. Their mounting extremism cooled the ardor of many influential men who had been eager to limit royal power but were not ready to upset the established order completely. The division in the parliamentary ranks emboldened Charles to try to restore his control; he went so far in early 1642 as to attempt to arrest the leaders of Parliament. This action was a call to arms, pitting against each other elements of a ruling class that had lost its community of interest, which had long focused on the king.

2. ENGLISH CIVIL WAR, COMMONWEALTH, AND PROTECTORATE (1642–1660)

The opening of armed strife led to confusing alliances. A considerable following, soon known as the Cavaliers, rallied around Charles, who represented himself as the champion of the established order against the political and religious radicals in Parliament. The backbone of the Cavalier forces came from the great noble families and their clientele among the country gentry living in the more backward areas of northern and western England. The opposition, called the Roundheads, drew support from lawyers, the gentry of the south and the east, and the commercial interests; many from these elements were Puritans. This core was soon reinforced by radical elements from the poor and oppressed, especially those living in London. In the intricate matter of choosing sides, there figured complex personal factors—family ties, friendships, personal loyalties—much after the fashion of the American Civil War.

The first phase of the civil war lasted through 1646. While neither side was prepared militarily, for a time the Cavaliers seemed to have the upper hand. But the Roundheads had forces working in their favor: support of the navy, domination of the richest part of England, control over the regular administrative system and Parliament, power to vote taxation. In 1643, the Roundhead cause was bolstered by an alliance with the Scots. But ultimately, the outcome of the struggle was determined by the success of the Roundheads in creating an effective army. The chief architect of the victorious army was a simple farmer with strong Puritan convictions, Oliver Cromwell. He organized a cavalry regiment of disciplined, deeply religious recruits who proved more than a match for the Cavalier forces they faced. His system was soon applied to the entire Roundhead force to create the New Model Army, made up of selected troops paid and equipped in a businesslike fashion. Upon this force was imposed a strict discipline, strongly colored by Puritan ideas of godliness and sobriety. It quickly proved itself superior to the Cavalier army, so that by 1646, the Cavalier army was crushed and Charles was forced to surrender to the Scots.

However, with victory in their grasp, the Roundheads split into factions. The course of the struggle slowly transferred Roundhead leadership from moderate parliamentarians with a leaning toward Presbyterianism and a willingness to accept limited monarchy to more radical leaders. The emerging leaders were advocates of the abolition of the state church, the end of monarchy, democratic elections, and the redistribution of property. The strength of the radicals was located in the New Model Army.

Fearful that the radicals would assume complete control, the moderate Roundheads turned back toward the king, who suddenly discovered considerable enthusiasm for parliamentary control over the monarchy and for Presbyterianism. The Independents—as the radicals were called—were brilliantly led by Cromwell. They destroyed Charles' hopes in a single battle in 1648 and, along with it, the cause of the Cavaliers and the moderate Roundheads. Backed by the New Model Army, Cromwell acted decisively to ensure the position of the Independents. He purged the Long Parliament of all members not dedicated to his cause and gave to the so-called Rump Parliament chief authority in the land. It immediately legislated out of existence the Anglican Church, the House of Lords, and the monarchy. And, at Cromwell's urging, it decreed the execution of the king in 1649 on the grounds that he was "a tyrant, traitor, and murderer."

For eleven years after Charles I's death, Cromwell's forces sought to rule England without a king. Always in a minority and dependent on the army, their desperate experimentation failed to establish a stable order.

The first experiment sought to create a republican form of government called the Commonwealth. A one-house Parliament was made the supreme authority, with a state council of forty-one members charged with conducting the daily affairs of government. Led by Cromwell, the men who controlled the Commonwealth tried to steer England into constructive ways acceptable to most people. The political and religious extremists in the army were curbed, and considerable toleration was extended to all Protestants. Severe measures were taken to subdue the rebellious Irish and the Scots. An aggressive foreign policy, aimed at promoting English commercial and colonial interests, was undertaken. Navigation acts were passed to ensure that trade within England's emerging empire would be monopolized by England. War was waged on the Dutch, England's chief commercial rival. None of these policies, however, helped to popularize the Commonwealth. The Cromwellians could not shed their image as regicides and Puritan extremists. Resistance to the Commonwealth grew steadily.

"Oliver Cromwell," by Peter Lely. This portrait of the stern and godly hero of the Puritans in their struggle against Stuart absolutism suggests Cromwell's strength of purpose and will. *Photo: Snark International/EPA, Inc.*

Cromwell ultimately blamed the failure of the Commonwealth on what he considered the self-seeking leaders of the Rump Parliament. Finally, in 1653, he dissolved the Rump by force and tried to replace it with a hand-picked body (called the Barebones Parliament, in honor of Praise-God Barebones, the first name on its roll). This body failed to distinguish itself in any way, and it too was dissolved. Finally, the very instrument that had stood against tyranny—Parliament—was gone. The tide of revolution had peaked, leaving Cromwell and his army in complete control.

The Cromwellian forces tried one more experiment, called the Protectorate. A written constitution was formulated entrusting power to a protector, who was to be advised by a council and guided by a one-house Parliament elected by property holders from districts of approximately equal population. Cromwell was selected as the first Protector. From the beginning, he was unable to agree with Parliament on most issues, and he seldom heeded parliamentary advice.

Oliver seeking God while the K. is murthered by his order.

The deep religious fervor of the Puritans and the taint of regicide that lingered throughout the Commonwealth and the Protectorate are satirized here as Oliver Cromwell is shown at prayer while Charles I is being executed. *Photo: NYPL Picture Collection*

tion of monarchy. In 1657, Parliament asked Cromwell to become king, an honor he declined, but he did agree to remain Protector for life. Thus, when he died in 1658, the wheel had come nearly full circle: A man who had led his soldiers to the abolition of monarchy was himself king without title. Whether Cromwell had served England well or ill will probably always be debated. He has been called everything from a tyrannical religious bigot to a champion of democracy. Unquestionably, he was a man of great talent, especially capable in warfare and administration. He was driven by strong religious convictions that persuaded him of his duty to purify England of what he believed to be its sins — gambling, drinking, swearing, ostentatious living, staying away from church. Yet he generally favored a religious settlement for England that would allow broad freedom to most Protestants. Although compelled to rule autocratically, he believed in parliamentary government and tried until his dying day to establish it. Certainly England had few greater patriots. His ultimate failure was perhaps quite simple: Only a minority of Englishmen were willing to accept what he cherished most, Puritanism and republicanism.

At Cromwell's death, his son, Richard, became Protector. This weak figure was soon swept aside by forces favoring the restoration of monarchy. By 1660, elements in the New Model Army joined with men of property and commerce to end the Protectorate. A new Parliament was elected and immediately opened negotiations with Charles Stuart, the son of Charles I, living in exile awaiting the day of reckoning with those who had killed his father. In May 1660, all parties were satisfied, and Charles appeared in London, triumphantly greeted by a happy people weary of political experimentation.

3. THE ENGLISH RESTORATION (1660–1688)

The Restoration of the Stuarts by no means resolved the basic problems that had divided England since 1603, particularly those involving the relationship between king and Parliament and the religious establishment. Between 1660

For what he found was that Parliament reflected political and religious positions that ran contrary to the convictions of those who alone could sustain him in power, the "godly" men of the New Model Army. Despite his realization that civilian control of the state alone would assure stability, Cromwell was forced to rely on the army. To curb disorder, he finally had to impose martial law in England. The rule of his puritanical army officers was detested by most Englishmen, and so increasingly was their leader.

Opinion began to run in favor of the restora-

and 1688, these problems continued to disturb England. However, the struggles of the Restoration era were more moderate than had been the case in the preceding two decades. Most Englishmen were weary of the dogmatism, the violence, the tampering with ancient institutions, and the burden of godliness that had plagued national life between 1640 and 1660. They were ready for "a very merry, dancing, quaffing and unthinkable time." For all his faults, Charles II proved to be a king who won the hearts of his subjects, something the austere, godly Cromwellians had failed to do.

The reign of Charles II began in a climate of forgiving compromise. The king and Parliament joined in repealing all the acts of the Commonwealth and the Protectorate. Only a few Cromwellians were punished by execution; the spirit of vengeance was slaked by digging up and hanging Cromwell's body. Generous arrangements were made for restoring to original owners the property confiscated during the civil war, a great boon to England's wealthy landowners. The king was assured of a sizable income on a regular basis, but he was deprived of many ancient feudal rights that had allowed his predecessors to exact taxes without approval of Parliament. Not only was control of taxation reserved to Parliament, but the Triennial Act was passed to ensure that it would meet every three years whether or not the king so wished. However, this settlement did not get to the basic political issue: where ultimate authority rested.

Even less satisfactory was the religious settlement embodied in a series of parliamentary acts passed in 1661 and 1662 and known as the Clarendon Code after Charles II's chief adviser, the Earl of Clarendon. These acts not only reestablished the Anglican Church but also threatened to destroy the Independents and Presbyterians. The Act of Uniformity required all clergymen to abide by the Book of Common Prayer. The Corporation Act ruled that all members of city governments worship in the Anglican Church. The Conventicle Act made religious meetings other than Anglican illegal, and the Five Mile Act forbade all preachers who were not Anglican to come within five miles of any city. In brief, the Clarendon Code promised to nonconformists (that is, non-Anglicans) little better than criminal status.

These troublesome issues soon began to surface, to divide opinion and generate conflict. They were intensified by a series of disasters that befell England during the early years of Charles' reign. He involved England in a war with the Dutch which led to a humiliating defeat. In 1665, a plague struck England, to be followed the next year by a fire which destroyed most of London. Many god-fearing Englishmen felt that these misfortunes were divine retribution for the immorality of the royal court, where the model of profligacy was set by the king himself.

Parliament again became the focus of dissatisfaction. It reacted to public wrath by forcing Clarendon out of office and by becoming stingier in its grants of taxation. Charles responded by turning to Louis XIV of France for help. In an alliance of 1670, Louis promised him a sizable subsidy provided that Charles join Louis in a war on the Dutch and work for the restoration of Roman Catholicism in England. When in 1672 Charles tried to set aside laws against Catholics, an outraged Parliament passed the Test Act (1673), excluding Catholics from all public offices. And when the king joined France in a war against the Dutch in 1672–1674, Parliament blocked him by refusing financial aid.

Charles showed considerable ingenuity in neutralizing Parliament. He minimized its power to coerce the king through its control over taxation by relying on Louis XIV for subsidies. More significantly, he skillfully built a parliamentary party devoted to strong monarchy and Anglicanism. Its members, scornfully dubbed *Tories* (a term used to designate Irish bandits) by the opposition, could often control Parliament in support of the king. An opposing party, committed to parliamentary supremacy and religious tolerance for all Protestants, was also formed; its members were called *Whigs* (after a term used to designate Scottish horse thieves and murderers). By skillful use of the Tories and French money, Charles enjoyed considerable freedom during his last years. However, fear that he would use this freedom to restore Catholicism grew steadily, fanned by the Whigs, who saw a "popish plot" in almost everything the king did. The Whigs bent their main efforts to the enactment of an Exclusion Act which would have barred Charles' Catholic brother, James, from the throne. Charles defeated their effort, but his methods convinced the despairing Whigs that tyranny—even worse, popish tyranny—had returned to England.

James II (1685–1688) inherited a strong position from his brother, based in large part on the Tory majority in Parliament. But he soon dissipated this strength by his open avowal of Roman Catholicism, the one thing that neither Tories nor Whigs would tolerate. From the beginning of his reign, James began to fill key positions in the army and the civil administration with avowed Catholics. In 1687, he issued the Declaration of Indulgence. Although this move relaxed restrictions on all religious groups, Protestant dissenters and Roman Catholics alike, most Protestants viewed it as a concession to Catholicism. Finally, in 1688, a son born to James by his Roman Catholic wife was baptized in the Catholic faith, ensuring that the Stuart dynasty would be perpetuated by a Catholic successor.

This was the last straw. Tory and Whig leaders set aside their rivalries long enough to invite James' Protestant daughter, Mary, and her husband, William of Orange, the rulers of the Dutch Netherlands, to assume England's throne. William, eager to ensure England's support against the French threat to his country, accepted. When he invaded England in late 1688, the great majority of the people rallied to his side; James II fled to France. For a second time, the unhappy Stuarts had been forced off England's throne, but this time the revolution was bloodless.

4. ENGLAND'S GLORIOUS REVOLUTION AND ITS CONSEQUENCES

The flight of James II, unlike the execution of Charles I, did not lead to radical political experimentation. Instead, what the English call a Glorious Revolution was carried through in the form of several fundamental legal enactments that pacified England and established the basis for her future political system.

Immediately after the triumph of William and Mary, Parliament declared James deposed by reason of abdicating his office. The new rulers were required to take a coronation oath which bound them to abide by the decisions of Parliament and the ancient laws of England. The Bill of Rights was passed in 1689. This fundamental charter laid down Parliament's authority to depose a king and choose a new one. It assured to the members of Parliament the right of free speech, immunity from prosecution for statements made in debate, and freedom from royal intervention in elections. It forbade a variety of acts that had long been the basis for royal absolutism: taxation without consent of Parliament, dispensing with laws, maintaining a standing army in peacetime, requiring excessive bail, depriving citizens of the right to trial in the regular courts, interfering with jurors, and denying people the right to petition the king. A Toleration Act was also enacted, allowing religious freedom to Puritans and Independents, although non-Protestants were still denied freedom.

Launched on this positive note, the reign of William and Mary was marked by other successes that proved popular. William led an army into Ireland, where discontent had long festered and which now became a center of Stuart intrigue aimed at recovering the throne. Having established control by force, he launched a policy which aimed at reducing Ireland to colonial status—a policy that provided splendid opportunities for English landlords to uproot Irish Catholic landowners and take possession of their lands. He began negotiations with the Scots that bore fruit after his death. In 1707, Parliament passed the Act of Union which joined the two kingdoms into a political unit henceforth known as the United Kingdom of Great Britain, gave Scotland a liberal number of seats in Parliament, and guaranteed her Presbyterian religious establishment. Most significant was the new orientation which William gave to England's foreign policy. In essence, he threw all of England's resources into the struggle to prevent Louis XIV from establishing French dominance in Europe. This action was decisive. Not only were Louis XIV's ambitious plans foiled, but England emerged from the wars caused by the

French threat as a major power well on the way to acquiring a world empire.

There remained one other question to settle — the succession problem. The immediate succession to William and Mary was clear enough; the crown would fall to Anne, another Protestant daughter of James II. But it was apparent that she would have no heirs, raising the specter that the crown would again fall to the Roman Catholic branch of the Stuart family. To avoid this possibility, Parliament in 1701 enacted the Act of Settlement, which provided that none but Protestants could inherit the throne. On the basis of this principle, Parliament designated the Protestant granddaughter of James I, Sophia of Hanover, and her heirs as successors to Anne. Despite considerable sentiment in favor of restoring the dynasty of James II, this act was honored at the death of Queen Anne (1702–1714), and George of Hanover became King George I of Great Britain.

The establishment of parliamentary supremacy in the wake of the Glorious Revolution left unresolved one major constitutional issue — that of the exact nature of the executive power responsible for the conduct of the routine affairs of state. Many feared trusting this responsibility to the king lest he find new opportunities to regain control over political life. Yet Parliament was in no position to take up this burden. During the half century after 1688, a solution was found that permitted Parliament to control the executive branch while still assuring the effective conduct of state business. The answer lay in the emergence of the *cabinet system*.

For centuries, English kings had relied on powerful ministers to assist in conducting government affairs and in shaping policy. Until 1688, these ministers had usually been chosen by the king and were responsible to him. Although there were often bitter complaints about the conduct of these bulwarks of royal authority, there usually was little that could be done to control them — short of violence. After the supremacy of Parliament was established in 1688–1689, this began to change. From the reign of William and Mary on, royal ministers were increasingly chosen on the basis of their ability to influence Parliament, especially the House of Commons. Since Commons tended to divide into parties that controlled large blocs of votes, it proved wisest for the rulers to seek out party leaders from that body for appointment as ministers responsible for exercising executive functions.

With the accession of Anne, this trend developed rapidly. Neither she nor the first Hanoverians, George I (1714–1727) and George II (1727–1760), were especially qualified for or interested in the rigorous tasks of administration. As a consequence, the direction of the government and the formulation of policy fell into the hands of royal ministers able to secure from Parliament approval to carry on the affairs of state in the name of the monarch. This *cabinet* of ministers slowly learned to accept mutual responsibility for the total operation of the government, which required that they all be members of the same party and that they use their collective influence in Parliament to assure approval of their program. If they failed to command a majority in that body, then they had to surrender their positions as ministers in favor of a new cabinet that did have a parliamentary majority. One member of the cabinet, the *prime minister*, came to be recognized as the leader and spokesman of the whole group; a major qualification for this designation was leadership of the majority party in Commons.

Although Queen Anne relied heavily on John Churchill, Duke of Marlborough, to conduct her government, the first real prime minister and architect of the cabinet system was Robert Walpole. A long-time member of Commons, he became George I's chief minister in 1721, chiefly because of his leadership of the dominant Whig party in Commons. From then until 1742, he virtually ran England by surrounding himself with fellow ministers who could control votes in Parliament. A coarse, hard-drinking country squire, Walpole was not above bribery and the shameless use of patronage to keep his party strong and to run England in a way that served Whig interests. But he did conduct an orderly administration. Not until he lost control of Commons over a foreign policy issue was he forced to relinquish his position as prime minister. However, the king had little choice but to appoint another prime minister and cabinet that could command a majority in Parliament. Henceforth

This scene shows Robert Walpole, who served as prime minister of England from 1721 to 1742, presiding over a session of the Cabinet. Walpole and the other Cabinet members shown here all were members of Parliament and belonged to the majority party in that body. In sessions such as this they decided upon the major policies to be followed by the government; their control of Parliament allowed them to enact their decisions. Thus, the Cabinet became the effective executive power in Great Britain, a position that it still holds today. The emergence of the Cabinet system was one of the major outcomes of the bitter political struggle in seventeenth-century England. *Photo: The Bettmann Archive*

to the present, the executive functions of government in Great Britain would be carried out in the name of the monarch by a circle of party leaders who could command a majority in the House of Commons but who were likewise required to render account to that body for their conduct of public affairs.

The Glorious Revolution and the settlement that followed marked a turning point in England's history. Two great decisions had been worked out to the satisfaction of most Englishmen. First, royal absolutism had been repudiated in favor of a limited monarchy entrusting ultimate authority to an elected Parliament. Second, religious uniformity had given way to religious toleration for all Protestants. The resolution of these issues restored England's internal stability and provided a basis for her rapid advance to the status of world power. Hardly less important, the English revolution and English system of constitutional monarchy were destined to serve as models for other nations impatient with absolutist government.

5. THE DUTCH NETHERLANDS: ECONOMIC AND POLITICAL ACHIEVEMENTS

Across the narrow waters of the English Channel, an even more exciting chapter in the drama of man's endless struggle for freedom was being enacted throughout the seventeenth century. There the Dutch people succeeded in setting up the freest society anywhere in the world. They also led the world in commerce, banking, and the arts and sciences. Numbering approximately one million and living mostly on islands, peninsulas, and land reclaimed from the sea with a total area about the size of the state of Maryland, the Dutch enjoyed a world-wide hegemony, filling a power vacuum that began with the death of Philip II of Spain in 1598 and ended with the coming to power of Louis XIV of France in 1661.

It will be recalled (see pp. 374–375) that the Dutch had won their independence from Spain as a result of Philip II's crusade to crush Protestantism in Europe. The ten southern provinces of the Netherlands (now Belgium) were overrun and submitted to Spanish and Roman Catholic rule, but the seven northern (Dutch) provinces, taking advantage of their geography, their superior navy, and the brilliant leadership of William (the Silent) of Orange and his sons, fought on to victory against the world's mightiest military power. When the long and costly war finally ended in 1609, the Dutch, far from being exhausted, exhibited a phenomenal burst of energy.

The seafaring economy of the Dutch had been founded originally upon the fishing industry. In the fourteenth century great shoals of herrings migrated from the Baltic to waters north of the Netherlands, and the Dutch discovered a secret formula for preserving them. By the time of their revolt from Spain, their fishing activities employed some twelve thousand ships and one hundred fifty thousand people. Their experienced sailors played a vital role in the struggle for independence. They also plundered Spain's commerce and overseas colonies. When Spain, in the midst of the war, temporarily annexed Portugal, the Dutch took advantage of Portugal's misfortune to seize most of her vast and lucrative Eastern empire. Throughout the seventeenth century, the Dutch East India Company, set up in 1602 to monopolize trade with the East Indies, paid annual dividends of up to 200 and 300 percent. The Dutch traders also took advantage of their favored geographical position at the mouth of the Rhine and its tributaries, and their excellent harbors along the east-west trade routes of Northern Europe, to gain a near monopoly of the carrying trade of Europe. At the time the Dutch gained their independence, more than half the water-borne commerce of Europe was carried in the broad-bellied Dutch ships, and more than half the ships of Europe were built in Dutch shipyards.

To handle the huge cash flow this commerce engendered, the Dutch set up the Bank of Amsterdam in 1609. This was a seminational bank—a private joint stock company closely supervised by the government. This bank served as Europe's chief money exchange during the seventeenth and eighteenth centuries. It became a model for the Bank of England, which was founded nearly a century later; for the Bank of France, which Napoleon established two hundred years later; and, indeed, for the United States Federal Reserve System. Amsterdam replaced Antwerp (in the Southern Netherlands) as the world's busiest port and financial center.

The economy of the United Provinces, as the Dutch Republic was called in the seventeenth century, determined in large measure the nature

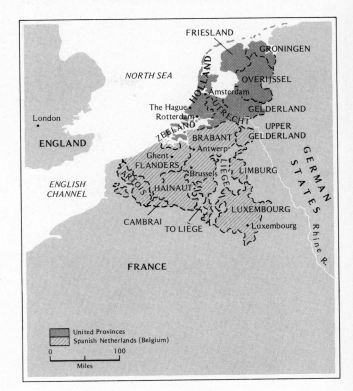

THE UNITED PROVINCES IN 1609

of their political life. Nowhere else in Europe were the nobility so overshadowed in wealth and influence by the bourgeoisie. The strength of the bourgeoisie lay in the commercial centers, particularly the cities of Holland and Zeeland. These commercial and financial leaders, fearing the establishment of a strong central government under the influence of the feudal nobility—particularly the House of Orange—saw to it that the government remained highly decentralized. Only a weak States General exercised some supervision over the country as a whole. Holland, the richest and the most populous of the seven provinces, was essentially a merchant oligarchy. Under this political system, the people of the Dutch Netherlands enjoyed a greater amount of freedom than the people of any other European country. The Dutch Declaration of Independence of 1581 contains many ideas and phrases that were to be found in the English Bill of Rights a

century later and in the American and French Declarations — of Independence and of the Rights of Man and the Citizen, respectively — approximately two centuries later. Religious freedom also prevailed. The Reformed (Calvinist) Church was established by law, but other churches and religious minorities were treated with toleration.

"Syndics of the Cloth Guild," by Rembrandt. In the Dutch Netherlands of the seventeenth century, commerce was king. Under the leadership of men like these, the tiny Dutch Netherlands attained a first-rank position in the world of science, philosophy, and trade. Rembrandt, one of the greatest portrait painters of all time, was probably also the greatest of the baroque painters. *Photo: Fotocommissie Rijksmuseum Amsterdam*

6. THE DUTCH NETHERLANDS: INTELLECTUAL AND ARTISTIC ACHIEVEMENTS

Such political freedom and religious toleration attracted some of the greatest intellects of Europe, who found refuge in the United Provinces and contributed to their intellectual vigor. Notable examples are René Descartes from France, John Locke from England, and Baruch Spinoza, whose Jewish family had fled religious persecution in Portugal. A free press enabled the

Dutch Netherlands to become the world's chief publisher of books.

But the Dutch during the seventeenth century were producing an impressive array of writers, artists, and scientists of their own. Hugo Grotius' *On the Law of War and Peace* was the first great treatise on international law and has remained a classic on the subject ever since. Joost van den Vondel was the greatest of all Dutch poets. His epic poem *Lucifer* is believed to have served as a model for Milton's *Paradise Lost*. This was the golden age of Dutch painters. While the baroque painters in other countries were glorifying the royalty and the nobility, Jan Vermeer, Franz Hals, and, above all, Rembrandt van Rijn were revealing the nature of Dutch society by dignifying — sometimes glamorizing — the middle and lower classes. Dutch scientists invented the telescope and the microscope. The first great microscopist, Anton van Leeuwenhoek, discovered blood corpuscles, the cellular structure of living tissue, and bacteria (two hundred years before Pasteur learned how to combat them). The most renowned scientist in the Western world in the seventeenth century was Christian Huygens. Among other things he invented the pendulum clock, man's first means of accurately measuring short intervals of time, and introduced the wave theory of light.

Such material and cultural achievements, of course, excited the envy of the United Provinces' larger neighbors. But it required several decades of all-out fighting by Cromwellian and Stuart England by sea and Louis XIV's France by land to break the power of the Dutch, near the close of the seventeenth century. Even then, Amsterdam remained Europe's financial capital for another hundred years.

Suggested Reading

General Treatments

R. Lockyer, *Tudor and Stuart Britain* (1964). A brilliant survey of the entire period.

*G. M. Trevelyan, *England Under the Stuarts* (21st ed., 1949). An older work, deeply sympathetic with the parliamentary cause and anti-Stuart, but exciting to read and full of information concerning social history.

*C. Hill, *The Century of Revolution, 1607–1714* (Norton). A treatment of the period from a Marxist perspective providing fresh insight into economic factors involved in the English Revolution.

J. R. Tanner, *English Constitutional Conflicts in the Seventeenth Century* (1928). Provides an excellent description of the major constitutional issues surrounding the English Revolution.

*W. Haller, *The Rise of Puritanism* (Pennsylvania). A perceptive treatment of the religious forces at work in seventeenth-century England.

*L. Stone, *The Causes of the English Revolution, 1529–1642* (Harper Torchbook). An excellent review of modern interpretations of the causes of the English Revolution.

The First Stuarts, the Civil War, the Age of Cromwell

*C. V. Wedgwood, *The King's Peace, 1637–1641* (Collier); *The King's War, 1641–1647* (Collier); and *A Coffin for King Charles* (Collier). Masterful treatments of the crucial years of the English civil war, distinguished by brilliant writing.

C. V. Wedgwood, *Oliver Cromwell* (rev. ed., 1973).

*Christopher Hill, *God's Englishman: Oliver Cromwell and the English Revolution* (Harper Torchbook). This and the preceding title are excellent studies of Cromwell's life written from differing points of view.

R. E. Boyer, ed., *Oliver Cromwell and the Puritan Revolution: Failure of a Man or a Faith?* (1966). A collection of essays representing the conflicting views of modern historians concerning Cromwell's accomplishments.

Michael Walzer, *The Revolution of the Saints: A Study of the Origins of Radical Politics* (1965). An excellent account of the radical elements that played a part in the English Revolution.

*C. Hill, *The World Turned Upside Down: Radical Ideas During the English Revolution* (Penguin). A brilliant treatment of the "lunatic" fringe of the seventeenth-century England and the special influence this element had on the course of the English Revolution.

The Restoration, the Glorious Revolution, and the Aftermath

*G. M. Trevelyan, *The English Revolution, 1688–1689* (Galaxy). A penetrating analysis of the events of 1688–1689 and their significance.

*G. Straka, ed., *The Revolution of 1688; Whig Triumph or Palace Revolution* (2nd ed., Heath). A good collection of conflicting interpretations of the Glorious Revolution.

*P. Laslett, *The World We Have Lost* (Scribner). A splendid evocation of English society about 1700.

The Dutch Netherlands

S. Baxter, *William of Orange and the Defense of Europe, 1650–1702* (1966). The best biography of the great Dutchman who became King of England and led the defense of Europe against Louis XIV.

P. Geyl, *The Netherlands in the Seventeenth Century, 1609–1715* (2 vols., 1961–1964). Sound survey by a leading Dutch scholar.

*C. Wilson, *The Dutch Republic and the Civilization of the Seventeenth Century* (World University Library). Excellent brief account, charmingly written.

Sources

Carl Stephenson and Frederick George Marcham, eds., *Sources of English Constitutional History* (1937). A rich collection of key political documents, including the Petition of Right and the Bill of Rights, which spell out the issues of the English Revolution.

*John Locke, *Two Treatises of Government* (many editions). The classic statement of the political ideology that inspired the English Revolution and especially the Glorious Revolution.

*Samuel Pepys, *Diary* (Harper Torchbook). A fascinating eyewitness picture of English social life during the Restoration period.

34

THE RISE OF PRUSSIA AND RUSSIA

The most significant political developments in Central and Eastern Europe during the seventeenth and eighteenth centuries were the rise of Prussia and Russia. At the opening of the seventeenth century, the two chief powers in Central and Eastern Europe were the Ottoman and Hapsburg empires. Although the Moslem Ottoman Turks had been restrained by Hapsburg military power in the sixteenth century on both land and sea, they were about to renew their effort to conquer Christian Europe. The Austrian Hapsburgs, in addition to disputing the control of Southeastern Europe with the Turks, dominated the Holy Roman Empire, which included all the German states. In Northeastern Europe, Sweden, Prussia, Poland, and Russia competed for hegemony. Among all these powers, Prussia and Russia had hitherto been the least conspicuous in world affairs.

1. THE EARLY HOHENZOLLERNS

The history of Prussia is in large measure the history of the Hohenzollern family. This aggressive and prolific dynasty was first heard of in the tenth century. At that time the Hohenzollerns were obscure counts ruling over the castle of Zollern and a tiny bit of surrounding territory in southwest Germany just north of the Swiss border. In the twelfth century they became burgraves of Nuremberg, an important commercial city in Bavaria. Early in the fifteenth century the Holy Roman Emperor, looking for an able ruler for the mark of Brandenburg, a military province near the exposed northeastern border of the empire, chose the head of the house of Hohenzollern. Although its ruler was one of the seven electors of the Holy Roman Emperor, Brandenburg was a bleak and thinly populated little province. Yet around this nucleus the Hohenzollerns built the important state of Prussia, and later the German Empire—the world's most powerful and feared nation.

From the time the Hohenzollerns became margraves of Brandenburg (1415) until they were finally overthrown at the end of World War I in 1918, they followed a threefold policy from which they never veered: militarism and territorial aggrandizement, paternal despotism, and centralized bureaucracy. No state in modern times has been so wedded to militarism as a cardinal feature of national life and policy as that of the Hohenzollerns, and few modern states have been more autocratic in their government and society.

Early in the seventeenth century Brandenburg began to expand. In 1609 the Hohenzollerns inherited three little provinces in and near the Rhine Valley far to the west, and nine years later they inherited East Prussia, a fief of Poland on the Baltic Sea far to the east. In 1640 Frederick William, the Great Elector, one of the ablest of all

This photo illustrates some of the military vigor and discipline that made Prussia an important European power, and the German nation, for many decades, one of the most dangerous and feared military powers in the world. *Photo: Culver Pictures*

the Hohenzollerns, became margrave and began filling in the territorial gaps. His first move was to take Brandenburg out of the Thirty Years' War, which had been devastating the Germanies for the past twenty-two years. While the other adversaries, France, Sweden, the Hapsburgs, and many of the small German states, exhausted themselves in eight more years of struggle, Brandenburg recouped her strength and resources. Reentering the war shortly before its end, she was in a position to demand and get valuable

territories. According to the terms of the Treaty of Westphalia (1648), Brandenburg received Eastern Pomerania, a sizable strip of territory that gave her valuable frontage on the Baltic, the large bishopric of Magdeburg, which straddled the Elbe, and several smaller bishoprics. Shortly afterward Frederick William gained the independence of East Prussia from Poland.

The Great Elector centralized and administered the governments of his scattered territories with energy and skill. He protected the native industries, improved communications, and aided agriculture. In a most intolerant age he followed a policy of religious toleration. When Louis XIV revoked the Edict of Nantes in 1685, Frederick William welcomed thousands of industrious Huguenots to Brandenburg. At the death of the Great Elector in 1688, Brandenburg was on the road to becoming a great power.

The next Hohenzollern, Frederick I (1688–1713), acquired the title of king for the dynasty. The Hapsburg Holy Roman Emperor in 1701 granted Frederick the title in return for aid against Louis XIV in the War of the Spanish Succession. Frederick I chose Prussia rather than Brandenburg for the name of his kingdom, since Prussia was outside the Holy Roman Empire and a free sovereign state. Hence Brandenburg became Prussia.

From 1713 to 1740 Prussia was ruled by a vigorous militaristic autocrat, Frederick William I (since he was the first Frederick William to be king). Unquestioned absolutism, machinelike centralized bureaucratic administration, and above all militarism were his obsessions. He built the Prussian army into the most efficient and one of the largest fighting forces in Europe. And yet Frederick William was so efficient and miserly that he was also able to pass along to his talented son a well-filled treasury.

The talented son, the future Frederick the Great, was a "problem" child. An ardent lover of music, literature, and philosophy, young Frederick hated militarism and governmental details. He even attempted to flee the country to escape the stern discipline of his disgruntled father. Arrested, he was forced to undergo exceptionally rigorous training from the bottom up in the army and the government services. Eventually Frederick became enamored of both, and Frederick William I died happy, sure that the Hohenzollern state would pass into good hands.

2. THE EMERGENCE OF PRUSSIA AS A GREAT POWER UNDER FREDERICK THE GREAT, 1740–1786

In the same year that Frederick II became king of Prussia (1740), the beautiful and gracious young Maria Theresa became archduchess of the Austrian Hapsburg dominions. These dominions included, in addition to the Austrian lands, the Kingdom of Hungary and the triune crown of Bohemia, Moravia, and Silesia. Maria Theresa's father, Emperor Charles VI, had spent much time in his last years attempting to safeguard his daughter's accession to the Hapsburg throne. He succeeded in obtaining the signatures of virtually every European sovereign, including the king of Prussia, to a document called the Pragmatic Sanction, which guaranteed the integrity of Maria Theresa's crown and territories. Two months after Charles VI died, however, Frederick II, without a declaration of war, marched his troops into and seized Silesia, one of the richest of the Hapsburg provinces. This Machiavellian act of the young Prussian king plunged most of the major European states into a series of wars for the mastery of Central Europe. Bavaria, Saxony, France, and Spain rushed in to despoil Maria Theresa of her territories. Only Great Britain and the Dutch Netherlands took the side of Austria. Great Britain was a bitter rival of France in India and North America, and she was also concerned for the Austrian Netherlands, with which she enjoyed a profitable trade, and for Hanover, whose ruling family now sat on the British throne. The Dutch were fearful of renewed French aggression in their direction.

The War of the Austrian Succession lasted for eight years (1740–1748). Maria Theresa successfully repelled the Bavarians, Saxons, French, and Spaniards, but she was unable to dislodge Frederick II from Silesia. Frederick, on his part, cynically deserted his allies as soon as he had achieved his own purposes. The Treaty of Aix-la-Chapelle in 1748 brought the hostilities to an end. Frederick retained Silesia, and Maria Theresa's husband, Francis of Lorraine, was recognized as Holy Roman Emperor. The only real gainer from the war was Frederick II. Silesia, a fertile province inhabited by more than a million German-speaking people, nearly doubled the population and resources of Prussia.

The Hapsburgs, however, had no intention of being thus despoiled of one of their fairest provinces by the upstart Hohenzollerns. Proud rulers over territories many times the size and population of Prussia and for centuries emperors of the Holy Roman Empire, of which Prussia was but a member state, they viewed the Hohenzollerns with condescension. Maria Theresa's able diplomat, Count Kaunitz, was soon at work lining up allies. Saxony, Sweden, Russia, and even France were won over. Spain, now ruled by the Bourbons, later followed France into the alliance. This time, however, Great Britain took the side of Prussia. She did this in order to oppose her archenemy France, with whom she was already at war in India and North America, and to safeguard Hanover. This double shifting of alliances came to be called the Diplomatic Revolution. Since Great Britain was Prussia's only ally and since her aid was limited to subsidies and to tying down French forces overseas, the opposition was certain of victory over Frederick II. They were already dividing up his territories, leaving him only the little original Hohenzollern province of Brandenburg.

But Frederick was not one to wait for his enemies to strike first. As soon as he became aware of their designs, he opened hostilities by overrunning Saxony. Thus began the Seven Years' War (1756–1763), the bloodiest war in history up to that time. Frederick, with his slender resources, soon found himself at bay; the four greatest military powers on the continent of Europe were closing in on him from all directions. The Austrians advanced from the south, the Russians from the east, the Swedes from the north, and the French from the west. Hurling his disciplined but ever-dwindling army against first one and then another of his enemies, Frederick held them off for seven years. His lightning

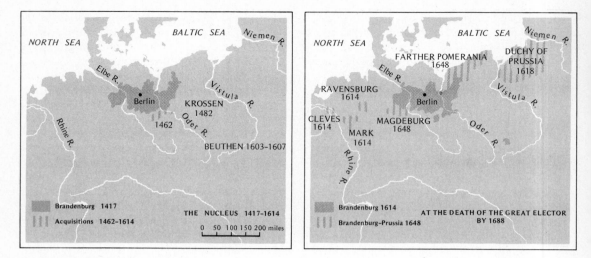

THE GROWTH OF PRUSSIA 1417–1807

marches, tricky maneuvers, and indefatigable tenacity in the face of seemingly hopeless odds won for him the title, "the Great." But after six years the end appeared to be near. His treasury was empty, his manpower exhausted, much of his territory laid waste. The Russians even captured and burned his capital, Berlin. Then suddenly fortune changed. In 1762 the Russian Tsarina Elizabeth, one of his bitterest enemies, died and was succeeded by the weakling Peter III, who was an ardent admirer of Frederick II and who put Russia's forces at the disposal of Prussia. Although Peter III was soon murdered by a group of his own officers and court nobility and Russia withdrew from the war, the remaining allies had no further stomach for the fight. The Peace of Hubertusburg in 1763 left things as they were at the beginning of the war, Prussia retaining the controversial Silesia. In the same year the Treaty of Paris brought to a close the colonial struggle between Great Britain and France in India and North America, leaving Great Britain master of both.

Having so narrowly escaped destruction, Frederick the Great spent the remaining twenty-three years of his life reconstructing his war-ravaged territories. His career as an enlightened despot will be surveyed in Chapter 37. He encouraged agriculture, subsidized and protected industry, and invited immigrants into his well-governed territories. At no time, though, did he neglect his war machine. In 1772 he joined Austria and Russia in the first partition of Poland. Frederick took West Prussia, thus joining East Prussia with the main body of the Prussian state. When Frederick II died in 1786, Prussia had been raised to the status of a great power, sharing equally with Austria the leadership of Central Europe. During his reign Prussia's size and population had more than doubled, and her military exploits pointed to a spectacular future.

3. RUSSIA BEFORE PETER THE GREAT

While Prussia was becoming a great power in Central Europe, Russia was rising to prominence to the east. The first shaping of some of the Slavic tribes of Eastern Europe into what eventually became the Russian national state was begun by Viking invaders in the ninth century. These intrepid seamen moved out from their Scandinavian homes in all directions—across the Atlantic, into the Mediterranean, and up the rivers of what are now England, France, Germany, and Russia (the word *Russia* is apparently derived from the Swedish word for rower). Their most important commercial and political center in Eastern Europe was Kiev, which became Rus-

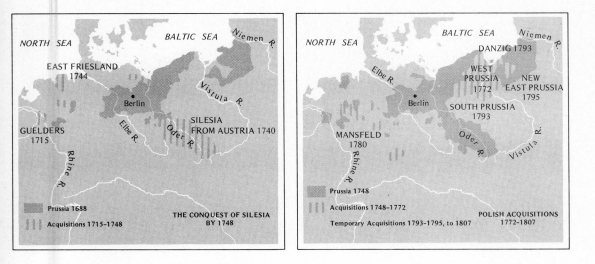

sia's first capital. Eventually the Norse invaders adopted the Slavic culture of their subjects.

In the tenth century Christianity was brought to Russia by missionaries from Constantinople. This is probably the most significant development in Russian history, for through the influence of the Greek Orthodox Church, whose headquarters were in Constantinople, Russia became a semi-Oriental Byzantine civilization and was cut off from the Greco-Roman and Roman Catholic culture common to the countries of Central and Western Europe. English, Spanish, Polish, and Swedish churchmen were constantly traveling to Rome, where they associated with churchmen from Italy, Hungary, France, and Germany. Russian churchmen, on the other hand, traveled to Constantinople, where they encountered only Greek, Serbian, Bulgarian, and Rumanian churchmen of the Balkan Peninsula.

Second in importance only to Greek Orthodox Christianity in the infusion of Oriental influence into Russian civilization was the Tartar conquest of the thirteenth century. Around the turn of the thirteenth century the Mongol conqueror Genghis Khan (1162–1227) had established a vast empire in Eastern Asia. Shortly after his death the Golden Horde, as the Mongol warriors were called, swept westward into Christian Europe. The thirteenth-century Europeans were

no match for the Tartars. Russia was easily overrun, and in 1241 a combined German and Polish army was defeated at Liegnitz in the heart of Central Europe. All Christian Europe appeared to be at the mercy of the invaders. At that moment, however, the great khan died in Eastern Asia, and the Tartar commander withdrew his forces to Russia and hastened back to seize his share of the spoils. The Golden Horde never resumed its triumphal surge westward, but for two and a half centuries it inundated Russia. Although there was little mixing of blood between the Mongol Tartars and the Caucasian Russians, there was considerable mixing of cultures. When the Mongol tide finally receded near the end of the fifteenth century, a deposit of such characteristically Oriental traits as backward-looking conservatism, fatalism, female seclusion, and absolutism in government had been added to the Byzantine cultural influence.

During the Tartar occupation the grand dukes of Muscovy managed to ingratiate themselves with their Mongol masters and build up their own influence and power. Moscow replaced Kiev as the political center of Russia. The first of the grand dukes of Muscovy under whom Russia took on the shape of a modern national state was Ivan III (1462–1505). In 1480 Ivan III defeated the rapidly declining Tartars and lim-

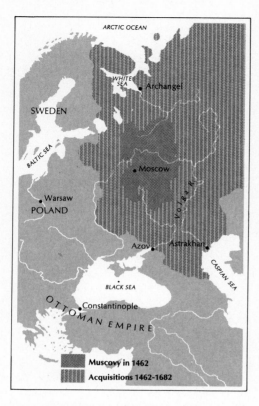

THE GROWTH OF RUSSIA IN THE WEST

ited their power in Russia to the southeastern area. Ivan greatly extended his sway both to the north and to the west by military conquest. A momentous event in Ivan III's reign was his marriage to Sophia Palaeologus, heiress to the now-defunct Byzantine (Eastern Roman) Empire. Ivan immediately declared himself successor to the Eastern Roman Caesars—hence the title Tsar. When he died, the foundations of a Russian national state had been laid.

Ivan IV (1533–1584) the Terrible added both to the authority of the Russian tsars and to the territories over which they ruled. He destroyed the remaining power of the Tartars in southeastern Russia and annexed most of their territory. The Ottoman Turks, however, seized the strategic Tartar territory north of the Black Sea. Although Ivan IV established trade relations with England by way of the White Sea and the Arctic Ocean,

his efforts to gain a foothold on the Baltic were frustrated by Sweden and Poland. It was during Ivan IV's reign that Russia's conquest of Siberia was begun. Half a century later the Russian flag was planted on the shores of the Pacific.

The twenty-nine years following the death of Ivan IV are known as the Time of Troubles (1584–1613). Weak rulers and disputed successions resulted in such anarchy that the Poles were able to capture Moscow and hold it briefly. To end the political chaos, a group of leading nobles in 1613 chose Michael Romanov as tsar. The Romanov dynasty was to rule Russia until the Communist revolution of 1917. Throughout the seventeenth century, Russia under the early Romanovs slowly but gradually established commercial and cultural contacts with the West. Increasing numbers of traders, craftsmen, and adventurers from Central and Western Europe,

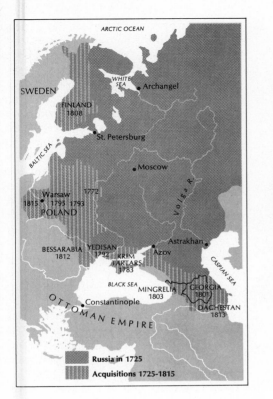

particularly Germany, came to Russia to seek their fortunes. Thus the stage was set for Russia to become Westernized and a first-rate European power. This was done during the reign of Peter the Great.

4. RUSSIA UNDER PETER THE GREAT, 1689–1725

Peter I (1689–1725)[1] was a physical giant full of mental vitality and primitive animal instincts and emotions. At the age of seventeen he seized the reins of government from his elder sister. For

the next thirty-six years he devoted his boundless energy to the twofold policy of Westernizing Russia and of gaining windows to the West on the Baltic and Black seas.

During Peter's youth he had come in contact with foreign craftsmen in Moscow and had become enamored of Western technology, particularly shipbuilding. In 1697 the twenty-five-year-old tsar made a grand tour of Western Europe, seeking allies against the Turks and firsthand knowledge of Western ways. He failed to gain any allies, but he learned a great deal about Western customs and techniques, which he proceeded to introduce into Russia. In Prussia, Peter studied one of the world's most efficient military organizations; in the Dutch Netherlands, shipbuilding; in England, shipbuilding, commerce, and finance.

On his way to Italy from Vienna he was sud-

---

[1] In 1682 Peter I, at the age of ten, technically became joint ruler with his elder brother, Ivan V, who was mentally incompetent. Until 1689, however, his rule was only nominal, and that date is usually considered to be the beginning of his reign.

Peter the Great was a physical giant. This portrait gives us a hint of the vigor and forcefulness which he put to use in Westernizing and modernizing Russia, making her a military power to be reckoned with. *Photo: Culver Pictures*

denly called home by the revolt of his bodyguard. Slicing off hundreds of heads by his own hand, he crushed the revolt with a ruthlessness that cowed all potential troublemakers. To make his authority as absolute as that of the most autocratic Western European monarchs, he adopted their bureaucratic system in both central and local government. Western technicians were brought to Russia in large numbers and new industries were subsidized and protected by mercantilist policies. Western, particularly French, social customs were introduced to the upper and middle classes of Russian society. Women were brought out of seclusion, and the long beards and flowing Oriental robes of the men were banned. These reforms hardly touched the peasant masses, who were increasingly tied down in a system of serfdom border-

ing on slavery—a process that had been going on in Russia throughout the sixteenth and seventeenth centuries. When the patriarch of the Russian Orthodox Church opposed the tsar's authority and some of his Westernizing policies, Peter abolished the patriarchate. He placed at the head of the church a Holy Synod composed of a committee of bishops and presided over by a lay procurator-general, all appointed by the tsar. Henceforth, the Orthodox Church was a powerful instrument of the Russian government. But Peter the Great's chief concern was always his military establishment. He built a navy and patterned his conscript army after that of Prussia. By the end of his reign, Russia had one of the major fighting forces of Europe.

When Peter became tsar, Russia had no warm-water access to the West. Sweden held the coveted shores of the Baltic Sea, and the Ottoman Turks occupied the territory north of the Black Sea. Peter's efforts to dislodge these "natural" enemies were only partly successful. He did manage to seize Azov on the Black Sea from the Turks and hold it for fourteen years, but the Turks were still too strong for the Russians. Against Sweden Peter was more successful. In 1697 the fifteen-year-old Charles XII came to the throne of Sweden, which since the reign of Gustavus Adolphus in the early seventeenth century had been the greatest military power in Northern Europe. Hoping to take advantage of Charles XII's youth, Peter formed an alliance with Denmark and Poland for the purpose of despoiling Sweden of valuable territories. Charles, however, proved to be a first-rate military genius. Not waiting for his enemies to ready their plans, he struck first at Denmark and forced her to sue for peace. Marching rapidly into Russia, he crushed a Russian army much larger than his own at Narva. Instead of pursuing the demoralized forces of Peter, however, he turned to Poland, defeated the Polish army, and placed a puppet king on the Polish throne. After spending seven years rearranging the affairs of Poland, Charles, known as the "Madman of the North," at last turned his attention once more to Russia. But Peter had used the seven years of grace to rebuild his forces. He retreated before the advancing Swedes deep into the vast interior of

L'ENJAMBÉE IMPERIALE.

Constantinople

Russie

Catherine the Great's territorial ambitions are satirized in this cartoon, which shows her leaping toward her coveted goal, Constantinople, as the pope and other European leaders look on in dismay.
Photo: NYPL Picture Collection

Russia, scorching the earth behind him. In 1709 the forces of Charles XII, decimated by hunger and disease, were brought to bay and shattered at Poltava, in southern Russia. Charles escaped with a remnant of his army to Turkey, but the military strength of Sweden was spent. Nine years later Charles XII was killed fighting in Norway. By the Treaty of Nystad in 1721, Russia received the Swedish Baltic provinces of Livonia, Estonia, Ingria, and Karelia. On the Neva River near the Baltic Peter built a new modern capital, St. Petersburg, facing the West. At his death in 1725, Russia was a great and growing power ready to play a major role in European affairs.

5. RUSSIA UNDER CATHERINE THE GREAT, 1762–1796

Peter the Great was followed by a succession of weak or mediocre rulers. After an interval of thirty-seven years, Catherine the Great (1762–1796) ascended the Russian throne. Catherine was an obscure princess from one of the little German states. She had been married for political reasons to young Peter III, grandson of Peter the Great, while he was still heir to the Russian crown. After he became tsar, Peter III, a weakling, quickly alienated all classes of his subjects. The astute Catherine, meanwhile, was be-

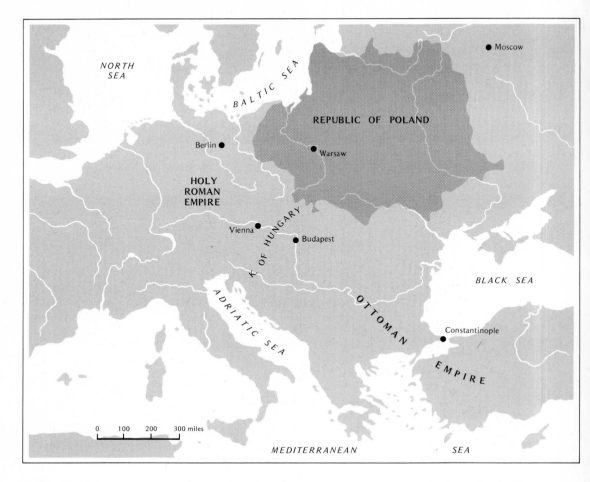

AGING EMPIRES (HOLY ROMAN EMPIRE, POLAND, OTTOMAN EMPIRE) AND NEW POWERS (AUSTRIA, PRUSSIA, RUSSIAN EMPIRE)

coming a good Russian, popularizing herself with her people. She was also reading widely from classical and French eighteenth-century authors. Less than a year after her husband became tsar, Catherine conspired with a group of aristocratic army officers, who murdered Peter and declared Catherine tsarina of Russia.

The Machiavellian tsarina prided herself on being an enlightened despot, as was fashionable in the late eighteenth century. She carried on a lively correspondence with Voltaire, D'Alembert, Frederick the Great, and other leading members of the eighteenth-century intelligentsia. She invited Diderot to St. Petersburg and

became his friend and patron. She talked learnedly about freedom, education, and reform, and soon after her seizure of the throne, she called a commission to study the question of reforms. All this made good salon talk, but none of it was translated into deeds. No one knew better than Catherine, as she admitted to a confidant, that an enlightened populace would endanger the position of all despots. The desperation of the peasants led to one of the greatest "slave" insurrections in history. Under the able leadership of a Don Cossack, Pugachev, hundreds of thousands of peasants rose against their masters. The rebellion was put down with

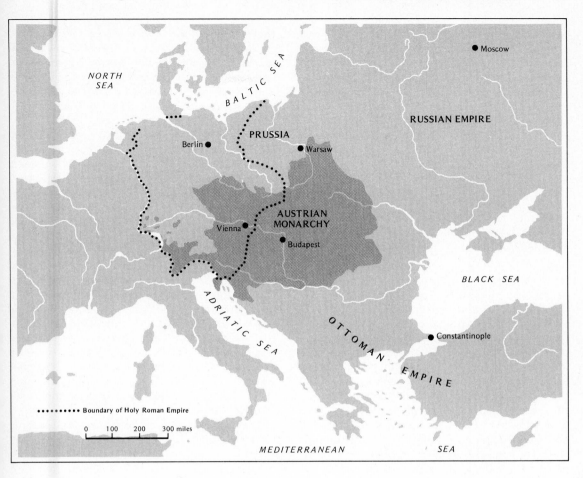

NORTH SEA

BALTIC SEA

Moscow

RUSSIAN EMPIRE

PRUSSIA

Berlin

Warsaw

AUSTRIAN
MONARCHY

Vienna

Budapest

BLACK SEA

ADRIATIC SEA

OTTOMAN EMPIRE

Constantinople

•••••••• Boundary of Holy Roman Empire

0   100   200   300 miles

MEDITERRANEAN   SEA

difficulty. The cruel repression left the Russian serf really a slave.

The chief significance of Catherine the Great in history lies in her aggressive foreign policy. Peter the Great had reached the Baltic by despoiling the Swedes. Catherine reached the Black Sea, the Balkan Peninsula, and the heart of Europe by defeating the Turks and destroying Poland. In two major wars between 1768 and 1792 Catherine defeated the Turks and seized all of their territory north of the Black Sea as far west as the Balkan Peninsula. Russia also gained a vague protectorate over the Christians in the Ottoman Empire, which gave her a standing op-

portunity to meddle in the internal affairs of the Turks. But Catherine fell short of her real goal, Constantinople. So certain was she of winning the old Byzantine capital on the Bosporus, which the Russian tsars had coveted since the days of Ivan III, that she named her second grandson Constantine. However, turning aside to join Prussia and Austria in the partitioning of the remainder of the Polish state, Catherine died before she could resume her drive on Constantinople. Already in 1772 Russia, Prussia, and Austria had seized strips of Poland. In 1793 Russia and Prussia enlarged their holdings, and in 1795 the three powers divided among themselves the remainder of the once huge Poland. Catherine's share, which was about two-thirds of the total, brought Russia's western boundary deep into Central Europe. The second and third partitions of Poland and concern over the French Revolution, which began in 1789, absorbed Catherine's energies during the last years of her life. When she finally died in 1796, Russia was a nation ominous in size and power, and a major factor in European and world affairs.

6. THE DISAPPEARANCE OF POLAND AND THE DECLINE OF SWEDEN AND THE OTTOMAN EMPIRE

Poland, at the opening of the eighteenth century, was the third largest country in Europe, exceeded in size only by Russia and Sweden. In the sixteenth and seventeenth centuries it had appeared that she would become a major power. Taking advantage of Russia's Time of Troubles (1584–1613), the Poles had captured Moscow. In the latter part of the century they had saved Vienna from the Turks.

Actually, however, the Polish nation was far from strong. Sprawling over a large area between Russia and the German states, she enjoyed no natural boundaries either in the east or the west. The eastern half of her territory was inhabited by Russian-speaking people. Her northern provinces were peopled largely by Latvians, Lithuanians, and Germans. There were also many Germans in the west. Religious cleavages followed the language lines. The Poles themselves were militantly Roman Catholic under strong Jesuit influence. Some of the Russians were Orthodox and some were Uniates (orthodox Christians who recognized the headship of the Roman pope). The Latvians and Germans were mostly Lutherans, as were some of the Lithuanians. In the cities lived many Jews.

Moreover, there was no strong middle class to vitalize Poland's economy. In the Late Middle Ages a sizable overland commerce between the Black and the Baltic seas had flowed across Poland. But with the shifting of commercial routes and centers to the west in the early sixteenth century, Poland's commerce had withered like

that of Italy and the German states. Furthermore, the Polish nobility, jealous of its own power and fearful of an alliance between the bourgeoisie and the king, deliberately penalized commerce with severe restrictions. The great mass of the people were serfs, tilling the soil of the powerful nobility.

In the face of so many divisive forces, only a strong central government could have made Poland a stable national state. But here lay Poland's greatest weakness. The kingship was elective, and the great nobles who held the elective power saw to it that no strong king ever came to the throne. During the eighteenth century the kings were all foreigners or puppets of foreign powers. The legislative Diet was completely monopolized by the nobility. In order to safeguard each nobleman's rights, unanimity was required for the passage of every measure. This meant that any nobleman could veto any proposed law (*liberum veto*). In addition, any nobleman could disband ("explode") the Diet and cancel all its acts. This system guaranteed virtual political anarchy. National spirit was weak. The all-powerful nobles were far more concerned for their own private interests than for the well-being of the nation.

It would have been surprising had such a power vacuum as eighteenth-century Poland not invited the aggression of her ambitious neighbors. In 1772 Catherine the Great and Frederick the Great bargained to take slices of Polish territory. The somewhat less greedy Maria Theresa of Austria, fearful of being outdistanced by Russia and Prussia, joined them, although her slice was beyond the Carpathian Mountains. Russia took a strip occupied by White Russians, and Prussia took West Prussia, joining up East Prussia with Brandenburg. This aggression at long last stirred the Poles to action. Sweeping reforms were passed improving the condition of the peasants and the bourgeoisie and giving the king and the Diet power to act effectively. But it was too late. Russia and Prussia were determined to prevent the emergence of a vigorous Polish nation. In 1793 they marched in and seized additional slices of territory. The Poles, under the leadership of Thaddeus Kosciusko, now flew to arms, although the arms were often only agricultural implements. They were no match for the professional armies of Russia, Prussia, and Austria, who in 1795 divided the remainder of Poland among themselves. Russia's share of Poland, about two-thirds of the total, was inhabited largely by Russian-speaking people. Austria's share was inhabited by Roman Catholics, as was Austria itself. Prussia's share, however, except for part of West Prussia, was inhabited for the most part by people who were neither linguistically nor religiously akin to the Prussians and who proved to be a fruitful source for future trouble.

Poland was not the only victim in Eastern Europe of the rise of Prussia and Russia. Sweden and the Ottoman Empire declined, both relatively and actually. Sweden had become the dominant military power in Northern and Eastern Europe under Gustavus Adolphus in the early seventeenth century. At the opening of the eighteenth century she was second only to Russia in size among the nations of Europe, holding large areas east and south of the Baltic in addition to the homeland. However, her population and resources were too small to hold for long such far-flung territories, which were coveted by ambitious and growing Prussia and Russia. Charles XII made a spectacular effort to hold them, but in the end he lost all his trans-Baltic territories except Finland, and dissipated Sweden's strength in so doing. Sweden has never been a major power since.

The Ottoman Turks, after reaching the gates of Vienna early in the sixteenth century and again late in the seventeenth century, weakened rapidly. The Treaty of Karlowitz in 1699 limited their power in Europe to the Balkan Peninsula and a strip of territory north of the Black Sea. Their two serious defeats at the hands of Catherine the Great marked the beginning of the breakup of the Ottoman Empire. By the end of the eighteenth century, the three dominant powers in Central and Eastern Europe were the relatively static Austrian Hapsburg Empire and the two rapidly rising military despotisms — Prussia and Russia.

Suggested Reading

General
*J. B. Wolf, *The Emergence of the Great Powers, 1685–1715* (Torch).
*P. Roberts, *The Quest for Security, 1715–1740* (Torch).
*W. L. Dorn, *Competition for Empire, 1740–1763* (Torch).
*L. Gershoy, *From Despotism to Revolution, 1763–1789* (Torch). All four are scholarly volumes in the Rise of Modern Europe series.

Rise of Prussia
*S. B. Fay, *The Rise of Brandenburg-Prussia to 1786* (Berkshire). Good brief survey.
H. Holborn, *A History of Modern Germany 1648–1840* (1966). Volume II of Holborn's history of modern Germany. Best on the subject.
G. P. Gooch, *Frederick the Great, the Ruler, the Writer, the Man* (1947). Probably the best all-around biography of Frederick the Great.

Rise of Russia
M. T. Florinsky, *Russia: A History and an Interpretation*, 2 vols. (1953). Best survey of Russian history to 1917.
*V. Klyuchevsky, *Peter the Great* (Vintage). Probably the best biography of Peter I.
*G. S. Thomson, *Catherine the Great and the Expansion of Russia* (Collier). Brief but scholarly.

Disappearance of Poland and Decline of Sweden and Ottoman Empire
O. Halecki, *A History of Poland*, rev. ed. (1961). Sound coverage of the partitions.
J. A. Gade, *Charles the Twelfth* (1916). Best biography.
*L. S. Stavrianos, *The Balkans Since 1453* (Holt, Rinehart and Winston). Brief but sound account of the decline of the Ottoman Empire.

35

OVERSEAS COLONIZATION AND COMPETITION FOR EMPIRE

During the age of royal absolutism, the European nations intensified their competition for overseas possessions and commerce, spurred on in large part by the riches that flowed to Europe from these possessions. Whereas Spain and Portugal had led the way beyond the Atlantic frontier during the sixteenth century, England, France, and the Netherlands threw themselves vigorously into colonizing and commercial expansion in various quarters of the globe during the seventeenth and eighteenth centuries. The newcomers indeed outstripped their older rivals and established themselves as the leading European colonial powers. As large as the world beyond Western Europe was, the competition for it led to struggles among the leading European powers; the outcome of these struggles decisively affected the power relationships among the competing nations. And while the Europeans colonized, traded, and competed around the globe, European civilization spread with them, impacting with varying results on the native populations encountered by the Europeans. The seventeenth and eighteenth centuries marked a decisive turning point in the establishment of Western European domination over much of the world.

1. THE NEW WORLD: THE ENGLISH, THE FRENCH, AND THE DUTCH

One of the areas attracting the English, French, and Dutch was the New World, where all three nations established thriving colonies during the seventeenth century and eventually became embroiled in bitter rivalry for dominance. The Northern European nations had their appetites whetted by the fabulous profits reaped from the New World by the Spanish and the Portuguese during the sixteenth century. These two powers retained their vast empires in Central and South America during the seventeenth and eighteenth centuries and continued to earn a rich reward from their enterprises. But the days of vast gold and silver hauls were soon over, and the Spanish and Portuguese turned their energies toward creating large plantations worked by oppressed natives and imported African slaves to produce products marketable in Western Europe. Their presence in South and Central America forced the attention of the English, French, and Dutch toward North America and the Caribbean area.

The English were the most successful colonizers in North America. The initial ventures were undertaken by joint stock companies specifically chartered by the royal government to plant settlements in the New World. The first English colony was established at Jamestown, Virginia, in 1607. It soon attracted a large population and developed a thriving economy based on tobacco growing. Only a little later, in 1620, a group of Puritans, despairing of finding religious freedom in Stuart England, founded a colony at Plymouth. This struggling colony was quickly overshadowed by the efforts of the Massachusetts Bay Company. Its first colony was located at Salem. However, the Puritan-dominated company soon moved its head-quarters from England to Boston, around which there developed a vigorous community, made up largely of small farmers and traders from England. New colonizing ventures, often inspired by resentment against the strong-handed political and religious dictates of the governors of the company, were undertaken from the Massachusetts base. Independent colonies were founded in Connecticut and Rhode Island, the latter under the leadership of Roger Williams, an especially strong advocate of religious freedom. Migrants from Massachusetts, reenforced by increasing numbers of Englishmen, also settled in New Hampshire and Maine.

Other colonies were established by proprietors, that is, individuals to whom the English king gave large grants of land. Maryland was established in 1632 through the efforts of Lord Baltimore, who tried to make his colony a refuge for Catholics. In 1663 eight English gentlemen were given proprietary rights over Carolina, and two centers of colonization were established shortly thereafter. In 1664 the English captured the Dutch colony of New Netherland, whereupon Charles II made his brother, the duke of York, its proprietor. Thus New York came into existence as an English colony. In 1681 William Penn received a grant from which grew the colony of Pennsylvania, where Penn hoped Quakers would find refuge. New Jersey and Delaware grew out of grants to various other proprietors. When in 1733 a colony was established in Georgia, England controlled the Atlantic seaboard from Maine to the Spanish colony in Florida. Her seaboard colonies, established under a variety of circumstances, very quickly began to enjoy a considerable independence that permitted them to take advantage of local circumstances and to develop a stable, prosperous order which showed remarkable potential for growth. Expansion was promoted by a steady flow of emigrants from not only England but also other northern European nations.

The English were also active elsewhere in the Western Hemisphere. English explorers and traders, seeking to establish a profitable trade in furs, penetrated into the Hudson Bay area in Canada. Flourishing colonies were established in the West Indies, the chief ones being Barbados, Jamaica, and Bermuda. In this area the English concentrated on developing highly profitable sugar plantations utilizing African slaves as a labor supply. At first, these Caribbean colonies appeared more valuable than did the seaboard colonies to the north.

Although no less interested and ambitious, France was not so successful as England in colonizing North America. Her first American colony was established by Samuel de Champlain at Quebec on the St. Lawrence River in 1608, only a year after the founding of Jamestown. Although Champlain explored the whole St. Lawrence Valley to the Great Lakes, settlers were slow to come from France to live in Canada. Most of those who did leave France preferred to settle in the West Indies, where France had also established enterprising colonists on Martinique and Guadeloupe. Here, sugar production gave France virtual control of the lucrative sugar market in Europe. Not until the reign of Louis XIV did the French turn to a more vigorous policy. Colbert, Louis' economic minister, put all of New France under royal administration and sent the Comte de Frontenac off to the New World as governor. Frontenac exerted every effort to increase France's possessions. During the last quarter of the seventeenth century, explorers and missionaries such as La Salle, Joliet, and Marquette explored the Mississippi Valley, allowing France to claim a huge territory, called Louisiana, which stretched from the Great Lakes to the Gulf of Mexico and included extensive lands on either side of the Mississippi. Territorially, the French holdings in North America were much larger than those of the English.

Efforts to attract settlers to this rich territory were unsuccessful. France closed her empire to non-Catholics, thus excluding the element that had been so important in populating England's colonies—the religiously dissatisfied. The French government, by making extensive grants to aristocrats, made it difficult for the lower classes to get land overseas. The excellent opportunities offered by the fur trade attracted more attention than the less profitable pursuit of agriculture. French settlements were thus few and far between in the territory stretching from the

St. Lawrence Basin across the rich lands around the Great Lakes and southward through the Mississippi Valley to New Orleans. When England seized France's American empire in 1763, perhaps no more than eighty thousand people lived in New France, and most of these were in the St. Lawrence Valley. By that time the inhabitants of the English colonies in the New World numbered at least 1.5 million.

Even this sparse population left its mark. The Roman Catholic Church was established firmly in New France. Missionaries were active converting the Indians. The French language was spoken everywhere. Larger communities, such as Quebec and New Orleans, imitated the ways of French society. Even today the influence of these early French colonists can be seen along the St. Lawrence Valley and in Louisiana.

The Dutch attempted to join the other powers in colonizing the North American wilds. In 1621 the Dutch West India Company was chartered to undertake colonization and commerce in the New World. In 1624 a colony was planted on Manhattan Island. Soon other Dutch communities were established in the Hudson Valley and on the Connecticut and Delaware rivers. The Dutch enjoyed only limited success, since Dutch interest and effort were concentrated chiefly on the more profitable East Indies. And in 1664 the English seized New Netherland during a war with the Dutch, ending Dutch colonization in North America. However, the Dutch influence on this area, especially the Hudson Valley, lasted almost to the present.

2. EUROPEAN PENETRATION OF THE FAR EAST

The nations that colonized North America in the seventeenth and eighteenth centuries—England, France, and the Netherlands—were equally aggressive in the Far East (see map, p. 434). Portugal had established her supremacy there in the sixteenth century, building a commercial empire based upon control of a few key ports. Spain had sought to enter the Far East, but had not progressed beyond the Philippines.

By 1600 Portugal had begun to lose her dominant position. Ruled by Spain from 1580 to 1640,

she was unable to protect her empire. The enterprising Dutch, who were successfully freeing themselves from Spanish control, were the chief beneficiaries. In 1602 all the competing Dutch companies interested in Far Eastern trade were joined into a single Dutch East India Company, to which the Dutch government gave almost complete freedom of action. The company soon drove the Portuguese out of the Spice Islands, which became the center of the Dutch Empire. In 1641 Malacca on the Malay Peninsula was seized, giving the Dutch control of the seas around the East Indies. Ceylon and the Celebes were also captured. The English tried to seize a share of this rich area, but were driven out by the Dutch as early as 1623. To safeguard the sea route to the Indies, the Dutch established a colony at the Cape of Good Hope in South Africa. Its growth was slow, but the Dutch influence was eventually strong enough to influence the history of South Africa to the present. To watch its interest in the Indies, the Dutch East India Company established a governor-general in Java, who in turn set up several other fortified governmental centers in the island empire.

For years after, the Dutch continued to profit from their holdings in the Indies. They demonstrated remarkable skill in utilizing the native agricultural economy to produce commodities such as spices that were in great demand in Western Europe. Consequently, their presence disturbed very little the existing patterns of life in the area. The Dutch also made attempts to penetrate China and Japan, but both countries refused to deal with them and were too strong to permit entrance by force.

The English, although shut out of the East Indies by the Dutch, made rapid progress toward replacing the Portuguese in India. The English East India Company was chartered in 1600 and given a monopoly of English trade in the East. This company concentrated chiefly on India, slowly forcing the Portuguese to let English traders into that rich land. The company founded its own "factories" (trading posts) at key locations—Surat, Madras, Bombay, and Calcutta. For a long time the East India Company was content to exploit the trading opportunities available in these cities; the merchants interfered little with Indian affairs and had little influence on Indian society.

Rather belatedly, the French entered the competition in the Far East. Again it took the far-sighted Colbert to see what France was missing. He organized a French East India Company (1664), which soon established a French outpost at Pondicherry in India. From this center the French company built up a prosperous trade that returned large profits.

3. THE IMPACT OF EUROPEAN EXPANSION: THE NATIVE AMERICANS

The increasing presence of European colonists and traders around the world during the seventeenth and eighteenth centuries had a significant impact on the native populations of the areas to which Europeans went. In many ways these encounters between Europeans and natives set a pattern that was destined to impose a bitter heritage on the modern world.

Of all the non-Europeans who felt the impact of the white man, the native Americans—the American Indians—were perhaps most immediately and directly affected. Their patterns of life,

This drawing shows a European factory, or trading settlement, built by the Western Europeans in seventeenth-century India. Within its confines were included warehouses, places of residence, market facilities, and even a church. Obviously, the structure was built to provide defense. From such factories Western European entrepreneurs were able to extend influences that allowed them not only to make huge economic profits but also to establish control over local political life. *Photo: The Bettmann Archive*

ranging from the highly sophisticated civilizations of the Incas in Peru and the Aztecs and Mayas in Mexico and Central America to the simple pastoral and hunting cultures of the North American Indians, were irreparably disrupted by the onslaught of the intruders.

We have already seen the destructive impact of the Spanish and Portuguese *conquistadors* on the Aztecs, Mayas, and Incas. During the seventeenth and eighteenth centuries, the dislocation continued. Spanish and Portuguese mercantilist policies cast the Indians into the role of laborers on the expanding plantation system and in the mining enterprises from which the Europeans drew huge profits. Although the native Europeans were few in number, they dominated political, economic, and social life with little respect for the established practices of native life. However, the new masters were not totally insensitive to their new minions. Especially through their missionary activities, they gave the native Americans not only a new religion but also an introduction to advanced technical skills and even access to a rudimentary education. The paternalistic policy of the Spanish and the Portuguese had the long-range effect of imposing a semblance of Iberian and Catholic culture on the native Indians; a living monument of this process is the language structure of modern Latin America.

Despite their indifference to established native American culture, the Europeans in Latin America were never numerous enough to exterminate the native Americans or their cultures. Inexorably, their blood and their culture intermingled with those of the native Americans. As a result, significant elements of native American culture survived, especially in family structure, agricultural techniques, art motifs, and even religion. Although the ancient Indian civilizations of Central and South America were forever disrupted, enough Indian culture survived to give Latin American society a special hybrid character that has survived to this day. This uniqueness will forever constitute a monument to native Americans.

The Indians of North America suffered a less dramatic but perhaps ultimately more ignominious fate at the hands of the Europeans than did the native Americans of Central and South America. Generally speaking, they were fewer in number and less advanced than were the Indians of Latin America. Their meager economic resources, their simple political and social institutions, and their ancient tribal rivalries limited their capacity to resist the onslaught of the French and English intruders.

On the whole, the French policy toward the Indians that inhabited their vast North American empire was not particularly disruptive, chiefly because there were not many French settlers in the New World. The chief French encounter with the Indians centered in the fur trade, a process that enticed the Indians into a new kind of economic activity and introduced into their world such European products as guns and liquor but that did not usually result in French control of their lives. The French also expended great efforts to Christianize the Indians. In general, the French and the Indians lived peaceably together to the point where the Indians joined the French as allies in the Anglo-French struggle for dominance in North America, a choice that boded ill for the Indians in the wake of the French defeat in the mid-eighteenth century.

The English settlers pursued a more ruthless policy toward the native Americans. From the beginning the English came to occupy and exploit the land of North America. Their intent demanded that they displace the natives by whatever means possible. Although English-Indian relationships were occasionally marked by friendliness and mutual assistance, a harsher pattern evolved as the number of white settlers increased. The burgeoning seaboard population began to assert inexorable pressure on the Indians aimed at exterminating them or driving them from their lands. As a consequence, the Indians began to disappear from the "new" America; their demise was often accompanied by brutality and every form of conniving on the part of their tormenters, who began to call themselves "Americans." In an effort to protect their lands, the Indians often fought back savagely. Their resistance nourished a feeling among the white men that the native Americans were bloodthirsty, inferior savages whose extermi-

This representation of the first settlement at Jamestown, Virginia, suggests something of the drastic changes that affected those who left European society — symbolized by the great ship standing at anchor — to face the wilds of the New World. *Photo: Culver Pictures*

nation would best serve everyone's interest. The British government struggled from afar to establish an enlightened Indian policy aimed at respecting Indian rights to their lands and at dealing with them honorably in resolving conflicts; this effort was especially intense after the French and Indian War, which resulted in English control of the vast Indian stronghold lying between the Appalachians and the Mississippi. But the westward bound, land-hungry Americans paid little heed to the Indian policy of the British government and proceeded with the grim business of displacing or exterminating the Indians. After the American Revolution there was nothing to restrain the movement of the white men into the huge Indian world west of the Appalachians. As the frontier moved West, the native American was progressively driven ahead of it or exterminated.

4. THE IMPACT OF EUROPEAN EXPANSION: INDIAN CIVILIZATION

In contrast with the New World, the impact of the Europeans was minimal on the peoples of the Far East. Few Europeans went to that part of the world as colonists. Those few who did isolated themselves in a few trading depots located in the seaboard cities of India and the East Indies, where their contacts with the natives were slight. The limited impact of the Europeans on the Far East resulted primarily from the fact that there they encountered ancient cultures, solidly founded and not inferior to those of Western Europe. A brief discussion of Indian civilization will illustrate why the European impact was minimal.

When the Europeans first began their penetration of India, they were confronted by a situation rare in her long history: the presence of a unified political system embracing almost the entire subcontinent. Political unity had been imposed by the Moguls, a branch of the Mongol horde of Tamerlane that had begun to penetrate India about 1500. By the reign of Akbar (1556–1605), the Moguls had subdued most of the petty principalities into which India had long been divided. Moslem by faith and the bearers of a foreign culture, the Mogul emperors held their power throughout the seventeenth century chiefly because of their tolerant attitude toward native Indian civilization. But their success represented a relatively rare episode in Indian history. Since the beginnings of Indian civilization in the third millennium B.C., foreign invaders had repeatedly tried to unite the peninsula, only to be frustrated by the racial, linguistic, and geographical barriers that fragmented this vast and populous land. For long stretches of time, Indian political life was dominated by numerous petty princes. A tradition of strong political organization was therefore not a decisive element in Indian civilization. Its strength lay elsewhere, in institutions and beliefs that were affected very little by the presence of outsiders, including Europeans.

Indian society in the sixteenth and seventeenth centuries gained its cohesion primarily from three interrelated and very ancient institutions—the village, the family, and the caste system. With the exception of a small minority of the population living in the coastal cities, the great mass of Indians lived in self-sufficient agricultural villages under the authority of the Brahmins (priests), whose role we will examine in a moment. Each village was made up of several families. Every family was a tightly knit unit held together by blood ties, common ownership and exploitation of the land, and religion. Each village had its own government, often involving the village inhabitants in significant ways in reaching decisions. The villages sometimes had to pay taxes to a faraway central authority, but seldom did that authority significantly influence the course of village life.

Even more fundamental in the life of each Indian was the caste system. Its origins were ancient and are still poorly understood. Long before the beginning of the Christian era, Indian society had been stratified into groups, each with its own customs, responsibilities, and rights. The system steadily became more complicated and more rigid. In ancient times there were four broad castes: the priests, the aristocratic warriors, the small landowners and ar-

tisans, and the laborers. The untouchables were those having no caste. As the centuries passed, numerous subgroups were created within each broad caste, and the rules regulating the conduct of each group became constantly more elaborate. By the time Europeans became acquainted with Indian society, there were hundreds of caste groups. Almost every occupational group in India constituted a special caste. Elaborate rules defining every detail of life within the caste and of relationships with other groups had been evolved. A member of a caste had his life clearly cut out for him from birth. Education, marriage, occupation, manners, dress, and nearly everything else were clearly defined. Obviously, this institution gave the individual little freedom, but just as obviously it provided him with a definite place in society and established a remarkably stable and unchanging social order.

The strength of the Indian caste system lay in the religious sanctions that stood behind it; every Indian accepted the system that bound him to his present lot because he believed that that system was the earthly embodiment of the divine order of the universe. More than anything else, religion gave Indian civilization its distinctive qualities and made most Indians immune to Western influences.

That religious system was already ancient when the Europeans first began settling in India. Several religious traditions, some dating back to the beginnings of Indian civilization, had merged to create the main body of Indian religious thought and practice. By 500 B.C. a basic set of assumptions had been clearly formulated by religious and philosophical leaders and set down in a body of philosophical literature called the Upanishads. From the Upanishads later developed the chief religious systems of India (except Mohammedanism, which entered India from the outside). A brief description of the basic ideas contained in the Upanishads is the best starting place for an understanding of Indian religion.

The ancient Indian thinkers agreed that the universe is permeated by a spiritual force that creates and animates everything. This spiritual force (called Brahma) is the only thing that is real. The world that man sees and experiences is merely an illusion, representing the spirit entrapped in material things. The destiny of spirits born to the flesh is to escape back to the perfect world of pure spirit.

At a certain stage on their way to perfection spirits are born into the material world. Once made flesh, spirits become excessively attached to earthly existence, piling up a record of activities not befitting a pure spirit. This record must be atoned for before a spirit achieves its ultimate perfection. When death parts the spirit from its earthly prison, the soul carries its record with it. Therefore, the spirit must be reincarnated in some earthly form to continue its purification. The form that rebirth takes depends on the record of a spirit's previous activities; forces beyond man's control assign him to a status in this world and demand that he keep that status. Rebirth may occur many times, each time putting the spirit in a different shape and presenting it with new tests. Eventually, the spirit will end its dependence on the material world and be freed from reincarnation. Toward that perfect state all things are destined.

Hinduism was by far the most significant religion that grew out of these basic concepts. The great spiritual force, which the philosophers said directed the universe, was redefined in terms of a variety of deities, each conceived in concrete form. Among the Hindu gods, three were predominant: Brahma the Creator, Vishnu the Preserver, and Siva the Destroyer. No matter how many different gods are worshiped, the Hindu believes they are all part of a single spiritual order and thus in no sense competitive. To honor these gods, an elaborate set of rituals has developed over the centuries, chiefly under the guidance of the Brahmins, or priests, who play a leading role in Indian society because they are necessary to approach the gods in the proper way.

Hindus take literally the idea that a part of the divine spirit dwells in every creature. This has led to the development of a complicated list of prohibitions against killing and eating animals, doing violence to other men, and mistreating one's own body. Since detachment from the world is a way of freeing the spirit, Hindus are strongly ascetic, often withdrawing from daily life for fasting, prayer, and chastisement of the

The flowering of Indian civilization under the Mogul emperors is revealed in splendid architectural monuments such as the Taj Mahal, in glorious poetry, and in exquisite painted miniatures such as this one, which shows the emperor Akbar on a hunt.
Photo: The Victoria and Albert Museum, London

flesh. All Hindus believe in reincarnation, and consider the caste system to be the earthly form of this truth. Each caste is a kind of religious order representing a stage into which spirits are born on the path to perfection. It becomes every Hindu's religious duty to accept his caste and fulfill all the obligations attached to it. In the ascending structure of the caste system, each grade represents a step nearer to spiritual perfection and liberation from the material world. The untouchable is the least pure of all humans and must suffer burdens equal to his impurity. The Brahmin at the top of the caste system is nearest to perfection and is about to end the cycle of rebirth, a status that gives Brahmins the wisdom to control earthly society. The orthodox Hindu therefore accepts the established social system and the rituals and elaborate laws it imposes on him as a vital part of his religion and feels that to change it would be to tamper with the divine order.

However, the powerful stream of Indian religious life did not confine itself to that one channel. Buddhism, for example, illustrates how the basic set of beliefs that we have just noted could produce a different religion. Buddhism drew its original inspiration from the teachings of Siddharta Gautama (ca. 563–483 B.C.), soon to be known as the Buddha (which means "the awakened one"). The son of a prince and well educated in the philosophical and religious teachings of the Upanishads, Buddha rejected his princely heritage and much of the religious practice of his day to seek a new vision through fasting and contemplation. His ultimate answer to life's travails was detachment from all things on this earth. He believed that all suffering, including the cycle of reincarnation, was caused by human desire for worldly things that did not befit the human spirit. To help men free themselves from their desires, Buddha laid down an enlightened and practical moral code, called the Eightfold Path, which stressed love of others, good works, right thinking, and rejection of sensual pleasures. He taught that by following this code an individual could help himself to achieve the perfect state of *nirvana*, a condition of freedom from desire and passion and of union with the great world spirit. Buddha did not reject re-

incarnation; instead, he insisted that the morally strong person willing to work at the extinction of the self could hasten deliverance.

Buddha's teachings, originally an ethical protest against Hindu religious practices, were soon turned into a religion. His disciples, organizing themselves into monastic groups, turned Buddha into a god, began worshiping his statues, and devised rituals to give expression to his teachings. The new religion took deep roots in India and flourished for many centuries. Eventually, it fell into decline and by 1500 virtually disappeared there. In part this was due to the fact that several foreign invaders of India were converts to Buddhism, causing it to gain a reputation as a foreign religion. However, before it died in India, Buddhism had gained a foothold abroad, especially in China and Southeast Asia. In its new homes it flourished and spread, until today it is one of the major religions of the world, practiced nearly everywhere in the Far East except India. Buddhism left its mark on India despite its disappearance there. Its moral earnestness, its explanation of suffering, and its denial of this world all became part of the Indian religious tradition.

Indian religion accounted for many things about the civilization that the Europeans met in India in the early modern period. Indians were inclined to accept this world passively, feeling that the individual's destiny lay elsewhere. Progress, competition for wealth, and the search for new things were not attractive to them. The good Indian took what life gave him reverently and humbly. He was not impressed by the Europeans, for he was convinced that he had reflected as keenly and deeply as they about human problems and had arrived at answers superior to theirs. He could point to a remarkable art and literature to prove (to his own satisfaction, at least) the superiority of his way of life. Nothing the European could bring him would, in his mind, improve upon his institutions and ideas. He therefore refused to be agitated by the advent of the Europeans. They, in turn, found that a few hundred soldiers and a few cannon could not shake the Indian's confidence in his village and family life, his caste system, and his religion. Only slowly and almost imperceptibly did the European way of life make any significant impression on the East.

5. THE IMPACT OF EUROPEAN EXPANSION: SUB-SAHARAN AFRICA

Too infrequently noted is the fact that the expansion of Europe in the seventeenth and eighteenth centuries had a significant impact on sub-Saharan Africa. On that vast continent the European influence was exercised by a tiny number of white men who changed the course of African history chiefly by enticing the Africans to serve their interests through trade — especially traffic in human beings.

The centuries prior to 1500 had been highly significant in shaping the destiny of sub-Saharan Africa. That period witnessed the formation of a number of prosperous states spread across a wide belt of territory south of the Sahara from the Atlantic to the Indian Ocean and then far southward along that inviting sea. These states — Ghana, Mali, Songhay, the kingdoms of Hausaland, and the Swahili city-states — were strongly influenced by Moslem religion, culture, and technology from North Africa; however, in all of them the imprint of much older native African cultures was also strongly felt, producing an amazingly cosmopolitan culture, especially in the brilliant cities that dominated these states. The remarkable affluence of these states depended on a vigorous trans-Saharan and Indian Ocean trade that carried gold, ivory, slaves, and many other products northward to the Moslem world and Europe and eastward to India. In fact, many of these states were brought into existence by enterprising native chieftains who organized extensive realms so as to control more effectively the trading ventures that brought such great riches. Because their existence depended so heavily on trade and because the techniques their rulers borrowed to assert their power had little impact on the great bulk of the native population, these African states tended to be unstable. Nonetheless, their creation and their active intercourse with outside cultures marked an important stage in the development of Africa and its involvement with the larger world. Farther to the south, beyond the sphere of Moslem influence, the native population continued its simple agricultural existence according to ancient customs, as yet little touched by developments to the north.

These developments in pre-1500 sub-Saharan Africa created a situation that made Africa particularly susceptible to the onslaught of the Western Europeans, chiefly because the destiny of so many African states was tied directly to trade with the outside world. Coming by sea to the coastal areas of sub-Saharan Africa, the Europeans almost instantly caused a redirection of trade routes from the traditional trans-Saharan routes toward Western Europe and the expanding European empires in the New World and the Far East. The newcomers made little effort to settle in sub-Saharan Africa, partly because the Africans resisted their settlement but more importantly because they could get what they wanted by doing little more than establishing a few trading posts in the coastal cities of Africa. What they wanted were the valuable raw materials of Africa and then before long the Africans themselves — as slaves to perform the arduous labor of creating a rich agricultural establishment in the New World. Throughout the seventeenth and eighteenth centuries massive numbers of black Africans — perhaps as many as 9 or 10 million — were uprooted from their native soil, often as a result of the efforts of their black compatriots, sold into the hands of English, French, Dutch, Portuguese, Spanish, and American slave traders, and distributed under inhuman conditions far and wide to toil as chattels in the service of white landowners intent on exploiting the vast agricultural potential of the New World.

As the Europeans opened slave stations along the coasts of sub-Saharan Africa, significant political alignments occurred in Africa. African kingdoms along the Gold Coast flourished as a result of their domination of trade flowing from inland into the hands of European traders. Often the ruling elements of these kingdoms became prime agents in supplying slaves to the Europeans, leading them to intervene among inland tribes to find slaves to sell. Native chiefs living inland likewise became caught up in the slave trade. Armed with deadly weapons from Europe, the native tribes began to wage war on one another as a means of procuring slaves. The Europeans asserted subtle influences on the coastal states in order to enhance their own trading interests, thus promoting a slow deterioration of the capability of the Africans to control their own destiny. As the demand for slaves increased and the prices commanded by the African slave suppliers rose, European traders moved farther and farther south along the west coast of Africa to turn the attention of more and more native Africans toward serving European trading interests, especially slavery, with the same disruptive consequences. European influences, especially Portuguese, on the east coast of Africa were equally disruptive of the brilliant Swahili civilization flourishing there. Only deep in the central part of Africa did the native population remain relatively free of the impact of European intrusion.

On the whole, the development of sub-Saharan Africa was seriously impeded by the encounter of its peoples with the Western Europeans during the seventeenth and eighteenth centuries. Africa's human resources were depleted, her natural resources plundered, and her political and social structures disoriented. The Europeans gave little in return, especially when compared to what the Moslems of North Africa had contributed to the enrichment of sub-Saharan Africa prior to 1500. Despite the traumatic consequences of European expansion in this era, the Africans retained many elements of their native tradition, which would later reassert itself as a significant aspect of the revival of Africa. And those who were uprooted from Africa in this period took much with them to add important elements to the civilization that was forming in the New World, where they were laboring as slaves.

6. THE STRUGGLE FOR OVERSEAS EMPIRE

In spite of nearly empty continents to occupy in the New World and rich trading opportunities to exploit in the highly civilized East and in sub-Saharan Africa, the aggressive European nations could not keep out of one another's way in their overseas expansion. In the sixteenth century the competition had begun with Dutch and English assaults on the Spanish and Portuguese empires. By the end of the seventeenth century the struggle for overseas empires entered a critical phase and progressed rapidly toward a decision in the eighteenth.

This struggle did not arise because the world overseas had become too crowded with Europeans or because the potential wealth of that world was being depleted. It was rooted in the policy of mercantilism practiced by most of the European powers of this age. Mercantilist policy was based on the conviction that national economic well-being depended on directing the total national economy in a way that would produce a favorable balance of money coming into the economy. Among other things, this policy saw colonies as a source of cheap food and raw materials and an outlet for manufactured goods that would return a profit to the mother country. Such a view made the accession and the careful management of the colonies crucial to each nation that aspired to be powerful. Likewise, it dictated that every effort be made to restrict the colonizing ventures of rival nations and to deprive them of their colonial possessions whenever possible. Thus, every conflict among the major European nations in the seventeenth and eighteenth centuries was extended to their colonies, and every major peace settlement included a redistribution of overseas possessions.

The Dutch were extremely active in engaging in serious competition for the purpose of expanding overseas holdings at the expense of other nations. As we have previously noted, they began to dismember the Portuguese Empire in the Far East in the sixteenth century. England soon followed the Dutch lead. Although her attacks on the Spanish Empire in the New World were not especially profitable, England did succeed in seizing most of Portugal's Indian holdings during the seventeenth century.

By the middle of the seventeenth century, the rivalry between the English and the Dutch began to increase. As early as 1651 England passed her first Navigation Act, providing that all goods coming to and from England and her overseas possessions would be carried in English ships. This struck a blow at Dutch commercial power, which concentrated on providing shipping services for other nations. It also encouraged the growth of the English navy, badly neglected by the first two Stuart kings. On three different occasions between 1651 and 1688 England engaged the Dutch in warfare. In general, these wars were not decisive. England did annex New Netherland in 1664, but gave the Dutch territory elsewhere. Probably the chief result of the wars was to add to the growing strength of the English navy. Eventually, the English and the Dutch began to see that France was the chief threat to both. The result was an alliance in 1689, when William of Orange became king of England. By that time the Netherlands was no longer the major sea power in Europe. The Dutch were content to keep their already established holdings and their still profitable carrying trade, letting the other nations compete for the rest of the world.

The Dutch and the English had real cause for alarm. Louis XIV threw France wholeheartedly into the competition for overseas possessions in Canada, Louisiana, the West Indies, and India — all areas near to England's centers of operation. From 1689 until 1763 England and France fought each other regularly in Europe, and each engagement had its repercussions abroad.

Several times during the War of the League of Augsburg (1688–1697), the English and the French engaged forces in North America, where the war was called King William's War. Neither in Europe nor in America was the action decisive, and no changes were made in the holdings of either combatant. England had more success during the War of the Spanish Succession (1702–1713). In North America, where the struggle was called Queen Anne's War, England captured Acadia (Nova Scotia) and received recognition of her claims to Newfoundland and Hudson Bay. From France's ally, Spain, she received Gibraltar and Minorca, assuring her entrance into the Mediterranean. Spain also granted to England the right to supply Spain's colonies with slaves (the *asiento*) and the privilege of sending one ship a year to the Spanish colonies in America. These concessions ended Spain's long effort to close her empire to outsiders and gave England the advantage over other nations in exploiting trading opportunities provided by the Spanish overseas holdings.

From 1713 to 1740 England and France remained at peace. During this calm neither nation was idle in overseas matters. France, realizing the weakness of her position, was especially active in North America. She tried to protect her holdings from English sea power by building a strong fort at Louisburg at the mouth of the St. Lawrence. She also began constructing a series of forts in her territories west of the Appalachians designed to keep the English colonists pinned to the Atlantic seaboard. England concentrated her efforts on widening the commercial breach she had made in Spain's empire in 1713. A new European war in 1740, the War of the Austrian Succession, led to a sharp conflict between England and France in America (King George's War) and in India. At the end of the war in 1748 each power restored its spoils to the other, England giving up Louisburg and France restoring Madras.

An eight-year truce ensued in Europe, each side preparing desperately for the struggle that everyone knew would soon reopen. In North America, France went back to her policy of building a barrier against the westward expansion of the English colonies. Already the colonists were pushing across the Appalachians into the Ohio Valley, claiming the territory as part of their original grants from the English crown. The inevitable clash came in 1755, when the British tried to stop the French from occupying Fort Duquesne at the present site of Pittsburgh. The issue was clearly joined; one power must destroy the other in America.

In India a no less dramatic struggle was shaping. France had entered the scene later than England but had made steady progress up to 1740. Growing English sea power then made France's position precarious. To offset this disadvantage, the French governor of Pondicherry, François Dupleix, decided to take advantage of the internal chaos in India resulting from the decline of Mogul authority. In return for concessions favorable to France, he supplied troops and made promises to whatever political faction in India gave him the best advantage. The policy

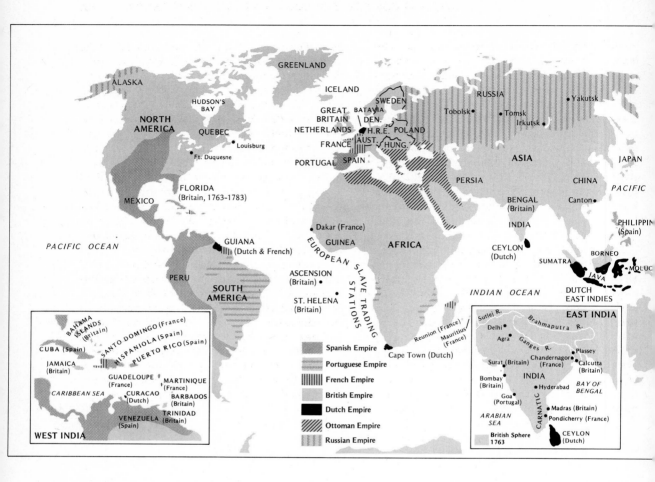

OVERSEAS POSSESSIONS 1763

Map labels:

ALASKA · GREENLAND · ICELAND · HUDSON'S BAY · NORTH AMERICA · QUEBEC · Louisburg · Ft. Duquesne · FLORIDA (Britain, 1763-1783) · MEXICO · PACIFIC OCEAN · GUIANA ‖‖ (Dutch & French) · PERU · SOUTH AMERICA · SWEDEN · GREAT BRITAIN · BATAVIA · DEN. · NETHERLANDS · H.R.E. · POLAND · FRANCE · AUST. · HUNG. · PORTUGAL · SPAIN · RUSSIA · Tobolsk · Tomsk · Irkutsk · Yakutsk · ASIA · JAPAN · PERSIA · CHINA · PACIFIC · BENGAL (Britain) · Canton · INDIA · PHILIPPIN (Spain) · CEYLON (Dutch) · BORNEO · SUMATRA · MOLUC · JAVA · DUTCH EAST INDIES · INDIAN OCEAN · Dakar (France) · GUINEA · AFRICA · EUROPEAN SLAVE TRADING STATIONS · ASCENSION (Britain) · ST. HELENA (Britain) · Reunion (France) · Mauritius (France) · Cape Town (Dutch)

Legend:
- Spanish Empire
- Portuguese Empire
- ‖‖ French Empire
- British Empire
- Dutch Empire
- ╱╱ Ottoman Empire
- Russian Empire

WEST INDIA inset:
BAHAMA ISLANDS (Britain) · SANTO DOMINGO (France) · HISPANIOLA (Spain) · PUERTO RICO (Spain) · CUBA (Spain) · JAMAICA (Britain) · GUADELOUPE (France) · MARTINIQUE (France) · CURACAO (Dutch) · BARBADOS (Britain) · CARIBBEAN SEA · TRINIDAD (Britain) · VENEZUELA (Spain)

EAST INDIA inset:
Sutlej R. · Brahmaputra R. · Delhi · Agra · Ganges R. · Plassey · Chandernagor (France) · Calcutta (Britain) · Surat (Britain) · INDIA · Bombay (Britain) · Hyderabad · BAY OF BENGAL · Goa (Portugal) · CARNATIC · Madras (Britain) · ARABIAN SEA · Pondicherry (France) · British Sphere 1763 · CEYLON (Dutch)

netted France a claim to most of southern India. Dupleix soon found his match in a lowly clerk of the British East India Company named Robert Clive, who began to fight fire with fire. Spending money liberally and making even greater promises to the Indian princes, Clive built a counteralliance of these princes and wrung generous concessions from them for his company. Soon an undeclared war was on in India. Dupleix was recalled to France in 1754, chiefly because his company did not trust his high-handed methods. The showdown began in 1756, when an Indian prince attacked the British garrison in Calcutta. Having captured the garrison,

the prince put 146 Englishmen into a tiny cell; by the next morning 123 were dead in this "Black Hole" of Calcutta. Clive decided to avenge this atrocity.

Thus, at the opening of the Seven Years' War (French and Indian War in America) in 1756 France and England were pitted against each other on three continents. We have previously examined the course of that war in Europe (see Chapter 34). England, led by William Pitt, threw her chief efforts into the naval and colonial war and won a smashing victory. In North America the French held their own until 1757. The superior British forces, supported by the navy, overpowered the French outposts one by one. The decisive blow came in 1759, when the British captured Quebec, opening all Canada to the British. British naval units captured the chief French holdings in the West Indies. In India, Robert Clive gave the British as great a victory as Quebec. Using his military resources brilliantly and gaining invaluable help from the navy, he smashed France's Indian allies and captured her trading centers. When Pondicherry fell in 1761, France was ruined in India. Perhaps even more important, Clive had added large territories to England's sphere of influence by conquering several native Indian states.

The Seven Years' War ended in 1763 with the Treaty of Paris. France surrendered Canada and all Louisiana east of the Mississippi (except New Orleans) to England. Spain, who had been an ally of France, ceded Florida to England. By a special treaty France compensated Spain for this loss by giving her the rest of Louisiana (west of the Mississippi). All French possessions in the West Indies except Guadeloupe and Martinique also fell to England. France's empire in India likewise went to Britain. The French were permitted to enjoy trading privileges in India and to keep Pondicherry, but Britain controlled the chief centers of trade, ending any hope of a French recovery of power there.

The Treaty of Paris closed an era in European expansion. Although the Dutch and the Spanish still had extensive holdings abroad, Great Britain had fought her way to supremacy in colonial and commercial affairs. She could now turn to the exploitation of her empire.

Since Columbus' voyage the Europeans had wrought an important change around the world. Energetic colonizers had planted European civilization on the soil of the New World. Enterprising merchants had begun to tap the wealth of a considerable part of the Far East and of sub-Sahara Africa, creating for the first time a global economy in which the level of prosperity in European nations was directly related to their access to the labor and products of peoples all over the earth. European patterns of civilization had begun to alter the lives of peoples who had developed their own cultures long before the Europeans came. For good or bad, the Europeanization of the world had begun. And European history never again ceased to have a world-wide scope.

Suggested Reading

European Overseas Colonization

J. H. Parry, *The Establishment of European Hegemony, 1415–1715: Trade and Exploration in the Age of the Renaissance* (3rd ed., rev., 1966). A thorough general treatment.

H. E. Bolton and T. M. Marshall, *The Colonization of North America* (1924). A careful, balanced study of the colonizing efforts of the European powers in North America.

*C. H. Haring, *The Spanish Empire in America* (Harcourt Brace Jovanovich). A splendid picture of the Spanish role in the New World.

*Ralph Davis, *The Rise of the Atlantic Communities* (Cornell). A good overview of the economic impact of colonization.

*C. M. Cipolla, *Guns, Sails and Empires: Technological Innovation and the Early Phases of European Expansion, 1400–1700* (Funk and Wagnalls). Provides interesting insights toward explaining the successes of Europeans in their overseas ventures.

The Impact of European Expansion

P. Radin, *The Story of the American Indian* (rev. ed., 1944). A good introduction.

*W. R. Jacobs, *Dispossessing the American Indians: Indians and Whites on the Colonial Frontier* (Scribners). An objective account of an unpleasant subject.

*Stanley Wolpert, *A New History of India* (Oxford). A well-written, perceptive survey.

*R. Thapar and P. Spear, *A History of India*, 2 vols. (Penguin). An excellent detailed survey.

H. G. Rawlinson, *India, A Short Cultural History* (rev. ed., 1954).

*A. L. Basham, *The Wonder that Was India* (Everest). Either this or the preceding title will provide a good general introduction to the main features of India's rich cultural traditions.

J. S. Hutton, *Caste in India: Its Nature, Function and Origins* (4th ed., 1963). A straightforward description of a complex institution.

*K. M. Sen, *Hinduism* (Penguin). An excellent introduction.

*E. Conze, *Buddhism: Its Essence and Development* (Harper Torchbook). A good introduction.

*Harry A. Gailey, *History of Africa: From the Earliest Times to 1800* (Holt, Rinehart and Winston).

Robert W. July, *A History of the African People* (2nd ed., 1974). Two well-written general surveys which succeed in making sense out of a confusing story.

*J. Maquet, *Civilization of Black Africa* (Oxford). Provides a sense of the unique and significant features of the cultures of the native Africans.

Imperial Rivalry

W. L. Dorn, *Competition for Empire, 1740–1763* (1940). A splendid treatment of the conflict for control of the world in a critical period.

Francis Parkman, *Parkman Reader*, ed. S. Morison (1955). This work will provide a good introduction to the work of the nineteenth-century American historian, whose many works provide a vivid picture of the Anglo-French struggle for dominance in North America.

36

CLASSICISM, BAROQUE, PIETISM

The spirit of royal absolutism, with its exaltation of kings, princes, and attendant nobility,
and also its concern for order and form, was
reflected in the literature, the arts, and certain
religious movements of the seventeenth and
eighteenth centuries. The prevailing styles were
classicism in literature and music and baroque
in painting and architecture. Pietistic religious
movements passively accepted royal absolutism
as a form of government. Absolutism had its
direct apologists in the field of political theory.

1. THE PHILOSOPHY OF ABSOLUTISM

In our twentieth-century concern for popular
government we sometimes forget the service
performed in early modern times by the royal
monarchs. It was they who suppressed feudal
turbulence, established law and order, and
molded the first national states. Some were incompetent and some were predatory. However,
the tragic example of Poland and the Holy
Roman Empire, where the monarchs were dominated by the nobility and the local princes,
would seem to indicate that in the first three
centuries of the modern era, the absolutist kings
generally served a useful, and possibly necessary, function. Their role was appreciated and
defended by many of their subjects. We have already encountered Bishop Bossuet's eloquent
defense of Louis XIV's claims to be God's duly
ordained vicegerent on earth, and James I's es-
pousal of divine right monarchy.

The seventeenth-century thinker Thomas
Hobbes, dismayed by the civil strife then raging
in England (the Puritan Revolution), decided
that only absolute government could maintain
law and order. In his *Leviathan* (1651), Hobbes
theorized that basically selfish men for their own
protection contracted with a prince to rule them;
but, once having made the compact, they could
not revoke it.[1] To be effective, the prince must be
all-powerful, controlling even the religion of his
subjects. The great Dutch political theorist Hugo
Grotius argued not only for absolute governmental authority within the state, but also for
absolute sovereignty and equality of all states
large and small. His chief work, *The Law of War
and Peace* (1625), was one of the earliest and
probably the most influential of all treatises on
international law. It was the outgrowth of Grotius' experiences during the revolt of the Netherlands against Spain and of his observation of
some of the horrors of the Thirty Years' War in
Germany. Both Hobbes and Grotius believed
royal absolutism to be in accordance with the
natural law.

2. THE GOLDEN AGE OF FRENCH LITERATURE

The reign of Louis XIV (1643–1715), which
marked the apogee of royal absolutism in France

---

[1] While proffering the social-contract theory of government, Hobbes did not believe that it actually occurred as a historical event.

This photo is of the interior of the basilica St. Andrea della Valle, which was built in the latter part of the seventeenth century. It well illustrates the elaborate, gaudy splendor of the baroque style, the hallmark of the age of royal absolutism and affluence. In this case the royal monarch was the pope, ruler of a Church reinvigorated by the Roman Catholic Reformation. The dome of this basilica is second in height only to St. Peter's among Roman edifices. This view will be familiar to many readers as the scene of the first act of the grandiloquent opera "Tosca." *Photo: Alinari/Scala/EPA, Inc.*

and indeed in all Europe, was also the golden age of French literature. The elegance, the sense of order, and the formalism of the court of the Grand Monarch were all reflected in the literature of the period, sometimes called the Augustan or the classical period of French literature. It was in the field of the drama that the French writers attained their greatest success. Corneille wrote elegant tragedies in the style of and often on the same subjects as the ancient Greek tragedies. The struggles of man against himself and against the universe furnish the dramatic conflicts. Corneille's craftsmanship and style are handsomely polished, though often exalted and exaggerated.

Even more exquisitely polished were the perfectly rhymed and metered couplets of Racine's tragedies: *Andromaque* relates the tragic story of Hector's wife after the death of her husband at the hands of Achilles and the ensuing fall of Troy. *Phèdre* is about the wife of the legendary Greek king Theseus who falls in love with her stepson. This story had also been the subject of plays by Euripides, Sophocles, and Seneca. As with the Greek and Roman dramatists, abnormal love was a favorite theme with the French playwrights of the seventeenth century. Racine, an ardent Jansenist, turned later in life to religious subjects.

One of the greatest of all the French dramatists was Molière. In his charming and profound comedies — such as *Tartuffe, Le Misanthrope*, and *Les Femmes Savantes (The Learned Ladies)* — Molière devastatingly portrays and satirizes the false, the stupid, and the pompous among men: egotists, pedants, social climbers, false priests, quack physicians. The tragic conflicts and the personality types of Corneille, Racine, and Molière are universal and eternal.

Other major French writers of the age of Louis XIV were Blaise Pascal, the scientist and mathematician who also wrote the marvelously styled *Provincial Letters* against the Jesuits and the deeply reflective *Pensées (Thoughts)*; Madame de Sévigné, who wrote almost two thousand letters to her daughter, each a work of art; and the Duke de Saint-Simon, who spent the latter part of his life writing forty volumes of *Mémoires*. Madame de Sévigné and the Duke de Saint-Simon, both of whom were eyewitnesses of the court of Louis XIV, constitute two of the most important sources we have for the history and the life of that period.

The common denominator among all these writers is their emphasis upon and mastery of elegant and graceful form. In this they reflect the spirit of royal absolutism at its height. However, the form is valued not merely for its own sake, but as an artistic clothing for subtle and critical thought. French literature in the late seventeenth century overshadowed that of all other countries of Europe, much as did French military and political influence. The lucid and graceful French language became the fashionable language of most of the royal courts and courtiers on the European continent.

French literature in the eighteenth century continued for the most part in the classical vein. Voltaire wrote dramas and poems carefully tailored to the dictates of classical formalism. His prose works exalted logic and the ideals of Greece and Rome. Only Rousseau among the major eighteenth-century French writers departed from the classical spirit to anticipate the romanticism of a later era. Voltaire and Rousseau, however, are much more important for the philosophic content of their works than for their literary artistry, and will be more fully examined

in the following chapter, "The Intellectual Revolution."

3. THE ENGLISH CLASSICAL WRITERS

Next to France, England produced the most important literature in the seventeenth and early eighteenth centuries, and like the French the English authors generally wrote in the classical vein. The giant of English letters in the mid-seventeenth century was John Milton. This learned Puritan was steeped in the literature of ancient Greece and Rome. His exquisite lyrics *L'Allegro* and *Il Penseroso* and incomparable elegy, *Lycidas*, are thickly strewn with references to classical mythology. The conscientious Milton contributed much of his great talent and energy to public affairs. During the Puritan Revolution he went blind working as pamphleteer for the Puritan cause and as secretary for Oliver Cromwell. The chief literary product of this period of his life is *Areopagitica*, probably the noblest defense of freedom of the press ever penned. Milton's masterpiece is *Paradise Lost*, written in his blindness and after the restoration of the Stuart kings had ruined his public career. *Paradise Lost* is a poem of epic proportions based on the Genesis account of the rebellion of Satan against God and the temptation and fall of man. This majestic theme is treated in stately blank verse of formal elegance. Even in this deeply religious work, holy writ is interwoven with classical pagan myth.

The two greatest poets to succeed Milton were John Dryden in the late seventeenth century and Alexander Pope in the early eighteenth century. Both were satirists, both displayed a massive knowledge of Greek and Roman lore, and both wrote chiefly in the formal rhymed couplets typical of the classical period. In the precision of their form, as in the sharpness of their satire, their appeal was to reason rather than to emotion. In these respects they resemble the great French classicist Voltaire, whom they preceded by a few decades.

The eighteenth century in English literature was an age of great prose. Following the upheavals of the seventeenth century, the Puritan and Glorious revolutions, it was a time of political and religious bitterness and bickering. In pungent and incisive prose Jonathan Swift, in his *Gulliver's Travels* and political essays, and Richard Sheridan in his numerous dramas, pilloried the fops, pedants, bigots, and frauds of the day, much as Molière had done a century earlier across the channel. It was in the eighteenth century that the English novel was born. Samuel Richardson, in *Clarissa Harlowe*, and Henry Fielding, in *Tom Jones*, used this medium to analyze human personality, emotions, and psychology, just as Corneille and Racine had used the poetic drama in France for the same purpose.

In the eighteenth century several writers — Robert Burns in Great Britain, Rousseau in France, Schiller and Goethe in Germany — anticipated romanticism (see pp. 511–519). But the prevailing spirit in eighteenth- as in seventeenth-century literature was classical. Precision, formalism, and ofttimes elegance marked the style. Ancient Greece and Rome furnished the models. The appeal was generally to reason. The royal monarchs and their courts had little to fear from this literature, even from the poetic and dramatic works of Voltaire. They could derive comfort from its formal order and laugh with the rest of the world at its satire, which was aimed at mankind in general rather than at ruling regimes.

4. BAROQUE PAINTING AND ARCHITECTURE

If the literature of the seventeenth and eighteenth centuries did not offend the absolutist kings and their aristocratic courtiers, the visual arts of the period usually glorified them. The dominant style of painting and architecture was the baroque, which was an elaboration of the classical style of the Renaissance. The baroque style was originally a product of the Roman Catholic Reformation and reflected the resurgence of a revitalized Roman Catholic Church led by the militant Jesuits. Later its massive and ornamental elegance reflected the wealth and power of the absolutist monarchs and their courts, then at the peak of their affluence.

The most popular of the baroque painters of the early seventeenth century was the Fleming Peter Paul Rubens. After studying the work of the Italian High Renaissance masters, Rubens returned to Antwerp and painted more than two thousand pictures, many of them huge in size. He operated what amounted to a painting factory, employing dozens of artists who painted in the details designed and sketched by the master. Rubens, a devout Roman Catholic, first painted religious subjects. His sculpturesque and sensational *Descent from the Cross* undoubtedly reveals the influence of Michelangelo. His later subjects were pagan mythology, court life, and especially voluptuous nude women — all painted in the most brilliant and sensuous colors. All these subjects appear in his most ambitious work — twenty-three colossal scenes (mostly imaginary) from the life of Marie de Médicis, widow of King Henry IV of France. Seldom, if ever, has a dull and colorless woman been more glamorized in paint.

Spain boasted two of the greatest seventeenth-century baroque painters: El Greco and Velásquez. El Greco, whose real name was Domenikos Theotokopoulos, was a native of the Greek island of Crete (hence "The Greek"). After studying the Italian Renaissance masters, he settled down in Toledo and developed a style of his own, usually called mannerism or expressionism. By deliberate distortion and exaggeration he achieved sensational effect. *View of Toledo*, *St. Jerome in His Study*, and *Christ at Gethsemane* illustrate his genius. El Greco's favorite subject was the reinvigorated Church of the Roman Catholic Reformation. Considered to be a madman by his contemporaries, he is now regarded as the forerunner, if not the founder, of several schools of nineteenth- and twentieth-century painting. Velásquez was a painter of great versatility. Although much of his earlier work was of a religious nature, he also painted genre subjects (depicting the life of the common people) and, later, portraits. He is considered one of the greatest of portrait painters. As official court painter, he exalted and glorified the Spanish royalty and ruling classes at a time when they had really passed their peak in world affairs. Velásquez was one of the chief pioneers of modern art; it was from him that the nineteenth-century impressionists and realists received much of their inspiration.

"Christ at Gethsemane," by El Greco. Baroque art was originally a product of the Roman Catholic Reformation, and this painting by the great Spanish baroque artist reveals the religious intensity engendered by the Catholic revival. El Greco deliberately distorted to attain a powerful effect. His work assumed great influence on nineteenth- and twentieth-century painting, despite the fact that he was regarded as insane by his contemporaries.
Photo: Toledo Museum of Art, Gift of Edward Drummond Libbey, 1946

France's chief contribution to baroque painting was Nicolas Poussin, who spent most of his life in Italy studying the Renaissance masters. Although his biblical and mythological scenes are much more serene and subtle than the works of Rubens and El Greco, they are more vibrant and pulsating than the Italian Renaissance paintings that inspired them. They must, therefore, be classified as baroque in style. Some critics think that Poussin's magnificent landscapes have never been surpassed.

In eighteenth-century Great Britain Reynolds, Gainsborough, Romney, and Lawrence (who lived and painted well into the nineteenth century) vied with each other for commissions to paint the portraits of royalty and aristocracy. The results were plumes, jewels, buckles, silks, brocades, and laces in dripping profusion. This flattering of royalty and aristocracy, however, did not go unchallenged. Hogarth in Great Britain

Rembrandt's "The Polish Rider" (ca. 1655), a work of the later life of this great baroque artist, has a moving depth and subtlety: The rider, alert to dangers we can only imagine, seems about to move past our view as he follows a curving path across the canvas. *Photo: Copyright The Frick Collection, New York*

and Goya in Spain in the eighteenth and early nineteenth centuries pitilessly satirized the excesses and abuses of aristocratic society. Their brushes matched the pens of Swift and Sheridan.

Only in the Dutch Netherlands did the age of the baroque fail to reflect the ascendancy of royalty. Here in the busy ports and marketplaces commerce was king, and the great Dutch painters of the seventeenth century, notably Frans Hals and Rembrandt van Rijn, portrayed the bourgeoisie and the common people. Hals was one of the first great realistic genre painters. Rembrandt is universally recognized as one of the greatest artistic geniuses of all time. One of his favorite subjects was the Dutch bourgeoisie. He was not a popularizer, however, and he suffered many personal hardships rather than compromise the sincerity of his art. The tragic toll of these hardships is strikingly revealed in a series of magnificent self-portraits. As a portrayer of character he has never been surpassed, perhaps not even equaled. His mastery of light and shade (*chiaroscuro*) made it seem as if the very souls of his subjects were illumined. *Syndics of the Cloth Guild, Night Watch,* and *Anatomy Lesson of Dr. Tulp* are among his most powerful portrait studies. These three paintings also vividly depict the commercial prosperity, the festive urban life, and the growing interest in natural science, respectively, in the seventeenth-century Dutch Netherlands. Rembrandt's glowing idealization of people and landscapes anticipates the age of romanticism of the early nineteenth century.

Baroque architecture, like baroque painting, was an elaboration and ornamentation of the classical style of the Renaissance, and a product of the Roman Catholic Reformation. In the late sixteenth, seventeenth, and eighteenth centuries Jesuit churches sprang up all over the Roman Catholic world. The most important and one of the best examples of the baroque style is the Jesuit parent church, Il Gesù, in Rome. Also, like the painting, baroque architecture was later used to represent the gaudy splendor of the seventeenth- and eighteenth-century absolute monarchs and their courts.

Towering over all other monuments of baroque architecture, much as did St. Peter's over all other Renaissance structures, was the Versailles Palace of Louis XIV. The exterior of Versailles is designed in long, horizontal classic lines. The interior is lavishly decorated with richly colored marbles, mosaics, inlaid woods, gilt, silver, silk, velvet, and brocade. The salons and halls are lighted with ceiling-to-floor windows and mirrors and crystal chandeliers holding thousands of candles. The palace faces hundreds of acres of groves, walks, pools, terraces, fountains, statues, flowerbeds, and clipped shrubs—all laid out in formal geometric patterns.

So dazzling was this symbol of royal absolutism that many European monarchs attempted to copy it. The most successful attempt was Maria Theresa's Schönbrunn Palace in Vienna. As late as the mid-nineteenth century, mad King Ludwig of Bavaria was building three palaces in the style of Versailles. One, Herrenchiemsee, is a remarkable duplication.

Two other notable examples of baroque architecture, seen by thousands of tourists in Paris, are the Hôtel des Invalides (Old Soldiers' Home) with its magnificent dome, and the Luxembourg Palace and Gardens. In England Sir Christopher Wren was the greatest architect of the baroque period. The great fire that destroyed most of the heart of London in 1666 provided Wren with an

"Miss Catherine Tatton," by Gainsborough. Thomas Gainsborough drew his chief inspiration from the Dutch and Flemish masters of the seventeenth century. His elegant portraits glorified the members of the upper classes. *Photo: Scala/EPA, Inc.*

opportunity to build numerous baroque structures. His masterpiece is St. Paul's Cathedral, with its lofty dome and columns.

In the eighteenth century, architecture tended to become more feminine and less massive, relying heavily upon multiple curves and lacy shell-like ornamentation. This style is usually referred to as rococo. One of the best examples is Frederick the Great's Sans Souci Palace at Potsdam. The rococo style, like the baroque, represented an age of royal and aristocratic affluence.

5. THE GREAT AGE OF CLASSICAL MUSIC

The classical spirit pervaded the music of the seventeenth and eighteenth centuries as it did the literature and the visual arts; and, like the literature and the visual arts, seventeenth- and eighteenth-century music was an outgrowth of Renaissance developments.[2] The piano and the violin family of instruments, whose forebears appeared in the sixteenth century, developed rapidly in the seventeenth. In the late seventeenth and early eighteenth centuries, three Italian families, the Amati, the Guarneri, and the Stradivari, fashioned the finest violins ever made. The seventeenth century was also marked by the rise of the opera. Alessandro Scarlatti in Italy, Lully in France, and Purcell in England popularized this grandiose combination of music and drama. The eighteenth was the great century of classical music — the age of Bach, Handel, Haydn, Mozart, and Beethoven.

Johann Sebastian Bach (1685–1750) was a member of a German family long distinguished in music. Noted in his own lifetime chiefly as an organist, he composed a vast array of great music for organ, harpsichord and clavichord (forerunner of the piano), orchestra, and chorus, much of which has been lost. Most of Bach's compositions were religiously inspired, and he holds the same position in Protestant music that the sixteenth-century Palestrina does in music of the Roman Catholic Church. Bach was not widely appreciated in his own day. It was not until Felix Mendelssohn in the nineteenth century "discovered" him that he became widely known. Today Bach is considered one of the greatest creative geniuses of all time — comparable to Leonardo da Vinci, Shakespeare, and Cervantes.

George Frederick Handel (1685–1759) was born in central Germany in the same year as Bach and not many miles distant. He studied Italian opera in Germany and Italy, and wrote forty-six operas himself. He became court musician of the elector of Hanover. Later he made his home in England, as did the Elector, who became King George I of England. Handel wrote an enormous quantity of music, both instrumental

and vocal. All of it is marked by dignity, formal elegance, and melodious harmony — fitting for and appreciated in an age of royal splendor. His best-known work is the majestic oratorio The Messiah, heard every Christmas season.

Franz Joseph Haydn (1732–1809), unlike Handel, was primarily interested in instrumental music; he was the chief originator of the symphony. During his long career in Vienna, which he helped to make the music capital of the world, he wrote more than a hundred symphonies in addition to scores of compositions of other forms of music, particularly chamber music. It was in his hands that orchestral music really came into its own. All his work is in the formal, classical style. He became a friend and an important source of inspiration for the younger Mozart.

Wolfgang Amadeus Mozart (1756–1791) is regarded by many students as the greatest musical genius of all time. Born in Salzburg, he spent most of his adult life in Vienna. Mozart began composing at the age of five (possibly four), and gave public concerts on the harpsichord at the age of six. At twelve he wrote an opera. Before his untimely death at the age of thirty-five, he wrote more than six hundred compositions in all the known musical forms. Symphonies, chamber music, and piano sonatas and concertos were his favorite forms. His best-known operas are The Marriage of Figaro, Don Giovanni, and The Magic Flute. In the masterful hands of Mozart the classical style reached the peak of its perfection. Never was music so clear, melodic, elegant, and graceful. However, Mozart's material rewards in this world were few. Although the courts of many kings, princes, and aristocrats were graced by his marvelous music, his opulent patrons gave him little money or honor. Even their servants looked down on him, and he was buried in a pauper's grave.

Upon the stage set by Bach, Handel, Haydn, and Mozart emerged the most titanic figure in the history of music, Ludwig van Beethoven (1770–1827). Beethoven's dynamic genius overflowed the bounds of any school or style. However, his training, his earlier work, and his fundamental style and form were classical. Beethoven, like so many geniuses, lived a tem-

---

[2] Some music historians designate the music of the seventeenth and early eighteenth centuries, including that of Bach and Handel, as baroque, which was a forerunner of the classical.

This painting of the Mozart family shows the great musical genius as a boy with his sister and his father. His mother's picture hangs on the wall. The original illustration is in Mozart's Wohnhaus, Salzburg. Many critics consider Mozart to be the greatest musical genius of all time. *Photo: Internationale Stiftung Mozarteum, Salzburg.*

pestuous, trouble-filled life. He was born in Bonn in the German Rhineland of Flemish ancestry (hence the "van"). High-strung, poor, unsocial, and frustratingly ambitious, he suffered in his early prime the greatest calamity that could befall a musical genius—deafness. At the age of twenty-two, he went to Vienna, where he lived the rest of his life. Although Beethoven studied under Haydn, the greatest influence in his life was Mozart, to whose work his earlier compositions bear a marked resemblance. To the classical style, however, the mature Beethoven added spontaneous and sometimes noisy emotion, thereby becoming the founder of the romantic style of a later generation. Beethoven

lived through the upheavals of the French Revolution, Napoleon, and the surge of nationalism that overthrew the Napoleonic dictatorship. His keen interest in these dramatic events is revealed in his music (see p. 517). Beethoven's nine symphonies, chamber music, and numerous piano sonatas and concertos constitute probably the best-known and the best-loved body of music in history.

6. PIETISM IN RELIGION

Royal political authority was passively accepted by a number of pietistic religious sects that arose during the seventeenth and eighteenth centuries.

We have already observed the Jansenist movement within the Roman Catholic Church in France in the seventeenth century (see p. 392). Although the Jansenists were by no means oblivious to the political and social issues of the day and actually participated in the Fronde uprising against Mazarin's tyranny, they were fundamentally a Puritanical pietistic group, seeking communion with God through prayer, meditation, and mild asceticism. Early in the eighteenth century Louis XIV, under the influence of the Jesuits, outlawed the Jansenists and destroyed their buildings. At the same time the pope declared them to be heretics. However, the spirit of Jansenism continued to exist.

In Germany Philipp Spener (1635–1705) and Count Zinzendorf (1700–1760) became leaders of pietist movements of considerable dimensions. Spener, a Lutheran pastor, recoiled from the formal officiousness that his church had fallen into after the heated religious strife of the sixteenth and early seventeenth centuries. He minimized dogma and external forms in favor of inner piety and holy living. His largely Lutheran following included some of the leading intellects of Germany. Count Zinzendorf, a well-to-do Saxon nobleman, undertook to restore the Bohemian Brethren, the persecuted and scattered followers of the early fifteenth-century reformer John Huss. He called his group the Moravian Brethren. The Moravians, too, shunned intricate dogma and formal ritual. They set up model communities based upon brotherly love, frugal living, hard work, and inner piety. Count Zinzendorf migrated to America and founded Moravian communities at Bethlehem and other Pennsylvania towns. Later many Moravian ("Pennsylvania Dutch") Germans migrated southward along the Appalachian piedmont as far as Georgia, planting settlements, such as Winston-Salem in North Carolina, along the way.

In Lutheran Sweden, Emanuel Swedenborg (1688–1772), a distinguished scientist, inventor, and public servant, founded a movement somewhat like the Moravian Brethren, based upon his visions, which he took to be direct revelations of God. Swedenborg wrote several learned theological works stressing inner and outward piety and individual communion with God. His followers, who called themselves the Church of the New Jerusalem, also came in considerable numbers to America.

England, however, was the seat of the most widespread and influential pietistic movements of the seventeenth and eighteenth centuries. The first was the Society of Friends, or the Quakers, as they were generally called, founded by George Fox (1624–1691). Fox, a man of great energy and stubborn independence, detested formalism in religion as well as in society and government. He believed that true Christianity is an individual matter—a matter of plain, pious living and of private communion with God under the guidance of divine "inner light." Opposed to war, to rank, and to intolerance, the Quakers refused military service, the use of titles, and the taking of oaths. In these respects the Quakers were different from most of the other pietists. They were considered dangerous to the established order and were severely persecuted. Probably the most prominent of the early Quakers was William Penn, a wealthy aristocrat, who in 1682 founded Pennsylvania as a refuge for members of the sect. Pennsylvania and the Quakers both prospered.

A more moderate and popular pietist movement was Methodism. The prime mover in Methodism was John Wesley (1703–1791). While studying for the Anglican ministry at Oxford, John Wesley and a little band of his fellow students became disillusioned at the coldness and spiritual emptiness that had fallen upon the Anglican Church following the exciting religious controversies of the seventeenth century. They also deplored its subservience to the government and to the aristocracy. Wesley's little group began holding prayer meetings and visiting the poor and the sick. Their lives were such examples of piety and moderate regularity that their fellow students branded them "Methodists" in derision. After leaving Oxford, John Wesley and his brother, Charles, spent two years in the newly founded American colony of Georgia, trying unsuccessfully to convert the Indians. In Georgia they came in contact with some German pietists and became converted to a more fervent, evangelical type of Christianity. This they took with them back to England. When the Anglican churches closed their doors to John Wesley, he preached emotional sermons to huge throngs in the streets and fields. A tireless and dynamic soul-stirrer, he rode horseback from one end of England to the other until well into his eighties. Charles Wesley wrote more than 6,500 hymns. George Whitefield, the most eloquent of all the early Methodists, electrified tens of thousands in England and America and converted many to pietistic Christianity. The real founder of Methodism in the American colonies was Francis Asbury (1745–1816), who duplicated in many respects the work of John Wesley in England. The Methodists played a prominent part in the two "Great Awakenings" in America — the first in the 1730s and 40s and the second at the opening of the nineteenth century. In both England and America the Methodists grew rapidly in numbers, mostly among the middle and lower classes.

The various pietist groups were definitely not political revolutionaries. They were intensely interested in social reform — in education, health and sanitation, temperance, penal reform, and abolition of the slave trade. But they hoped to achieve these reforms by private charity rather than political action. They tended to accommodate themselves to absolute monarchy in the belief that spiritual and social conditions could be improved within that framework of government. John Wesley, for instance, though deeply interested in social reform in the American colonies, did not sympathize with their struggle for independence. It was not the pietists, but their contemporary rationalistic philosophers of the Enlightenment (see the following chapter), who helped to bring on the revolutionary era that toppled the thrones of many absolute monarchs and chastised or frightened the rest.

Suggested Reading

General
*C. J. Friedrich, *The Age of the Baroque, 1610–1660* (Torch). In Rise of Modern Europe series. Good chapters on the arts in the seventeenth century.
A. Guérard, *The Life and Death of an Ideal: France in the Classical Age* (1928). Well written.

Philosophy of Idealism
J. N. Figgis, *The Divine Right of Kings*, 2nd ed. (1922).
*H. Rosenberg, *Bureaucracy, Aristocracy, and Autocracy, the Prussian Experience, 1660–1815* (Beacon).

Classical Literature
C. H. C. Wright, *French Classicism* (1970).
*R. F. Jones, *The Seventeenth Century* (Stanford University). Good survey of English literature.

Baroque Art
D. N. Robb and J. J. Garrison, *Art in the Western World*, 3rd ed. (1953). Excellent survey. Well illustrated.

Classical Music
E. J. Stringham, *Listening to Music Creatively*, 2nd ed. (1959). Written by a learned musicologist for the layman.

Pietism
W. C. Braithwaite, *The Beginnings of Quakerism* (1912).
*F. J. McConnell, *John Wesley* (Apex). Popularly written by a leading scholar.

Sources
*J. B. Racine, *Three Plays* (Phoenix).
*Molière, *Eight Plays* (Modern Library).
*H. Fielding, *Tom Jones* (Modern Library).

Retrospect
The seventeenth and eighteenth centuries were the apogee of royal absolutism as a form of government in the Western world. With few exceptions, it was the nations ruled by absolutist kings that achieved the greatest successes during those two centuries. The most noteworthy exceptions were England and the Dutch Netherlands.

Under Henry IV, Richelieu, Mazarin, and Louis XIV, the Bourbon monarchy achieved a degree of absolutism in France that was virtually complete and a hegemony in Europe that has seldom, if ever, been equaled. European history during the years 1661–1715 has come to be called the age of Louis XIV. Louis and his court were the envy of all other monarchs, who sought to emulate them. France possessed a military strength so great that the major states of Western and Central Europe working in combination held her in check only with difficulty.

France's only real military rival for European and world hegemony in the seventeenth century was England. There royal absolutism had reached its peak during the sixteenth century under the vigorous and politically crafty Tudor rulers. The Stuart kings, who came to the throne in 1603 when Elizabeth I died childless, were full of fine absolutist theories but were politically inept. They soon found themselves in a running fight, mostly over money matters, with Parliament, stronghold of the landed and commercial interests. In a showdown—the Puritan Revolution—the parliamentary forces, under the able leadership of Oliver Cromwell, triumphed. Before the century had ended one Stuart king had been executed, another invited to the throne on terms, and a third driven out of the country. During the course of the seventeenth and eighteenth centuries England's parliamentary and cabinet system gradually took shape. The landed and commercial interests now in control of the English government, however, were no less aggressive in foreign and colonial affairs than had been the royal monarchs. In fact, they were more so.

The Dutch Netherlands in the seventeenth century were a case apart. Lacking the military sources and potential of their bigger neighbors, France and England, the Dutch nevertheless achieved a phenomenal commercial and financial dominance in the Western world. Their economic exploits were accompanied by a preeminence in the fields of painting and philosophy. The Dutch lived under a republican form of government and enjoyed a degree of individual freedom that could not be matched in Europe.

The most significant political developments in Central and Eastern Europe during the seventeenth and eighteenth centuries were the rise of two military despotisms—Prussia and Russia. The Hohenzollerns of Prussia, consistently pursuing the policies of royal absolutism, militarism, and territorial aggrandizement, more than doubled their territory and population and challenged Austria for the leadership of the German-speaking world. Russia under Peter the Great and Catherine the Great became more Westernized, decisively defeated Sweden and the Ottoman Turks, and gained valuable territory facing the West. Poland disappeared from the map, carved up by Russia, Prussia, and Austria.

While Prussia, Russia, and Austria were struggling for the mastery of Central and Eastern Europe, the French, the English, and the Dutch were competing for dominance in North America and Asia. In this contest the English emerged victorious in North America and India, and the Dutch in the East Indies. The English found it relatively easy to drive the primitive Indians out of eastern North America and colonize the continent with Europeans. In Asia the English and the Dutch easily defeated the technologically backward natives, but found it next to impossible to Europeanize peoples steeped in cultures and religions more ancient than those of the West.

The baroque and the classical styles prevailed in literature and the arts in Western Europe throughout most of the seventeenth and eighteenth centuries. These styles generally harmonized with and often exalted the absolutist monarchs and their courts. And the numerous pietist and quietist religious sects that arose during this period passively accepted, for the most part, the political authority of the absolutist governments.

But it would be a mistake to assume that the European masses were participating in and enjoying so much affluence and glamour, which were limited almost entirely to the royalty and to the landed and commercial aristocracy. The lower classes whose labor and blood made so much regal and military splendor possible received few benefits. By the middle of the eighteenth century critics of royal absolutism were reaching more receptive ears.

INDEX

ABOUT THE AUTHORS

John B. Harrison was born in Lawrenceville, Virginia, and grew up in Rich Square, North Carolina. He received his B.A. and M.A. at the University of North Carolina, and his Ph.D. at the University of Wisconsin. He also studied at the Sorbonne. He taught history at Lees Junior College, Jackson, Kentucky, the University of Wisconsin extension, Ohio Northern University, and since 1942 has been teaching at Michigan State University where he is now Professor Emeritus of History. He was Visiting Professor at the University of North Carolina, 1963–1964. Professor Harrison is a member of the American Historical Association and the Society for French Historical Studies. During seven trips to Europe he has visited twenty-one countries. He has also traveled in the Far and the Middle East, Africa, and Latin America. He is the author of *This Age of Global Strife* (1952), and of a number of articles and book reviews.

Richard E. Sullivan was born and raised near Doniphan, Nebraska. He received a B.A. degree from the University of Nebraska in 1942, and an M.A. degree and a Ph.D. degree from the University of Illinois in 1947 and 1949 respectively. His doctorate was earned in the field of medieval history. He has taught history at Northeast Missouri State Teachers' College (1949–1954) and at Michigan State University (1954 to the present). While at Michigan State University he has served as chairman of the Department of History (1967–1970) and Dean of the College of Arts and Letters (1970–1979). Professor Sullivan held a Fulbright Research Fellowship and a John Simon Guggenheim Fellowship to Belgium in 1961–1962. He is the author of *Coronation of Charlemagne* (1959), *Heirs of the Roman Empire* (1960), and *Aix-la-Chapelle in the Age of Charlemagne* (1963). His articles have appeared in many scholarly journals.

A NOTE ON THE TYPE

The text of this book was set by means of modern photocomposition in a text type called PALATINO. The display types are MICHELANGELO and POST ROMAN BOLD. MICHELANGELO is a companion titling to PALATINO and both are contemporary creations of the German type designer Hermann Zapf. PALATINO is distinguished by broad letters and vigorous, inclined serifs typical of the work of a sixteenth century Italian master of writing. MICHELANGELO expresses the simplicity and clarity of the classic form. Both PALATINO and MICHELANGELO reflect the early Venetian scripts influencing Zapf's creations. POST ROMAN BOLD, a display roman with slight variation of colour, designed by Herbert Post, distinguishes itself by capitals almost without serifs, most of them wide, and a lower case of small, strong horizontal serifs and short descenders.

This book was composed by Ruttle, Shaw & Wetherill, Inc., Philadelphia, Pa. It was printed and bound by Halliday Lithograph, West Hanover, Mass.